D0884141

Second Edition

Annotated Teacher's Edition

Writers
Rolando Castellanos
Paul J. Hoff
Charisse Litteken

ST. PAUL • INDIANAPOLIS

Editorial Director
Alejandro Vargas Bonilla

Associate Editors
Tanya Brown
Kimberly Rodrigues

Production Specialists
Jaana Bykonich
Julie Johnston

Cover Design
Leslie Anderson

ISBN 978-0-82196-251-0

875 Montreal Way
St. Paul, MN 55102
E-mail: educate@emcp.com
Web site: www.emcp.com

Printed in the United States of America

16 15 14 13 12 11 1 2 3 4 5 6 7 8 9 10

Contents

From the Authors

Greetings fellow teachers!

Welcome to the Second Edition of *¡Aventura!* We believe knowledge of languages is more important than ever before. Information-based technology and globalization require a skillful workforce in the area of interpersonal communication. Such a dynamic environment calls for the instruction of world languages and cultural sensitivity.

¡Aventura! is a Spanish series designed to make language instruction a rewarding experience. This product embeds the five C's of communication, cultures, connections, comparisons and communities that are promoted by the National Standards for Foreign Language Learning. Our program empowers students to learn how to speak, read, write and comprehend Spanish within diverse cultural contexts. Textbook activities and readings help motivate students to explore the Spanish-speaking world that lies beyond the classroom.

The extensive set of components that complement the textbooks is described in this Annotated Teacher's Edition to allow instructors to develop an effective and flexible curriculum geared to fulfill their particular classroom needs. Whether teachers want to address their students' learning needs through Web-based interaction, listening practice, grammar and vocabulary activities, software or audiovisual aids, *¡Aventura!* includes all the resources necessary to reinforce, recycle and expand upon the textbook content. In our Second Edition, we've made it easier to access these resources and have added helpful review content and cultural facts.

¡Aventura! offers scores of exciting opportunities for teachers and pupils to mutually tackle multiple intelligences, career skills, critical thinking, cross-curricular scholarship, creative problem solving and teamwork environments. Welcome to the *¡Aventura!* family.

Scope and Sequence

Level 1, Chapters 1-10

	Capítulo 1	Capítulo 2	Capítulo 3	Capítulo 4	Capítulo 5
Objectives	**Lecciones A & B** • ask for and give names • ask or tell where someone is from • ask for and state age • ask and tell how someone is feeling • express courtesy • ask for and state the time	**Lecciones A & B** • identify people and classroom objects • ask for and give names • ask or tell where someone is from • discuss school schedules and daily activities • describe classroom objects and clothing • say some things people do • state location • talk about how someone feels	**Lecciones A & B** • talk about places in the city • make introductions and express courtesy • ask and answer questions • discuss how to go somewhere • say some things people do • say where someone is going • talk about the future • order food and beverages	**Lecciones A & B** • talk about family and relationships • seek and provide personal information • express possession • say some things people do • express an opinion • state likes and dislikes • describe people and things	**Lecciones A & B** • describe everyday activities • say what someone is going to do • seek and provide personal information • write about everyday life • say what someone likes or dislikes • express strong feelings • talk about dates and holidays
Topics	**Lección A** greetings farewells alphabet names numbers 0–20 Spanish-speaking countries benefits of learning Spanish **Lección B** greetings farewells health formal and informal time numbers 21–100 courtesy Spanish-speaking countries	**Lección A** identifying people where a person is from Spanish influence in the United States classroom objects **Lección B** school subjects class schedule days of the week colors clothing school life in the United States and in Spanish-speaking countries technology	**Lección A** Mexico City places in a city courtesy transportation **Lección B** Mexico places in a city foods restaurant dining	**Lección A** Puerto Rico family relationships possession descriptions **Lección B** Dominican Republic leisure-time activities relationships with friends likes and dislikes descriptions	**Lección A** Costa Rica electronic equipment weekly schedule leisure-time activities **Lección B** Nicaragua dates special days numbers (101-999,999) months
Cultura viva	**Lección A** Saludos y despedidas Los cumpleaños **Lección B** Más sobre los saludos Con cortesía	**Lección A** La influencia hispana en los Estados Unidos El español en los Estados Unidos **Lección B** Los colegios en el mundo hispano Las notas	**Lección A** De visita en la Ciudad de México ¿Cómo viajamos en el D.F.? **Lección B** El Distrito Federal (el D.F.) Salir a comer en México	**Lección A** Puerto Rico ¿Cómo se llama? **Lección B** La República Dominicana El merengue	**Lección A** Costa Rica ¡Pura vida! **Lección B** Nicaragua Los días de fiesta
Idioma	**Lección A** Punctuation Definite articles and countries Cognates **Lección B** Formal/Informal Time	**Lección A** Subject pronouns and the verb *ser* Using definite articles with nouns Using indefinite articles with nouns **Lección B** *Repaso rápido:* Nouns Using adjectives to describe Saying what someone does: present tense of *-ar* verbs Talking about schedules: *¿A qué hora?* Talking about location or how someone feels: *estar*	**Lección A** Making introductions: *te, le, les* *Repaso rápido:* Question-asking words Asking questions Saying where someone is going: *ir* **Lección B** Talking about the future: *ir a* + infinitive Saying what someone does: present tense of *-er* verbs	**Lección A** *Repaso rápido:* Adjectives Expressing possession: possessive adjectives Saying what you do: present tense of *-ir* verbs Describing people and things with *estar* **Lección B** Using *gustar* to state likes and dislikes Using *a* to clarify or emphasize what you are saying *Ser* vs. *estar*	**Lección A** Saying what someone has: *tener* Expressing strong feelings with *¡Qué* (+ adjective/noun)*!* Direct object pronouns **Lección B** Telling where someone is coming from: *venir* *Repaso rápido:* Present tense to indicate the future Using the numbers 101-999,999 Asking for and giving the date
Tú lees	Estrategia: *Using cognates to understand Spanish* El mundo hispanohablante	Estrategia: *Activating background knowledge* Puentes y fronteras	Estrategia: *Anticipating special vocabulary* Frida Kahlo, una artista universal	Estrategia: *Skimming* El béisbol y la familia Martínez	Estrategia: *Scanning for details before reading* Hacer un viaje a Costa Rica El mundo hispanohablante
Tú escribes	Estrategia: *Using the dictionary*	Estrategia: *Writing a dialog journal*	Estrategia: *Combining images to build word pictures*	Estrategia: *Creating an outline*	Estrategia: *Brainstorming*

Capítulo 6	Capítulo 7	Capítulo 8	Capítulo 9	Capítulo 10
Lecciones A & B • identify items in the kitchen and at the dinner table • express obligations, wishes and preferences • talk about everyday activities • state an opinion • discuss food and table items • point out people and things • describe a household • tell what someone says • say how someone is doing	**Lecciones A & B** • talk about leisure-time activities • discuss sports • say what someone can do • discuss length of time • describe what is happening • talk about the seasons and weather • indicate order	**Lecciones A & B** • talk about household chores • say what just happened • ask for and offer help • talk about the past • identify and describe foods • discuss food preparation • make comparisons	**Lecciones A & B** • describe clothing • identify parts of the body • express disagreement • talk about the past • discuss size and fit • discuss price and payment	**Lecciones A & B** • discuss past actions and events • talk about everyday activities • express emotion • indicate wishes and preferences • write about past actions • talk about the future • make polite requests • describe personal characteristics
Lección A Venezuela objects in a kitchen table setting and cleanup foods at the dinner table **Lección B** Colombia rooms and floors of a house describing a home how someone is doing	**Lección A** Argentina leisure-time activities entertainment sports time expressions **Lección B** Chile seasons weather sports leisure-time activities ordinal numbers	**Lección A** Spain household chores **Lección B** foods shopping in a market comparisons preparing paella eating in Spain	**Lección A** Panama clothing shopping in a department store parts of the body bargaining **Lección B** Ecuador shopping in a department store gift ideas jewelry size and fit at the cash register	**Lección A** Peru school likes and dislikes travel **Lección B** Guatemala plans for the future vacations careers
Lección A Explorando Venezuela Las arepas venezolanas **Lección B** Colombia ¡Hogar, dulce hogar!	**Lección A** Argentina Che, bailá conmigo... **Lección B** Chile ¿Farenheit o centígrados?	**Lección A** España: país multicultural Los quehaceres en una casa española **Lección B** La paella ¡Cómo se come en España!	**Lección A** Panamá, el cruce del mundo También se dice **Lección B** Ecuador, país de maravillas naturales De compras en Guayaquil	**Lección A** El Perú, centro del imperio inca **Lección B** Guatemala, tierra maya
Lección A Expressing obligations with *tener que* and *deber* Stem-changing verbs: *e* → *ie* Pointing out someone or something: demonstrative adjectives **Lección B** Telling what someone says: *decir* Expressing wishes with *querer* or *gustaría* *Repaso rápido:* Regular present-tense verbs Stem-changing verbs: *e* → *i*	**Lección A** Stem-changing verbs: *o* → *ue* and *u* → *ue* Expressions with *hacer* Saying what is happening: present progressive *Repaso rápido:* Direct object pronouns Using the present progressive with direct object pronouns **Lección B** Verbs that require special accentuation Present tense of *dar* and *poner* Describing people using *-dor* or *-ista* Using ordinal numbers	**Lección A** *Repaso rápido:* Direct object pronouns Indirect object pronouns Saying what just happened with *acabar de* Present tense of *oír* and *traer* Talking about the past: preterite tense of *-ar* verbs **Lección B** Making comparisons *Repaso rápido:* Preterite tense of regular *-ar* verbs Preterite tense of *dar* and *estar*	**Lección A** Adjectives as nouns Talking about the past: preterite tense of *-er* and *-ir* verbs Preterite tense of *ir* and *ser* Affirmative and negative words **Lección B** Diminutives Preterite tense of *leer, oír, ver, decir, hacer* and *tener* *Repaso rápido:* Prepositions Using prepositions	
Estrategia: *Using graphics to understand a reading* La casa de mis sueños	Estrategia: *Previewing* El mundo de los deportes	Estrategia: *Gathering meaning from context* Ir de tapas y a merendar	Estrategia: *Using visual format to predict meaning* La tienda por departamentos Danté	Estrategia: *Applying your skills* Es sólo una cuestión de actitud
Estrategia: *Connecting phrases*	Estrategia: *Questioning*	Estrategia: *Using graphic organizers*	Estrategia: *Indicating sequence*	Estrategia: *Defining your purpose for writing*

Middle School: Level 1A

	Capítulo 1	Capítulo 2	Capítulo 3	Capítulo 4	Capítulo 5
Objectives	**Lecciones A & B** • ask for and give names • ask or tell where someone is from • ask for and state age • ask and tell how someone is feeling • express courtesy • ask for and state the time	**Lecciones A & B** • identify people and classroom objects • ask for and give names • ask or tell where someone is from • discuss school schedules and daily activities • describe classroom objects and clothing • say some things people do • state location • talk about how someone feels	**Lecciones A & B** • talk about places in the city • make introductions and express courtesy • ask and answer questions • discuss how to go somewhere • say some things people do • say where someone is going • talk about the future • order food and beverages	**Lecciones A & B** • talk about family and relationships • seek and provide personal information • express possession • say some things people do • express an opinion • state likes and dislikes • describe people and things	**Lecciones A & B** • describe everyday activities • say what someone is going to do • seek and provide personal information • write about everyday life • say what someone likes or dislikes • express strong feelings • talk about dates and holidays
Topics	**Lección A** greetings farewells alphabet names numbers 0–20 Spanish-speaking countries benefits of learning Spanish **Lección B** greetings farewells health formal and informal time numbers 21–100 courtesy Spanish-speaking countries	**Lección A** identifying people where a person is from Spanish influence in the United States classroom objects **Lección B** school subjects class schedule days of the week colors clothing school life in the United States and in Spanish-speaking countries technology	**Lección A** Mexico City places in a city courtesy transportation **Lección B** Mexico places in a city foods restaurant dining	**Lección A** Puerto Rico family relationships possession descriptions **Lección B** Dominican Republic leisure-time activities relationships with friends likes and dislikes descriptions	**Lección A** Costa Rica electronic equipment weekly schedule leisure-time activities **Lección B** Nicaragua dates special days numbers (101-999,999) months
Cultura viva	**Lección A** Saludos y despedidas Los cumpleaños **Lección B** Más sobre los saludos Con cortesía	**Lección A** La influencia hispana en los Estados Unidos El español en los Estados Unidos **Lección B** Los colegios en el mundo hispano Las notas	**Lección A** De visita en la Ciudad de México ¿Cómo viajamos en el D.F.? **Lección B** El Distrito Federal (el D.F.) Salir a comer en México	**Lección A** Puerto Rico ¿Cómo se llama? **Lección B** La República Dominicana El merengue	**Lección A** Costa Rica ¡Pura vida! **Lección B** Nicaragua Los días de fiesta
Idioma	**Lección A** Punctuation Definite articles and countries Cognates **Lección B** Formal/Informal Time	**Lección A** Subject pronouns and the verb *ser* Using definite articles with nouns Using indefinite articles with nouns **Lección B** *Repaso rápido:* Nouns Using adjectives to describe Saying what someone does: present tense of *-ar* verbs Talking about schedules: *¿A qué hora?* Talking about location or how someone feels: *estar*	**Lección A** Making introductions: *te, le, les* *Repaso rápido:* Question-asking words Asking questions Saying where someone is going: *ir* **Lección B** Talking about the future: *ir a* + infinitive Saying what someone does: present tense of *-er* verbs	**Lección A** *Repaso rápido:* Adjectives Expressing possession: possessive adjectives Saying what you do: present tense of *–ir* verbs Describing people and things with *estar* **Lección B** Using *gustar* to state likes and dislikes Using *a* to clarify or emphasize what you are saying *Ser* vs. *estar*	**Lección A** Saying what someone has: *tener* Expressing strong feelings with *¡Qué* (+ adjective/noun)*!* Direct object pronouns **Lección B** Telling where someone is coming from: *venir* *Repaso rápido:* Present tense to indicate the future Using the numbers 101-999,999 Asking for and giving the date
Tú lees	Estrategia: *Using cognates to understand Spanish* El mundo hispanohablante	Estrategia: *Activating background knowledge* Puentes y fronteras	Estrategia: *Anticipating special vocabulary* Frida Kahlo, una artista universal	Estrategia: *Skimming* El béisbol y la familia Martínez	Estrategia: *Scanning for details before reading* Hacer un viaje a Costa Rica El mundo hispanohablante
Tú escribes	Estrategia: *Using the dictionary*	Estrategia: *Writing a dialog journal*	Estrategia: *Combining images to build word pictures*	Estrategia: *Creating an outline*	Estrategia: *Brainstorming*

Middle School: Level 1B

Capítulo 6	Capítulo 7	Capítulo 8	Capítulo 9	Capítulo 10
Lecciones A & B • identify items in the kitchen and at the dinner table • express obligations, wishes and preferences • talk about everyday activities • state an opinion • discuss food and table items • point out people and things • describe a household • tell what someone says • say how someone is doing	**Lecciones A & B** • talk about leisure-time activities • discuss sports • say what someone can do • discuss length of time • describe what is happening • talk about the seasons and weather • indicate order	**Lecciones A & B** • talk about household chores • say what just happened • ask for and offer help • talk about the past • identify and describe foods • discuss food preparation • make comparisons	**Lecciones A & B** • describe clothing • identify parts of the body • express disagreement • talk about the past • discuss size and fit • discuss price and payment	**Lecciones A & B** • discuss past actions and events • talk about everyday activities • express emotion • indicate wishes and preferences • write about past actions • talk about the future • make polite requests • describe personal characteristics
Lección A Venezuela objects in a kitchen table setting and cleanup foods at the dinner table **Lección B** Colombia rooms and floors of a house describing a home how someone is doing	**Lección A** Argentina leisure-time activities entertainment sports time expressions **Lección B** Chile seasons weather sports leisure-time activities ordinal numbers	**Lección A** Spain household chores **Lección B** foods shopping in a market comparisons preparing paella eating in Spain	**Lección A** Panama clothing shopping in a department store parts of the body bargaining **Lección B** Ecuador shopping in a department store gift ideas jewelry size and fit at the cash register	**Lección A** Peru school likes and dislikes travel **Lección B** Guatemala plans for the future vacations careers
Lección A Explorando Venezuela Las arepas venezolanas **Lección B** Colombia ¡Hogar, dulce hogar!	**Lección A** Argentina Che, bailá conmigo... **Lección B** Chile ¿Farenheit o centígrados?	**Lección A** España: país multicultural Los quehaceres en una casa española **Lección B** La paella ¡Cómo se come en España!	**Lección A** Panamá, el cruce del mundo También se dice **Lección B** Ecuador, país de maravillas naturales De compras en Guayaquil	**Lección A** El Perú, centro del imperio inca **Lección B** Guatemala, tierra maya
Lección A Expressing obligations with *tener que* and *deber* Stem-changing verbs: *e* → *ie* Pointing out someone or something: demonstrative adjectives **Lección B** Telling what someone says: *decir* Expressing wishes with *querer* or *gustaría* *Repaso rápido:* Regular present-tense verbs Stem-changing verbs: *e* → *i*	**Lección A** Stem-changing verbs: *o* → *ue* and *u* → *ue* Expressions with *hacer* Saying what is happening: present progressive *Repaso rápido:* Direct object pronouns Using the present progressive with direct object pronouns **Lección B** Verbs that require special accentuation Present tense of *dar* and *poner* Describing people using *-dor* or *-ista* Using ordinal numbers	**Lección A** *Repaso rápido:* Direct object pronouns Indirect object pronouns Saying what just happened with *acabar de* Present tense of *oír* and *traer* Talking about the past: preterite tense of *-ar* verbs **Lección B** Making comparisons *Repaso rápido:* Preterite tense of regular *-ar* verbs Preterite tense of *dar* and *estar*	**Lección A** Adjectives as nouns Talking about the past: preterite tense of *-er* and *-ir* verbs Preterite tense of *ir* and *ser* Affirmative and negative words **Lección B** Diminutives Preterite tense of *leer, oír, ver, decir, hacer* and *tener* *Repaso rápido:* Prepositions Using prepositions	
Estrategia: *Using graphics to understand a reading* La casa de mis sueños	Estrategia: *Previewing* El mundo de los deportes	Estrategia: *Gathering meaning from context* Ir de tapas y a merendar	Estrategia: *Using visual format to predict meaning* La tienda por departamentos Danté	Estrategia: *Applying your skills* Es sólo una cuestión de actitud
Estrategia: *Connecting phrases*	Estrategia: *Questioning*	Estrategia: *Using graphic organizers*	Estrategia: *Indicating sequence*	Estrategia: *Defining your purpose for writing*

Scope and Sequence

Level 2, Chapters 1-10

	Capítulo 1	Capítulo 2	Capítulo 3	Capítulo 4	Capítulo 5
Objectives	**Lecciones A & B** • talk about ecology • discuss technology • talk about everyday activities • seek and provide personal information • state what is happening right now • talk about the future • talk about the past • express negation or disagreement	**Lecciones A & B** • identify objects in a bathroom • discuss daily routine • discuss personal grooming • seek and provide personal information • point out someone or something • talk about the past • discuss health • identify parts of the body • give and take instructions	**Lecciones A & B** • talk about places in a city • ask for and give directions • tell others what to do or not to do • give advice and make suggestions • discuss what is sold in specific stores • talk about everyday activities • discuss whom and what people know • identify parts of a car	**Lecciones A & B** • discuss activities at a special event • describe in the past • identify animals • discuss details about the past • express past intentions • talk about nationality • add emphasis to a description • discuss size • indicate possession	**Lecciones A & B** • name some foods • talk about the past • talk about what someone remembers • express an opinion • describe clothing • ask for advice • state what was happening at a specific time • describe how something was done • express length of time
Topics	**Lección A** Spanish-speaking world Technology and communication Environmental issues **Lección B** Spanish-speaking world Current events, vacations, everyday activities	**Lección A** Spanish in the United States Daily routines **Lección B** Spanish in the United States Parts of the body Activities and health	**Lección A** Places in the city Stores Directions **Lección B** Directions Neighborhood and neighbors Everyday activities Driving; parts of a car Traffic signs	**Lección A** Amusement parks Zoo animals Nationalities **Lección B** The circus Wild and farm animals	**Lección A** Supermarket, fish, meats and seafood Metric system Menu **Lección B** Clothing Everyday activities Food and dining
Cultura viva	**Lección A** El mundo es un pañuelo Un problema de todos **Lección B** Los cibercafés Novios y novias	**Lección A** En los Estados Unidos hay nombres en español Comer bien es salud **Lección B** Aquí se habla español Minoría mayoritaria	**Lección A** México, país con un pasado diverso De compras en México **Lección B** México, país de contrastes Por un aire más puro	**Lección A** El Salvador Sopa de iguana, por favor **Lección B** Honduras Gestos y palabras para describir animales	**Lección A** El Caribe, islas de encanto Las paladares **Lección B** La República Dominicana y su diseñador estrella La comida criolla
Idioma	**Lección A** *Repaso rápido:* present tense of *-ar, -er* and *-ir* verbs *Repaso rápido:* present tense of verbs with irregularities *Repaso rápido:* the present progressive *Repaso rápido: ir a* *Repaso rápido:* preterite tense of *-ar* verbs Talking about the past: preterite tense of *-er* and *-ir* verbs **Lección B** *Repaso rápido:* the preterite tense Irregular preterite-tense verbs Negative and affirmative expressions *Repaso rápido:* direct and indirect object pronouns Using direct and indirect object pronouns together	**Lección A** Reflexive verbs The word *se* Preterite tense of reflexive verbs *Repaso rápido:* demonstrative adjectives Demonstrative pronouns **Lección B** Verbs that are similar to *gustar* More on reflexive verbs Prepositions	**Lección A** Telling someone what to do: informal affirmative commands Formal and plural commands Suggesting what to do: *nosotros* commands **Lección B** Talking about whom and what you know: *conocer* and *saber* Telling someone what not to do: negative commands	**Lección A** Talking about the past: imperfect tense Irregular imperfect tense verbs: *ser, ir* and *ver* *Repaso rápido: ser* vs. *estar* Adjectives of nationality **Lección B** Special endings: *-ísimo/a* and *-ito/-ita* Adjective placement Possessive adjectives: long forms *Lo* with adjectives/adverbs	**Lección A** *Repaso rápido:* the preterite tense Preterite vs. imperfect tense Present tense of *reír* and *freír* Irregular preterite-tense verbs **Lección B** The imperfect progressive tense Adverbs ending in *-mente* *Repaso rápido: Hace* (+ time) *que* *Hacía* (+ time) *que*
Tú lees	Estrategia: *Using cognates to determine meaning* En la red	Estrategia: *Drawing on background knowledge* Los atletas profesionales	Estrategia: *Using format clues to predict meaning* ¡Viva México!	Estrategia: *Contextual cues* ¡El gran Circo de los Hermanos Suárez!	Estrategia: *Using a combination of reading strategies* El Caribe
Tú escribes	Estrategia: *Keeping your reader in mind*	Estrategia: *Stating chronological information*	Estrategia: *Providing details to appeal to your reader*	Estrategia: *Writing a poem*	Estrategia: *Concept maps*

Capítulo 6	Capítulo 7	Capítulo 8	Capítulo 9	Capítulo 10
Lecciones A & B • describe a household • talk about family • tell someone what to do • state wishes and preferences • talk about everyday activities • invite someone to do something • make a request • express doubt, emotion and uncertainty • state hopes and opinions	**Lecciones A & B** • say what has happened • discuss the news • talk about a television broadcast • describe people and objects • identify sections of newspapers and magazines • relate two events in the past • talk about a radio broadcast • talk about soccer	**Lecciones A & B** • express emotion • talk about everyday activities • talk about the future • plan a vacation • state what is probable • make travel and lodging arrangements • use the twenty-four-hour clock • talk about schedules • express logical conclusions • talk about hopes and dreams	**Lecciones A & B** • discuss careers • express events in the past • relate two past events • talk about hopes and dreams • state wishes and preferences • discuss the future • express uncertainty • express doubt • advise and suggest • express emotion • identify and locate countries	**Lecciones A & B** • talk about past actions and events • apply technology to find information on the Spanish-speaking world • talk about art in some Spanish-speaking countries • discuss contemporary Hispanic culture • talk about the future • discuss travel and employment opportunities • state wishes and preferences
Lección A Home and family Household items and everyday activities Household chores **Lección B** Household rules and expectations Household appliances	**Lección A** News, television programs and everyday activities **Lección B** Newspapers, radio, soccer	**Lección A** Vacations, travel agencies and food Emotions and dreams **Lección B** Airports and hotels The twenty-four-hour clock	**Lección A** Careers and jobs Problems of the world Hopes and dreams Personal relationships **Lección B** Body language Nationalities Future plans	
Lección A Bolivia, país de quechuas y aymaras Las casas coloniales **Lección B** Bolívar y los países bolivarianos Las celebraciones familiares	**Lección A** Uruguay, el país más pequeño de América del Sur La televisión uruguaya **Lección B** Paraguay, corazón de América del Sur El fútbol y la radio en Paraguay	**Lección A** De vacaciones en España ¡Olé! **Lección B** España ¡Viajando por España!	**Lección A** Nuestro planeta Las universidades latinoamericanas **Lección B** Los gestos El ecoturismo	**Lección A** Minneapolis y Santiago: ciudades hermanas **Lección B** Después del colegio
Lección A *Repaso rápido:* stem-changing verbs The subjunctive Irregular subjunctive verbs Using an infinitive instead of the subjunctive **Lección B** The subjunctive with verbs of emotion and doubt The subjunctive with impersonal expressions	**Lección A** The present perfect tense and past participles The present perfect tense of reflexive verbs Participles as adjectives **Lección B** The past perfect tense *Repaso rápido:* the passive voice More on the passive voice	**Lección A** *Repaso rápido:* the future tense with *ir a* The future tense The future tense: irregular forms **Lección B** The twenty-four-hour clock The conditional tense The conditional tense of irregular verbs	**Lección A** *Repaso rápido:* uses of *haber* Present perfect subjunctive More on the subjunctive **Lección B** *Repaso rápido:* the subjunctive *Repaso rápido:* the future tense *Repaso rápido:* the conditional tense	
Estrategia: *Skimming* La familia hispana	Estrategia: *Determining the main theme of a reading* Gran exhibición de artistas latinoamericanos	Estrategia: *Combining reading strategies* Lázaro cuenta su vida y de quién fue hijor	Estrategia: *Predict content using supporting visuals* Lázaro cuenta su vida y de quién fue hijo (continuación)	Estrategia: *Word families* ¿Estudiar o trabajar?
Estrategia: *Comparing and contrasting*	Estrategia: *Modeling a style of writing*	Estrategia: *Creating a chronological itinerary*	Estrategia: *Graphic organizers*	Estrategia: *Similes, metaphors and symbols*

Scope and Sequence

Level 3, Chapters 1-10

	Capítulo 1	Capítulo 2	Capítulo 3	Capítulo 4	Capítulo 5
Objectives	**Lecciones A & B** • greet friends • talk about school classes and schedules • describe others in terms of personality • talk about after-school jobs • talk about sports and after-school activities • ask for information • describe occupations • describe movies and programs • talk about likes and dislikes • express an opinion	**Lecciones A & B** • describe family members • express negation or disagreement • name different areas of a house and household items • talk about activities in progress • make generalized statements • talk about daily routine • describe emotions and relationships • talk about house chores • tell others what to do	**Lecciones A & B** • classify news in corresponding sections • talk about activities of the media • talk about how long something has been going on • comment on news and events in the media • recall and talk about events in the past • react to news events • link parts of sentences	**Lecciones A & B** • describe your personality and that of your friends • talk about personal relationships • make apologies • express events in the past • describe people and things • talk about family relationships • give recommendations and advice • receive and place phone calls • talk about actions that lasted for an extended time	**Lecciones A & B** • give advice about driving in the city • identify road signs • tell others what to do • ask for and give directions • make generalizations about what's important, useful and necessary • talk about train travel • talk about camping activities • make requests, suggestions and demands
Topics	**Lección A** Colombia greetings school-related activities descriptions **Lección B** Venezuela after-school activities, jobs asking for information types of movies likes and dislikes	**Lección A** United States family members celebrations household items parts of a house **Lección B** United States daily routine household chores emotions	**Lección A** Spain sections of a newspaper activities of the media events in the past **Lección B** Spain news events in the past	**Lección A** Puerto Rico descriptions feelings apologies **Lección B** Dominican Republic family relationships giving orders and advice using the phone	**Lección A** Argentina driving road signs giving directions **Lección B** Chile train travel the country camping activities
Cultura viva	**Lección A** Colombia y los famosos ¿Qué se puede hacer en Bogotá? **Lección B** Béisbol en Venezuela Venezuela y la industria de la telenovela	**Lección A** El *Spanglish* en los Estados Unidos La Fiesta de San Antonio **Lección B** Anuncios comerciales para los hispanos La Gran Manzana	**Lección A** Un *Aula* muy especial El Festival Internacional de Cine de San Sebastián **Lección B** Almería, el Hollywood español Sevilla: 3000 años de historia	**Lección A** La herencia taína Los jóvenes y la salsa **Lección B** Juan Luis Guerra, un canto de esperanza Los jóvenes dominicanos de hoy	**Lección A** ¿En subte o en colectivo? El transporte público en Buenos Aires El mundo de Mafalda **Lección B** El Tren de la Poesía Los parques nacionales de Chile
Idioma	**Lección A** *Repaso rápido:* El presente del indicativo Los verbos que terminan en *-cer, -cir* Usos del presente *Repaso rápido:* Número y género de los adjetivos Usos de *ser* y *estar* con adjetivos Learning irregular verb forms **Lección B** Palabras interrogativas: *¿Qué es?* o *¿Cuál es?* El verbo *ser* para describir ocupaciones o profesiones Para hablar de gustos y preferencias: el verbo *gustar* Para expresar su opinión: otros verbos como *gustar*	**Lección A** *Repaso rápido:* Palabras afirmativas y negativas Más sobre expresiones afirmativas y negativas *Repaso rápido:* Los complementos El presente progresivo El uso de *se* en expresiones impersonales **Lección B** Las construcciones reflexivas para hablar de la rutina diaria Otros usos de las construcciones reflexivas Acciones recíprocas Los mandatos informales afirmativos *Repaso rápido:* Las preposiciones de lugar	**Lección A** *Repaso rápido:* El pretérito Verbos irregulares en el pretérito I Verbos irregulares en el pretérito II *Repaso rápido:* Expresiones de tiempo con hace El imperfecto **Lección B** Usos del pretérito y del imperfecto Cambios de significado en el pretérito y en el imperfecto El participio pasado y el pretérito pluscuamperfecto Los pronombres relativos *que, quien(es)*	**Lección A** *Repaso rápido:* Más sobre verbos y pronombres Los complementos directos e indirectos en una misma oración Los participios pasados y el pretérito perfecto La posición del adjetivo y su significado **Lección B** Los mandatos negativos informales Los usos de la preposicióna El imperfecto progresivo	**Lección A** Los mandatos formales y plurales Los mandatos con nosotros *Repaso rápido: Preguntar* y *pedir* El subjuntivo: verbos regulares y con cambios ortográficos **Lección B** El subjuntivo: verbos irregulares y más expresiones impersonales El subjuntivo: verbos con cambios de raíz *Por* y *para* El subjuntivo con verbos de obligación
Tú lees	Estrategia: *Rhythm and rhyme* Versos sencillos (*AP Selection*)	Estrategia: *Visualizing* ¿No oyes ladrar los perros? *(AP Selection)*	Estrategia: *Use prior knowledge* De la segunda salida de don Quijote *(AP Selection)*	Estrategia: *Inferring the poet's attitude* "A Julia de Burgos" *(AP Selection)*	Estrategia: *Identifying symbols* El Sur *(AP Selection)*
Tú escribes	Estrategia: *Organize the main ideas*	Estrategia: *Combining sentences*	Estrategia: *Use snappy introductions*	Estrategia: *Transitions*	Estrategia: *Comparing and contrasting*

Capítulo 6	Capítulo 7	Capítulo 8	Capítulo 9	Capítulo 10
Lecciones A & B • make travel plans • make weather predictions • talk about events that will take place in the future • express doubt or certainty about certain facts • make lodging arrangements • state wishes and preferences • make requests in a polite manner • describe a visit to a national park • express emotions, likes and dislikes	**Lecciones A & B** • talk about grocery shopping • describe foods in terms of flavor and freshness • make comparisons • single out something • discuss food preparations • express accidental occurrences • talk about good manners • order food in a restaurant • make complaints • avoid using a word already mentioned	**Lecciones A & B** • inquire and give advice about health • express future events • talk about situations that would have happened • talk about symptoms and remedies • ask for and provide medical information • express length of time • discuss ways to stay fit • express what someone would do in a specific situation • talk about a healthy diet	**Lecciones A & B** • describe hairstyles • express hypothetical situations • describe clothes and accessories • describe colors • talk about the cleaning and tailoring of clothing items • specify conditions under which things will be done • say to whom things belong • talk about handicrafts	**Lecciones A & B** • talk about projects for the future • talk about careers • prepare for a job interview • evaluate work conditions • refer to indefinite or unknown subjects • talk about future technologies • express wishes and hopes for the future • discuss environmental problems, their causes and solutions
Lección A Panama travel plans weather airport **Lección B** Costa Rica lodging arrangements national parks outdoor activities wildlife	**Lección A** eating in Bolivia food shopping in an outdoor market comparisons cooking **Lección B** Peru good manners at a party ordering food	**Lección A** Guatemala emergencies at a clinic parts of the body at the hospital symptoms remedies **Lección B** Honduras fitness nutrition	**Lección A** Mexico hairstyles clothes colors **Lección B** Mexico at the dry cleaner sewing notions handicrafts	**Lección A** Spain professions plans for the future job interview **Lección B** Spain future technologies space and science the environment
Lección A Panamá, tres ciudades en una San Blas, un viaje al pasado **Lección B** El volcán Arenal El viaje de las tortugas verdes	**Lección A** El carnaval de Oruro Yuca, el tubérculo andino Los dos capitales de Bolivia **Lección B** Inti Raymi, la Fiesta del Sol Una receta peruana	**Lección A** Remedios de la medicina maya Baños termales en Guatemala **Lección B** Los Juegos Deportivos Estudiantiles La cocina hondureña	**Lección A** Trajes tradicionales aztecas De compras por los tianguis **Lección B** Entrevista con Macario, diseñador mexicano Revistas para chavos y chavas	**Lección A** Las primeras universidades de la Península Ibérica Cómo se hace un currículum en España **Lección B** Pedro Duque, un español en la Estación Espacial Internacional Ayudando a combatir una marea negra
Lección A El subjuntivo con cláusulas adverbiales El futuro El subjuntivo para expresar duda y negación **Lección B** El condicional Otros usos del condicional El subjuntivo con verbos que expresan emoción	**Lección A** *Repaso rápido:* El comparativo El comparativo de igualdad El superlativo La voz pasiva *Estar* y el participio pasado Más usos de *se* **Lección B** El imperfecto del subjuntivo El subjuntivo después de pronombres relativos La nominalización y el pronombre relativo *que*	**Lección A** *Repaso rápido:* El verbo *doler* Los tiempos compuestos: el futuro perfecto y el condicional perfecto Expresiones con *hace / hacía... que* **Lección B** El imperfecto del subjuntivo con *si* *Repaso rápido:* Preposiciones y pronombres Preposiciones seguidas de infinitivo	**Lección A** El presente perfecto del subjuntivo El pluscuamperfecto del subjuntivo *Cualquiera* Adjetivos para describir colores *Repaso rápido:* Los diminutivos y los aumentativos **Lección B** *Repaso rápido:* Los adjetivos y pronombres posesivos El subjuntivo en cláusulas adverbiales Otros usos del infinitivo Usos del gerundio y del participio pasado	**Lección A** Verbos que terminan en *-iar, -uar* Usos del subjuntivo y del indicativo *Repaso rápido:* El subjuntivo con sujeto indefinido **Lección B** *Repaso rápido:* El futuro perfecto Más sobre el imperfecto del subjuntivo Repaso de las formas del subjuntivo Repaso de los usos del subjuntivo I Repaso de los usos del subjuntivo II
Estrategia: *Interpreting figurative language* En una tempestad *(AP Selection)*	Estrategia: *Using your senses* Oda a la alcachofa (*AP Selection*)	Estrategia: *Using context clues to clarify meaning* Un día de éstos *(AP Selection)*	Estrategia: *Imagining the action* El delantal blanco *(AP Selection)*	Estrategia: *Understanding the author's purpose* Vuelva usted mañana *(AP Selection)*
Estrategia: *Organizing information*	Estrategia: *Using sensorial details*	Estrategia: *Describing a process*	Estrategia: *Turning point in a story*	Estrategia: *Present the pros and cons*

Scope and Sequence

Level 4, Chapters 1-10

	Capítulo 1	Capítulo 2	Capítulo 3	Capítulo 4	Capítulo 5
Objectives	• greet friends • analyze the importance of friendship • ask questions and express emotion • describe people and things • point out someone or something • divide words into syllables • obtain information to write an article about a friend • understand cultural perspectives of Cuba	• use words and terms related to traveling • make travel plans • identify people • talk about present activities • talk about the future • compare and contrast • understand cultural perspectives of Spain	• describe daily activities • utilize vocabulary related to school • discuss the school enrollment process • learn about studying abroad • talk about present activities • express obligations and probability • understand cultural perspectives of *Perú*	• use words and terms associated with the home • describe household chores • discuss rites of passage in the Spanish-speaking world • talk about events in the past • narrate events in the past • explain how long something has been occurring • understand cultural perspectives of Bolivia	• use words and terms associated with banking and the business world • discuss trade and job opportunities in Spanish-speaking countries • refer to people and objects • talk about situations that have and had happened • make generalized statements • understand cultural perspectives of *México*
Topics	greetings farewells introductions office expressions to ask for information to ask for help courtesy expressions expressions of excitement and disappointment	airport expressions travel customs train station at a hotel traveling in Spain horoscope planets	Peru daily routines school subjects being a student homework people in a school professions and careers school buildings schedules roommates	Bolivia rooms and objects in the house floor plan meals family and relatives last names family tree uses of *saber* and *conocer*	Mexico business people transactions with money at the bank loans office lingo business expressions
Cultura viva	Nuevas amistades ¿Necesita Ud. más amistades? Ibrahim Ferrer	En el aeropuerto de Barajas La vida nocturna madrileña Un puesto de botones	El proceso de matrícula ¿Quiere estudiar en el extranjero? Hay distintas opciones. Un semestre en Perú ¡Piensa en tu futuro!	En Bolivia La sociedad de los antiguos incas Una boda boliviana	Las Pymes mexicanas México Breve historia de la Ciudad de México
Idioma	Los interrogativos y las exclamaciones Los sustantivos y artículos Los adjetivos Los demostrativos	Los pronombres personales El presente del indicativo El tiempo futuro Las comparaciones	Los verbos reflexivos Los usos de *ser* y *estar* Los verbos *haber, hacer, tener, nevar* y *llover* Expresiones de obligación y probabilidad Las preposiciones *en* y *de*	Las formas del pretérito Las formas del imperfecto El pretérito vs. El imperfecto El verbo *hacer* en expresiones temporales	Las formas del presente perfecto y del pluscuamperfecto Los pronombres en función de complemento directo, indirecto o de preposición El verbo *gustar* y verbos similares Usos especiales del pronombre *se* Las preposiciones *a* y *con*
Ud. lee	*Sensemayá* por Nicolás Guillén	*Caminante, son tus huellas* y *He andado mucho caminos* por Antonio Machado	*El alacrán de Fray Gómez* por Ricardo Palma	*Las medias rojas* por Emilia Pardo Bazán	*Autorretrato* por Rosario Castellanos
Ud. escribe	Las palabras en español	La acentuación	El uso de la *b* y la *v*	Las letra *c (ce, ci), s* y *z*	Las combinaciones *ca, que, qui, co, cu*
Ud. escucha	*La muchacha de la película*	*El problema de una turista*	*Milagro de la dialéctica*	*Un original día de campo*	*Las gafas*

Capítulo 6	Capítulo 7	Capítulo 8	Capítulo 9	Capítulo 10
• talk about health • identify body parts • talk about alternative ways to manage illness and stress • make requests, suggestions and demands • indicate ownership • understand cultural perspectives of Chile	• use terms and words associated with shopping in the city • identify foods and clothing items • discuss hypothetical situations • talk about situations that would have happened • describe actions • discuss issues related to living in a big city • understand cultural perspectives of Argentina	• use terms and words associated with geography, the environment and current events • express hypothetical situations • make positive and negative statements • avoid using a word already mentioned • analyze social and environmental issues • understand cultural perspectives of Puerto Rico	• use terms and words associated with celebrations • incorporate infinitive verb forms • decide which preposition to use in specific situations • add emphasis to a description • discuss holidays in Colombia and the Spanish-speaking world • understand cultural perspectives of Colombia	• use terms and words associated with print and electronic communication • talk about what is currently happening • say what will have and would have happened • express hypothetical and contrary past actions • avoid using a word already mentioned • understand cultural perspectives of Honduras
Chile health parts of the body expression in the hospital health symptoms treatments emergency room waiting room stress and tension	Argentina in the city in the street types of fabric fashion foods	Puerto Rico geography natural phenomena the economy ethnic groups politics	Colombia at a party celebrations holidays traditions legends artisans	Honduras types of communication expressions on the telephone at the post office the press film and theater computer radio television video
La medicina alternativa Termas de Chillán	En Mendoza se soluciona un problema urbano Ir de compras en Buenos Aires	En Puerto Rico... El alcohol: un problema grave La contaminación en Puerto Rico El elemento indígena	Juanes Las navidades en Colombia La piñata Halloween en Colombia	En Honduras ¡Volveré a Honduras! Más sobre Honduras Un reportaje inolvidable
El subjuntivo El imperativo formal de *Ud.* y *Uds.* El imperativo familiar de *tú* y *vosotros* El imperativo de *nosotros*	El subjuntivo en cláusulas adjetivales El subjuntivo en cláusulas adverbiales El imperfecto del subjuntivo El subjuntivo en oraciones independientes Los adverbios	El tiempo condicional Las cláusulas condicionales con *si* El presente perfecto del subjuntivo Expresiones afirmativas y negativas La voz activa y pasiva	Los usos del infinitivo Las preposiciones *por* y *para* Los usos de algunas preposiciones Los diminutivos y los aumentativos	El gerundio El futuro perfecto y el condicional perfecto El pluscuamperfecto del subjuntivo Los usos de los pronombres relativos *que* y *quien(es)*
Walking Around por Pablo Neruda	*La muerte y la brújula* por Jorge Luis Borges	*Dos patrias* por José Martí	*Un señor muy viejo con unas alas enormes* por Gabriel García Márquez	*Peso ancestral* por Alfonsina Storni *Sátira filosófica* por Sor Juana Inés de la Cruz
El verbo *haber*	Las letras *g (ge, gi)* y *j*	Las combinaciones *ga, gue, gui, go, gu*	El uso de la letra *h*	Las letras *ll* e *y*
El triste futuro de Jacinta	*La mano*	*Isapí: La leyenda del sauce llorón*	*El secreto de la viña*	*En las sombra del cinematógrafo*

¡Aventura! Components

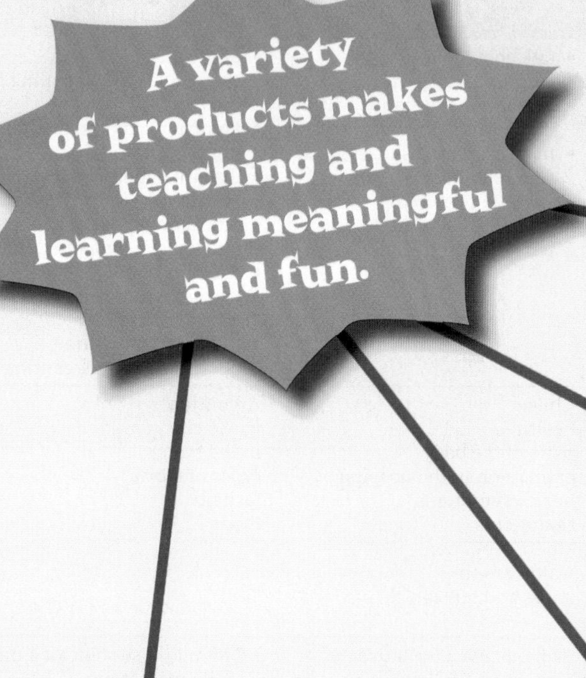

A variety of products makes teaching and learning meaningful and fun.

For the Teacher

 Annotated Teacher's Edition (Hardcover)

 EMCLanguages.net

 Teacher Resources DVD, which includes:

- Annotated Teacher's Edition
- Workbook Teacher's Edition*
- Grammar and Vocabulary Exercises Teacher's Edition*
- Interactive Lesson Planner
- Textbook Audio Program Manual* and Audio (MP3 format)
- Test Booklet with Answer Key*
- Quizzes with Answer Key*
- Assessment Audio (MP3 format)
- Examview® Assessment Program
- Portfolio Assessment
- Internet Activities Answer Key
- *Materiales para hispanohablantes nativos* Package*
- *Las aventuras de la familia Miranda* Reader*
- Communicative Activities
- Activities for Proficiency
- TPR Storytelling Manual
- Listening Activities Manual and Audio (MP3 format)
- Transparencies with audio
- *¡Otra Vez!* Electronic Flash Card Maker
- *El cuarto misterioso* Videos and DVD Manual
- *¡Aventureros!* Videos
- *Juegos*
- All Middle School Resources from Levels 1A and 1B

**Items are available in Print and in PDF format on the Teacher Resources DVD*

For the Student

 Textbook + Aventureros CD (Hardcover, CD and online)

 Workbook (softcover and online)

 Grammar and Vocab Activity Book (softcover and online)

 Internet Activities (online)

 Repaso Activities (online)

 EMCLanguages.net (online)

Go online **EMCLanguages.net**

EMCLanguages.net

Additional materials help you meet the needs of your diverse learners.

EMCLanguages.net is EMC Publishing's online resource center for many of the *¡Aventura!* ancillary materials. Online delivery of classroom materials allows students to access them in an electronic, interactive format and connect to the classroom in new ways. EMCLanguages.net includes additional Internet activities that correspond to each chapter's content, and *Repaso* activities are included for students to apply their newly acquired knowledge. EMCLangauges.net also allows students to access critical listening and textbook audio from home.

Student Resources include:

- eBook Standard Edition
- Workbook
- Grammar and Vocabulary Exercises
- Flash Card Maker
- Transparencies
- *Juegos*
- Textbook and Listening Activities Audio
- DVD Program: *El cuarto misterioso*
- Self-review: *Autoevaluación*
- Review: *Repaso*
- Internet Activities

Teacher Resources include:

- Annotated Teacher's Edition
- Workbook Teacher's Edition
- Grammar and Vocabulary Exercises Teacher's Edition
- Portfolio Assessment
- Internet Activities Answer Key
- Assessment Audio
- Student Workbook Exercises
- Student Grammar and Vocabulary Exercises
- Flash Card Maker
- Transparencies
- *Juegos*
- Textbook and Listening Activities Audio
- DVD Program: *El cuarto misterioso*
- Student Self-review: *Autoevaluación*
- Student Review: *Repaso*
- Student Internet Activities

i-Culture

Web-based activities give students an authentic connection to the Spanish-speaking world!

i-News Daily news articles keep students up-to-date with what's happening in the Spanish-speaking world at a level they can understand.

i-Videos Monthly videos show Spanish-speaking youth demonstrating their unique hobbies and interests.

i-Songs Monthly karaoke songs allow students to sing the most popular Spanish-language songs.

i-Passport Monthly videos take students on a journey around the world to experience Spanish-speaking countries.

Multimedia Technology

DVD and CD formats offer students a multisensory Spanish language experience.

DVD program: *El cuarto misterioso* incorporates chapter learning objectives into an intriguing teen-centered adventure.

***¡Aventureros!* CD** compiles 10 i-Catcher videos that complement instructional content with additional vocabulary and electronic activities.

Electronic Flash Card Maker provides color images of vocabulary words that students can use to make their own flash cards.

***¡Aventura! Juegos* CD** contains electronic games that practice each chapter's vocabulary and grammatical objectives.

The National Standards and Philosophy behind *¡Aventura!*

National Standards

The *Goals 2000: Educate America Act* of 1994 provided funding for improving education. One result of this funding was the establishment of content standards in foreign language education as determined by a K-12 Student Standards Task Force. The new framework, revised and expanded in 1999, *Standards for Foreign Language Learning in the 21st Century including Chinese, Classical Languages, French, German, Italian, Japanese, Portuguese, Russian, and Spanish,* includes information about standards application in specific languages. The main points of the National Standards are listed here. More information can be found at www.actfl.org.

Communication

Communicate in Languages Other Than English

Standard 1.1: Students engage in conversations, provide and obtain information, express feelings and emotions and exchange opinions.

Standard 1.2: Students understand and interpret written and spoken language on a variety of topics.

Standard 1.3: Students present information, concepts and ideas to an audience of listeners or readers on a variety of topics.

Cultures

Gain Knowledge and Understanding of Other Cultures

Standard 2.1: Students demonstrate an understanding of the relationship between the practices and perspectives of the culture studied.

Standard 2.2: Students demonstrate an understanding of the relationship between the products and perspectives of the culture studied.

Connections

Connect with Other Disciplines and Acquire Information

Standard 3.1: Students reinforce and further their knowledge of other disciplines through the foreign language.

Standard 3.2: Students acquire information and recognize the distinctive viewpoints that are only available through the foreign language and its cultures.

Comparisons

Develop Insight into the Nature of Language and Culture

Standard 4.1: Students demonstrate understanding of the nature of language through comparisons of the language studied and their own.

Standard 4.2: Students demonstrate understanding of the concept of culture through comparisons of the cultures studied and their own.

Communities

Participate in Multilingual Communities at Home and around the World

Standard 5.1: Students use the language both within and beyond the school setting.

Standard 5.2: Students show evidence of becoming lifelong learners by using the language for personal enjoyment and enrichment.

Correlations with standards and extensive research create the framework for *¡Aventura!*

Philosophy behind *¡Aventura!*

¡Aventura! is a reflection of extensive research and the work of many dedicated professionals in foreign language education. This research, the National Standards and best instructional practices helped define the philosophy that led the creation of the *¡Aventura!* series. Guiding principles, like the ones that follow, are included throughout the book to enrich the classroom experience and expand it beyond your classroom walls.

Cross-curricular Learning

In the *¡Aventura!* classroom, students can understand and enjoy the real-life application of their language learning as they relate the study of other academic disciplines. The student textbook includes *Conexión con otras disciplinas,* and the ATE margins provide activities titled Connections.

Career Awareness/Workplace Readiness Skills

The global economy has made it more important than ever for individuals to develop their language skills to be able to compete in the international marketplace. Suggested activities can be found in the margins of the ATE.

Service Learning/Mentor Programs

Teachers can help students connect with service learning opportunities and mentor programs to gain firsthand experience while learning about themselves and their communities.

Parental Involvement

The benefits of having students, parents, teachers and the community involved in supporting one another are undeniable. The margins of the *¡Aventura!* ATE give teachers ideas about how to encourage parental support for classroom learning, and promote parental awareness of student progress and goals.

Spanish for Spanish-Speaking Students

The *¡Aventura!* ATE includes a variety of activities and suggestions for teaching Spanish to Spanish-speaking students.

The Multiple Intelligences

Howard Gardner's theory of multiple intelligences suggests that people have different abilities in many different areas of thought and learning. *¡Aventura!* has utilized Gardner's research to provide teachers with a plethora of learning activities. Teachers can create innovative lessons using the textbook and ancillary materials to address diverse learning styles so that each student can maximize his or her individual potential.

The general characteristics associated with each of these eight identified intelligences are described below.

Bodily-Kinesthetic: These students learn best by doing. They learn through movement and touch, and express their thoughts with body movement. They are good with hands-on activities, such as dancing, athletics and crafts.

Interpersonal: These students are natural leaders who communicate well, empathize with others and often intuit what someone is thinking or feeling.

Intrapersonal: People with intrapersonal intelligence may appear to be shy but are self-motivated and aware of their own thoughts and feelings about a given subject.

Linguistic: This type of student appreciates and is fascinated with words and language. These students enjoy writing, reading, word searches, crossword puzzles and storytelling.

Logical-Mathematical: This type of student likes establishing patterns and categorizing words and symbols. These students enjoy mathematics, experiments and games that involve strategy or rational thought.

Musical: Musical students can be observed singing or tapping out a tune on a desk or other object. These students are discriminating listeners who catch what is said the first time.

Naturalist: Students with naturalist intelligence might have a special ability to observe, understand and apply learning to the natural environment.

Spatial (Visual): These students think in pictures and can conceptualize well. They like complicated puzzles, drawing and constructing.

Textbook and Teacher's Edition Tour

Margin Activities

Margin activities offer additional opportunities to address an individual learner's needs.

- **Communities.** These activities connect students to the community through Spanish and provide them with suggestions on how they may participate in service learning.
- **Connections.** Cross-curricular activities included here are opportunities to use Spanish in conjunction with other subject areas.
- **Cooperative Learning.** These activities offer students additional opportunities for cooperative learning beyond the textbook content. The activities require students to cooperate with one another in pairs or small groups, using Spanish for authentic communication.
- **Critical Listening.** These activities promote listening comprehension. They require that students learn not only the sounds of the language, but also the meaning behind them. Ultimately, students will reach a point where they are able to correct their own errors.
- **Critical Thinking.** These activities develop higher-order thinking skills. Critical thinking is an essential part of the total academic development of students. *¡Aventura!* includes a thorough and systematic program of higher-order thinking activities that address comprehension, application, analysis, synthesis and evaluation.
- **Expansion.** Expansion activities offer enrichment opportunities. They allow students' personal interests and creativity to take over, empowering them to discover a wealth of information about the language and the cultures studied in *¡Aventura!*
- **Language through Action.** These activities require students to combine Spanish-speaking or listening skills with physical movement.
- **Multiple Intelligences.** The multiple intelligences are addressed through activities focused on the eight areas identified by brain research: linguistic intelligence, logical-mathematical intelligence, spatial intelligence, bodily-kinesthetic intelligence, musical intelligence, interpersonal intelligence, intrapersonal intelligence and naturalist intelligence.
- **Prereading Strategy.** These questions about the subject matter prepare students for what they are about to read. Students might be asked to look at an illustration and suggest the theme of the accompanying dialog. Students are encouraged to guess the meanings of words they do not recognize and are taught that they need not understand all the vocabulary to discern the main theme of an activity.
- **Prior Knowledge.** Students will be asked to apply what they already know. Students will recall the Spanish that they have learned and draw on personal experiences that will help them comprehend and process the information that they are about to learn.
- **Pronunciation.** These activities allow students to practice pronunciation. Have students break down sentences into individual words and sounds and then have them use the words you have practiced in meaningful sentences. In addition, after presenting the initial dialog (or other expository material) and accompanying activities, have students work in pairs practicing the activity and focusing on the new pronunciation point. Circulate and assist with pronunciation and intonation.
- **Spanish for Spanish Speakers.** These activities are designed especially for students who are native speakers of Spanish. They allow students to examine their cultural heritage and to increase their Spanish skills.

- **Students with Special Needs.** These activities are for students who need extra help. They allow students to practice areas in which they are having difficulty and facilitate the acquisition of new skills and the comprehension of various subject matters.
- **Technology.** These activities require students to use the Internet, e-mail or another electronic medium in combination with their knowledge of Spanish to complete an activity.
- **TPR.** These activities involve Total Physical Response (TPR). Whereas many teachers have used TPR either extensively or on a limited basis, these activities often require an extra effort on the part of the teacher to prepare for and use TPR in the classroom.

The contents and special features of *¡Aventura!* make teaching and learning effective and fun.

Margin Icons

Margin icons denote additional ancillaries that support the contents of that page.

 *Materiales para hispanohablantes nativos*

TPRS TPR Storytelling Manual

 DVD Program

 Audio Program

 Transparencies

 Workbook

 Grammar and Vocabulary Exercises Manual

 Activities for Proficiency Manual

 Communicative Activities Manual

 *Las aventuras de la familia Miranda*

 Listening Activities

 *Juegos*

Flash Cards *¡Otra Vez!* Electronic Flash Card Maker

 Repaso

 *¡Aventureros!*

 Internet Activities

 i-Culture

 *Speaking Spanish Confidently*

 Quizzes

Assessment Program

Tour

The **chapter opener** prepares students for the cultural and communicative content of the thematic lesson that follows.

Refer to this section as a guide to analyze the contents and special features of *¡Aventura!*

Margin icons denote additional ancillaries that support the contents of that page.

Answers of the close-ended activities appear in the left- and right-hand margins of the ATE.

Questions that accompany the ***El cuarto misterioso*** DVD program ask students to review what has happened in the drama and predict what will happen in the current chapter episode.

Objectives encourage students to anticipate the chapter's content. ATE notes include questions that can be used to initiate reflection and discussion.

Margin activities offer additional opportunities to address individual learner's needs.

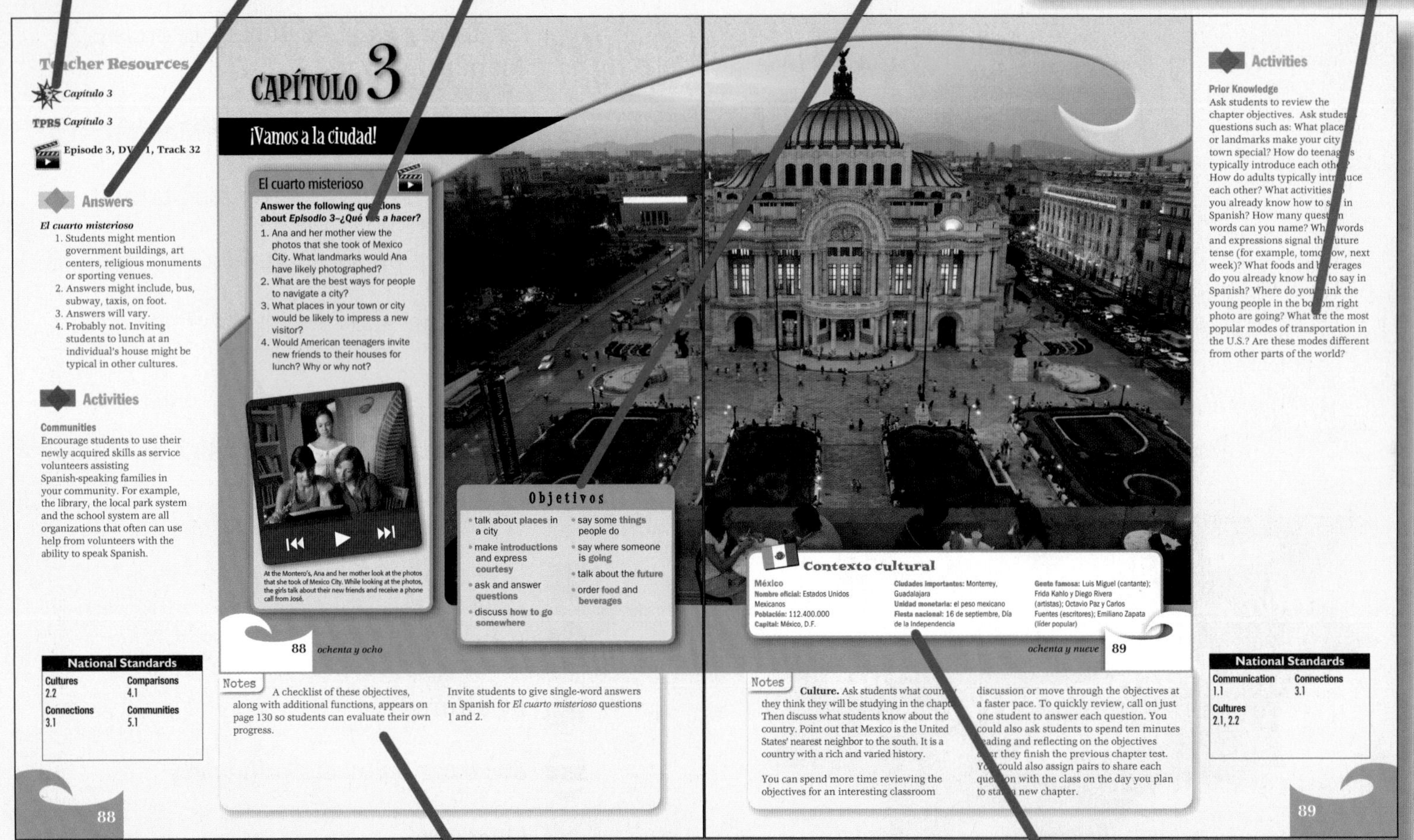

Teacher Resources

Capítulo 3

TPRS *Capítulo 3*

Episode 3, DVD 1, Track 32

Answers

El cuarto misterioso

1. Students might mention government buildings, art centers, religious monuments or sporting venues.
2. Answers might include, bus, subway, taxis, on foot.
3. Answers will vary.
4. Probably not. Inviting students to lunch at an individual's house might be typical in other cultures.

Activities

Communities

Encourage students to use their newly acquired skills as service volunteers assisting Spanish-speaking families in your community. For example, the library, the local park system and the school system are all organizations that often can use help from volunteers with the ability to speak Spanish.

National Standards	
Cultures 2.2	Comparisons 4.1
Connections 3.1	Communities 5.1

CAPÍTULO 3

¡Vamos a la ciudad!

El cuarto misterioso

Answer the following questions about *Episodio 3–¿Qué vas a hacer?*

1. Ana and her mother view the photos that she took of Mexico City. What landmarks would Ana have likely photographed?
2. What are the best ways for people to navigate a city?
3. What places in your town or city would be likely to impress a new visitor?
4. Would American teenagers invite new friends to their houses for lunch? Why or why not?

At the Montero's, Ana and her mother look at the photos that she took of Mexico City. While looking at the photos, the girls talk about their new friends and receive a phone call from José.

Objetivos

- talk about places in a city
- make introductions and express courtesy
- ask and answer questions
- discuss how to go somewhere
- say some things people do
- say where someone is going
- talk about the future
- order food and beverages

88 *ochenta y ocho*

Notes A checklist of these objectives, along with additional functions, appears on page 130 so students can evaluate their own progress.

Invite students to give single-word answers in Spanish for *El cuarto misterioso* questions 1 and 2.

88

Contexto cultural

México
Nombre oficial: Estados Unidos Mexicanos
Población: 112.400.000
Capital: México, D.F.

Ciudades importantes: Monterrey, Guadalajara
Unidad monetaria: el peso mexicano
Fiesta nacional: 16 de septiembre, Día de la Independencia

Gente famosa: Luis Miguel (cantante); Frida Kahlo y Diego Rivera (artistas); Octavio Paz y Carlos Fuentes (escritores); Emiliano Zapata (líder popular)

ochenta y nueve 89

Notes **Culture.** Ask students what country they think they will be studying in the chapter. Then discuss what students know about the country. Point out that Mexico is the United States' nearest neighbor to the south. It is a country with a rich and varied history.

You can spend more time reviewing the objectives for an interesting classroom discussion or move through the objectives at a faster pace. To quickly review, call on just one student to answer each question. You could also ask students to spend ten minutes reading and reflecting on the objectives after they finish the previous chapter test. You could also assign pairs to share each question with the class on the day you plan to start a new chapter.

Activities

Prior Knowledge

Ask students to review the chapter objectives. Ask students questions such as: What places or landmarks make your city or town special? How do teenagers typically introduce each other? How do adults typically introduce each other? What activities do you already know how to say in Spanish? How many question words can you name? What words and expressions signal the future tense (for example, tomorrow, next week)? What foods and beverages do you already know how to say in Spanish? Where do you think the young people in the bottom right photo are going? What are the most popular modes of transportation in the U.S.? Are these modes different from other parts of the world?

National Standards	
Communication 1.1	Connections 3.1
Cultures 2.1, 2.2	

89

Margin notes provide additional teaching suggestions and cultural notes that expand on the lesson's content.

Contexto Cultural provides basic information of the country or region where each chapter takes place. Each chapter focuses on a different Spanish-speaking country or region.

Each chapter is divided into ***Lección A*** and ***Lección B***. Each chapter of *¡Aventura!* contains two lessons that follow an identical format, which makes teaching and learning meaningful, effective, and fun!

Vocabulario I introduces lessons with a colorful one- or two-page presentation of new vocabulary and grammatical structures in a meaningful context. Two or three activities, including one listening activity, follow.

Speaker icons next to some activities indicate that the Textbook Audio Program is required to complete the activity. Transcripts can be found on pages TE46-55.

The **EMCLanguages.net** icon indicates that more support or ancillary activities related to the page's content can be found online.

Diálogo I uses the recently presented vocabulary and expressions in an interesting and authentic depiction of everyday life in the Spanish-speaking world. The dialog is followed by a comprehension activity, personal application, and listening comprehension activities.

Cultura viva I explains the cultural theme of the lesson and provides historical, geographical, and political information about the country or countries featured in the chapter. Comprehension and personal application questions follow.

Diálogo I En la Ciudad de México

MARISOL: ¡Hay una fiesta fantástica en la ciudad!
TOMÁS: ¿Cuándo es la fiesta?
PILAR: Es mañana en el Zócalo. ¿Por qué no vamos?
TOMÁS: ¡Claro! ¡Vamos!

TOMÁS: Y... Olga va también, ¿no? Es muy simpática.
PILAR: Sí, ella va.
TOMÁS: ¡Ah, muy bien!

PILAR: Allí está mi amiga. ¡Hola, Ana! Te presento a Tomás.
TOMÁS: Tanto gusto.
ANA: Encantada. ¿Por qué no caminamos al parque?
TOMÁS: Sí, quiero caminar.

3 ¿Qué recuerdas?

1. ¿Dónde están los muchachos?
2. ¿Dónde hay una fiesta?
3. ¿Cómo es Olga?
4. ¿Va Tomás al Zócalo?
5. ¿Adónde quiere ir Ana?

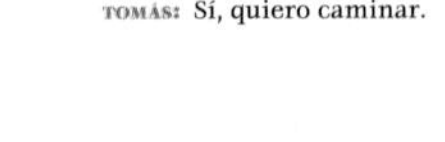

4 Algo personal

1. ¿Eres tú simpático/a? ¿Y tus amigos/as?
2. ¿Hay un parque en tu ciudad? ¿Cómo se llama?
3. ¿Caminas a la escuela?

5 Presentaciones

Indica la letra de la foto que corresponde con lo que oyes.

A

B

C

D

Cultura viva I

Go online EMCLanguages.net

El Parque de Chapultepec, México, D.F.

De visita en la Ciudad de México

When you are in Mexico, you may hear the terms *México, La República* or *los Estados Unidos Mexicanos*, all of which are used interchangeably to refer to the country. Similarly, when you are planning to travel to the capital, you may say you are going to visit Mexico City. However, according to Mexicans, you will be in *el D.F. (Distrito Federal), la Ciudad de México* or just in *México*. Once there, start your sightseeing in the center of the city—the *Zócalo*—or main plaza. Mexico was once the center of the ancient Aztec capital *Tenochtitlán*. Today the site offers visitors a view of the excavated ruins of the *templo mayor* (main temple). Walk a short distance and you will find the wide and elegant *Paseo de la Reforma*. This street was built by the emperor Maximilian to join his palace at Chapultepec with his office in the National Palace (where works by one of Mexico's most famous artists, Diego Rivera, are on display) in the *Zócalo*. Chapultepec today is a large park where you can enjoy *el zoológico* (zoo), *las atracciones* (amusement park rides) or *el Castillo* (castle). Transportation inside the park is limited to walking and biking, so many people come just to enjoy the outdoors. The park also includes the world-famous *Museo Nacional de Antropología*, which contains three miles of exhibits of art, architecture and culture of the ancient civilizations that existed in Mexico before Spanish colonization.

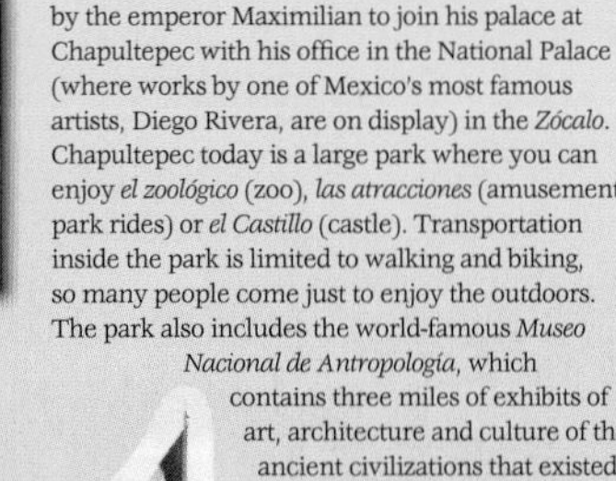

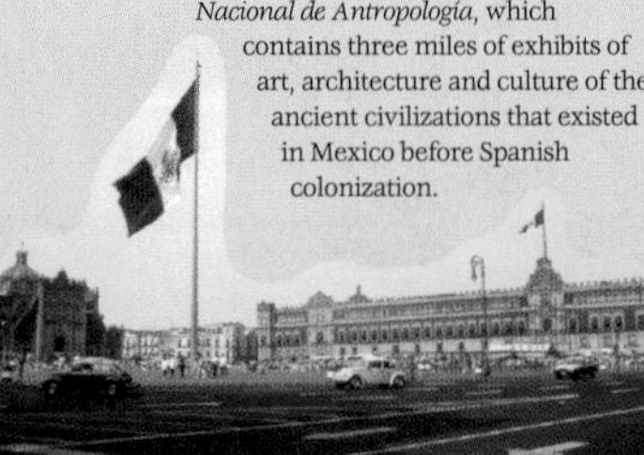
El Zócalo.

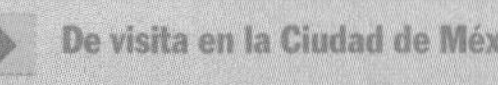

6 De visita en la Ciudad de México

¿Sí o no?

1. Los mexicanos llaman a la capital La República.
2. D.F. quiere decir *Distrito Federal*.
3. El Zócalo es una biblioteca.
4. El Paseo de la Reforma es una avenida elegante.
5. En el Parque de Chapultepec hay un zoológico, atracciones y un castillo.
6. En el Museo Nacional de Antropología hay exhibiciones de arquitectura y cultura.

7 En el D.F.

Make a list of four places mentioned in *Cultura viva* that you might visit on a trip to Mexico City. Search the Internet or go to the library and describe what you would see or do at one of the places you listed.

Headphone icons indicate that the section or activity has been recorded by a native speaker and can be found in the Textbook Audio Program.

Subdivided and titled, ***Estructura***, the ***Idioma*** section explains grammatical concepts clearly and concisely and helps students learn grammar content in small chunks.

The ***¡Extra!*** section provides additional related vocabulary, notes, tips, and suggestions to help students feel successful. The section gives students extra information, much like the margin notes for teachers in the ATE. The content of the *¡Extra!* features is not required and thus is not addressed in the accompanying Assessment Program.

Idioma

Estructura

Making introductions: *te, le, les*

Follow these guidelines when you wish to introduce people:

te	**(to one person, informal)**	*Laura, **te presento a** Gabriel.*
le	**(to one person, formal)**	*Sra. Durán, **le presento a** María.*
les	**(to two or more people, informal and formal)**	*Luis y José, **les presento a** Margarita y a Pablo.*

Note: When the definite article *el* (the) follows *a* or *de*, the two words combine to form *al* or *del*.

a + el = al   de + el = del

*Tomás y Pilar, les presento **al** señor Rojas.*
*Te presento **al** amigo del estudiante nuevo.*

You have several responses to choose from when meeting someone, among them: ***Mucho gusto***, ***Tanto gusto*** or ***El gusto es mío***. In addition, males can say ***Encantado***, while females may wish to say ***Encantada***.

¡Extra!

Títulos de cortesía

You have already learned to use *señorita, señora, señor, profesora, profesor* in face-to-face conversation. However, if you are talking about someone, these titles of respect are preceded by the definite articles *la, el, las* or *los*: ***El señor Díaz** es mi profesor.*

Two additional titles of respect, ***don*** (masculine) and ***doña*** (feminine), do not require a definite article and are used with a person's first name when talking to adults you know very well: ***Don** Diego, le presento a **doña** Teresa.*

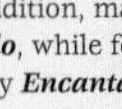

Práctica

8 Presentaciones

Completa las siguientes oraciones con palabras de la lista.

de	te	a	al
les	le	del	a

MODELO ¡Ay, Rosario! Te presento a mi amigo Iván.

1. Jorge, __ presento __ señor Francisco Ortiz.
2. Rodolfo y Ana, __ presento __ amigo __ Sr. Rodríguez.
3. Paco y Antonio, __ presento __ señor Pedraza.
4. Profesor Vallejo, __ presento __ doña Marina.
5. Rodrigo y Pablo, __ presento __ Diana y a Catalina.
6. Sr. y Sra. Gaviria, __ presento __ profesora __ historia.
7. Rosario, __ presento __ don Carlos y __ Ernesto.

Encantada.

9 En la fiesta del Zócalo

Go online EMCLanguages.net

Completa los diálogos.

Roberto: Sr. y Sra. Ortega, (1) presento (2) mi amiga Estefanía.
Sr. Ortega: Tanto (3), Estefanía.
Sra. Ortega: Encantada, Estefanía.
Sra. Tovar: Sra. Santos, (4) presento a Felipe, mi amigo de Acapulco.
Sra. Santos: (5), Felipe.
Felipe: El (6) es mío, Sra. Santos.
Sofía: Marcos, te (7) a Pilar y a Daniel. Marcos es el estudiante nuevo de Veracruz.
Marcos: ¡(8) gusto! Me llamo Marcos Castilla.
Pilar: (9).
Iván: ¿(10) estás?
Daniel: Bien, gracias.

¡Mucho gusto!

10 En la Ciudad de México

You and two classmates are greeting some friends and family who have decided to visit Mexico City. Introduce everyone using the words shown.

MODELO Hernando / presento a / el profesor de música, el señor Villamil
Hernando, te presento al profesor de música, el señor Villamil.

1. Maribel / presento a / mi amigo, Jorge Contreras
2. Carmen y Gabriel / presento a / Edgar
3. Sra. Giraldo / presento a / la señora Suárez
4. Sr. y Sra. Ruiz / presento a / el profesor de historia de / el colegio, el señor Botero
5. Enrique y Sonia / presento a / el amigo de / el profesor Osorio, el señor Jaramillo
6. Sr. y Sra. Reyes / presento a / la amiga de Silvia, Juliana
7. Isabel / presento a / el amigo de / el señor Rueda, don Carlos

Comunicación

11 En el Zócalo

You are with some friends and classmates at the Zócalo while on a study abroad program in Mexico City. In small groups, act out these introductions. Take turns playing the part of each person.

1. Your friend Miguel meets your friend Margarita for the first time.
2. Your classmate Pedro sees one of his neighbors *la señora Carvajal* whom you do not know.
3. Two other students you know from the exchange program pass by while you are with your other friends.
4. The mother of one of your friends, *la señora García*, is crossing the Zócalo and runs into you and your friends.

The ***Práctica*** section provides activities that increase in difficulty and scope, from mechanical to meaningful to communicative.

Pair or ***group*** activities icons indicate that two or more students are required to complete an activity.

The ***Comunicación*** section provides open-ended practice.

Repaso rápido reviews previously taught grammatical topics.

Vocabulario II is a second presentation of new and review vocabulary. As in *Vocabulario I*, two or three activities, including one listening activity, follow.

12 En una fiesta de bienvenida

In groups of three or four, pretend you are guests at a *quinceañera* party at the home of the study abroad program director. Practice introducing one another in Spanish and then start conversations with the other guests: ask where they are from, how they are, if they speak Spanish and English and so on. Exchange phone numbers with at least one other person. Remember to use appropriate greetings, gestures and responses in your conversations.

Repaso rápido

Question-asking words

You are already familiar with several words used for asking information questions:

*¿**Cómo** estás?*	**How** are you?
*¿**Cuál** es tu cuaderno?*	**Which (one)** is your notebook?
*¿**Cuáles** son?*	**Which (ones)** are they?
*¿**Cuándo** es la clase de español?*	**When** is the Spanish class?
*¿**Cuánto** es?*	**How much** is it?
*¿**Cuántos** hay?*	**How many** are there?
*¿**Dónde** están ellos?*	**Where** are they?
*¿**Por qué** está ella allí?*	**Why** is she there?
*¿**Qué** es?*	**What** is it?
*¿**Quién** es de Cancún?*	**Who** is from Cancún?
*¿**Quiénes** son ellos?*	**Who** are they?

Note: Unlike *qué, cuál* (or *cuáles*) may never be followed by a noun: *¿Qué autobús tomas?* (What bus are you taking?); *¿Cuál de los autobuses tomas?* (Which of the buses are you taking?).

13 Unas preguntas

Escribe preguntas usando cada una de las palabras interrogativas del Repaso rápido. ***(Write questions using each of the question-asking words in the Repaso rápido.)***

¿Dónde está el Museo de Bellas Artes?

96 *noventa y seis* **Lección A**

Diálogo II provides additional exposure to authentic Spanish. As in *Diálogo I*, a comprehension activity, personal application and listening comprehension activities follow.

Cultura viva II offers a second, more personal glimpse into everyday life in the Spanish-speaking world.

Diálogo II ¿Qué?

TOMÁS: Hola, Olga, tú vas mañana a la fiesta, ¿verdad?
OLGA: ¿Cómo? Estás muy lejos.
TOMÁS: Lo siento.

TOMÁS: ¿Vas tú mañana a la fiesta en el Zócalo?
OLGA: Estás muy cerca, Tomás.
TOMÁS: Perdón.

OLGA: No, no voy porque no tengo transporte.
TOMÁS: Bueno, no hay problema.
OLGA: ¿Por qué no hay problema?
TOMÁS: Porque yo tengo carro para ir a la fiesta.

24 ¿Qué recuerdas?

1. ¿Quién está lejos?
2. ¿Con quién habla Tomás?
3. ¿Por qué no va Olga a la fiesta?
4. ¿Por qué no hay problema?

25 Algo personal

1. ¿Qué transporte tomas para ir a la escuela?
2. ¿Qué tomas para ir al parque? ¿Está lejos o cerca?
3. ¿Vas a fiestas con amigos? Explica.

26 ¿Qué transporte toman?

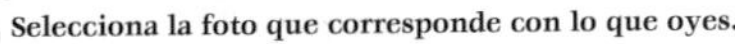

Selecciona la foto que corresponde con lo que oyes.

A

B

C

D

E

Cultura viva II

Nosotros viajamos en metro.

Taxis are numerous and usually relatively inexpensive compared to the United States. In Mexico City, governmental regulations require taxi drivers to be licensed and that each taxi operate with a working meter and a driver's picture identification placed in a visible location inside the cab.

The buses in Mexico are clean and reasonably priced. The best public transportation bargain in Mexico City is undoubtedly its subway system (*el metro*), which allows a rider to travel from one area of the city to another with a single ticket. For this reason, the metro can be a little overcrowded during rush hours.

¿Cómo viajamos en el D.F.?

Transportation options in Mexico are varied and abundant. One option, owning a car and driving in Mexico, can present challenges. Cars are expensive to purchase and maintain since taxes are steep. In addition, finding parking can be difficult and is expensive when available. Most people prefer to use the excellent public transportation that is available.

¡Hay mucho tráfico en el D.F.!

27 Comparando

Compara el transporte en México con el transporte en tu ciudad.

México	Mi ciudad
1. owning a car presents challenges	1. driving a car also presents challenges
2.	2.
3.	3.

A Spanish reading, ***Lectura cultural***, concludes Lección A and takes a more extensive look at the Spanish-speaking world.

Lectura cultural

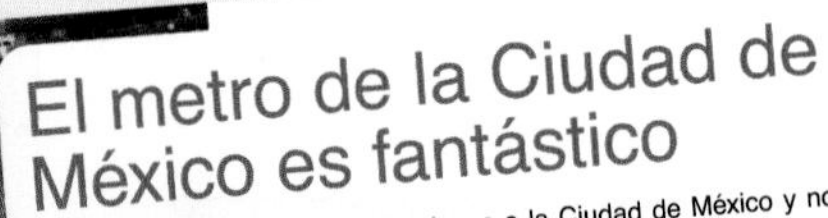

El metro de la Ciudad de México es fantástico

¿Vas de vacaciones a la Ciudad de México y no sabes qué hacer? ¿Por qué no pasas[1] un día fantástico usando[2] el metro? Toma la línea 2 a Chapultepec y camina por el parque. O toma la línea 3 a la estación de Pino Suárez y mira la pirámide azteca descubierta[3] en 1968 durante la construcción del metro. O toma la línea 4 a la estación de Talismán y mira los restos de un mamut[4] que tiene 13.000 años. Todos los días[5], cinco millones de personas toman el metro para ir al trabajo[6] o la escuela. Tú y tus amigos pueden[7] tomar el metro para divertirse[8]. El metro es un transporte moderno, limpio[9], seguro[10] y eficiente. ¡Vamos en metro!

La pirámide azteca en la estación de Pino Suárez.

Datos interesantes del metro de México, D.F.:

- Es el primer sistema que usa símbolos y colores para identificar las estaciones.
- Es el metro más barato[11] del planeta porque sólo cuesta[12] US $0,20.
- La estación Pantitlán es la estación de transbordo[13] más grande del planeta.

[1]spend [2]using [3]discovered [4]mammoth [5]Every day [6]work [7]can [8]have fun [9]clean [10]safe [11]cheapest [12]costs [13]transfer

¿Qué recuerdas?

1. ¿Cómo es el metro de la Ciudad de México?
2. ¿Cómo identifican las estaciones del metro?
3. ¿Qué hay en la estación de metro Pino Suárez?
4. ¿Qué hay en la estación de metro Talismán?
5. ¿Cuántas personas toman el metro todos los días?

Algo personal

1. ¿Hay un sistema de metro en tu ciudad?
2. ¿Cuánto cuesta el transporte público en tu ciudad?
3. ¿Cómo son las estaciones (de metro o de bus) en tu ciudad?

- **Have you ever taken the subway? Describe your experience. How did it compare with the Mexican subway described in the article?**
- **Why do you think they built stations around the Aztec pyramid and the remains of the mammoth instead of transferring these discoveries to a museum? Is that a good idea?**

108 *ciento ocho* **Lección A**

The ***Estrategia*** section offers communicative strategies for learning. Included are pointers on topics such as how to be successful learning Spanish vocabulary and how to improve skills in reading, speaking, writing, and listening.

26 ¿Qué ves?

Go online EMCLanguages.net

Say what these people do, see or know, according to what you see in each illustration.

1. Gabriel y María

2. ellos

3. Mónica

4. Diego

5. los Montoya

6. la Sra. Ruiz

Comunicación

27 En El Charro

In groups of four, two students play the role of friends who are considering going to a popular restaurant in town, El Charro. The other two students should pretend they often go to eat at El Charro. Then, four of you meet on the street and discuss the restaurant (the restaurant's name, if it is new, where it is, etc.). Be sure to ask your friends what they eat when they go to El Charro. Then say what you are going to eat when you go there. Switch roles.

Estrategia

The importance of reviewing
Whenever you do an activity that requires you to be creative, look at previous activities, dialogs, readings, etc. for words, grammar and cultural information you have already learned that may be useful in the new activity (e.g., the word *nuevo* in activities 9 and 22, asking for or giving names in activities 27 and 28, the question-asking words for activities 27 and 28). This recombining of old and new content will help you remember what you learned. It will also help you express yourself naturally in ever more complex situations.

28 ¿Qué leen los estudiantes en la clase?

Survey your classmates to find out how many are reading a book right now. Next, find out the names of the books and how many students are reading each one. Finally, summarize your findings in a short paragraph.

Hay seis estudiantes que leen libros. Uno lee Marianela. Dos leen

Comunicación

10 En el Distrito Federal

As part of a summer study program, you have the opportunity to take classes at *la UNAM* and a classmate has prepared a list to help you find your way around the city. Answer the questions about places to go in the city.

1. ¿Cómo vas a ir a los museos de Chapultepec?
2. ¿Qué museo de arte está en Chapultepec?
3. ¿A qué museos vas a ir?
4. Tomas un taxi a la Calle 16 de Septiembre. ¿De qué plaza vas a estar cerca?
5. ¿Dónde está el restaurante con "mole fantástico"?
6. ¿Dónde está el Palacio de Bellas Artes? ¿Cómo vas a ir allí?
7. Quiero ir al Museo de Arte Moderno. ¿Sabes el número de teléfono del museo?

Adónde ir en el D.F.

Parque de Chapultepec (ir en metro):
- Museo Nacional de Antropología
- Museo Nacional de Historia (en el Castillo)
- Casa del Lago (parque de atracciones)
- Museo Tecnológico
- Museo de Arte Moderno (en Av. Reforma): 776-83-41
- Museo de Historia Natural

Otros lugares interesantes:
- Palacio de Bellas Artes (museo y teatro en el Centro Histórico)
— Está en la Alameda Central y la Avenida Juárez. (camiones Nº 16 ó 52) Información: 683-48-05

- El Zócalo (plaza central)
— Calle 16 de Septiembre (cerca de la Calle Seminario)

Restaurantes:
- La Bodega (¡Mole fantástico!)
Popocatépetl 25, Colonia Hipódromo Condesa, Zona Centro
Teléfono: 525-84-73

- SpaceNet Café
Calz. del Hueso 160 local 3-B Fuentes Plaza Ex Hacienda Coapa, Zona Sur
Teléfono: 567-35-52

11 Sus propios planes

Working in pairs, use the list from the previous activity to make your own plans for what you are going to do while in Mexico City.

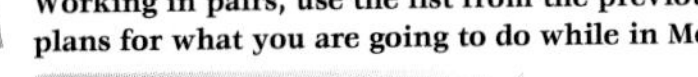

MODELO **A:** ¿Vamos a ir al Museo de Antropología?
B: Sí. Vamos a ir allí en taxi.

12 ¿Qué van a hacer mañana?

Talk with two classmates about going downtown tomorrow. Start by asking each other what you are going to do. Then ask where you are going to go, how you are going to get there, etc. Use a variety of expressions and as many new words as you can.

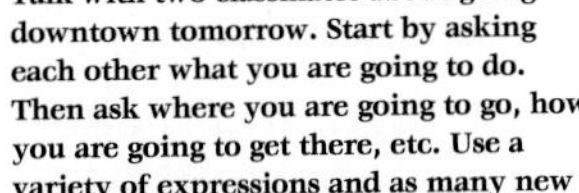

MODELO **A:** ¿Qué van a hacer mañana?
B: Voy a ir al centro.
C: ¿Cómo vas a ir?
B: Voy a ir en metro.

¡Oportunidades!

Se habla español en México y en tu ciudad
It is not always necessary to travel to Mexico or to go a great distance in order to use Spanish. In the United States, nearly every community offers opportunities to apply language skills you are learning this year. Many American cities have large Spanish-speaking populations, so you may find yourself using your new language skills in a restaurant, at a museum, in a store or while you are simply strolling along a city street. Knowing Spanish opens doors and offers opportunities you might otherwise never experience!

The ***Oportunidades*** section provides thoughtful insights about the advantages that students will have because they know Spanish and are familiar with the culture of the Spanish-speaking world. The section addresses issues such as careers, travel, college, and lifelong study in the field of languages and cultures.

The ***Lectura personal*** follows members of the fictional rock group *La Ola* as its members relate their experiences while touring the Spanish-speaking world.

Autoevaluación helps students assess what they have learned. Activity answers are available online

¿Qué aprendí? offers students an opportunity to reflect upon what they have learned in the lesson.

In the **EMCLanguages.net Center**, students can check the *autoevaluación* questions, complete additional *repaso* activities, and extend their learning with thematic Internet activities.

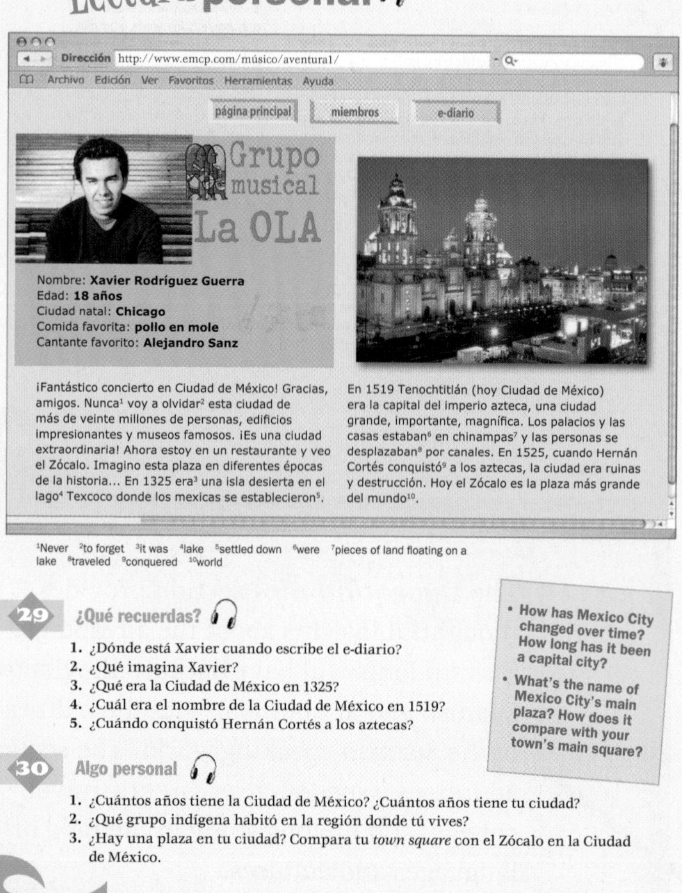

Lectura personal

Dirección http://www.emcp.com/músico/aventura1/

Archivo Edición Ver Favoritos Herramientas Ayuda

página principal | miembros | e-diario

Grupo musical La OLA

Nombre: **Xavier Rodríguez Guerra**
Edad: **18 años**
Ciudad natal: **Chicago**
Comida favorita: **pollo en mole**
Cantante favorito: **Alejandro Sanz**

¡Fantástico concierto en Ciudad de México! Gracias, amigos. Nunca[1] voy a olvidar[2] esta ciudad de más de veinte millones de personas, edificios impresionantes y museos famosos. ¡Es una ciudad extraordinaria! Ahora estoy en un restaurante y veo el Zócalo. Imagino esta plaza en diferentes épocas de la historia... En 1325 era[3] una isla desierta en el lago[4] Texcoco donde los mexicas se establecieron[5].

En 1519 Tenochtitlán (hoy Ciudad de México) era la capital del imperio azteca, una ciudad grande, importante, magnífica. Los palacios y las casas estaban[6] en chinampas[7] y las personas se desplazaban[8] por canales. En 1525, cuando Hernán Cortés conquistó[9] a los aztecas, la ciudad era ruinas y destrucción. Hoy el Zócalo es la plaza más grande del mundo[10].

[1]Never [2]to forget [3]it was [4]lake [5]settled down [6]were [7]pieces of land floating on a lake [8]traveled [9]conquered [10]world

29 ¿Qué recuerdas?

1. ¿Dónde está Xavier cuando escribe el e-diario?
2. ¿Qué imagina Xavier?
3. ¿Qué era la Ciudad de México en 1325?
4. ¿Cuál era el nombre de la Ciudad de México en 1519?
5. ¿Cuándo conquistó Hernán Cortés a los aztecas?

- How has Mexico City changed over time? How long has it been a capital city?
- What's the name of Mexico City's main plaza? How does it compare with your town's main square?

30 Algo personal

1. ¿Cuántos años tiene la Ciudad de México? ¿Cuántos años tiene tu ciudad?
2. ¿Qué grupo indígena habitó en la región donde tú vives?
3. ¿Hay una plaza en tu ciudad? Compara tu *town square* con el Zócalo en la Ciudad de México.

124 *ciento veinticuatro* **Lección B**

¿Qué aprendí?

Go online EMCLanguages.net

Autoevaluación

As a review and self-check, respond to the following:

1. Ask a friend what he or she is going to do today.
2. If you were in Mexico City, name some things you might see.
3. Tell a friend what you are going to do this week (go to school at 8:00 A.M. on Monday, study in the library on Tuesday, etc.).
4. What opportunities does knowing Spanish offer you?
5. Name four or five things you can order from a menu in Spanish.
6. Imagine you are driving around town. Name in Spanish two or three buildings you see.

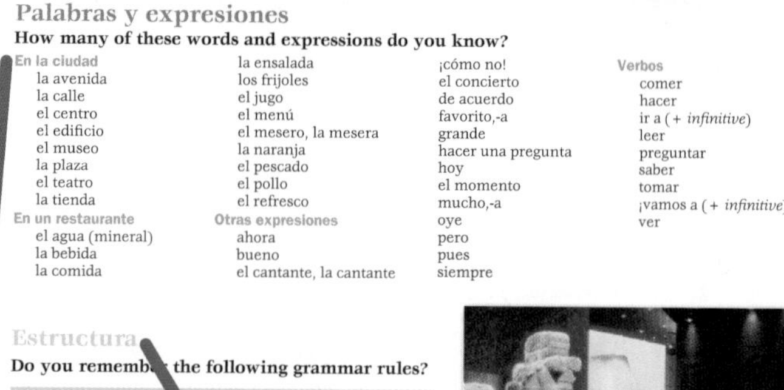

Palabras y expresiones

How many of these words and expressions do you know?

En la ciudad
la avenida
la calle
el centro
el edificio
el museo
la plaza
el teatro
la tienda

En un restaurante
el agua (mineral)
la bebida
la comida
la ensalada
los frijoles
el jugo
el menú
el mesero, la mesera
la naranja
el pescado
el pollo
el refresco

Otras expresiones
ahora
bueno
el cantante, la cantante
¡cómo no!
el concierto
de acuerdo
favorito,-a
grande
hacer una pregunta
hoy
el momento
mucho,-a
oye
pero
pues
siempre

Verbos
comer
hacer
ir a (+ *infinitive*)
leer
preguntar
saber
tomar
¡vamos a (+ *infinitive*)!
ver

Estructura

Do you remember the following grammar rules?

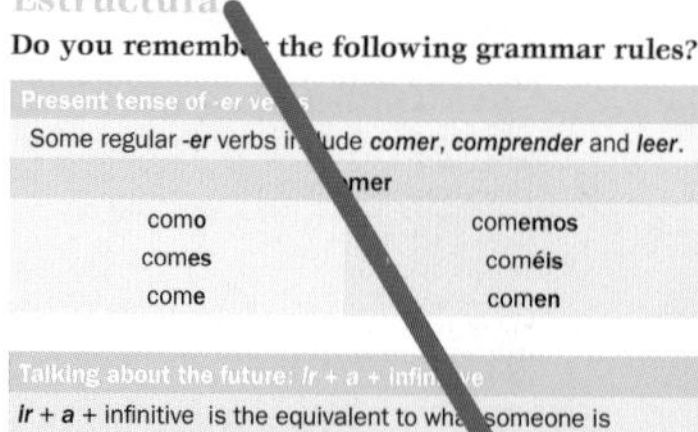

Present tense of -er verbs

Some regular **-er** verbs include ***comer, comprender*** and ***leer***.

comer	
como	comemos
comes	coméis
come	comen

Talking about the future: *Ir + a + infinitive*

Ir + *a* + infinitive is the equivalent to what someone is "going" to do in the near future.
Voy a ir a la fiesta. **I am going to go to the party.**

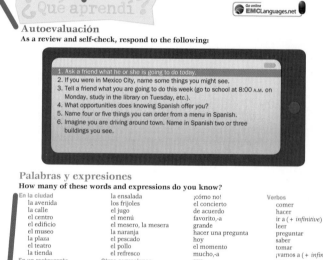

Museo de Antropología.

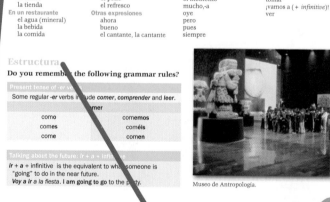

Capítulo 3 *ciento veinticinco* 125

Estructura provides a brief review of grammar concepts introduced in the lesson.

Palabras y expresiones includes active vocabulary from the lesson.

Tú lees contains a reading that is followed by two activities: comprehension-based and personalized.

The end-of-the-chapter section ***¡Viento en popa!*** (Full speed ahead! Literally, "Wind to the stern") helps students increase reading proficiency.

Tú lees

Conexión con otras disciplinas: arte

Estrategia

Anticipating special vocabulary It will be easier for you to read and understand specialized subject matter if you try anticipating some of the words and expressions you may encounter. Identifying specialized vocabulary beforehand will help you zero in on what a writer is saying since your mind will already be thinking about the topic. For example, in this reading you will learn about the famous Mexican artist Frida Kahlo. What words would you anticipate might appear in the reading?

Preparación

Selecciona las palabras de la columna I que van con las palabras en inglés de la columna II.

I	II
1. un estilo	A. a painting
2. un autorretrato	B. a style
3. una pintora	C. a painter, artist
4. un tema	D. a self-portrait
5. un cuadro/ una pintura	E. a theme

Frida Kahlo, una artista universal

Frida Kahlo es una de las pintoras más importantes de México. Como[1] su esposo[2], Diego Rivera, ella comprendió[3] el impacto social de combinar el arte y la política, pero sus temas son más universales. Por ejemplo[4], ella trató[5] los aspectos negativos de la industrialización como la contaminación del aire y de la naturaleza[6]. Otros temas que trató son los problemas de la vida[7]. Frida siempre tuvo[8] problemas físicos. De muchacha, ella tuvo polio. A los dieciocho años, tuvo un accidente terrible de tráfico en la Ciudad de México. Después[9] del accidente, sufrió mucho dolor[10] porque tuvo muchas operaciones. Frida muestra[11] su dolor en muchas de sus pinturas.

La pintora Frida Kahlo en 1931.

Un tema que Frida y Diego tienen en común es el orgullo[12] de la cultura indígena[13] de México. Frida tenía raíces[14] indígenas y adoptó el estilo de la ropa y del pelo[15] de una india para expresar su orgullo indígena. Además[16], sus autorretratos representan la cultura indígena mediante el uso de[17] plantas, animales y colores de la naturaleza.

[1]As, Like [2]her husband [3]understood [4]For example [5]dealt with [6]nature [7]life [8]had [9]After [10]pain [11]shows [12]pride [13]native [14]roots [15]hair [16]In addition [17]by means of

Autorretrato con mono (Self-Portrait with Monkey), Frida Kahlo, 1938. Albright-Knox Art Gallery, Buffalo, N.Y.

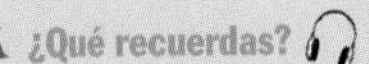

A ¿Qué recuerdas?

1. ¿Qué comprendió Frida Kahlo?
2. ¿Cuáles son los temas de los cuadros de Frida?
3. ¿Por qué sufrió Frida mucho dolor?
4. ¿Qué representa Frida en su autorretrato?

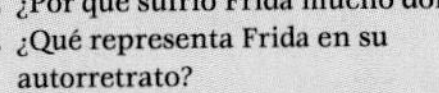

B Algo personal

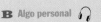

1. ¿Es importante el arte de Frida Kahlo? ¿Por qué?
2. ¿Cuál te gusta más, la foto de Frida Kahlo o su autorretrato? ¿Por qué?

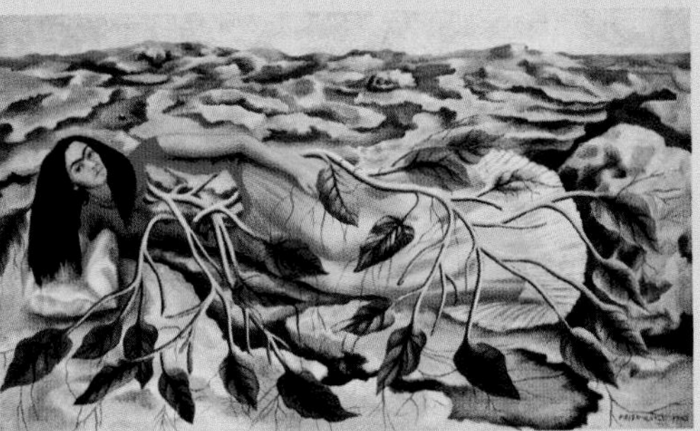

Raíces (Roots), Frida Kahlo, 1943. Private collection.

Tú escribes contains a writing strategy that encourages students to apply what they learned in the chapter.

Proyectos adicionales presents additional opportunities to synthesize knowledge through technology projects and cooperative learning activities that address the National Standards. Students work individually, in pairs, or in small groups.

Tú escribes

Estrategia

Combining images to build word pictures

Poems make pictures out of your words that can be seen by the mind's eye. They can be about any theme and can appear in any form. For example, a stair poem permits you to build up ideas one on another following a stair pattern. Just as the Aztecs built their pyramids layer upon layer, you can construct a poem in the shape of stairs using your knowledge of Spanish, following these steps:

Step 1: State the main idea (usually composed of just one word).

Step 2: List two or three words that describe the topic. (Use adjectives or nouns.)

Step 3: Name a place or time connected with the topic.

Step 4: Summarize the main idea with a phrase that expresses your feelings about the topic.

Write a stair poem about any topic you choose, such as school, a class, a city, a person, etc. Follow the "steps" to build your poem. When you finish constructing your stair poem, add artwork or graphics to make it visually appealing.

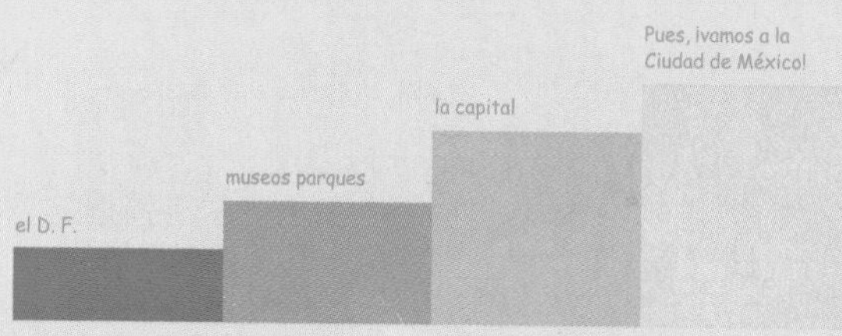

Proyectos adicionales

Go online EMCLanguages.net

A Conexión con la tecnología

In pairs or in small groups, search the Internet and complete one of the following activities:

1. Find a restaurant in Mexico City. Then, write down the name, say where the restaurant is, describe the menu selection and prices, etc.
2. Research Mexican food and then describe a dish that sounds good to you. Try to name the ingredients, say what the food looks like, discuss how it is prepared and tell what state/region of Mexico the dish is from.
3. Find a map of Mexico City and locate major landmarks *(el Zócalo, el Palacio Nacional, la Catedral, el Palacio de Bellas Artes, la Zona Rosa, el parque de Chapultepec, etc.)*. Say what each site offers that makes it special.

www

B Conexión con otras disciplinas: matemáticas

You are going out to dine at the *Restaurante Danubio* in Mexico City. Choose what you would like to eat. Then calculate the total price of the food items you ordered, add 7 percent in taxes, 10 percent in tips and convert the total amount from pesos into U.S. dollars. Obtain the current exchange rate from the Internet or from a newspaper.

Restaurante Danubio
Cocina Internacional

Ensaladas	
Ensalada mixta	44 pesos
Ensalada especial Danubio	61 pesos
Para comer	
Mojarra	95 pesos
Calamares	99 pesos
Ostras	92 pesos
Filete con champiñones	98 pesos
Filete a la parrilla	92 pesos
Pollo frito	44 pesos
Pollo a la cacerola	53 pesos
Bebidas	
Refrescos	16 pesos
Jugo de naranja	13 pesos
Limonada	12 pesos

C Conexión con otras disciplinas: historia

Prepare a tourist guide for Mexico City. Include information about history, the main tourist attractions, museums, places to shop, places to eat and transportation in the city. Be sure to use photos or illustrations to illustrate your guide.

The ***Repaso*** checklist allows students to evaluate their progress with the objectives presented at the beginning of the chapter.

Trabalenguas presents a fun tongue twister challenge.

This Spanish-English ***Vocabulario*** contains the active vocabulary for the chapter and is a useful reference tool.

REPASO

Now that I have completed this chapter, I can...	Go to these pages for help:
talk about places in a city.	90
make introductions and express courtesy.	94
ask and answer questions.	97
discuss how to go somewhere.	100
say some things people do.	100
say where someone is going.	110
talk about the future.	114
order food and beverages.	116
I can also...	
identify some things to do in Mexico.	93
state personal benefits to learning Spanish.	115
use pause words in conversation.	118
talk about food and drink in Mexico.	119
recognize the importance of review.	123
read in Spanish about Mexican artists.	126
write a simple poem in Spanish.	128

Trabalenguas

Erre con erre pizarra, erre con erre barril.
Rápido corren los carros, los carros del ferrocarril.

Resolviendo el misterio

After watching Episode 3 of *El cuarto misterioso*, answer the following questions.

1. What did José discover about Francisco and Ana?
2. Do José and Francisco gain entrance to the secret room? Why or why not?
3. What will José and Francisco serve Ana and Conchita for lunch?

Vocabulario

Go online EMCLanguages.net

a **caballo** on horseback *3A*
a pie on foot *3A*
¿adónde? (to) where? *3A*
el **agua (mineral)** (mineral) water *3B*
ahora now *3B*
al to the *3A*
el **autobús** bus *3A*
la **avenida** avenue *3B*
el **avión** airplane *3A*
el **banco** bank *3A*
el **barco** boat, ship *3A*
la **bebida** drink *3B*
la **biblioteca** library *3A*
la **bicicleta** bicycle *3A*
bueno well, okay *3B*
el **caballo** horse *3A*
la **calle** street *3B*
caminar to walk *3A*
el **camión** truck *3A*
el **cantante,** la **cantante** singer *3B*
el **carro** car *3A*
el **centro** downtown, center *3B*
cerca (de) near *3A*
el **cine** movie theater *3A*
la **ciudad** city *3A*
¡claro! of course! *3A*
comer to eat *3B*
la **comida** food *3B*
¡cómo no! of course! *3B*
el **concierto** concert *3B*
¿cuándo? when? *3A*
de acuerdo agreed, okay *3B*
del of the, from the *3A*
el **dentista,** la **dentista** dentist *3A*
el **edificio** building *3B*
El gusto es mío. The pleasure is mine. *3A*
en *(means of transportation)* by *3A*
en carro by car *3A*
encantado,-a delighted, the pleasure is mine 3A
la **ensalada** salad *3B*
la **escuela** school *3A*
fantástico,-a fantastic, great *3A*
favorito,-a favorite *3B*
la **fiesta** party *3A*
los **frijoles** beans *3B*
grande big *3B*
hacer to do, to make *3B*
hacer una pregunta to ask a question *3B*
el **hotel** hotel *3A*
hoy today *3B*
ir to go *3A*
ir a *(+ infinitive)* to be going to (do something) *3B*
el **jugo** juice *3B*
le/les/te presento a let me introduce you to *3A*
leer to read *3B*
lejos (de) far (from) *3A*
el **médico, la médica** doctor *3A*
el **menú** menu *3B*
el **mesero, la mesera** food server *3B*
el **metro** subway *3A*
el **momento** moment *3B*
la **moto(cicleta)** motorcycle *3A*
el **museo** museum *3B*
la **naranja** orange *3B*
la **oficina** office *3A*
oye hey, listen *3B*
el **parque** park *3A*
para for, to, in order to *3A*
pero but *3B*
el **pescado** fish *3B*
la **plaza** plaza, public square *3B*
el **pollo** chicken *3B*
¿por qué? why? *3A*
porque because *3A*
preguntar to ask *3B*
el **problema** problem *3A*
pues thus, well, so, then (pause in speech) *3B*
¿quiénes? who? (pl.) *3A*
quiero I want, I love *3A*
el **refresco** soft drink, refreshment *3B*
el **restaurante** restaurant *3A*
saber to know *3B*
sabes you know *3A*
siempre always *3B*
simpático,-a nice, pleasant *3A*
también also, too *3A*
Tanto gusto. So glad to meet you. *3A*
el **taxi** taxi *3A*
el **teatro** theater *3B*
la **tienda** store *3B*
tomar to take; to drink; to have *3B*
el **transporte** transportation *3A*
el **tren** train *3A*
¡vamos a *(+ infinitive)*! let's *(+ infinitive) 3B*
¡vamos! let's go! *3A*
ver to see; to watch *3B*
¿verdad? right? *3A*

Cómo viajar
por México
gastando menos

The ***Resolviendo el misterio*** section asks students to recall the story line of *El cuarto misterioso*.

Planning and Pacing

Teaching Notes and Tips

- The authors recommend that you complete the first nine chapters of the book in order to prepare students to use *¡Aventura! 2* at the beginning of the next school year. Chapter 10 does not present any new vocabulary or grammar, but it does contain valuable recycled content.
- Don't do every exercise on every page. Gauge how easily students grasp a topic and what interests them.
- Expose students to vocabulary, grammar and culture every day.
- Challenge students to listen to, speak, read and write Spanish every day.
- Provide more or less practice on a specific topic according to the mastery level of your students.
- At the beginning of each daily lesson, review what you did the day before.
- At the end of each daily lesson, review what learning was accomplished during class.
- Always prepare an activity for students to complete after they have finished a test or quiz.
- Use the *¡Aventura!* electronic supplements to bring the Spanish-speaking world into your classroom daily.
- Assign small amounts of homework often. (Requiring students to practice independently what they learned in class will help them retain information.)
- Warm-up your students each day with a homework check or a review of the previous day's activities.
- The Electronic Lesson Planner will help you organize your teaching calendar.

Traditional Schedule (50-minute classes)

9 essential *¡Aventura!* chapters
× 19 days per chapter

+ 9 flexible days (expansion, Chapter 10, projects, the unexpected)

---

180 days of instruction

Block Schedule (90-minute classes)

9 essential *¡Aventura!* chapters
× 9 blocks per chapter

+ 9 flexible blocks (expansion, Chapter 10, projects, the unexpected)

---

90 blocks of instruction

¡Aventura! **allows you to focus on your instructional goals with a flexible and fun program.**

Sample Chapter Lesson Plan

The chart that follows illustrates how to pace one chapter of *¡Aventura!* All chapters contain the same instructional components. Based on Chapter 3, this chapter lesson plan can be applied to all chapters.

Traditional Schedule (50 minutes)	Block Schedule (90 minutes)	Page(s)	Chapter Content	Practice, Review and Recycle
Day 1	Day 1	88-89 90-91	Chapter Opener *El cuarto misterioso* *Vocabulario I*	
Day 2		92-93	*Diálogo I* and *Cultura viva I*	Review *Vocabulario I* with transparencies or flash cards.
Day 3	Day 2	94-96	*Estructura*	
Day 4		97-99	*Estructura*	Review *Vocabulario I* and *Estructura*.
Day 5	Day 3	100-1 102	*Vocabulario II* *Diálogo II*	Review *Estructura*.
Day 6	Day 4	103 104-5	*Cultura viva II* *Estructura*	Review *Vocabulario II* with transparencies or flash cards.
Day 7		106-7	*Estructura*	Review *Cultura viva II*.
Day 8		108-9 109	*Lectura cultural* *¿Qué aprendí?*	Review *Estructura*. Review *Vocabulario*.
Day 9	Day 5	110-1	*Lección A quiz* *Begin Lección B* *Vocabulario I*	Review for quiz.
Day 10		112 113	*Diálogo I* *Cultura viva I*	Check quiz. Review *Vocabulario*.
Day 11	Day 6	114-5 116-7	*Estructura* *Vocabulario II*	Review *Estructura* and *Cultura viva I*.
Day 12		118 119	*Diálogo II* *Cultura viva II*	Review *Vocabulario*.
Day 13		120-1	*Estructura*	Review *Vocabulario* and *Estructura*.
Day 14	Day 7	122-3	*Estructura* Review for Quiz B	Review *Vocabulario* and *Estructura*.
Day 15		 124 125	Quiz B *Lectura personal* *¿Qué aprendí?*	Integrate all content.
Day 16	Day 8	 126-27	*¡Viento en popa!* *Tú lees*	Integrate all content.
Day 17		128 129	*Tú escribes* *Proyectos adicionales*	Prepare review actitivities using leftover ancillary activities.
Day 18		130-1	Repaso Resolviendo el misterio	Have students correct review activities.
Day 19	Day 9		Chapter Test	After test, ask students to explore upcoming chapter objectives and *Vocabulario* words.

First Day of School Activities

The first day of school is always an exciting and challenging time! We have included a few useful and interesting tools to help you and your students enter into the new academic year.

- **So many faces, so many names.** Take pictures of your students. If you take digital images, you can put them in a PowerPoint presentation. Use the PowerPoint to review names. Later in the week you can use the PowerPoint to give a name quiz. Students will be tested on the names of their classmates.
- **Let the crying begin?** Maybe this is the thought on the minds of some of your students. Pass around a role of toilet paper. Tell students to take as much as they think that they will need. For each piece of toilet paper they have, they must tell the class something about themselves.
- **Set the record straight!** Instead of telling the students what the rules and procedures of the classroom are, have them do it! Have the students number off into groups of four or five. Tell them that "Respect" is the number one rule of the class, and have each group define the word "respect." Then give the groups time to come up with a list of five classroom rules by answering the following questions: What do you need in our class to be successful? What kind of rules do you want in our classroom? The teacher can also ask open-ended questions to groups as they are brainstorming such as: Can you turn in late homework? If so, what is the limit for late homework? Should you raise your hand to be called on? After students have created their rules, have one representative from each group read their definition of "respect," then have another representative read their rules. The teacher should write the defnninitions and rules on the board for everyone to see. In the end, have a large group discussion to consolidate the rules, reject the ones that are inappropriate or that the class doesn't agree with, then create a final statement. It should read:

  "Respect is our number one rule. In order to practice respect I will: *(insert the class' definition of respect*). In order for me to be successful in my Spanish class I will be respectful, (*insert the class' rules*)."

  Ask the class if the statement accurately reflects the brainstorming work and list they created. Once it's approved, go over the class procedures for such things as where to hand in homework, how to ask for the bathroom pass, borrowing pencils/pens, etc. (The teacher can also incorporate these topics into the class rules discussion, if desired, by asking the students what they think is reasonable for each point during the brainstorming session). For the next class period, print out individual copies of the class rules as they were created by the students, in addition to the classroom procedures for the students to sign and bring home for parent signatures. The teacher can also hand-write the rules contract with the class' period number on an oversized piece of paper or poster board and have it ready the next day for all students to sign. Then post it in the classroom wall for the duration of the school year to remind the students that they all agreed to abide by the rules *they* created.
- **Create your own classroom CSI.** Each student must tell two truths and a lie. Students must guess which statements are true and which statement is a lie. The last student standing wins.
- **Happiness runs in circular motion!** Have students say their first names and something else that starts with the same letter. Each student must repeat the names that were said previously before they add their names. This activity has a lot of repetition that can help students learn something about all of their classmates.

Additional Tips for the Upper Levels

- **Step it up!** The previous activities can be altered for the more advanced levels by having the students participate with their classmates in the target language.
- **Let the cat out of the bag!** Students must bring a paper bag to class that contains at least three items that are important to them. They will explain the importance of each item to the class in the target language.
- **If you could, would you...?** Each student is given a card with an "If.../then..." situation. They must complete the situations in the target language and share them with the class.

Organizing Pairs and Groups for Games and Activities

Providing opportunities for students to work cooperatively with others is important in the language classroom. When students work together with classmates of varying abilities and personalities, they enhance their classroom experience by creating a community of learners, challenging their comfort levels and language skills and having fun in the meantime.

Match 'em up quickly

Sometimes, students struggle sitting in the same spot for an entire class period. Getting them up and moving will refresh their minds while motivating them to use the target language.

Cut index cards in half and put them in pairs, based on the number of students you have in your largest class. At the beginning of class, count how many students are present. Create that many pairs of cards and distribute them. Students should circulate around the room asking questions in Spanish to find their partners.

They should quickly find two desks together and sit down. Offer a prize to the first pair. The noise level may rise momentarily. Once students get in the habit of finding partners, they will move more quickly and efficiently. Collect the cards in pairs once the activity has begun. Circulate around the room after giving instructions. Use odd-numbered students to help you monitor the pairs or make a group of three. Possible partner-finding questions: *¿Quién está ____?* or *¿Quién tiene_____?* Or *¿Quién es mi compañero? Tengo ______.*

1. Use stickers or photos of vocabulary that students need to know. Students match picture to picture, or picture to Spanish (for example, J with J, or J with *contenta*).
2. Use countries and their capitals (for example, Tegucigalpa with Honduras or Lima with Peru).
3. Use opposites (for example, *alto* with *bajo* or *contento* with *triste*).
4. Use numerals and numbers spelled out (for example, *un mil* with *1,000* or *ochenta y ocho* with *88*).

A Month's Worth of Partners

Get students up and moving while they schedule partners for several weeks. Students refer to their organizational partner sheet for a few weeks at a time.

Partner of the day. Students receive an index card on which they write the days of the week down the left-hand side starting with *el domingo.* Students find partners for each day of the week, asking *¿Quieres bailar conmigo el lunes? ¿Tienes planes el martes? ¿Estás libre el miércoles?* (To utilize non-school days, the teacher announces that students should use their Saturday and Sunday partners and pretend that it's already the weekend.)

12 meetings. The teacher distributes a clock face. Students set up meetings at every hour of the day. Possible questions: *¿Estás ocupado/a a la una? Estoy libre a las 4. ¿Te gustaría reuinirte?*

Traveling the world. The teacher distributes a map of Central America. Students set up meeting locations with their partners. For example, *¿Te gustaría ir a Tegucigalpa? ¿Quieres visitar la capital de Nicaragua conmigo?*

Inner/outer circles. Get students up and moving with this fast-paced question and answer activity. Create 10-15 open- or closed-ended questions for students to answer. Have students find a partner. Partners should face each other, one member in the inside circle, the other partner in the outside circle. The teacher asks a question and gives 30 seconds for each partner to answer. Students refrain from talking after they are finished answering or until the teacher cues for silence. The teacher directs the outer circle to move one person to the right while the inner circle remains in place. The teacher asks a new question, each student answers his/her new partner, and the outer circle rotates one student to the right while the inner circle remains in the same place. Once students get used to the circles, they move into formation quickly. They also become accustomed to listening for the teacher silence cue and the next question. Mix it up by directing the inner circle to move one person to the left.

Names and Expressions

Spanish Names

When students choose a Spanish name for Spanish class, your classroom can provide a more authentic forum for lively communication.

Muchachos

Adán	David	Gustavo	Leonardo	Pepe
Agustín	Diego	Homero	Lorenzo	Rafael
Alberto	Eduardo	Horacio	Luis	Ramón
Alejandro	Emilio	Humberto	Manuel	Raúl
Alfonso	Enrique	Hugo	Marcos	Ricardo
Andrés	Eugenio	Ignacio	Mario	Roberto
Angel	Federico	Isidro	Martín	Rodrigo
Antonio	Felipe	Jaime	Miguel	Rubén
Armando	Fernando	Javier	Nicolás	Samuel
Arturo	Franco	Jesús	Norberto	Santiago
Benito	Francisco	Jorge	Oscar	Sergio
Benjamín	Gabriel	José	Pablo	Timoteo
Carlos	Gerardo	Juan	Paco	Tomás
César	Gilberto	Joaquín	Pancho	Vicente
Daniel	Guillermo	Julio	Pedro	Victor

Muchachas

Alana	Clara	Graciela	Margarita	Raquel
Alejandra	Claudia	Guadalupe	María	Rebeca
Alicia	Cristina	Inés	Mariana	Rita
Amalia	Diana	Irene	Marisol	Rosa
Ana	Dolores	Isabel	Marta	Sandra
Angela	Elena	Jimena	Mercedes	Sara
Beatriz	Elisa	Josefina	Mónica	Selena
Camila	Emilia	Juana	Natalia	Shakira
Carmen	Enriqueta	Julieta	Olivia	Silvia
Carlota	Esperanza	Laura	Paloma	Sofía
Carolina	Eulalia	Lourdes	Paquita	Soledad
Casandra	Eva	Lucía	Patricia	Susana
Catalina	Florencia	Luisa	Paulina	Verónica
Cecilia	Francisca	Luz	Paz	Victoria
Chavela	Gabriela	Magdalena	Pilar	Yolanda

Classroom Expressions

Tips

- Beginning on the first day of class, speak Spanish as much as possible. Use gestures and act out expressions to convey meaning so that you and your students avoid overusing English. It can be challenging at first, but your students will follow your lead as you strive to use Spanish as the primary means of communication.
- Encourage students to respond to directions and give answers in Spanish. Encourage them to use only Spanish with you and with their classmates.
- Point out that the more students use Spanish, the more natural it will become as a means of communication.

Student Survival

Estuve ausente.	I was absent.
Necesito ayuda.	I need help.
No comprendo/entiendo.	I don't understand.
No recuerdo.	I don't remember.
No sé.	I don't know.
No tengo la tarea.	I don't have the homework.
Necesito...	I need...
un lápiz.	a pencil.
un bolígrafo.	a pen.
el papel.	A piece of paper.
la tarea.	the homework assignment.
Necesito ir al enfermero/a.	I need to go to the nurse.
Necesito ver a mi consejero/a.	I need to see my counselor.
¿Puedo usar el teléfono?	May I use the telephone?
¿Puedo ir al baño?	May I go to the restroom?
¿Puedo ir a mi depósito de libros?	May I go to my locker?
Se me olvidó.	I forgot. (Literally, it forgot me.)
Tengo una pregunta.	I have a question.

Gentle Reminders

Continúa/Sigue (Continúen Uds./Sigan Uds.).	Continue.
Piensa (Piensen Uds.).	Think.
Presta (Presten Uds.) atención a...	Pay attention to...
Recuerda (Recuerden Uds.).	Remember.
Trata (Traten Uds.).	Try.

Listening and Speaking

¿Alguien?	Anyone?
Contesta/Responde (Contesten Uds./Responden Uds.).	Answer.
Cuenta (Cuenten Uds.)...	Tell (a story)...
Dime (Díganme Uds.)...	Tell me...
Escucha (Escuchen Uds.).	Listen.
Habla (Hablen Uds.) en español.	Speak Spanish.
Lee (Lean Uds.)...en voz alta.	Read...aloud.
Levanta (Levanten Uds.) la mano (para contestar).	Raise your hand (to answer).
Oye (Oigan Uds.).	Listen.
Más alto/bajo.	Louder. / Softer.
Pronuncia (Pronuncien Uds.)...	Pronounce...
Repite (Repitan Uds.).	Repeat.
Silencio.	Silence.
Otra vez.	Again.
Todos juntos.	Everyone together.

Moving and Doing

Abre (Abran Uds.) el libro/cuaderno en la página...	Open your book/workbook to page...
Apunta/Señala (Apunten Uds./Señalen Uds.)...	Point at...
Borra (Borren Uds.) la pizarra.	Erase the board.
Cierra (Cierren Uds.) el libro/cuaderno.	Close your book/workbook.
Copia (Copien Uds.)...	Copy...
Da (Den Uds.) la vuelta.	Turn around.
Dibuja (Dibujen Uds.)...	Draw...
Levántate (Levántense Uds.).	Stand up.
Llévate (Llévense Uds.)...	Carry/bring...
Pasa (Pasen Uds.) a la pizarra.	Go to the board.
Pon (Pongan Uds.)...	Put...
Quita (Quiten Uds.) todo de encima de sus pupitres.	Clear your desks.
Recoge (Recojan Uds.)...	Pick up...
Saca (Saquen Uds.) una hoja de papel/un bolígrafo/ un lápiz.	Take out a piece of paper/pen/pencil.
Siéntate (Siéntense Uds.).	Sit down.
Toca (Toquen Uds.)...	Touch...
Trae (Traigan Uds.)...	Bring...
Ve (Vayan Uds.) a...	Go...
Ven (Vengan Uds.) aquí.	Come here.

These expressions will help you and your students communicate in Spanish.

Activity Directions

Empieza (Empiecen Uds.) ahora.	Begin now...
Entrégame (Entréguenme Uds.) la tarea.	Turn in the homework.
Escoge (Escojan Uds.)...	Choose...
Escribe (Escriban Uds.)...	Write...
Escribe (Escriban Uds.) a máquina...	Type...
Estudia (Estudien Uds.)...	Study...
Inserta (Inserten Uds.) el CD en la computadora.	Insert the CD in the computer.
Mira (Miren Uds.)...	Look...
Para mañana...	For tomorrow...
Revisa (Revisen Uds.)...	Check over...

Pair and Group Work

Formen Uds. grupos de...	Form groups of... (# of students)
Para (Paren Uds.).	Stop.
Trabajen Uds. en parejas en...	Work in groups of... (# of students)

Inquiry

¿Cómo se dice...(en español)?	How do you say...in Spanish?
¿Cómo se escribe...?	How do you spell...?
¿Hay preguntas?	Are there any questions?
¿Qué quiere decir...?	What does...mean?
¿Quién sabe (la respuesta)?	Who knows (the answer)?

Praise

Bien hecho.	Well done.
Fabuloso.	Fabulous.
Muy bien.	Very good.
Excelente.	Excellent.

Classroom Fun for Pairs and Groups

Having fun is a key component to a student's language learning experience.

Games

Use these games and activities to promote active communication and make Spanish class the highlight of every student's day.

Battleship

This game makes verb conjugation fun and competitive.

Create a worksheet with two identical 12 x 6 grids and three types of boats. In the left hand column of the grid make a list of twelve verbs, across the top label the boxes *yo, tú, él/ella/Ud., nosotros, vosotros, ellos/ellas/Uds.* The top grid is the student's game board where they will place their boats. The bottom grid is where each student will keep track of the other player's board. Students should place boats on the grid to highlight three conjugated verbs. To find boats, students need to conjugate the verb from the left hand column in any form from the top row. *Yo oigo*. If the student has placed their ship in this location, it is a hit. If not, it is a miss. Students will continue playing until one player's ships have all been hit.

Concentration

This game can be used for practicing numbers or for reviewing or practicing verbs.

The same rhythm is maintained: students tap the tops of their desks twice, clap their hands twice and snap their fingers twice. Words may be called out only during the snapping of fingers. For verb practice, for example, the first student in each row gives an infinitive *(hablar)* on the first snapping of fingers, the next student gives a subject pronoun *(tú)* on the second, and the third student must respond with the appropriate answer *(tú hablas)* on the third snapping of fingers. Students who make an error move to the end of the row and the other students move up. Try to have an uneven number of students in each row so that every student will have an opportunity to match the subject pronoun and verb ending. All the students in each row monitor each other for errors. You may also have the entire class participate rather than play the game by rows. In this case, you may want to point to students for a verb infinitive, subject pronoun, and response.

Caramba

This game reinforces correct verb conjugation and encourages peer editing.

Create a list of infinitives with subjects and the word *Caramba* five times. Print the sheet, cut it into pieces and place the pieces in an envelope. Have students form groups and give each group an envelope. Have students take turns pulling out a verb to conjugate. If they conjugate the verb correctly, they get to keep the paper and earn one point. If they do not conjugate the verb correctly, they do not get a point and they should put the paper back in the envelope. If students pull out the word *Caramba*, they lose all of their points. Encourage students to self-correct or correct each other while playing *Caramba*.

El detective

This game may be played with a number of different objectives, for example, to help students get to know one another, to practice specific vocabulary or to practice different verb tenses.

Make a number of lists with five to ten different items on each list. If the object is for students to get to know each other, include items such as *le gusta el fútbol, el béisbol* (a different sport on each list); *come pollo, ensalada, hamburguesas* (a different food on each list); *mañana va a la playa, al concierto, al cine* (a different place on each list). Include an unusual category to make the activity more interesting. Copy the lists to equal the number of students you have, so that each member of a group has the same list and different groups have different lists. *El detective* must fill in his or her list by asking fellow students if certain categories apply to them, and if so, they sign the appropriate list beside the category. Students will practice the *tú* form while asking classmates questions *(¿Juegas al fútbol?)*. Have them follow up by using the third-person singular to report their findings to the class after all students have completed the activity.

Dice Game

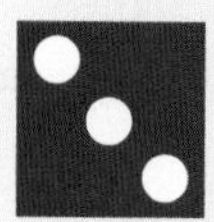

This game helps students conjugate verbs in any tense the teacher would like to practice.

Put students in small groups and provide each group with a pair of dice. One die should be red and the other green. Create an overhead with two columns. The first column should be a list of six subjects in the color red (1. *yo*, 2. *tú*, 3. *ella*, 4. *nosotros*, 5. *vosotros*, 6. *ellos*). The second column in green is a list of 6 verbs (1. *ir*, 2. *buscar*, 3. *traer*, 4. *andar*, 5. *preferir*, 6. *contar*). Each group should take turns rolling the dice and conjugating the verbs aloud according to the numbers that they roll, The red die is the subject of the verb and the green die is the verb that needs to be conjugated. If the students conjugate the verb correctly, they will receive points from each roll. If you roll a two and a three, you would receive five points for a correct answer. Encourage students to self-correct or correct each other while playing the dice game.

Dibujos

This game is designed to review vocabulary while allowing students to use their artistic abilities.

The class is split into teams. Give one member of each group a word or phrase. The team member with the word or phrase then draws clues for his or her team members. Each team has one minute to guess the word or phrase from the drawn clues. Award points to the fastest team and continue with different vocabulary and artists until a team reaches a point total determined in advance.

¿Dónde está?

This game practices directional vocabulary and commands.

Choose a small object such as a piece of chalk, show it to the students and ask them to hide it somewhere in the room. Go out of the room for a few minutes while they hide the item. When you return, they will help you find it by giving you directional commands or indicating direction *(Doble a la derecha, está cerca, mire al suelo*, etc.*)*. Next, divide the class into groups of four or five, choose one person from each group to leave the room and then repeat the game, this time with familiar commands.

Hot Potato

This simple game will help beginning students gain confidence in speaking, because it occupies students with a physical activity while they are conversing in Spanish, thus reducing their inhibitions about making an error.

Students stand in a circle in the classroom. One student, who is holding a soft rubber ball, asks a question and then gently tosses the ball to the second student, who must answer the question. Allow students 10 to 15 seconds to answer each question. The student who catches the ball and answers a question then asks a question and passes the ball to another student, and so on. If a student misses a question, he or she must sit down. The last person standing wins the game.

Jeopardy

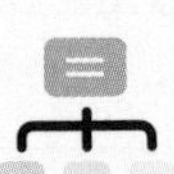

This game is especially good as a general review before an exam, but it can be used at almost any time in many different ways. Similar to the television game show, it involves writing a series of categories horizontally on the board.

Write the numbers 10 through 50 by tens under each category. Prepare questions in advance. Unlike the television game show, students need not respond with a question. Categories may be completions, synonyms or antonyms, translations, direct questions, matching and so forth. Divide the class into three or four teams and tell students that each person on the team must make a buzzer sound to indicate that he/she is able to answer. (You may wish to use an actual buzzer.)

To determine which team will go first, ask a question that may be answered by any student. The first student who sounds the buzzer gets a chance to answer. The team that correctly answers the opening question has the opportunity to choose a category and a dollar amount. Read the question, allowing that team to respond within a time limit (10 or 15 seconds). If not answered within the specified time limit, the question is open to the entire class, but buzzers must be used; students should not randomly blurt out answers.

Prepare several *Daily Double* questions as well. Use these when enthusiasm for the game wanes. Whatever the dollar amount in the chosen category, double it. These questions may be answered by any team, not just the team that chose the category.

When a question is answered correctly, write the answer in the space left by the erased dollar amount as you keep score. This will provide students with visual reinforcement of the material. When the entire board is filled with answers, total the scores. You may wish to offer prizes as an incentive.

El mensaje

This activity is useful for reviewing vocabulary and reinforces listening, writing, reading and speaking skills.

In advance, provide students with a list of the names of all students in class. The list can be in alphabetical or random order. As you hand out the list of names, inform students that they will be leaving phone messages with one another in Spanish and should hold on to this phone list to know whom to call with messages. Then, on a day when you would like to review vocabulary (or just to vary the routine), start several phone calls by whispering to several students a word or expression in Spanish that they must write down and then whisper to the next student on the list. Give students a set time when you will be collecting all phone messages (five minutes, for example). Compare what the final person wrote down with the "phone message" you whispered to the first person for each vocabulary word or expression.

Spelling Bee

This game is a fun way to practice the spelling of Spanish words, including accent marks.

To play Spelling Bee, place desks in rows. Encourage students to have paper and pecils on their desks. The students in the row cannot communicate with each other during the activity. Call out a word in Spanish that the row must spell (for example, *decir*). Have the first person in the row say the first letter "d," the second person "e," until the row has spelled the word correctly. If the row does not spell the word correctly, go to the next row and start the word over with the first person. Encourage students to write the letters that they have heard. Remind students they must include appropriate accents for the letter to be correct.

Stop the Clock

This fast-paced game helps student review vocabulary by quickly recalling object names upon seeing a picture.

Make up a series of small cards with pictures on one side and their Spanish equivalents on the other, and distribute them to the class. Divide the class into two groups and choose one person to be "it" for each group (you will have two games going at once). The rest of the students sit at their desks (or stand in front of them) in a circle, holding their cards with the pictures facing out. The person who is "it" stands in the center.

To begin the game, pick one student in each group. Each of those students must say the name in Spanish of the object on his or her card card and name of the picture on another student's card. (It makes it harder for the person who is "it" to not see the person whose card is named. Thus, you may wish to advise students to name a second card that is to the side of or behind the person who is "it.") The person in the center of the circle must find the second person and point at the corresponding picture, thus "stopping the clock," before the second student can name both his or her picture and another person's picture. Make sure the person in the center is accurately pointing at, or preferably touching, the picture. If someone's clock is stopped, that person is then "it."

Streetcar

This game keeps students involved as they move from seat to seat practicing vocabulary.

Prepare file cards with the words you want to practice in Spanish on one side and in English on the reverse side. It may be helpful to indicate infinitives with an asterisk and include articles with the Spanish nouns. You may extend this game by using synonyms and antonyms. Your list could be based on the active vocabulary words listed at the end of each lesson. Decide whether you want the students to produce the English or the Spanish. Students should study the lesson's vocabulary before playing Streetcar. The object of this game is to get all the way back to one's seat. Every time a student answers correctly, he or she moves forward one seat. The teacher or a student may direct the game.

Begin on the left side of class with the first row. The first student stands up next to the second, who remains seated. Show a card to these students while saying the word. The first student to respond correctly moves on to compete with the third student. Whoever answers correctly stands next to the third student. If the second student wins the round, he or she moves on to the third student and the first student sits down in the second student's seat. If neither of the first two students can answer after five seconds, the third student is given an opportunity to respond. If there is still no answer, use the card as a free review, ask the class to define the problem word and choose a new card. This should be a relatively fast-paced game. By saying the target word as you show it, students assign sounds to visual cues.

Transcripts for Textbook Listening Activities

Note: Reproducible answer sheets have been provided for these activities and can be found at the end of the Audio Program Manual in the Teacher Resources DVD or online at EMCLanguages.net.

Available on the Teacher Resources DVD, textbook listening comprehension activities in *¡Aventura!* are indicated by the icon (🔊).

Capítulo 1 (Lección A)

1. ¿Cómo se escribe? Escribe los nombres que oyes.

MODELO Me llamo Carlos. Carlos se escribe con c mayúscula, a, ere, ele, o, ese.

1. Me llamo Ana. Ana se escribe con a mayúscula, ene, a.
2. Me llamo José. José se escribe con jota mayúscula, o, ese, e con acento.
3. Me llamo María. María se escribe con eme mayúscula, a, ere, i con acento, a.
4. Me llamo Paz. Paz se escribe con pe mayúscula, a, zeta.
5. Me llamo Raúl. Raúl se escribe con ere mayúscula, a, u con acento, ele.
6. Me llamo Verónica. Verónica se escribe con ve mayúscula, e, ere, o con acento, ene, i, ce, a.

7. ¿Cuál es la respuesta correcta? Escoge una respuesta correcta a lo que oyes.

1. ¿Cómo se escribe Hugo? ¿Con hache?
2. Yo me llamo Hugo. ¿Y tú?
3. Me llamo Carmen.
4. Hasta luego.

12. Los países. Practice saying the names of the Spanish-speaking countries you hear.

1. Argentina
2. Bolivia
3. Colombia
4. Costa Rica
5. Chile
6. Cuba
7. Ecuador
8. El Salvador
9. España
10. Guatemala
11. Guinea Ecuatorial
12. Honduras
13. México
14. Nicaragua
15. Panamá
16. Paraguay
17. Perú
18. República Dominicana
19. Uruguay
20. Venezuela

18. ¿Cuántos años tienes? Escribe los números que oyes.

MODELO Soy de Bogotá, la capital de Colombia. Tengo dieciséis años.

1. Soy de Santiago, la capital de Chile. Tengo veinte años.
2. Soy de la Ciudad de México, la capital de México. Tengo quince años.
3. Soy de La Paz, la capital de Bolivia. Tengo diez años.
4. Soy de Washington, la capital de Estados Unidos. Tengo ocho años.

Capítulo 1 (Lección B)

1. ¿Saludo o despedida? Di si lo que oyes es: un saludo; una despedida; un saludo y una despedida.

1. Hasta mañana.
2. Buenos días.
3. Hola.
4. Buenas tardes.
5. Buenas noches.

6. ¿Cuál es una respuesta correcta? Escoge una respuesta correcta a lo que oyes.

1. Hola.
2. ¿Qué tal?
3. Adiós.

13. Los números hasta cien. Escribe los números que oyes.

MODELO Me llamo Raúl Varese. Tengo treinta años.

1. Me llamo Gabriela Cervantes. Tengo veintiséis años.
2. Soy el señor Carlos Eduardo Ramírez. Tengo setenta y nueve años.
3. Soy Amalia de la Torre. Tengo treinta y cuatro años.
4. Me llamo Ángela Torres. Tengo quince años.
5. Me llamo Dolores López Cruz. Tengo cien años.

17. ¿Qué hora es? Escribe la hora que oyes.

MODELO Son las nueve y veinticinco.

1. Son las seis.
2. Es la una y media.
3. Son las tres y diez.
4. Son las cuatro y veinte.
5. Son las cinco y cuarto.
6. Es la una menos veinte.

Capítulo 2 (Lección A)

1. ¿Quién? Selecciona la foto de la(s) persona(s) apropiada(s).

1. Ellas son de Minnesota.
2. Ellos son de Texas.
3. Ella es de Colorado.
4. Él es de Nueva York.

5. ¡No es lógico! Escucha la información y corrige lo que no es lógico.

1. Ella se llama Raúl.
2. Ellos son Laura y Diana.
3. Él es de Los Ángeles.

16. ¿Qué es? Identifica los objetos que oyes.

1. la regla
2. el bolígrafo
3. el libro
4. el cesto de papeles
5. el cuaderno
6. el lápiz

20. ¿Sí o no? ¿Son lógicos los diálogos?

1. ¿Quién es la chica con la mochila?
   Ella es la estudiante nueva de Los Ángeles.
2. ¿Qué quiere decir la palabra *mochila*?
   Quiere decir *chair*.
3. ¿Cómo se llama la chica nueva?
   Se llama Raúl y es mi amiga.
4. ¿Cómo se dice *clock* en español?
   Se dice *reloj*.

Capítulo 2 (Lección B)

1. ¿Qué día es mañana? Contesta la pregunta *¿Qué día es mañana?* según lo que oyes.

MODELO *You hear:* Es lunes. ¿Qué día es mañana?
You write: martes

1. Es jueves. ¿Qué día es mañana?
2. Es viernes. ¿Qué día es mañana?
3. Es martes. ¿Qué día es mañana?
4. Es domingo. ¿Qué día es mañana?
5. Es sábado. ¿Qué día es mañana?
6. Es miércoles. ¿Qué día es mañana?

6. ¿Qué clase es? Escribe la letra que identifica cada clase que oyes.

1. Hay una clase de arte el jueves a las ocho y cuarto.
2. La clase de español es a la una y cuarto de la tarde.
3. La clase de historia termina a las tres menos cinco.

4. La señora Valdés es la profesora de matemáticas.
5. Hay un estudiante nuevo en mi clase de inglés.

26. ¿Qué necesitan? Write the names Julio and Pilar. Next, listen and list under each of their names what Julio and Pilar need before they leave for college. Then circle any items on the lists that they both need.

1. Necesito una computadora nueva.
2. Necesito unos diskettes.
3. Necesito un ratón nuevo.
4. Necesito la dirección de correo electrónico de Julio.
5. Necesito unos CDs.
6. Necesito una impresora láser.
7. Necesito unos diskettes.
8. Necesito un teclado nuevo.
9. Necesito el número de celular de Pilar.
10. Necesito unos CDs.

35. Conexión con otras disciplinas: geografía. Say where each of these cities is located.

MODELO Malabo
Malabo está en Guinea Ecuatorial.

1. San Antonio y Santa Fe
2. Sevilla y Madrid
3. Santiago
4. Managua
5. Maracaibo
6. Montevideo
7. Potosí
8. La Plata
9. Cali
10. Concepción

Capítulo 3 (Lección A)

1. La ciudad. Selecciona la foto que corresponde con lo que oyes.

1. Rosa está en el dentista.
2. Los Ortega están en el hotel.
3. Belia y Jeff están en el parque.
4. Tomás está en la biblioteca.
5. La señora Elvira está en el médico.
6. Los chicos están en el restaurante.

5. Presentaciones. Indica la letra de la foto que corresponde con lo que oyes.

1. Sra. Gómez, le presento a Diana.
2. Mauricio y Armando, les presento a Carmen.
3. Alicia, te presento a Gonzalo.
4. Gloria, te presento al Sr. Iglesias.

21. ¿Qué medio de transporte es? Selecciona la foto que corresponde con lo que oyes.

1. Voy a México en avión.
2. Van a la oficina en autobús.
3. ¡Vamos al parque en bicicleta!
4. ¿Tomamos el tren a Guadalajara?
5. Es el caballo de mi amiga Inés.
6. ¿Por qué no vamos a la biblioteca en taxi?
7. Ellos van a pie.
8. ¡El lunes vamos en barco a Puerto Rico!

26. ¿Qué toman para ir? Selecciona la foto que corresponde con lo que oyes.

1. Tomás toma el carro para ir a la fiesta.
2. Yo tomo un taxi para ir al centro.
3. Los muchachos toman el autobús para ir a la escuela.
4. Mi profesora de inglés toma un barco para ir a Dominica y Barbados.
5. Mi profesor de biología toma el avión para ir a Cancún.

Capítulo 3 (Lección B)

1. En el centro. Selecciona la ilustración del lugar apropiado, según lo que oyes.

1. Es un museo.
2. Es un teatro.
3. Es un edificio.
4. Es una ciudad.
5. Es una plaza.
6. Es una calle.
7. Es una tienda.
8. Es un cine.

6. ¿Qué vas a hacer hoy? Indica la letra de la ilustración que corresponde con lo que oyes.

1. Qué vas a hacer hoy?
   Voy a ir con Juana al nuevo restaurante El Charro.

2. ¿Dónde está?
   Está en la Avenida de la Independencia.
3. ¿No van a ir Uds. al Museo de Arte Moderno también?
   Sí. Vamos a la exhibición de Picasso.
4. ¿Qué van a hacer Uds. el sábado?
   Vamos a ir al concierto de Luis Miguel en el Teatro Arlequín.

13. ¿Dónde está? Di si lo que oyes está en un restaurante o en un colegio.

1. La chica con la tiza y el borrador se llama Marta.
2. Aquí está el menú.
3. El mesero está allí con las ensaladas y las bebidas.
4. Hay un cuaderno blanco allí en el pupitre.
5. La profesora de matemáticas está en la pizarra.
6. No veo pollo en mole en el menú.

18. ¿Cuál es la respuesta correcta? Escoge la letra de la respuesta correcta.

1. ¿Dónde está el restaurante?
2. ¿Qué vas a comer?
3. Siempre comes pollo en mole, ¿no?
4. ¿Qué vas a tomar?

Capítulo 4 (Lección A)

1. ¿Cierto o falso? Di si lo que oyes es cierto o falso, según la información en el Vocabulario I. Si es falso, di lo que es cierto.

1. Los padres de Pepe se llaman Rodrigo y Mónica.
2. Rosa es una tía de Pepe.
3. Enrique, Nancy y Carmen son los primos de Pepe.
4. Las abuelas de Pepe se llaman Gloria y Pedro.
5. Álvaro es el tío de Pepe.
6. Mónica es el hermano de Pepe.

5. ¿Quién es? Escucha la información y, luego, escoge la letra de la respuesta correcta.

1. Es el hijo de mi abuelo y el esposo de mi madre.
2. Es el padre de mi madre.
3. Es la madre de mi prima.
4. Es la hija de mi tía.

19. ¿Cómo están? Selecciona la letra de la ilustración que corresponde con lo que oyes.

1. Está apurada.
2. Está nerviosa.
3. Está cansado.
4. Está triste.

23. ¿Cómo están todos? Listen as several people talk about how they are feeling. Then match the names with the description that fits each person.

1. Hoy voy a hacer mucho. Salgo para el colegio a las siete. Estoy en el colegio hasta las tres. Luego, voy al museo de arte en Ponce con unos amigos.
2. No estoy bien. Estoy mal, muy mal. Me duele el estómago.
3. El avión que voy a tomar sale pronto y yo estoy en casa.
4. Voy a un concierto con todos mis amigos. ¡Qué divertido!
5. Mi tío favorito va a estar en casa mañana pero yo voy a estar en clases.
6. Voy al dentista pero no quiero.

Capítulo 4 (Lección B)

1. ¿Quién es? Selecciona la foto apropiada a lo que oyes.

1. Me gusta nadar.
2. Me gusta patinar sobre ruedas.
3. Quiero tocar el piano.
4. Voy a ir a un partido de fútbol.
5. Me gusta jugar al tenis.
6. Quiero ver la televisión.

5. ¿Qué les gusta? Write the names Natalia and Andrés. Next, listen and list under each person's name what he or she likes to do. Then circle any item on the lists that they both like to do.

1. Me gusta ir de compras con mis amigas.
2. También me gusta ir a la playa.
3. Me gusta mucho bailar.
4. Me gusta tocar el piano.
5. Me gusta jugar al tenis.
6. Me gusta jugar al béisbol.
7. Me gusta ir a la playa.

8. Me gusta bailar.
9. También me gusta patinar sobre ruedas.
10. Me gusta nadar.

18. ¿Cómo es? Mira las fotos y contesta las preguntas con *sí* o *no*, según lo que oyes.

1. ¿Es morena?
2. ¿Es calvo?
3. ¿Es bajo?
4. ¿Es delgado?
5. ¿Son guapas?
6. ¿Es fácil?
7. ¿Es pelirroja?
8. ¿Son canosos?

22. ¿Cuál es el opuesto? You will hear some descriptions of people and objects. Give the opposite of each adjective you hear.

MODELO Guillermo y Margarita son delgados. ¿Cuál es el opuesto de **delgados**?

1. Mi hermana, Teresita, siempre es buena. ¿Cuál es el opuesto de **buena**?
2. Yolanda es baja. ¿Cuál es el opuesto de **baja**?
3. Ellas están muy contentas. ¿Cuál es el opuesto de **contentas**?
4. Mi carro es rápido. ¿Cuál es el opuesto de **rápido**?
5. La clase de español es difícil. ¿Cuál es el opuesto de **difícil**?
6. Mis primos son inteligentes. ¿Cuál es el opuesto de **inteligentes**?
7. Su esposo es feo. ¿Cuál es el opuesto de **feo**?
8. Es un programa aburrido. ¿Cuál es el opuesto de **aburrido**?

Capítulo 5 (Lección A)

1. ¿Qué buscan? Selecciona la ilustración que corresponde con lo que oyes.

1. Buscamos un casete de música rock.
2. Busco una grabadora de casetes.
3. Busco un disco compacto con música de piano.
4. Buscamos un reproductor de CDs.
5. Busco un equipo de sonido.
6. Buscamos un reproductor de MP3.

5. ¿Lo tienen? Write the names Marta and Sofía. Next, listen and list under their names what they are looking for at an electronics store. Then circle any items on the lists that are the same.

1. Busco unos DVDs.
2. Busco unos CDs.
3. Busco un reproductor de CDs.
4. Busco un quemador de CDs.
5. Busco una computadora.
6. Busco un equipo de sonido.
7. Busco un reproductor de MP3.
8. Busco unos DVDs.
9. Busco unos CDs.
10. Busco una impresora láser.

16. Las actividades de Javier la semana que viene. Selecciona la letra de la foto que corresponde con lo que oyes.

1. El lunes tengo práctica de tenis.
2. El martes voy a llevar al perro a caminar al parque.
3. El miércoles tengo que estudiar para un examen de historia.
4. El jueves voy a llamar a mis abuelos.
5. El viernes voy a montar en bicicleta.
6. El sábado voy a hacer la maleta para mi viaje a Puntarenas.

21. ¿Cuándo? Marta dice lo que tiene que hacer. Indica el día en que va a hacerlo, según el diálogo.

1. Tengo práctica de fútbol.
2. Voy a hacer un viaje.
3. Voy a estudiar para el examen de biología.
4. Voy a la librería.
5. Tengo práctica de tenis.

22. Las actividades de Tomás. Escribe en una hoja de papel lo que vas a escuchar.

El lunes voy a la tienda a buscar un disco compacto. Busco el CD de Alejandro Sanz. El martes voy a clase de piano en un edificio en el centro. El miércoles voy a montar en bicicleta con un compañero en el parque. El fin de semana que viene voy de viaje.

Capítulo 5 (Lección B)

1. **¿Qué día es? Escoge una respuesta correcta a cada pregunta que escuchas.**
   1. Hoy es el primero de enero. ¿Qué día es hoy?
   2. Hoy es miércoles y pasado mañana voy de compras. ¿Qué día voy de compras?
   3. Hoy es lunes y mi cumpleaños fue anteayer. ¿Cuándo fue mi cumpleaños?
   4. Ayer fue viernes y mañana es el cumpleaños de mi tía. ¿Qué día es su cumpleaños?
   5. Hoy es mi día favorito. Es Navidad. ¿Cuál es la fecha?

6. **¿Cuál es la respuesta? Escoge una respuesta correcta a lo que escuchas.**
   1. Yo tengo dieciséis años. Mi hermano Javier tiene doce. ¿Qué es Javier?
   2. Mi cumpleaños es pasado mañana y hoy es martes. ¿Qué día es mi cumpleaños?
   3. Mi hermano mayor viene el día de Noche Vieja. ¿En qué fecha viene?
   4. Mi hermano tiene veinticinco años. Yo tengo diecisiete. ¿Qué soy yo?
   5. Hoy jueves es mi cumpleaños, pero voy a celebrar mañana. ¿Cuándo voy a celebrar?
   6. Hoy es el veinticinco de diciembre. ¿Qué día es hoy?

14. **¿Cuándo cumplen años? Selecciona la letra de la fecha que corresponde con lo que escuchas.**
   1. Mi cumpleaños es el doce de noviembre.
   2. El dos de marzo es mi cumpleaños.
   3. Mario y yo cumplimos años el veintitrés de enero.
   4. Cumplo años el veinte de mayo.
   5. Mi cumpleaños fue el dieciséis de junio.
   6. Nuestro cumpleaños es el treinta de agosto.

19. **¡Feliz cumpleaños, Sergio! Di si lo que oyes es cierto o falso, según el Diálogo II. Si es falso, corrige la información.**
   1. Hoy es el veinticinco de octubre.
   2. ¡Hoy es el cumpleaños de Sergio!
   3. Sergio es viejo.
   4. Sergio cumple veintisiete años.
   5. En dos meses llega la Navidad.
   6. A Darío no le gusta la idea de la Navidad ni un poquito.

Capítulo 6 (Lección A)

1. **¿Qué tenemos que hacer en la cocina? Selecciona la ilustración que corresponde con lo que oyes.**
   1. ¿Por qué no enciendes el lavaplatos?
   2. Debes cerrar la puerta del refrigerador.
   3. ¿Por qué no enciendes la lámpara del comedor?
   4. Debes poner la mesa del comedor con aquellos platos.
   5. ¿Por qué no enciendes la estufa?
   6. Debes poner la mesa con aquellas servilletas.

5. **¿Qué hacen para ayudar? Mira las palabras de la lista. Di la que corresponde con lo que oyes.**
   1. Tu cuarto tiene buena luz.
   2. Tu comida está fría aquí.
   3. Tu comida está caliente aquí.
   4. Tus platos están limpios aquí.
   5. Tu plato con comida está aquí.
   6. Tu refresco está aquí.

15. **¿Qué necesitas?**
   Di lo que necesitas para hacer lo que oyes.
   MODELO Para tomar sopa.
   1. Para poner mantequilla en el pan.
   2. Para tomar agua.
   3. Para comer el postre.
   4. Para tomar café o té.
   5. Para comer la ensalada.
   6. Para tomar jugo.

21. **Yo necesito.... Selecciona la letra de la frase que completa lógicamente cada oración que oyes.**
   1. Para comer pescado y una ensalada, voy a necesitar un....
   2. Para la sopa, necesito....
   3. No quiero café, gracias. Prefiero un vaso....
   4. Por favor, pásame las....
   5. Voy a poner los platos en....
   6. Voy a poner un poco de mantequilla....
   7. Necesito la pimienta y la....
   8. Para la mesa voy a necesitar un....

Capítulo 6 (Lección B)

1. **Dictado. Escucha la información y escribe lo que oyes.**

   Hola papás,

   ¿Qué tal? Escribo desde Cartagena. Cartagena es una ciudad muy bonita e interesante. Cada día le gusta más a Daniela la idea de vivir aquí, pero también le gustaría vivir con Uds. en Caracas.

   La casa del primo Julián es muy cómoda. Aquí va el dibujo de la casa donde vive él. Entramos en la casa por una puerta en el patio. El cuarto de Daniela está al lado de la cocina. Tiene unas ventanas pequeñas. Yo estoy en el cuarto de Julián. Cuando yo estoy aburrido, voy a la sala a ver televisión. Por las noches siempre comemos en el patio.

   El tío dice que en dos semanas vamos a ir a Barranquilla. Vamos a pasar siete u ocho días allí en la casa de su tía Isabel. Allá vamos a aprender a montar a caballo. Tenemos muchas ganas de ir.

   A Daniela no le gusta escribir cartas. Entonces, ella los va a llamar por teléfono en estos días.

   Un abrazo,

   Santiago

7. **¿Está en la casa, en el colegio o en el parque? Di dónde están las siguientes personas según lo que oyes.**
   1. Veo televisión en la sala con mis padres.
   2. Rodrigo habla con su profesora de historia, en la planta baja.
   3. Mi profesor de español lee un libro en el cuarto de su hija.
   4. Allí patina sobre ruedas Esperanza con sus amigas todos los sábados.
   5. La Sra. Durán prepara la comida en la cocina al lado del garaje.
   6. Pedrito juega con su perro en el patio que está al lado de la piscina.
   7. Natalia toma un refresco en la cafetería del primer piso.
   8. Rafael limpia el baño del cuarto de sus padres.

18. **¿Cierto o falso? Di si lo que oyes es cierto o falso, según la información en el *Vocabulario II*. Si es falso, di lo que es cierto.**
    1. Nicolás no tiene sueño.
    2. Mateo tiene ganas de correr.
    3. El abuelo dice que tiene calor.
    4. Los tíos dicen que tienen frío.
    5. Verónica tiene mucha hambre.
    6. Cristina tiene prisa.

22. **¿Qué tienen? Selecciona la ilustración apropiada que corresponde con lo que oyes.**
    1. Ellas tienen frío.
    2. Tienen hambre.
    3. Ella tiene calor.
    4. Él tiene ganas de correr.
    5. Tengo sed.
    6. ¿Tienes sueño?

Capítulo 7 (Lección A)

1. **¿Qué actividad es? Identifica la actividad que oyes.**
   1. Vamos a jugar al básquetbol.
   2. Vamos a jugar al fútbol americano.
   3. Vamos a jugar al ajedrez.
   4. Vamos a jugar al béisbol.
   5. Vamos a jugar a las cartas.
   6. Vamos a jugar al voleibol.

5. **¿Qué comprendiste? Di si lo que oyes es cierto o falso, según el diálogo *¿No quieres jugar al ajedrez?***
   1. Luz quiere jugar al tenis.
   2. Hugo mira una telenovela en la televisión.
   3. Hugo no quiere jugar al ajedrez.
   4. Luz no recuerda cómo jugar al ajedrez.
   5. Los chicos juegan a videojuegos.

13. **El tiempo libre. Selecciona la ilustración que corresponde con lo que oyes.**
    1. Es tarde.
    2. Está durmiendo.
    3. Hace una hora que está viendo televisión.
    4. Quiere alquilar una película nueva.
    5. ¿Jugamos ajedrez?
    6. Es casi mediodía.

17. Dictado
Escucha la información y escribe lo que oyes.

Hugo: ¿Estás durmiendo?
Luz: No. Estoy viendo televisión. ¿Por qué?
Hugo: Porque quiero ir a alquilar una película.
Luz: ¿Ahora mismo?
Hugo: Sí, quiero ir antes de comer. ¿Quieres ir?
Luz: Un segundo.... Ya voy.
Luz: No quiero ver las mismas películas otra vez.
Hugo: ¿Cuánto tiempo hace que no ves una película?
Luz: ¡Uy! Hace mucho tiempo. Casi dos meses.
Hugo: ¡Entonces no vas a ver las mismas películas!

Capítulo 7 (Lección B)

1. Las estaciones. Escoge la estación correcta, según lo que oyes.

1. Hace frío y puedes patinar sobre hielo.
2. Hay flores por todos lados y llueve mucho.
3. Hace sol y mucho calor.
4. No hace mucho calor.

5. ¿Qué actividades puedes hacer? Escucha la información y di qué actividad o actividades puedes hacer.

MODELO Es el otoño y hace sol.

1. Es invierno y hace mucho frío.
2. Es verano y hace mucho calor.
3. Es primavera y llueve.
4. Es otoño y no hace calor.
5. Es primavera y hace sol.

16. ¿Quién es? Selecciona la foto de la persona apropiada.

1. Soy tenista.
2. Soy futbolista.
3. Soy esquiadora.
4. Soy patinador.
5. Soy corredora.
6. Soy jugadora de fútbol.

21. ¿Qué tiempo hace? Selecciona la ilustración que corresponde con lo que oyes.

1. Hace calor.
2. Está nublado.
3. Hace viento.
4. Llueve mucho.
5. Hay neblina.
6. Nieva ahora.

Capítulo 8 (Lección A)

1. ¿Qué tienen que hacer? Write the names Julia and Enrique. Next, listen and list under each of their names what chores each of them has to do. Then circle any items on the lists that they both have to do. The first one has been done for you.

1. Tengo que adornar la sala para la fiesta de cumpleaños de mi tía.
2. Tengo que cocinar el pollo.
3. Tengo que trabajar en el jardín.
4. Tengo que hacer mi cama.
5. Tengo que limpiar la cocina.
6. Tengo que adornar la sala para la fiesta de cumpleaños de mi tía.
7. Tengo que preparar la ensalada.
8. Tengo que doblar la ropa.
9. Tengo que hacer mi cama.
10. Tengo que limpiar la cocina.

6. ¿Me ayudas?
Mira las tres fotos que van con el diálogo y di si lo que oyes va con la primera, la segunda o la tercera foto.

MODELO La Sra. Zea está hablando con Inés y Víctor.

1. Inés le dice a la Sra. Zea que la cocina está limpia.
2. Víctor dice que está haciendo unos quehaceres.
3. Inés está colgando su abrigo.
4. La cocina ya está limpia.
5. Víctor le dice a Inés que tiene que terminar de limpiar la casa.

19. Los quehaceres. Selecciona la foto de la persona que corresponda con lo que oyes.

1. Pasa la aspiradora.
2. Arregla el cuarto.
3. Barre.
4. Lava las ollas.

23. ¿Vais a hacer un quehacer o un deporte? Las siguientes personas van a hablar de sus actividades de hoy. Di si lo que oyes es *un quehacer* o *un deporte*.

1. Hola. Me llamo Tomás. Voy a jugar al fútbol hoy.
2. Soy Ramón. Tengo que pasar la aspiradora por la sala hoy.
3. Me llamo Roberto. Voy a lavar las ollas esta noche para ayudar a mis padres.
4. Hola. Yo soy Verónica. Voy con unos amigos a esquiar.
5. Me llamo Margarita. Voy a buscar leche y pan en la tienda hoy.

Capítulo 8 (Lección B)

1. En el supermercado. Selecciona la ilustración que corresponde con lo que oyes.

1. Los aguacates parecen muy maduros.
2. Los tomates están frescos.
3. Aquellos son los mejores pimientos.
4. Necesitamos el ingrediente más importante, el ajo.
5. Éstos son los peores guisantes.
6. Voy a llevar un kilo de pescado.

5. ¿Qué les hace falta? Di la letra de la ilustración que identifica lo que les hace falta comprar a las siguientes personas, según lo que oyes.

1. Ayer compré el pollo. Me hace falta comprar un kilo de arroz.
2. A nosotros nos hace falta comprar unas cebollas.
3. Yo necesito comprar una lechuga para la ensalada.
4. A mi madre le hace falta comprar unos pimientos y una lata de tomates.
5. Yo tengo todas las verduras, sólo me hace falta comprar un pollo.

20. En el mercado. Selecciona la ilustración que corresponde con lo que oyes.

1. Les di las mejores manzanas.
2. ¿A qué precio tiene las habichuelas?
3. Ayer estuve en el mercado y compré fresas.
4. Las zanahorias están a un euro el kilo.
5. Éstas son las mejores naranjas.
6. Este maíz es tan bueno como aquel maíz.

25. ¿Qué comprendiste? Escucha lo que dicen las personas del diálogo *Comprando chorizo* y di si lo que oyes es cierto o falso. Corrige lo que no es cierto.

1. Ayer estuve con Víctor en el supermercado.
2. Compramos los ingredientes para hacer una ensalada.
3. Quiero comprar queso.
4. El chorizo del supermercado no me gusta.
5. Éste es el peor supermercado de la ciudad.
6. El chorizo está a € 4,00 el kilo.

Capítulo 9 (Lección A)

1. Comprando ropa. Selecciona la ilustración que corresponde con lo que oyes.

1. Quiero una blusa de seda rosada.
2. Busco una corbata morada.
3. Necesito unas botas marrones.
4. Busco un traje de baño anaranjado.
5. Quiero un pijama de algodón azul.
6. Necesito un vestido verde.

6. ¿Cuál prefieres? Selecciona la letra de la ilustración que corresponde con lo que las siguientes personas prefieren.

1. Prefiero el traje negro.
2. El negro no me gusta. Prefiero el marrón.
3. Prefiero los zapatos bajos.
4. Prefiero la camisa morada.
5. La morada no me gusta ni un poquito. Prefiero la anaranjada.
6. Yo prefiero los zapatos de tacón.
7. Prefiero el vestido rosado.
8. Prefiero las medias azules.

20. ¿Qué es? Escribe el artículo de ropa que oyes.

MODELO Me gustó el sombrero rojo.

1. Preferí los guantes negros.
2. Quiero comprar un abrigo de lana.
3. Voy a buscar una chaqueta nueva.
4. Necesitas un impermeable porque va a llover.
5. ¿Llevas tu suéter de algodón?
6. Escogí el pantalón verde.

25. *¿Cuándo?* Listen carefully to statements made by several people. Indicate whether each sentence you hear is in the past *(pretérito)* or in the present *(presente)*.

1. ¿Te conté que ayer fui a una tienda por departamentos?
2. Puedes comprar ese abrigo nuevo, si quieres.
3. No me queda ninguno de lana.
4. Te prometí llevarte al centro comercial ayer, ¿verdad?
5. Te compré algo nuevo.
6. No quiero ni la chaqueta ni el impermeable.
7. Es un suéter para tus vacaciones.

Capítulo 9 (Lección B)

1. ¿Qué les gustaría recibir de regalo? Selecciona la letra de la ilustración que corresponde con lo que oyes.

1. A mí me gustaría recibir una billetera.
2. A mí me gustaría recibir una pulsera de oro.
3. De regalo, a mí me gustaría recibir un paraguas.
4. Yo quiero recibir de regalo unos aretes de plata.
5. Yo quiero recibir un cinturón de cuero.
6. A mí me gustaría recibir un anillo de oro.

6. Bueno, bonito y barato. Selecciona la letra de la ilustración que corresponde con lo que buscan las siguientes personas.

1. Busco un bolsito de material sintético barato.
2. Busco una bufanda larga para usar todos los días.
3. Busco un paraguas bueno, bonito y barato.
4. Buscamos unos pañuelos de seda.
5. Busco un collar y unos aretes de perlas.
6. Buscamos una chaqueta de cuero corta.

18. ¿Cuál es la respuesta correcta? Escoge la letra de la respuesta correcta a lo que oyes.

1. ¿Cómo va a pagar?
2. ¿Quieres venir conmigo a la tienda?
3. ¿Qué necesito para cambiar este paraguas?
4. ¿Cuánto es mi cambio?
5. ¿Te gusta la calidad de la blusa?
6. ¿Es caro el collar?

22. ¿Sí o no? ¿Son lógicos los diálogos? Corrige lo que no es lógico.

1. ¿Cuánto cuesta el perfume?
   Cuesta veinte dólares.
2. ¿Está en oferta el perfume?
   Sí, es muy caro.
3. ¿Cómo va a pagar?
   Voy a pagar con recibos.
4. Aquí tiene su recibo y dos dólares de cambio.
   No, no lo voy a cambiar.
5. ¿Cómo puedo ahorrar dinero?
   Puedes ahorrar dinero si compras lo barato.

Capítulo 10 (Lección A)

3. ¡Fue un año divertido! Di si lo que oyes es cierto o falso, según el Diálogo. Si es falso, corrige la información.

1. Silvia dijo que el año fue muy aburrido.
2. Mario dijo que le gusta la historia.
3. Silvia dijo que le gusta la geografía.
4. Mario dijo que no le gusta la biología.

Capítulo 10 (Lección B)

3. ¿Quién dijo qué? ¿Quién dijo lo siguiente, Inés o Luis?

1. Tuve que ayudar a mis padres.
2. Vamos a ir a las ruinas de Tikal.
3. Fui a Tikal el año pasado.
4. Me gustaría ir a California.
5. Pienso que debes ir a California.

Activities for Substitutes and Rainy Days*

¿Adónde?

This civilization and culture resource focuses on Spain and the Spanish-speaking world. It provides students with opportunities to improve their reading, writing, speaking and listening skills. The book includes readings supported by photographs and graphs and includes historical and cultural topics such as music, sports and cinema. Current affairs, social customs, the environment and globalization issues are among topics explored. An audio CD reinforces content.

Pasatiempos en español Volumenes 1 and 2

Each volume includes crossword puzzles and word searches that allow for students to practice vocabulary words in 16 categories. Vocabulary words are introduced with lively, colorful illustrations.

Use this chart to find materials that can save the day.

Activity Books

Supplemental Title / 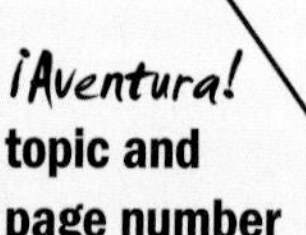 ¡Aventura! topic and page number					
Capítulo 1 ¿Cómo te llamas?					
Greetings	8				
Time	84, 85				
Numbers 21-100	29				
Capítulo 2 En mi colegio					
School subjects	32	14		70	
Days of the week			22		
Spanish influence in the U.S.	8, 9, 34, 72				
Present tense *-ar* verbs		62	62	76	82

*EMC offers this supplemental package to enhance classroom instruction. Visit the EMC website at www.emcp.com for ordering information.

El español en crucigramas Volumenes 1, 2 and 3

Beginning, intermediate and advanced students practice a wide variety of vocabulary sets. Students grow their vocabularies by incorporating the illustrated words in crossword puzzles.

Vocabulario activo Volumenes 1 and 2

The 60 reproducible worksheets in each volume are organized around approximately 40 themes. A variety of activity formats provide students the opportunity to develop reading, writing and higher-level thinking skills.

Prácticas de audición Volumenes 1 and 2

Each reproducible volume offers a wide range of listening activities to supplement text work and helps students develop listening comprehension and speaking skills. Thirty realistic and stimulating situations apply essential grammatical concepts. Students practice comprehension skills through question and answer, fill-in-the-blanks, note taking and other activity formats.

El español en crucigramas 3	ELI Diccionario Ilustrado Español Junior	Vocabulario activo 1	Vocabulario activo 2	Prácticas de audición 1	Prácticas de audición 2
		8	11	31	8, 29
	44	21		12	10
	9	28	54	15	
	12, 14, 16, 17, 30	15			17, 26
	68	22		20	10, 18
76	72, 73, 74, 75	32, 47, 48, 63, 66	30	17	22, 32

Activity Books

Supplemental Title / *¡Aventura!* topic and page number				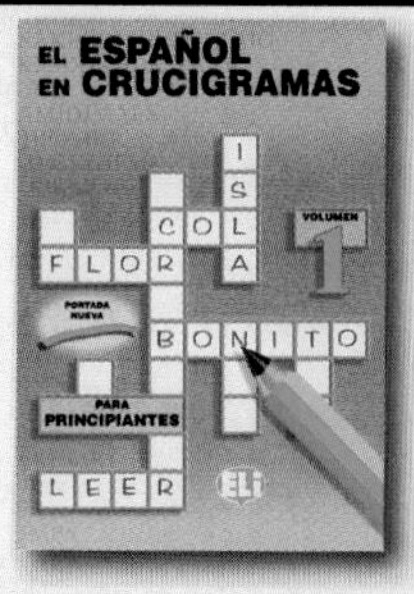	
Capítulo 3 ¡Vamos a la ciudad!					
Places in the city	22, 24, 118, 120, 122	22	38	46	22, 46, 64
Transportation		26		82	16, 58
Present tense *-er* verbs		62		76	82
The verb *ir*		62		76	82
Capítulo 4 Mi familia y mis amigos					
Family	56		10 , 11		
El merengue and dancing	66, 68, 70		70		70
The verb *estar*					
Ser vs. *estar*					
The verb *gustar*					
Capítulo 5 Una semana típica					
Leisure activities	68, 70		54		
Tener and *venir*					
Capítulo 6 En casa					
Kitchen objects		18	18	16	46
Food	36, 58, 60, 62, 64	46, 50		28, 34	
The home		18	14	10, 16	

	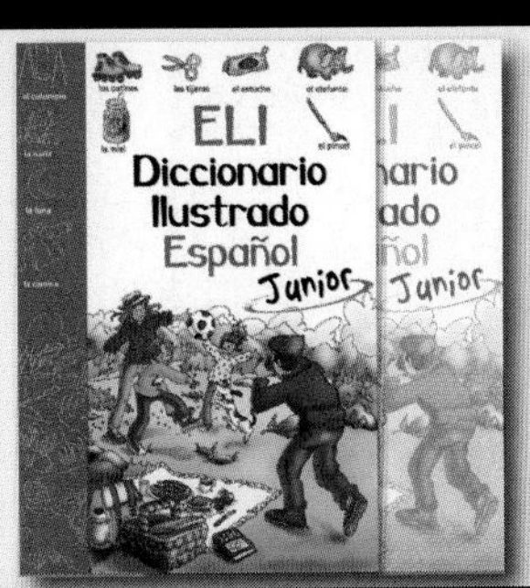				
	26			14, 21	14, 18
	54	44, 46	45, 46, 62	26	
76	72, 74	47, 48, 58	30, 51	17	32
	74	58, 59		16, 22	16
	4	36	41	11	
40	14, 15	60			
		12, 32, 47, 66, 67		24	
		12	48	10	
		55, 64	59	19	28
40, 46	40, 41, 72, 73, 74, 75	32, 35, 59	40, 64	21, 25	32, 34
				10,11, 30	
	28, 32, 33	25	22, 23	34	15
	18,19, 33, 42, 43	33, 34	37, 38	18, 34	25
	28, 29	25, 26		30	

Activity Books

Supplemental Title / *¡Aventura!* topic and page number					
Capítulo 7 El tiempo libre					
Leisure activities	68, 70		54		
Sports	112, 114, 116		54	22	
Weather and seasons		34	26		
Present progressive					
Capítulo 8 Mis quehaceres					
Household chores					
Comparisons					
Spain	16-24, 30-36, 52-56, 86-96				
Direct and indirect object pronouns					
Preterite tense *-ar* verbs		62	62	76	82
Capítulo 9 La ropa					
Clothing	92, 93	58		52	
Body parts		54			22, 28
Department store	60				
Capítulo 10 Un año más					
Future plans					
Vacations	118, 120, 122		50	4	
Leisure activities	32				
Past tense verbs					

	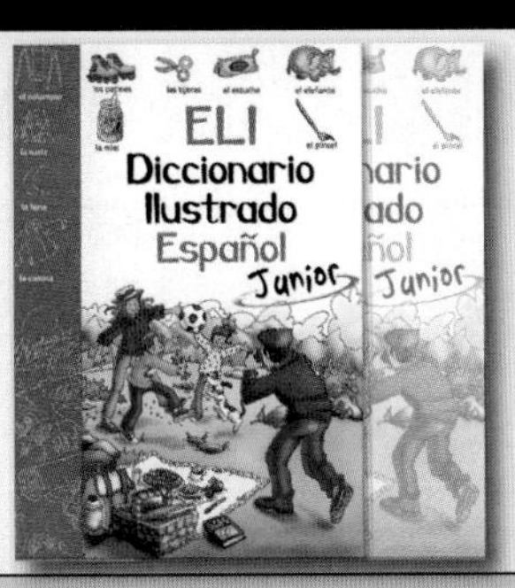				
40, 46	40, 41, 72, 73, 74, 75	32, 35, 59	40, 64	21, 25	32, 34
52	24, 25		20		
	62, 63, 64, 65	23, 24	42	13	
		11, 47		24	
			50, 51	9	30
		11, 56	41, 57	26	24
		65		8	12, 28, 29
				34	27, 37
76	72, 73, 74, 75	32, 47, 48, 63, 66	19, 30	17	22, 32
	38, 39	37, 38	26	25	21
16	20, 21	11, 30, 31	33, 34		
22	40, 41	29, 35	36	15	11
		44, 66		22, 25	32
	56, 57, 60, 62, 64	45		22	16
		58, 59, 63		16, 20	10
		64, 65		29, 35, 36	17

Speaking Spanish Confidently Correlation*

Speaking Spanish Confidently is an instructional resource that teachers can use to introduce and reinforce 20 useful Spanish language concepts in a unique way.

Speaking Spanish Confidently motivates learners to attach lexical meaning to visual symbol cards. When placed side by side, the symbol cards create an easy way for students to master Spanish syntax, for even the trickiest grammatical structures.

With frequent repetition of individual words and sentence patterns by the teacher, then by individuals and finally by the whole class, students begin speaking with confidence during the first unit.

The visual symbols, paired with audio references, become effectively stored in students' long-term memory banks.

Speaking Spanish Confidently is an entertaining and effective classroom tool that will add excitement and meaningful content to your daily lessons.

Symbol Card Categories

Adjectives and adverbs
Affirmatives and negatives
Clothes
Colors
Days of the week, times of day, weather
Foods
Objects
People
Places
Possessive adjectives
Prepositions and connecting words
Questions
Reflexive verbs and pronouns
Sports, entertainment and music
Subjects
Transportation

When to use Speaking Spanish Confidently during your *¡Aventura!* lessons

Topic / *¡Aventura!* chapter	Unit 1 Emerging Fluency	Unit 2 Subject Pronouns	Unit 3 Conjugating Skills	Unit 4 Expressions with *hacer* and *tener*	Unit 5 Question Formation	Unit 6 Adjective Agreement	Unit 7 Adjectives and the Verb *ser*	Unit 8 Adjectives and the Verb *estar*	Unit 9 Possessive Adjectives
Capítulo 1	X						X		
Capítulo 2	X	X	X			X	X	X	
Capítulo 3	X		X	X	X				
Capítulo 4			X			X		X	X
Capítulo 5			X	X		X			
Capítulo 6			X	X					
Capítulo 7			X	X					
Capítulo 8			X					X	
Capítulo 9									
Capítulo 10									

*EMC offers this supplemental product to enhance classroom instruction.
Visit the EMC website at www.emcp.com for ordering information.

265 Symbol Cards (Symbol cards representing various parts of speech and abstract concepts allow you to create thousands of sentence combinations.)

Teacher's Guide (Each unit of the guide includes learning objectives, symbol cards needed, step-by-step lesson design, helpful hints, expansion activities, and symbol card games.)

Training DVD (This teacher reference tool introduces the Symtalk philosophy and how to use the symbol cards effectively with students. In the DVD, a teacher models how to present the key elements of the 20 units to students.)

Unit 10 Direct Object Pronouns	Unit 11 Indirect Object Pronouns	Unit 12 Using *gustar* and *molestar*	Unit 13 Negative and Affirmative Expressions	Unit 14 Comparisons	Unit 15 Verbs Followed by an Infinitive	Unit 16 Immediate Future	Unit 17 Present Progressive	Unit 18 Preterite	Unit 19 Imperfect	Unit 20 Present Subjunctive
						x				
		x	x							
x			x							
					x					
x	x									
x	x		x	x			x	x		
			x		x			x		

Tips for Internet Use

Teacher Resources on the World Wide Web

¡Aventura! creators frequent the following sites. (**Note:** These addresses may change at any time. Visit sites to verify they are active before using them in class.)

Travel and Tourism
http://www.embassyworld.com
http://www.embassy.org
http://www.travelchannel.com
http://virtualtourist.com
http://www.towd.com
http://www.lonelyplanet.com

Radio and Television News
http://www.bbc.co.uk/mundo
http://voanews.com/Spanish
http://www.zonalatina.com/Radio.htm
http://radio-locator.com
http://www.univision.com

Suggested Sites for e-mail projects
http://www.epals.com
http://linguistic-funland.com/penpalpostings.html
http://www.worldwide.edu/index.html

Weather
http://www.eltiempo.es
http://cnn.com/weather
http://intellicast.com

Newspapers and Magazines
http://www.zonalatina.com/
http://www.elpais.com
http://cnnespanol.com
http://libguides.mit.edu/flnewspapers
http://es-us.yahoo.com
http://www.editorandpublisher.com

Culture
http://lanic.utexas.edu
http://www.mcu.es/cooperacion
http://www.everyculture.com

Grammar Practice
http://www.verbix.com
http://www.vocabulix.com
http://www.studyspanish.com

Text accompanied by audio
http://www.elmundo.es
http://www.palabravirtual.com

Education and Teaching sites
http://www.worldwide.edu
http://www.cehd.umn.edu/PPG
http://www.miscositas.com
http://www.teachers.net
http://www.cla.net/lessons/topspanish.html
http://www.actfl.org

Language Professionals

The Foreign Language Teaching Forum is an integrated service for language teachers. The organization includes an Internet site (http://www.cortland.edu/FLTEACH), e-mail LISTSERV Academic Discussion List (FLTEACH@listserv.buffalo.edu), archives and the FLNEWS server at the State University of New York College at Cortland. The sites facilitate networking and dialog among language professionals. Topics include language teaching methods, school/college articulation, training of student teachers, classroom activities, curriculum and syllabus design.

The Internet holds much promise as a tool for teaching and learning by providing up-to-date and culturally-authentic information.

Policy and Guidelines for Computer Users

It is essential to create an acceptable use policy before allowing student access to the Internet. The development of such a policy should include all interested parties, such as school administrators, faculty, students, parents and members of the school board. The following policy and guidelines are examples created by one school. This "working document" allows for revisions and additions.

Acceptable Use Policy

¡Aventura!

The major school rules provide the basic structure for the Acceptable Use Policy. All users must be honest and respectful of others. Their work must meet the schoolwide guidelines for appropriate language and subject matter; it must not violate the school's harassment policy.

All use of the computers must be within the law. Copyright laws must be observed. Only software licensed to the school may be put in school computers. Copyrighted files cannot be sent from or received by school computers without permission of the copyright owner.

Users may access only their own files and programs or those intended for their use. Access to another's account or files without authorization is forbidden. Students must not attempt to access administrative files.

Those using the school's computing resources for classroom use and school-related projects have priority for use of the lab and/or equipment. School facilities may not be used for commercial purposes. Individuals are expected to use the resources thoughtfully. Use that unnecessarily slows access to the network, wastes storage or wastes other resources is forbidden.

Students who violate these policies will be subject to the school's disciplinary process.

Students will be asked to read and sign a list of additional guidelines before being given access to the school's computers. These guidelines will give students additional information about safe and respectful use of the school's computing resources.

Guidelines for Computer Users

Permission to use the school's computing facilities is granted to those who agree to use them thoughtfully and respectfully. The following guidelines should be followed:

- All use of school's computers must be consistent with the school's Acceptable Use Policy. You are expected to be honest, respect others, follow the school's rules about harassment and do nothing illegal.
- Access only those files for which you are authorized. You must not use or attempt to use any other person's files or programs without permission. Attempting to access administrative files, even for fun, will be viewed as a serious offense.
- Do not use offensive language, which includes both vulgar or insulting language and derogatory language.
- Do not monopolize the use of the equipment. Users working on class-related projects have priority for the use of the facilities.
- Do not give your home address or phone number over the Net. If you need to give someone an address or phone number, use the school's. If in doubt, check with a teacher.
- Be a positive member of the school's computer-using community. Be helpful to those less knowledgeable than you. Avoid activities that earn some computer users bad reputations: Do not "hack," "spam," "flame," introduce viruses and so on.
- Keep the system running legally and efficiently. Get rid of unwanted programs, files, and e-mail that take up valuable storage. "Unsubscribe" from mail lists that no longer interest you. Do not use illegal software. Do not store your own personal software at school.
- Student use of the Internet is limited to the computers in the student computer lab unless they are working under the supervision of a faculty member.

EMC *Español*

¡Aventura!

¡Aventura! is a ***flexible, focused*** and ***fun*** Spanish program created to allow you and your students to meet the challenges of varied teaching and learning styles. Take your students on an adventure into the Spanish-speaking world. Culture, vocabulary, grammar, technology—it's all here waiting to be discovered!

Second Edition
Five-level
Spanish Program
© 2013

Flexible!

Focused!

Fun!

Go to
www.emcp.com/aventura
to review sample pages of all
five levels!

Second Edition

Author

Alejandro Vargas Bonilla

Contributing Writers

Belia Jiménez Lorente

Karin Fajardo

Rolando Castellanos

Consultants

Paul J. Hoff
University of Wisconsin—Eau Claire
Eau Claire, Wisconsin

Heidi Oshima
Parsippany High School
Parsippany, New Jersey

Marne Patana
Middle Creek High School
Apex, North Carolina

Anne Marie Quihuis
Paradise Valley High School
Phoenix, Arizona

Ana Selvás Watson
Henrico High School
Richmond, Virginia

Nancy Wrobel
Champlin Park High School
Champlin, Minnesota

ST. PAUL • INDIANAPOLIS

Associate Editors
Tanya Brown
Kimberly Rodrigues

Editorial Consultants
Judy Cohen, Lori Coleman, Sharon O'Donnell, David Thorstad, Sarah Vaillancourt

Readers
Pat Cotton, Mónica Domínguez, Barbary Forney, Daniela Guzmán, Barbara Peterson, Roy Sweezy, Beth Verdin

Proofreaders
Susana Petit, Mercedes Roffé, Gilberto Vázquez

Production Specialist
Jaana Bykonich, Julie Johnston

Illustrators
Ron Berg, Kristen Copham, Chris Dellorco, Len Ebert, Julia Green, Susan Jaekel, Katherine Hanley Knutson, Nedo Kojic, Jeff Mangiat, Mendola Artists, Hetty Mitchel, Tom Newsom, D.J. Simison, Scott Youtsey/Miracle Studios, Gregg Zamora

Text Design
Leslie Anderson

Cover Design
Leslie Anderson

ISBN 978-0-82196-245-9 (Text + CD)
ISBN 978-0-82196-293-0 (Text)

875 Montreal Way
St. Paul, MN 55102
E-mail: educate@emcp.com
Web site: www.emcp.com

Printed in the United States of America

16 15 14 13 12 11 1 2 3 4 5 6 7 8 9 10

¡Saludos!

You are about to embark on an adventure that will take you to many countries and that will open doors you may never have imagined. Whether you are drawn to Spanish because of your interest in travel or your desire to learn how to communicate with others, this year offers you rewarding possibilities as you navigate your way through the Spanish-speaking world. This sense of real-life adventure and travel is reflected in the covers of the *¡Aventura!* series.

Learning a language has always meant more than merely memorizing words and grammar rules and then putting them together, hoping to actually be able to communicate. Just as language is inseparable from culture, so is it inseparable from the authentic communication of thoughts and emotions. The culture of the Spanish-speaking world varies from one country to another. In *¡Aventura!*, you will navigate your way, learning about others while at the same time learning how to share your ideas and feelings. These real-life learning experiences will introduce you to and expand your knowledge of language, geography, history and the arts. In *¡Aventura!* you will learn not only fascinating information, but also problem-solving, survival and employment skills so that when you leave the classroom you can step right into the real world.

Are you ready to learn to use Spanish in the real world? Experience the authentic: *¡Aventura!*

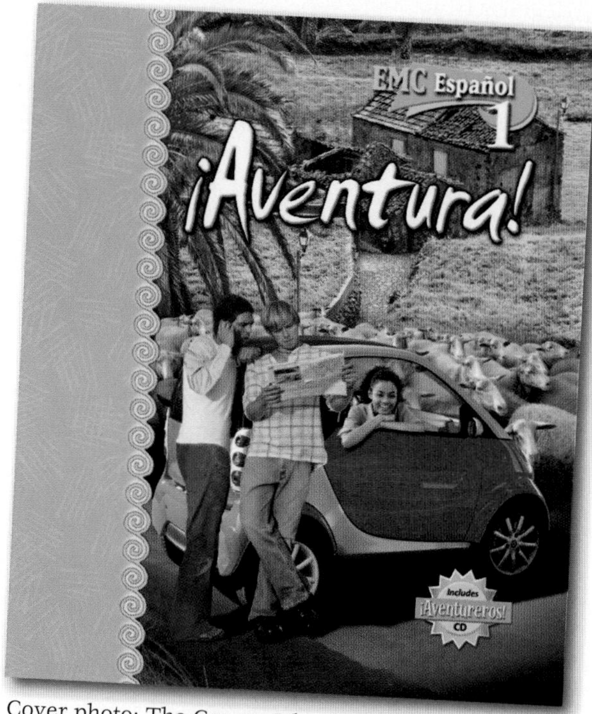

Cover photo: The Canary Islands, Spain

Contents

Capítulo 1 ¿Cómo te llamas? 1

iv

v

vi

vii

Capítulo 5 Una semana típica 180

viii

Capítulo 6 En casa 224

ix

xi

xii

xiii

MAPA
La lengua espa
Groenlandia (Din.)
Alaska (EE.UU.)
CANADÁ
ESTADOS UNIDOS
Denver
Chicago
Nueva York
Los Ángeles
San Diego
San Antonio
Miami
MÉXICO
C. de México
La Habana
CUBA
BAHAMAS
Trópico de Cáncer
REPÚBLICA DOMINICANA
HAITÍ
JAMAICA
Santo Domingo
Puerto Rico (EE. UU.)
BELIZE
Belmopán
GUATEMALA
Guatemala
HONDURAS
Tegucigalpa
EL SALVADOR
San Salvador
NICARAGUA
Managua
COSTA RICA
San José
PANAMÁ
Panamá
TRINIDAD Y TOBAGO
Puerto España
Caracas
VENEZUELA
GUYANA
SURINAM
Guayana Francesa (Fr.)
Bogotá, D.C.
COLOMBIA
Quito
ECUADOR
Ecuador
Is.Galápagos (Arch. de Colón) (Ec.)
Is. Hawai (EE. UU.)
BRASIL
Lima
PERÚ
La Paz
BOLIVIA
Sucre
PARAGUAY
Asunción
ARGENTINA
CHILE
Santiago
URUGUAY
Montevideo
Buenos Aires
I. Malvinas
OCÉANO PACÍFICO
OCÉANO ATLÁNTICO
OCÉANO GLA
ISLANDIA
NORUEGA
REINO UNIDO
IRLANDA
DINAMARCA
ALEMANIA
FRANCIA
ANDORRA
PORTUGAL
ESPAÑA
Madrid
ITALIA
MARRUECOS
TUNICIA
I. Canarias
ARGELIA
Sahara Occidental
MAURITANIA
MALI
NÍGER
CABO VERDE
SENEGAL
GAMBIA
GUINEA-BISSAU
GUINEA
BURKINA FASO
NIGERIA
SIERRA LEONA
LIBERIA
COSTA DE MARFIL
GHANA
TOGO
BENIN
Malabo
CAMERÚN
GUINEA ECUAT.
SANTO TOMÉ Y PRÍNCIPE
GABÓN
REP. POP. CONGO
Nº PAIS
1 ST. CRISTÓBAL Y NEVIS
2 SAN VICENTE Y LAS GRANADINAS
3 DOMINICA
4 BARBADOS
5 PAÍSES BAJOS
6 BÉLGICA
7 LUXEMBURGO
8 REP. CHECA
9 AUSTRIA
10 SUIZA
11 MÓNACO
12 SAN MARINO
13 LIECHTENSTEIN
14 HUNGRÍA
15 ESLOVENIA
16 CROACIA
17 BOSNIA-HERZEGOVINA
18 YUGOSLAVIA
19 MACEDONIA
Nº PAIS
20 ALBANIA
21 LÍBANO
22 JORDANIA
23 LESOTHO
24 SWAZILANDIA
25 BAHREIN
26 ESTONIA
27 LETONIA
28 LITUANIA
29 MOLDAVIA
30 GEORGIA
31 ARMENIA
32 AZERBAIDZHÁN
33 KIRGUIZISTÁN
34 TADZHIKISTÁN
35 ESLOVAQUIA
36 DJIBOUTI
37 RUANDA
38 BURUNDI
©edigol ediciones,s.a.
Oeste de Greenwich 0° Este de Greenw

xiv

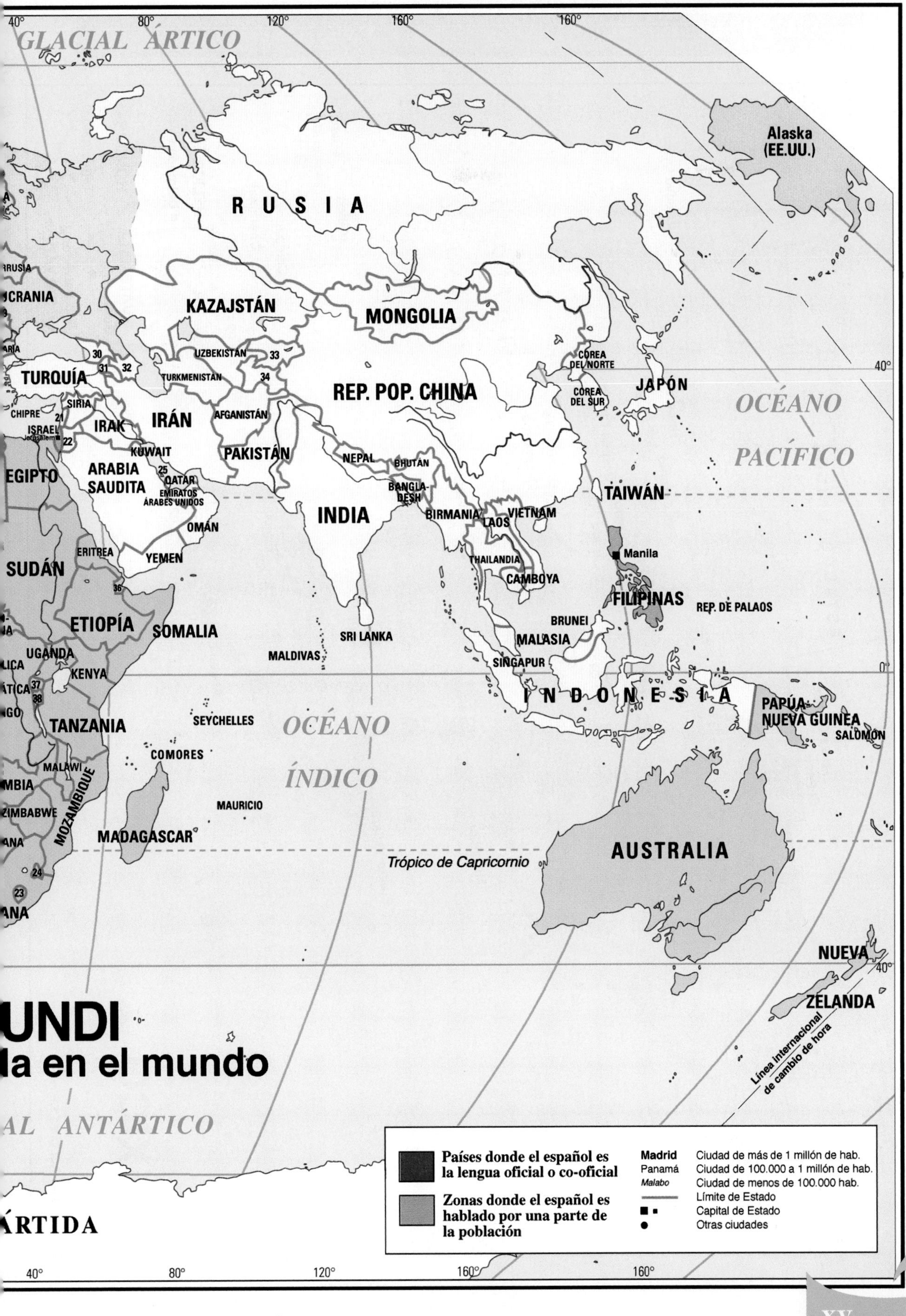
GLACIAL ÁRTICO
RUSIA
Alaska (EE.UU.)
BIELORRUSIA
UCRANIA
KAZAJSTÁN
MONGOLIA
UZBEKISTÁN
TURKMENISTÁN
TURQUÍA
COREA DEL NORTE
COREA DEL SUR
JAPÓN
REP. POP. CHINA
SIRIA
CHIPRE
ISRAEL
Jerusalem
IRAK
IRÁN
AFGANISTÁN
PAKISTÁN
KUWAIT
ARABIA SAUDITA
QATAR
EMIRATOS ÁRABES UNIDOS
OMÁN
YEMEN
EGIPTO
NEPAL
BHUTAN
BANGLADESH
INDIA
BIRMANIA
LAOS
VIETNAM
TAIWÁN
OCÉANO PACÍFICO
Manila
FILIPINAS
REP. DE PALAOS
THAILANDIA
CAMBOYA
BRUNEI
MALASIA
SINGAPUR
INDONESIA
PAPÚA NUEVA GUINEA
SALOMÓN
SUDÁN
ERITREA
ETIOPÍA
SOMALIA
UGANDA
KENYA
TANZANIA
MALAWI
MOZAMBIQUE
ZIMBABWE
MADAGASCAR
SEYCHELLES
COMORES
MAURICIO
MALDIVAS
SRI LANKA
OCÉANO ÍNDICO
AUSTRALIA
Trópico de Capricornio
NUEVA ZELANDA
Línea internacional de cambio de hora
UNDI
la en el mundo
AL ANTÁRTICO
ÁRTIDA
40°
80°
120°
160°
0°
Países donde el español es la lengua oficial o co-oficial
Zonas donde el español es hablado por una parte de la población
Madrid — Ciudad de más de 1 millón de hab.
Panamá — Ciudad de 100.000 a 1 millón de hab.
Malabo — Ciudad de menos de 100.000 hab.
Límite de Estado
Capital de Estado
Otras ciudades

XV

MÉXICO
©edigol ediciones,s.a.
ESTADOS UNIDOS
MISSISSIPPI
COLORADO
BRAZOS
RÍO GRANDE
San Diego
Tijuana
Mexicali
Las Cruces
El Paso
Ciudad Juárez
Hermosillo
SONORA
YAQUI
RÍO DEL FUERTE
Chihuahua
San Antonio
Houston
Nueva Orleans
Laredo
Nuevo Laredo
Corpus Christi
Culiacán
La Paz
Brownsville
Matamoros
Monterrey
Saltillo
Trópico de Cáncer
Golfo de California
Cabo San Lucas
Mazatlán
Ciudad Victoria
Zacatecas
Aguascalientes
Tepic
San Luís Potosí
Tampico
Puerto Vallarta
León
Guanajuato
Querétaro
Guadalajara
Morelia
Ciudad de México
Toluca
Colima
Tlaxcala
Puebla
Cuernavaca
Jalapa Enríquez
Veracruz
Chilpancingo
Acapulco
Oaxaca
COLOTOPEC
Villahermosa
Palenque
USUMACINTA
Mérida
Cancún
Uxmal
Chichén Itzá
Tulum
Campeche
Chetumal
BELICE
Belmopán
GUATEMALA
Guatemala
HONDURAS
Tegucigalpa
San Salvador
EL SALVADOR
Sierra Madre Occidental
Sierra Madre Oriental
Sierra Madre del Sur
Sierra Madre de Chiapas
Golfo de México
OCÉANO PACÍFICO
Golfo de Tehuantepec
110°
100°
90°
30°
20°

xvi

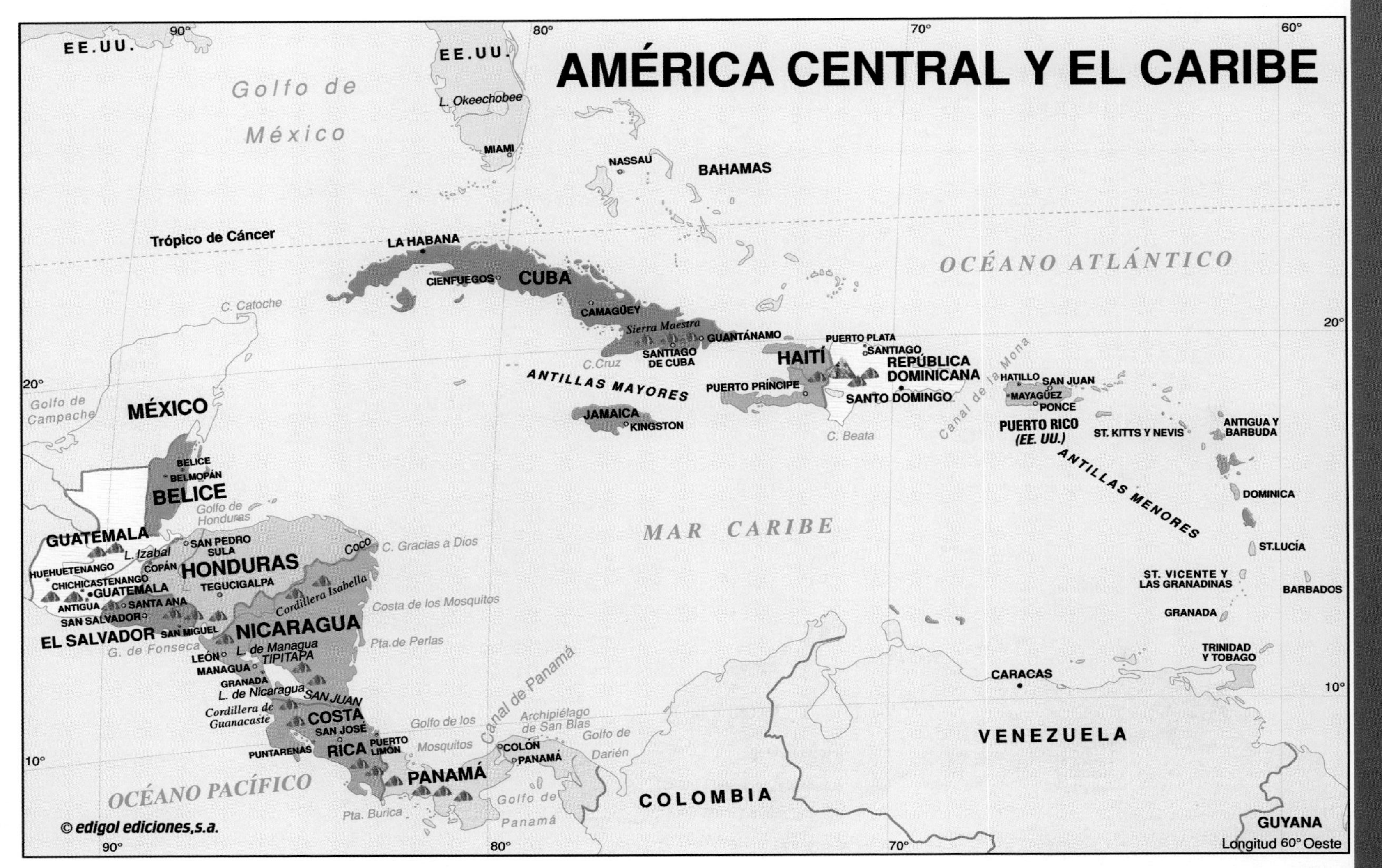
AMÉRICA CENTRAL Y EL CARIBE
EE.UU.
EE.UU.
Golfo de México
L. Okeechobee
MIAMI
NASSAU
BAHAMAS
Trópico de Cáncer
LA HABANA
CIENFUEGOS
CUBA
CAMAGÜEY
Sierra Maestra
GUANTÁNAMO
SANTIAGO DE CUBA
C. Catoche
C.Cruz
ANTILLAS MAYORES
JAMAICA
KINGSTON
HAITÍ
PUERTO PRÍNCIPE
PUERTO PLATA
SANTIAGO
REPÚBLICA DOMINICANA
SANTO DOMINGO
C. Beata
Canal de la Mona
HATILLO
SAN JUAN
MAYAGÜEZ
PONCE
PUERTO RICO (EE. UU.)
ST. KITTS Y NEVIS
ANTIGUA Y BARBUDA
ANTILLAS MENORES
DOMINICA
ST.LUCÍA
ST. VICENTE Y LAS GRANADINAS
BARBADOS
GRANADA
TRINIDAD Y TOBAGO
OCÉANO ATLÁNTICO
MAR CARIBE
Golfo de Campeche
MÉXICO
BELICE
BELMOPÁN
BELICE
Golfo de Honduras
GUATEMALA
L. Izabal
SAN PEDRO SULA
HUEHUETENANGO
COPÁN
HONDURAS
CHICHICASTENANGO
GUATEMALA
TEGUCIGALPA
ANTIGUA
SANTA ANA
SAN SALVADOR
EL SALVADOR
SAN MIGUEL
G. de Fonseca
Coco
C. Gracias a Dios
Cordillera Isabella
Costa de los Mosquitos
NICARAGUA
Pta.de Perlas
LEÓN
L. de Managua
TIPITAPA
MANAGUA
GRANADA
L. de Nicaragua
SAN JUAN
Cordillera de Guanacaste
COSTA RICA
SAN JOSÉ
PUNTARENAS
PUERTO LIMÓN
Golfo de los Mosquitos
Canal de Panamá
Archipiélago de San Blas
Golfo de Darién
COLÓN
PANAMÁ
PANAMÁ
Golfo de Panamá
Pta. Burica
OCÉANO PACÍFICO
COLOMBIA
CARACAS
VENEZUELA
GUYANA
Longitud 60° Oeste
90°
80°
70°
60°
20°
10°
© edigol ediciones,s.a.

xvii

ESPAÑA
MAR CANTÁBRICO
FRANCIA
ANDORRA
Andorra la Vella
Pirineos
OCÉANO ATLÁNTICO
PORTUGAL
MAR MEDITERRÁNEO
GOLFO DE CÁDIZ
Estrecho de Gibraltar
MARRUECOS
GALICIA
La Coruña
Lugo
Orense
Pontevedra
MIÑO
ASTURIAS
Oviedo
Cordillera Cantábrica
CANTABRIA
Santander
PAÍS VASCO
Bilbao
Vitoria
San Sebastián
NAVARRA
Pamplona
LA RIOJA
Logroño
ARAGÓN
Huesca
Zaragoza
Teruel
EBRO
Montes Ibéricos
CATALUÑA
Lérida
Gerona
Barcelona
Tarragona
TER
CASTILLA Y LEÓN
León
Palencia
Burgos
Soria
Valladolid
Zamora
Salamanca
Ávila
Segovia
DUERO
Sistema Central
MADRID
Madrid
Guadalajara
CASTILLA-LA MANCHA
Cuenca
Toledo
Ciudad Real
Albacete
TAJO
JÚCAR
COMUNIDAD VALENCIANA
Castellón de la Plana
Valencia
Alicante
TURIA
MURCIA
Murcia
SEGURA
EXTREMADURA
Cáceres
Badajoz
GUADIANA
ANDALUCÍA
Huelva
Sevilla
Córdoba
Jaén
Granada
Málaga
Almería
Cádiz
GUADALQUIVIR
Sierra Morena
Sierra Nevada
Mulhacén 3478
Gibraltar (R.U.)
Ceuta
Melilla
Lisboa
ISLAS BALEARES
MALLORCA
Palma de Mallorca
MENORCA
IBIZA
FORMENTERA
CABRERA
CANARIAS
LANZAROTE
FUERTEVENTURA
GRAN CANARIA
Las Palmas de Gran Canaria
TENERIFE
Santa Cruz de Tenerife
Teide 3715
LA PALMA
LA GOMERA
EL HIERRO
OCÉANO ATLÁNTICO
10°
6°
2°
42°
38°
14°
16°
18°
28°
©edigol ediciones,s.a.

xviii

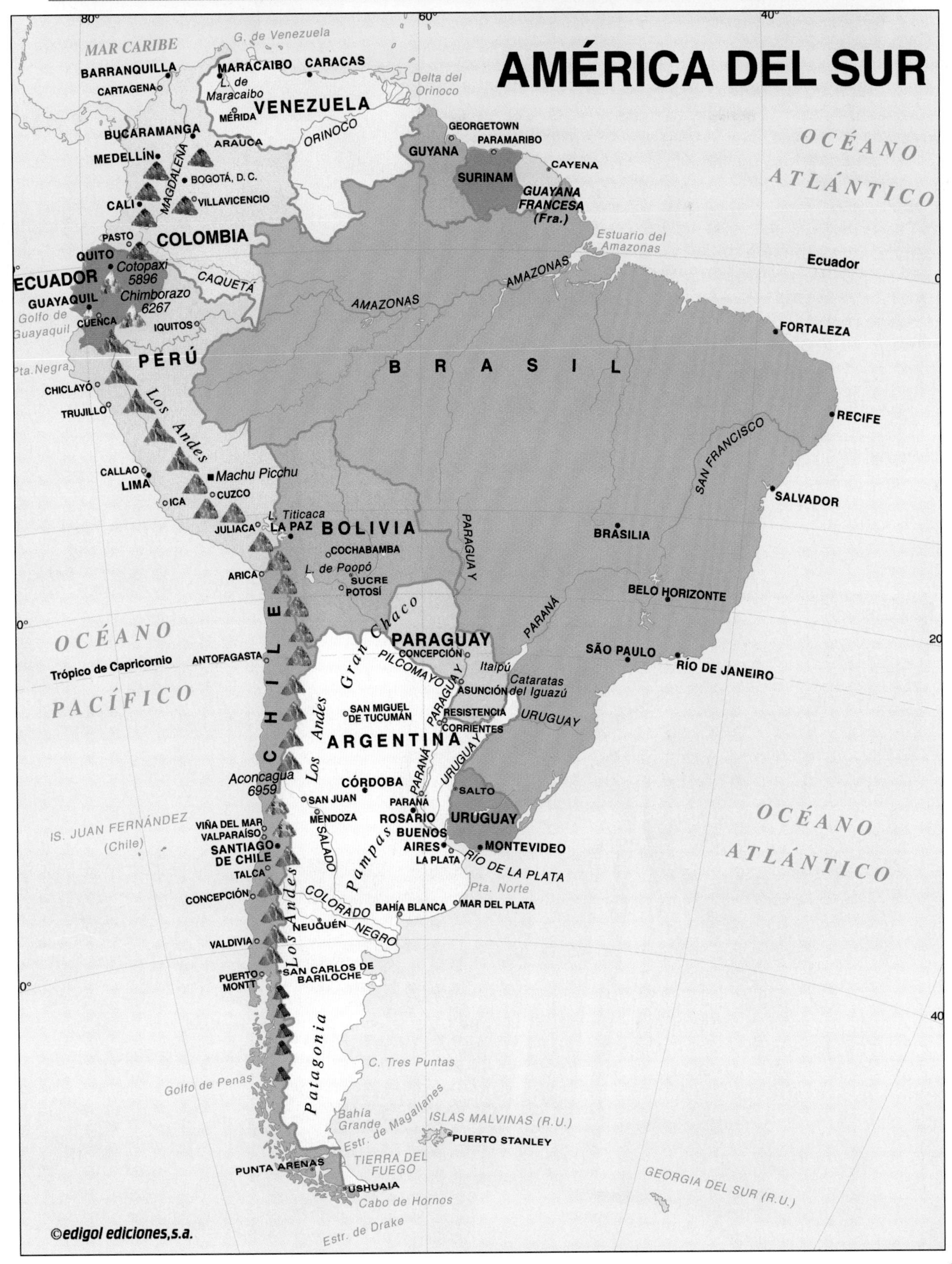

AMÉRICA DEL SUR
80°
60°
40°
MAR CARIBE
G. de Venezuela
BARRANQUILLA
CARTAGENA
MARACAIBO
CARACAS
L. de Maracaibo
MÉRIDA
VENEZUELA
Delta del Orinoco
ORINOCO
BUCARAMANGA
ARAUCA
MEDELLÍN
MAGDALENA
BOGOTÁ, D. C.
VILLAVICENCIO
CALI
PASTO
COLOMBIA
QUITO
ECUADOR
Cotopaxi 5896
Chimborazo 6267
GUAYAQUIL
Golfo de Guayaquil
CUENCA
CAQUETÁ
IQUITOS
GEORGETOWN
PARAMARIBO
GUYANA
SURINAM
CAYENA
GUAYANA FRANCESA (Fra.)
OCÉANO ATLÁNTICO
Estuario del Amazonas
Ecuador
AMAZONAS
FORTALEZA
Pta. Negra
PERÚ
B R A S I L
CHICLAYO
TRUJILLO
Los Andes
RECIFE
SAN FRANCISCO
CALLAO
LIMA
Machu Picchu
CUZCO
ICA
SALVADOR
L. Titicaca
JULIACA
LA PAZ
BOLIVIA
PARAGUAY
BRASILIA
COCHABAMBA
L. de Poopó
SUCRE
POTOSÍ
ARICA
BELO HORIZONTE
Gran Chaco
PARANÁ
OCÉANO PACÍFICO
Trópico de Capricornio
ANTOFAGASTA
PARAGUAY
CONCEPCIÓN
PILCOMAYO
Itaipú
Cataratas del Iguazú
ASUNCIÓN
SÃO PAULO
RÍO DE JANEIRO
CHILE
SAN MIGUEL DE TUCUMÁN
RESISTENCIA
CORRIENTES
URUGUAY
ARGENTINA
Los Andes
Aconcagua 6959
CÓRDOBA
SAN JUAN
PARANÁ
SALTO
IS. JUAN FERNÁNDEZ (Chile)
VIÑA DEL MAR
VALPARAÍSO
SANTIAGO DE CHILE
MENDOZA
ROSARIO
URUGUAY
SALADO
Pampas
BUENOS AIRES
LA PLATA
MONTEVIDEO
RÍO DE LA PLATA
OCÉANO ATLÁNTICO
TALCA
CONCEPCIÓN
COLORADO
Pta. Norte
BAHÍA BLANCA
MAR DEL PLATA
NEUQUÉN
NEGRO
VALDIVIA
PUERTO MONTT
SAN CARLOS DE BARILOCHE
Patagonia
C. Tres Puntas
Golfo de Penas
Bahía Grande
Estr. de Magallanes
ISLAS MALVINAS (R.U.)
PUERTO STANLEY
TIERRA DEL FUEGO
PUNTA ARENAS
USHUAIA
Cabo de Hornos
GEORGIA DEL SUR (R.U.)
Estr. de Drake
©edigol ediciones,s.a.

xix

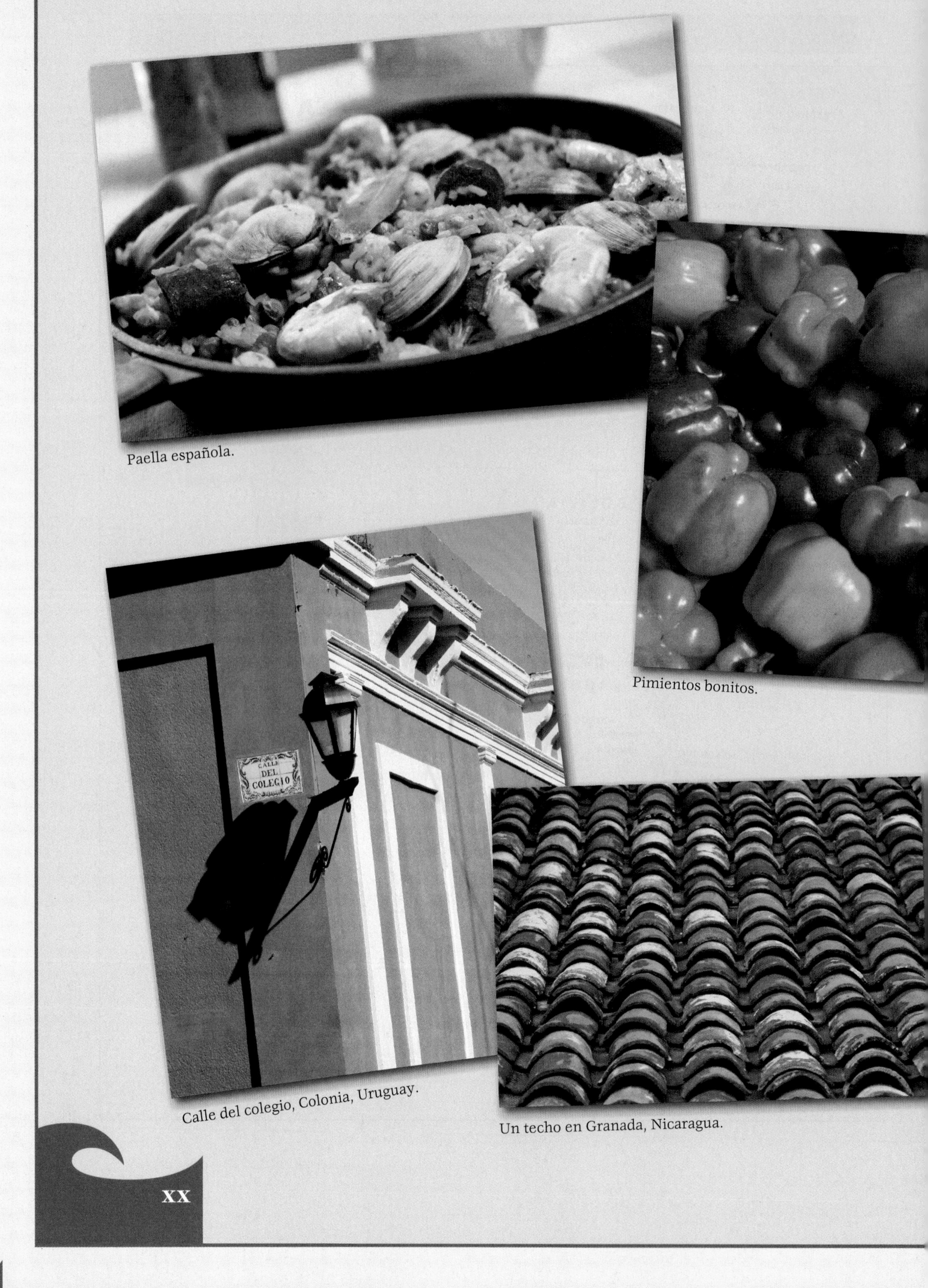

Paella española.

Pimientos bonitos.

Calle del colegio, Colonia, Uruguay.

Un techo en Granada, Nicaragua.

Me gusta la música de Cuba.

Mariana y Luciana son gemelas.

Emiliano toca la guitarra.

Alcázar, Sevilla, España

xxi

Mi papá juega al fútbol los domingos.

Agave, de México.

Valle Nevado, Chile.

Escalones a la Ciudad Perdida, Santa Marta, Colombia.

xxii

El tren a Machu Picchu.

Parque Cachamy, Venezuela.

Una rana arborícola, Costa Rica.

Olivas de España.

xxiii

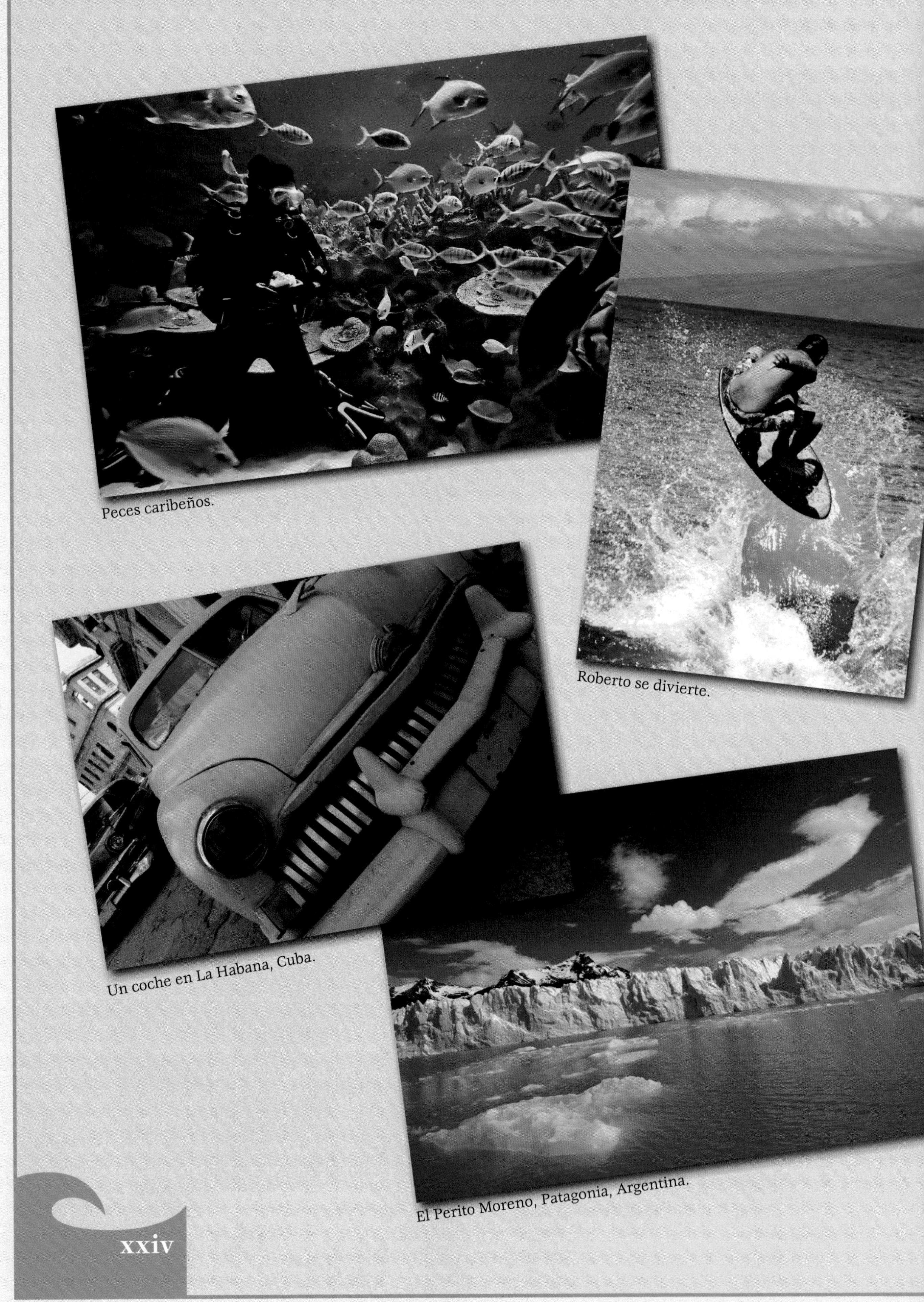

Peces caribeños.

Roberto se divierte.

Un coche en La Habana, Cuba.

El Perito Moreno, Patagonia, Argentina.

xxiv

La Boca, Buenos Aires, Argentina.

Museo de arte contemporánea de Barcelona, España.

Chiles en Oaxaca, México.

Él es de Uruguay.

XXV

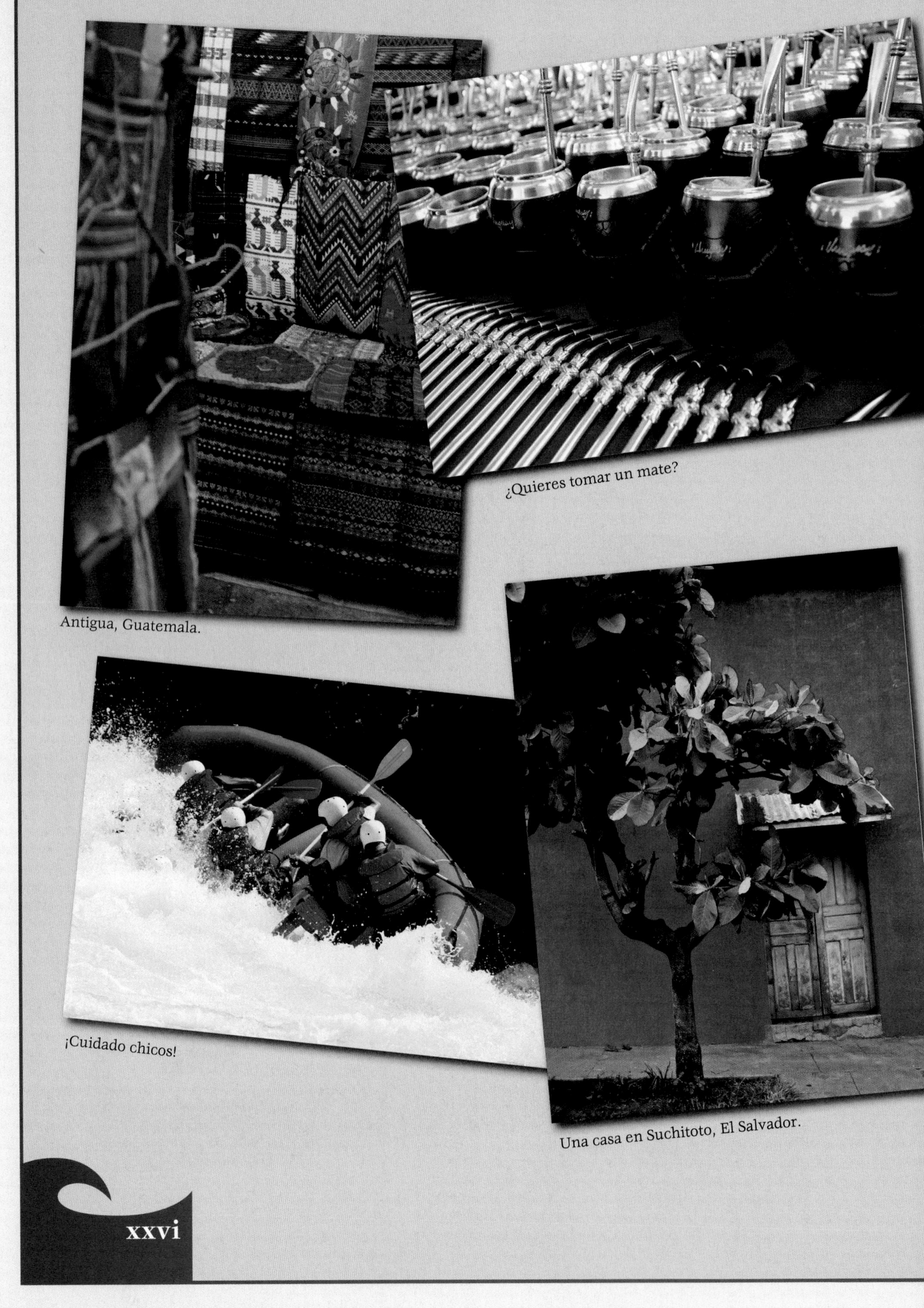
¿Quieres tomar un mate?

Antigua, Guatemala.

¡Cuidado chicos!

Una casa en Suchitoto, El Salvador.

xxvi

Amatista de Bolivia.

Ellas llevan ropa tradicional.

¡Vamos al carnaval!

xxvii

Teacher Resources

 *Capítulo 1*

TPRS *Capítulo 1*

 Episode 1, DVD 1, Track 4

 Activities 1–10

 pp. 25, 27

Connections with Parents

During the first few days of class, you might wish to send a letter home explaining objectives and expectations for the course.

Answers

El cuarto misterioso

1. Answers will vary.
2. Answers will vary.
3. Answers will vary.
4. Answers will vary.

Activities

Critical Thinking

The opening spread of each chapter highlights a scene from the video/DVD series, *El cuarto misterioso*. The series is centered around the lives of Spanish-speaking teenagers who find themselves in mysterious circumstances in their Mexico City suburb. The video script follows the order of presentation of vocabulary and grammatical structures as they are introduced in each chapter.

CAPÍTULO 1

¿Cómo te llamas?

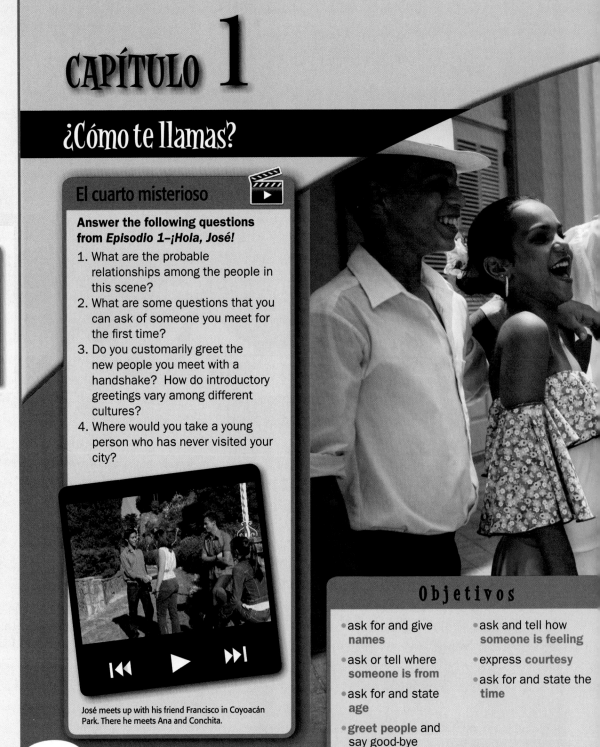

El cuarto misterioso

Answer the following questions from *Episodio 1–¡Hola, José!*

1. What are the probable relationships among the people in this scene?
2. What are some questions that you can ask of someone you meet for the first time?
3. Do you customarily greet the new people you meet with a handshake? How do introductory greetings vary among different cultures?
4. Where would you take a young person who has never visited your city?

José meets up with his friend Francisco in Coyoacán Park. There he meets Ana and Conchita.

Objetivos

- ask for and give **names**
- ask or tell where **someone is from**
- ask for and state **age**
- **greet people** and say good-bye
- ask and tell how **someone is feeling**
- express **courtesy**
- ask for and state the **time**

Notes

Icons in the side margins of the ATE indicate components with additional activities to reinforce and expand upon the content taught in *¡Aventura!*. These icons are explained in the ATE Introduction.

Students acquire new material in a variety of ways and at different speeds. Numerous activities in the left and right margins of this ATE have been provided to address students' multiple intelligences and to help meet the needs of individuals who require additional help in order to reach their maximum potential. Related activities can be found in the *¡Aventura!* ancillaries.

Activities

Prior Knowledge
The learning objectives of each chapter are accompanied by a photo or illustration from the chapter of study. Students should review the objectives and analyze the accompanying images. In the beginning, students will obviously use English to express themselves. Many times, students will make comparisons between English and Spanish. As students gain more vocabulary, expressions, structures and confidence in the language, they will begin to reflect more and more in Spanish. For these objectives, ask questions such as: What is happening in the picture? Who appears in the picture? Where do you think those people are from? What are some ways that we express courtesy in English? A checklist of these objectives, along with additional functions, appears on page 36 so students can evaluate their own progress.

Contexto cultural

El mundo hispano
Spanish is the official language of Spain, eighteen Latin American countries, Ecuatorial Guinea and Puerto Rico. Although many more use Spanish daily for both business and pleasure, more than 450 million people throughout the world consider Spanish as their official language.

Notes After students have analyzed the *El cuarto misterioso* screenshot and have answered the questions, you could show the video of the specific scene or even the whole episode. The end of the chapter activities include a *Resolviendo el misterio* activity that checks students' comprehension of the episode. The episode can be viewed again at the end of the chapter as well. The *El cuarto misterioso* video manual provides additional activities that reinforce vocabulary and grammatical structures that appear in the *¡Aventura!* textbook.

National Standards
Cultures 2.1, 2.2
Comparisons 4.2

Teacher Resources

 **Vocabulario I**
¿Cómo te llamas?
Alfabeto

 **Activity 11**

 **Activities 1–2**

 **Activity 1**

 **Activity 1**

 **Activities 1–2**

Activities

Critical Thinking
Have students point out the letters that are not in the English alphabet: *ñ* and *rr*.

Pronunciation *(el alfabeto)*
Point out that words that begin with the letters *k* and *w* are foreign.

TPR
Use this TPR (Total Physical Response) activity to practice the alphabet: Tell students that you will call out letters. If the letter you call appears in their first or last name, they should stand up quickly. The first student to stand when a letter from his or her name is called gets a point.

National Standards

Communication
1.1, 1.2, 1.3

Vocabulario I
¿Cómo te llamas?

El alfabeto

a	a	h	hache	ñ	eñe	t	te
b	be	i	i	o	o	u	u
c	ce	j	jota	p	pe	v	ve
d	de	k	ka	q	cu	w	doble ve
e	e	l	ele	r	ere	x	equis
f	efe	m	eme	rr	erre	y	i griega
g	ge	n	ene	s	ese	z	zeta

Hasta luego, Susana.
Me llamo Raúl.
¡Hola! ¿Cómo te llamas?
Adiós, Marcos.
Yo me llamo Ana.
¡Mucho gusto!
Me llamo Juan. ¿Y tú?
Sí, con hache mayúscula, e, ere, ene, a con acento, ene.
¿Cómo se escribe Hernán? ¿Con hache?

H → mayúscula
h → minúscula

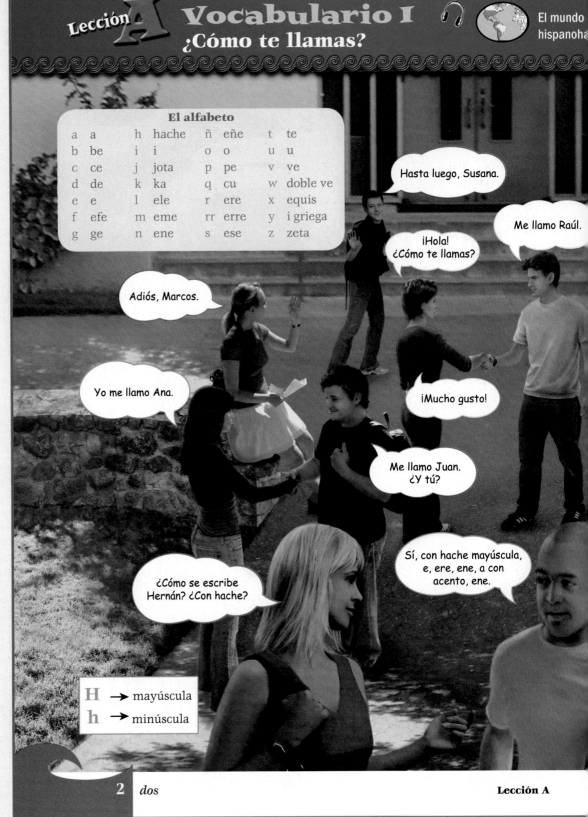

Notes Another word for *alfabeto* is *abecedario*. Several letters have different names in different parts of the Spanish-speaking world. For example, the letter *w* may become *doble v*, *v doble*, *doble u* or *uve doble*.

It is interesting to note that the Association of Spanish Language Academies met in Madrid for its annual conference in April of 1994 and voted to eliminate the letters *ch* and *ll* from the Spanish alphabet.

Inform students that a letter may be *mayúscula (A)* or *minúscula (a)*. In addition to teaching a letter *con acento (á)*, you may wish to teach *con tilde (ñ)*.

1 ¿Cómo se escribe?

Go online EMCLanguages.net

Escribe los nombres que oyes.

MODELO Carlos

muchachos

Alberto	Ernesto	José	Ramón
Alejandro	Esteban	Juan	Raúl
Andrés	Felipe	Julio	Ricardo
Ángel	Francisco	Lorenzo	Roberto
Antonio	Gerardo	Luis	Rodrigo
Benjamín	Guillermo	Marcos	Rogelio
Carlos	Héctor	Martín	Santiago
Daniel	Hernán	Miguel	Timoteo
David	Hugo	Nicolás	Tomás
Diego	Jaime	Pablo	Víctor
Eduardo	Jesús	Pedro	
Enrique	Jorge	Rafael	

muchachas

Alicia	Dolores	Laura	Pilar
Ana	Elena	Luisa	Raquel
Ángela	Elisa	Luz	Rosa
Bárbara	Esperanza	Margarita	Sandra
Blanca	Eva	María	Sara
Carlota	Gabriela	Marta	Susana
Carmen	Gloria	Mercedes	Teresa
Carolina	Inés	Mónica	Verónica
Catalina	Isabel	Natalia	Virginia
Claudia	Josefina	Patricia	Yolanda
Cristina	Juana	Paula	
Diana	Julia	Paz	

2 Me llamo....

Write the words *muchacho* and *muchacha* on a piece of paper. In the appropriate column, list any names from activity 1 of people you know. Then, list up to five names of your friends or family and write the name that you think is the Spanish equivalent. Can you find your own name or one that is similar to yours?

3 ¡Mucho gusto!

Contesta las siguientes preguntas. *(Answer the following questions.)*

1. How would you greet someone in Spanish?
2. What would you say to find out a person's name?
3. What would you answer if someone asked *¿Cómo te llamas?*
4. How might you politely tell someone you are pleased to meet him/her?
5. How do you say **Good-bye** in Spanish? And **See you later**?

4 ¿Cómo se escribe?

With a classmate, read aloud at least five male and five female names from activity 1 as your partner writes the names in Spanish. Next, take turns asking one another how to spell the names on the lists.

MODELO **A:** ¿Cómo se escribe *(name from list)?*
B: Se escribe con *(spell name).*
A: *¿(Spell name)?*
B: Sí.

¡Extra!

Los apodos

Nicknames *(apodos)* are common in Spanish. Examples include ***Isa*** (for *Isabel*), ***Fina*** or ***Pepa*** (for *Josefina*), ***Lola*** (for *Dolores*), ***Lupe*** (for *Guadalupe*), ***Paco*** or ***Pancho*** (for *Francisco*), ***Pepe*** (for *José*) and ***Quique*** (for *Enrique*). Personal characteristics are also used for nicknames in Spanish: ***Flaco*** (Slim).

Teacher Resources

Los nombres Activity 1

Activity 3

GV Activities 2–3

Answers

1 1. Ana
2. José
3. María
4. Paz
5. Raúl
6. Verónica

2 Creative self-expression.

3 1. Hola.
2. ¿Cómo te llamas?
3. Me llamo....
4. Mucho gusto.
5. Adiós. Hasta luego.

4 Answers will vary.

Activities

Spanish for Spanish Speakers
For different letters of the alphabet, ask students to think of other Spanish names. Write them on the board under the headings *Muchachas/Muchachos.*

National Standards

Communication
1.1, 1.2

Cultures
2.1

Comparisons
4.1, 4.2

Notes

The script for all *¡Aventura! 1* recorded content is provided in the Audio Program Manual.

For teacher convenience, student answer sheets have been provided for the activities indicated in the student textbook by the audio speaker icon (the first activity after *Vocabularios I* and *II* and the third activity after *Diálogos I* and *II*). These reproducible answer sheets can be found at the end of the Audio Program Manual.

The section *¡Extra!* offers additional vocabulary, notes, and suggestions to students. It is not required content.

Teacher Resources

 Diálogo I
¡Hola!
Activity 7

 p. 3

Answers

5 1. B
2. D
3. F
4. A
5. C
6. E

6 Answers will vary.

7 1. Sí, con hache.
2. Me llamo Carmen.
3. ¡Mucho gusto, Carmen!
4. Adiós.

Activities

Prereading Strategy
Instruct students to cover up the dialog with one hand and look at the photographs. Ask them to imagine where the conversation takes place and what the people are saying to one another.

National Standards
Communication 1.1, 1.2
Comparisons 4.1

Diálogo I ¡Hola!

CARMEN: ¡Hola! ¿Cómo te llamas?
HUGO: Yo me llamo Hugo. ¿Y tú?
CARMEN: Me llamo Carmen.

HUGO: ¡Mucho gusto, Carmen!
CARMEN: ¿Cómo se escribe Hugo?
HUGO: Se escribe con hache mayúscula, u, ge, o.

HUGO: Hasta luego.
CARMEN: Adiós.

5 ¿Qué recuerdas?

Completa las frases de la izquierda con una de las frases de la derecha, según el diálogo ¡Hola! ***(Complete the sentences on the left with the appropriate sentence on the right, according to the dialog*** **¡Hola!*)***

1. ¡Hola! ¿Cómo...	**A.** ...gusto, Carmen!
2. Yo me...	**B.** ...te llamas?
3. Me llamo...	**C.** ...escribe Hugo?
4. ¡Mucho...	**D.** ...llamo Hugo. ¿Y tú?
5. ¿Cómo se...	**E.** ...hache mayúscula, u, ge, o.
6. Se escribe con...	**F.** ...Carmen.

6 Algo personal

1. ¿Cómo te llamas?
2. ¿Cómo se escribe *(your name)*?

7 ¿Cuál es la respuesta correcta? 

Escoge una respuesta correcta a lo que oyes. ***(Choose a correct response to what you hear.)***

Adiós. Me llamo Carmen.
¡Mucho gusto, Carmen! Sí, con hache.

Notes

¡Aventura! stresses the use of authentic Spanish. Therefore, vocabulary is introduced in context, along with appropriate cultural notes.

The *Diálogos I* and *II* are intended to apply the vocabulary presented in the *Vocabularios I* and *II*. Students thus have the opportunity to see new words and expressions applied immediately in a functional context with follow-up factual and personal questions for practice.

Dialogs have been recorded by native speakers. The recordings are included in the *¡Aventura!* Audio Program.

Cultura  

Saludos y despedidas

¡Mucho gusto!

Learning how to speak Spanish involves more than just learning vocabulary and grammar. Gestures *(los gestos)* go hand in hand with speaking, which makes conversation in Spanish seem much more animated than in English. Spanish-speaking people commonly greet one another with a quick, relaxed handshake, which may be followed by a hug *(un abrazo)* as they pat each other on the back. Often women and young girls greet each other with a light kiss on the cheek. In some countries, men and women who know each other well also greet one another with a kiss on the cheek (or on both cheeks in Spain). These same gestures are often repeated when saying good-bye. The next time you see people speaking Spanish, watch how they use their hands, eyes and bodies to communicate.

¡Hola!

8 Comparando

In two columns (labeled *Similar* and *Diferente*) compare how you think the gestures and body language of a native Spanish speaker are similar to or different from yours when greeting someone or saying good-bye.

MODELO

Similar	Diferente
1. We shake hands sometimes.	1. We do not kiss on the cheeks.
2.	2.

Me llamo Juan.

Teacher Resources

Activity 4

Answers

8 Answers will vary.

Activities

Critical Thinking

Ask how students feel about the use of gestures, the embrace or a kiss on the cheek for greeting others or for saying farewell.

Notes

Tell students that in Hispanic countries people tend to stand closer to the person they are addressing than people do in the United States.

You may wish to have students use a Venn diagram to do activity 8. (Refer to the *Estrategia* on page 358 in *Capítulo 8* for ideas on how to use this graphic organizer.)

National Standards

Cultures
2.1

Connections
3.2

Comparisons
4.1, 4.2

Teacher Resources

 *Estrategia*

 Activity 5

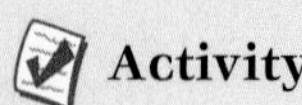 Activity 3

Answers

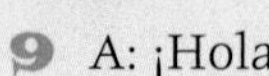

9 A: ¡Hola!
B: ¡Hola! ... llamas?
A: ... ¿Y tú?
B: *No punctuation is missing.*
A: ¡Mucho ...!
B: ¿Con ...?
A: ... ese.
B: ..., Inés!

Activities

Cooperative Learning

After practicing the expressions in *Estrategia*, ask students to use the expressions with one another in pairs or in small groups. Select several pairs of students to demonstrate their use at the front of the class.

TPR

Practice the expressions in *Estrategia*. Say several expressions and call on students to respond to your instructions. Observe to see that students respond appropriately.

National Standards

Communication
1.1, 1.2

Comparisons
4.1

Estructura

Punctuation ¡Mucho gusto! ¿Y tú? ¡Hola! ¿Cómo te llamas?

Have you noticed any punctuation marks in Spanish that are not used in English? Written Spanish requires two question marks and two exclamation points, one at the beginning and the other at the end of the sentence. The first is written upside down and tells you that a question or an exclamation will follow. No other punctuation (e.g., period, comma) follows this pattern.

Práctica

9 Puntuación

Señala la puntuación que falta en el siguiente diálogo. ***(Point out the missing punctuation marks in the following dialog.)***

A: Hola!
B: ¡Hola ¿Cómo te llamas
A: Me llamo Inés. Y tú?
B: Yo me llamo Andrés.
A: Mucho gusto, Andrés!
B: Mucho gusto. ¿Cómo se escribe Inés? Con i?
A: Sí, con i mayúscula, ene, e con acento, ese
B: ¡Adiós, Inés

Estrategia

Learning tip: Recognizing classroom expressions

You will see and hear many of the following common expressions. You do not have to memorize them, but learning to recognize them will help you understand instructions and complete activities in class during this school year. Look through the textbook to find examples of these expressions. Do they help you understand instructions?

Abre/Abran (el libro).	Open (your book).
Busca/Busquen... en la página....	Look for... on page....
Cierra/Cierren (el libro).	Close (your book).
Contesta/Contesten....	Answer....
Da/Den....	Give....
Di/Digan....	Say (or tell)....
Escoge/Escojan....	Choose....
Escribe/Escriban....	Write....
Escucha/Escuchen.	Listen.
Habla/Hablen en español.	Speak in Spanish.
Haz/Hagan....	Make (or do)....
Lee/Lean....	Read....
Levanta/Levanten (la mano).	Raise (your hand).
Mira/Miren.	Look.
Pasa/Pasen a (la pizarra).	Go to (the board).
Responde/Respondan....	Respond....
Saca/Saquen (una hoja de papel).	Take out (a sheet of paper).
Señala/Señalen (el mapa).	Point at (the map).
Siéntate/Siéntense.	Sit down.

Notes Point out to students that learning common classroom expressions will help them function and succeed in Spanish class. In order to demonstrate this, give examples of the expressions listed in *Estrategia*. The word *señala* is used in activity 9, and *haz* is used in activity 10. Ask if students can understand instructions after learning these expressions.

Explain that this list offers two forms of some common expressions. The first form (the singular form before the slash) is used informally for talking with one person who is the students' age or younger, or a close friend or family member, whereas the second form (the plural form after the slash) is used when talking to more than one person.

¿En qué orden?

Haz oraciones lógicas usando las siguientes pistas. ***(Make complete sentences using the following cues.)***

MODELO llamo / Me / Alejandro / .
Me llamo Alejandro.

1. ¡ / ! / Hola
2. llamas / ? / te / ¿ / Cómo
3. Carlota / . / llamo / Me / ¿ / tú? / Y
4. Yo / Carlota / Jaime / . / me / gusto, / ! / llamo / ¡Mucho
5. se / ¡Mucho / ¿ / Cómo / Jaime? / gusto / ! / escribe
6. escribe / Se / jota / i, / con / eme, / mayúscula, / a, / e / .

Comunicación

A escribir

Imagine you are a scriptwriter for a video that is being produced in Spanish. Write a scene in which two Spanish-speaking teenagers meet. They should: 1) greet one another; 2) ask each other's name and how to spell it; 3) say good-bye. Be sure to add director's notes, where appropriate, suggesting gestures and body language the actors should use.

SCENE ONE: THEY MEET
Boy: Hola. ¿Cómo te llamas?
Girl: Me llamo Claudia.
Boy: Yo me llamo Daniel.
(They shake hands.)
Mucho gusto.

Answers

10 1. ¡Hola!
2. ¿Cómo te llamas?
3. Me llamo Carlota. ¿Y tú?
4. Yo me llamo Jaime. ¡Mucho gusto, Carlota!
5. ¡Mucho gusto! ¿Cómo se escribe Jaime?
6. Se escribe con jota mayúscula, a, i, eme, e.

11 Creative writing practice.

Activities

Language through Action
Pair students up and have them play the role of one of the people in the video they wrote for activity 11. Inform students that if they are uncomfortable, they can pretend they are kissing one another on the cheek instead of actually touching one another.

Notes Some of the more common classroom expressions are taught in this lesson. For a complete list of classroom expressions, refer to the ATE Introduction.

Other useful classroom expressions: *¿Cómo se dice...en español?* (How do you say...in Spanish?); *¿Qué quiere decir...?* (What does... mean?); *No sé.* (I don't know.); *No comprendo.* (I don't understand.); *Tengo una pregunta.* (I have a question.)

National Standards

Communication
1.1, 1.3

Connections
3.1

Communities
5.1

Teacher Resources

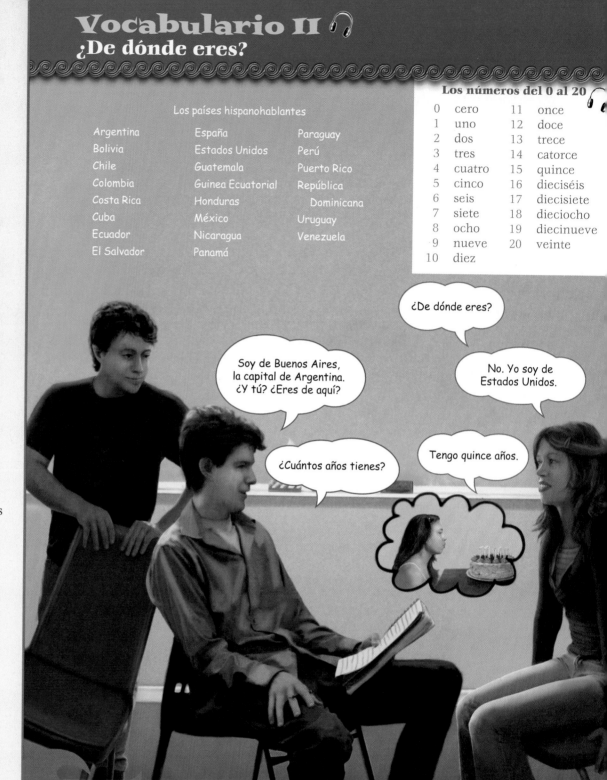

Vocabulario II
¿De dónde eres?
Los números del 0 al 20

 **Activity 12**

 **Activities 6–10**

 **Activities 4–8**

 **pp. 33–34**

Activity 2
Activity 3
Activity 4

 **Activities 4–5**

Activities

Critical Thinking

Provide students with blank map outlines of the Spanish-speaking parts of the world (or have students prepare the maps) on which they can write the names of the countries and capitals they know. Extend the activity by having students add the names of non-Spanish-speaking countries and their capitals.

Multiple Intelligences (logical-mathematical)

Help students with conversion rates for different currencies to American dollars.

National Standards

Communication
1.2

Cultures
2.1

Connections
3.1

Vocabulario II

¿De dónde eres?

Los países hispanohablantes

Argentina	España	Paraguay
Bolivia	Estados Unidos	Perú
Chile	Guatemala	Puerto Rico
Colombia	Guinea Ecuatorial	República Dominicana
Costa Rica	Honduras	Uruguay
Cuba	México	Venezuela
Ecuador	Nicaragua	
El Salvador	Panamá	

Los números del 0 al 20

0	cero	11	once
1	uno	12	doce
2	dos	13	trece
3	tres	14	catorce
4	cuatro	15	quince
5	cinco	16	dieciséis
6	seis	17	diecisiete
7	siete	18	dieciocho
8	ocho	19	diecinueve
9	nueve	20	veinte
10	diez		

Notes

The numbers 21–100 are presented with time on pages 24–25. For students asking for a comprehensive reference list of the numbers, and for teachers wishing to teach all the numbers at once, turn to the Appendices at the back of the book.

Use transparencies or a wall map to show students where Spanish is spoken in the world.

12 Los países

Practice saying the names of the Spanish-speaking countries you hear. Write the name of each country after it is repeated.

Soy de Honduras.

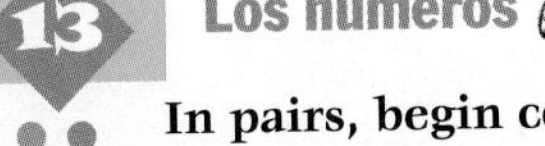

13 Los números

In pairs, begin counting with *cero* and continue by twos to *veinte*. Start over, beginning with *uno*, and count by twos to *diecinueve*.

14 Del cero al veinte

Create your own pattern of at least four numbers from zero to twenty. Then with a classmate, read the numbers aloud as your partner writes them down. Next, have your partner spell aloud the numbers from the list while you write them. Compare the lists and make any needed corrections. Switch roles.

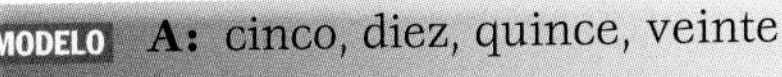

MODELO **A:** cinco, diez, quince, veinte
B: *(Write* cinco.*)*
B: ce, i, ene, ce, o
A: *(Write* cinco.*)*
(Compare the numbers you have written.)

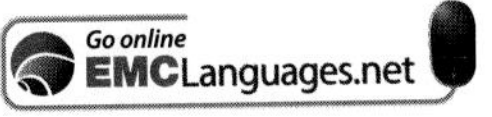

15 Una encuesta

Survey classmates to find out the range of ages in your Spanish class. Begin by preparing a chart. Then ask ten classmates how old they are in Spanish, filling in the blank space with their age and adding a mark in the column underneath for each person who is the same age. Summarize your findings for the class.

Encuesta				
14	15			
||	|||			

¿Cuántos años tienes?

Teacher Resources

Activity 12
Activity 13

Answers

12 Check for correct pronunciation.
13 Check pronunciation and make sure students are saying the numbers in the correct order.
14 Numbers will vary. Check for correct pronunciation and spelling.
15 Creative self-expression.

Activities

Connections

Ask students to draw a map of the world without using any reference materials. They should then share their maps with others and discuss the following: What did they draw first? What parts of the world are they most/least familiar with? Where did they put the United States? Is a certain area too large or too small? Which Spanish-speaking areas/countries are included?

Cooperative Learning

Working in groups of three or four, students can practice counting aloud in Spanish from zero to ten, one number at a time. They must continue until everyone has said each number at least once. Have them practice the numbers through twenty in the same way.

National Standards

Communication
1.1, 1.2

Connections
3.1, 3.2

Notes

Standards for Foreign Language Learning in the 21st Century discusses philosophical issues, implications and strategies for maximizing proficiency and for empowering all students to become successful learners and users of world languages. *¡Aventura!* is designed to support and advance the vision described by the authors of the national standards, blending the five Cs of communication, cultures, connections, comparisons and communities with pedagogically sound content, fun activities and an ongoing discussion of the wealth of opportunities that learning a world language creates for students.

Teacher Resources

Diálogo
¿De dónde eres, Hugo?
Activity 17
Activity 18

p. 4

Answers

16 1. E
2. C
3. A
4. F
5. B
6. D

17 Answers will vary.

18 1. veinte
2. quince
3. diez
4. ocho

19 Refer to the map at the front of the book for capital names.

Activities

Cooperative Learning
Have students work in groups to complete an unlabeled map of the Spanish-speaking world. See how many countries and capitals they can name in four minutes.

Critical Thinking
Provide students with a list of countries and capitals. Then have them match the capitals to the appropriate countries.

National Standards

Communication
1.1, 1.2

Connections
3.1

Diálogo II ¿De dónde eres, Hugo?

CARMEN: ¿De dónde eres, Hugo?
HUGO: Soy de Bogotá, la capital de Colombia.

HUGO: ¿Y tú? ¿Eres de aquí?
CARMEN: No. Yo soy de México.

CARMEN: ¿Cuántos años tienes, Hugo?
HUGO: Tengo dieciséis años. ¿Y tú?
CARMEN: Yo tengo quince años.

16 ¿Qué recuerdas?

Completa las frases de la izquierda con una de las frases de la derecha, según el diálogo *¿De dónde eres, Hugo?*

1. ¿De dónde...
2. Soy de Bogotá,...
3. ¿Y tú? ¿Eres...
4. No. Yo soy...
5. ¿Cuántos años...
6. Tengo...

A. ...de aquí?
B. ...tienes, Hugo?
C. ...la capital de Colombia.
D. ...dieciséis años.
E. ...eres, Hugo?
F. ...de México.

17 Algo personal

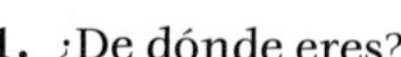

1. ¿De dónde eres?
2. ¿Cuántos años tienes?

18 ¿Cuántos años tienes?

Escribe los números que oyes.

1

3

2

4

19 Conexión con otras disciplinas: geografía

Using the map at the front of the textbook, identify the capitals of the Spanish-speaking countries.

Notes

Dialogs in *¡Aventura!* provide exposure to authentic spoken Spanish in specific contexts. Explain to students that they will hear audio recordings of Spanish speakers. They are not expected to understand everything they hear. However, students should listen carefully to the sounds, tone and rhythm of the language while determining what topics are being discussed.

Note for students, before assigning activity 19, that Bolivia has the rare distinction of having two capitals: *Sucre* is the constitutional capital, but *La Paz* is the actual governmental center.

Cultura viva II

Las damas en mi cumpleaños.

Mi madre y mi padre.

Los cumpleaños

Birthdays *(los cumpleaños)* are important events throughout the Spanish-speaking world. Carmen's fifteenth birthday *(la quinceañera)* was a big occasion since the event often symbolizes that a girl is ready to date. Traditionally, this coming-of-age celebration begins with a religious ceremony followed by a fancy reception at home or in a local banquet hall. The festivities include food, music and, often, a choreographed dance performed by the birthday girl and her court, which is composed of male escorts *(chambelanes)* and maids of honor *(damas)*. It takes a lot of time, money and effort to plan a fiesta de quinceañera. Today, instead of the traditional party, a growing number of fifteen-year-old girls *(quinceañeras)* prefer to receive a special gift. Spanish-speaking males, on the other hand, celebrate their fifteenth birthday *(el quinceañero)* like any other *cumpleaños* with a small party, an informal dance, a trip to the beach or a special dinner with their family.

Soy quinceañera y bailo.

20 Comparando

Is the way Latin American teenagers celebrate their birthdays different from what you and your friends do? If you were a *quinceañero* or *quinceañera* in Mexico, how would you choose to celebrate your coming of age? Explain.

Notes The section *Cultura viva* contains interesting and useful cultural information that will help students understand how life in the many Spanish-speaking parts of the world may be similar to or different from what they are used to in their community.

Students are invited to broaden their learning to include subject matter that reaches beyond just the language skills they are learning in Spanish class.

¡Aventura! provides cross-curricular connections to mathematics, history, geography, science and other disciplines, as seen in activity 19.

Teacher Resources

Activity 6

Answers

20 Answers will vary.

Activities

Communities

Discuss the *Cultura viva* and activity 20 on page 11 with students. Ask if students know anyone who has celebrated a *quinceañera*. Ask them to describe what it was like. Then have students share with the class any celebrations they have in their home that may seem out of the ordinary to others.

National Standards	
Communication 1.3	**Communities** 5.1
Cultures 2.1	
Comparisons 4.1, 4.2	

Teacher Resources

Activities 11–13

Activity 7

Answers

21 There are twenty-one countries where Spanish is the official language. Refer to the maps at the front of the book for country names.

22 1. D
2. E
3. C
4. B
5. A

23 Answers will vary.

National Standards

Communication
1.1, 1.2, 1.3

Connections
3.1

Comparisons
4.1

Estructura

Definite articles and countries

Some Spanish speakers use the definite articles *(artículos definidos) el, la* and *los* with these country names, whereas others prefer to omit the articles. Their use is optional.

la	Argentina	→	Argentina
el	Ecuador	→	Ecuador
los	Estados Unidos	→	Estados Unidos
el	Paraguay	→	Paraguay
el	Perú	→	Perú
la	República Dominicana	→	República Dominicana
el	Uruguay	→	Uruguay

Práctica

21 Los países hispanohablantes

Working in pairs, list as many Spanish-speaking countries as you can in three minutes. Check your work by looking at the map in the book. How many are there?

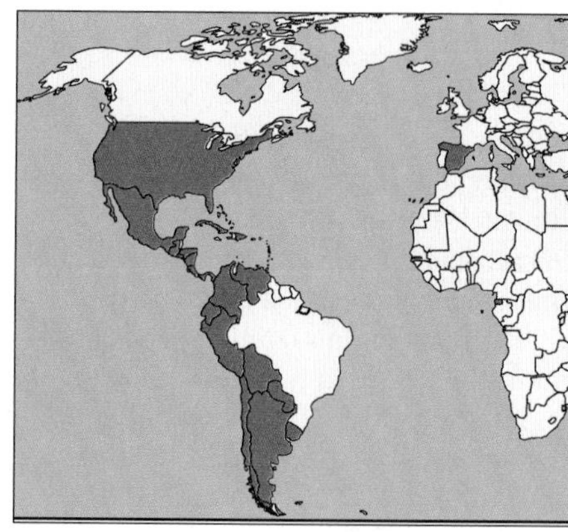

22 Soy de la capital

Selecciona la respuesta más apropiada. ***(Select the most appropriate response.)***

1. ¿Eres de Venezuela?
2. ¿Eres de la Argentina?
3. ¿Eres de España?
4. ¿Eres de Ecuador?
5. ¿Eres de El Salvador?

A. Sí, soy de la capital, San Salvador.
B. Sí, soy de la capital, Quito.
C. Sí, soy de la capital, Madrid.
D. Sí, soy de la capital, Caracas.
E. Sí, soy de la capital, Buenos Aires.

23 ¿Qué países quieres visitar?

What countries in the Spanish-speaking world would you like to visit? Why?

Notes Inform students they will learn more about the use of articles in *Capítulo 2.*

The icon indicates activities that students perform orally with a partner.

The icon indicates interation with a group. You may want to have students prepare the content in advance or follow up by writing a summary of their oral work.

Comunicación

24 ¿De dónde eres?

With a classmate, take turns asking for one another's names and where each of you is from. In your answer, choose a city and country from one of the Spanish-speaking countries you have studied.

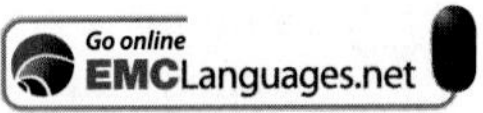

Estructura

Cognates

Words in Spanish often resemble English words you already know (e.g., *acento* looks similar to the English word **accent**). Words that resemble one another and that have the same meaning in two languages are called **cognates** *(cognados)*. Do you recognize these cognates?

Argentina *capital* *diálogo* *persona* *teléfono* *vocabulario*

When words look similar but have entirely different meanings in Spanish and English, they are called **false cognates**. Here are a few examples: *colegio* (school), *éxito* (success), *lectura* (reading), *sin* (without).

Buenos Aires, la capital de Argentina.

Teacher Resources

Activity 14

Activity 5

Answers

24 Role-playing activity.

Activities

Critical Thinking

It is always exciting for students to see how their vocabulary seems to grow after they learn about cognates. As a simple demonstration, ask students to name the Spanish-speaking countries that are cognates. Then have students classify the countries according to the following categories: 1) countries that appear exactly the same; 2) countries that are the same except for an accent mark; 3) countries that have a spelling change. Finally, ask if students can name a country that is not a cognate: *los Estados Unidos*. Other examples that students have not yet learned include Germany *(Alemania)* and England *(Inglaterra)*.

Notes

Encourage students to refer to the maps at the beginning of the book to see where the places mentioned in the textbook are located.

Whereas the *Práctica* activities offer basic mechanical and/or meaningful practice on structures, the *Comunicación* activities provide open-ended opportunities for self-expression.

National Standards
Communication 1.1
Connections 3.1
Comparisons 4.1

Teacher Resources

 Activity 25

 Activity 15

Answers

25 Pronounce the words in the list for students or play the audio for students. Point out that although these cognates are similar in both languages, they are pronounced differently. Check pronunciation and correct words that students are mispronouncing.

26 1. C
2. B
3. A
4. D

Activities

Communities
Invite a professional who uses Spanish in his or her work to talk to the class.

Critical Thinking
Ask students how they think the people mentioned in activity 26 might use Spanish in their daily lives.

Technology
Have students who have access to a computer do an Internet search of occupations that require bilingual employees.

National Standards	
Communication 1.2	**Communities** 5.1
Connections 3.1	
Comparisons 4.1	

Práctica

Go online EMCLanguages.net

25 Los cognados

Practice pronouncing these cognates. Try to guess the meaning of the words as you say them.

1. favorito
2. estudiar
3. el chocolate
4. formal
5. México
6. el actor
7. la persona
8. la capital
9. el animal
10. la televisión
11. el restaurante
12. el teléfono
13. la posibilidad
14. el diálogo
15. el vocabulario

¡Oportunidades!

¿Por qué estudiar español?
Knowing Spanish offers you opportunities to communicate with people throughout the Spanish-speaking world. In addition, learning Spanish will…

- help you understand other cultures.
- offer you insights into and a better understanding of your own culture.
- improve your English skills.
- increase employment opportunities.

26 ¡Varias profesiones son cognados!

Indica la letra de la foto que corresponde con la profesión de las siguientes personas.

A B C D

1. Es veterinario.
2. Es actor de televisión.
3. Es profesora.
4. Es policía.

Notes

Have students compare English and Spanish using cognates introduced in this lesson.

Companies are requiring more from their workforce than mere rote knowledge of facts. The pages of *¡Aventura!* reflect these changing requirements by preparing students for the many opportunities and challenges they will face in the ever-expanding international market.

If students have trouble with photograph B in activity 26, explain that the person shown is Wilmer Valderrama, from Venezuela, one of the stars of the television program *That '70s Show*.

 Comunicación

27 A conversar

Working with a classmate, read and discuss this article. Do not use a dictionary to look up words. Then, prepare a list of the cognates. Finally, write a short summary of what you understood.

WWW

www.mrshowbiz.go.com/celebrities/people

Si deseas ver la historia, la biografía, las fotos más recientes y las anécdotas de tus artistas favoritos, entra en esta página Web. Aquí encuentras toda la información sobre las estrellas; noticias y novedades de los famosos de Hollywood, así como enlaces que te llevan a los sitios personales de numerosos personajes.

Penélope Cruz

28 ¡Mucho gusto!

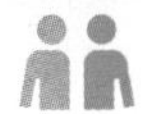

Working with a partner, create a dialog in which you ask for one another's names and ages, and where each of you is from. Each person should prepare at least four lines. Practice the dialog and then present it in class. Remember to shake hands when appropriate.

¿De dónde eres tú?

Teacher Resources

 **Activity 6**

Answers

27 Cognates: *historia* (history); *biografía* (biography); *fotos* (photos); *recientes* (recent); *anécdotas* (anecdotes); *artistas* (artists); *favoritos* (favorite); *información* (information); *famosos* (famous); *personales* (personal); *numerosos* (numerous)

28 Creative self-expression.

Activities

Cooperative Learning

Have students practice the question *¿Qué país hispanohablante te gustaría visitar?* Then have them conduct a survey of at least ten classmates to find out which Spanish-speaking country they would most like to visit. Procedure: 1) First, create a chart listing all the Spanish-speaking countries; 2) In Spanish, ask at least ten students which Spanish-speaking country they would like to visit (using *¿Qué país hispanohablante te gustaría visitar?*); 3) Record the results on the chart.

País	Número de personas
Argentina	| |
Bolivia	|
Chile	|
Colombia	| |
Costa Rica	| | | |

National Standards

Communication
1.1, 1.2, 1.3

Connections
3.1

Comparisons
4.1

Notes

As part of your classroom management, consider setting a time limit for each pair or group activity. You can hold students accountable by selecting pairs or groups to perform the task they are practicing or by having students select one person from each group to give a summary of the activity to the class.

The word *actriz* is used by many people as the feminine for *actor*.

Teacher Resources

Lectura cultural
¡Visita las diez maravillas del mundo hispanohablante!
Activity 29

Answers

29 1. El desierto más árido del planeta está en Chile.
2. La capital más alta del planeta es La Paz, Bolivia.
3. La universidad más antigua de América está en la República Dominicana.
4. Ojos del Salado es el volcán activo más alto del planeta.
5. La pirámide más grande del planeta está en México.

30 Answers will vary.

Activities

Critical Thinking
Using a map for visual reinforcement, discuss what students know about the Spanish-speaking world. Ask both general and specific questions about geography, history, current events, etc. Name and point out the location of each site you mention. Then compare how each place is similar to or different from the United States.

National Standards	
Communication 1.1, 1.2	**Comparisons** 4.2
Cultures 2.2	
Connections 3.1	

Lectura cultural

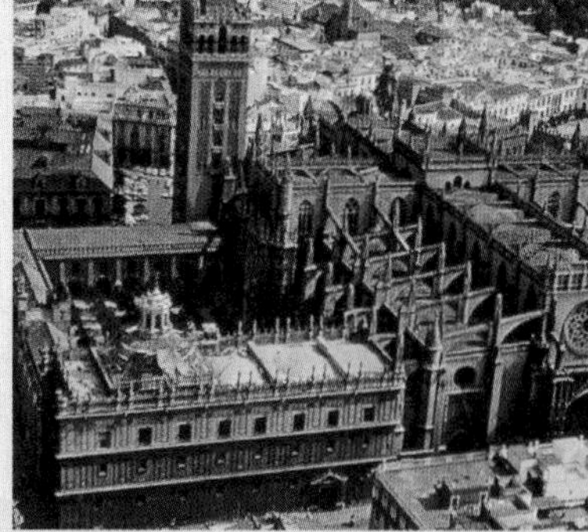

La Catedral de Sevilla, España.

¡Visita las diez maravillas del mundo hispanohablante!

Si estás buscando[1] un destino diferente para tus próximas[2] vacaciones, te invitamos[3] a visitar los sitios de nuestro[4] "tour de los récords del mundo hispanohablante[5]". El tour incluye[6] diez maravillas fascinantes en diferentes lugares[7] del mundo: España, la república africana de Guinea Ecuatorial, América del Sur, América Central, México y el Caribe.

Diez maravillas para visitar:

1. La **Catedral** en Sevilla, España, el edificio[8] gótico[9] más grande[10] de Europa.
2. **Guinea Ecuatorial**, uno de los países más húmedos del planeta.
3. **Ojos del Salado**, Argentina, el volcán activo más alto[11] del planeta.
4. El **Desierto de Atacama**, Chile, el desierto más árido del planeta.
5. **La Paz**, Bolivia, la capital más alta del planeta.
6. **Cuzco**, Perú, la ciudad más antigua[12] habitada de forma continua[13] del continente.
7. El **Salto del Ángel**, Venezuela, la catarata[14] más alta del planeta.
8. **Granada**, Nicaragua, la ciudad colonial más antigua de América Central.
9. La **pirámide Quetzalcóatl** en Cholula, México, la pirámide más grande del planeta.
10. La **Universidad Autónoma de Santo Domingo**, la República Dominicana, la universidad más antigua de América.

[1]If you are looking for [2]for your next [3]we invite you [4]our [5]Spanish-speaking world [6]includes [7]places [8]building [9]Gothic (style of architecture) [10]biggest [11]highest [12]oldest city [13]continuously inhabited [14]waterfall

El Salto del Ángel, Venezuela.

29 ¿Qué recuerdas?

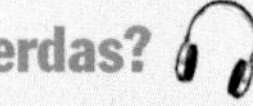

Corrige las siguientes oraciones. ***(Correct the following sentences.)***

1. El desierto más árido del planeta está en Guinea Ecuatorial.
2. La capital más alta del planeta es Cuzco, Perú.
3. La universidad más antigua de América está en México.
4. El Salto del Ángel es el volcán activo más alto del planeta.
5. La pirámide más grande del planeta está en Egipto.

30 Algo personal

1. Name three facts that you learned in this reading. What is the most surprising one? Which world records, if any, did you already know about?
2. If you took this trip around the Spanish-speaking world, which of the ten places would you like to visit the longest? Explain why.

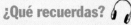

Notes

The section *¿Qué aprendí?* that appears at the end of lessons (pp. 17, 31, etc.) enables students to check their own progress. The section provides a self-test *(Autoevaluación)* they can use to measure their progress in learning the main elements of the lesson when preparing for the lesson test. It also has a thematic vocabulary list students can use to evaluate which words they recognize and which words they should review.

The *Lectura cultural* offers students the opportunity to use newly acquired skills in Spanish to learn about the culture of the Spanish-speaking world.

Autoevaluación

As a review and self-check, respond to the following:

1. Answer the question *¿Cómo te llamas?*
2. Say hi to someone in Spanish.
3. How can you ask where someone is from?
4. What do you say to find out how old someone is? How would you answer that question?
5. How can you tell someone in Spanish that you are pleased to meet them?
6. How will learning Spanish be beneficial to you in the future?

¡Extra!

¡Ojo!

The section *Palabras y expresiones* lists vocabulary that you are responsible for knowing how to use. Words and expressions that are for recognition only are not included here. Refer to the *Vocabulario* at the end of *Capítulo 1* for a reference list of definitions or learn to use the Spanish/English dictionary at the back of this book to look up any words and expressions you cannot figure out.

Palabras y expresiones

How many of these words and expressions do you know?

Despedidas
Adiós.
Hasta luego.

Números
cero
uno
dos
tres
cuatro
cinco
seis
siete
ocho
nueve
diez
once
doce
trece
catorce
quince
dieciséis
diecisiete
dieciocho
diecinueve
veinte

Países
la Argentina
Bolivia
Chile
Colombia
Costa Rica
Cuba
el Ecuador
El Salvador
España
los Estados Unidos
Guatemala
Guinea Ecuatorial
Honduras
México
Nicaragua
Panamá
el Paraguay
el Perú
Puerto Rico
la República Dominicana
el Uruguay
Venezuela

Palabras interrogativas
¿cómo?
¿(de) dónde?

Personas
tú
yo

Saludos
Hola.
Mucho gusto.

Verbos
eres
me llamo
se escribe
soy
te llamas
tengo
tienes

Otras expresiones
el acento
aquí
la capital
¿Cómo te llamas?
con
¿Cuántos años tienes?
de
¿Eres (tú) de...?
la mayúscula
la minúscula
el muchacho, la muchacha
no
el país
sí
Tengo (number) años.
y

Estructura

Do you remember the following grammar rules?

Punctuation

Written Spanish requires two questions marks and two exclamation points, one at the beginning (written upside down) and the other at the end of the sentence.

Definite articles and countries

Some Spanish speakers use the definite articles, *el, la, los* and *las*, with country names.

la Argentina *los Estados Unidos*
el Ecuador *las Filipinas*

Cognates

Words in Spanish and English that resemble one another and that have the same meaning are cognates. For example, *accento* in Spanish looks similar to the English word **accent**. When a word in Spanish looks similar to a word in English but they do not have the same meaning they are false cognates. For example, *colegio* means school, not **college**.

Notes Begin a discussion about student answers for *Autoevaluación* activity 6 by pointing out that the international marketplace demands that employees demonstrate a wide range of competencies and knowledge. Today's student must develop the ability to adapt quickly to new workplace requirements to compete and excel. Encourage students to explore what opportunities learning Spanish will provide them in the areas of work, travel, college, personal fulfillment, etc.

Teacher Resources

 Activity 16

 Activity 9

 p. 79

 Juegos

Flash Cards

Answers

Autoevaluación

Possible answers:

1. Me llamo....
2. ¡Hola!
3. ¿De dónde eres?
4. ¿Cuántos años tienes?/ Tengo...años.
5. ¡Mucho gusto!
6. Answers will vary.

Activities

Spanish for Spanish Speakers

Tell students to imagine being the minister of tourism for their country of origin or for that of their relatives. They have to produce a brochure to encourage tourists from the United States to visit their country. What information and photos would they include in their brochure?

National Standards

Communication
1.2, 1.3

Connections
3.1

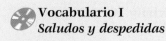

Teacher Resources

Vocabulario I
Saludos y despedidas

Activity 13

Activities 1–4

GV **Activities 1–2**

P **p. 12**

Activity 1
Activity 2

Activity 1

Content reviewed in *Lección B*

- greeting people and saying good-bye
- Spanish speaking countries
- numbers 1–20

Connections with Parents

Success during the first couple of weeks can lead to positive results throughout the rest of the year. If you have not yet done so, send a letter home with the students explaining your grading policy and your classroom management expectations.

National Standards

Comparisons
4.1

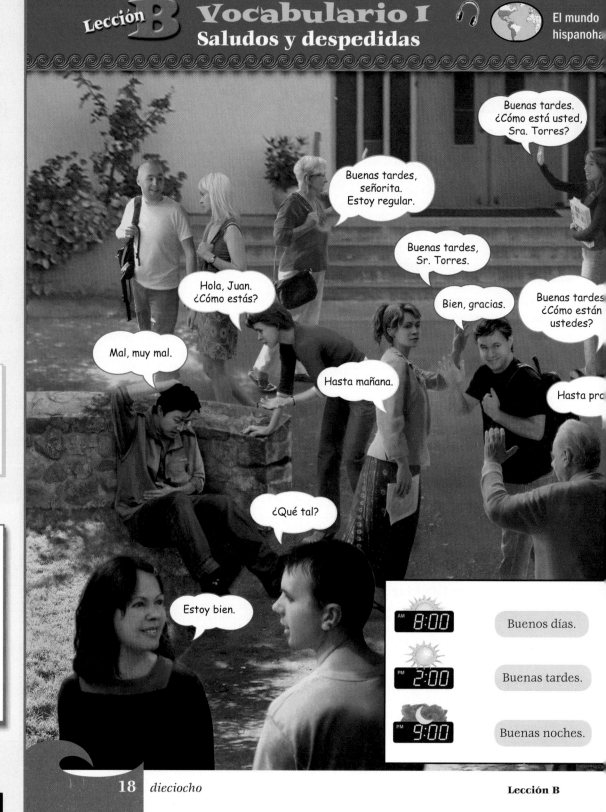

Lección B Vocabulario I
Saludos y despedidas

El mundo hispanoha

Buenas tardes. ¿Cómo está usted, Sra. Torres?

Buenas tardes, señorita. Estoy regular.

Buenas tardes, Sr. Torres.

Hola, Juan. ¿Cómo estás?

Bien, gracias.

Buenas tardes ¿Cómo están ustedes?

Mal, muy mal.

Hasta mañana.

Hasta pro

¿Qué tal?

Estoy bien.

AM 8:00	Buenos días.
PM 2:00	Buenas tardes.
PM 9:00	Buenas noches.

Notes

The script for all *¡Aventura! 1* recorded content is provided in the Audio Program Manual. This includes the *Vocabulario I* on page 18 and activity 1 on page 19. In addition, student answer sheets have been provided for the activities indicated in the student textbook by the audio speaker icon , such as activity 1, for teachers who wish to use them. These reproducible answer sheets can be found at the end of the Audio Program Manual.

¿Saludo o despedida?

Di si lo que oyes es: *un saludo; una despedida; un saludo y una despedida.* (*Say if what you hear is:* a greeting, a farewell or a greeting and a farewell.)

Es un saludo.

Es un saludo y una despedida.

Es una despedida.

¡Hola!

Completa los siguientes diálogos de una manera lógica. *(Complete the following dialogs logically.)*

A: ¡Hola! ¿Qué (1)?
B: Estoy (2).

A: Buenos días, Sra. Fernández. ¿Cómo (3) Ud.?
B: Estoy bien, (4).

A: ¿(5) tal?
B: (6), muy (7).

A: ¿(8) estás, Julia?
B: Estoy (9) mal, Pedro.

Las abreviaturas

Just as **Mr.** is a shortened form of the word **mister** in English, *Sr.* is an abbreviation *(abreviatura)* for *señor* in Spanish. Other abbreviations: *Srta. (señorita), Sra. (señora), Ud. (usted), Uds. (ustedes), Dr. (doctor)* and *Dra. (doctora).*

¿Adiós?

Escoge la despedida apropiada para las siguientes situaciones.

Hasta luego. Buenas noches. Adiós. Hasta mañana. Hasta pronto.

1. A friend's family is moving away to live in Madrid.
2. It is Monday morning and you are leaving home to go to school.
3. You are leaving friends at the end of the school day.
4. It is Saturday night and you are leaving your friends to go home after a basketball game.

Notes Clarify that the expression *mal* is seldom used to say how you are feeling unless the speaker wants to convey an illness or a personal catastrophe, such as the death of a close friend or family member.

Inform students that another way to express *regular* (okay or average) is *así así.*

Activity 1

Answers

1 1. Es una despedida.
2. Es un saludo.
3. Es un saludo.
4. Es un saludo.
5. Es un saludo y una despedida.

2 1. tal
2. (muy) bien/(muy) mal/ regular
3. está
4. gracias
5. Qué
6. Bien/Mal
7. bien/mal
8. Cómo
9. muy

3 Possible answers:
1. Adiós.
2. Hasta luego./Hasta pronto./ Adiós.
3. Hasta mañana./Hasta luego./ Hasta pronto./Adiós.
4. Buenas noches./ Adiós./ Hasta mañana.

Activities

Prereading Strategy
Ask students to think of a variety of questions they might ask when greeting someone. Then instruct students to cover up the words in *Vocabulario I* and look at the illustration. Call on students to guess what each person is saying.

National Standards

Communication
1.2

Comparisons
4.1

Teacher Resources

Diálogo I
Buenos días
Activity 6

Answers

4 1. C
2. A
3. F
4. B
5. E
6. D

5 Creative self-expression.

6 1. Buenos días.
2. Bien, gracias.
3. Adiós, no. Hasta pronto.

Activities

Critical Thinking

In groups of four, have one student act out how he or she is feeling, while the others guess what that feeling is. Make sure all students have an opportunity to act out their feelings.

Language through Action

Have students write their own dialog and present it to the class, incorporating appropriate gestures.

Prereading Strategy

Instruct students to cover up the dialog with one hand and look at the photographs. Ask them to imagine where the conversation takes place and what the people are saying to one another.

National Standards
Communication 1.1, 1.2, 1.3
Comparisons 4.1

Diálogo I — Buenos días

ALICIA: Buenos días, Quique. ¿Cómo estás?
QUIQUE: Estoy muy bien.

QUIQUE: ¿Y tú? ¿Qué tal?
ALICIA: Bien, gracias.

ALICIA: Adiós, Quique.
QUIQUE: Adiós, no. Hasta pronto.

4 ¿Qué recuerdas?

Completa las frases de la izquierda con una de las frases de la derecha, según el diálogo *Buenos días*.

1. ¿Cómo...	**A.** ...muy bien.
2. Estoy...	**B.** ...gracias.
3. ¿Y tú? ¿Qué...	**C.** ...estás?
4. Bien,...	**D.** ...pronto.
5. Adiós,...	**E.** ...Quique.
6. Hasta...	**F.** ...tal?

5 Algo personal

Greet four or five students in class and ask how each one is. Your classmates then answer and ask how you are.

MODELO
A: Buenos días/Buenas tardes, *(name of student B)*. ¿Qué tal?
B: Mal. ¿Y tú?
A: Muy bien, gracias.

¡Extra!

¡Estoy muy mal!

¿Por qué?	*Why?*
Me duele la cabeza.	*I have a headache./ My head hurts.*
Me duele el estómago.	*My stomach hurts.*
Me duele la garganta.	*I have a sore throat.*
Tengo catarro.	*I have a cold.*

6 ¿Cuál es una respuesta correcta?

Escoge una respuesta correcta a lo que oyes.

Bien, gracias.
BUENOS DÍAS.
Adiós, no. Hasta pronto.

Notes

Point out for students that the expression *¿Qué tal?* is provided as an equivalent for *¿Cómo estás?*. Both *¿Cómo estás?* and *¿Qué tal?* are commonly used in informal conversation.

While teaching the expression *Me duele...* teach students some additional body parts in Spanish: *el brazo* (arm), *la mano* (hand), *la boca* (mouth), *el ojo* (eye), *la oreja* (ear), *la pierna* (leg), *el pie* (foot), *la cara* (face).

Cultura viva

Más sobre los saludos

Spanish is the official language in Spain, in eighteen Latin American countries, in the African nation of Equatorial Guinea and in the Commonwealth of Puerto Rico. Spanish is also used extensively in the United States, in Europe and elsewhere for both business and pleasure. Because so many people speak Spanish in so many places around the world, you can well imagine that the words and expressions people use vary a great deal. For example, the most common Spanish greetings are the informal *hola* and the more formal *buenos días* (which is used until around noon), *buenas tardes* (which is used until around dusk) and *buenas noches* (which can be used as an evening greeting or as another way to take leave of someone). However, *buenas* is sometimes used by itself as a short form of either *buenas tardes* or *buenas noches*. The word *muy* can then be added to these expressions for emphasis, as in *muy buenos días* or *muy buenas*.

Buenos días.

Buenas tardes.

7 Los saludos en el mundo hispano

¿*Sí o no*? Corrige lo que no es lógico.

1. *Hola* and *Buenos días* are both formal ways to say good-bye.
2. *Buenas tardes* is used to greet someone in the morning.
3. *Buenas noches* is used to greet someone in the evening.
4. You may hear *Buenas* or *Muy buenas* when someone is greeting you in the afternoon or in the evening.

8 Saludos y despedidas

Haz una lista en español de saludos y una lista de despedidas.

MODELO	Saludos	Despedidas
	Muy buenas.	Hasta pronto.

Notes Point out that in many situations, native Spanish-speakers may seem to be very expressive using body language. Shaking hands when greeting, kissing when taking leave of one another, signaling with thumbs up, gesticulating while making a point are all part of communication for many people throughout the world who use Spanish every day.

Answers

7
1. No. Both are greetings. *Hola* is used casually; *Buenos días* is more formal.
2. No. *Buenas tardes* is used to greet someone in the afternoon.
3. Sí.
4. Sí.

8 Answers will vary.

Activities

Critical Thinking

Call on three students to go to the board (or ask for volunteers). One student writes the word *Saludo*, another writes the word *Despedida* and the third student writes *Saludo y despedida*. Say several greetings and farewells aloud: *hasta luego, hola, adiós, buenas tardes, hasta mañana, buenas noches, hasta pronto*, etc. Students must write the word under the appropriate column. When a student answers by spelling the word correctly and placing it into the correct column, he or she gets to call on a classmate to come to the board and continue the game.

National Standards

Communication
1.2

Connections
3.1

Comparisons
4.1, 4.2

Teacher Resources

 Activities 5–6

 Activity 3

 Activity 3

 Activity 2

Answers

9 1. tú; 2. tú; 3. Ud.; 4. Uds.; 5. Ud.; 6. Uds.; 7. vosotras; 8. vosotros

Activities

Critical Thinking

After students complete activity 9, ask them to come up with a list of other people in their lives. Call on students to share their lists with the class as a volunteer writes the list on the board. Then call on individuals to say whether they would use *tú*, *usted*, *ustedes*, *vosotros* or *vosotras* with the people on the list.

National Standards
Communication 1.2
Cultures 2.1
Comparisons 4.1

Idioma

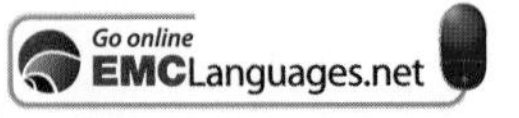

Estructura

Formal/Informal

Spanish has several words for **you**. Use the informal *tú* when talking to someone you refer to by a first name. Use the more formal *usted* (abbreviated *Ud.*) when talking to someone you would address using a title (*señor Torres, señorita Jiménez*).

Although throughout the Spanish-speaking world the plural **you** is *ustedes* (abbreviated *Uds.*), in Spain you have two choices for **you** when speaking to more than one person: 1) use the informal *vosotros* (for males or a combination of males and females) or *vosotras* (for females) with two or more friends, family members or younger people; 2) use the more polite and formal *ustedes* (or *Uds.*) when talking with two or more people you address using a title.

	singular	plural
informal	tú	ustedes (*Uds.*) vosotros (*masculine*)/vosotras (*feminine*)
formal	usted (*Ud.*)	ustedes (*Uds.*)

Práctica

9 A saludar

How would you address these people? Choose either *tú*, *Ud.*, *Uds.*, *vosotros* or *vosotras*.

1. a friend at school
2. your sister
3. your teacher
4. an elderly couple you have just met
5. the principal at your school
6. two close friends (Latin America)
7. two close female friends (Spain)
8. two close male friends (Spain)

Estrategia

Learning from mistakes

Do not be afraid to make mistakes when you use Spanish. They are a natural part of learning a language. By using Spanish every day and by completing assignments, gradually you will notice that you are able to say and understand more and more as the year continues. Of course, there will be challenges throughout the year, but one result of your effort will be a profound sense of accomplishment as your skills and knowledge improve.

Notes Inform students that *vosotros/vosotras* is used in Spain. Although the subject pronouns *vosotros* and *vosotras* are introduced here, you should decide what role these words will have in your class. In *¡Aventura!*, verb paradigms include the *vosotros/vosotras* verb forms for recognition. However, activities do not require students to practice the *vosotros/vosotras* verb forms.

Point out that in some Latin American countries, such as Argentina, *vos* is used instead of *tú*.

¿Tú, usted, ustedes, vosotros o vosotras?

Would you use *tú*, *usted*, *ustedes*, *vosotros* or *vosotras* when talking to these people?

1. María y Lupe (México)

2. Amalia y José (España)

3. la Sra. Sánchez (República Dominicana)

4. Paz, Mercedes y Marta (España)

5. Pepe (Ecuador)

6. el Sr. Fernández y el Sr. García (España)

¿Cómo están?

Greet these people in Spanish and ask how they are feeling.

MODELO

Paula
Hola, Paula. ¿Cómo estás?/¿Qué tal?

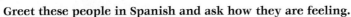

1. Sr. y Sra. Uribe

2. Antonio

3. Jaime y Marta

4. Srta. Sosa

5. Teresa y Raquel

Comunicación

Estoy...

You have just walked up to some friends. In groups of three, talk about how you are feeling. Be sure everyone in the group practices each of the roles shown (*A*, *B* and *C*).

MODELO **A:** *(Greet two classmates and ask how they feel.)*
B: *(Say how you feel.)*
C: *(Say how you feel and ask how student A feels.)*
A: *(Say how you feel.)*

Answers

10 1. ustedes
2. vosotros
3. usted
4. vosotras
5. tú
6. ustedes

11 Possible answers:
1. Buenas tardes, señor y señora Uribe. ¿Cómo están Uds.?
2. Buenas noches, Antonio. ¿Cómo estás?/¿Qué tal?
3. Buenos días, Jaime y Marta. ¿Cómo están Uds.?/¿Qué tal?
4. Hola, señorita Sosa. ¿Cómo está Ud.?
5. Buenas tardes, Teresa y Raquel. ¿Cómo están Uds.?

12 Creative self-expression.

Activities

Expansion
Have students walk around the room and introduce themselves to classmates. Then, as a follow-up to activity 12, they can ask questions using what they have learned in this lesson and have a conversation with one or more of the people they meet.

Spanish for Spanish Speakers
Pair bilingual and nonbilingual students for activity 12.

National Standards

Communication
1.1, 1.2, 1.3

Cultures
2.1

Comparisons
4.1

Teacher Resources

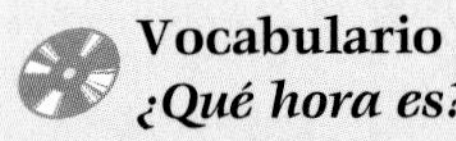

Vocabulario II
¿Qué hora es?

Activities 14–15

Activities 7–10

Activities 4–6

pp. 35–37

pp. 5–6

Activity 4
Activity 5

Activity 3

Activities

Connections
For additional practice on the numbers, have students count backwards in Spanish, one number at a time, by twos, by threes, etc.

Expansion
Try holding up a card with a number on it while saying a number and have your students say out loud the words *sí* or *no* to indicate if you are holding up the number you have said. As a variation, call on students to identify the number orally in Spanish or have a student go to the board and write the numeral you are holding.

National Standards
Communication 1.2
Connections 3.1
Comparisons 4.1

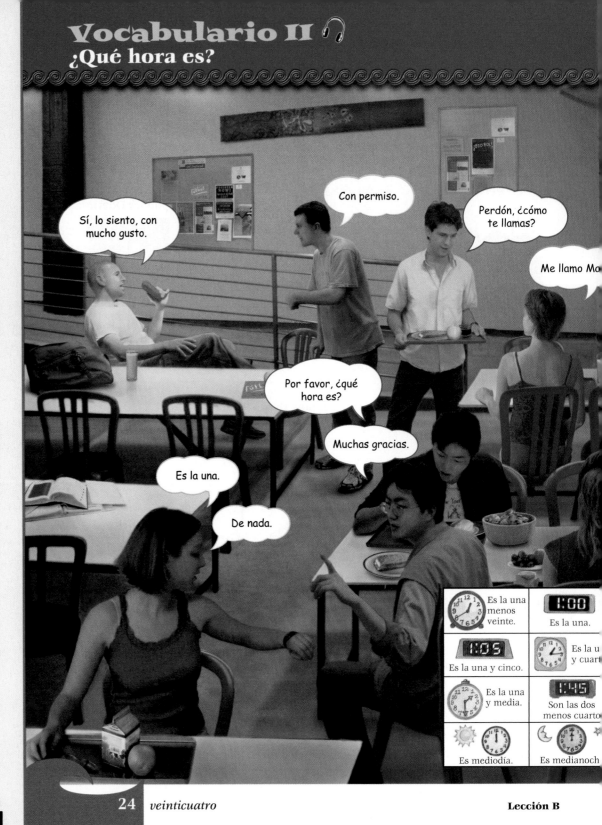

Vocabulario II
¿Qué hora es?

Sí, lo siento, con mucho gusto.
Con permiso.
Perdón, ¿cómo te llamas?
Me llamo Ma
Por favor, ¿qué hora es?
Muchas gracias.
Es la una.
De nada.

Es la una menos veinte.	1:00 Es la una.
1:05 Es la una y cinco.	Es la u y cuart
Es la una y media.	1:45 Son las dos menos cuarto
Es mediodía.	Es medianoch

Notes Review the numbers 1–20 before presenting 21–100. The numbers 101 to 999,999 are taught in *Capítulo 5.*

Explain that the numbers beginning with *treinta y uno* may require the combination of three words, even though the numbers *cero* through *treinta* are written as one word. Likewise, your students may find it useful if you point out the spelling change that occurs in the combination of three words in the numbers *dieciséis (diez y seis)* through *veintinueve (veinte y nueve).*

Los números del 21 al 100			
21	veintiuno	31	treinta y uno
22	veintidós	32	treinta y dos
23	veintitrés	40	cuarenta
24	veinticuatro	50	cincuenta
25	veinticinco	60	sesenta
26	veintiséis	70	setenta
27	veintisiete	80	ochenta
28	veintiocho	90	noventa
29	veintinueve	100	cien
30	treinta		

13 Los números hasta cien

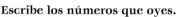

Escribe los números que oyes.

MODELO treinta

14 Conexión con otras disciplinas: matemáticas

Completa de forma lógica las siguientes series de números hasta 100.

1. cero, cinco, diez...
2. cero, siete, catorce...
3. cero, once, veintidós...
4. cero, trece, veintiséis, treinta y nueve...

Nueve por nueve, ochenta y uno.

Notes Ask students to identify the many ways they use numbers on a daily basis. Then they should identify numbers that are especially important to them (phone numbers, ages, etc.).

The Appendices at the back of the book provide all the numbers in one place if you choose to teach them all at the same time or if students ask about the numbers after 100.

Activities with the title *Conexión con otras disciplinas* are intended specifically to offer cross-curricular learning opportunities.

Teacher Resources

Los números del 21 al 100
Activity 13
Activity 14

pp. 38–39, 51

Answers

13 1. veintiséis; 2. setenta y nueve; 3. treinta y cuatro; 4. quince 5. cien

14 1. quince, veinte, veinticinco, treinta, treinta y cinco, cuarenta, cuarenta y cinco, cincuenta, cincuenta y cinco, sesenta, sesenta y cinco, setenta, setenta y cinco, ochenta, ochenta y cinco, noventa, noventa y cinco, cien
2. veintiuno, veintiocho, treinta y cinco, cuarenta y dos, cuarenta y nueve, cincuenta y seis, sesenta y tres, setenta, setenta y siete, ochenta y cuatro, noventa y uno, noventa y ocho
3. treinta y tres, cuarenta y cuatro, cincuenta y cinco, sesenta y seis, setenta y siete, ochenta y ocho, noventa y nueve
4. cincuenta y dos, sesenta y cinco, setenta y ocho, noventa y uno

National Standards

Communication
1.2

Connections
3.1

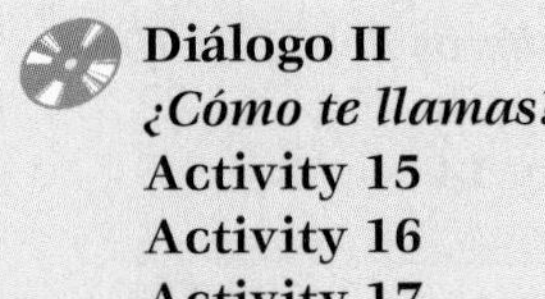

Teacher Resources

Diálogo II
¿Cómo te llamas?
Activity 15
Activity 16
Activity 17

Answers

15 1. Son las tres y diez.
2. Dice *Perdón.*
3. Se llama Paloma.
4. Se llama Quique.
5. Dice *Con permiso.*

16 Answers will vary.

17 1. 6:00
2. 1:30
3. 3:10
4. 4:20
5. 5:15
6. 12:40

Activities

Expansion

Have students identify words from the dialog that they already know.

Prereading Strategy

Instruct students to cover up the dialog with one hand and look at the photographs. Then play the recorded version of the dialog as students listen without looking at the words. Ask them to imagine where the conversation takes place and what the people are saying to one another.

National Standards

Communication
1.2

Connections
3.1

Diálogo II ¿Cómo te llamas?

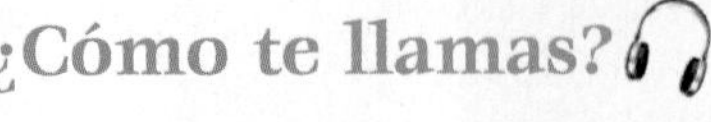

QUIQUE: Por favor, ¿qué hora es?
PALOMA: Son las tres y diez.
QUIQUE: Muchas gracias.

QUIQUE: Perdón, ¿cómo te llamas?
PALOMA: Me llamo Paloma.
QUIQUE: Mucho gusto. Me llamo Quique.

PALOMA: Con permiso.
QUIQUE: Sí, lo siento.

15 ¿Qué recuerdas?

1. ¿Qué hora es en el diálogo?
2. ¿Qué dice el muchacho antes de preguntar el nombre a la muchacha? (What does the boy say before asking the girl's name?)
3. ¿Cómo se llama la muchacha?
4. ¿Cómo se llama el muchacho?
5. ¿Qué dice la muchacha antes de bajar del autobús? (What does the girl say before getting off the bus?)

16 Algo personal

1. ¿Qué hora es?
2. ¿Cómo te llamas?

17 ¿Qué hora es?

Escribe la hora que oyes. ***(Write the time you hear.)***

MODELO 9:25

3:10 1:30 6:00 4:20
9:25 12:40 5:15

Notes

A recorded version of this dialog is provided in the *¡Aventura!* Audio Program. If possible, use the audio before exposing students to the written version of the dialog. Play the audio version of the dialog as students listen and repeat, practicing their pronunciation.

Cultura viva II

Con cortesía

The expressions *Perdón* and *Con permiso* are equivalent to "Excuse me." However, these expressions are used in different situations. Use *Perdón* to interrupt a conversation, to get someone's attention, to indicate you do not understand what someone said or to excuse yourself if you bump into someone. *Con permiso,* on the other hand, is used more specifically to ask someone to let you pass by or to politely let someone know you are about to leave.

Perdón, ¿qué hora es?

18 Lo cortés no quita lo valiente

Selecciona la respuesta más apropiada para cada *(each)* situación en la ilustración.

- De nada.
- Muchas gracias.
- Perdón, ¿qué hora es?
- Con permiso.
- Cuatro, por favor.
- Perdón.
- Con mucho gusto.
- Perdón. Lo siento.

19 ¿Qué dices?

Indicate which of these expressions you would use in the following situations.

Con permiso.	Perdón.	Dos, por favor.
De nada.	Con mucho gusto.	No, gracias.
Muchas gracias.	Perdón. Lo siento.	Perdón, ¿qué hora es?

1. You want to politely refuse an offer to do something.
2. A friend asks you for help.
3. Someone thanks you for doing something.
4. You step on someone's foot.
5. You are on an elevator standing behind other people and you want to exit.
6. You politely ask for two movie tickets.
7. Someone speaks to you so quickly in Spanish that you cannot understand what the person is saying.

Notes Point out that when they travel, students may meet people who seem overly polite and more formal. Explain that their familiarity with the expressions in activity 19 will come in handy when talking with others in Spanish.

Teacher Resources

Activity 4

Answers

18
1. Con mucho gusto.
2. Cuatro, por favor.
3. Perdón. Lo siento.
4. Muchas gracias.
5. De nada.
6. Con permiso./Perdón.
7. Perdón, ¿qué hora es?

19
1. No, gracias.
2. Con mucho gusto.
3. De nada.
4. Perdón. Lo siento.
5. Con permiso.
6. Dos, por favor.
7. Perdón.

Activities

Language through Action
Have students walk around the room and practice the courtesy expressions they have learned in short conversations. For example, they may interrupt someone to ask for the time, thank someone for information provided, say they are sorry to hear someone doesn't feel well, etc.

National Standards

Communication	Comparisons
1.1, 1.2	4.2
Cultures	
2.1	
Connections	
3.2	

Teacher Resources

 Activities 11–13

 Activity 7

 Activity 6

 Activity 5

Answers

20 1. Es la una menos diez.
2. Son las once y veinticinco.
3. Son las dos menos cuarto (menos quince).
4. Son las tres y media (y treinta).
5. Son las seis y cinco.
6. Es la una y cuarto (y quince).
7. Son las doce./ Es mediodía./ Es medianoche.
8. Son las siete menos veinte.

Activities

Connections

In many countries where Spanish is spoken, people use the twenty-four-hour clock to tell time. For example, tell students they are visiting Spain during their summer vacation. Have them convert the following times to A.M. and P.M.: 1. 18:00 (6:00 P.M.); 2. 23:00 (11:00 P.M.); 3. 13:00 (1:00 P.M.); 4. 19:00 (7:00 P.M.); 5. 21:00 (9:00 P.M.).

National Standards

Communication
1.2

Cultures
2.1

Connections
3.1

Idioma

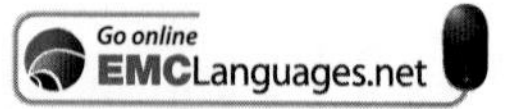

Estructura

Time

- You can find out what time it is by asking *¿Qué hora es?* When giving the time in Spanish, use *Es la una* to refer to one o'clock and *Son las* (+ number) to indicate any other hour.

  1:00 *Es la una.* 2:00 *Son las dos.*

- Use *y* (+ number of minutes through *veintinueve*) to add minutes after the hour or *menos* (+ number of minutes through *veintinueve*) to indicate time before the hour.

  2:29 *Son las dos y veintinueve.* 2:31 *Son las tres menos veintinueve.*

- Add *y cuarto* for a quarter past the hour, *y media* for half past the hour and *menos cuarto* for a quarter to the hour.

  4:15 *Son las cuatro y cuarto.* 4:30 *Son las cuatro y media.*
  4:45 *Son las cinco menos cuarto.*

- In Spanish, the expression A.M. is equivalent to *de la mañana* (in the morning). Morning goes from midnight to noon. P.M. is equivalent to *de la tarde* (in the afternoon) or to *de la noche* (at night). Afternoon is from noon to around 6:00 P.M., and night extends from 6:00 P.M. to midnight.
- Two additional useful expressions: *Es mediodía* (It is noon) and *Es medianoche* (It is midnight).

Práctica

20 La hora

Indica qué hora es.

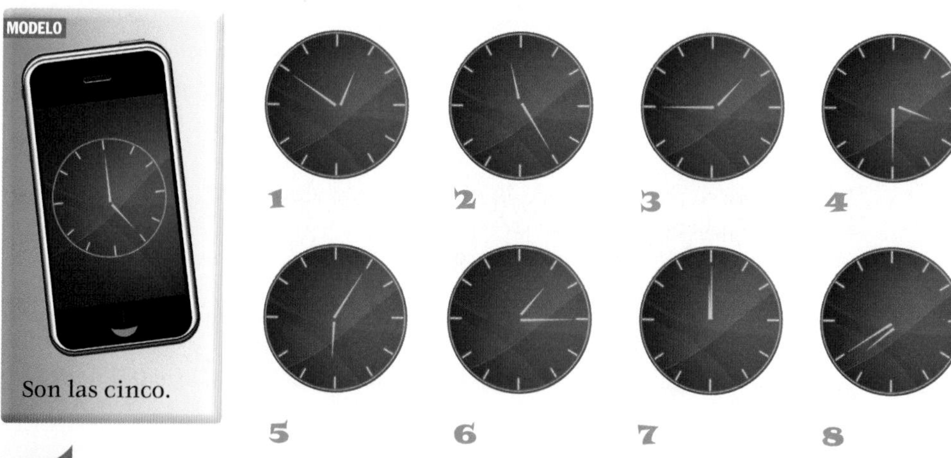

Notes Tell your students that **o'clock** can be conveyed in Spanish as *en punto* when you want to emphasize the exact hour on the hour (e.g., It's three o'clock. *Son las tres en punto.*).

Es mediodía and *Es medianoche* can also be expressed by *Son las doce.*

21 La entrevista

Completa el siguiente diálogo de una manera lógica.

LORENZO: Buenos (1), Sra. Vargas.
SRA. VARGAS: ¡Hola, Lorenzo! ¿Cómo (2)?
LORENZO: Estoy bien, (3). ¿Y (4)?
SRA. VARGAS: (5) muy bien.
LORENZO: (6), ¿(7) hora es?
SRA. VARGAS: (8) las diez y media de la (9).
LORENZO: ¿No son (10) nueve y media?
SRA. VARGAS: No.
LORENZO: ¡Uy! Tengo clase de español. Hasta (11).
SRA. VARGAS: Adiós, hasta (12).

¡Extra!

Los gestos

Gestures and other non-spoken language are important when talking with people in Spanish about how they feel: In several countries, turning your thumb up indicates you feel well, whereas turning your thumb down signals you do not feel well.

bien  **mal** 

Comunicación

22 Por favor, ¿qué hora es?

Imagine you have stopped someone on the street to politely ask what time it is. Take turns asking for and stating the indicated time.

MODELO

A: Por favor, ¿qué hora es?
B: Son las siete y cuarto (y quince) de la mañana.
A: Muchas gracias.

1

2

3

4

5

6

7

8

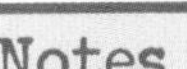

Notes Point out that *Es mediodía* and *Es medianoche* are not modified by a number of minutes or by the expressions *y cuarto, menos cuarto or y media.*

Mention that *quince* may be used instead of *cuarto.*

Answers

21 Possible answers:
1. días
2. estás
3. gracias
4. usted/Ud.
5. Estoy
6. Perdón
7. qué
8. Son
9. mañana
10. las
11. luego/pronto/mañana
12. luego/pronto/mañana

22
1. Son las tres y cuarto (y quince) de la tarde.
2. Son las once y veintinueve de la mañana.
3. Es la una de la tarde.
4. Son las doce y diez de la mañana.
5. Son las ocho y veinte de la noche.
6. Son las cinco de la tarde.
7. Son las nueve y veinticinco de la noche.
8. Son las once menos cuarto (quince) de la noche.

National Standards

Communication
1.1, 1.2

Cultures
2.1

Connections
3.1, 3.2

Teacher Resources

 Lectura personal

Answers

23 1. D
2. C
3. E
4. A
5. F
6. B

24 Answers will vary.

National Standards

Cultures
2.2

Connections
3.1, 3.2

Lectura personal

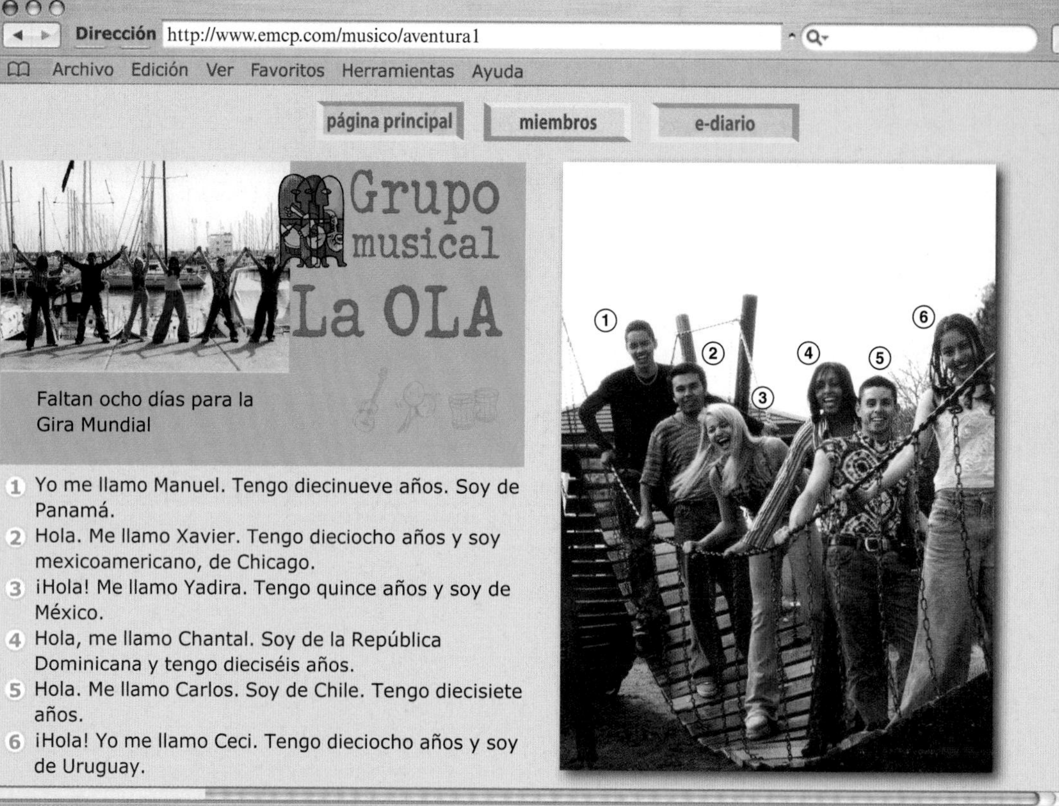

Dirección http://www.emcp.com/musico/aventura1
Archivo Edición Ver Favoritos Herramientas Ayuda
página principal
miembros
e-diario
Grupo musical
La OLA
Faltan ocho días para la Gira Mundial
1 Yo me llamo Manuel. Tengo diecinueve años. Soy de Panamá.
2 Hola. Me llamo Xavier. Tengo dieciocho años y soy mexicoamericano, de Chicago.
3 ¡Hola! Me llamo Yadira. Tengo quince años y soy de México.
4 Hola, me llamo Chantal. Soy de la República Dominicana y tengo dieciséis años.
5 Hola. Me llamo Carlos. Soy de Chile. Tengo diecisiete años.
6 ¡Hola! Yo me llamo Ceci. Tengo dieciocho años y soy de Uruguay.
1
2
3
4
5
6

23 ¿Qué recuerdas?

Match the person on the right with the information on the left.

1. 19 años	**A.** Yadira
2. Uruguay	**B.** Xavier
3. 17 años	**C.** Ceci
4. México	**D.** Manuel
5. 16 años	**E.** Carlos
6. Chicago	**F.** Chantal

24 Algo personal

1. What kind of music do you think the band La Ola plays? Do you listen to music in Spanish? If so, what is the name of the band or singer?
2. You have now seen pictures of people who are from various Spanish-speaking countries. Do you think you can tell what language someone speaks just by looking at the person?

Notes *La Ola* is the name for the singing group depicted in the *Lectura personal* that concludes each even-numbered lesson. Explain that the word *ola* means **wave**. Students will enjoy band members' personal viewpoints as they reflect on the many cultures of the Spanish-speaking world during their travels.

The accompanying audio concludes with the song *Es sólo una cuestión de actitud,* which was written by Rodolfo "Fito" Páez. You may wish to play the audio recording of the song so students can hear the kind of music the band performs. Students will see the lyrics and hear the entire song again in *Capítulo 10.*

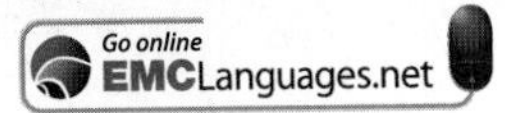

Autoevaluación

As a review and self-check, respond to the following:

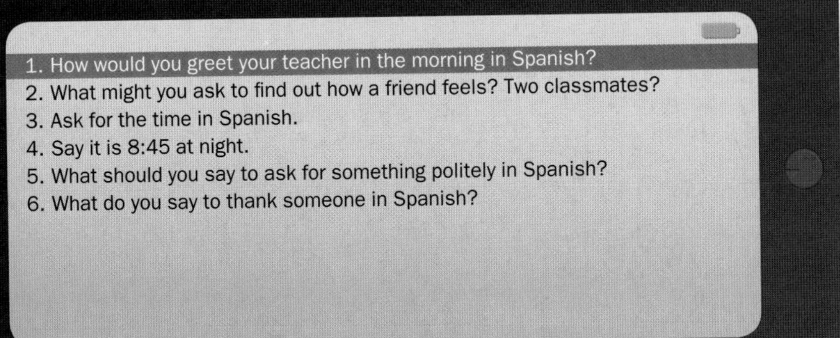

1. How would you greet your teacher in the morning in Spanish?
2. What might you ask to find out how a friend feels? Two classmates?
3. Ask for the time in Spanish.
4. Say it is 8:45 at night.
5. What should you say to ask for something politely in Spanish?
6. What do you say to thank someone in Spanish?

Palabras y expresiones

How many of these words and expressions do you know?

Cortesía
- con mucho gusto
- con permiso
- de nada
- (muchas) gracias
- lo siento
- perdón
- por favor

Gente
- el señor (Sr.)
- la señora (Sra.)
- la señorita (Srta.)
- usted (Ud.)
- ustedes (Uds.)
- vosotros,-as

La hora
- de la mañana
- de la noche
- de la tarde
- Es la.... / Son las....
- Es medianoche.
- Es mediodía.
- la hora
- la mañana
- menos
- la noche
- ¿Qué hora es?
- la tarde
- y cuarto
- y media

Números
- veintiuno
- veintidós
- veintitrés
- veinticuatro
- veinticinco
- veintiséis
- veintisiete
- veintiocho
- veintinueve
- treinta (y uno, etc.)
- cuarenta
- cincuenta
- sesenta
- setenta
- ochenta
- noventa
- cien

Saludos y despedidas
- Buenas noches.
- Buenas tardes.
- Buenos días.
- Hasta mañana.
- Hasta pronto.

Verbos
- es
- está (él, ella)
- está (Ud.)
- están (Uds.)
- estás (tú)
- estoy
- son

Otras expresiones
- bien
- mal
- muy
- pronto
- ¿Qué tal?
- regular

Estructura

Do you remember the following grammar rules?

Formal/Informal = you

	singular	plural
informal	tú	ustedes (Uds.) vosotros/vosotras (Spain)
formal	usted	ustedes (Uds.)

Time

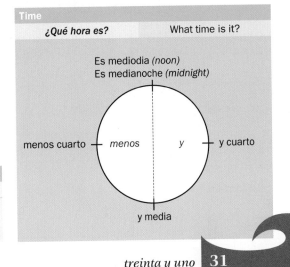

¿Qué hora es?	What time is it?

Es mediodía *(noon)*
Es medianoche *(midnight)*

menos cuarto — *menos* — *y* — y cuarto

y media

Notes The *Autoevaluación* provides several self-check activities students can use for evaluating their own progress. Assign them as time and your own judgment allow.

Have students check their own understanding of the vocabulary by reviewing the list of *Palabras y expresiones*. Then have them find the words they do not recognize where they are first presented in the lesson.

Teacher Resources

 Activity 14

 p. 46

 Juegos

Flash Cards

Answers

Autoevaluación

Possible answers:

1. Buenos días, Sr./Sra./Srta. ¿Cómo está Ud.?
2. ¿Cómo estás? (¿Qué tal?)/ ¿Cómo están Uds.?
3. ¿Qué hora es?
4. Son las nueve menos cuarto de la noche.
5. Por favor.
6. Gracias.

Activities

Expansion

Add additional activities or questions to the *Autoevaluación* as you see fit: How would students greet a best friend? How would they say good-bye to several friends as they leave school Monday or Tuesday afternoon? What can students say to thank someone in Spanish? Can students identify a popular Hispanic musician/singer? Can they say what kind of music they perform?

National Standards

Communication
1.2

Connections
3.1

Teacher Resources

 *El mundo hispanohablante*

Answers

Preparación

1. Answers will vary.
2. Possible answers: *oficial*, *República*, names of countries, *capital*, *persona*, *famosa*, etc.

Activities

Expansion

In groups of three or four, have students pass around a piece of paper while each group member adds the name of a famous person who speaks Spanish. After two minutes, add up the number of names each group has listed.

Multiple Intelligences (bodily-kinesthetic)

Have students create an autobiographical poster/collage that includes some of the following information in Spanish: name, place of origin, age, a favorite greeting, a Spanish-speaking place of interest and three cognates that describe him/her.

National Standards

Communication
1.3

Cultures
2.2

Connections
3.1

Tú lees

Estrategia

Using cognates to understand Spanish

Spanish will be more enjoyable to read if you learn some techniques that will help you recognize cognates. For example, many words that end in *-ión* have English counterparts that end in **-tion,** such as *información* (information). Look at the endings in these words: *adicional, biología.* Can you guess what they mean? What would be the endings of their English equivalents?

Preparación

Contesta a las siguientes preguntas como preparación para la lectura:

1. Give five examples of cognates you have seen in *Capítulo 1.*
2. Find at least five cognates in the country information that follows.

El mundo hispanohablante

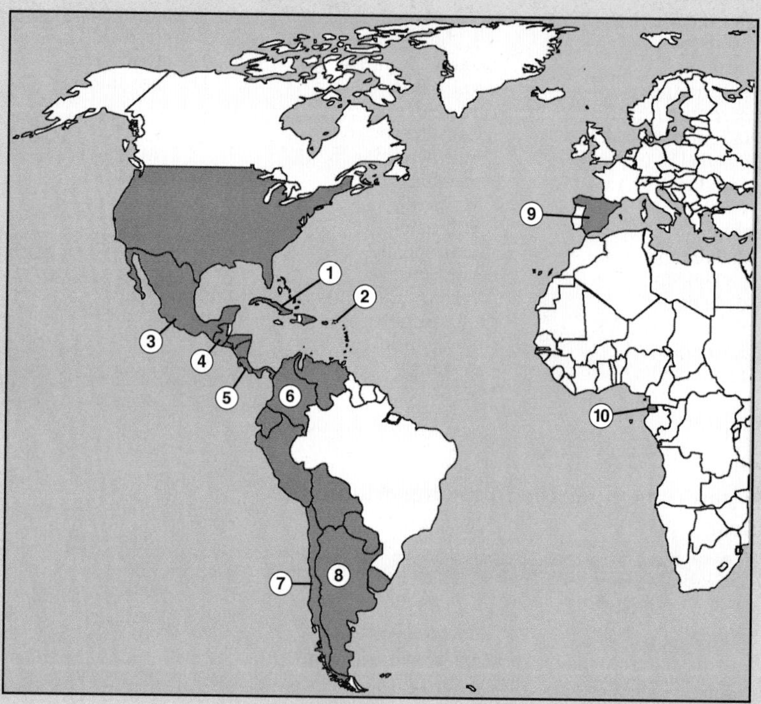

Notes

Chapters in *¡Aventura!* conclude with *¡Viento en popa!* (Full speed ahead!), a selection of activities that combine the themes and content of the lesson.

The *Tú lees* provides a formal opportunity for students to improve their ability to read in Spanish. Note for students that it is not essential to understand every word in order to read in Spanish. Equivalents for most of the unfamiliar words have been provided to help students enjoy reading without having to look up important but passive vocabulary. Be sure to go over *Estrategia* and *Preparación* prior to beginning the *Tú lees* reading.

(1) **Nombre oficial:** República de Cuba
Capital: La Habana
Poblacion aproximada: 11,2 millones
Moneda: el peso cubano
Persona famosa: José Martí (escritor, revolucionario)

(2) **Nombre oficial:** Puerto Rico
Capital: San Juan
Población aproximada: 3,7 millones
Moneda: el dólar (EE.UU.)
Persona famosa: Ricky Martin (cantante)

(3) **Nombre oficial:** Estados Unidos Mexicanos
Capital: México, D.F.
Población aproximada: 112,4 millones
Moneda: el peso mexicano
Persona famosa: Octavio Paz (escritor, Premio Nobel de Literatura)

(4) **Nombre oficial:** República de El Salvador
Capital: San Salvador
Poblacion aproximada: 7,2 millones
Moneda: el colón el dólar (EE.UU)
Persona famosa: Francisco Gavidia (dramaturgo)

(5) **Nombre oficial:** República de Costa Rica
Capital: San José
Población aproximada: 4,5 millones
Moneda: el colón
Persona famosa: Óscar Arias Sánchez (ex-presidente, Premio Nobel de la Paz)

(6) **Nombre oficial:** Colombia
Capital: Bogotá
Población aproximada: 44,9 millones
Moneda: el peso colombiano
Persona famosa: Gabriel García Márquez (escritor, Premio Nobel de Literatura)

(7) **Nombre oficial:** República de Chile
Capital: Santiago
Población aproximada: 17 millones
Moneda: el peso chileno
Persona famosa: Isabel Allende (escritora)

(8) **Nombre oficial:** República Argentina
Capital: Buenos Aires
Población aproximada: 41 millones
Moneda: el peso argentino
Persona famosa: Jorge Luis Borges (escritor, poeta)

(9) **Nombre oficial:** España
Capital: Madrid
Población aproximada: 46,9 millones
Moneda: el euro
Persona famosa: Pablo Picasso (pintor)

(10) **Nombre oficial:** Guinea Ecuatorial
Capital: Malabo
Población aproximada: 668.000
Moneda: el franco CFA
Persona famosa: Teodoro Obiang (presidente)

A ¿Qué recuerdas?

Match the famous person named in column A with the country he or she is from under column B.

Column A	Column B
1. Jorge Luis Borges	**A.** México
2. Isabel Allende	**B.** Costa Rica
3. Pablo Picasso	**C.** Chile
4. Octavio Paz	**D.** Guinea Ecuatorial
5. Teodoro Obiang	**E.** Argentina
6. Óscar Arias	**F.** España
7. José Martí	**G.** El Salvador
8. Francisco Gavidia	**H.** Cuba

B Algo personal

1. Can you name any famous Hispanic people? Who? Name four or five people, if you can, and say why they are well known.
2. If you could have a conversation with one of the famous people mentioned above, who would it be? Why?

Answers

A 1. E
2. C
3. F
4. A
5. D
6. B
7. H
8. G

B Answers will vary.

*Note: The audio for *El mundo hispanohablante* does not include the population estimates.

Notes

Other countries:

Nombre oficial: República de Honduras
Capital: Tegucigalpa
Población aproximada: 8,1 millones
Moneda: el lempira
Persona famosa: José Antonio Velázquez (pintor)

Nombre oficial: Bolivia
Capitales: La Paz, Sucre
Población aproximada: 10,1 millones
Moneda: el boliviano
Persona famosa: Nataniel Aguirre (dramaturgo)

National Standards

Cultures
2.2

Connections
3.1

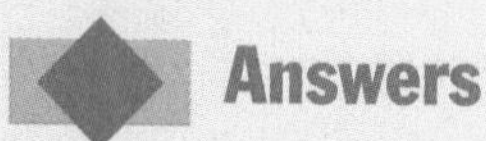

Answers

A False cognates: *lectura* (reading), *largo* (long), *sopa* (soup), *vaso* (glass), *dinero* (money), *pariente* (relative), *ropa* (clothing).

B Answers will vary.

Activities

Expansion

Extend activity A by offering some additional words and having students determine whether they are cognates or false cognates. Cognates: *banco, color, curva, divorcio, especial, farmacia, geografía, hospital, policía, solución, taxi, tropical*. False cognates: *colegio* (school), *dato* (fact), *disgusto* (displeasure), *embarazada* (pregnant), *fútbol* (soccer), *librería* (bookstore), *dirección* (address), *saludar* (to greet), *simpático* (nice), *sin* (without).

Spanish for Spanish Speakers

Ask native speakers to compile a list of ten false cognates and present it to the class as a mini-lesson.

Tú escribes

Estrategia

Using the dictionary

In addition to checking how words are spelled, you can use a dictionary to get a clearer and more accurate understanding of what words mean and to avoid misunderstandings. For example, you have already learned the difference between cognates and false cognates. A good way to make sure that a word is not a false cognate is to look it up in a dictionary.

A How many of these words can you recognize?

Look them up in the dictionary and decide which are cognates *(cognados)* and which are false cognates *(cognados falsos)*.

pariente
parque
practicar
dinero
sopa
ropa
CHOCOLATE
largo
pasaporte
programa
lectura
estudiante
vaso

B Make a list of some cognates you have learned.

Use what you know about word endings to think of words that might have cognates in Spanish. Then check your guesses in the dictionary. Find at least three new cognates.

National Standards

Communication
1.2, 1.3

Comparisons
4.1

Notes

The section *Tú escribes* is not required content. It offers a formal opportunity for students to improve their ability to write in Spanish. The *Estrategia* provides helpful tips that students must practice in the activities provided. You may choose to skip the section based upon your professional observation about how well student writing skills are progressing and as your school's curriculum dictates.

Rubrics for written evaluation. Portfolio assessment in Appendix H offers rubrics for written evaluation.

Proyectos adicionales

A Conexión con la tecnología

Research one of the countries where Spanish is the official language. You might surf the Web to try to find a home page that provides information on festivals, holidays, restaurants, maps and so forth. Then create your own travel brochure that features that country.

B Comunidades

You have already learned where Spanish is spoken in the world. Working in groups of three or four, prepare a list of several famous people *(las personas famosas)* who speak Spanish and say where they are from.

Estrategia

Recognizing community connections

As you learn Spanish this year, you will also learn about the culture of the people who speak Spanish. Who are they? Where do they live? What is their history? What contributions have they made to the world? Read newspapers, watch television, search the Internet and try to find out more about the influence Spanish has on the world today.

C Conexión con otras disciplinas: geografía

Draw your own map of the Spanish-speaking world. Include the names of the Spanish-speaking countries, their capital cities, major bodies of water, large mountain chains, etc. Make the finished map attractive by adding color and any other details you wish. Present the map to the class.

Teacher Resources

p. 67

Answers

A Creative self-expression.
B Answers will vary.
C Creative self-expression.

Activities

Communities

Suggest to students that they talk to their parents or guardians about ways they may use the Spanish skills they are developing by volunteering in the community. For example, students may wish to volunteer at the local library and use Spanish to work with Spanish-speaking customers. Brainstorm with the class other ways in which students might participate in community service.

Technology

To help students in their search for information about Spanish-speaking countries, suggest these Web sites as a starting point: **The Electronic Embassy** offers addresses, telephone numbers and additional links (http://www.embassy.org); the **Mexican Foreign Ministry** (http://embamex.sre.gob.mx/usa); (http://consulmexny.org); the **Tourism Office of Spain** (http://www.spain.info). Additional Web sites can be found by using a search engine and entering a keyword such as the name of a city, country or region.

National Standards

Communication	Connections
1.1, 1.3	3.1
Cultures	**Communities**
2.1, 2.2	5.1, 5.2

Notes

Many activities in *¡Aventura!* provide an opportunity for students to learn about where Spanish is spoken and to begin to make comparisons between the students' knowledge and the reality of what life is like in the Spanish-speaking world. Other activities provide an opportunity for students to establish connections with their communities that will encourage them to become lifelong learners.

The National Standards are practiced throughout the chapter. The projects that appear at the end of every chapter offer additional standards practice you may or may not choose to use, depending on student needs.

Teacher Resources

 *Trabalenguas*

 Episode 1, DVD 1, Track 4

Answers

Resolviendo el misterio

1. José lives with his uncle, Mr. Juárez.
2. Ana and Conchita are sisters from Spain who go to school with Francisco.
3. José is studying history.

Activities

Multiple Intelligences (linguistic)
You may choose to have students begin to create a Writer's Journal consisting of student writing activities. The Writer's Journal offers appropriate portfolio activities for addressing student writing skills and is an ideal opportunity for an ongoing dialog with students about their writing progress. How to create a Writer's Journal is addressed more thoroughly in the *Tú escribes* at the end of *Capítulo 2*.

Trabalenguas
Assign days when students have to recite the *Trabalenguas* as a ticket to enter or exit the classroom.

Repaso

Now that I have completed this chapter, I can ...	Go to these pages for help:
ask for and give names.	2
ask or tell where someone is from.	8
ask for and state age.	8
greet people and say good-bye.	18
ask and tell how someone is feeling.	18
express courtesy.	24
ask for and state the time.	24
I can also ...	
spell words in Spanish.	2
use appropriate gestures to greet people.	5
identify where Spanish is spoken.	8
state why learning Spanish may be beneficial in one's life.	14
recognize the difference between informal and formal in Spanish.	22
read a simple narrative in Spanish.	30

Trabalenguas

Tres tristes tigres tragaban trigo en tres tristes trastos sentados tras un trigal.

Resolviendo el misterio

After watching Episode 1 of *El cuarto misterioso*, answer the following questions.

1. With whom does José live?
2. Who are the girls that José meets?
3. What is José studying?

National Standards

Communication
1.2

Notes

Through the *Repaso*, students can measure their own progress in learning the main elements of the chapter.

Review the functions and other objectives in the *Repaso* and assign the activities. Answer questions so students can prepare for the chapter test. Follow up by reviewing the activities as a class.

Loose translation of the *Trabalenguas*: Three sad tigers swallowed wheat out of three sad bowls, sitting behind a wheat field.

Vocabulario

Go online EMCLanguages.net

el **acento** accent *1A*
Adiós Good-bye. *1A*
aquí here *1A*
la **Argentina** Argentina *1A*
bien well *1B*
Bolivia Bolivia *1A*
Buenas noches Good night *1B*; *Buenas tardes.* Good afternoon *1B*
Buenos días Good morning *1B*
la **capital** capital *1A*
catorce fourteen *1A*
cero zero *1A*
Chile Chile *1A*
cien one hundred *1B*
cinco five *1A*
cincuenta fifty *1B*
Colombia Colombia *1A*
¿cómo? how?, what? *1A*; *¿Cómo te llamas?* What is your name? *1A*
con with *1A*; *con mucho gusto* I would be very glad to *1B*; *con permiso* excuse me, may I *1B*
Costa Rica Costa Rica *1A*
¿Cuántos años tienes? How old are you? *1A*
cuarenta forty *1B*
cuatro four *1A*
Cuba Cuba *1A*
de from *1A*; *(¿de) dónde?* (from) where? *1A*; *de la mañana* in the morning, A.M. *1B*; *de la noche* at night, P.M. *1B*; *de la tarde* in the afternoon, P.M. *1B*; *de nada* you are welcome *1B*
diecinueve nineteen *1A*
dieciocho eighteen *1A*
dieciséis sixteen *1A*
diecisiete seventeen *1A*
diez ten *1A*
doce twelve *1A*
dos two *1A*
el **Ecuador** Ecuador *1A*
El Salvador El Salvador *1A*
eres you (informal) are *1A*; *¿Eres (tú) de...?* Are you from...? *1A*
es you (formal) are, he/she/it is *1B*; *Es la una.* It is one o'clock. *1B*; *Es medianoche.* It is midnight. *1B*; *Es mediodía.* It is noon. *1B*
España Spain *1A*
está (él, ella) you are *1B*; *está (Ud.)* you (formal) are *1B*
los **Estados Unidos** United States *1A*
están (Uds.) you are (pl.) 1B
estás (tú) you (informal) are 1B
estoy I am 1B
Guatemala Guatemala *1A*
Guinea Ecuatorial Equatorial Guinea *1A*
Hasta luego See you later. *1A*; *Hasta mañana.* See you tomorrow. *1B*; *Hasta pronto.* See you soon. 1B
Hola Hello. *1A*
Honduras Honduras *1A*
hora hour *1B*
lo siento I am sorry *1B*
mal badly *1B*
mañana tomorrow *1B*
la **mañana** morning *1B*
la **mayúscula** capital letter *1A*
me llamo my name is *1A*
menos (cinco, cuarto, etc.) minus, to, until, before (to express time) *1B*
México Mexico *1A*
la **minúscula** lowercase *1A*
la **muchacha** girl, young woman *1A*
el **muchacho** boy, guy *1A*
(muchas) gracias thank you (very much) *1B*
¡Mucho gusto! Glad to meet you! *1A*
muy very *1B*
Nicaragua Nicaragua *1A*
no no *1A*
la **noche** night *1B*
noventa ninety *1B*
nueve nine *1A*
ochenta eighty *1B*
ocho eight *1A*
once eleven *1A*
el **país hispano** Hispanic country *1A*
Panamá Panama *1A*
el **Paraguay** Paraguay *1A*
perdón excuse me, pardon me *1B*
el **Perú** Peru *1A*
por favor please *1B*
pronto soon, quickly *1B*
Puerto Rico Puerto Rico *1A*
¿Qué hora es? What time is it? *1B*
¿Qué tal? How are you? *1B*
quince fifteen *1A*
regular average, so-so, regular *1B*
la **República Dominicana** Dominican Republic *1A*
se escribe it is written *1A*
seis six *1A*
el **señor (Sr.)** gentleman, sir, Mr. *1B*
la **señora (Sra.)** lady, madame, Mrs. *1B*
la **señorita (Srta.)** young lady, Miss *1B*
sesenta sixty *1B*
setenta seventy *1B*
sí yes *1A*
siete seven *1A*
son they are *1B*; *Son las* (+ number). It is (+ number) o'clock. *1B*
soy I am *1A*
la **tarde** afternoon *1B*
te llamas your name is *1A*
tengo I have *1A*; *Tengo* (number) *años.* I am (number) years old. *1A*
tienes you have *1A*
trece thirteen *1A*
treinta (y uno, etc.) thirty (one, etc.) *1B*
tres three *1A*
tú you (informal) *1A*
uno one *1A*
el **Uruguay** Uruguay *1A*
usted (Ud.) you (s.) *1B*
ustedes (Uds.) you (pl.) *1B*
veinte twenty *1A*
veinticinco twenty five *1B*
veinticuatro twenty four *1B*
veintidós twenty two *1B*
veintinueve twenty nine *1B*
veintiocho twenty eight *1B*
veintiséis twenty six *1B*
veintisiete twenty seven *1B*
veintitrés twenty three *1B*
veintiuno twenty one *1B*
Venezuela Venezuela *1A*
vosotros,-as you (Spain, pl.) *1B*
y and *1A*; *y cuarto* quarter past, quarter after *1B*; *y media* half past *1B*
yo I *1A*

Estrategia

Learning vocabulary

Try to learn new vocabulary in a context (illustration, dialog, word groupings, etc.), since that will help you to use Spanish without having to translate word for word. Look at the words and expressions in the *Vocabulario* to see how many you remember. Say them aloud. If you have forgotten a word, return to where it was first introduced in order to check its meaning.

Notes This *Vocabulario* provides a reference list of new words and expressions that students are required to know for the chapter test and for future chapters.

Teacher Resources

Repaso

***¡Aventureros!*, Ch. 1**

Internet Activities

i-Culture

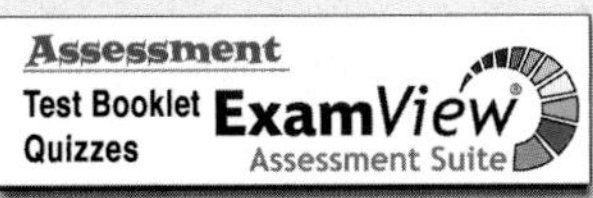

Activities

Expansion

Model each word or expression and have students repeat. Then call on students to use the word or expression in a sentence. This activity would be appropriate for all lists of vocabulary found in *¡Aventura!*.

Students with Special Needs

Help students practice the numbers by having them count around the class, each person saying one number. Go front to back, back to front or across the rows. When students are comfortable with numbers, use the same technique to have them count by 5s, 3s, 2s. You may also wish to have students count off in order numbers containing a 3 (for example, 3, 13, 23).

National Standards

Communication
1.2

Connections
3.1

Teacher Resources

 *Capítulo 2*

TPRS *Capítulo 2*

 Episode 2, DVD 1, Track 16

Connections with Parents

Establish parental support early in the school year. Send a note home or place a phone call to parents/guardians sharing something positive about their child. If an unfortunate circumstance does arise, it will be easier to resolve because you have already established a positive, caring connection.

Answers

El cuarto misterioso

1. In the city, perhaps outside of José's school.
2. Answers will vary.
3. Answers will vary.
4. Answers will vary but might include going to the movies, sporting events, restaurants or coffee shops and other people's houses.

National Standards
Communication 1.1

CAPÍTULO 2

En mi colegio

El cuarto misterioso

Answer the following questions about *Episodio 2–¿Qué hora es?*

1. Where does this scene take place?
2. What are the names of some classes that José and Conchita probably take?
3. What conversation do you think will take place between José and Conchita?
4. What are some activities that young people do to have fun?

José invites Conchita for a soda after Ana claims that she is too busy. During their conversation, José and Conchita discover that they have many things in common.

Objetivos

- identify **people** and **classroom objects**
- ask for and give **names**
- ask or tell **where someone is from**
- discuss **school schedules** and **daily activities**
- describe **classroom objects** and **clothing**
- say some **things people do**
- state **location**
- talk about **how someone feels**

Notes

Students should look at the screenshot and answer the questions that appear above the video clip. You may direct your students to work individually or in pairs, recording their answers on paper. You may also conduct this exercise as a full class activity asking individual students to share their answers.

As students watch each episode of *El cuarto misterioso,* they will begin to recall events from prior episodes. Ask a student to be a scribe and record the class's initial reactions to the screen shots that appear at the beginning of each chapter. At the end of each chapter, the class can review the notes to see how well it evaluated the specific screen shot before viewing the episode.

Contexto cultural

Estados Unidos

More than thirty million people in the United States use Spanish every day. In fact, in some parts of the United States—such as Florida, California, New Mexico and Texas—knowing Spanish proves very advantageous because Spanish is spoken by so many people for both pleasure and business.

Activities

Prior Knowledge

Take a few minutes to let students reflect on the chapter objectives. Ask students what classroom objects might be universal to all middle or high schools in the United States. Do U.S. classrooms require more gadgets than classrooms around the world? Why or why not? Ask students if they can easily remember the names of the people they meet. How does knowing where someone is from shape how we think about him or her? What categories of descriptions might students expect to learn in this chapter (for example, size, color, and so on)?

Notes

A checklist of these objectives, along with additional functions, appears on page 86 so students can evaluate their own progress.

National Standards	
Communication 1.1	**Comparisons** 4.1
Cultures 2.2	
Connections 3.1	

Teacher Resources

Vocabulario I
¿Quién es?

Activity 16

Activities 1–2

p. 8

Activity 1
Activity 2

Activity 1

Content reviewed in *Lección A*

- asking for and giving names
- talking about where someone is from
- Spanish-speaking countries

Lección A Vocabulario I
¿Quién es?

¿Quién es él?
Él es Daniel.
¿Cómo se llama ella?
Se llama Teresa.
¿De dónde es él?
Él es de California.
¿De dónde son ellos?
Ellos son de Colorado.

National Standards

Cultures
2.2

Connections
3.1

Comparisons
4.1

Notes

Names for states and cities often reflect the rich Hispanic heritage in the United States. Ask students to name several such locations and identify them on a map. Point out how the pronunciation of the names changes when students say them in Spanish (*e.g.*, *California*, *Texas*).

An alternative spelling for *Texas* is *Tejas*.

1 ¿Quién?

Selecciona la foto de la(s) persona(s) apropiada(s).

A

B

C

D

2 Minidiálogos

Completa los minidiálogos con las palabras apropiadas. ***(Complete the mini-dialogs with appropriate words.)***

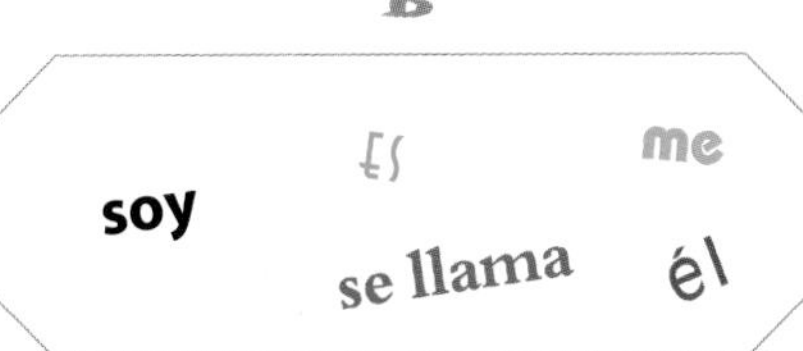

A

eres quién él dónde es te llamas ella

B

soy es me se llama él

MODELO **A:** ¿Quién es él?
B: Él es José.

A: ¿Cómo se llama (1)?
B: (2) Alejandro.

A: ¿(3) es?
B: ¿Ella?
A: No, (4) no. ¿Quién es él?

A: ¿De (5) es Daniel?
B: (6) de Miami.

A: Y, ¿cómo (7) tú?
B: Yo (8) llamo Marta.

A: ¿De dónde (9) tú?
B: (10) de El Paso.

Él es José.

Teacher Resources

Activity 1

Answers

1 1. C
2. A
3. D
4. B

2 1. él
2. Se llama
3. Quién
4. ella
5. dónde
6. Es
7. te llamas
8. me
9. eres
10. Soy

Notes Reproducible answer sheets have been provided for the activities indicated in the student textbook by the audio speaker icon. These reproducible answer sheets can be found at the end of the Audio Program Manual.

National Standards
Communication 1.2

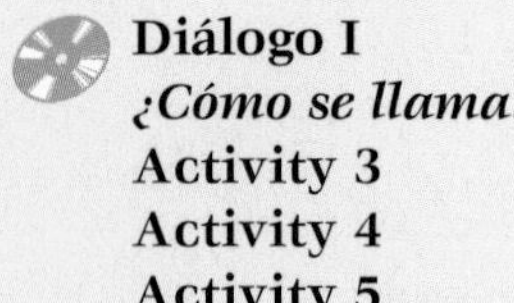

Teacher Resources

Diálogo I
¿Cómo se llama?
Activity 3
Activity 4
Activity 5

Answers

3 1. El muchacho es Raúl.
2. No, Laura es una muchacha.
3. Se llama Diana.

4 1. Answers will vary.
2. Washington, D.C.

5 Possible answers:
1. Él se llama Raúl.
2. Ellas son Laura y Diana.
3. Ella es de Los Ángeles.

Activities

Prereading Strategy
Have students cover up the dialog with one hand and look at the photographs. Ask them to imagine where the conversation takes place and what the people are saying to one another.

Pronunciation *(las vocales cerradas: i, u)*
Encourage students to focus on the correct Spanish pronunciation of Spanish geographical names (*Los Ángeles*, *Colorado*, etc.).

National Standards
Communication 1.2
Comparisons 4.1

Diálogo I ¿Cómo se llama ella?

RAÚL: Laura, ¿quién es?
LAURA: ¿Él?
RAÚL: No, ella.

RAÚL: ¿Cómo se llama ella?
LAURA: Se llama Diana.
RAÚL: ¿Es de aquí?
LAURA: No, ella es de Los Ángeles.

DIANA: ¿Quién eres tú?
RAÚL: Perdón. Me llamo Raúl.
DIANA: Mucho gusto, Raúl.
RAÚL: Mucho gusto, Diana.

3 ¿Qué recuerdas? 

1. ¿Quién es el muchacho?
2. ¿Es Laura un muchacho?
3. ¿Cómo se llama la muchacha de Los Ángeles?

4 Algo personal

1. ¿Eres tú de California? ¿De dónde eres?
2. ¿Cómo se llama la capital de los Estados Unidos?

5 ¡No es lógico! 

Escucha la información y corrige lo que no es lógico. ***(Listen to the information and correct what is not logical.)***

1. Raúl

2. Laura y Diana

3. María

Notes The *Diálogos I* and *II* contextualize the new words and expressions that are introduced in the *Vocabularios I* and *II*, allowing students to practice the new vocabulary in complete-sentence answers to activities.

The activities that follow the dialog are recorded in *Lección 2A* of the Audio Program. Student answer sheets for activity 5 can be found in the back of the Audio Program Manual.

Comparisons. Point out how the pronunciation of the city and state names in the dialog and in activity 6 changes when students say them in Spanish.

La influencia hispana en los Estados Unidos

Have you been to a Mexican or Spanish restaurant? Do you recognize the names Sammy Sosa or Shakira? Perhaps you have studied art by famous Latino/Hispanic artists. Examples of how the Hispanic culture has influenced daily life in the United States abound. Words that have Spanish origins are one example that you experience every day of the strong influence that Spanish cultures have probably had in your community. Have you ever sat outside on a *patio* or taken a *siesta* in your free time? If so, then you have enjoyed some of the rich Hispanic heritage that exists in the United States today. Here are other words that have been borrowed from Spanish:

Adobe en Santa Fe, Nuevo México.

adobe *rodeo* *plaza* *mosquito* *chile*

The Spaniards explored and settled parts of America years before the arrival of the pilgrims on the *Mayflower*. Thanks to these early settlers, communities throughout the United States today reflect their rich Spanish colonial architecture, delicious foods, interesting geographical names and much more.

6 Conexión con otras disciplinas: geografía

Using a dictionary, encyclopedia or the Internet, research these geographical names that have come to the English language from the Spanish language. Give the English equivalent for each word. Then find each place on a map.

1. Los Ángeles
2. Las Vegas
3. Amarillo
4. Boca Ratón
5. Florida
6. Río Grande
7. Colorado
8. Alcatraz
9. Nevada

7 Conexión con la comunidad

Tell where Spanish is used in your community or state. Are you aware of any other Hispanic influences in your community?

Teacher Resources

 **Activities 3–4**

 **pp. 42–43**

Answers

6
1. the angels
2. the fertile lowlands
3. yellow
4. mouth of the mouse
5. full of flowers
6. big river
7. red-colored
8. pelican
9. snow-covered

7 Answers will vary.

Activities

Cooperative Learning
Have students work in groups to identify ten cities/states in the United States with Spanish names. Each group should share its list with the class.

Expansion
Bring to class some newspapers or magazines published in Spanish. Ask students to look at the advertisements to identify cognates. Next ask students to identify three Hispanics mentioned in the newspapers or magazines. Who are they? Where are they from? Why are they in the news?

Notes

Cultures. In Santa Fe, New Mexico (shown in the photograph on the left side of the *Cultura viva*), some descendants of the Spaniards who founded the city in 1610 still speak Spanish today.

Some additional words that have come to the English language from the Spanish language include: lasso, from *lazo* (slipknot); maize, from *maíz* (corn); poncho, from *poncho* (blanket-like cloak); and bronco, from *bronco* (rough, wild).

National Standards

Communication	Comparisons
1.1, 1.3	4.1, 4.2
Cultures	**Communities**
2.2	5.1
Connections	
3.1, 3.2	

Teacher Resources

 Activities 5–8

 Activities 1–3

 Activity 3

 Unit 2

 Activity 2

 Activities

Cooperative Learning

Have your students pretend to be from one of the Spanish-speaking countries (other than the United States). Then have students ask three other students near them in Spanish for their name (*¿Cómo te llamas?*) and where they are from (*¿De dónde eres?*). Finally, test how much information the students obtained by asking them to report to the class what they learned (*Se llama...y es de...*).

Estructura

Subject pronouns and the verb *ser*

- You will often use subject pronouns *(pronombres personales)* when discussing people in Spanish. You have already used subject pronouns with the following forms of the verb *ser* (to be) to identify people and to say where someone is from.

ser					
yo	**soy**	*I am*	nosotros nosotras	**somos**	*we are*
tú	**eres**	*you are*	vosotros vosotras	**sois**	*you are*
Ud. él ella	**es**	*you are* *he (it) is* *she (it) is*	Uds. ellos ellas	**son**	*you are* *they are* *they are*

- Make a sentence negative in Spanish by placing *no* before the verb.

Alicia es de Arizona. → *Alicia **no** es de Arizona.*

- Subject pronouns may be used with or without a verb. They may not be needed if the subject is already known or if the verb form itself identifies the subject.

*¿De dónde eres **(tú)**?*	Where are **you** from?
***(Yo)** Soy de Indiana. ¿Y **él**?*	**I** am from Indiana. And **he**?
***(Él)** Es de Virginia.*	**He** is from Virginia.

- The plural forms *nosotras*, *vosotras* and *ellas* refer only to females, while the subject pronouns *nosotros*, *vosotros* and *ellos* are used to refer either to males only or to a mixed group of both males and females.

***Ellos** son de Miami.*	**They (the boys)** are from Miami.
***Ellas** son de Charleston.*	**They (the girls)** are from Charleston.

but:

***Ellos** son de los Estados Unidos.*	**They (the boys and girls)** are from the United States.

National Standards

Communication
1.1, 1.3

Comparisons
4.1

Notes

Point out that in Spanish the subject pronouns are often unnecessary unless the speaker wishes to add emphasis or clarity to a sentence.

Explain that *tú* is the singular familiar form of **you** and is used with family, friends, children and others with whom you have informal relationships.

Point out for students that the subject pronoun *ellos* may refer to more than one boy, to a boy and a girl or to a group of boys and girls.

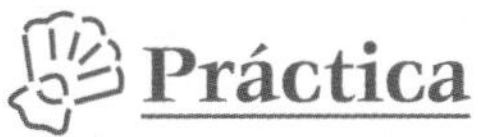

Práctica

8 En tu colegio

Complete this conversation with your teacher as you review a list of people who speak Spanish. Use the appropriate subject pronoun.

MODELO A: ¿Felipe?
B: No, él no.

1. **A:** ¿Yo?
   B: Sí, __ sí.
2. **A:** ¿La Srta. Barnés?
   B: No, __ no.
3. **A:** ¿Paul y Luisa?
   B: Sí, __ sí.
4. **A:** ¿David y Ud.?
   B: Sí, __ sí.
5. **A:** ¿La profesora de música?
   B: No, __ no.
6. **A:** ¿Uds.?
   B: Sí, __ sí.
7. **A:** ¿Teresa, Daniel y yo?
   B: Sí, __ sí.
8. **A:** ¿Miguel y Jaime?
   B: Sí, __ sí.
9. **A:** ¿Tú y yo?
   B: Sí, __ sí.

9 Los estudiantes de mi colegio

Completa las oraciones de una manera lógica con la forma correcta del verbo ser. ***(Complete the sentences logically with the correct form of the verb ser.)***

1. ¿Tú __ de South Bend, Indiana?
2. Él __ de Seattle, Washington.
3. Ellas __ de San Antonio, Texas.
4. Ella __ de Denver, Colorado.
5. Ellos __ de San Diego, California.
6. Yo __ de *(name of your city and state)*.
7. Nosotros __ de (los)....

Ser

Ser is irregular, which means its six different forms do not follow the same predictable pattern that regular verbs do. Also, although the subject pronouns *Ud., él* and *ella* are different in meaning, they share the same verb form, as do *Uds., ellos* and *ellas*.

10 ¡No!

Show that you disagree with these statements by making them negative.

MODELO Teresa y Daniel son de España.
Teresa y Daniel no son de España.

1. Soy de París.
2. Diana es de Nueva York.
3. Ella es de aquí.
4. Me llamo Hernán.
5. Se llama Luz.
6. Nosotros somos de la Argentina.

Teresa y Daniel no son de España.

Teacher Resources

Activity 10

Answers

8
1. tú/Ud.
2. ella
3. ellos
4. nosotros
5. ella
6. nosotros,-as
7. Uds./vosotros
8. ellos
9. nosotros,-as

9
1. eres
2. es
3. son
4. es
5. son
6. soy
7. somos

10
1. No soy de París.
2. Diana no es de Nueva York.
3. Ella no es de aquí.
4. No me llamo Hernán.
5. No se llama Luz.
6. Nosotros no somos de la Argentina.

National Standards

Connections
3.1

Comparisons
4.1

Notes With the exception of activity 8, the *vosotros/vosotras* verb forms are included in *¡Aventura!* for passive recognition only. However, you may choose to require students to learn and use the *vosotros* and *vosotras* pronouns and verb forms.

Clarify for students that questions like *¿Cómo se llama?* can be the English equivalent of "What is your/his/her name?" Eliminate confusion by adding *Ud., él* or *ella* to the end of the question. In the same way they can clarify a statement such as *Se llama...* by placing *Ud., él* or *ella* at the beginning of the sentence.

Answers

11 1. ¿...Penélope Cruz y Antonio Banderas?/Ellos son de España.
2. ¿...Jimmy Smits y Christina Aguilera?/Ellos son de (los) Estados Unidos.
3. ¿...Don Francisco?/Él es de Chile.
4. ¿...Pedro Martínez y Sammy Sosa?/Ellos son de (la) República Dominicana.
5. ¿...Juan Pablo Montoya y Carlos Vives?/Ellos son de Colombia.
6. ¿...Rubén Blades?/Él es de Panamá.
7. ¿...Daisy Fuentes y Gloria Estefan?/Ellas son de Cuba.
8. ¿...Salma Hayek?/Ella es de México.

12 1. Jimmy Smits, Penélope Cruz y Salma Hayek son actores.
2. Shakira, Enrique Iglesias y Ricky Martin son cantantes.
3. Sergio García, Sammy Sosa y Juan Pablo Montoya son atletas.
4. Fernando Botero, Pablo Picasso y Diego Rivera son pintores.

13 1. Isabel Allende (Chile), José Martí (Cuba)
2. Jimmy Smits (Estados Unidos), Penélope Cruz (España), Salma Hayek (México)
3. Shakira (Colombia), Enrique Iglesias (España), Ricky Martin (Puerto Rico)
4. Sergio García (España), Sammy Sosa (República Dominicana), Juan Pablo Montoya (Colombia)
5. Fernando Botero (Colombia), Pablo Picasso (España), Diego Rivera (México)

National Standards

Communication
1.1

Cultures
2.2

11 La influencia hispana

Your class is studying Hispanic influence in the United States. With a classmate, take turns asking and answering where some well-known people are from.

Shakira es de Colombia.

MODELO Shakira / Colombia
A: ¿De dónde es Shakira?
B: Ella es de Colombia.

1. Penélope Cruz y Antonio Banderas / España
2. Jimmy Smits y Christina Aguilera / Estados Unidos
3. Don Francisco / Chile
4. Pedro Martínez y Sammy Sosa / la República Dominicana
5. Juan Pablo Montoya y Carlos Vives / Colombia
6. Rubén Blades / Panamá
7. Daisy Fuentes y Gloria Estefan / Cuba
8. Salma Hayek / México

12 ¿Por qué son famosos?

You are going to do a report about famous Spanish-speaking people. Find out who these people are and say what field of expertise they have in common.

MODELO Jorge Luis Borges, Isabel Allende, José Martí
Ellos son escritores.

cantantes *(singers)* atletas *(athletes)* actores *(actors)* pintores *(painters)* escritores *(writers)*

1. Jimmy Smits, Penélope Cruz, Salma Hayek
2. Shakira, Enrique Iglesias, Ricky Martin
3. Sergio García, Sammy Sosa, Juan Pablo Montoya
4. Fernando Botero, Pablo Picasso, Diego Rivera

Comunicación

13 ¡Son de muchos países!

With a classmate, talk about where the famous people mentioned in activity 12 are from. Then look up a few other Spanish-speaking celebrities, indicating their profession and/or where they are from.

MODELO Jorge Luis Borges
A: ¿De dónde es Jorge Luis Borges?
B: Es de Argentina.

Notes **Cultures.** Suggest that students use one of many available Internet search engines to do research about the famous Spanish-speaking individuals mentioned in activity 11.

Es de...

With a partner, discuss where the following people are from, according to the illustration.

MODELO Alicia
A: ¿De dónde es Alicia?
B: Es de (los) Estados Unidos.

1. Pablo
2. Luis
3. tú
4. Jorge y Luisa
5. Daniel, tú y yo
6. la Srta. Muñoz
7. yo
8. el Sr. y la Sra. Vargas

EE.UU.

Can you guess the abbreviation *(abreviatura)* in Spanish for *Estados Unidos?* It is *EE.UU.* As in English, some proper nouns are abbreviated in Spanish. Although most abbreviations use only one letter, this Spanish abbreviation uses double letters because *Estados Unidos* is a plural noun.

Juego: ¿De dónde es?

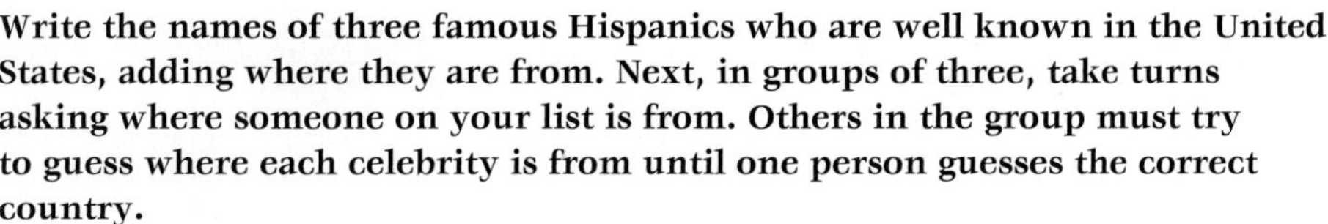

Write the names of three famous Hispanics who are well known in the United States, adding where they are from. Next, in groups of three, take turns asking where someone on your list is from. Others in the group must try to guess where each celebrity is from until one person guesses the correct country.

MODELO
A: ¿De dónde es Jennifer López?
B: Es de Ecuador.
A: No, no es de Ecuador.
C: Es de Estados Unidos.
A: Sí, es de Estados Unidos.

Notes Another abbreviation that requires double letters is *JJ.OO.* for *Juegos Olímpicos.*

Using a wall map or maps from the *¡Aventura! 1* set of transparencies, talk with students about where the places mentioned in activities 13, 14 and 15 are located.

Answers

14 1. ¿...es...?/Es de México.
2. ¿...es...?/Es de Honduras.
3. ¿...eres...?/Soy de (los) Estados Unidos.
4. ¿...son...?/Son de Puerto Rico.
5. ¿...somos...?/Somos de (los) Estados Unidos.
6. ¿...es...?/Es de Panamá.
7. ¿...soy...?/Eres de (los) Estados Unidos.
8. ¿...son...?/Son de Colombia.

15 Names and answers will vary.

Activities

Connections
Show a representative sample of works of art made by the artists mentioned in activity 12. Then have students make a drawing or painting in the same style as that of one of the artists. Display the paintings or drawings in class.

Expansion
Make a bulletin board of famous Spanish speakers, using pictures and other items that students bring in.

Language through Action
Have students point out the countries mentioned on maps in your classroom.

National Standards	
Communication 1.1, 1.2, 1.3	**Comparisons** 4.1
Cultures 2.2	
Connections 3.1	

Teacher Resources

 **Vocabulario II**
¿Qué hay en la clase?

 **Activities 17–18**

 **Activities 9–11**

 **Activity 4**

 **pp. 48–49**

 **p. 7**

 **Activity 4**
Activity 5

 **Activity 3**

Activities

Critical Thinking
Have students name classroom items that are also found in their homes.

Pronunciation
Have students practice pronouncing in Spanish the names of the objects that are in the illustration of a classroom. Check for correct pronunciation.

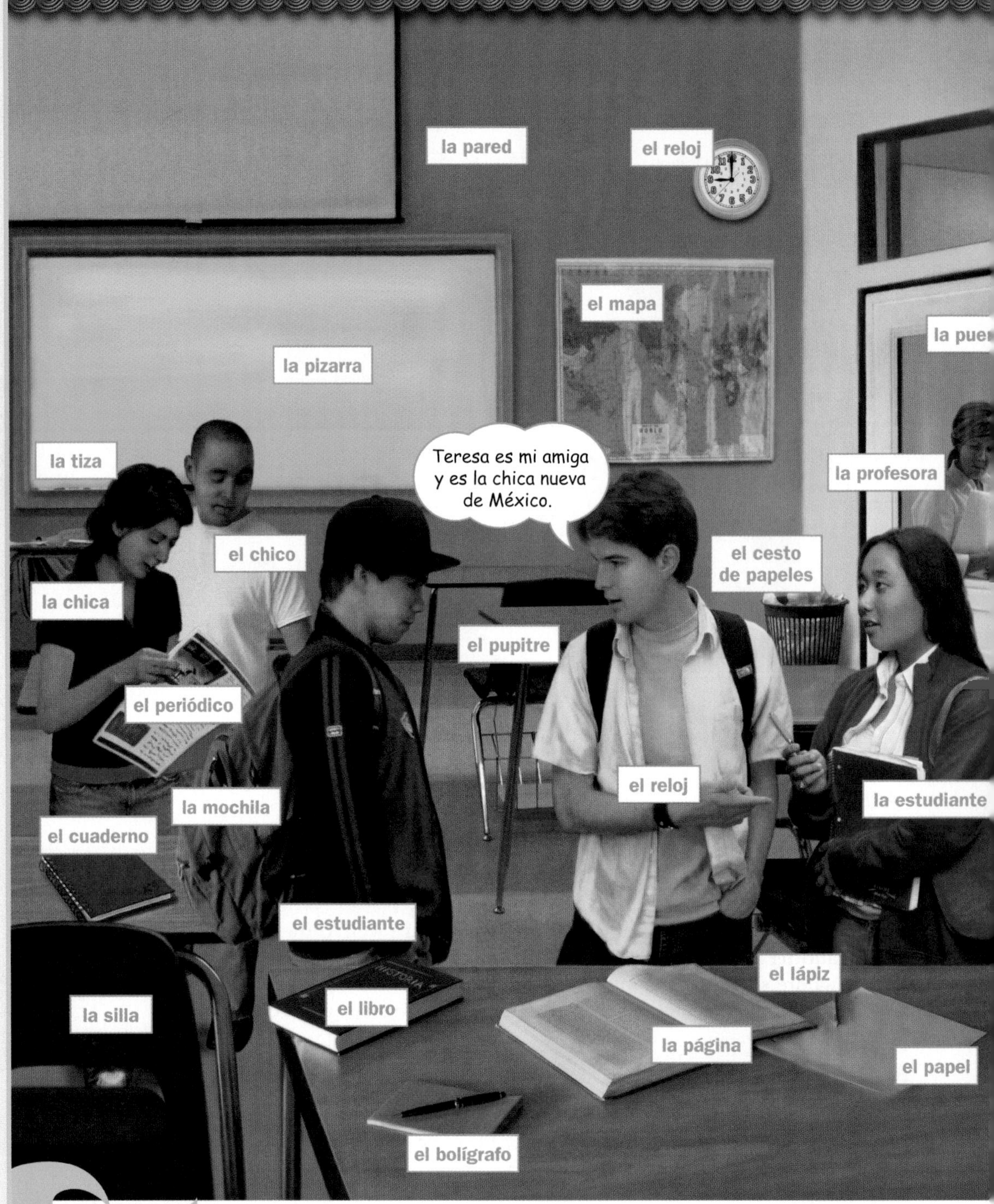

National Standards

Communication
1.1

Vocabulario II
¿Qué hay en la clase?

la pared
el reloj
el mapa
la puer
la pizarra
la tiza
Teresa es mi amiga y es la chica nueva de México.
la profesora
el chico
el cesto de papeles
la chica
el pupitre
el periódico
el reloj
la mochila
la estudiante
el cuaderno
el estudiante
el lápiz
la silla
el libro
la página
el papel
el bolígrafo

Notes Explain to students that synonyms exist in Spanish just as they are common in English. Then ask if students can remember the synonyms for *chico* and *chica* that they saw in *Capítulo 1: muchacho, muchacha*. Point out that students now know two terms for **boy** and **girl**: *chico* is an alternate form of *muchacho*; *chica* is an alternate form of *muchacha*.

¿Qué es?

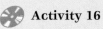

Identifica los objetos que oyes. *(Identify the objects you hear.)*

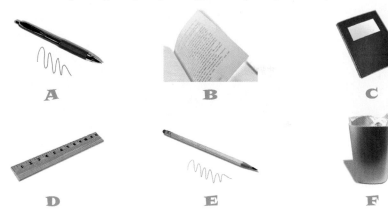

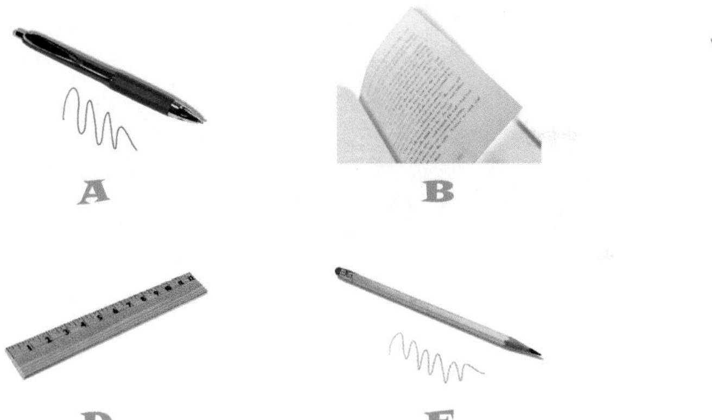

No comprendo una palabra

With a classmate, take turns pretending you do not know the word in Spanish to identify various objects in your classroom. Ask one another *¿Cómo se dice* (plus a word in English)? as you point to an object. Your partner must then tell you how to say the word in Spanish using *Se dice* (plus the word in Spanish).

MODELO **A:** ¿Cómo se dice *wall?*
B: Se dice *pared.*

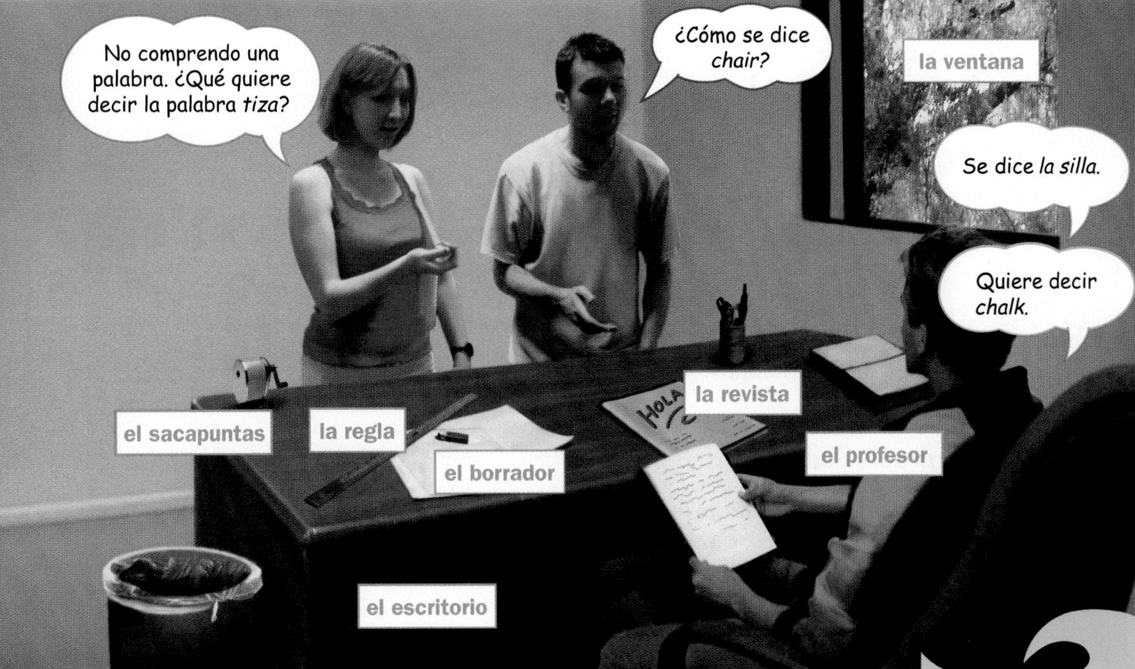

Notes The following are additional classroom vocabulary terms you may wish to introduce: *el resaltador* (highlighter), *el gancho/la grapa* (clip), *la calculadora* (calculator), *el calendario* (calendar), *el cartel* (poster), *la computadora/el computador/el ordenador* (computer), *la impresora* (printer), *el mapa* (map).

Teacher Resources

Activity 16

Answers

16 1. D
2. A
3. B
4. F
5. C
6. E

17 Role-playing activity.

Activities

TPR

Use TPR in order to reinforce classroom vocabulary: *señala el mapa*, etc.

National Standards

Communication
1.1, 1.2

Teacher Resources

 **Diálogo II**
La nueva estudiante de Los Ángeles
Activity 18
Activity 19
Activity 20

 **p. 53**

Answers

18 1. La palabra mochila quiere decir ***backpack.***
2. Es de Los Ángeles.
3. Es Diana.
4. No. Es amiga de Raúl.
5. Se dice reloj.
6. Sí, hay un reloj en la clase.

19 Answers will vary.

20 1. Sí.
2. No. ...***backpack.***
3. No. ...Diana...
4. Sí.

21 Role-playing activity.

Activities

Expansion
Additional questions (*¿Qué recuerdas?*): *¿De dónde es la estudiante nueva?*; *¿Cómo se llama ella?*; *¿Es Diana la amiga de Raúl?*

Spanish for Spanish Speakers
Ask students to write a short composition about a new student during the first day of class. Ask that they include what it would feel like to be new in school, as well as some of the fears and hopes they might have.

National Standards
Communication 1.1, 1.2

Diálogo II La nueva estudiante de Los Ángeles

CARLOS: ¿Quién es la chica con la mochila?
RAÚL: ¿Qué quiere decir la palabra *mochila?*
CARLOS: Quiere decir *backpack*.

RAÚL: Ella es la estudiante nueva de Los Ángeles.
CARLOS: ¿Cómo se llama?
RAÚL: Se llama Diana y es mi amiga.

DIANA: Perdón, chicos. ¿Cómo se dice *clock* en español?
CARLOS: Se dice reloj.
DIANA: Muchas gracias.

18 ¿Qué recuerdas?

1. ¿Qué quiere decir la palabra *mochila?*
2. ¿De dónde es la chica con la mochila?
3. ¿Quién es la estudiante nueva?
4. ¿Es la estudiante nueva amiga de Carlos?
5. ¿Cómo se dice *clock* en español?
6. ¿Hay un reloj en la clase?

¡Extra!

En otras palabras

As in English, Spanish words and expressions can vary according to where the speaker has lived. Look at these examples:

el bolígrafo	*el boli, la pluma, el lapicero, el estilo*
el borrador	*la goma*
el cesto de papeles	*la papelera, la caneca, el basurero*
el escritorio	*el buró*
el estudiante	*el alumno, el compañero (de clase)*
la estudiante	*la alumna, la compañera (de clase)*
la mochila	*la bolsa, el bulto*
el sacapuntas	*el afilalápices, el cortalápices*

19 Algo personal

1. ¿Tienes una mochila?
2. ¿Tienes un reloj? ¿Qué hora es?

20 ¿Sí o no?

¿Son lógicos los diálogos? Corrige lo que no es lógico.

21 Tu propio diálogo

With a partner, use the previous dialog as a model to create your own dialog. Use your own names, change the italicized words and make any other changes you feel are appropriate.

Notes If students ask about *nuevo/nueva*, explain that *nuevo* is used with masculine nouns much as *el* accompanies masculine nouns, and *nueva* is used with feminine nouns much as *la* accompanies feminine nouns. Adjective/noun agreement will be taught in *Lección 2B*.

Point out the accent mark on *Los Ángeles* in *Diálogo II*. Then have students practice pronouncing the Spanish equivalent of several cities in the United States: *San Antonio*, *Miami*, *Chicago*, *Santa Cruz*.

Cultura 

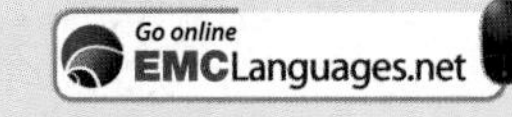

El español en los Estados Unidos

In the United States, over thirty million people use Spanish daily for business or pleasure. Many American cities are becoming bilingual because of their large Spanish-speaking communities. In fact, Spanish is the second language of the United States. Los Angeles, Miami, San Antonio, New York and numerous other cities across the United States have Spanish television and radio stations, Spanish newspapers and magazines and bilingual signs in most public places. The Hispanic presence is increasing rapidly in the United States and influencing many aspects of the American culture and economy. Look around, you may find you can experience more Spanish than you ever realized!

22 Oportunidades de trabajo

Answer the questions below based on the following classified advertisements.

Compañía multinacional ubicada en Chicago
busca
Secretario/a bilingüe Español-inglés
Responsabilidades: mantener archivos, contestar teléfonos y escribir cartas para los clientes hispanohablantes.
Experiencia mínima: 1 año
Salario: $30.000 anuales
Para mayor información llame al (312) 100-7799.

BANCO CAMINO REAL
necesita
Director(a) de Servicio al Cliente
Se prefiere persona bilingüe (español e inglés), con fluidez y excelentes habilidades de escritura en ambas lenguas, buen manejo de las relaciones personales e impecable presentación. Se requiere experiencia mínima de 3 años. Interesados por favor enviar curriculum vitae a: Banco Camino Real, 201 SW Black Rd., Austin, TX 78701-6384.

Se requieren profesores para Español y Literatura
Prestigiosa escuela privada busca profesores de español y literatura para la primavera. Los interesados deben tener un Masters en educación y tener licencia para enseñar en el estado de New Mexico. Se requiere un mínimo de dos años de experiencia.
Candidatos favor enviar su CV con carta de presentación a P.O Box 75634, Albuquerque, NM 87106.

1. How much experience is needed for the job as a bilingual secretary? For the position as a teacher? For the position as the director of customer service at the bank?
2. How do you find out about the *secretario/a bilingüe* job? About the other two jobs?
3. Where is the company located that is looking for a bilingual secretary?
4. What type of business do you think *Banco Camino Real* is?
5. Which job includes keeping archives, answering phones and writing letters?
6. Which job requires a college degree? Why do you think a degree is important for this job?

¡Oportunidades!

Las ventajas de ser bilingüe

Many American companies today are searching for bilingual employees who can expand their market and increase sales to the growing population of Spanish speakers in the United States. Being bilingual may be the advantage you need to compete in the job market.

Teacher Resources

 p. 54

 Activity 6

 Activity 4

Answers

22
1. One year; two years; three years.
2. Call 312-100-7799. Send curriculum vitae (résumé) to the addresses listed.
3. Chicago.
4. A bank.
5. The bilingual secretary job.
6. The teaching job. Answers will vary.

Activities

Spanish for Spanish Speakers

Have students write a short composition in Spanish listing three or four benefits available to them because they know Spanish.

Notes

Communities. The choices for obtaining information in Spanish about the Spanish-speaking world (and news and entertainment in general) are growing every year. Television stations that broadcast in Spanish around the world include cable stations such as *Univision, CBS Telenoticias* and *CNN en Español.*

Cultures. Job listings in activity 22 are for cities in the United States with large Hispanic populations.

The section *¡Oportunidades!* gives students an opportunity to see how learning Spanish is beneficial now and in the future.

National Standards	
Cultures 2.1, 2.2	**Communities** 5.1
Connections 3.1, 3.2	
Comparisons 4.2	

Teacher Resources

 Activities 12–13

 Activities 5–7

 p. 137

 Activity 7

 Activities 5–6

Activities

Multiple Intelligences (linguistic)
Divide students into small groups. Provide each group with one copy of a "Masculine/Feminine Noun Concept Development Sheet." On the sheet of paper provide a list of ten or more masculine nouns ending in *-o*, each one listed with the definite article *el* in front of each noun. On the same sheet, provide a list of feminine nouns grouped according to the endings *-a*, *-ción*, *-sión* and *-dad*, with the definite article *la*. Then have students compare and contrast the lists to identify which nouns are ***masculino*** and which are ***femenino***. Each group should make a hypothesis about how to determine which nouns are masculine and which are feminine based on their observations and discussions. Each group should present their hypotheses to the class.

National Standards

Comparisons
4.1

Estructura

Using definite articles with nouns

- Nouns refer to people, places, things or concepts. All nouns in Spanish have a gender: They are either masculine or feminine. Nouns that end in *-o* are generally masculine and are often used with the definite article *el* (the), whereas nouns that end in *-a*, *-ción*, *-sión* or *-dad* are usually feminine and are often used with the definite article *la* (the).

masculino: ***el*** *chic**o***
femenino: ***la*** *chic**a*** ***la*** *pronuncia**ción*** ***la*** *mi**sión*** ***la*** *posibili**dad***

- Some nouns do not follow these patterns.

masculino: *el día* ***femenino:*** *la noche*

- Also, some nouns that refer to people have only one form and the gender of the person being referred to is indicated by the definite article.

masculino: ***el*** *estudiante* ***femenino:*** ***la*** *estudiante*

- Make most nouns in Spanish plural by adding *-s*. The accompanying plural of the definite articles are *los* (masculine) or *las* (feminine).

masculino: *el amigo* → ***los*** *amigo**s*** *el libro* → ***los*** *libro**s***
femenino: *la amiga* → ***las*** *amiga**s*** *la revista* → ***las*** *revista**s***

- Make nouns that end with a consonant plural by adding *-es*.

el papel → ***los*** *papel**es*** *la actividad* → ***las*** *actividad**es***
el reloj → ***los*** *reloj**es*** *la pared* → ***las*** *pared**es***

- Nouns that end in *-z* change the *-z* to *-c* in the plural.

*el lápi**z*** → *los lápi**ces***

- It may be necessary to add or remove an accent mark when making a noun plural.

*el ex**a**men* → ***los*** *ex**á**men**es*** *la lec**ción*** → ***las*** *lec**ciones***

¿Masculino o femenino?
Remember . . . use the masculine form of the noun when you refer to males and females as a group or to masculine and feminine objects simultaneously.

los chicos the boys
the boys and the girls

Notes You may wish to tell students that the gender of nouns has nothing to do with the nature of an object. Gender has grammatical significance because it determines the form of articles and adjectives that accompany the noun.

Práctica

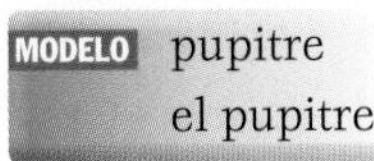

23 Objetos en la clase

Da cada sustantivo con su artículo definido. Sigue el modelo. ***(Give each noun with its definite article. Follow the model.)***

MODELO pupitre
el pupitre

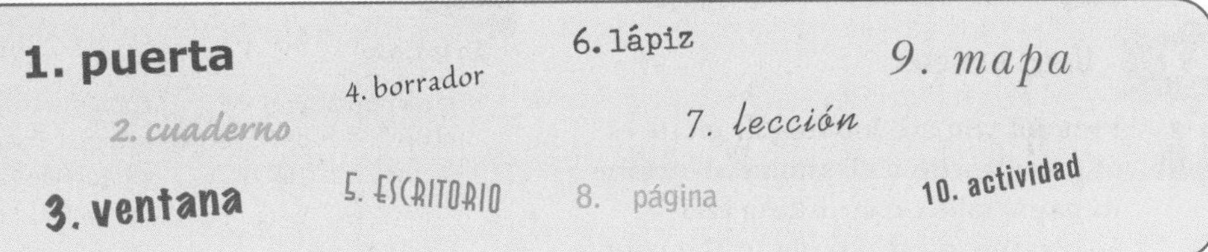

1. puerta
2. cuaderno
3. ventana
4. borrador
5. ESCRITORIO
6. lápiz
7. lección
8. página
9. mapa
10. actividad

24 Más de uno

Da la forma plural de cada palabra de la actividad anterior. ***(Give the plural of each word in the preceding activity.)***

MODELO el pupitre
los pupitres

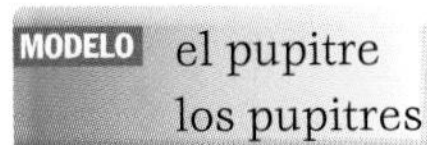

25 Periódicos en la clase de español

Identify the nouns in these magazine and newspaper headlines and ads and tell which ones are masculine *(masculino)* and which are feminine *(femenino)*.

1.

2.

3.

4.

5. Los lápices PRISMACOLOR
Dan color a tu clase

6. Todo está en las Páginas Amarillas

7.
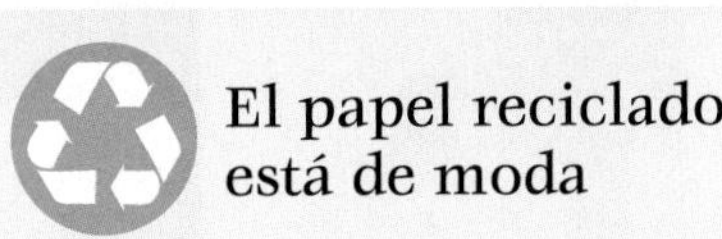

Teacher Resources

Activity 23

Answers

23 1. la puerta; 2. el cuaderno; 3. la ventana; 4. el borrador; 5. el escritorio; 6. el lápiz; 7. la lección; 8. la página; 9. el mapa; 10. la actividad

24
1. las puertas
2. los cuadernos
3. las ventanas
4. los borradores
5. los escritorios
6. los lápices
7. las lecciones
8. las páginas
9. los mapas
10. las actividades

25 Students should not be expected to find all nouns.

Probable common answers:
1. la puerta (femenino)
2. la hora (femenino)
3. la pared (femenino)
4. el reloj (masculino), la hora (femenino)
5. los lápices (masculino)
6. las páginas (femenino)
7. el papel (masculino)

Other nouns include the following: *cultura (femenino), exposición (femenino), opinión (femenino), color (masculino), clase (femenino), moda (femenino).*

Activities

Critical Thinking

For activity 23, have students explain how they know which nouns are *masculino* and which are *femenino.*

National Standards

Communication
1.2

Connections
3.1

Notes Before beginning activity 24, note for students that there are certain exceptions to the rules for making nouns plural. For example, many words ending in *-es* and *-is* do not change in the plural, such as the days of the week *(el lunes, los lunes)*; *la crisis, las crisis.*

Have students look at the clippings that appear in activity 25. Then ask if they recognize any of the words. Are they able to understand any of these advertisements?

Answers

26 Answers will vary.

27 Possible answers:

1. ¿Quién es el chico con los libros?/Se llama Felipe y es mi amigo.
2. ¿Quién es la chica con el periódico?/Se llama Rosa y es mi amiga.
3. ¿Quién es la mujer con la tiza y el borrador?/Se llama Doris y es mi amiga.
4. ¿Quién es el chico con los cuadernos?/Se llama Luis y es mi amigo.
5. ¿Quién es la chica con el profesor?/Se llama Sandra y es mi amiga.
6. ¿Quién es el chico con el reloj?/Se llama Daniel y es mi amigo.

Activities

Critical Thinking

Have students return to previous dialogs and practice identifying masculine and feminine words. Inform students that the ending *-ción* is the equivalent of **-tion** at the end of many English words and the *-dad* ending on many Spanish words appears as **-ty** in English. Then ask if students can guess the meaning of *presentación, pronunciación, actividad, posibilidad* and *realidad.*

Spanish for Spanish Speakers

Give students a few paragraphs from a newspaper or magazine article written in Spanish and have them find all the nouns.

National Standards

Communication
1.1

Comparisons
4.1

26 Juego

Working in pairs, take two minutes to list in Spanish everything you can see in your classroom.

MODELO el papel
la tiza

¡Extra!

En la clase

la computadora	*computer*
el disco compacto (el CD)	*compact disc (CD)*
el disco DVD (el DVD)	*digital video disc (DVD)*
la pantalla	*computer screen*
el proyector	*overhead projector*
el reproductor de discos compactos	*CD player*
el reproductor de DVDs	*DVD player*
la videocasetera	*VCR*

Comunicación

27 Unos amigos

Pretend you are looking at pictures of friends with a classmate. Working in pairs, take turns asking and answering questions about the people shown. For each question, mention what the person is holding or whom the person is with. Answer by giving the person's name and then say he or she is your friend.

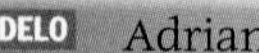

MODELO Adriana

A: ¿Quién es la chica con la profesora?

B: Se llama Adriana y es mi amiga.

Adriana

1. Felipe

2. Rosa

3. Doris

4. Luis

5. Sandra

6. Daniel

Notes

Words ending in *-ista* are invariable and the same form is used for both masculine and feminine. The distinction is made with the appropriate definite article: *el violinista/la violinista, el dentista/la dentista.*

Inform students that many Spanish nouns ending in *-ma, -pa* and *-ta* are derived from Greek and are usually masculine: *el problema, el poema, el drama, el mapa, el telegrama, el planeta.*

28 Objetos en la clase

Working in pairs, take turns telling one another to point at an object in the classroom. Use the phrase *Señala...* and add any of the classroom objects you have learned. Check to be sure your partner has pointed at the correct object before continuing.

MODELO Señala la puerta.

29 En la clase

Identify and talk about the people and objects in your classroom with another student. You may wish to use some of the words shown and add some of your own as needed.

MODELO
A: ¿Quién es el chico con la *mochila*?
B: Es Pablo.
A: ¿Cómo se dice *pencil sharpener*?
B: Se dice sacapuntas.

¿cómo? la pizarra ¿qué? el chico se escribe ¿quién? se dice es quiere decir

Estructura

Using indefinite articles with nouns

Whereas the definite articles *el, la, los* and *las* (the) are used to designate a specific person or thing, indefinite articles refer to nonspecific people or things (e.g., **a**, **an**, **some** or **a few**). The singular forms of the indefinite articles are *un* (masculine) and *una* (feminine).

el lápiz (the pencil)	→	***un*** *lápiz* (**a** pencil)	*la página* (the page)	→	***una*** *página* (**a** page)

The plural forms of the indefinite articles are *unos* (masculine) and *unas* (feminine).

los lápices (the pencils)	→	***unos*** *lápices* (**a few/some** pencils)	*las páginas* (the pages)	→	***unas*** *páginas* (**a few/some** pages)

Las palabras *un, una* y *uno*

The words *un* and *una* can also mean **one** when used before a singular noun. *Uno* (the number **one**) is never used before a noun.

dos cuadernos y ***un*** *libro* *tres chicos y* ***una*** *chica*

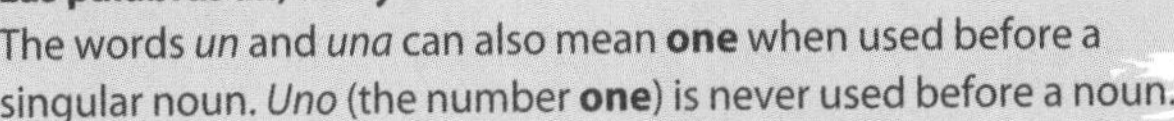

Go online EMCLanguages.net

Notes Several nouns in Spanish at first glance may appear to be masculine or feminine by their endings but are in fact just the opposite: *el día, la mano, el programa*.

Teacher Resources

 Activities 14–16

 Activity 8

 Activity 8

Activity 7

Answers

28 Answers will vary.
29 Answers will vary.

Activities

Cooperative Learning
Working in pairs, students should name aloud a classroom object they have learned in Spanish. Each student's partner then spells the word. Have pairs check their spelling and then switch roles. This will reinforce vocabulary to be used with indefinite articles.

Critical Thinking
Say aloud several nouns and ask students to provide the appropriate indefinite article and repeat the noun that you give. Then give students several words with definite articles *(el chico, la amiga)* and ask them to give the corresponding indefinite article with the same noun *(un chico, una amiga)*.

Multiple Intelligences (linguistic)
Have students make a copy of a news article in Spanish and bring it to class. Working in pairs, students should identify and circle the definite and indefinite articles.

National Standards

Communication
1.1, 1.2

Connections
3.1

Answers

30 1. Es un mapa.
2. Son unos muchachos.
3. Es una estudiante/chica.
4. Es un cesto de papeles.
5. Son unas revistas.
6. Son unas sillas.
7. Es una mochila.
8. Es un reloj.

31 1. un
2. un
3. unas
4. unos
5. unos
6. unos
7. unos
8. un
9. un
10. una

Activities

Expansion

Have one student ask *"¿Qué es?"* while holding up one of the vocabulary items learned in this lesson. A second student then answers, identifying the item with *"Es un/una* (item)."

National Standards

Communication
1.1

Práctica

30 ¿Qué ves?

Di lo que ves en las fotos. ***(Say what you see in the photos.)***

MODELO

Es un escritorio.

Son unos estudiantes.

1

2

3

4

5

6

7

8

31 En la clase hay...

Completa el párrafo con un, una, unos o unas para indicar qué hay en la clase. ***(Complete the paragraph with a, an or some/a few to indicate what is in the classroom.)***

La clase tiene cuatro paredes y dos ventanas. La profesora es la Sra. Martínez. En la clase hay (1) escritorio, (2) cesto de papeles, (3) sillas y (4) pupitres con (5) libros, (6) lápices y (7) bolígrafos. En las paredes hay (8) reloj, (9) sacapuntas y (10) pizarra.

En la clase hay pupitres y estudiantes

Notes This may be a good time to use transparencies 17 and 18 for *¡Aventura! 1*, if you have not already done so, to teach or reinforce the new vocabulary for *Vocabulario II*. As an alternative, try using transparency 17 (without labeled words) and quiz students on the classroom vocabulary. Have students answer your questions orally or have them write their answers and turn them in for a grade.

Conexión con otras disciplinas: matemáticas

Go online EMCLanguages.net

Create a shopping list of some school supplies you would like to buy. Write the prices offered at *Papelería Nueva Era* next to the items on your list. Then, add up the total cost of your purchases and write a complete sentence stating the total in dollars *(dólares)* and cents *(centavos)*. You only have $40.00, so be careful not to spend more than you have!

una mochila "Mochil-In"	$25,00
unos bolígrafos "Bolimétrico"	$ 2,22
un lápiz "Trazo"	$ 0,10
Total	$27,32

Comunicación

Es.../Son...

In pairs, take turns identifying people or objects in class using the expressions *¿Qué es?/¿Quién es?* and adding any new words from this lesson. Point out where each person or object is located.

MODELO **A:** *(Point to a chair.)* ¿Qué es?
B: Es una silla.
A: *(Point to a student.)* ¿Quién es?
B: Es mi amigo Rafael.

¿Qué hay en la clase de español?

In pairs, talk about what is or is not in the Spanish class. Make sure to ask about the meaning of words you do not remember.

MODELO **A:** ¿Hay una ventana en la clase?
B: ¿Qué quiere decir *ventana*?
A: Quiere decir *window*.
B: No, no hay una ventana en la clase.

Notes Before beginning activity 32, check student comprehension of the advertisement on page 57 for *Nueva Era* stationary store by giving a price and asking students to identify the corresponding items in Spanish using indirect object pronouns. You say: *Cuesta cuatro dólares con noventa y cinco.* Student says: *Es una pizarra.*

Teacher Resources

 p. 110

Answers

32 Answers will vary.
33 Answers will vary.
34 Creative self-expression.

Activities

Critical Thinking
Have students put the plural forms of a set number (two, for example) of classroom objects into the following categories: things made of paper, things for writing, things for finding information, parts of a room and classroom furniture. You may want to make this into a game (such as Password) or a contest in which the first person to include all items in the correct categories wins a prize.

National Standards

Communication
1.1

Connections
3.1

Teacher Resources

Lectura cultural
La Ola de gira
Activity 35

Answers

35 1. no
2. sí
3. sí
4. no
5. sí

36 Answers will vary.

Activities

Expansion
Conduct a discussion about singers and musicians who perform in Spanish: Ask students which singers and groups are popular; find out which individuals and groups they think will be popular in the future; ask students if they can name anyone who won a Latin Grammy Award the last time the show aired.

Prereading Strategy
Have students look quickly through the *Lectura cultural* to find cognates and other words they recognize.

Spanish for Spanish Speakers
Have students do a report about one of their favorite singers or musical groups. Then ask them to bring in examples of the person's best work to share with the class.

National Standards

Communication
1.1

Cultures
2.2

Connections
3.1, 3.2

Lectura cultural

La Ola de gira

La gira[1] mundial[2] de La Ola arranca[3] con un concierto en Los Ángeles

La Ola, el nuevo grupo juvenil de rock en español, lanza[4] su CD con una serie de conciertos en todo el continente y España. Sus fans pueden ver[5] el primer concierto en el Greek Theatre en Los Ángeles, California a las ocho de la noche del 20 de septiembre. ¿Por qué[6] La Ola empieza[7] su gira en Los Ángeles? ¿Qué quiere decir esto? ¿Es Los Ángeles la capital de la música latina en los Estados Unidos? Muchos opinan que sí. Después de todo[8], los Premios Grammy de la música latina se celebran en Los Ángeles. Con cinco millones de latinos, Los Ángeles es la ciudad con la mayor[9] concentración de latinos en los Estados Unidos. Es la segunda ciudad con mayor población mexicana después[10] de la Ciudad de México. Tiene una población salvadoreña mayor que[11] la población en San Salvador, la capital de El Salvador.

[1]tour [2]world [3]starts off [4]launches [5]can see [6]Why [7]starts [8]After all [9]the highest [10]after [11]larger than

¿Qué recuerdas? 

¿Sí o no?

1. El primer concierto del grupo La Ola es en España.
2. Los Premios Grammy de la música latina se celebran en Los Ángeles.
3. La mayor concentración de latinos en los Estados Unidos está en Los Ángeles.
4. Hay un millón de mexicanos en Los Ángeles.
5. Hay una mayor población salvadoreña en Los Ángeles que en San Salvador.

Algo personal

1. Have you ever seen the Latin Grammy Awards on television? What did you like about it? Why do you think the Latin Grammy Awards are celebrated in Los Angeles?
2. You can see Hispanic influences all over the United States, not only in large cities like Los Angeles. Discuss the Hispanic influence in your own community.

Notes

The choice of which words to define or leave for students to discern the meaning of is a subjective one. Words that your students are unable to recognize are glossed at the end of the reading or can be found in the glossary that appears at the end of the book.

Communities. Due to its significant Hispanic population, Los Angeles is one of the largest Spanish-speaking cities in the world.

Connections. Activities 35 and 36 make the cross-curricular connection to geography.

Autoevaluación

As a review and self-check, respond to the following:

1. How might you ask who your classmates are and where they are from during the first day of school?
2. Name two Spanish-speaking celebrities and tell where they are from.
3. Identify objects in your classroom in Spanish.
4. Ask someone how to say "computer" in Spanish.
5. What are the benefits of learning Spanish?

Palabras y expresiones

How many of these words and expressions do you recognize?

La clase
el bolígrafo
el borrador
el cesto de papeles
el cuaderno
el escritorio
el lápiz
el libro
el mapa
la mochila
la página
el papel
la pared
el periódico
la pizarra
la puerta
el pupitre
la regla
el reloj
la revista
el sacapuntas
la silla
la tiza
la ventana

Gente
el amigo, la amiga
el chico, la chica
él
ella
ellas
ellos
el estudiante, la estudiante
nosotros,-as
el profesor, la profesora

Palabras interrogativas
¿qué?
¿quién?

Verbos
comprendo (comprender)
hay
se dice
sé
ser

Otras expresiones
hay
¿Cómo se dice...?
¿Cómo se llama (Ud./él/ella)?
el, la
en la clase
la palabra
los, las
mi
nuevo,-a
¿Qué quiere decir...?
quiere decir
(Ud./Él/Ella) se llama...
un, una
unos, unas

Estructura

Do you remember the following grammar rules?

The verb ser	
soy	somos
eres	sois
es	son

Definite and indefinite articles with nouns

In Spanish definite and indefinite articles match nouns in number and gender.

		definite article	noun	indefinite article	noun
masculine	singular	el	chico	un	chico
	plural	los	chicos	unos	chicos
feminine	singular	la	chica	una	chica
	plural	las	chicas	unas	chicas

Notes

Have students check their own understanding of the *Palabras y expresiones.* Point out that the active vocabulary on this page is vocabulary that will be used throughout the book and that it will appear on the chapter test. Words appear again with English equivalents in the end-of-chapter *Vocabulario* and in the vocabulary glossary at the end of *¡Aventura! 1.*

Teacher Resources

Activity 17

pp. 47, 81

Juegos

Flash Cards

Answers

Autoevaluación

Possible answers:

1. ¿Quién es? ¿Cómo se llama el/la estudiante nuevo/a? ¿De dónde es?
2. Daisy Fuentes (Cuba), Juan Luis Guerra (República Dominicana), Antonio Banderas (España), Salma Hayek (México), Jimmy Smits (Estados Unidos), Isabel Allende (Chile), Edgar Rentería (Colombia), Rubén Blades (Panamá), Gloria Estefan (Cuba)
3. Hay un escritorio, unos libros, unos bolígrafos, un cesto de papeles, unas chicas, unos chicos y una pizarra.
4. ¿Cómo se dice *computer*?
5. Answers will vary.

Activities

Multiple Intelligences (musical)

Ask for volunteers to play a popular musical selection for the class using a guitar or other instrument. As a simpler alternative, ask for volunteers to bring in CDs of popular musicians who perform in Spanish. Then conduct a class discussion about what they do or do not like about the music.

National Standards
Communication 1.1
Cultures 2.2
Connections 3.1

Teacher Resources

Vocabulario I
Las clases

Activity 19

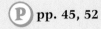

Activities 1–3

GV Activities 1–5

P pp. 45, 52

p. 9

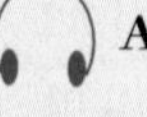

Activity 1

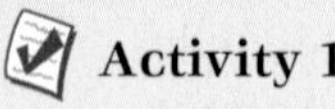

Activity 1

Content reviewed in *Lección B*

- classroom objects
- asking for and stating the time
- numbers 0–100
- expressing courtesy
- noun recognition and plural of nouns

Activities

Cooperative Learning
While introducing the topic of school schedules, ask small groups of students to brainstorm an ideal schedule by noting favorite classes and times of day. They should use their imagination, and their ideas should then be shared with the class.

National Standards

Communication
1.1

Connections
3.1

Cultures
2.1

Lección B

Vocabulario I
Las clases

Estad... Unid...

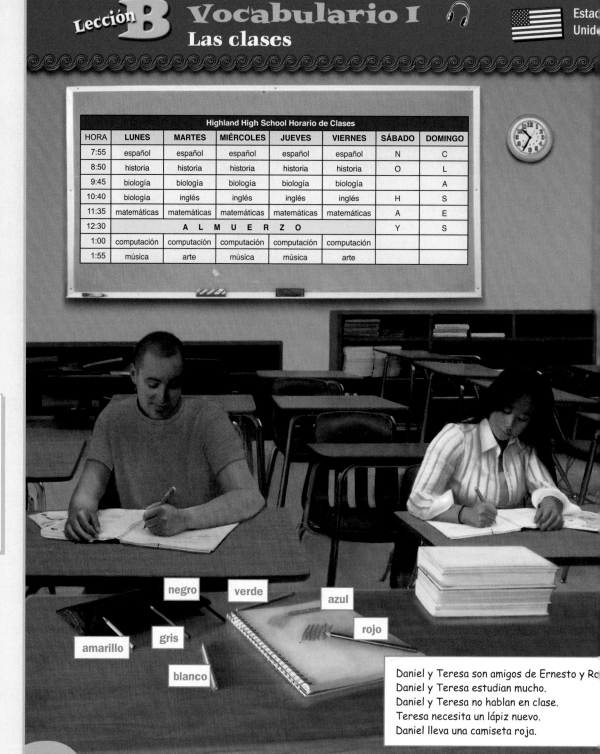

Highland High School Horario de Clases

HORA	LUNES	MARTES	MIÉRCOLES	JUEVES	VIERNES	SÁBADO	DOMINGO
7:55	español	español	español	español	español	N	C
8:50	historia	historia	historia	historia	historia	O	L
9:45	biología	biología	biología	biología	biología		A
10:40	biología	inglés	inglés	inglés	inglés	H	S
11:35	matemáticas	matemáticas	matemáticas	matemáticas	matemáticas	A	E
12:30	A L M U E R Z O					Y	S
1:00	computación	computación	computación	computación	computación		
1:55	música	arte	música	música	arte		

negro
verde
azul
rojo
amarillo
gris
blanco

Daniel y Teresa son amigos de Ernesto y Ro...
Daniel y Teresa estudian mucho.
Daniel y Teresa no hablan en clase.
Teresa necesita un lápiz nuevo.
Daniel lleva una camiseta roja.

Notes Explain to students that school schedules vary greatly throughout the Spanish-speaking world. For example, classes in some countries begin at 8:00 in the morning and end at 2:00. Elsewhere, students may go home for lunch and then return to continue classes until 4:30 or 5:30. Many schools in South America and in Mexico have begun to move to a system consisting of *horario de la mañana* (7:00 to 12:00) and *horario de la tarde* (12:00 to 5:00) to deal with traffic, rush-hour congestion and overcrowding.

¡Aló! ¿Ernesto?
Soy yo, Rosa.
¿Perdón? ¿Cómo?
¿A qué hora terminan las clases en tu colegio? ¿A las tres o a las tres y media?
Terminan a las tres de la tarde.
la blusa
la ropa
la camisa
el pantalón
la camiseta
los jeans
la falda
los calcetines

1 ¿Qué día es mañana?

Contesta la pregunta *¿Qué día es mañana?* según lo que oyes. *(Answer the question* ¿Qué día es mañana? *according to what you hear.)*

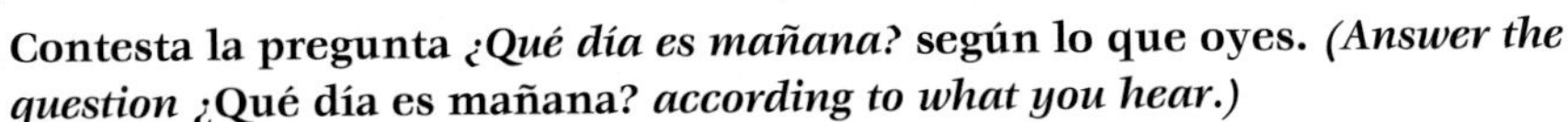

MODELO *You hear:* Es lunes. ¿Qué día es mañana?
You write: martes

2 A corregir

Corrige la información incorrecta, según el Vocabulario I. *(Correct the incorrect information, using Vocabulary I.)*

MODELO La clase de español es a las doce menos cinco.
La clase de español es a las ocho menos cinco.

1. La clase de inglés es lunes, martes, miércoles, jueves y viernes a las diez menos cuarto de la mañana.
2. La clase de computación es a la una y cinco de la mañana.
3. Hay clases de música martes y viernes a las dos menos cinco de la tarde.
4. La clase de historia es a las doce y media.
5. No hay clases los jueves y los viernes.
6. Daniel y Teresa son amigos de Eduardo y Amalia.

¡Extra!

La palabra *de*

The word *de* (of, from) has several different uses in Spanish. For example, *de* can be used to talk about where someone is from *(¿De dónde eres?/Soy de...)* or to describe someone or something *(la clase de español)*. Several expressions use *de (de nada, de la mañana)*. In addition, *de* takes the place of the English apostrophe and the letter *s* ('s) to indicate possession or relationships.

*Es la mochila **de** Marta.*	It is Marta**'s** backpack.
*Son los amigos **de** Sara y **de** Rodrigo.*	They are Sara and Rodrigo**'s** friends.

3 ¿Qué llevan?

Name five people in class and say what each is wearing.

MODELO La profesora lleva una falda.

Notes Encourage students to use *¿Cómo?*, *¿Perdón?* or a similar expression of your choosing when they do not understand what has been said, as Ernesto does at the top of this page.

Activity 1 is recorded and is part of the Audio Program. Reproducible answer sheets have been provided at the end of the Audio Program Manual.

Teacher Resources

Activity 1

Answers

1. 1. viernes
   2. sábado
   3. miércoles
   4. lunes
   5. domingo
   6. jueves
2. 1. La clase de biología
   2. a la una de la tarde
   3. lunes, miércoles y jueves
   4. El almuerzo
   5. los sábados y los domingos
   6. son amigos de Ernesto y Rosa
3. Answers will vary.

Activities

Critical Thinking
Have students identify which of the listed classes they have in their schedule. Then give an English equivalent for one of the classes shown on the schedule and have students give the Spanish for each class you say.

Expansion
Give the time for a class listed on the schedule. Call on students to state what class is at the time stated.

National Standards

Communication
1.2

Connections
3.1

Comparisons
4.1

Teacher Resources

Diálogo I
El horario de clases
Activity 4
Activity 5
Activity 6

Answers

4 1. No, no es nuevo el pantalón. Los zapatos son nuevos.
2. No, no hay.
3. Sí, sí hay.
4. Es el viernes.
5. Necesita unos lápices rojos y verdes.
6. Es a las once y cinco.

5 Answers will vary.

6 1. A
2. D
3. E
4. G
5. F

Activities

Critical Listening

Play the audio version of the dialog. Tell students to look only at the photographs while they listen. Then ask several individuals to state what they believe the main theme of the conversation is.

Prereading Strategy

Instruct students to look only at the photographs. Ask them to imagine where the conversation takes place and what the people are saying to one another. Ask students to find cognates and other words they recognize.

National Standards	
Communication	**Connections**
1.1, 1.2	3.1

Diálogo I El horario de clases

RAÚL: Laura, ¿es nuevo tu pantalón?
LAURA: No, pero los zapatos son nuevos.

LAURA: Oye, Raúl, ¿hay clase de música mañana martes?
RAÚL: No, mañana no hay clase de música, mañana hay clase de arte. La clase de música es el viernes.
LAURA: ¡Ah, sí! Mañana hay clase de arte y necesito unos lápices rojos y verdes.

RAÚL: ¿Qué hora es?
LAURA: Son las once. ¿A qué hora es la clase de historia?
RAÚL: Es a las once y cinco.
LAURA: Bueno, es la hora de la clase.

4 ¿Qué recuerdas?

1. ¿Es nuevo el pantalón de Laura?
2. ¿Hay clase de música el martes?
3. ¿Hay clase de arte el martes?
4. ¿Cuándo es la clase de música?
5. ¿De qué colores necesita unos lápices Laura?
6. ¿A qué hora es la clase de historia?

5 Algo personal

1. ¿De qué color es tu ropa?
2. ¿Qué clases hay en tu colegio?
3. ¿Cuántas clases hay en tu horario en un día?
4. ¿Hay clase de arte en tu horario?
5. ¿Tienes lápices de colores? ¿De qué colores son?
6. ¿A qué hora es tu clase de español?
7. ¿A qué hora terminan tus clases?

¡Extra!

Las clases: un poco más

el álgebra	*algebra*
las asignaturas	*subjects*
las ciencias naturales	*earth sciences*
la educación física	*physical education*
la geografía	*geography*
la geometría	*geometry*
la literatura	*literature*

6 ¿Qué clase es?

Escribe la letra que identifica cada clase que oyes.

A. arte
D. español
F. inglés
B. biología
G. matemáticas
C. computación
E. historia
H. música

Notes

When talking about daily schedules, remind students they may wish to use the following expressions to indicate time of day: *de la mañana, de la tarde* and *de la noche.*

The activities that follow the dialog are recorded and can be found in the Audio Program. Student answer sheets for activity 6 are located in the back of the Audio Program Manual.

Cultura ¡viva! • • • Go online EMCLanguages.net

Los colegios en el mundo hispano

What do you think schools are like in Spanish-speaking countries? The options include either public schools or somewhat expensive but numerous private schools. In addition, some teenagers attend technical institutes instead of traditional high schools. Secondary schools in Spanish-speaking countries are often very rigorous. Schools do not offer many extracurricular activities, such as clubs or sports, nor do they have a wide selection of elective courses to choose from. Instead, all students follow the same demanding curriculum consisting of courses such as calculus, chemistry, physics and philosophy.

The classroom atmosphere is different, too. In Spain, for example, students do not actively participate in class as much as in the United States since courses are usually taught through lectures. Students have few tests, must complete several projects and take a comprehensive exam at the end of the year to determine whether they will pass or fail. In many South American countries, however, quizzes and exams are more common, and a student's grade is determined by participation and achievements over the course of the entire grading period.

7 Los colegios en el mundo hispano

¿Sí o no?

1. Students in Spanish-speaking countries may choose from many extracurricular school activities.
2. Students in schools in many Spanish-speaking countries often follow the same demanding curriculum.
3. In Spain, courses are usually taught through lectures and students do not participate in class as much as in the United States.
4. In South America, quizzes and exams are not common, and a student's grade is based upon classroom participation and achievements during an entire grading period.

¡Extra!

En otras palabras

There are several words in Spanish that mean **school.** You have already learned *el colegio,* but here are a few additional words you might hear Spanish speakers use to talk about school: *la escuela, la preparatoria, la academia, el instituto, el liceo, la secundaria, el plantel.*

8 Comparando

Compare the schools in your community with what you know about schools elsewhere in Spanish-speaking countries of the world. What do you consider to be the advantages and disadvantages of the school system you attend? What would you change?

Notes **Comparisons.** Ask students to investigate school life in one of the Spanish-speaking countries they have studied. Then ask them to compare some aspect of school in that country with their school. Topics may include the calendar year, vacation schedule, school activities, classes offered, etc. Suggest that students obtain information on the Internet, at the library or from Spanish-speaking members of the community.

Use a Venn diagram to complete activity 8.

Teacher Resources

Activity 4

p. 55

Answers

7 1. no
2. sí
3. sí
4. no

8 Creative problem solving.

Activities

Spanish for Spanish Speakers

Have students make a detailed report of the educational system of a Spanish-speaking country of their choice. Then have students present their findings to the class and contrast them to the school system in the United States.

National Standards

Communication	Comparisons
1.3	4.1, 4.2
Cultures	Communities
2.2	5.1
Connections	
3.2	

Teacher Resources

 Activity 9

 Activity 5

 Activities 6–8

 pp. 137, 140

 p. 10

 Activity 2

 Activity 2

Answers

9 1. masculino, el colegio, los colegios
2. masculino, el día, los días
3. femenino, la falda, las faldas
4. masculino, el lápiz, los lápices
5. femenino, la camiseta, las camisetas
6. masculino, el papel, los papeles
7. masculino, el mapa, los mapas
8. masculino, el zapato, los zapatos
9. masculino, el calcetín, los calcetines

Activities

Cooperative Learning
Have students describe several common objects (a pen, newspaper, the door, paper, etc.). Then ask them to pair up and take turns reading their descriptions to see if their partner can guess the object.

Communication	Comparisons
1.1	4.1

Idioma

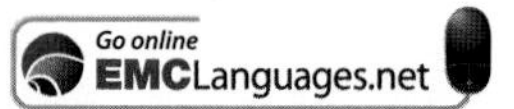

Repaso rápido

Nouns

Nouns in Spanish are either masculine or feminine. Many masculine nouns end in *-o* and many feminine nouns in *-a*. Make most nouns plural by adding *-s*.

	masculino	femenino
singular	*un bolígrafo*	*una silla*
plural	*unos bolígrafos*	*unas sillas*

Remember that some nouns may require you to add or remove an accent mark in their plural form.

el examen* → *los exámenes   *el calcetín* → *los calcetines*

9 ¿Qué sabes sobre los sustantivos? 

Say if the following nouns are masculine *(masculino)* or feminine *(femenino)* by giving the corresponding definite article. Then, give the plural form of each.

MODELO clase
femenino, la clase, las clases

1. colegio
2. día
3. falda
4. lápiz
5. camiseta
6. papel
7. mapa
8. zapato
9. calcetín

Hay unos cuadernos rojos.

Estructura

Using adjectives to describe

Adjectives *(adjetivos)* describe (or modify) nouns. In Spanish, they must match the gender (masculine or feminine) and number (singular or plural) of the nouns they describe. Singular masculine adjectives often end in *-o (rojo)*, singular feminine adjectives often end in *-a (roja)* and either form can be made plural by adding *-s (rojos, rojas)*.

Hay un cuaderno amarillo.	There is one yellow notebook.
Hay una regla amarilla.	There is one yellow ruler.
Hay dos cuadernos amarillos.	There are two yellow notebooks.
Hay dos reglas amarillas.	There are two yellow rulers.

Notes The section *Repaso rápido* provides a review of previously learned grammar and is intended to help prepare students for a related grammar point, in this case adjective-noun agreement.

Have students name several objects in the classroom and then tell whether each is masculine or feminine.

- Adjectives that end in *-e* generally have only one singular form, which can be made plural by adding *-s*.

singular	plural
Hay un bolígrafo verde.	Hay dos bolígrafos verdes.
Hay una puerta verde.	Hay dos puertas verdes.

- Adjectives that end with a consonant usually have only one singular form, which can be made plural by adding *-es*.

singular	plural
Hay un cuaderno azul.	Hay dos cuadernos azules.
Hay una puerta azul.	Hay dos puertas azules.

- Although Spanish adjectives generally follow the nouns they modify, adjectives of quantity such as numbers *(dos, tres)* and question-asking words are exceptions. They precede their nouns.

Tengo ***dos*** *cuadernos verdes.* — I have two green notebooks.
*¿****Cuántas*** *sillas hay?* — How many chairs are there?

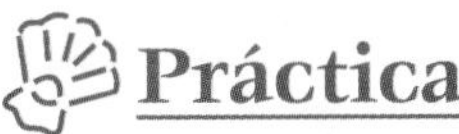

Práctica

10 ¡No estoy de acuerdo!

Correct these descriptions by replacing the underlined words with the words in parentheses. Remember to make all the nouns and adjectives agree and to change the verb forms when necessary.

MODELO Es una camisa azul. (verde)
No, es una camisa verde.
Julia es la estudiante nueva. (Armando y Juan)
No, Armando y Juan son los estudiantes nuevos.

1. El chico nuevo se llama Julián Fernández. (el profesor)
2. Marta lleva la camiseta gris. (el pantalón)
3. Hay dos zapatos nuevos en el pupitre. (una revista)
4. Hay un cuaderno blanco en el escritorio. (una tiza)
5. Son unos calcetines verdes. (negro)
6. Belia lleva los zapatos blancos. (negro)

Julia es la estudiante nueva.

Notes Ask students to identify several adjectives in Spanish that are cognates: *moderno, natural, artificial, personal, ideal.*

When an adjective modifies two or more nouns, one of which is masculine, use the masculine form of the adjective.

Teacher Resources

 Activity 10

Answers

10
1. No, el profesor nuevo se llama Julián Fernández.
2. No, Marta lleva el pantalón gris.
3. No, hay una revista nueva en el pupitre.
4. No, hay una tiza blanca en el escritorio.
5. No, son unos calcetines negros.
6. No, Belia lleva los zapatos negros.

National Standards

Comparisons
4.1

Answers

11 Answers should match the colors of these items in your classroom. Check to be sure students use the correct forms of the adjectives.

12 1. El color negro quiere decir horrible o fatal. El color amarillo quiere decir excelente. El color azul quiere decir regular.
2. No, es un día superior para el romance.
3. El domingo es fatal para la energía física. El jueves y el viernes son superiores para la energía física.
4. El domingo es excelente en las categorías de familia y también de dinero.
5. La profesión es azul.
6. No, no tengo energía física el martes. Sí, tengo energía física el lunes.
7. *Possible answer:* El mejor día es el (viernes).

13 Conversations may include the questions *¿Qué es/son?*, *¿De qué color es?* or *¿De qué colores son?* (to review the forms of *ser*). Possible descriptions include the following:
1. Es un libro de historia. Es gris.
2. Es una mochila. Es verde.
3. Es una puerta. Es amarilla.
4. Es una pizarra. La pizarra es blanco.
5. Es un mapa. Es verde y azul.
6. Es un periódico. Es blanco y negro.
7. Es un bolígrafo. Es rojo.

National Standards

Communication
1.1

Connections
3.1

11 ¿De qué color es?

Describe objects in your classroom by combining words from the two columns.

MODELO Los bolígrafos de Laura son verdes.

1. el escritorio
2. la puerta
3. la pizarra
4. los lápices
5. las sillas
6. los libros
7. las revistas
8. los bolígrafos

A. verde
B. negro
C. gris
D. amarillo
E. rojo
F. azul
G. blanco

12 Los colores de tu día

Imagine you are reading a newspaper in Spanish and you see this horoscope. How much can you understand? Pretend it pertains to your sign and answer the questions.

1. ¿Qué quiere decir el color negro? ¿El color amarillo? ¿El color azul?
2. ¿Es el jueves un día malo para el romance?
3. ¿Qué día es fatal para la energía física?
4. ¿Es el domingo un día excelente?
5. En general, ¿de qué color es la profesión?
6. ¿Tienes energía física el martes? ¿Y el lunes?
7. En tu opinión, ¿qué día es el mejor *(best)*?

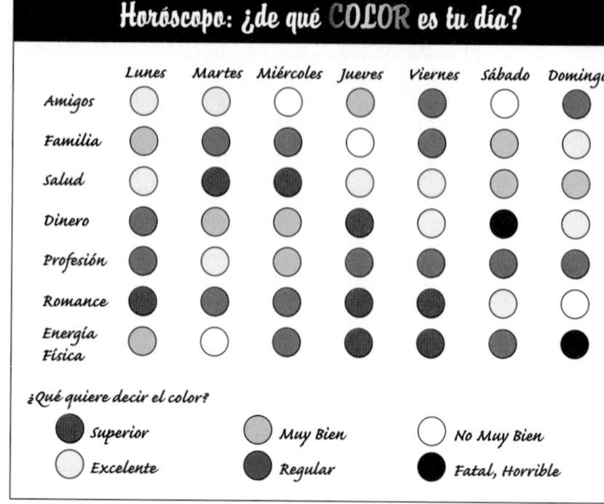

Comunicación

13 Los objetos en la clase

En parejas, hablen Uds. de los siguientes objetos en la clase. ***(In pairs, talk about the following objects in the classroom.)***

MODELO
A: ¿Qué es?
B: Es una silla.
A: ¿De qué color es la silla?
B: Es azul.

1

2

3

4

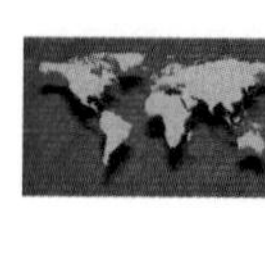
5

6

7

Notes

Point out that colors can act as nouns *(El azul es un color.)* or adjectives *(Es una camisa azul.)*.

Remind students that colors are descriptive adjectives and that like other descriptive adjectives they usually follow the noun they describe.

Consider teaching students the following colors: *beige, café, rosado, morado, anaranjado.*

You may wish to introduce the following: *¿Cuál es tu color favorito?* (What is your favorite color?); *Mi color favorito es azul/amarillo/blanco.* (My favorite color is blue/yellow/white.).

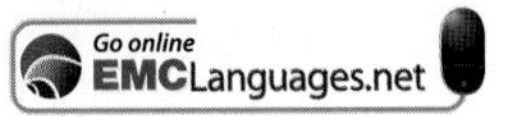

14 Juego

Working in pairs, take turns describing three or four people and three or four objects in the classroom. See how quickly you can communicate to your partner what you are describing.

Estructura

Saying what someone does: present tense of *-ar* verbs

- Verbs express actions (to do something) or states of being (to be). The form of the verbs found in Spanish dictionaries is called an **infinitive**. In English, an infinitive generally is used with the word **to** (to study, to eat, to live). Spanish infinitives end with *-ar*, *-er* or *-ir*.
- Spanish verbs are considered regular if their various forms follow a predictable pattern. To form the present tense of a regular *-ar* verb, such as *hablar* (to speak), remove the *-ar* ending. Then attach the endings that correspond to each of the subject pronouns.

hablar			
yo	habl**o**	nosotros nosotras	habl**amos**
tú	habl**as**	vosotros vosotras	habl**áis**
Ud. él ella	habl**a**	Uds. ellos ellas	habl**an**

- A present-tense Spanish verb may have several different equivalents in English.

Hablo *español.*	I **speak** Spanish. I **do speak** Spanish. I **am speaking** Spanish.

- Other useful *-ar* verbs that follow the same pattern are: *estudiar* (to study), *llevar* (to wear), *necesitar* (to need) and *terminar* (to end, to finish).

Notes Model correct pronunciation several times to ensure that students accentuate the correct syllable of the verb forms.

You may wish to tell students that the present tense can also express an action intended or planned for the near future: *Hablamos mañana.*

Teacher Resources

Activities 6–8

GV Activities 9–10

P pp. 146–147

 Activity 3

 Unit 3

 Activity 3

Answers

14 Creative self-expression.

Activities

Critical Thinking

Have students identify several infinitives in a Spanish dictionary or the glossary at the end of the textbook. You should provide or ask students to prepare a written list of infinitives. As an extension, have students find additional infinitives in dialogs and reading passages.

Multiple Intelligences (spatial)

Ask students to look carefully at several well-known paintings by Spanish and Latin American artists. What colors can they identify? What other words can they use to describe what they see? Encourage interested students to learn more about the paintings and artists via the Internet.

TPR

Many *-ar* verbs are easily dramatized through total physical response. Use TPR to reinforce verbs, such as *hablar*, that appear in this chapter and to preview others that will be learned later.

National Standards	
Communication 1.1	**Connections** 3.1, 3.2
Cultures 2.2	**Comparisons** 4.1

Teacher Resources

Activity 16

Answers

15 The *-ar* infinitives: *pasar, terminar, descansar, quedar, regresar, entrar, estar, jugar, cantar, levantar, buscar, encontrar, comprar, disfrutar, quedar, aguantar*.

16
1. Sí, yo hablo español.
2. Sí, mis amigos hablan español.
3. Sí, mi amiga habla español.
4. Sí, mi amigo y yo hablamos español.
5. Sí, Uds. hablan español.
6. Sí, el estudiante nuevo habla español.

Activities

Spanish for Spanish Speakers

Have Spanish-speaking students pair up with nonbilingual students to talk about the poem that appears on page 68. As an alternative, ask for a Spanish-speaking student to teach the poem to the class.

National Standards

Communication
1.1

Connections
3.1, 3.2

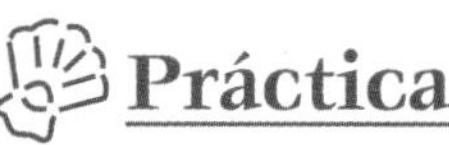

Práctica

15 Un poema sobre el colegio

Busca los infinitivos que terminan en *-ar* en este poema.

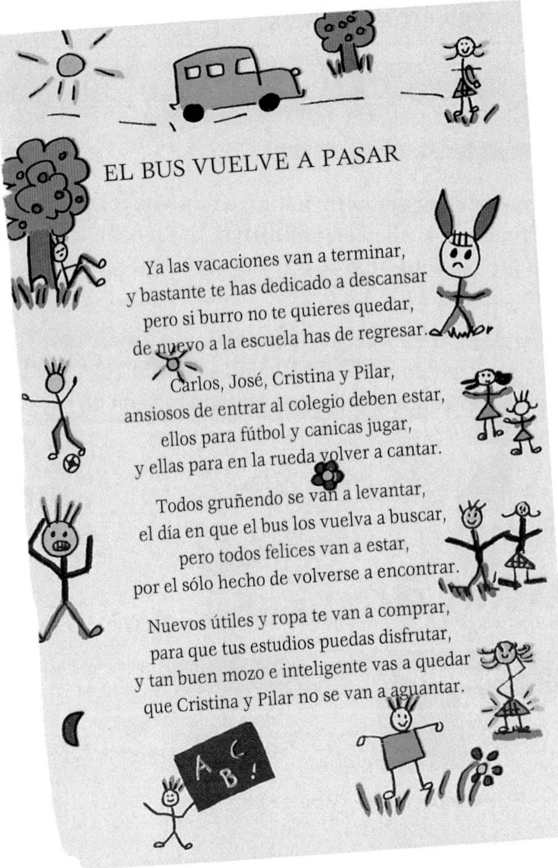

EL BUS VUELVE A PASAR

Ya las vacaciones van a terminar,
y bastante te has dedicado a descansar
pero si burro no te quieres quedar,
de nuevo a la escuela has de regresar.

Carlos, José, Cristina y Pilar,
ansiosos de entrar al colegio deben estar,
ellos para fútbol y canicas jugar,
y ellas para en la rueda volver a cantar.

Todos gruñendo se van a levantar,
el día en que el bus los vuelva a buscar,
pero todos felices van a estar,
por el sólo hecho de volverse a encontrar.

Nuevos útiles y ropa te van a comprar,
para que tus estudios puedas disfrutar,
y tan buen mozo e inteligente vas a quedar
que Cristina y Pilar no se van a aguantar.

Estrategia

Scanning

Scanning is a quick way to get the main idea of what you are about to read. You can increase your understanding of this poem by first scanning the text for cognates (words with similar spelling and meaning in two languages). Also, by scanning headings, boldface words and lists, you are focusing on the important information that will help you get the main point of the text you are about to read.

Before doing activity 15, scan the poem *El bus vuelve a pasar* and jot down all the cognates you recognize. Can you understand the poem more easily now?

16 ¿Hablan español?

Di que las siguientes personas hablan español. ***(Say that the following people speak Spanish.)***

MODELO ¿Tú?
Sí, tú hablas español.

1. ¿Yo?
2. ¿Mis amigos?
3. ¿Mi amiga?
4. ¿Mi amigo y yo?
5. ¿Uds.?
6. ¿El estudiante nuevo?

Hablamos español.

Notes

Have students find words they recognize in the poem *El bus vuelve a pasar*. Then have them apply the scanning strategy to try and discern the meaning of lines of the poem. Finally, discuss the poem so students have a general idea of what the poem is about.

Consider having students memorize the poem on page 68. You may want to give a grade for their work or offer extra credit.

Un día típico en el colegio

Di lo que ocurre en un día típico en el colegio, usando los verbos indicados. ***(Say what happens on a typical day at school, using the indicated verbs.)***

MODELO Carolina y Víctor necesitan papel en la clase de historia. (necesitar)

1. Yo __ español con mi profesor. (hablar)
2. La clase de historia __ a las ocho menos cinco. (terminar)
3. Paz y Ricardo __ computación. (estudiar)
4. Tú y yo __ español en la clase de español. (hablar)
5. Rosita __ un bolígrafo en la clase de matemáticas. (necesitar)
6. Tú __ con una amiga. (estudiar)
7. Uds. __ biología con unos amigos. (estudiar)
8. Las clases de mi colegio __ a las tres de la tarde. (terminar)
9. Nueve o diez estudiantes __ jeans. (llevar)
10. Un estudiante o una estudiante __ ropa nueva. (llevar)

En el colegio

Haz siete oraciones lógicas usando palabras de las tres columnas.

1.	una estudiante	terminar	con el profesor de arte
2.	mi amigo y yo	estudiar	unos cuadernos amarillos
3.	unos estudiantes	necesitar	a las tres
4.	la clase de español	hablar	unos jeans y zapatos negros
5.	el estudiante nuevo	llevar	una mochila nueva
6.	tú		arte y computación
7.	yo		inglés y español

Comunicación

Una encuesta

Working in groups of three, complete a survey of your classmates to find out what they are studying in school. Each person should select one subject (choosing from *arte, biología, computación, historia, matemáticas* or *música*). Then find out how many boys and how many girls in class study the subject you are investigating. Record the results under the headings *Chicos* and *Chicas*. Summarize your findings for the members of your group.

MODELO **A:** Mario, ¿estudias computación?
B: Sí, estudio computación.

Computación	
Chicos	Chicas

Sí, estudio computación.

Notes Have students create their own sentences about what happens during a typical day at school, similar to activity 17.

Explain to students that some of their sentences for activity 18 will use the same verb more than once.

Answers

17 1. hablo
2. termina
3. estudian
4. hablamos
5. necesita
6. estudias
7. estudian
8. terminan
9. llevan
10. lleva

18 Answers will vary.

19 Creative self-expression.

Activities

Students with Special Needs

As preparation or warm-up before assigning activity 17, do a quick verb conjugation "round-robin" activity with the class. Give students a subject pronoun and an *-ar* infinitive to be conjugated appropriately: *yo/necesitar (yo necesito), tú/hablar (tú hablas)* and so on.

National Standards

Communication
1.1, 1.3

Connections
3.1

Teacher Resources

 Activity 22

 Activity 9

 Activity 11

 p. 56

 Activity 4

Answers

20 Have students report their findings in Spanish (e.g., *Veinticinco estudiantes estudian arte*). They should then listen to compare their summary results with the results of other students who asked the same question.

21 Role-playing activity.

22 Answers will vary.

National Standards

Communication
1.1, 1.3

Los resultados de la encuesta

While working with the same students as in activity 19, tabulate the results of the three surveys each of you completed in the previous exercise. One member of each group should then report the findings to the class. Compare what you learned from the survey results of other students in the class to determine if your survey is accurate.

MODELO Veinticuatro estudiantes estudian computación. Son doce chicos y doce chicas.

¿Qué necesitan Uds.?

Pretend you are in a bookstore. Working in groups of four or five, take turns playing the roles of the clerk and customers. Find out which item(s) your customers need. If you would like, you may answer with *Aquí está* (Here it is) or *Aquí están* (Here they are).

Estructura

Talking about schedules: *¿A qué hora?*

To ask when something is going to occur ask ***¿A qué hora* (+ verb + event)?** Answer with the following: **Verb + *a la/las* (+ time)** or simply with ***A la/las* (+ time).**

¿A qué hora es *la clase de español?*	When (At what time) is Spanish class?
Es a la *una.*	It is at one o'clock. At one o'clock.

Note: The twenty-four hour clock (i.e., military time) often appears in railroad, airline and bus timetables or in movie and theater advertising. When expressing time this way, the day begins at one minute after midnight. The numbers one to twelve refer to the time of day between midnight and noon. After noon, each hour is added to twelve: 13:00 hours would be the equivalent of 1:00 P.M. *(Es la una de la tarde.)*.

Práctica

Mi horario en el colegio

Contesta las siguientes preguntas.

1. ¿A qué hora es tu clase de español? ¿A qué hora termina?
2. ¿A qué hora es tu clase de inglés? ¿A qué hora termina?
3. ¿A qué hora es tu clase de historia? ¿A qué hora termina?
4. ¿A qué hora es tu clase de matemáticas? ¿A qué hora termina?

¿Qué hora es?

Notes When students discuss their own schedules, be sure they use *mi/tu clase* rather than *la clase* in their questions and answers.

Select one or two groups to present their skits from activity 21. As an alternative, have all groups present their skits over several days and assign grades.

23 En la televisión

Contesta las siguientes preguntas, según el horario de Telemundo.

1. ¿A qué hora es *De Mañanita?*
2. ¿A qué hora termina *Cotorreando?*
3. ¿Qué hay a las cinco de la tarde?
4. ¿A qué hora es *La Corte de Familia?*
5. ¿*Laura* termina a las siete de la noche?
6. ¿Es *Pobre Pablo* una telenovela *(soap opera)*?

HORARIO	PROGRAMA	GÉNERO
6:00	Noticiero Telemundo	Noticias
6:30	Noticiero Telemundo	Noticias
7:00	De Mañanita	Noticias
10:00	Pobre Pablo	Novela
10:30		
11:00	¿Sabía usted?	Variedad
11:30	¡Ay Caramba!	Comedia
12:00	Maritere	Talk Show
12:30		
13:00	Cotorreando	Variedad
13:30		
14:00	Sala de Parejas	Variedad
14:30		
15:00	La Corte de Familia	Variedad
15:30	La Corte del Pueblo	Variedad
16:00	Laura	Talk Show
16:30		
17:00	Al Rojo Vivo con María Celeste	Noticias
17:30		
18:00	La Corte del Pueblo	Variedad
18:30	Noticiero Telemundo	Noticias

Comunicación

24 ¿A qué hora?

Ask several classmates about their school schedules. Discuss what they are studying and when each class is.

25 El horario de clases de Mónica

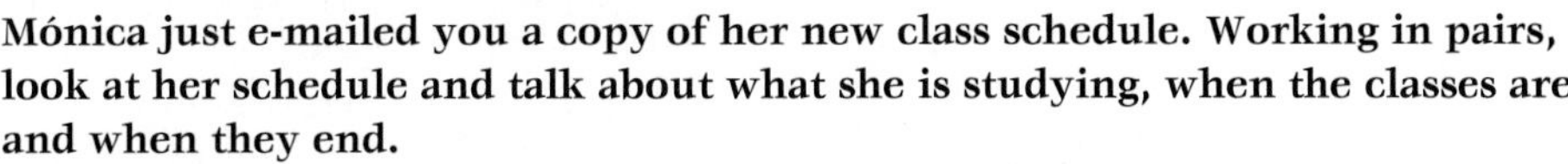

Mónica just e-mailed you a copy of her new class schedule. Working in pairs, look at her schedule and talk about what she is studying, when the classes are and when they end.

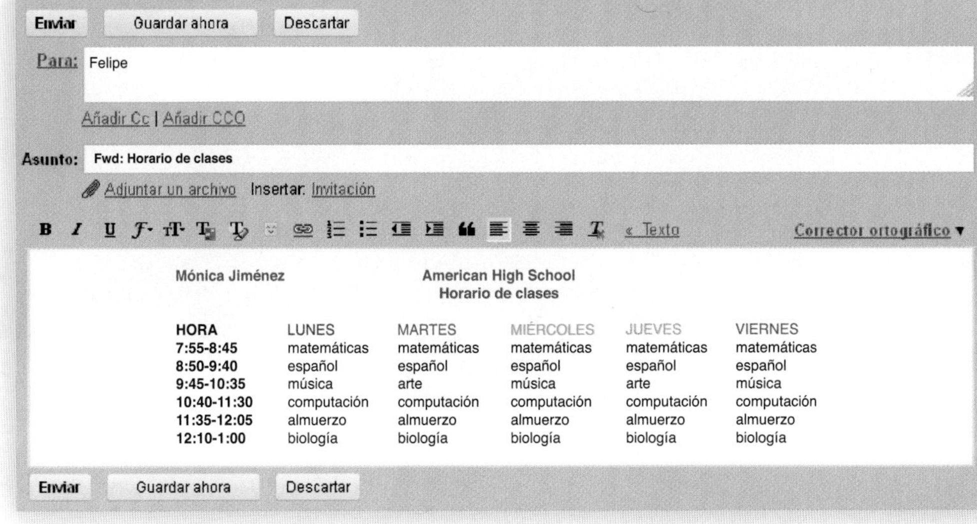

Enviar | Guardar ahora | Descartar

Para: Felipe

Añadir Cc | Añadir CCO

Asunto: Fwd: Horario de clases

Adjuntar un archivo Insertar: Invitación

« Texto Corrector ortográfico ▾

Mónica Jiménez

American High School
Horario de clases

HORA	LUNES	MARTES	MIÉRCOLES	JUEVES	VIERNES
7:55-8:45	matemáticas	matemáticas	matemáticas	matemáticas	matemáticas
8:50-9:40	español	español	español	español	español
9:45-10:35	música	arte	música	arte	música
10:40-11:30	computación	computación	computación	computación	computación
11:35-12:05	almuerzo	almuerzo	almuerzo	almuerzo	almuerzo
12:10-1:00	biología	biología	biología	biología	biología

Enviar | Guardar ahora | Descartar

Answers

23 1. Es a las siete de la mañana.
2. Termina a las dos de la tarde.
3. Hay Al Rojo Vivo con María Celeste.
4. Es a las tres de la tarde.
5. No, Laura termina a las cinco de la tarde.
6. Sí.

24 Creative self-expression.

25 Creative self-expression.

Activities

Cooperative Learning

Have students work in pairs, writing their actual schedules (help them with Spanish words for subjects they take). They should exchange schedules and ask *¿A qué hora es tu clase de...?*. (Because A has B's schedule, A can verify if B answers correctly.)

Spanish for Spanish Speakers

Have students write a short composition about their favorite class. Ask them to explain why they like it. Students should also discuss their least favorite class.

Technology

If you have located a class with which to do e-mail projects in a Spanish-speaking country or in another city in the United States, have students exchange and compare their schedules. You may wish to try the following sources before assigning the activity to students: Intercultural E-mail Exchanges and Intercultural E-mail Connections. Also, the State Department is a good source for American schools abroad.

National Standards

Communication
1.1, 1.3

Connections
3.1

Comparisons
4.1

Notes

Comparisons. After completing activity 23, ask similar questions in relation to television shows popular with your students.

Just as **TV** is a common abbreviation in English, *televisión* is often shortened to *tele* in informal conversations in Spanish.

Teacher Resources

Vocabulario II
¿Dónde está?

Activity 20

Activities 10–11

Activities 12–13

p. 47

Activity 5
Activity 6

Activity 4

Activities

Critical Listening
Say aloud several telephone or fax numbers. Have students write the number they hear. Then call on students to write the numbers on the whiteboard.

Multiple Intelligences (bodily-kinesthetic/linguistic)
Have students draw and label the parts of a computer with all peripherals (mouse, mouse pad, etc.). Display the drawings around the room or use them to review vocabulary.

Students with Special Needs
Create labels for classroom objects, and attach the labels to the objects with string or tape. This can be a good opportunity to enrich student vocabulary by adding words that are not yet active in *¡Aventura!*, for example: *la bandera, el calendario, el diccionario.*

National Standards
Communication 1.2
Connections 3.1

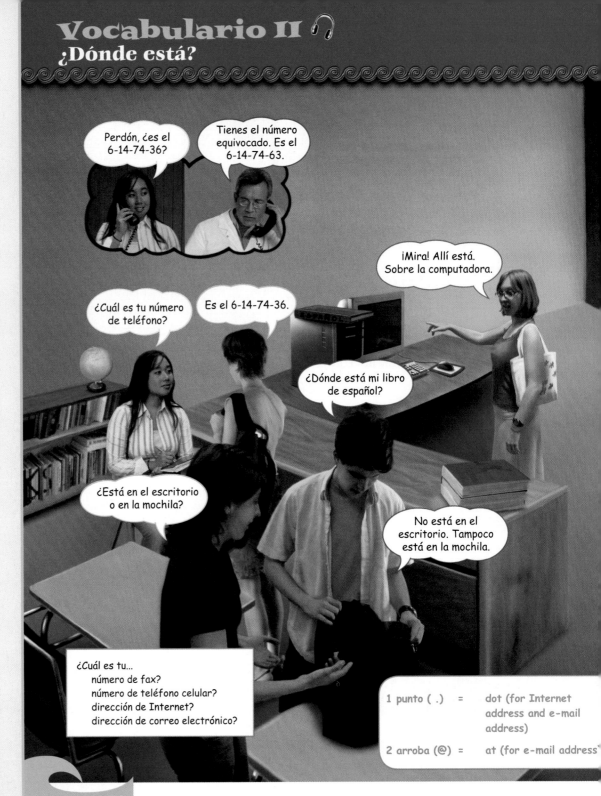

Vocabulario II
¿Dónde está?

Perdón, ¿es el 6-14-74-36?
Tienes el número equivocado. Es el 6-14-74-63.
¿Cuál es tu número de teléfono?
Es el 6-14-74-36.
¡Mira! Allí está. Sobre la computadora.
¿Dónde está mi libro de español?
¿Está en el escritorio o en la mochila?
No está en el escritorio. Tampoco está en la mochila.

¿Cuál es tu...
número de fax?
número de teléfono celular?
dirección de Internet?
dirección de correo electrónico?

1 punto (.)	=	dot (for Internet address and e-mail address)
2 arroba (@)	=	at (for e-mail address)

Notes

Point out the article *el* is needed in a complete-sentence response to *¿Cuál es tu número de teléfono?*.

Tell students that the plural form of *la impresora láser* is *las impresoras láser*.

Help students with the meanings of some of the new words and expressions.

In Spain, the term *móvil* is used instead of *celular*.

26 ¿Qué necesitan?

Write the names Julio and Pilar. Next, listen and list under each of their names what Julio and Pilar need before they leave for college. Then circle any items on the lists that they both need.

27 Información personal

In groups of four, take turns asking for your classmates' phone numbers, fax numbers and e-mail addresses. (You may invent any of the information you wish.)

28 La computadora

Mira la ilustración y contesta las siguientes preguntas en español.

1. ¿De qué color es la pantalla?
2. ¿Hay dos teclados?
3. ¿Dónde está la computadora?
4. ¿Dónde está el papel?
5. ¿Hay un ratón?
6. ¿Cuántos diskettes hay en el escritorio?

¡Extra!

El plural de algunas palabras

Note that the word *ratón* changes when it is plural. The accent on the *o* disappears *(ratones)*. Words ending in *-ón, -ión, -és* and *-án* lose the accent when the plural ending *-es* is attached: *ratón* ⟶ *ratones; dirección* ⟶ *direcciones.*

Teacher Resources

Activity 26

Answers

26 Pilar

1. una computadora nueva
2. (circled) unos diskettes
3. un ratón nuevo
4. la dirección de correo electrónico de Julio
5. (circled) unos CDs (unos discos compactos)

Julio

6. una impresora láser
7. (circled) unos diskettes
8. un teclado nuevo
9. el número de celular de Pilar
10. (circled) unos CDs (unos discos compactos)

27 Creative self-expression.

28
1. La pantalla es negra.
2. No, hay un teclado.
3. La computadora está en el escritorio.
4. El papel está en la impresora.
5. Sí, hay un ratón.
6. Hay cuatro diskettes en el escritorio.

Notes

You may wish to have students use a Venn diagram to do activity 26.

Activity 26 is intended to practice listening comprehension. Play the audio of the activity that is part of the Audio Program.

Instead of having students list the names Pilar and Julio, you may wish to use the student answer sheet for activity 26, which can be found at the end of the Audio Program Manual.

National Standards

Communication
1.1, 1.2

Connections
3.1

Teacher Resources

 Diálogo II
¿Cuál es tu dirección de correo electrónico?
Activity 29
Activity 30

Answers

29 1. Carlos habla con Diana.
2. En clase de computación.
3. No, no está en la mochila. No, no está sobre el pupitre tampoco.
4. Está sobre el escritorio del profesor.
5. Es dianavelez, arroba, latinored, punto, com.

30 Answers will vary.

31 Role-playing activity.

Activities

Prereading Strategy
Before students open their books, have them brainstorm in Spanish different objects that can be found in a classroom. Then instruct students to cover up the dialog with one hand and look at the photographs. Ask them to imagine where the conversation takes place and what the people are saying to one another. Finally, have students look through the dialog quickly to find cognates and others words they already know.

National Standards

Communication
1.1

Connections
3.1

Diálogo II ¿Cuál es tu dirección de correo electrónico?

CARLOS: Diana, necesito una nota de ocho en computación. ¿Estudiamos?
DIANA: Sí, Carlos.
CARLOS: Muy bien... ¿Cuál es tu dirección de correo electrónico?
DIANA: Es dianavelez@....
CARLOS: ¡Ay, perdón!

CARLOS: ¿Dónde está mi bolígrafo?
DIANA: No sé. ¿No está en tu mochila?
CARLOS: No, no está y tampoco está sobre mi pupitre.

DIANA: ¡Mira! Allí hay un bolígrafo sobre el escritorio del profesor. ¿Es tu bolígrafo?
CARLOS: ¡Ay, sí! Muchas gracias. ¿Cuál es tu correo electrónico?
DIANA: Es dianavelez, arroba, latinored, punto, com.

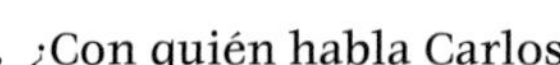

29 ¿Qué recuerdas?

1. ¿Con quién habla Carlos?
2. ¿En qué clase necesita Carlos una nota de ocho?
3. ¿Está el bolígrafo de Carlos en la mochila? ¿Sobre el pupitre?
4. ¿Dónde está el bolígrafo de Carlos?
5. ¿Cuál es la dirección de correo electrónico de Diana?

30 Algo personal

1. ¿Qué tienes en tu mochila?
2. ¿Cuál es tu dirección de correo electrónico?
3. ¿Cuál es tu dirección de internet favorita?

31 En la clase

Trabajando en parejas, haz el papel de una de las personas del diálogo anterior. ***(Working in pairs, play the part of one of the people in the preceding dialog.)***

¡Extra!

Más sobre la tecnología

la almohadilla	*mouse pad*
el archivo	*file*
el disco duro	*hard drive*
la Internet/la Red	*Internet*
el micrófono	*microphone*
navegar por Internet/la Red	*to surf the Web*
los parlantes	*speakers*
la unidad CD-ROM	*CD-ROM drive*
el software	*software*
la Web/la Red	*World Wide Web*

¿Qué tienes en tu mochila?

Notes

If students ask about *¡Mira!* in the dialog, remind them they have already seen the expression in *Capítulo 1* and need only to recognize how to use this command naturally in conversation. Commands are addressed in the Appendices at the back of this book.

Activity 31 is a pair activity. As such, it has not been recorded as part of the Audio Program for listening comprehension practice.

Cultura viva II

¡Qué notas!

Las notas

Schools in many Spanish-speaking countries often base report card grades *(las notas)* on a numerical scale such as 1-10 instead of using the letter grades *A-F*. Descriptive categories sometimes accompany the number grade to further clarify the numerical values. In general, cinco or seis is the minimum passing grade, while *un/una estudiante de diez* (an *A* student) is a very difficult distinction to achieve.

If you were a student in Mexico or the Dominican Republic and your report card contained the grades *EX* and *MB*, would you be pleased? Would the parents of a student from Chile or Honduras be happy with a B? Look at this grading scale found at the bottom of a report card and determine what grades they would be equivalent to at your school.

Escala:

10	Superior (S)
9	Excelente (EX)
8	Muy Bueno/Muy Buena (MB)
7-6	Bueno/Buena (B)
5	Necesita Mejorar (NM)
4-0	Deficiente (D)

¿Soy una estudiante excelente?

32 ¿Qué nota?

Using the scale from the *Cultura viva* reading, what grade would you assign the following students based upon the comments about their work?

MODELO Paquito does okay in biology, but he does not study enough.
Cinco. Necesita mejorar en biología.

1. Sara is a computer genius. She aces every assignment!
2. Jaime scores 100 on every English test.
3. Luisa is an average student in history.
4. Julio didn't turn in three math assignments.
5. Teresa is a good singer and enjoys music class.
6. The average of Daniel's quizzes in Spanish is 84.
7. Laura likes to draw. Her artwork is good, but she does not pay attention to the instructor.

Notes

Students have already seen the words *bueno (buenos días)* and *buena (buenas tardes)*. Ask if the students know the meaning of these terms as they refer to grades.

Another way of referring to grades is: *Sobresaliente* (9/10); *Notable* (7/8); *Bien* (6); *Suficiente* (5); *Insuficiente* (3/4); *Deficiente* (0/2).

Teacher Resources

 **Activity 12**

 **p. 46**

 **Activity 5**

Answers

32 Answers will vary. Students should give a reasonable grade. Possible answers:

1. ¡Diez! Es superior en computación.
2. ¡Diez! Es superior en inglés.
3. Siete. Es buena en historia.
4. Cinco. Necesita mejorar en matemáticas.
5. ¡Nueve! Es excelente en música.
6. Ocho. Es muy bueno en español.
7. Seis. Es buena en arte.

National Standards

Cultures
2.1, 2.2

Comparisons
4.1, 4.2

Teacher Resources

Activities 13–14

Activities 14–15

Activity 7

Activity 6

Activities

Expansion

Ask students to identify several people at your school and explain where they are at a given time (*La Sra. Codina está en la clase de inglés.*).

Multiple Intelligences (bodily-kinesthetic/linguistic)

Have students draw a map of the United States that includes seven cities with Spanish names. Then they must explain where each city is located. (*San Antonio está en Texas.*)

National Standards

Connections
3.1

Comparisons
4.1

Estructura

Talking about location or how someone feels: *estar*

The verb *estar* (to be) is irregular in the present tense. You already have seen several forms of this verb.

estar					
yo	**estoy**	*I am*	nosotros nosotras	**estamos**	*we are*
tú	**estás**	*you are*	vosotros vosotras	**estáis**	*you are*
Ud. él ella	**está**	*you are* *he (it) is* *she (it) is*	Uds. ellos ellas	**están**	*they are*

Estar indicates location or a state of being or a condition at a given moment.

location:	*¿Dónde* ***está*** *el profesor?* ***Está*** *en clase.*	Where is the teacher? He is in class.
state of being or condition:	*¿Cómo* ***estás****?* ***Estoy*** *bien, gracias.*	How are you? I am well, thanks.

¿Cómo estás?

¿Dónde está El Alamo?

Notes Explain that although both *es* and *está* can mean **is** in English, their usage is quite different. For example, *está* has been used to express health and is also used here to indicate location, whereas *es* conveys existence. Forms of the verb *ser* are used to describe more permanent, basic characteristics of a person, place or thing, whereas forms of *estar* are used to describe more changeable aspects of a person, place or thing. Some examples of changeable aspects include emotions, feelings, locations and temporary conditions.

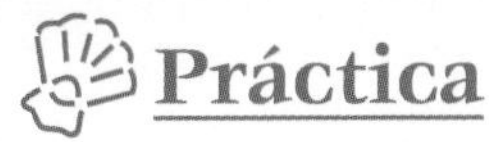

Práctica

33 Un mensaje para Felipe

Complete María's e-mail message to Felipe with the appropriate words before she sends him the message.

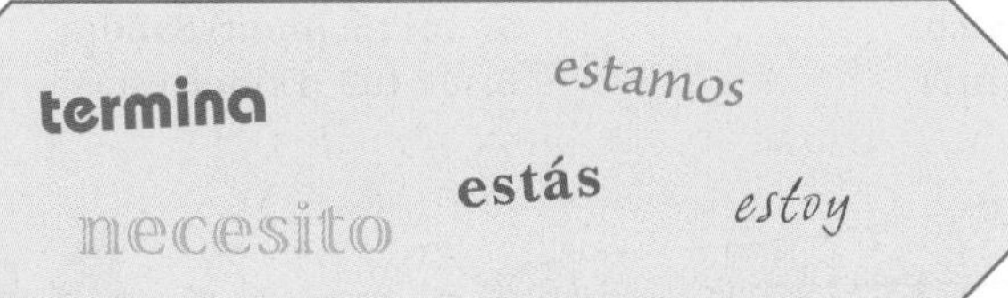

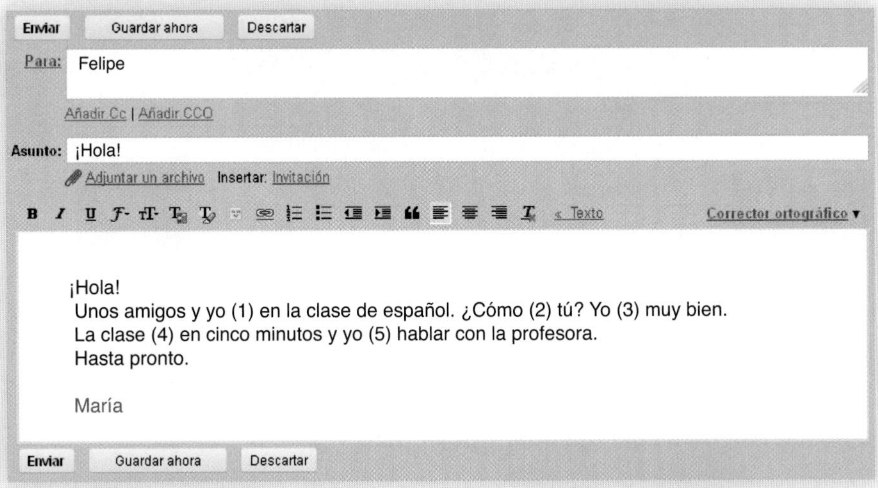

Enviar
Guardar ahora
Descartar
Para: Felipe
Añadir Cc | Añadir CCO
Asunto: ¡Hola!
Adjuntar un archivo Insertar: Invitación
« Texto
Corrector ortográfico ▾
¡Hola!
Unos amigos y yo (1) en la clase de español. ¿Cómo (2) tú? Yo (3) muy bien.
La clase (4) en cinco minutos y yo (5) hablar con la profesora.
Hasta pronto.
María
Enviar
Guardar ahora
Descartar

Estoy bien, gracias.

Notes **Comparisons.** Have students compare English and Spanish: Explain that words such as *yo* and *tú* are often omitted when the subject of the sentence is understood. Similarly, the English subject **it** seldom requires a Spanish equivalent: *¿Dónde está el lápiz?* (Where is the pencil?); *Está aquí.* (**It is** here.).

Answers

33
1. estamos
2. estás
3. estoy
4. termina
5. necesito

National Standards

Comparisons
4.1

Teacher Resources

 Activity 35

Answers

34 1. Felipe está en Los Ángeles.
2. Pedro y Francisco están en Denver.
3. Amalia y Virginia están en Atlanta.
4. Josefina, Kathy y yo (Nosotras) estamos en Santa Fe.
5. Mi tía Sandra está en Miami.
6. Yo estoy en *(name of city)*.

35 1. San Antonio y Santa Fe están en Estados Unidos.
2. Sevilla y Madrid están en España.
3. Santiago está en Chile.
4. Managua está en Nicaragua.
5. Maracaibo está en Venezuela.
6. Montevideo está en Uruguay.
7. Potosí está en Bolivia.
8. La Plata está en Argentina.
9. Cali está en Colombia.
10. Concepción está en Paraguay.

National Standards

Connections
3.1

Communities
5.1

34 En EE.UU.

María is sending e-mail messages to family and friends across the United States. Tell where she and her acquaintances are located according to the illustration.

MODELO María está en Dallas.

1. Felipe
2. Pedro y Francisco
3. Amalia y Virginia
4. Josefina, Kathy y yo
5. mi tía *(aunt)* Sandra
6. ¿Y tú? ¿Dónde estás?

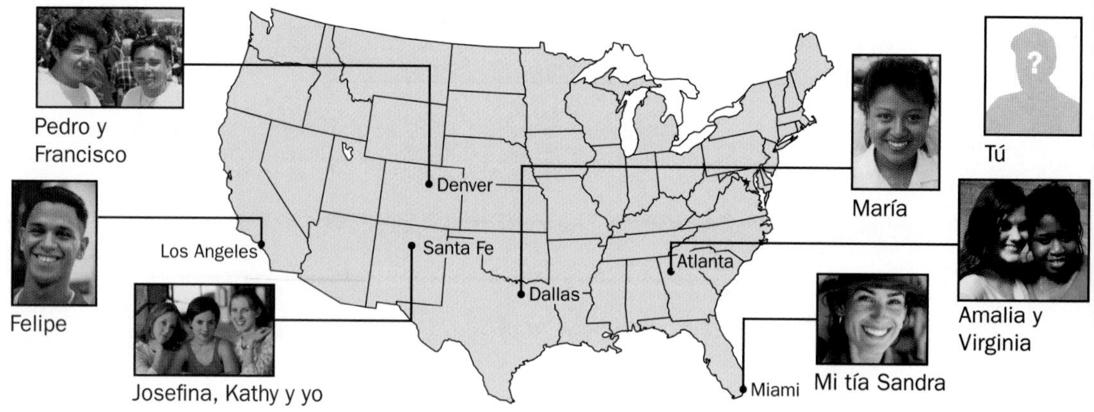

35 Conexión con otras disciplinas: geografía

Amalia is studying for a geography quiz. Can you tell her where each of the following Spanish-speaking cities is located?

MODELO Malabo
Malabo está en Guinea Ecuatorial.

1. San Antonio y Santa Fe
2. Sevilla y Madrid
3. Santiago
4. Managua
5. Maracaibo
6. Montevideo
7. Potosí
8. La Plata
9. Cali
10. Concepción

Malabo está en Guinea Ecuatorial.

Notes

Connections. The verbs *ser* and *estar* can serve to reinforce the geography of the Spanish-speaking world that was emphasized in *Capítulo 1*. Remind students that ser is used for origin, whereas *estar* is used for location.

Communities. Just as many young people in the United States study Spanish, many students in Spain and Latin America study English. Encourage students to consider ways they may learn more about people throughout the Spanish-speaking world (e-mail, partnerships, study abroad, exchanges), make friends and practice what they are learning in Spanish class.

36 En la clase del Sr. Ardila

Mira la ilustración y contesta las preguntas en español.

MODELO ¿Dónde está el profesor Ardila?
Está en clase.

1. ¿Dónde está el reloj?
2. ¿Dónde está Sarita Ortíz?
3. ¿Dónde están los libros verdes?
4. ¿Dónde está el mapa de México?
5. ¿Dónde está la revista Shock?
6. ¿Dónde están las sillas?
7. ¿Dónde está el periódico?
8. ¿Dónde están los libros de biología?
9. ¿Dónde está el colegio Highland High School?
10. ¿Dónde está Mazatlán?

Comunicación

37 Después de las clases

Pretend you are looking for someone or something. Working with a classmate, take turns asking about where several people and objects are. Be sure to be polite and say "please" and thank the other person for information about each person or object you are trying to find.

38 Mi colegio

Create your ideal schedule for next year. Include six classes and a lunch. Then, in pairs, create a telephone conversation in which you discuss your schedules. Find out who has math, times for classes, if you have the same lunch period, how many books each of you will need and so forth.

Notes

Have students work together in small groups and take turns asking and answering where several objects or people in activity 36 are located.

Remind students before assigning activity 38 that the questions containing the possessive adjective *tu (tu clase)* have answers that contain the word *mi*.

As part of your classroom management, set a time limit for activity 38.

You may wish to obtain several play or real telephones for students to use as they present the conversation for activity 38 in front of the class.

Answers

36 Possible answers:
1. Está en la pared.
2. Está en la clase (en la silla azul).
3. Están en el escritorio.
4. Está en la pared.
5. Está en la mochila.
6. Están en la clase.
7. Está en el cesto de papeles.
8. Están sobre el escritorio.
9. Está en Dallas, Texas.
10. Está en México.

37 Creative self-expression.
38 Creative self-expression.

Activities

Cooperative Learning
Have students work in pairs, asking and answering questions about their school for activity 38. They should say where the school is, when classes are, what their schedule is like and who their teachers are.

Expansion
Conduct a class discussion about students' classes. Start with Spanish class: when the class starts and ends, who the teacher is, who is in the class, what objects are in the class, etc. Then continue on to include other classes and other topics.

Language through Action
Have students describe what they see in the illustration that accompanies activity 36. Then they should find and identify similar items or people in the classroom as they point to each and describe it.

National Standards

Communication
1.1, 1.2

Teacher Resources

Lectura personal
Activity 39

Answers

39
1. Se llama Preparatoria Benito Juárez.
2. Son de las 2:00 P.M. a las 8:00 P.M.
3. Es inglés.
4. Hay cuarenta estudiantes.
5. Estudia con un profesor particular.

40 Answers will vary.

Activities

Cooperative Learning

Have students work in pairs to create a dialog, using the Spanish they have learned in this lesson. Each student should prepare four to eight lines. Ask them to be as creative as possible! Then ask for volunteers to present their dialog in class. All students should speak Spanish and work cooperatively to prepare for this activity. Students who have completed the lesson successfully will be able to do what is requested and should demonstrate creative self-expression.

Prereading Strategy

Have students look quickly through the *Lectura cultural* about the musical group La Ola to find cognates and other words they recognize.

National Standards

Communication
1.1, 1.3

Cultures
2.2

Lectura personal

Mañana viernes tengo que decir[1] adiós a mi colegio. Se llama Preparatoria Benito Juárez. Tiene dos horarios: el horario de la mañana y el horario de la tarde. Yo tengo[2] el horario de la tarde, de las 2:00 P.M. a las 8:00 P.M. En mi clase hay cuarenta estudiantes. Los estudiantes y los profesores son buena onda[3]. ¡Los echaré de menos![4] Durante[5] la gira, estudio con un profesor particular[6]. No sé cómo se llama. Tampoco sé de dónde es. ¡Ojalá sea[7] buena onda[8]! Bueno, amigos, ¡hasta pronto!

[1]I have to say [2]have [3]nice [4]I'll miss them [5]During [6]private [7]I hope he will be [8]lucky

39 ¿Qué recuerdas?

1. ¿Cómo se llama el colegio de Yadira?
2. ¿De qué hora a qué hora son sus clases?
3. ¿Cuál es su clase favorita?
4. ¿Cuántos estudiantes hay en su clase?
5. ¿Con quién estudia en la gira?

40 Algo personal

1. How many schedules does Yadira's school have? Why do you suppose many Latin American schools have more than one schedule? Which schedule would you choose? Explain why.
2. What are the advantages and disadvantages of studying with a private tutor? Do you think Yadira will like being tutored or will she miss being in a classroom with forty students?

Notes

Play the recorded version of the reading on page 80 that is part of the Audio Program.

Help students with the reading: Apply some of the strategies they have been learning such as scanning.

Use the questions for the *Algo personal* as the basis for a discussion with students about school life.

Autoevaluación

As a review and self-check, respond to the following:

1. Ask when Spanish class is.
2. How would you tell a friend that English ends at 2:15 P.M.?
3. Say you study art on Saturdays.
4. Identify differences between your high school and a high school in one of the Spanish-speaking countries.
5. Describe several objects around you by telling what color they are.
6. How would you ask a friend where the compact discs (CDs) are?
7. What might the person on the other end say to you in Spanish if you have dialed the wrong telephone number?

Palabras y expresiones

How many of these words and expressions do you recognize?

Clases
el arte
la biología
el colegio
la computación
el español
la historia
el horario
el inglés
las matemáticas
la música

Colores
amarillo,-a
azul
blanco,-a
gris
negro,-a
rojo,-a
verde

Días
el domingo
el jueves
el lunes
el martes
el miércoles
el sábado
el viernes

Por teléfono
aló
¿cuál?
la dirección (de correo electrónico)
el número de teléfono/de fax/de teléfono celular/equivocado
el teléfono

Ropa
la blusa
el calcetín
la camisa
la camiseta
la falda
los jeans
el pantalón
el zapato

Tecnología
la arroba
la computadora
el disco compacto (CD)
el diskette
la impresora (láser)
la pantalla
el punto
el ratón (pl. los ratones)
el teclado

Verbos
estar
estudiar
hablar
llevar
necesitar
terminar

Otras expresiones
a
allí
el almuerzo
¿a qué hora?
el color
¿Cómo?
¿cuánto,-a?
el día
el examen
¡mira!
o
sobre
tampoco
tu

Estructura

Do you remember the following grammar rules?

Noun-Adjective agreement

In Spanish adjectives must match the gender and number of the nouns they describe.

	masculine	feminine
singular	un cuaderno amarillo.	una regla roja.
plural	unos cuardernos amarillos.	unas reglas rojas.

Present tense of *-ar* verbs

hablar	
hablo	hablamos
hablas	habláis
habla	hablan

Talking about schedules: *¿A qué hora?*

To ask and answer when something is going to occur.
Question: ***¿A que hora es*** la clase de español?
Answer: ***Es a las*** dos.

The verb *estar*

estoy	estamos
estás	estáis
está	están

Teacher Resources

 Activity 15

 pp. 48, 82

 Juegos

Flash Cards

Answers

Autoevaluación

Possible answers:

1. ¿A qué hora es la clase de español?
2. La clase de inglés termina a las dos y cuarto de la tarde.
3. Estudio arte los sábados.
4. Hispanic high schools can be rigorous; there are not many extracurricular activities; there are not many elective courses; private schools are common; grades are often based upon a numerical scale.
5. Objects will vary. Be sure students match number and gender.
6. ¿Dónde están los discos compactos (CDs)?
7. Tienes el número equivocado.

Activities

Expansion

Model new words and expressions from the *Palabras y expresiones* and have students repeat after you. Then call on students to use the words or expressions in sentences.

National Standards

Communication
1.1

Notes

Assign the *Autoevaluación* to provide students with an opportunity to measure their own progress learning the main elements of the lesson and as preparation for the end-of-chapter test.

Have students work together in groups of three to create a dialog using the expressions and new vocabulary from the lesson. Remind students to be creative.

Answers

Preparación

1. Chicano literature is taught in states close to the Mexico-United States border in California, Texas, New Mexico and Arizona, but may also be offered elsewhere.
2. Possible answers: They would not be able to speak English, get a job, borrow money for a car or have a place to live.
3. Key vocabulary might include: *fronteras*/borders, *dividen*/divide, *puente*/bridge, *dos Californias*/two Californias, *pases*/you can cross, *sur*/south, *norte*/north.

Activities

Multiple Intelligences (bodily-kinesthetic/linguistic)

Have students write a four- or five-line poem in Spanish with an English equivalent about a theme of their choosing. They should try to choose from vocabulary and structures they have learned, but ambitious students may want to use a dictionary and create a more complex poem.

Technology

Many universities in the United States offer courses in Chicano literature. Students can surf the Web and find Chicano literature courses that can be taken via the Internet.

National Standards

Cultures
2.2

Connections
3.1, 3.2

¡Viento en popa!

Tú lees

Conexión con otras disciplinas: literatura

Estrategia

Activating background knowledge

Applying what you already know about a topic when you read will prepare you for the type of information and vocabulary that will likely appear in the reading. For example, in this chapter, you have become more aware of how the Hispanic culture has influenced the United States. Do you know Hispanic culture also enriches American literature? The themes of Chicano literature reflect the difficulties faced by Hispanics as they adjust to life in the United States. In her bilingual book of Chicano poetry, *Puentes y fronteras/Bridges and Borders,* Gina Valdés patterns her poems after one of the oldest styles of Spanish poetry, called a *copla*. The *coplas* were popular in medieval Spain (13th century) because they were composed of short lines of poetry that were easily memorized. Minstrels often sang *coplas* to villagers they encountered in their travels. This established an oral tradition that passed stories and information from one person to another for centuries.

Preparación

Contesta las siguientes preguntas como preparación para la lectura.

1. Where do you think courses on Chicano literature might be offered?
2. What difficulties might Hispanic immigrants face when they move to the United States?
3. What key words in the following poems do you think most likely reflect some of the issues found in Chicano literature?

Cruzando la frontera *(crossing the border).*

Notes

Ask students to identify factors that may influence immigration from Spanish-speaking nations to the United States. Then assign the strategy on activating background knowledge on this page. Next, ask the questions that appear in the *Preparación*.

Puentes y fronteras/*Bridges and Borders* (selecciones)
por Gina Valdés

Hay tantísimas fronteras **que dividen a la gente,** **pero por cada frontera** **existe también un puente.**	***There are so many borders*** ***that divide people,*** ***but for every border*** ***there is also a bridge.***
***	***
Entre las dos Californias **quiero construir un puente,** **para que cuando tú quieras** **te pases del sur al norte,** **caminando libremente** **no como liebre del monte.**	***Between the two Californias*** ***I want to build a bridge,*** ***so whenever you wish*** ***you can cross from south to north,*** ***walking freely*** ***not like a wild rabbit.***

A ¿Qué recuerdas?

1. What are the "two Californias" the poet talks about?
2. Whom is the author referring to that would cross the border "like a wild rabbit" *(como liebre del monte)*?
3. Which words rhyme in the two poems?

B Algo personal

1. Why do you think the author uses the old style of *coplas* to express her modern poetry?
2. Besides the physical border, in what other ways are the Mexican and American cultures divided?
3. Themes found in poetry are based upon human experiences. What themes are depicted in these poems?

Notes The two *coplas* presented here are individual poems from the same book of poetry.

Have students read these selections by Gina Valdés. Finally, discuss *Puentes y fronteras* (Bridges and Borders) using the questions in the activities *¿Qué recuerdas?* and *Algo personal.*

Teacher Resources

 ***Puentes y fronteras***

Answers

A 1. The two Californias refer to the state of California (United States) and Baja California (Mexico). They could also symbolize the Anglo California and the Hispanic California that coexist in the United States.
2. The author is referring to the illegal immigrants that cross the border between Mexico and California.
3. Possible answers include: *gente* and *puente*, *Californias* and *quieras*, *puente* and *libremente*, *norte* and *monte*.

B Answers will vary.

Activities

Expansion

Additional questions *(Algo personal)*: *¿Qué divide a la gente?; ¿Qué existe por cada frontera?; ¿Para qué quiere la poeta construir un puente?; ¿Tienes algún amigo de un país de habla hispana?; ¿Eres de algún país de habla hispana?*

National Standards
Communication 1.1
Cultures 2.2
Connections 3.1, 3.2

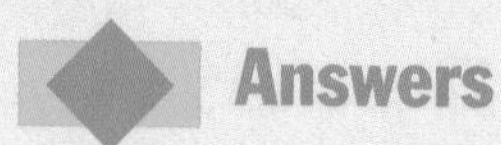

Answers

Creative writing practice.

Activities

Critical Thinking

As an alternative writing activity, have students write a five- or six-sentence paragraph in Spanish telling about themselves. Ask them to include such things as their name, where they are from, telephone number, family or friends' names and where they go to school. Have them add a visual element about themselves to decorate it. Display the final products on a bulletin board for parents to see when they visit the classroom.

Tú escribes

Estrategia

Writing a dialog journal

Whether you write in a spiral notebook, a composition book or a loose-leaf binder, writing your thoughts in a journal offers a written means of recording your experiences, wishes and dreams. In addition, keeping a journal offers a way for you as a student writer to respond personally to what you are reading or learning in class. You may even choose to create an electronic journal using a computer. Regardless of the format you choose, writing down your thoughts regularly and expressing yourself freely in a dialog journal can increase your motivation to write as you look back and reflect upon where you have been and as you consider where you are going. Communicating your thoughts and feelings through journal writing allows you and your teacher to get to know each other more rapidly on a deeper, more personal level.

Choose one of the topics below and write at least a paragraph to your teacher to express how you feel about it.

1. How will learning Spanish benefit you personally?
2. If you were attending school in a Hispanic country, what do you think you would like? What would you dislike?
3. How is the Hispanic culture evident in your community? What aspects of this culture would you like to learn more about?
4. What famous Spanish-speaking person would you like to interview? Why?
5. Imagine you are an immigrant who has just entered the United States to live. What is going through your mind?

El activista César Chávez.

La escritora Isabel Allende.

National Standards

Communication
1.2

Notes

The journal entries should pertain to the chapter content and should serve to provide feedback on the topic, to promote communication between you and your students and to give students grammar and vocabulary practice. Your purpose is not to correct the entry, but rather to comment on students' ideas and answer students' questions. You can model correct spelling and grammar in your return entry. The most important thing is to get to know one another and to motivate your students to keep writing.

Consider having students write journal entries every lesson.

Proyectos adicionales

A Conexión con la tecnología

Search the Internet for additional information about one of the famous Spanish speakers mentioned in *Capítulo* 2. Prepare a short report about the person and share the information with your classmates.

B Comparaciones

Imagine you are attending high school in a Spanish-speaking country and you are writing to a key pal in your Spanish class back home describing the experience. Compare what you know about school life in a Spanish-speaking country with school life in the United States. Create your class schedule based on what you have learned about the different systems of education and describe your daily routine. Use color and computer-generated artwork or designs to make the schedule appear interesting. Be prepared to discuss your schedule in class, naming similarities and differences between the different systems.

MODELO El colegio se llama....
Tengo la clase de... a las dos y media.

El artista Pablo Picasso.

C Comunidades

Do you know any people in your community who speak Spanish? Are there any restaurants, radio stations, grocery stores, etc. that are owned or run by a Spanish-speaking individual? Name some people and places in your community that have a connection to Spanish and the cultures of the Spanish-speaking world. If you can, interview someone on the list and find out more about that connection to Spanish (where the person is from, difficulties the person experienced coming to the United States, etc.).

Notes

Communities. Spanish is used extensively on Spanish radio and television programs, for business and for pleasure in such diverse places as California and the Southwest, Denver, Chicago, Miami, New York and numerous other major cities and small towns throughout the United States.

Teacher Resources

p. 68

Answers

A Creative self-expression.
B Creative self-expression.
C Creative self-expression.

Activities

Communities
Ask students to research their own family histories. When did their relatives come to the United States and why? Where were they originally from?

Expansion
Make a bulletin board of famous Hispanics with pictures and items students bring in.

Students with Special Needs
Select two or three students or have volunteers present to the class what they wrote for activity A.

National Standards	
Communication 1.2, 1.3	**Comparisons** 4.2
Cultures 2.2	**Communities** 5.1
Connections 3.2	

Teacher Resources

 *Trabalenguas*

 **Episode 2, DVD 1, Track 16**

Answers

Resolviendo el misterio

1. They both play the guitar, like music and history, and dislike math.
2. Answers will vary.
3. Answers will vary.

Activities

Communities

Have students investigate businesses in your community that require Spanish-speaking employees. Then discuss the results. As an alternative, have one or two students share their findings with the class.

Trabalenguas

See which student can say the *Trabalenguas* the most times in a row without making a mistake.

REPASO

Now that I have completed this chapter, I can...	Go to these pages for help:
identify people and classroom objects.	40, 48
ask for and give names.	40
ask or tell where someone is from.	40
discuss school schedules and daily activities.	60
describe classroom objects and clothing.	60
say some things people do.	67
state location.	76
talk about how someone feels.	76
I can also...	
identify Hispanic influences in the United States.	43
identify some well-known people who speak Spanish.	43
name places in the United States where Spanish is spoken.	51
name some ways learning Spanish can enhance career opportunities.	51
scan an article in Spanish for cognates.	68
talk about technology.	73
compare Hispanic and American school systems and grading scales.	75
read a poem in Spanish.	83
write in Spanish.	84

Trabalenguas
Teresa trajo tizas hechas trizas.
NO HAY TIZAS

PREPARATORIA
LA LUZ

Resolviendo el misterio

After watching Episode 2 of *El cuarto misterioso*, answer the following questions.

1. What do José and Conchita have in common?
2. Who is the mysterious man in the car?
3. Don Pedro says that there are rats behind the hidden door. What do you think is behind the door?

National Standards

Communication
1.2, 1.3

Cultures
2.1

Communities
5.1

Notes Talk with students about why it is important to know about the culture and other background information of a person with whom someone is establishing business relations. Explain that foreign businesspeople are much more willing to do business with people who respect their culture as well as their language. When doing business with someone in Spanish, they should remember the expression *la cortesía mucho vale y poco cuesta* (courtesy is worth a lot and costs little).

Loose translation of the *Trabalenguas:* Teresa brought broken-up chalk.

Vocabulario

a to, at, in *2B*
¿a qué hora? at what time? *2B*
allí there *2B*
el **almuerzo** lunch *2B*
aló hello (telephone greeting) *2B*
amarillo,-a yellow *2B*
el **amigo**, la **amiga** friend *2A*
la **arroba** at (the symbol @ used for e-mail addresses) *2B*
el **arte** art *2B*
¡ay! oh! *2A*
azul blue *2B*
la **biología** biology *2B*
blanco,-a white *2B*
la **blusa** blouse *2B*
el **bolígrafo** pen *2A*
el **borrador** eraser *2A*
el **calcetín** sock *2B*
la **camisa** shirt *2B*
la **camiseta** jersey, polo, t-shirt *2B*
el **cesto de papeles** wastebasket *2A*
el **chico**, la **chica** boy, girl *2A*
la **clase** class *2A*
el **colegio** school *2B*
el **color** color *2B*
¿Cómo se dice...? How do you say...? *2A*
¿Cómo se llama (Ud./él/ella)? What is (his/her) name? *2A*
¿Cómo? How? *2B*
comprendo (comprender) I understand (to understand) *2A*
la **computación** computer science *2B*
la **computadora** computer *2B*
el **cuaderno** notebook *2A*
¿cuál(es)? which one(s)? *2B*
¿cuánto,-a? how many? *2B*
el **día** day *2B*
la **dirección** *(de correo electrónico)* address (e-mail) *2B*
el **disco compacto** (CD) compact disc *2B*
el **diskette** diskette *2B*
el **domingo** Sunday *2B*
él he *2A*
el, la the *2A*
ella she *2A*
ellas they (f.) *2A*
ellos they (m.) *2A*
en in, on, at *2A*
el **escritorio** desk *2A*
el **español** Spanish *2B*
estar to be *2B*
el **estudiante**, la **estudiante** student *2A*
estudiar to study *2B*
el **examen** exam, test *2B*
la **falda** skirt *2B*
gris grey *2B*
hablar to speak *2B*
hay there is, there are *2A*
la **historia** history *2B*
el **horario** schedule *2B*
la **impresora (láser)** (laser) printer *2B*
el **inglés** English *2B*
los **jeans** jeans, blue jeans *2B*
el **jueves** Thursday *2B*
el **lápiz** pencil *2A*
el **libro** book *2A*
llevar to wear *2B*
los, las the (m.pl.), the (f.pl.) *2A*
el **lunes** Monday *2B*
el **mapa** map *2A*
el **martes** Tuesday *2B*
las **matemáticas** mathematics *2B*
mi my *2A*
el **miércoles** Wednesday *2B*
¡mira! look! *2B*
la **mochila** backpack *2A*
la **música** music *2B*
necesitar to need *2B*
negro,-a black *2B*
nosotros,-as we *2A*
nuevo,-a new *2A*
el **número de teléfono/de fax/de teléfono celular** phone number/fax number/cell phone number *2B*
la **página** page *2A*
la **palabra** word *2A*
la **pantalla** screen *2B*
el **pantalón** pants *2B*
el **papel** paper *2A*
la **pared** wall *2A*
el **periódico** newspaper *2A*
la **pizarra** blackboard *2A*
el **profesor**, la **profesora** teacher *2A*
la **puerta** door *2A*
el **punto** dot (term used in Internet address) *2B*
el **pupitre** desk *2A*
¿Qué quiere decir...? What does ... mean? *2A*
¿qué? what? *2A*
¿quién? who? *2A*
quiere decir it means *2A*
el **ratón** mouse *2B*
la **regla** ruler *2A*
el **reloj** clock, watch *2A*
la **revista** magazine *2A*
rojo,-a red *2B*
la **ropa** clothing *2B*
el **sábado** Saturday *2B*
el **sacapuntas** pencil sharpener *2A*
sé I know *2A*
se dice it is called *2A*
ser to be *2A*
la **silla** chair *2A*
sobre on, over, on top of *2B*
tampoco neither *2B*
el **teclado** keyboard *2B*
el **teléfono** telephone *2B*
terminar to finish *2B*
la **tiza** chalk *2A*
tu your *2B*
(Ud./Él/Ella) se llama... (you/his/her) name is ... *2A*
un, una a, an, one *2A*
unos, unas some, any, a few *2A*
la **ventana** window *2A*
verde green *2B*
el **viernes** Friday *2B*
el **zapato** shoe *2B*

Teacher Resources

Repaso

¡Aventureros!, Ch. 2

Internet Activities

i-Culture

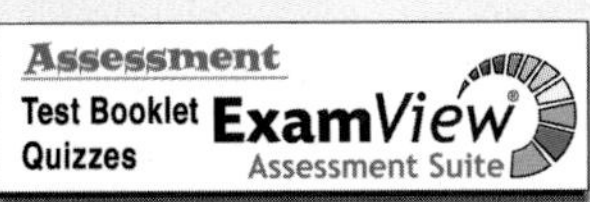

Activities

Critical Listening

Say several nouns aloud in Spanish and ask students to provide the appropriate definite article and repeat the noun that you give. First give words that students have seen, such as those on this page. Then give words that are unknown to students, including some ending in *-o*, *-a*, *-dad*. If necessary, point out to students that they should be able to give the appropriate definite article even if the word is unknown by generalizing about the information provided on noun gender.

Expansion

Model the words and expressions and have students repeat. Then call on students to make statements using the vocabulary from the chapter.

National Standards

Communication
1.2

Notes The words and expressions on this page are provided as a handy reference list with English equivalents of all active vocabulary. Encourage students to return to either *Lección 2A* or *Lección 2B* (as indicated after each English equivalent) to review words and expressions they do not recognize.

Quizzes have been formatted to allow teachers to evaluate how well students are learning key content. Teachers may opt to combine these quizzes at the end of a lesson as a comprehensive test over the contents of the entire lesson.

Teacher Resources

 *Capítulo 3*

TPRS *Capítulo 3*

 Episode 3, DVD 1, Track 32

Answers

El cuarto misterioso

1. Students might mention government buildings, art centers, religious monuments or sporting venues.
2. Answers might include, bus, subway, taxis, on foot.
3. Answers will vary.
4. Probably not. Inviting students to lunch at an individual's house might be typical in other cultures.

Activities

Communities

Encourage students to use their newly acquired skills as service volunteers assisting Spanish-speaking families in your community. For example, the library, the local park system and the school system are all organizations that often can use help from volunteers with the ability to speak Spanish.

National Standards	
Cultures 2.2	**Comparisons** 4.1
Connections 3.1	**Communities** 5.1

CAPÍTULO 3

¡Vamos a la ciudad!

El cuarto misterioso

Answer the following questions about *Episodio 3–¿Qué vas a hacer?*

1. Ana and her mother view the photos that she took of Mexico City. What landmarks would Ana have likely photographed?
2. What are the best ways for people to navigate a city?
3. What places in your town or city would be likely to impress a new visitor?
4. Would American teenagers invite new friends to their houses for lunch? Why or why not?

At the Montero's, Ana and her mother look at the photos that she took of Mexico City. While looking at the photos, the girls talk about their new friends and receive a phone call from José.

Objetivos

- talk about **places** in a city
- make **introductions** and express **courtesy**
- ask and answer **questions**
- discuss **how to go somewhere**
- say some **things** people do
- say where someone is **going**
- talk about the **future**
- order **food** and **beverages**

Notes A checklist of these objectives, along with additional functions, appears on page 130 so students can evaluate their own progress.

Invite students to give single-word answers in Spanish for *El cuarto misterioso* questions 1 and 2.

 Activities

Prior Knowledge
Ask students to review the chapter objectives. Ask students questions such as: What places or landmarks make your city or town special? How do teenagers typically introduce each other? How do adults typically introduce each other? What activities do you already know how to say in Spanish? How many question words can you name? What words and expressions signal the future tense (for example, tomorrow, next week)? What foods and beverages do you already know how to say in Spanish? Where do you think the young people in the bottom right photo are going? What are the most popular modes of transportation in the U.S.? Are these modes different from other parts of the world?

Contexto cultural

México
Nombre oficial: Estados Unidos Mexicanos
Población: 113.724.000
Capital: México, D.F.
Ciudades importantes: Monterrey, Guadalajara
Unidad monetaria: el peso mexicano
Fiesta nacional: 16 de septiembre, Día de la Independencia
Gente famosa: Luis Miguel (cantante); Frida Kahlo y Diego Rivera (artistas); Octavio Paz y Carlos Fuentes (escritores); Emiliano Zapata (líder popular)

National Standards

Communication	Connections
1.1	3.1
Cultures	
2.1, 2.2	

Notes

Culture. Ask students what country they think they will be studying in the chapter. Then discuss what students know about the country. Point out that Mexico is the United States' nearest neighbor to the south. It is a country with a rich and varied history.

You can spend more time reviewing the objectives for an interesting classroom discussion or move through the objectives at a faster pace. To quickly review, call on just one student to answer each question. You could also ask students to spend ten minutes reading and reflecting on the objectives after they finish the previous chapter test. You could also assign pairs to share each question with the class on the day you plan to start a new chapter.

Teacher Resources

 Vocabulario I *¿Adónde vamos en la ciudad?*

 Activities 21–22

 Activity 1

 Activities 1–2

 pp. 63, 58

 Activity 1

 Activity 1

Content reviewed in *Lección A*

- making introductions
- asking and answering questions
- expressing courtesy

Activities

Prereading Strategy

Have students look at *Vocabulario I* and identify cognates and other words they recognize. Then ask students to guess what the people along the bottom of pages 90 and 91 are saying to one another.

TPR

Using overhead transparencies 21 and 22, ask students to come up and point to the different places you name in Spanish.

National Standards

Communication
1.1, 1.2

Lección A Vocabulario I

¿Adónde vamos en la ciudad?

Méxi

HOTEL MARCO POLO

la médica

Biblioteca

la biblioteca

COLEGIO BILBOA

el hotel

el dentista

CINEPOLIS

la ofi

la escuela

BANCRECER

el banco

el cine

el restaurante

¿Cuándo es la fiesta?

Es mañana.

¿Por qué no vamos?

tomar el camión/ tomar el autobús

¡Claro! ¡Vamos! Yo quiero ir.

¿Sabes ir?

EL PARQUE

Hay una fiesta fantástica.
Natalia es simpática y va también.

Notes

Use transparencies 21 and 22 to introduce the new words and expressions in *Vocabulario I*. Begin by showing students transparency 21 and point to one of the buildings and identify it in Spanish. Students should repeat after you. Continue on to the next building and repeat the process. As a second step, show students transparency 22. Once again identify the buildings in Spanish, allowing students to see how each word is spelled.

La ciudad

Selecciona la foto que corresponde con lo que oyes. ***(Select the photo that matches what you hear.)***

A

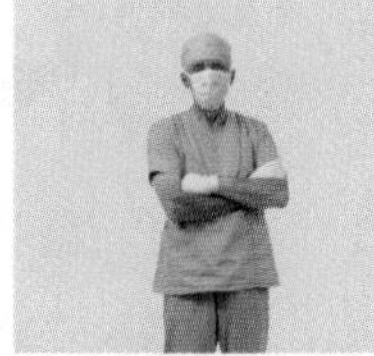

B

C

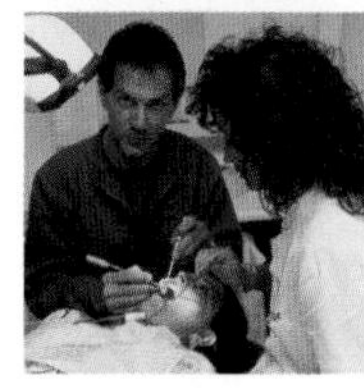

D

E

F

Juego

Haz una lista de tantos lugares en una ciudad como puedas en un minuto. ***(Make a list of as many places in a city as you can in one minute.)***

Go online
EMCLanguages.net

El gusto es mío.
Encantado, Laura.
Laura, te presento a Gabriel y a Jaime.
Tanto gusto.
caminar

Notes

Explain that the expression *El gusto es mío* is often used as a response to someone saying *Mucho gusto*, *Tanto gusto* or *Encantado/encantada*.

Activity 1 is intended for listening comprehension practice. Play the audio of the activity that is part of the Audio Program or use the transcript that appears in the ATE Introduction if you prefer to read the activity yourself.

Teacher Resources

 **Activity 1**

 **Activity 2**

Answers

1. 1. D
   2. E
   3. F
   4. A
   5. B
   6. C
2. Discuss the lists. Find out how many places students came up with in the time allotted and announce who has the longest list.

Activities

Pronunciation *(la letra e)*

Review the sound of *e* by practicing the following words: *problema, fiesta, también, en, nueve, es, noche, número, teléfono, ella, tres, seis, siete.* Point out that the sound of *e* in Spanish has two basic variations. In syllables that combine *e* with *d* (except a final *e* after a *d*), *m, n* and *s*, for example, the sound of *e* is similar to the sound of **e** in the English word **bet:** *cuaderno* (note the difference after a final *d: dónde*), *número, Inés, ser*. In syllables that combine *e* with any other consonant or diphthong, the sound is a little more open than the vowel sound in the English word **date:** *cero, colegio, bien, pues.*

National Standards
Communication 1.2

Teacher Resources

Diálogo I
En la Ciudad de México
Activity 3
Activity 4
Activity 5

Answers

3 1. Están en (la Ciudad de) México.
2. Hay una fiesta en la ciudad, en el Zócalo.
3. Olga es simpática.
4. ¡Claro! Tomás va al Zócalo.
5. Quiere ir al parque.

4 Answers will vary.

5 1. A; 2. D; 3. B; 4. C

Activities

Critical Listening
Tell students to look at only the photographs while they imagine what the people are saying to one another. Have several individuals state what they believe is the main theme of the conversation.

Prereading Strategy
Ask students to recall different ways to greet people in Spanish. Then instruct students to open their books and to cover up the dialog with one hand and look at the photographs. Ask them to imagine where the conversation takes place and what the people are saying to one another. Finally, have students look through the dialog quickly to find cognates.

National Standards
Communication 1.2
Cultures 2.2
Connections 3.1

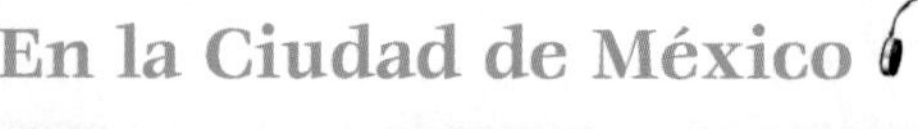

Diálogo I En la Ciudad de México

MARISOL: ¡Hay una fiesta fantástica en la ciudad!
TOMÁS: ¿Cuándo es la fiesta?
PILAR: Es mañana en el Zócalo. ¿Por qué no vamos?
TOMÁS: ¡Claro! ¡Vamos!

TOMÁS: Y... Olga va también, ¿no? Es muy simpática.
PILAR: Sí, ella va.
TOMÁS: ¡Ah, muy bien!

PILAR: Allí está mi amiga. ¡Hola, Ana! Te presento a Tomás.
TOMÁS: Tanto gusto.
ANA: Encantada. ¿Por qué no caminamos al parque?
TOMÁS: Sí, quiero caminar.

3 ¿Qué recuerdas?

1. ¿Dónde están los muchachos?
2. ¿Dónde hay una fiesta?
3. ¿Cómo es Olga?
4. ¿Va Tomás al Zócalo?
5. ¿Adónde quiere ir Ana?

4 Algo personal

1. ¿Eres tú simpático/a? ¿Y tus amigos/as?
2. ¿Hay un parque en tu ciudad? ¿Cómo se llama?
3. ¿Caminas a la escuela?

5 Presentaciones

Indica la letra de la foto que corresponde con lo que oyes.

A

B

C

D

Notes

Point out for students that the *Zócalo* (referred to in the dialog) is the nickname for the *Plaza de la Constitución* in Mexico City. The *Zócalo* is an open quadrangle built on the earlier central square of the Aztec capital. Here you can visit the largest cathedral in North America, see Diego Rivera's murals in the National Palace and view the excavation of a sacred Aztec temple *(templo mayor)*.

Play the audio version of activity 5 for listening comprehension practice.

Point out that the people are shaking hands in activity 5 as they meet one another.

Cultura  

El Parque de Chapultepec, México, D.F.

De visita en la Ciudad de México

When you are in Mexico, you may hear the terms *México, La República* or *los Estados Unidos Mexicanos*, all of which are used interchangeably to refer to the country. Similarly, when you are planning to travel to the capital, you may say you are going to visit Mexico City. However, according to Mexicans, you will be in *el D.F. (Distrito Federal), la Ciudad de México* or just in *México*. Once there, start your sightseeing in the center of the city—the *Zócalo*—or main plaza. Mexico was once the center of the ancient Aztec capital *Tenochtitlán*. Today the site offers visitors a view of the excavated ruins of the *templo mayor* (main temple). Walk a short distance and you will find the wide and elegant *Paseo de la Reforma*. This street was built by the emperor Maximilian to join his palace at Chapultepec with his office in the National Palace (where works by one of Mexico's most famous artists, Diego Rivera, are on display) in the *Zócalo*. Chapultepec today is a large park where you can enjoy *el zoológico* (zoo), *las atracciones* (amusement park rides) or *el Castillo* (castle). Transportation inside the park is limited to walking and biking, so many people come just to enjoy the outdoors. The park also includes the world-famous *Museo Nacional de Antropología*, which contains three miles of exhibits of art, architecture and culture of the ancient civilizations that existed in Mexico before Spanish colonization.

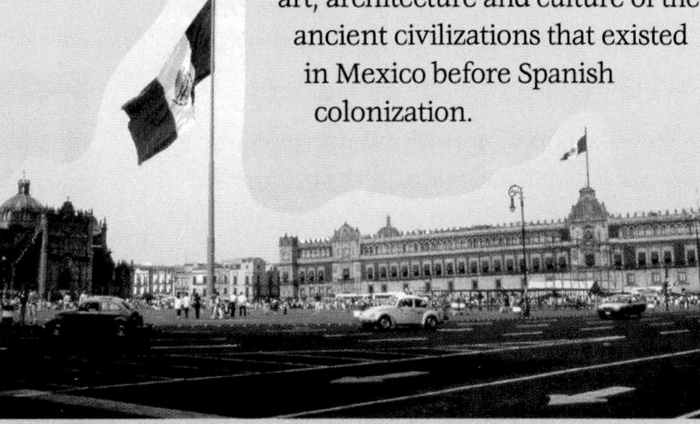
El Zócalo.

6 De visita en la Ciudad de México 

¿Sí o no?

1. Los mexicanos llaman a la capital La República.
2. D.F. quiere decir *Distrito Federal*.
3. El Zócalo es una biblioteca.
4. El Paseo de la Reforma es una avenida elegante.
5. En el Parque de Chapultepec hay un zoológico, atracciones y un castillo.
6. En el Museo Nacional de Antropología hay exhibiciones de arquitectura y cultura.

7 En el D.F.

Make a list of four places mentioned in *Cultura viva* that you might visit on a trip to Mexico City. Search the Internet or go to the library and describe what you would see or do at one of the places you listed.

Notes The official name for Chapultepec Park is *el Bosque de Chapultepec*, which includes several major attractions in addition to the park, such as the castle, museums, botanical gardens, amusement park and a lake. In Mexico, the word *bosque* is a synonym for *parque* since it refers loosely to an unpopulated outdoor or sanctuary area in an urban environment.

Chapultepec Park is popular throughout the week, but it is especially popular on weekends, when individuals, couples, families and groups congregate in the park to take advantage of the many sites and activities offered.

Teacher Resources

 **Activity 6**

 **Activity 3**

 **Activity 2**

Answers

6 1. No.; 2. Sí.; 3. No.; 4. Sí.; 5. Sí.; 6. Sí.

7 Possible answers: el Zócalo, el Templo Mayor, el Paseo de la Reforma, el Parque de Chapultepec, el Museo Nacional de Antropología.

Activities

Communities

Ask if students can name any well-known Mexicans or celebrities of Mexican descent. Then find out how many of the following figures students can identify: Frida Kahlo (painter); Octavio Paz (writer, winner of the Nobel Prize in literature); Selena Quintanilla (Grammy Award-winning singer); Emiliano Zapata (leader of the Mexican Revolution); Diego Rivera (muralist).

Technology

Have students search the Internet to research some well-known Mexicans or American celebrities of Mexican descent. Students should prepare a list of facts or summarize what they find and then share their findings with the class.

National Standards	
Communication 1.3	**Communities** 5.1
Cultures 2.1, 2.2	
Connections 3.1, 3.2	

Teacher Resources

 Activities 4–6

Activities 3–5

 p. 12

 Activity 3

 Activity 2

Answers

8 1. te, al; 2. les, al, del; 3. les, al; 4. le, a; 5. les, a; 6. les, a la, de; 7. te, a, a

Activities

Expansion
Have students introduce themselves to the teacher and each other in small groups.

Pronunciation *(la letra a)*
Write several sentences on the board. Break the sentences into individual words and sounds and then have students use the words you have practiced in meaningful sentences. *I: Tomás, a, amiga, Ana, caminamos* and *encantada*. Point out that the sound of *a* in Spanish is similar to the **a** of the English word **father**, but a little more open. (As an alternative, you may wish to provide your own list of words or have students find appropriate words.) After practicing the *a* sound, have students use the words by acting out the dialog or by creating their own dialogs.

National Standards

Communication
1.1, 1.3

Cultures
2.1

Comparisons
4.1

Idioma

Estructura

Making introductions: *te, le, les*

Follow these guidelines when you wish to introduce people:

te	**(to one person, informal)**	*Laura, **te presento a** Gabriel.*
le	**(to one person, formal)**	*Sra. Durán, **le presento a** María.*
les	**(to two or more people, informal and formal)**	*Luis y José, **les presento a** Margarita y **a** Pablo.*

Note: When the definite article *el* (the) follows *a* or *de*, the two words combine to form *al* or *del*.

a + el = al

de + el = del

*Tomás y Pilar, les presento **al** señor Rojas.*
*Te presento **al** amigo del estudiante nuevo.*

You have several responses to choose from when meeting someone, among them: ***Mucho gusto***, ***Tanto gusto*** or ***El gusto es mío***. In addition, males can say ***Encantado***, while females may wish to say ***Encantada***.

Títulos de cortesía

You have already learned to use *señorita, señora, señor, profesora, profesor* in face-to-face conversation. However, if you are talking about someone, these titles of respect are preceded by the definite articles *la, el, las* or *los*: ***El señor Díaz** es mi profesor.*

Two additional titles of respect, ***don*** (masculine) and ***doña*** (feminine), do not require a definite article and are used with a person's first name when talking to adults you know very well: ***Don** Diego, le presento a **doña** Teresa.*

Práctica

8 Presentaciones

Completa las siguientes oraciones con palabras de la lista.

de	te	a la	al
les	le	del	a

MODELO ¡Ay, Rosario! Te presento a mi amigo Iván.

1. Jorge, __ presento __ señor Francisco Ortiz.
2. Rodolfo y Ana, __ presento __ amigo __ Sr. Rodríguez.
3. Paco y Antonio, __ presento __ señor Pedraza.
4. Profesor Vallejo, __ presento __ doña Marina.
5. Rodrigo y Pablo, __ presento __ Diana y a Catalina.
6. Sr. y Sra. Gaviria, __ presento __ profesora __ historia.
7. Rosario, __ presento __ don Carlos y __ Ernesto.

Encantada.

Notes

Comparisons. The titles *don* and *doña* do not have English equivalents. They are used to show respect and closeness when addressing or speaking of a person with whom *señor* or *señora* would be too formal or with adults of the same age but of a higher social status or business rank. *Don* can be used when addressing or referring to any male, single or married; however, *doña* usually is reserved for older, married or widowed women. One exception is royalty, in which case *doña* can be used with the name of an unmarried woman such as *la princesa doña Isabel*. The abbreviations for *don (Dn. or D.)* and *doña (Dña. or D.ª)* are always capitalized.

9 En la fiesta del Zócalo

Completa los diálogos.

Roberto: Sr. y Sra. Ortega, (1) presento (2) mi amiga Estefanía.
Sr. Ortega: Tanto (3), Estefanía.
Sra. Ortega: Encantada, Estefanía.
Sra. Tovar: Sra. Santos, (4) presento a Felipe, mi amigo de Acapulco.
Sra. Santos: (5), Felipe.
Felipe: El (6) es mío, Sra. Santos.
Sofía: Marcos, te (7) a Pilar y a Daniel. Marcos es el estudiante nuevo de Veracruz.
Marcos: ¡(8) gusto! Me llamo Marcos Castilla.
Pilar: (9).
Iván: ¿(10) estás?
Daniel: Bien, gracias.

¡Mucho gusto!

10 En la Ciudad de México

You and two classmates are greeting some friends and family who have decided to visit Mexico City. Introduce everyone using the words shown.

MODELO Hernando / presento a / el profesor de música, el señor Villamil
Hernando, te presento al profesor de música, el señor Villamil.

1. Maribel / presento a / mi amigo, Jorge Contreras
2. Carmen y Gabriel / presento a / Edgar
3. Sra. Giraldo / presento a / la señora Suárez
4. Sr. y Sra. Ruiz / presento a / el profesor de historia de / el colegio, el señor Botero
5. Enrique y Sonia / presento a / el amigo de / el profesor Osorio, el señor Jaramillo
6. Sr. y Sra. Reyes / presento a / la amiga de Silvia, Juliana
7. Isabel / presento a / el amigo de / el señor Rueda, don Carlos

Comunicación

11 En el Zócalo

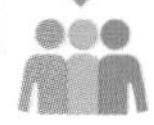

You are with some friends and classmates at the Zócalo while on a study abroad program in Mexico City. In small groups, act out these introductions. Take turns playing the part of each person.

1. Your friend Miguel meets your friend Margarita for the first time.
2. Your classmate Pedro sees one of his neighbors *la señora Carvajal* whom you do not know.
3. Two other students you know from the exchange program pass by while you are with your other friends.
4. The mother of one of your friends, *la señora García*, is crossing the Zócalo and runs into you and your friends.

Answers

9 1. les
2. a
3. gusto
4. le
5. Encantada/Mucho gusto/Tanto gusto
6. gusto
7. presento
8. Mucho/Tanto
9. Encantada/El gusto es mío
10. Cómo

10 1. Maribel, te presento a mi amigo, Jorge Contreras.
2. Carmen y Gabriel, les presento a Edgar.
3. Sra. Giraldo, le presento a la señora Suárez.
4. Sr. y Sra. Ruiz, les presento al profesor de historia del colegio, el señor Botero.
5. Enrique y Sonia, les presento al amigo del profesor Osorio, el señor Jaramillo.
6. Sr. y Sra. Reyes, les presento a la amiga de Silvia, Juliana.
7. Isabel, te presento al amigo del señor Rueda, don Carlos.

11 Creative self-expression.

Activities

Language through Action
Ask students to imagine they have invited a famous person (past or present) to a party. Working in groups of three, they should take turns introducing the person to their guests.

National Standards

Communication
1.1

Comparisons
4.1

Notes Remind students that *te* is used informally with one person (when referring to **you** informally), *le* is used formally with one person (when referring to **you** formally) and *les* is used both informally and formally when making introductions to two or more people (when referring to **all of you**).

Comparisons. Note for students that English has many possible contractions **(can't, won't, it's, we're)** but Spanish has only two: *al* and *del*.

Point out to students that, unlike the English title **Mrs.**, the word *señora (Sra.)* as it is used in activity 9 is a title of respect.

Answers

12 Creative self-expression.

13 Questions will vary.

Activities

Cooperative Learning

Have students pretend they are at a meeting where there are many people who do not know one another. They must walk around the room, asking for the names of other people at the meeting. They then must take turns introducing one another to other people nearby, using the expressions they have learned (*¿Cómo te llamas?; Me llamo...; ¡Mucho gusto!; Encantado/a; Perdón; Te/le/les presento a...*). Remind students to shake hands as they meet one another. You may wish to have students introduce their new acquaintances to you, too.

Students with Special Needs

Have students pair up to create questions for activity 13. Then review the questions students created as part of a class discussion about how students have learned to form questions and as part of your introduction to the *Estructura* on page 97.

National Standards

Communication
1.1, 1.3

Comparisons
4.1

12 En una fiesta de bienvenida

In groups of three or four, pretend you are guests at a *quinceañera* party at the home of the study abroad program director. Practice introducing one another in Spanish and then start conversations with the other guests: ask where they are from, how they are, if they speak Spanish and English and so on. Exchange phone numbers with at least one other person. Remember to use appropriate greetings, gestures and responses in your conversations.

Repaso rápido

Question-asking words

You are already familiar with several words used for asking information questions:

*¿**Cómo** estás?*	**How** are you?
*¿**Cuál** es tu cuaderno?*	**Which (one)** is your notebook?
*¿**Cuáles** son?*	**Which (ones)** are they?
*¿**Cuándo** es la clase de español?*	**When** is the Spanish class?
*¿**Cuánto** es?*	**How much** is it?
*¿**Cuántos** hay?*	**How many** are there?
*¿**Dónde** están ellos?*	**Where** are they?
*¿**Por qué** está ella allí?*	**Why** is she there?
*¿**Qué** es?*	**What** is it?
*¿**Quién** es de Cancún?*	**Who** is from Cancún?
*¿**Quiénes** son ellos?*	**Who** are they?

Note: Unlike *qué, cuál* (or *cuáles*) may never be followed by a noun: *¿Qué autobús tomas?* (What bus are you taking?); *¿Cuál de los autobuses tomas?* (Which of the buses are you taking?).

13 Unas preguntas

Escribe preguntas usando cada una de las palabras interrogativas del Repaso rápido. *(Write questions using each of the question-asking words in the Repaso rápido.)*

¿Dónde está el Museo de Bellas Artes?

Notes Have students role-play the *quinceañera* party in activity 12. Have a few students create signs with the word *Ud.* that they wear to play the part of adults so participants practice both *tú* and *Ud.* Next, have everyone prepare cards with questions they wish to ask others at the party. After asking a question on the card and receiving an answer, students should ask the person to sign the card.

Comparisons. Inform students that *¿Cómo?* used alone is a way of asking for clarification when one doesn't understand something that was said.

Estructura

Asking questions

- One way to ask a question is by making your voice rise at the end of the sentence.

  Hay un museo en Chapultepec. → *¿Hay un museo en Chapultepec?*

- Another way to ask a question in Spanish is to place the subject after the verb.

  ***Tomás está** en el museo.* → *¿**Está Tomás** en el museo?*
  1 2 → **2 1**

- You can also create a question by adding a tag word such as *¿no?* or *¿verdad?* to the end of a sentence, much as you might add **isn't she?** or **right?**, etc. in English.

  *Eva va al restaurante, **¿no?*** — Eva is going to the restaurant, **isn't she?**
  *Uds. van al Zócalo, **¿verdad?*** — All of you are going to the Zócalo, **right?**

- When forming information questions with interrogative words (*¿cómo?*, *¿cuál?*, *¿cuáles?*, and so forth), the verb precedes the subject, just as in English (*¿Cuándo es la fiesta?*). Some interrogative words may be used alone or in combination with various prepositions (*¿**De dónde** eres tú? ¿**A qué** hora termina?*).

14 En forma de pregunta

Cambia las siguientes oraciones a preguntas.

MODELO La amiga de Pilar es simpática.
¿Es la amiga de Pilar simpática?

1. Ana es la amiga de Pilar.
2. Ana y Tomás estudian música en la Ciudad de México con la señora Alvarado.
3. La señora y el señor Alvarado son de Puebla.
4. Los dos chicos caminan en el Parque de Chapultepec.
5. Ellos hablan con la señora Alvarado en el Museo de Antropología.
6. La señora Alvarado toma el camión a Puebla.

La amiga de Pilar es simpática.

15 A contestar

Working in pairs, take turns reading and answering the questions you created for the previous activity. Remember to answer each question with *Sí* or *No*, followed by a complete sentence.

MODELO **A:** ¿Es la amiga de Pilar simpática?
B: Sí, la amiga de Pilar es simpática./No, la amiga de Pilar no es simpática.

Notes Explain that learning to ask questions is an essential skill. For example, when they visit Mexico or another country, students will need to inquire about transportation, locations, lodging, schedules and more.

Teacher Resources

 Activity 14

 Activities 7–9

 Activities 6–9

 Activity 4

 Activities 3–4

Answers

14
1. ¿Es Ana la amiga de Pilar?
2. ¿Estudian Ana y Tomás música en la Ciudad de México con la señora Alvarado?
3. ¿Son la señora y el señor Alvarado de Puebla?
4. ¿Caminan los dos chicos en el Parque de Chapultepec?
5. ¿Hablan ellos con la señora Alvarado en el Museo de Antropología?
6. ¿Toma la señora Alvarado el camión a Puebla?

15 Check for correct intonation.

Activities

Pronunciation
Recycle the statements in activity 14 to model forming a question with inflection. Check to see that students use rising inflection correctly over the last word of the question.

National Standards

Communication
1.1

Comparisons
4.1

Answers

16 Possible answers:
1. Cuándo/Dónde; 2. Quién; 3. qué; 4. Por qué; 5. dónde; 6. qué; 7. Cuál; 8. Cómo

17 Possible answers:
1. ¿Qué necesita doña Cecilia?/¿Quién necesita el horario de camiones?
2. ¿Quién camina en el parque de Chapultepec?/¿Dónde está el señor Galindo?
3. ¿Qué está en el D.F.?/ ¿Dónde está el Paseo de la Reforma?
4. ¿Quiénes estudian en Mazatlán?/¿Qué hay en Mazatlán?/¿Dónde estudian César, Ignacio y Pedro?

18 Creative self-expression.

Activities

Critical Thinking

With only the interrogative as a prompt, students should be able to predict the type of information they are going to be asked. (This critical thinking activity will help students learn to anticipate forthcoming information.) Write the following question words and responses in random order on the board or on an overhead transparency. Have students match questions to responses: *¿Cómo...?/Muy bien; ¿Cuál...?/ 7-24-38-56; ¿Cuáles...?/Las chicas de Acapulco; ¿Cuándo...?/Por la mañana; ¿Cuánto...?/$79.40; ¿Cuántos...?/29 estudiantes; ¿Dónde...?/En la clase; ¿De dónde...?/De México; ¿Quién...?/ Cristina, la chica nueva.*

National Standards

Communication
1.1, 1.2

16 Palabras interrogativas

Completa las siguientes oraciones de una manera lógica.

1. ¿__ hay una fiesta fantástica?
2. ¿__ va a la fiesta?
3. ¿A __ hora es la fiesta?
4. ¿__ no vamos al parque?
5. ¿De __ es ella?
6. ¿De __ ciudad son?
7. ¿__ es tu número de teléfono?
8. ¿__ es ella? ¿Simpática?

17 Unas preguntas

Make as many different questions as you can for each of the following statements.

MODELO Mañana hay una fiesta fantástica en el Zócalo.
¿Qué hay mañana en el Zócalo?/¿Dónde hay una fiesta mañana?/ ¿Cuándo es la fiesta?

1. Doña Cecilia necesita el horario de camiones.
2. El señor Galindo camina en el Parque de Chapultepec.
3. El Paseo de la Reforma está en el D.F.
4. César, Ignacio y Pedro estudian en una escuela en Mazatlán.

Comunicación

18 México

Referring to *Cultura viva*, create five questions in Spanish about Mexico. Then, with a classmate, take turns asking and answering the questions.

¿Están en el Parque de Chapultepec?

Notes

Clarify that when a speaker is trying to determine which item or items are being discussed, he or she should use the word *cuál* if the next word is a verb and *qué* if the next word is a noun. Examples: *¿Cuál es tu cuaderno? ¿Qué cuaderno es?* Also, explain to the students that the word *porque* means **because** and *por qué* means **why?**

Asking questions. Note for students that question words require a written accent mark whether they are used in questions or in statements where a question is implied: *No sé dónde está* (in which the implied question is **Where is it?**).

Una entrevista

Write five or six questions you would like to ask a classmate. Then pair up with another student and take turns interviewing one another using the questions you prepared. Take notes during the interview and report your findings to the class. Be creative.

¿De dónde eres tú?

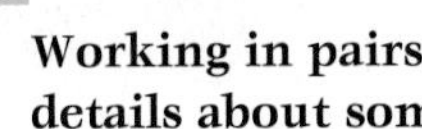

En el teléfono

Working in pairs, create a telephone conversation in which you discuss details about some future activity you are going to do together. Tell when, where and at what time the activity takes place.

¿Aló?

MODELO

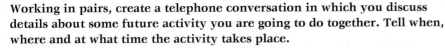

A: ¿Aló?
B: Hola, Pedro. ¿Vamos a la fiesta de Juan?

A: ¿Cuándo es?
B: Es el sábado.

A: ¿A qué hora es?
B: Es a las ocho.

Hay mucha gente en el D.F., ¿verdad?

Answers

19 Creative self-expression.
20 Creative self-expression.

Activities

Cooperative Learning
Have students work in pairs asking and answering questions about illustrations, photographs and realia found in this chapter.

Expansion
Show students several magazine or newspaper clippings and have them ask questions about each article.

Multiple Intelligences (spatial)
Creative visual learners will enjoy creating a pop-up version of a city. Have them label the buildings and any geographical features in Spanish.

Notes

Note for students that *bueno* is a common telephone greeting in Mexico. The greeting *aló* is used in activity 20 because it is more universal. Tell students which greeting you prefer they use.

Remind students to use correct Spanish punctuation (*¿ ?*) when writing questions.

National Standards

Communication
1.1, 1.3

Cultures
2.1

Connections
3.1, 3.2

Teacher Resources

 Vocabulario II *¿Cómo vamos?*

 Activities 23–24

 Activities 10–11

 pp. 59–60, 105–106

 p. 11

 Activity 5

 Activity 5

Activities

Expansion

Model new words and expressions and have students repeat them after you to improve their pronunciation. Then call on individuals to use the new words and expressions in sentences.

TPR

Using overhead transparencies 23 and 24, ask students to come up and point to the different means of transportation as you name them in Spanish.

National Standards

Communication
1.1

Connections
3.1

Vocabulario II

¿Cómo vamos?

BIBLIOTECA NACIONAL

COLEGIO BILBOA

a pie

en avión

en metro

en barco

en tren

a caballo

en moto(cicleta)

en taxi

en bicicleta

en camión

en autobús

en carro

Roberto está lejos de la escuela.
Roberto está cerca de la biblioteca.
Roberto tiene un problema porque no tiene transporte para ir a la escuela.
Tú tienes transporte para ir a la escuela, ¿verdad?

Notes Remind students that these words will change as they travel from one part of the Spanish-speaking world to another, just as expressions in English change from country to country and from one region to another.

The word *moto* is feminine because it is short for *la motocicleta*.

Mexicana and *Aeroméxico* are two airlines that fly to and from Mexico and the United States.

21 ¿Qué medio de transporte es? 

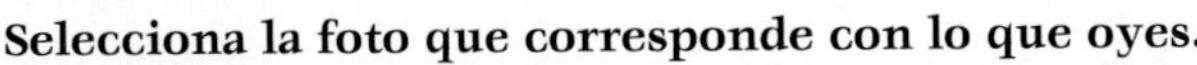

Selecciona la foto que corresponde con lo que oyes.

A

B

C

D

E

F

G

H

22 ¿Cómo vamos?

Cut photographs of various means of transportation from magazines. On the back of each cutout, identify what it is in Spanish. Working in pairs, take turns asking and answering what each item is.

¡Extra!

En otras palabras

el autobús	*el bus, la buseta, el camión, el colectivo, la flota, la guagua, el micro, el ómnibus*
el barco	*el buque, la nave*
la bicicleta	*la bici*
el carro	*el automóvil, el auto, el coche*
el metro	*el subterráneo (el subte)*

23 ¿Cómo vas?

Say which means of transportation you would use to go to the following places.

MODELO la oficina de tu padre
en autobús

1. la escuela
2. la biblioteca
3. el parque
4. México, D.F.
5. el dentista
6. el cinev
7. tu restaurante favorito
8. el médico

Teacher Resources

Activity 21

Answers

21 1. B
2. A
3. F
4. C
5. E
6. D
7. H
8. G

22 Tell students how many words they must find and identify in Spanish. Then, as students work in pairs, walk around the room to be sure they stay on task and are using good pronunciation.

23 Answers will vary.

Notes

The universally recognized word for **truck** is *camión*, although in Mexico, this word is widely used for **bus**. Whereas in Mexico the word for **bus** is *camión*, in other countries there are various words that refer to **bus**: *bus, colectivo, guagua, micro* and *ómnibus* to name a few. Decide if you want students to know *camión* as a term for **bus** or whether you want them to recognize *camión* only as **truck**. The more universally recognized word *autobús* will be taught later in this lesson.

National Standards

Communication
1.1, 1.2

Cultures
2.1

Teacher Resources

Diálogo II
¿Qué?
Activity 24
Activity 25
Activity 26

Answers

24 1. Tomás está lejos.
2. Habla con Olga.
3. Porque no tiene transporte.
4. Porque Tomás tiene carro.

25 Answers will vary.

26 1. B
2. A
3. C
4. D
5. E

Activities

Critical Listening
Tell students to look only at the photographs while they imagine what the people are saying to one another. Have several individuals state what they believe is the main theme.

Expansion
Additional questions *(Algo personal): ¿Vas a una fiesta mañana?; ¿Cuándo vas a una fiesta?*

Prereading Strategy
Ask students to look only at the photographs and imagine where the conversation takes place and what the people are saying. Finally, have students look through the dialog quickly to find cognates.

National Standards

Communication
1.2

Diálogo II ¿Qué?

TOMÁS: Hola, Olga, tú vas mañana a la fiesta, ¿verdad?
OLGA: ¿Cómo? Estás muy lejos.
TOMÁS: Lo siento.

TOMÁS: ¿Vas tú mañana a la fiesta en el Zócalo?
OLGA: Estás muy cerca, Tomás.
TOMÁS: Perdón.

OLGA: No, no voy porque no tengo transporte.
TOMÁS: Bueno, no hay problema.
OLGA: ¿Por qué no hay problema?
TOMÁS: Porque yo tengo carro para ir a la fiesta.

24 ¿Qué recuerdas?

1. ¿Quién está lejos?
2. ¿Con quién habla Tomás?
3. ¿Por qué no va Olga a la fiesta?
4. ¿Por qué no hay problema?

25 Algo personal

1. ¿Qué transporte tomas para ir a la escuela?
2. ¿Qué tomas para ir al parque? ¿Está lejos o cerca?
3. ¿Vas a fiestas con amigos? Explica.

26 ¿Qué transporte toman?

Selecciona la foto que corresponde con lo que oyes.

A

B

C

D

E

Notes

Activities 24, 25 and 26 have been recorded by professional native speakers and are recorded as part of the Audio Program.

Activity 26 is intended for listening comprehension practice. You may either use the audio of the activity or you may find a transcript for the recorded portion of the activity in the Introduction to the ATE if you choose to read it yourself.

Cultura viva II

Nosotros viajamos en metro.

¿Cómo viajamos en el D.F.?

Transportation options in Mexico are varied and abundant. One option, owning a car and driving in Mexico, can present challenges. Cars are expensive to purchase and maintain since taxes are steep. In addition, finding parking can be difficult and is expensive when available. Most people prefer to use the excellent public transportation that is available.

Taxis are numerous and usually relatively inexpensive compared to the United States. In Mexico City, governmental regulations require taxi drivers to be licensed and that each taxi operate with a working meter and a driver's picture identification placed in a visible location inside the cab.

The buses in Mexico are clean and reasonably priced. The best public transportation bargain in Mexico City is undoubtedly its subway system (*el metro*), which allows a rider to travel from one area of the city to another with a single ticket. For this reason, the metro can be a little overcrowded during rush hours.

¡Hay mucho tráfico en el D.F.!

27 Comparando

Compara el transporte en México con el transporte en tu ciudad.

México	Mi ciudad
1. owning a car presents challenges	1. driving a car also presents challenges
2.	2.
3.	3.

Notes Due to the smog in Mexico City, private cars can drive only during certain days of the week, according to the number on the license plate.

Have students create a Venn diagram for activity 27.

Consider conducting a follow-up discussion about driving in the United States and in Mexico, using information from the *Cultura viva* and activity 27 as a starting point.

Teacher Resources

 **Activity 6**

Answers

27 Answers will vary.

Activities

Connections
Tell students that in many ways the history of Mexico is closely connected to that of the United States. Have students choose one of the following topics and write a brief report (two to three paragraphs) to share with the class. They may use reference materials from the library or they may search the Internet to gather information for their reports. Some possible topics: Treaty of Guadalupe Hidalgo, Constitution of 1917, North American Free Trade Agreement (NAFTA), Battle of the Alamo.

Expansion
Have students identify various modes of transportation and say where they would go in each if they could.

National Standards

Communication 1.3
Comparisons 4.1, 4.2
Cultures 2.1
Connections 3.1

Teacher Resources

 Activities 12–15

 Activities 10–12

 Activity 6

 Activity 7

Answers

28 1. va
2. vamos
3. van
4. van
5. vamos
6. vas
7. voy

Activities

Critical Thinking

Say the various conjugated forms of the verb *ir* as students write the corresponding subject pronoun. Then say the subject pronouns and have the students write the corresponding verb forms.

Expansion

Review vocabulary for places people go and the means of transportation they use. Then ask questions using *ir a* followed by a place or a means of transportation: *¿Vas a un restaurante mañana? ¿Cómo vas a ir?; ¿Quién va a ir a la biblioteca? ¿Cómo vas a ir?*

National Standards

Communication
1.1

Comparisons
4.1

Idioma

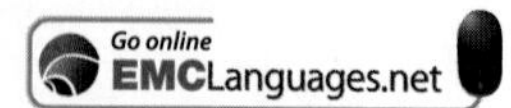

Estructura

Saying where someone is going: *ir*

- The verb *ir* (to go) is irregular in the present tense.

ir			
yo	**voy**	nosotros nosotras	**vamos**
tú	**vas**	vosotros vosotras	**vais**
Ud. él ella	**va**	Uds. ellos ellas	**van**

- The verb *ir* is usually followed by the preposition *a* (or the contraction *al*) and a destination.

*¿Por qué no vamos **a** la biblioteca?* — Why don't we go to the library?
*Voy **al** cine.* — I am going to the movies.

Note: When you want to suggest going somewhere or doing something ("Let's go somewhere/do something!"), use ***Vamos a*** **(+ a place or an infinitive)**.

¡Vamos a la ciudad hoy! — Let's go into town today!
¡Vamos a tomar el autobús! — Let's take the bus!

Práctica

28 ¿Adónde van mañana?

Completa las siguientes oraciones con la forma apropiada de *ir*.

MODELO Nuria y Rosario van al Museo Nacional de Antropología.

1. Tomás __ a la fiesta en el Zócalo, ¿no?
2. Nosotros __ a la fiesta con él, ¿verdad?
3. El señor y la señora Morales __ en avión a Veracruz.
4. Andrea y tú __ en metro a un restaurante en el D.F., ¿verdad?
5. ¡Claro! Andrea y yo __ con Mauricio al Paseo de la Reforma.
6. Tú __ a la Ciudad de México con ellos.
7. Yo __ a *(give a location)*.

Notes

Comparisons. Point out for students that in Spanish the subject can be omitted because the verb form implies who is doing the action. For example, the subject of *vamos* is understood to be *nosotros* or *nosotras*; the subject of *voy* is understood to be *yo*. Finally, explain that the word *a* is a necessary part of this expression in Spanish, but that it is not used in the English equivalent.

The preposition *a* used with the verb *ir* also contracts with the article *el*: *Voy al centro.*

29 ¿Adónde van en la ciudad?

With a classmate, take turns asking and answering questions about where these people are going in the city. You may answer either affirmatively or negatively.

MODELO Gloria / al banco
A: ¿Adónde va Gloria? Al banco, ¿verdad?
B: Sí, va al banco. / No, no va al banco.

1. don Francisco / la médica
2. los muchachos / el restaurante
3. nosotros / el dentista
4. el Sr. López / la oficina
5. tú / el parque
6. Uds. / la escuela

En la ciudad

la cafetería	*cafeteria, coffee shop*
el hospital	*hospital*
la iglesia	*church*
la oficina de correos	*post office*
el supermercado	*supermarket*

30 Todos vamos a lugares diferentes

Indica adónde van las siguientes personas.

MODELO Héctor
Héctor va a la oficina.

1. yo

2. tú

3. la señora Sabogal

4. las muchachas

5. Nicolás

6. Ud.

Answers

29
1. ¿Adónde va don Francisco? A la médica, ¿verdad?/Sí, (No, no) va a la médica.
2. ¿Adónde van los muchachos? Al restaurante, ¿verdad?/Sí, (No, no) van al restaurante.
3. ¿Adónde vamos? Al dentista, ¿verdad?/Sí, (No, no) vamos al dentista.
4. ¿Adónde va el Sr. López? A la oficina, ¿verdad?/Sí, (No, no) va a la oficina.
5. ¿Adónde vas? Al parque, ¿verdad?/Sí, (No, no) voy al parque.
6. ¿Adónde van Uds.? A la escuela, ¿verdad?/Sí, (No, no) vamos a la escuela.

30
1. ...voy al banco.
2. ...vas al cine.
3. ...va a la dentista.
4. ...van al restaurante.
5. ...va a la biblioteca.
6. ...va al médico.

Activities

Critical Thinking

Use pictures of places and of methods of transportation (overhead transparencies 23 and 24). Ask the question *¿Vas a... en...?*, according to the pictures. You may have one student ask the question and call on another for the response. If the response is not logical, a follow-up question might be *Entonces, ¿cómo vas a...?* Choose illogical methods of transportation for humor (*¿Vas a Puerto Rico en tren? Entonces, ¿cómo vas a Puerto Rico?*).

National Standards

Communication
1.1

Notes

Before beginning activity 29, remind students that they may make the sentences negative by placing the word *no* before the verb (see page 44 in *Lección 2A*). Point out also that *Sí* and *No* must be separated from the rest of the sentence by a comma.

When doing activity 29, inform students they may use *¿no?* as an alternative for *¿verdad?* in their questions.

Teacher Resources

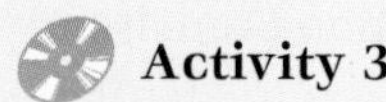

 Activity 31

Answers

31 1. ...van al parque a caballo.
2. ...vamos a la oficina en tren.
3. ...van al restaurante en bicicleta.
4. ...va al banco en moto(cicleta).
5. ...vas al Zócalo en metro.
6. ...voy a Isla Mujeres en barco.

32 Answers will vary.

Activities

Cooperative Learning

Have students bring in several magazine pictures of places they go *(el cine, el banco)*. Encourage them also to bring pictures of places they would like to go (beach, island, lake, mountains). Students should learn the words for these places before class. They should then use the pictures to discuss where various people are going (imaginary trips are fine): *Voy a la playa.; ¿Vas a la playa también?; ¿Tus amigos van a las montañas?* As a follow-up discussion, ask individual students where they are going. They should show the picture to the class as they respond.

National Standards
Communication 1.1
Connections 3.1
Comparisons 4.1

31 ¿Cómo van? 

Say how these people are going to arrive at the places indicated.

MODELO Ángela y Carlota / cine
Ángela y Carlota van al cine en autobús.

1. Uds. / parque

2. nosotros / oficina

3. Uds. / restaurante

4. Jaime / banco

5. tú / Zócalo

6. yo / Isla Mujeres

Comunicación

32 ¿Cómo vamos?

Working in pairs, alternate mentioning places in the city and suggesting how you might go to each one.

MODELO **A:** el banco
B: ¡Vamos al banco en bicicleta!

¡Vamos al banco en bicicleta!

Notes Before beginning activity 31, remind students that the bus shown in the model is commonly referred to as *el camión* in Mexico, although elsewhere in the Spanish-speaking world *camión* is the term used to refer to a truck.

For number 6, tell students that *Isla Mujeres* is an island north of Cancun just off the coast of Mexico.

Tell students that in Spanish, the contractions *al* and *del* are obligatory whenever *a* or *de* is followed by *el*, unlike in English, where it is a matter of choice whether to contract words (e.g., **can't** for **cannot**).

¡Vamos al Hotel San Gabriel!

This information card was left in your room at the Hotel San Gabriel in Mexico City. With a partner, answer the questions that follow. When you finish, ask each other two original questions.

1. ¿Dónde está el Hotel San Gabriel?
2. Necesitas transporte. ¿Cuál es el número de teléfono?
3. ¿Cómo se llama el cine? ¿Y el banco?
4. ¿Dónde está la Oficina de Turismo?
5. ¿Cuántos restaurantes hay cerca del hotel?
6. ¿La Cafetería Don Chang está cerca o lejos del hotel?
7. La Azteca es un restaurante fantástico. ¿Vas tú allí?
8. ¿Adónde van Uds. mañana?

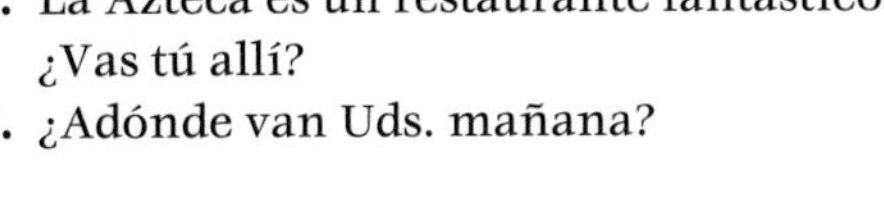

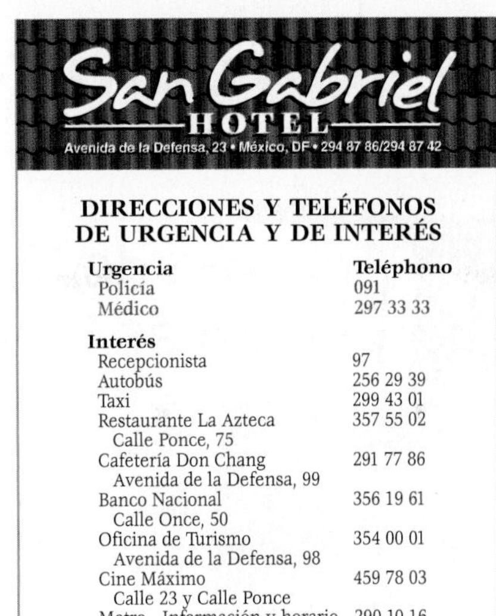

San Gabriel
HOTEL
Avenida de la Defensa, 23 • México, DF • 294 87 86/294 87 42

DIRECCIONES Y TELÉFONOS
DE URGENCIA Y DE INTERÉS

Urgencia	Teléphono
Policía	091
Médico	297 33 33
Interés	
Recepcionista	97
Autobús	256 29 39
Taxi	299 43 01
Restaurante La Azteca, Calle Ponce, 75	357 55 02
Cafetería Don Chang, Avenida de la Defensa, 99	291 77 86
Banco Nacional, Calle Once, 50	356 19 61
Oficina de Turismo, Avenida de la Defensa, 98	354 00 01
Cine Máximo, Calle 23 y Calle Ponce	459 78 03
Metro—Información y horario	290 10 16

PARA MÁS INFORMACIÓN, FAVOR LLAMAR AL/A LA RECEPCIONISTA AL 97.

Planeando un viaje a México

Plan a trip to Mexico with a classmate using the advertisements. Decide on places to visit, transportation options, schedules and other necessary details for the trip.

MODELO **A:** El lunes vamos de Tampico a Guanajuato en camión. ¿A qué hora vamos?
B: Vamos a las ocho de la mañana.
A: No, vamos a las once menos diez de la mañana.

CAMIONES TRANSMEX

Reservaciones, 965 99 88 — Información, 965 43 21

HORARIO: LUNES A VIERNES

de: a:	DF	Guadalajara	Guanajuato	Morelia	Tampico	Veracruz
DF		6:40, 9:25	7:05, 11:20	7:35, 10:00	8:00, 11:00	8:15
Guadalajara	7:20, 10:05		7:55, 12:00	8:20, 11:05	8:35, 10:40	9:25
Guanajuato	7:05, 9:15	7:35, 11:25		8:25, 11:50	8:00	No hay servicio.
Morelia	8:20, 10:00	6:40, 8:00	6:30, 7:55		7:50, 11:10	9:00, 12:00
Tampico	7:35	7:05, 9:15	8:00, 10:50	8:35, 11:25		7:20, 10:00
Veracruz	7:55, 9:00	8:20, 10:00	No hay servicio.	7:35, 10:20	7:05, 11:40	

¡TAXI YA!
Con servicio a toda la ciudad de México
• Conveniente • Cómodo
• Rápido • Y listo... ¡YA!
Llamar 24 horas . . . 577 36 79

Aerolínea Yucatecas — *Tu amigo en el aire*

Con servicio entre 12 ciudades mexicanas

• Acapulco • Chihuahua • Cuernavaca • Distrito Federal (México) • Guadalajara • Guanajuato • León • Mérida • Monterrey • Morelia • Tampico • Veracruz

los lunes - los viernes • 8 vuelos los sábados y domingos • entre Acapulco, DF, Mérida y Veracruz
Para reservaciones e información llamar al **480 12 17/482 08 19**

Notes Point out for students that daily hours for businesses and other services (such as bus and airline schedules in activity 34) may be very different from schedules students are used to in the United States.

Have students find on a map the sites mentioned in the realia on page 107.

Answers

33 1. Está en México en la Avenida de la Defensa, 23.
2. Es el dos, noventa y nueve, cuarenta y tres, cero, uno./Es el dos, cincuenta y seis, veintinueve, treinta y nueve.
3. El cine se llama Cine Máximo. El banco se llama Banco Nacional.
4. Está en la Avenida de la Defensa, 98.
5. Hay dos restaurantes.
6. Está muy cerca del hotel.
7. Sí, (No, no) voy allí.
8. Answers will vary.

34 Creative self-expression.

Activities

Expansion

Possible questions for activity 34: *Uds. están en Guanajuato y necesitan ir a Veracruz. Van en los camiones de Transmex, ¿verdad?; ¿A qué hora vamos de Guadalajara a Veracruz en camión (autobús)? Uds. están en la capital y necesitan ir a Tampico el viernes. ¿Cómo van Uds. a Tampico?; La señora Pérez necesita tomar un taxi. ¿Hay servicio de taxi en el D.F.? ¿Cómo se llama la compañía de taxis? ¿Sabes el número de teléfono?; Yo quiero ir de Monterrey a Nuevo Laredo en avión con la Aerolínea Yucatecas. ¿Hay un problema? ¿Cuál es?; ¿Cómo es el servicio de ¡Taxi Ya!?; El señor Pérez necesita ir de Veracruz al D.F. el viernes. ¿A qué hora va?; ¿Adónde vas en autobús (camión)? ¿en avión?*

National Standards

Communication
1.1, 1.2

Connections
1.3

Comparisons
4.1

Teacher Resources

Lectura Cultural
El metro de la Ciudad de México es fantástico
Activity 35
Activity 36

Answers

35 1. El metro de la Ciudad de México es moderno, limpio, barato, seguro y eficiente.
2. Identifican las estaciones del metro con símbolos y colores.
3. Hay una pirámide azteca.
4. Hay restos de un mamut.
5. Cinco millones de personas toman el metro todos los días.

36 Answers will vary.

Activities

Prereading Strategy
Have students look over the realia on page 108 and pick out cognates and other words they recognize before assigning activities 35 and 36.

Spanish for Spanish Speakers
Ask your native Spanish speakers to contribute any information they may know about Mexico, such as recent news stories, articles about celebrities and famous people and so on.

National Standards

Cultures
2.1, 2.2

Connections
3.1, 3.2

Comparisons
4.1, 4.2

Lectura cultural

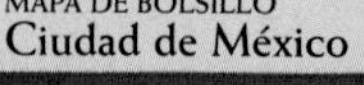

El metro de la Ciudad de México es fantástico

La pirámide azteca en la estación de Pino Suárez.

¿Vas de vacaciones a la Ciudad de México y no sabes qué hacer? ¿Por qué no pasas[1] un día fantástico usando[2] el metro? Toma la línea 2 a Chapultepec y camina por el parque. O toma la línea 3 a la estación de Pino Suárez y mira la pirámide azteca descubierta[3] en 1968 durante la construcción del metro. O toma la línea 4 a la estación de Talismán y mira los restos de un mamut[4] que tiene 13.000 años. Todos los días[5], cinco millones de personas toman el metro para ir al trabajo[6] o la escuela. Tú y tus amigos pueden[7] tomar el metro para divertirse[8]. El metro es un transporte moderno, limpio[9], seguro[10] y eficiente. ¡Vamos en metro!

Datos interesantes del metro de México, D.F.:
- Es el primer sistema que usa símbolos y colores para identificar las estaciones.
- Es el metro más barato[11] del planeta porque sólo cuesta[12] US $0,20.
- La estación Pantitlán es la estación de transbordo[13] más grande del planeta.

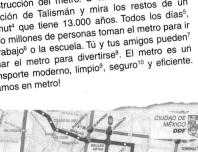

[1]spend [2]using [3]discovered [4]mammoth [5]Every day [6]work [7]can [8]have fun [9]clean [10]safe [11]cheapest [12]costs [13]transfer

35 ¿Qué recuerdas?

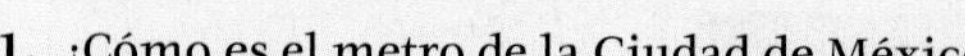

1. ¿Cómo es el metro de la Ciudad de México?
2. ¿Cómo identifican las estaciones del metro?
3. ¿Qué hay en la estación de metro Pino Suárez?
4. ¿Qué hay en la estación de metro Talismán?
5. ¿Cuántas personas toman el metro todos los días?

36 Algo personal

1. ¿Hay un sistema de metro en tu ciudad?
2. ¿Cuánto cuesta el transporte público en tu ciudad?
3. ¿Cómo son las estaciones (de metro o de bus) en tu ciudad?

- **Have you ever taken the subway? Describe your experience. How did it compare with the Mexican subway described in the article?**
- **Why do you think they built stations around the Aztec pyramid and the remains of the mammoth instead of transferring these discoveries to a museum? Is that a good idea?**

Notes

Connections. Note the cross-curricular connections to history in this reading about Mexico City.

Encourage students to visit the Web site for the Mexico City subway system:

http://www.metro.df.gob.mx

In Mexico the first two or three cars of *metro* trains are often reserved for senior citizens and mothers traveling with children. It is also interesting to note that indigenous ruins have been found when digging for the *metro*.

Autoevaluación

As a review and self-check, respond to the following:

1. In Spanish, identify five places in a city.
2. There is going to be a party in a nearby restaurant. Ask what time the party is.
3. A new girl who speaks Spanish has moved into your neighborhood. Tell her if the following places are near or far and what means of transportation you use to go to each place: la escuela, el parque, el cine.
4. What would you say in Spanish when introducing these people to your teacher: a friend named Diana? don Diego? two friends?
5. Give an example of a courteous response in Spanish when you are introduced.
6. How would you confirm that your friends are going to the movie theater near the library?
7. You are about to travel to Mexico. What would you like to see and do?

Palabras y expresiones

How many of these words and expressions do you know?

La ciudad
el banco
la biblioteca
el cine
el dentista, la dentista
la escuela
el hotel
el médico, la médica
la oficina
el parque
el restaurante

Palabras interrogativas
¿adónde?
¿cuándo?
¿por qué?
¿quiénes?

Transporte
a caballo
a pie
el autobús
el avión
el barco
la bicicleta
el caballo
el camión
el carro
en carro
en *(means of transportation)*
el metro
la moto(cicleta)
el taxi
el transporte
el tren

Verbos
caminar
ir
presento
quiero
sabes
tomar
¡vamos!

Otras expresiones
al
cerca (de)
¡claro!
del
El gusto es mío.
encantado,-a
fantástico,-a
la fiesta
lejos (de)
le/les/te presento a
porque
el problema
simpático,-a
también
Tanto gusto.
¿verdad?

Estructura

Do you remember the following grammar rules?

Making introductions: *te, le, les*

	to one person	to two or more people
informal	te	les
formal	le	les

Asking questions

- raise voice at the end of a sentence
- place a subject after the verb
- add a tag word, *¿no?* or *¿verdad?*
- use a question word *(¿cómo?, ¿cuál?, ¿qué?)* that precedes the subject

Irregular verb: *ir*

The verb *ir* is usually followed by the preposition *a* and a destination.

ir	
voy	vamos
vas	vais
va	van

Teacher Resources

 Activity 16

 pp. 49, 83

 Patinador, Escalador

Flash Cards

 **Answers**

Autoevaluación

Possible answers:

1. La biblioteca, el cine, el restaurante, el parque, la escuela, etc.
2. ¿A qué hora es la fiesta?
3. La escuela está cerca de aquí. Yo voy a la escuela a pie. El parque está cerca de aquí. Yo voy al parque en bicicleta. El cine está lejos. Yo voy al cine en metro.
4. Diana, te presento al profesor (a la profesora) de español. Don Diego, le presento al profesor (a la profesora) de español. (*Names of two friends*), les presento al profesor (a la profesora) de español.
5. Mucho gusto./Encantado (Encantada).
6. Van al cine cerca de la biblioteca, ¿verdad?/... ¿no?
7. Answers will vary.

 **Activities**

Expansion

Model the words and expressions on page 109 and have students repeat. Then call on students to use the words or expressions in sentences.

National Standards

Cultures
2.1

Connections
3.1

Notes

Extend number 7 of the *Autoevaluación* by having students locate additional information that will help them plan a trip, such as maps, restaurant names and locations, currency rates, etc.

If you have not yet done so, explain that various forms of physical contact may accompany greetings or introductions.

Depending on the participants, a handshake, hug or kiss(es) may be appropriate.

Teacher Resources

 Vocabulario I
En el centro

 Activity 25

 Activities 1–2

 Activities 1–2

 p. 62

 Activity 1

 Activity 1

Content reviewed in *Lección B*

- city destinations
- seeking and providing personal information
- transportation
- discussing schedules

 **Activities**

Critical Thinking
Ask students if the city is important in their lives. Is it a popular place to live? Does it offer important cultural events that they attend? Are there important places of interest they enjoy visiting? Discuss city life with the class and have students compare their city's downtown with what they are learning about life in Spanish-speaking cities of the world.

National Standards

Communication
1.1

Cultures
2.1

Comparisons
4.1, 4.2

Lección B Vocabulario I
En el centro

México

Museo de Arte Moderno
el museo
el edificio
METRO
El Charro
ALTO
las tiendas
ZAPATOEXPRESS
AVENIDA DE LA INDEPENDENCIA
CALLE VERSALLES
la plaza

En la ciudad hay muchos edificios grandes.
Los edificios están en el centro.
En el centro hay teatros, museos y tiendas.

Notes

Comparisons. In Spanish-speaking parts of the world, a city's downtown is often a popular place to live (in addition to offering cultural events and places of interest). Conduct a class discussion about how this compares with cities in the United States. Note that a main square *(plaza)* is often at the heart of a city or neighborhood in the Spanish-speaking world.

¿Qué vas a hacer hoy?
Voy a ir al concierto de mi cantante favorito.
ARLEQUIN
CONCIERTO: LUIS MIGUEL
LUIS MIGUEL
el teatro

1 En el centro 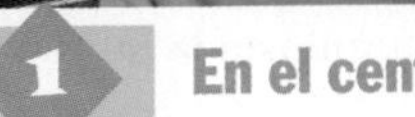

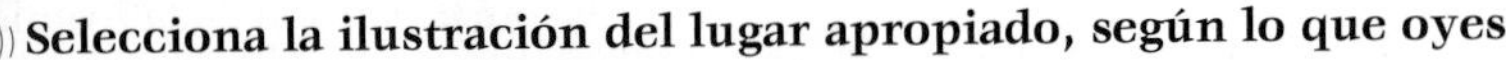
Selecciona la ilustración del lugar apropiado, según lo que oyes.

A

B

C

D

E

F

G

H

2 La ciudad

Completa las oraciones de acuerdo con las ilustraciones del Vocabulario I.

1. El autobús va por la __.
2. Gabriela y Ana van al __ de arte.
3. Luis Miguel va a estar mañana en el __ Arlequín.
4. El Museo de Arte Moderno está en la __ de la Independencia.
5. Moda In y Zapato Express son __ en la Calle Versalles.
6. Hay seis personas en la __.
7. En el __ hay muchas oficinas.
8. ¿Vamos al __ El Charro?

3 ¿Adónde vas?

Haz una lista de los lugares adónde vas.

Notes Inform students that it is not uncommon to meet someone who uses two names in Spanish (as the singer Luis Miguel, whose name appears on the marquee, does here).

Luis Miguel is one of the best-known Mexican singers of popular music. He has won the Latin Grammy award several times.

This would be a good time to play some of his music for the class if you have any of his CDs.

Teacher Resources

Activity 1

Answers

1
1. H
2. A
3. G
4. E
5. B
6. D
7. C
8. F

2
1. calle
2. museo
3. Teatro
4. Avenida
5. tiendas
6. plaza
7. edificio
8. restaurante

3 Answers will vary.

Activities

Critical Thinking
Ask students how the city shown on pages 110–111 is similar to or different from cities in the United States.

Multiple Intelligences (linguistic)
Play a CD of some of Luis Miguel's songs and have students identify and write down words they recognize.

National Standards	
Communication 1.2	Comparisons 4.1
Cultures 2.2	
Connections 3.1	

Teacher Resources

Diálogo I
Vamos al museo
Activity 4
Activity 5
Activity 6

Answers

4 1. Va al centro con Pilar.
2. No. Ella va al museo.
3. Es un edificio grande.
4. El restaurante está en la Avenida de la Independencia.

5 Answers will vary.

6 1. B
2. C
3. D
4. A

Activities

Critical Listening
Play the audio version of the dialog. Tell students to look only at the photographs while they imagine what the people are saying to one another. Have several individuals state what they believe is the main theme of the conversation.

Prereading Strategy
Instruct students to cover up the dialog with one hand and look at the photographs. Ask them to imagine where the conversation takes place and what the people are saying to one another.

National Standards

Communication
1.2

Cultures
2.1

Diálogo I Vamos al museo

TOMÁS: Olga, ¿qué vas a hacer el sábado?
OLGA: Voy a ir al centro con Pilar.

TOMÁS: ¿Van a las tiendas?
OLGA: No. Vamos al museo de arte.
TOMÁS: El museo está en un edificio grande.

OLGA: Sí, luego, vamos al restaurante El Charro. ¿Vas?
TOMÁS: ¡Claro! ¿Está el restaurante en la calle Versalles?
OLGA: No, está en la Avenida de la Independencia.

4 ¿Qué recuerdas?

1. ¿Qué va a hacer Olga el sábado?
2. ¿Va ella a las tiendas?
3. ¿Cómo es el edificio del museo?
4. ¿Dónde está el restaurante?

5 Algo personal

1. ¿Qué vas a hacer el sábado?
2. ¿Hay muchos edificios grandes en el centro de tu ciudad?
3. ¿En qué calle está tu colegio?

6 ¿Qué vas a hacer hoy?

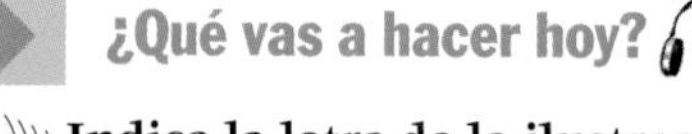

Indica la letra de la ilustración que corresponde con lo que oyes.

A

B

C

D

Notes

Native Spanish speakers tend to stand closer to one another than most people might in the United States. It is not unusual to see mothers and their teenage sons or daughters walking arm in arm as they tour ruins and museums in Mexico and throughout Europe. Also, two girls who are good friends may be walking around arm in arm in the parks or other public sites of interest. In addition, explain to students that because personal space is more limited in many Spanish-speaking countries, they should not find it particularly surprising when they are jostled a bit in lines where they are making a purchase such as admittance tickets to a museum.

Cultura viva

El Distrito Federal (el D.F.)

Mexico City is not only the capital of the country, the *Distrito Federal* is also the center of Mexico's government, economy, culture and educational system. Internationally known sites you may want to visit include *El Palacio Nacional, el Museo de Antropología* and one of the largest universities in the world, *la Universidad Autónoma de México (UNAM),* among others. Downtown, virtually every street offers an array of interesting sites and experiences, including Aztec ruins *(la Plaza de las Tres Culturas),* beautiful parks *(Alameda),* museums and art galleries *(el Palacio de Bellas Artes),* as well as many interesting colonial buildings.

Contaminación del aire (*air pollution*) en el D.F.

Mexico City also faces challenges. Like most large U.S. cities, downtown streets are crowded, noisy, polluted and frequently congested with traffic jams. In addition, early Spanish colonists constructed the city on top of the original Aztec capital, Tenochtitlán, which had been built on an island in the middle of Lake Texcoco. Consequently, parts of the city are now sinking because of this soft land, and this creates problems providing fresh drinking water to millions of residents.

When you travel to *el D.F.,* you will experience a cosmopolitan atmosphere that is both similar to and yet very different from other cities in the world. While there, you see why Mexicans take great pride in their heritage. Now they are focused on an even brighter future.

La Universidad Autónoma de México.

7 Un viaje a México

Plan an itinerary for a trip to Mexico. First, decide what you want to see and do and indicate why each site or activity interests you (e.g., *el Palacio Nacional* to see Diego Rivera's artwork in person). Next, list hotels (with addresses and rates) where you want to stay. Include in your travel plans flight schedules to and from the destinations you want to visit, including Mexico City. Finally, map out your daily schedule from beginning to end.

Está en la internet

You can find all of the information needed to complete a travel itinerary by searching the Internet. Alternative sources of information include travel agents, airlines and the library.

Answers

7 Creative self-expression.

Activities

Expansion
Select several students to share their trip preparations with the class.

Language through Action
As an optional cross-curricular activity, have students work with the school's art teacher to create a small mural in the style of Diego Rivera. Students can use long pieces of art paper and watercolors, oils, pastels or any medium available. Before assigning the project, have students research books on art at the library or search the Internet for examples of Rivera's art, especially as it relates to his murals, so students can become familiar with the artist's style. You might wish to suggest that students represent the past, the present and the future. After completing their *murales*, have students work in groups of three or four and talk in Spanish about their art. As an alternative, the activity could be done in groups.

Spanish for Spanish Speakers
Ask students to research and write an essay about the Aztec legend upon which the founding of *Tenochtitlán* is based. The report should address why an island in the middle of Lake Texcoco was chosen as the site of the Aztec capital.

Notes Another reason it is difficult to provide fresh drinking water to residents of Mexico City is that the pipes that transport the water are old and cracked by previous earthquakes the city has endured. The last major earthquake in Mexico City was in 1985.

In 1325 the Aztecs founded and began to inhabit *Tenochtitlán*, in what today is Mexico City.

National Standards	
Communication 1.1, 1.3	**Comparisons** 4.1, 4.2
Cultures 2.1, 2.2	
Connections 3.1, 3.2	

Idioma

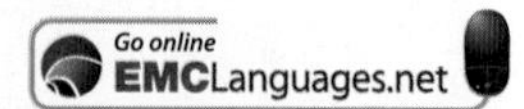

Estructura

Talking about the future: *ir a* + infinitive

Say what you are going to do or what is going to happen by using the present tense of *ir*, followed by *a* and an infinitive *(infinitivo)*.

ir + a + infinitive

*Laura **va a ser** médica.*	Laura is going to be a doctor.
*Uds. **van a estar** en México, ¿verdad?*	You are going to be in Mexico, right?

Práctica

8 Van a ir a diferentes lugares 

Ask where these people are going to go tomorrow in downtown Guadalajara, using tag questions.

MODELO Juán / restaurante El Amanecer
Juán va a ir al restaurante El Amanecer, ¿verdad?

1. Uds. / museo de arte
2. Manolo / fiesta en la plaza
3. Fabiola y Gerardo / teatro
4. nosotros / tiendas
5. Doris / oficina
6. Ud. / banco
7. tú / biblioteca
8. doña Ester / médico

¿Adónde van a ir chicas?

9 ¿Adónde van a ir en Cuernavaca?

Haz oraciones lógicas usando palabras y expresiones de cada columna.

MODELO Los Martínez van a ir al cine a las seis.

los Martínez	centro	el lunes
la Sra. Sandoval	concierto	en la tarde
nosotros	restaurante	a las seis
yo	tienda	a las 10:30 P.M.
doña Angelina	edificio nuevo	el domingo
Ariel Tovar	museo	al mediodía
tú	plaza	en la mañana
Mónica y Jairo Ruíz	teatro	
	cine	

Teacher Resources

 Activity 8

 Activities 3–4

 Activities 3–5

 p. 14

 Activity 2

 Activity 2

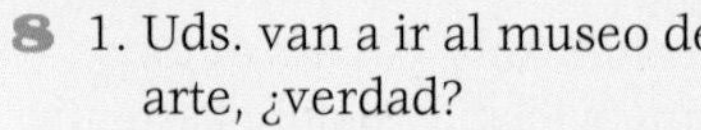

Answers

8
1. Uds. van a ir al museo de arte, ¿verdad?
2. Manolo va a ir a la fiesta en la plaza, ¿verdad?
3. Fabiola y Gerardo van a ir al teatro, ¿verdad?
4. Nosotros vamos a ir a las tiendas, ¿verdad?
5. Doris va a ir a la oficina, ¿verdad?
6. Ud. va a ir al banco, ¿verdad?
7. Tú vas a ir a la biblioteca, ¿verdad?
8. Doña Ester va a ir al médico, ¿verdad?

9 Answers will vary.

Activities

Expansion
After reviewing activity 9, ask students how people are going to go to the places named: *¿Cómo van los Martínez al centro?*

Students with Special Needs
Review the present tense of the verb *ir* before presenting the future with *ir* + *a* + infinitive.

National Standards

Communication
1.1

Comparisons
4.1

Notes

Comparisons. You may wish to tell students that in addition to being used to indicate a future action, *vamos a* + infinitive may also be used to express a suggestion similar to **let's** or **shall we?** in English.

Comunicación

10 En el Distrito Federal

As part of a summer study program, you have the opportunity to take classes at *la UNAM* and a classmate has prepared a list to help you find your way around the city. Answer the questions about places to go in the city.

1. ¿Cómo vas a ir a los museos de Chapultepec?
2. ¿Qué museo de arte está en Chapultepec?
3. ¿A qué museos vas a ir?
4. Tomas un taxi a la Calle 16 de Septiembre. ¿De qué plaza vas a estar cerca?
5. ¿Dónde está el restaurante con "mole fantástico"?
6. ¿Dónde está el Palacio de Bellas Artes? ¿Cómo vas a ir allí?
7. Quiero ir al Museo de Arte Moderno. ¿Sabes el número de teléfono del museo?

Adónde ir en el D.F.

Parque de Chapultepec (ir en metro):
- Museo Nacional de Antropología
- Museo Nacional de Historia (en el Castillo)
- Casa del Lago (parque de atracciones)
- Museo Tecnológico
- Museo de Arte Moderno (en Av. Reforma): 776-83-41
- Museo de Historia Natural

Otros lugares interesantes:
- Palacio de Bellas Artes (museo y teatro en el Centro Histórico)

— Está en la Alameda Central y la Avenida Juárez. (camiones Nº 16 ó 52) Información: 683-48-05

- El Zócalo (plaza central)

— Calle 16 de Septiembre (cerca de la Calle Seminario)

Restaurantes:
- La Bodega (¡Mole fantástico!)

Popocatépetl 25, Colonia Hipódromo Condesa, Zona Centro
Teléfono: 525-84-73

- SpaceNet Café

Calz. del Hueso 160 local 3-B Fuentes Plaza Ex Hacienda Coapa, Zona Sur
Teléfono: 567-35-52

11 Sus propios planes

Working in pairs, use the list from the previous activity to make your own plans for what you are going to do while in Mexico City.

MODELO
A: ¿Vamos a ir al Museo de Antropología?
B: Sí. Vamos a ir allí en taxi.

12 ¿Qué van a hacer mañana?

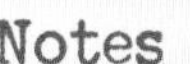

Talk with two classmates about going downtown tomorrow. Start by asking each other what you are going to do. Then ask where you are going to go, how you are going to get there, etc. Use a variety of expressions and as many new words as you can.

MODELO
A: ¿Qué van a hacer mañana?
B: Voy a ir al centro.
C: ¿Cómo vas a ir?
B: Voy a ir en metro.

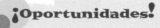

¡Oportunidades!

Se habla español en México y en tu ciudad

It is not always necessary to travel to Mexico or to go a great distance in order to use Spanish. In the United States, nearly every community offers opportunities to apply language skills you are learning this year. Many American cities have large Spanish-speaking populations, so you may find yourself using your new language skills in a restaurant, at a museum, in a store or while you are simply strolling along a city street. Knowing Spanish opens doors and offers opportunities you might otherwise never experience!

Notes Tell the class how addresses are generally given in Spanish-speaking countries: the street name is followed by the number. See if any student can guess that *Nº* is an abbreviation for *Número* before telling the class.

UNAM (activity 10) is the abbreviation for the *Universidad Nacional Autónoma de México* in Mexico City. *UNAM* offers virtually free public education to college students in Mexico. More than 300,000 students attend *UNAM*. The library, which features mosaic murals by Juan O'Gorman, is one of the most famous buildings on the campus. See page 113 for a photo.

Answers

10
1. Voy a ir a los museos en metro.
2. El Museo de Arte Moderno está en Chapultepec.
3. Answers will vary.
4. Voy a estar cerca del Zócalo.
5. Está en Popocatépetl 25 Hipódromo Condesa, Zona Centro.
6. El Palacio de Bellas Artes está en el Centro Histórico (en la Alameda Central y la Avenida Juárez). Voy a ir allí en el autobús (camión) número dieciséis o el autobús (camión) número cincuenta y dos.
7. Sí. El número de teléfono es el siete, setenta y seis, ochenta y tres, cuarenta y uno.

11 Creative self-expression.

12 Answers will vary.

Activities

Communities

Ask students to name businesses and organizations in your community where Spanish is commonly used on a daily basis. Then ask if they can name radio or television stations that use Spanish extensively. Finally, ask students what other opportunities they have to use Spanish in your community.

Prereading Activity

Before starting activity 10, be sure students understand the realia *Adónde ir en el D.F.* Ask what the places named are (Anthropology Museum, History Museum, etc.).

National Standards	
Communication 1.1	Comparisons 4.1
Cultures 2.1	Communities 5.1
Connections 3.1	

Teacher Resources

 **Vocabulario I**
En el restaurante

 **Activity 26**

 **Activity 5**

 **Activity 6**

 **pp. 61, 88**

 **p. 13**

 **Activity 3**

 **Activity 3**

Activities

Communities
Ask students for the name of a local restaurant that serves Mexican food. See if students know what the restaurant name means. Then ask what foods are served there.

Technology
Have students search the Internet for information about Mexican food. They may find restaurants, recipes, articles about Mexican cuisine or any other information of interest.

National Standards
Connections 3.1, 3.2

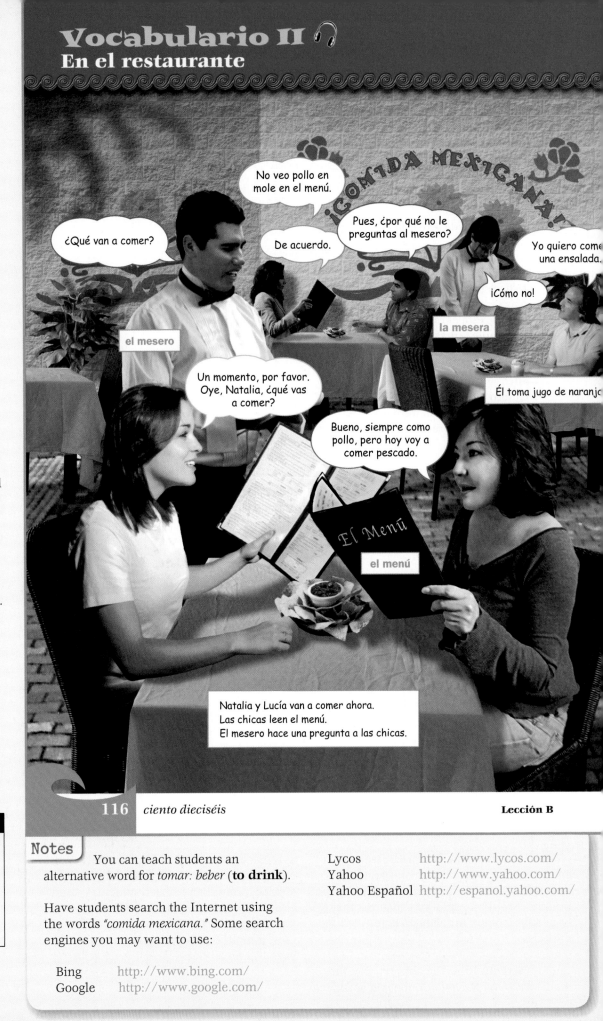

Vocabulario II
En el restaurante

¡COMIDA MEXICANA!

No veo pollo en mole en el menú.

¿Qué van a comer?

De acuerdo.

Pues, ¿por qué no le preguntas al mesero?

Yo quiero come
una ensalada.

¡Cómo no!

la mesera

el mesero

Él toma jugo de naranja

Un momento, por favor. Oye, Natalia, ¿qué vas a comer?

Bueno, siempre como pollo, pero hoy voy a comer pescado.

El Menú

el menú

Natalia y Lucía van a comer ahora.
Las chicas leen el menú.
El mesero hace una pregunta a las chicas.

Notes You can teach students an alternative word for *tomar: beber* (**to drink**).

Have students search the Internet using the words *"comida mexicana."* Some search engines you may want to use:

Bing	http://www.bing.com/
Google	http://www.google.com/
Lycos	http://www.lycos.com/
Yahoo	http://www.yahoo.com/
Yahoo Español	http://espanol.yahoo.com/

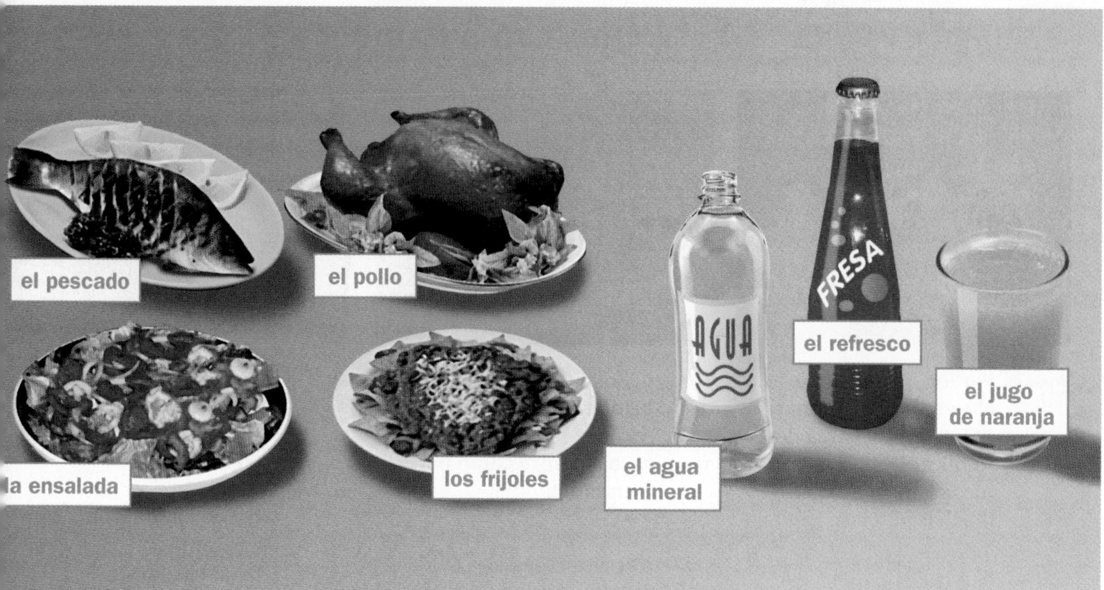

 ¿Dónde está? 

 Di si lo que oyes está en un restaurante o en un colegio.

Está en un restaurante.

Está en un colegio.

 ¿Qué sabes?

Haz una lista de tres comidas y tres bebidas.

15 En el restaurante

Completa las siguientes oraciones en forma lógica.

1. Las chicas leen en el __ lo que hay para comer y para tomar.
2. El __ pregunta a las chicas "¿Qué van a comer?".
3. Natalia y Lucía toman __ mineral.
4. La __ que toma el señor de camisa azul es un jugo de naranja.
5. La señora quiere pollo en mole de __ pero no está en el menú.
6. Lucía quiere pescado para __ .

¡Extra!

Más bebidas y comidas

Para tomar:

el café	*coffee*
el chocolate	*hot chocolate*
la gaseosa, el refresco	*soft drink*
la leche	*milk*
el té	*tea*

Para comer:

la carne	*meat*
la ensalada	*salad*
la hamburguesa	*hamburger*
el pan	*bread*
las papas fritas	*french fries*
el postre	*dessert*

Notes

Point out that the use of the definite article *el* with the feminine noun *agua* (shown in the illustration) is an exception to the rule that students have already learned. Also, inform the class that it is more common for diners in Spanish-speaking countries to have *agua mineral* with a meal than tap water.

Note that in Mexico, tortillas are eaten as much as bread is eaten in the United States.

Teacher Resources

 **Activity 13**

 **Activity 6**

Answers

13 1. Está en un colegio.
2. Está en un restaurante.
3. Está en un restaurante.
4. Está en un colegio.
5. Está en un colegio.
6. Está en un restaurante.

14 Discuss the lists. Find out if students can name other foods.

15 1. menú
2. mesero
3. agua
4. bebida
5. comida
6. comer

Activities

Multiple Intelligences (bodily-kinesthetic)

Give students a simple Mexican recipe. Then have students prepare the food and share it with the class. (You may want to make arrangements with a Family and Consumer Sciences instructor in the building to prepare the food during school hours.)

National Standards
Communication 1.2
Cultures 2.2
Connections 3.1

Teacher Resources

 **Diálogo II**
¿Qué van a comer?
Activity 16
Activity 17
Activity 18

Answers

16 1. Está cerca de la biblioteca, en la Avenida de la Independencia.
2. Tomás siempre come pollo en mole.
3. Olga va a comer pescado.
4. No, ella va a comer unos frijoles.

17 Answers will vary.

18 1. B
2. C
3. A
4. D

Activities

Critical Listening
Play the audio version of the dialog. Have students cover up the words with one hand to promote the development of good listening skills. Ask where the dialog takes place (nearby and inside *el restaurante El Charro*).

Prereading Strategy
Have students cover up the dialog with one hand and look at the photographs. Ask them to imagine where the conversation takes place and what the people are saying to one another.

National Standards
Communication 1.2
Comparisons 4.1

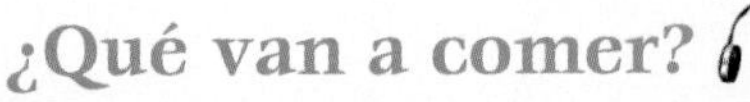

Diálogo II ¿Qué van a comer?

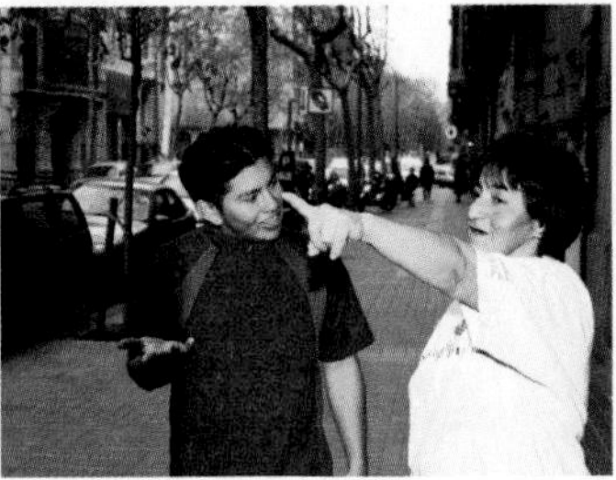

TOMÁS: Perdón, ¿sabe dónde está el restaurante El Charro?
SEÑORA: ¡Sí! Está allí, cerca de la biblioteca, en la Avenida de la Independencia.
TOMÁS: Muchas gracias.

TOMÁS: Hola, Olga. Hola, Pilar.
OLGA: ¡Hola, Tomás! Oye, ¿qué vas a comer?
TOMÁS: Yo siempre como pollo en mole.

MESERA: ¿Qué van a comer, señoritas?
OLGA: Este... quiero el pescado y un refresco.
PILAR: Yo voy a comer unos frijoles y a tomar un jugo de naranja.
MESERA: De acuerdo.

16 ¿Qué recuerdas?

1. ¿Dónde está el restaurante El Charro?
2. ¿Qué come Tomás siempre?
3. ¿Qué va a comer Olga?
4. ¿Va Pilar a comer una ensalada?

17 Algo personal 

1. ¿Dónde está tu restaurante favorito?
2. ¿Qué comida vas a comer allí?
3. ¿Tomas agua mineral, jugo de naranja o refresco?

18 ¿Cuál es la respuesta correcta? 

 **Escoge la letra de la respuesta correcta.**

A. Sí, pero hoy no quiero pollo en mole.
B. Está allí, cerca de la biblioteca.
C. Pues, un momento, por favor... Voy a comer pescado hoy.
D. Quiero tomar agua mineral, por favor.

¡Extra!

Para ser natural

Do you ever use a word while you are talking just to fill in the conversation while you are thinking, such as **well, um** or **hey**? Adding some of these pause words to conversations will make your speech sound more natural:

a ver	*let's see*
bueno	*okay, well*
este	*well, so*
mira	*look, hey*
oye	*hey, listen*
pues	*thus, well, so, then*
es que...	*well, it's just that...*

Notes A reproducible student answer sheet for activity 18 has been provided for your convenience if you choose to use it.

Cultura Viva II

Go online EMCLanguages.net

Unos tamales deliciosos.

Salir a comer en México

Mexican cuisine consists of much more than *enchiladas, tacos, tamales, quesadillas* and *burritos*. Each region of Mexico has its own particular type of food. In Mexico City, restaurants and cafés are everywhere. To eat well at reasonable prices, imitate the Mexicans and make your main meal *(la comida principal)* a large, late lunch *(el almuerzo)*.

Tacos en la taquería.

Mole is one of the most popular dishes, consisting of a thick, spicy, dark brown sauce of various chiles, sesame seeds, chocolate, herbs and spices. Served over chicken *(pollo)* or turkey *(pavo)*, it is called *mole poblano*. You can also eat crispy chicken in a rosticería, order standard Mexican cuisine such as *tacos* or *enchiladas* at a *taquería*, or try fruit shakes, sodas, ice cream or fruit salads at a juice *(jugo)* shop. Other eating choices range from inexpensive coffeehouses and pastry shops to international Chinese, Japanese, French and Middle Eastern restaurants. Beverage choices are varied, too, and consist of popular fruit drinks *(jugos)*, milk, bottled mineral waters *(aguas minerales)*, soft drinks with or without ice *(hielo)* and much more.

TIPOS DE PLATOS

Entrada

Es el primer plato de una comida. Usualmente es una sopa, una crema, un coctel de mariscos o de frutas, o un antipasto.

Ensalada

Puede servir de acompañamiento al plato fuerte, o como plato único cuando es con pollo o mariscos.

Plato fuerte

El pollo, las carnes y pescados son generalmente la base de esta parte de la comida.

Postre

Es el tercer o cuarto plato en una comida. Debe ser dulce y los cubiertos que se usan para comerlo son una cuchara pequeña y un tenedor, también pequeño.

19 Salir a comer en México 

Contesta las siguientes preguntas.

1. ¿Hay muchos restaurantes en el Distrito Federal?
2. ¿Qué comida es muy popular en México?
3. ¿Adónde vas a ir para comer pollo rostizado en México?
4. ¿Adónde vas a ir para comer tacos y enchiladas en México?
5. ¿Qué hay para tomar en México?
6. ¿Cuántos tipos de platos *(courses)* hay?

Notes Explain that shopping for food also entails cultural traditions. Most Mexican families buy fresh food daily, often at a local market *(mercado)* that features a great variety of produce and specialty items.

Corn tortillas are an important staple in nearly all Mexican meals. They can be eaten alone or with other ingredients in tacos, enchiladas, burritos and quesadillas.

Teacher Resources

 Activity 19

 Activity 4

 Activity 4

Answers

19
1. Sí, hay muchos restaurantes en el Distrito Federal.
2. El mole (poblano) es muy popular.
3. Voy a ir a la rosticería.
4. Voy a ir a la taquería.
5. Hay jugos, leche, aguas minerales, refrescos, etc. (Students may decide to add other nonactive vocabulary from the *¡Extra!*.)
6. Hay cuatro tipos.

Activities

Communities

Arrange a field trip to a local Mexican restaurant so students have an opportunity to try some of the foods they are learning about. While on the trip, require that everyone use Spanish to reinforce the value of the trip for both cultural and linguistic benefits.

Expansion

Have students create a list of all the foods they have learned in Spanish. Then have them use a dictionary and find five other words they would like to know.

National Standards
Cultures 2.1, 2.2
Connections 3.1
Comparisons 4.1, 4.2

Teacher Resources

 Activity 20

 Activities 7–11

 Activities 7–11

 p. 148

 Activity 5

 Activity 5

Answers

20 All questions begin with *¿Comes...?* and all answers begin with *Sí, (No, no) como....*

Activities

Critical Thinking
Have students find examples of several infinitives that end in *-er* in the Spanish/English glossary at the end of *¡Aventura! 1*. Supply a list or ask students to create one. As an extension to this, have students find additional infinitives in magazine or newspaper articles.

Students with Special Needs
Practice verb conjugation using choral response to each form of the verbs *comer, comprender* and *leer*. Start with the *yo* form of each verb. Then ask for the *tú* form of each verb, and so on, until students have practiced all forms of each verb.

National Standards

Communication
1.1

Connections
3.2

Idioma

Estructura

Saying what someone does: present tense of *-er* verbs

- Form the present tense of regular *-er* verbs, such as *comer* (to eat), *comprender* (to understand) and *leer* (to read), by first removing the *-er* ending and then attaching endings that correspond to each of the subject pronouns shown in this chart.

comer			
yo	com**o**	nosotros nosotras	com**emos**
tú	com**es**	vosotros vosotras	com**éis**
Ud. él ella	com**e**	Uds. ellos ellas	com**en**

- Three additional verbs that end in *-er*, *hacer* (to do, to make), *saber* (to know information) and *ver* (to see), are regular **except** for the yo forms.

hacer yo ***hago***   *saber yo* ***sé***   *ver yo* ***veo***

- In addition, the *vosotros* form of *ver* does not require an accent mark: *vosotros* ***veis***.

Veo *la calle Versalles.*
*¿****Veis*** *vosotros la Avenida Suárez en el mapa?*

Práctica

20 ¿Qué comes?

Working in pairs, take turns asking questions about whether each of you does or does not eat the items listed.

MODELO tacos
A: ¿Comes tacos?
B: Sí, (No, no) como tacos.

1. ensalada
2. frijoles
3. pescado
4. pollo

Notes This might be a good time to practice the conjugation of the verb *beber*.

Point out the similarities in forming regular *-ar* and *-er* verbs. Show students how to remove the infinitive ending and add endings that correspond with the subject pronouns, as indicated in the paradigm.

21 Tenemos mucho en común

Read the following statements and say who else does the same thing, according to the cue in parentheses. Add an expression such as *pues* before each sentence.

MODELO Leo periódicos en español y comprendo muy bien. (Elena)
Pues, Elena lee periódicos en español y comprende muy bien también.

1. Josefina lee una revista y toma jugo de naranja. (yo)
2. El señor y la señora Correa leen libros en español. (nosotros)
3. El profesor comprende inglés y español. (José y Ana)
4. Comemos pescado y ensalada en el centro hoy. (los Peña)
5. Roberto come tacos en el restaurante Los Rancheros. (tú)

Leo periódicos en español.

22 ¿Comprenden y hablan inglés y español?

Say that the following people all understand and speak English and Spanish.

MODELO Alejandro
Alejandro comprende y habla inglés y español.

1. yo
2. tú
3. mi amiga y yo
4. el profesor
5. los estudiantes en la clase de español
6. la chica nueva

23 En el restaurante El Charro

Complete the following paragraph with the present tense of the verbs in parentheses.

Los viernes, mi amiga Pilar y yo siempre *(1. comer)* en el restaurante El Charro. Hoy muchos chicos del colegio *(2. comer)* aquí. En la mesa número uno, Paco y María *(3. leer)* el menú. Paco no *(4. saber)* qué comer. María siempre *(5. comer)* pescado. En la mesa dos, el mesero pregunta a Jorge, Daniel y Patricia qué van a comer. Ellos *(6. hacer)* una pregunta al mesero: "Nosotros no *(7. ver)* tacos en el menú. ¿Hay tacos aquí?" "Sí, ¡cómo no!" responde el mesero. En la mesa tres estamos Graciela y yo. Graciela *(8. leer)* el menú. Yo siempre *(9. comer)* ensalada, pero no *(10. saber)* qué tomar hoy. Graciela dice "Un momento, por favor". Yo *(11. ver)* que ella no *(12. comprender)* una palabra del menú. Luego, ella dice "¡Ahora *(13. comprender)*! Yo quiero el pollo en mole y un refresco por favor". "De acuerdo".

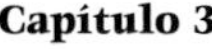

Notes Because the *vosotros/vosotras* verb forms are included in *¡Aventura!* for passive recognition only, you are free to determine whether students must learn the corresponding verb forms. If your students are going to learn to conjugate verbs with *vosotros* and *vosotras*, you may modify one of the existing sentences for activities such as 22 or simply add a sentence or two to each activity and have students use *vosotros* and *vosotras* when conjugating the corresponding verbs.

Teacher Resources

Activity 22

Answers

21 Possible answers:
1. Pues, yo leo una revista y tomo jugo de naranja también.
2. Bueno, nosotros leemos libros en español también.
3. Oye, José y Ana comprenden inglés y español también.
4. Bueno, los Peña comen pescado y ensalada en el centro hoy también.
5. Pues, tú comes tacos en el restaurante Los Rancheros también.

22
1. Yo comprendo y hablo inglés y español.
2. Tú comprendes y hablas inglés y español.
3. Mi amiga y yo comprendemos y hablamos inglés y español.
4. El profesor comprende y habla inglés y español.
5. Los estudiantes en la clase de español comprenden y hablan inglés y español.
6. La chica nueva comprende y habla inglés y español.

23 1. comemos; 2. comen; 3. leen; 4. sabe; 5. come; 6. hacen; 7. vemos; 8. lee; 9. como; 10. sé; 11. veo; 12. comprende; 13. comprendo

National Standards

Connections
3.1

Teacher Resources

Activity 25

Answers

24 Possible answers:

1. Graciela comprende las matemáticas.
2. Camilo come una ensalada.
3. Las muchachas leen el menú.
4. Ellos no comprenden el mapa.
5. Edgar y Vivian leen el periódico.
6. Monica come pescado.

25 Creative self-expression.

Activities

Cooperative Learning
In pairs, students should take turns inviting one another to do activities *(comer, estudiar, tomar el autobús,* etc.) and to go to various places *(cine, teatro, restaurante,* etc.). They may accept or refuse any invitation. Students should expand upon the conversation by saying how and when they are going to go and any other details they wish.

Students with Special Needs
Model another sentence for activity 24.

National Standards
Communication 1.1, 1.2

24 Unas personas en mi comunidad

Using the verbs *comer, comprender* and *leer*, tell what these people are doing.

MODELO el chico
El chico come pollo.

1. Graciela

2. Camilo

3. las muchachas

4. ellos

5. Edgar y Vivian

6. Mónica

25 ¿Qué hacen?

Working with a partner, read the following statements about Alfredo and his friends. Tell your partner that you do the same things as Alfredo, and then ask what your partner does.

MODELO **A:** Alfredo va a un colegio grande en el centro.
B: Pues, yo también voy a un colegio grande en el centro. ¿Y tú?
A: Yo (no) voy a un colegio grande en el centro.

1. Alfredo sabe historia.
2. Alfredo siempre lee muchas revistas y periódicos.
3. Las muchachas leen el menú.
4. Alfredo y Tomás hacen muchas preguntas en la clase de biología.
5. Alfredo comprende español.
6. Alfredo, Rebeca y Tomás comen pescado y pollo.

Alicia y Enrique van a un colegio grande en el centro.

Notes The Appendices contain a grammar review and a reference section on verb conjugations. Refer to the chart anytime you would like additional help explaining verb conjugation to students. The reference provides a concise and comprehensive review of both regular and irregular verb forms.

26 ¿Qué ves?

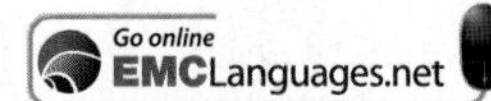

Say what these people do, see or know, according to what you see in each illustration.

1. Gabriel y María

2. ellos

3. Mónica

4. Diego

5. los Montoya

6. la Sra. Ruiz

Comunicación

27 En El Charro

In groups of four, two students play the role of friends who are considering going to a popular restaurant in town, El Charro. The other two students should pretend they often go to eat at El Charro. Then, four of you meet on the street and discuss the restaurant (the restaurant's name, if it is new, where it is, etc.). Be sure to ask your friends what they eat when they go to El Charro. Then say what you are going to eat when you go there. Switch roles.

Estrategia

The importance of reviewing

Whenever you do an activity that requires you to be creative, look at previous activities, dialogs, readings, etc. for words, grammar and cultural information you have already learned that may be useful in the new activity (e.g., the word *nuevo* in activities 9 and 22, asking for or giving names in activities 27 and 28, the question-asking words for activities 27 and 28). This recombining of old and new content will help you remember what you learned. It will also help you express yourself naturally in ever more complex situations.

28 ¿Qué leen los estudiantes en la clase?

Survey your classmates to find out how many are reading a book right now. Next, find out the names of the books and how many students are reading each one. Finally, summarize your findings in a short paragraph.

Hay seis estudiantes que leen libros. Uno lee Marianela. Dos leen

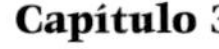

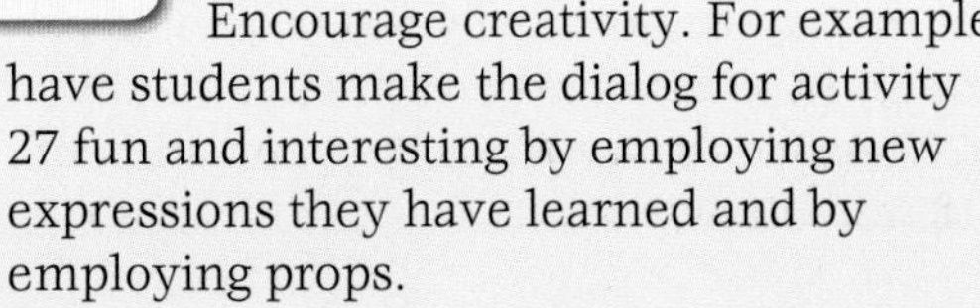

Notes Encourage creativity. For example, have students make the dialog for activity 27 fun and interesting by employing new expressions they have learned and by employing props.

Teacher Resources

Activity 6

Answers

26 1. Gabriel y María ven el autobús (camión).
2. (Ellos) no saben el número de teléfono de Juan.
3. Mónica hace una pregunta.
4. Diego hace la comida.
5. Los Montoya ven el edificio.
6. La Sra. Ruiz sabe la dirección del cine.

27 Creative self-expression.

28 Creative self-expression.

Activities

Cooperative Learning

As a follow-up and reinforcement to writing their answers, have students pair up to ask and answer questions about what the people in activity 26 do, see or know, according to the illustrations.

Multiple Intelligences (bodily-kinesthetic/linguistic)

Have students draw and label the objects from the lesson (e.g., places and foods). Display the drawings around the room or use them to review vocabulary.

National Standards

Communication
1.1

Connections
3.1

Communities
5.1

Teacher Resources

Lectura personal
Activity 29
Activity 30

Answers

29 1. Está en un restaurante de donde ve el Zócalo.
2. Imagina el Zócalo en diferentes épocas de la historia.
3. La Ciudad de México era una isla desierta en 1325.
4. El nombre de la Ciudad de México era Tenochtitlán.
5. Hernán Cortés conquistó a los aztecas en 1525.

30 Answers will vary.

Activities

Multiple Intelligences (musical)
Working with a music teacher, ask if students are interested in learning a musical piece by a Mexican singer or composer. Have students work in pairs and perform the piece in class.

Technology
Have students search the Internet to find out more about one of the points mentioned in the *Lectura personal* (Mexican museums, history of Mexico). They should then write a short summary about what they learned.

National Standards
Cultures 2.2
Connections 3.1, 3.2
Comparisons 4.1, 4.2

Lectura personal

Dirección http://www.emcp.com/músico/aventura1/

Archivo Edición Ver Favoritos Herramientas Ayuda

página principal | miembros | e-diario

Nombre: **Xavier Rodríguez Guerra**
Edad: **18 años**
Ciudad natal: **Chicago**
Comida favorita: **pollo en mole**
Cantante favorito: **Alejandro Sanz**

¡Fantástico concierto en Ciudad de México! Gracias, amigos. Nunca[1] voy a olvidar[2] esta ciudad de más de veinte millones de personas, edificios impresionantes y museos famosos. ¡Es una ciudad extraordinaria! Ahora estoy en un restaurante y veo el Zócalo. Imagino esta plaza en diferentes épocas de la historia... En 1325 era[3] una isla desierta en el lago[4] Texcoco donde los mexicas se establecieron[5].

En 1519 Tenochtitlán (hoy Ciudad de México) era la capital del imperio azteca, una ciudad grande, importante, magnífica. Los palacios y las casas estaban[6] en chinampas[7] y las personas se desplazaban[8] por canales. En 1525, cuando Hernán Cortés conquistó[9] a los aztecas, la ciudad era ruinas y destrucción. Hoy el Zócalo es la plaza más grande del mundo[10].

[1]Never [2]to forget [3]it was [4]lake [5]settled down [6]were [7]pieces of land floating on a lake [8]traveled [9]conquered [10]world

¿Qué recuerdas?

1. ¿Dónde está Xavier cuando escribe el e-diario?
2. ¿Qué imagina Xavier?
3. ¿Qué era la Ciudad de México en 1325?
4. ¿Cuál era el nombre de la Ciudad de México en 1519?
5. ¿Cuándo conquistó Hernán Cortés a los aztecas?

- How has Mexico City changed over time? How long has it been a capital city?
- What's the name of Mexico City's main plaza? How does it compare with your town's main square?

Algo personal

1. ¿Cuántos años tiene la Ciudad de México? ¿Cuántos años tiene tu ciudad?
2. ¿Qué grupo indígena habitó en la región donde tú vives?
3. ¿Hay una plaza en tu ciudad? Compara tu *town square* con el Zócalo en la Ciudad de México.

Notes

The Aztec capital *Tenochtitlán* was characterized by its canals. Mexico City's soft land base is one reason the city is susceptible to earthquakes.

Comparisons. Explain to students that *el D.F.* is a federal district and is comparable to the District of Columbia, or Washington, D.C.

Mexico City is growing by 50,000 people per month. Population experts predict that by 2020 Mexico City will reach a population of 21,8 million people.

Mexico City is located in the southern portion of the Valley of Mexico at an altitude of 7,349 feet.

¿Qué aprendí?

Autoevaluación

As a review and self-check, respond to the following:

1. Ask a friend what he or she is going to do today.
2. If you were in Mexico City, name some things you might see.
3. Tell a friend what you are going to do this week (go to school at 8:00 A.M. on Monday, study in the library on Tuesday, etc.).
4. What opportunities does knowing Spanish offer you?
5. Name four or five things you can order from a menu in Spanish.
6. Imagine you are driving around town. Name in Spanish two or three buildings you see.

Palabras y expresiones

How many of these words and expressions do you know?

En la ciudad
la avenida
la calle
el centro
el edificio
el museo
la plaza
el teatro
la tienda

En un restaurante
el agua (mineral)
la bebida
la comida
la ensalada
los frijoles
el jugo
el menú
el mesero, la mesera
la naranja
el pescado
el pollo
el refresco

Otras expresiones
ahora
bueno
el cantante, la cantante
¡cómo no!
el concierto
de acuerdo
favorito,-a
grande
hacer una pregunta
hoy
el momento
mucho,-a
oye
pero
pues
siempre

Verbos
comer
hacer
ir a (+ *infinitive*)
leer
preguntar
saber
tomar
¡vamos a (+ *infinitive*)!
ver

Estructura

Do you remember the following grammar rules?

Present tense of *-er* verbs

Some regular *-er* verbs include ***comer***, ***comprender*** and ***leer***.

comer	
como	comemos
comes	coméis
come	comen

Talking about the future: *ir* + *a* + infinitive

ir + *a* + infinitive is the equivalent to what someone is "going" to do in the near future.
***Voy a ir** a la fiesta.* **I am going to go** to the party.

Museo de Antropología.

Notes

Comparisons. Have students compare large cities in the United States and Mexico City.

Cultures. Two popular gathering places in Mexico City are the *Zona Rosa* and *Polanco.* Both offer an incredible variety of shops, sidewalk cafés and elegant restaurants. Another favorite weekend spot is the floating gardens called Xochimilco—a series of canals left over from the former Aztec capital.

Teacher Resources

 **Activity 12**

 **pp. 40, 12**

 **Castor, Parejas, Crucigrama**

Flash Cards

Answers

Autoevaluación

Possible answers:

1. ¿Qué vas a hacer hoy?
2. El teatro, la tienda, los edificios grandes, el restaurante, la plaza, el museo, el Palacio de Bellas Artes, el Zócalo, el Parque de Chapultepec, etc.
3. Voy a ir al colegio a las ocho de la mañana el lunes. Voy a estudiar en la biblioteca el martes. Voy a ir al cine el miércoles. Voy a comer en mi restaurante favorito el jueves. Voy a ir al centro el viernes. Voy a caminar en el parque el sábado. Voy a ir al museo el domingo.
4. Answers will vary. Whether traveling or staying in the United States, students may be able to communicate with someone in Spanish when ordering from a menu, when shopping in a store or strolling through their own hometown.
5. Ensalada, pollo, pescado, frijoles, un refresco, jugo de naranja, agua mineral, etc.
6. Veo un cine, un teatro, un restaurante, etc.

National Standards

Cultures
2.1, 2.2

Connections
3.1

Comparisons
4.1

Teacher Resources

 *Frida Kahlo, una artista universal*

Answers

Preparación

1. B
2. D
3. C
4. E
5. A

Activities

Critical Thinking

Have the students guess the meaning of *pintora*, pointing out the relationship to *pintar*. Then ask if students can guess what words ending in *-ora* mean (the word ending *-ora* signifies a person who does the activity indicated by the stem of the word).

Multiple Intelligences

Using visual examples, talk with students about Frida Kahlo's art. Ask questions about themes in her art, techniques and anything else that you or your students wish to discuss.

National Standards

Cultures
2.2

Connections
3.1, 3.2

Tú lees

Conexión con otras disciplinas: arte

Estrategia

Anticipating special vocabulary
It will be easier for you to read and understand specialized subject matter if you try anticipating some of the words and expressions you may encounter. Identifying specialized vocabulary beforehand will help you zero in on what a writer is saying since your mind will already be thinking about the topic. For example, in this reading you will learn about the famous Mexican artist Frida Kahlo. What words would you anticipate might appear in the reading?

Preparación

Selecciona las palabras de la columna I que van con las palabras en inglés de la columna II.

I	II
1. un estilo	A a painting
2. un autorretrato	B. a style
3. una pintora	C. a painter, artist
4. un tema	D. a self-portrait
5. un cuadro/ una pintura	E. a theme

Frida Kahlo, una artista universal

Frida Kahlo es una de las pintoras más importantes de México. Como[1] su esposo[2], Diego Rivera, ella comprendió[3] el impacto social de combinar el arte y la política, pero sus temas son más universales. Por ejemplo[4], ella trató[5] los aspectos negativos de la industrialización como la contaminación del aire y de la naturaleza[6]. Otros temas que trató son los problemas de la vida[7]. Frida siempre tuvo[8] problemas físicos. De muchacha, ella tuvo polio. A los dieciocho años, tuvo un accidente terrible de tráfico en la Ciudad de México. Después[9] del accidente, sufrió mucho dolor[10] porque tuvo muchas operaciones. Frida muestra[11] su dolor en muchas de sus pinturas.

La pintora Frida Kahlo en 1931.

Notes

Words presented in the *Preparación* are not glossed in this reading on Frida Kahlo in an effort to encourage students to apply new passive vocabulary.

The use of cognates in the readings requires students to use skills developed in reading strategies that have already been presented. This careful use of cognates enables students to read authentic Spanish without having to look up a large number of words.

Un tema que Frida y Diego tienen en común es el orgullo[12] de la cultura indígena[13] de México. Frida tenía raíces[14] indígenas y adoptó el estilo de la ropa y del pelo[15] de una india para expresar su orgullo indígena. Además[16], sus autorretratos representan la cultura indígena mediante el uso de[17] plantas, animales y colores de la naturaleza.

[1]As, Like [2]her husband [3]understood [4]For example [5]dealt with [6]nature [7]life [8]had [9]After [10]pain [11]shows [12]pride [13]native [14]roots [15]hair [16]In addition [17]by means of

Autorretrato con mono (Self-Portrait with Monkey), Frida Kahlo, 1938. Albright-Knox Art Gallery, Buffalo, N.Y.

A ¿Qué recuerdas?

1. ¿Qué comprendió Frida Kahlo?
2. ¿Cuáles son los temas de los cuadros de Frida?
3. ¿Por qué sufrió Frida mucho dolor?
4. ¿Qué representa Frida en su autorretrato?

B Algo personal

1. ¿Es importante el arte de Frida Kahlo? ¿Por qué?
2. ¿Cuál te gusta más, la foto de Frida Kahlo o su autorretrato? ¿Por qué?

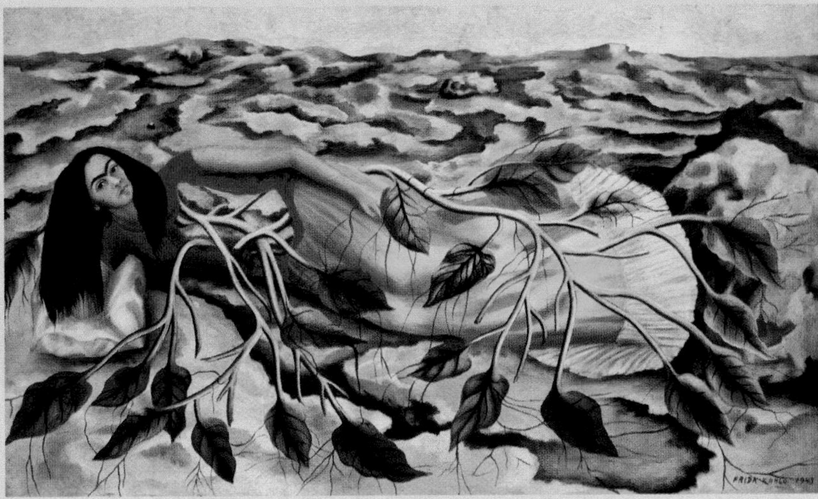

Raíces *(Roots)*, Frida Kahlo, 1943. Private collection.

Notes Students may learn more about Frida Kahlo via the following Web site:

Frida Kahlo Museum
http://www.mexconnect.com/articles/1379-the-frida-kahlo-museum

Teacher Resources

Activity A
Activity B

Answers

A
1. Comprendió el impacto de combinar el arte y la política.
2. Los temas son los aspectos negativos de la industrialización, los problemas de la vida y el orgullo de la cultura indígena.
3. Ella tuvo polio y tuvo un accidente de tráfico.
4. La cultura indígena.

B Answers will vary.

Activities

Connections
Have students do some research on some aspect of Frida Kahlo or her art. Then have them summarize what they found out and present the information to the class.

Expansion
Additional questions *(Algo personal): ¿Qué tipo de arte te gusta?; ¿Crees que la industrialización tiene aspectos negativos?; ¿Te gustan los autorretratos?; ¿Te gusta ir a exposiciones de arte?*

National Standards	
Communication 1.3	**Comparisons** 4.2
Cultures 2.2	
Connections 3.1, 3.2	

Activities

Multiple Intelligences (linguistic)
If you have not done so yet, have students begin to create a Writer's Journal consisting of student writing activities. The Writer's Journal offers appropriate portfolio activities for addressing student writing skills and is an ideal opportunity for an ongoing dialog with students about their writing progress. How to create a Writer's Journal is addressed more thoroughly in the *Tú escribes* at the end of *Capítulo 2*. Offer the following themes from this lesson for students' entries: Frida Kahlo, Diego Rivera, Mexican art, Mexican food, places to visit and sights in Mexico.

Tú escribes

Estrategia

Combining images to build word pictures

Poems make pictures out of your words that can be seen by the mind's eye. They can be about any theme and can appear in any form. For example, a stair poem permits you to build up ideas one on another following a stair pattern. Just as the Aztecs built their pyramids layer upon layer, you can construct a poem in the shape of stairs using your knowledge of Spanish, following these steps:

Step 1: State the main idea (usually composed of just one word).

Step 2: List two or three words that describe the topic. (Use adjectives or nouns.)

Step 3: Name a place or time connected with the topic.

Step 4: Summarize the main idea with a phrase that expresses your feelings about the topic.

Write a stair poem about any topic you choose, such as school, a class, a city, a person, etc. Follow the "steps" to build your poem. When you finish constructing your stair poem, add artwork or graphics to make it visually appealing.

el D. F.

museos parques

la capital

Pues, ¡vamos a la Ciudad de México!

National Standards

Connections
3.1

Notes Display some of the poems students created on a bulletin board in class or arrange to publish a few poems in the school newspaper.

Go online EMCLanguages.net

Proyectos adicionales

A Conexión con la tecnología

In pairs or in small groups, search the Internet and complete one of the following activities:

1. Find a restaurant in Mexico City. Then, write down the name, say where the restaurant is, describe the menu selection and prices, etc.
2. Research Mexican food and then describe a dish that sounds good to you. Try to name the ingredients, say what the food looks like, discuss how it is prepared and tell what state/region of Mexico the dish is from.
3. Find a map of Mexico City and locate major landmarks *(el Zócalo, el Palacio Nacional, la Catedral, el Palacio de Bellas Artes, la Zona Rosa, el parque de Chapultepec, etc.)*. Say what each site offers that makes it special.

B Conexión con otras disciplinas: matemáticas

You are going out to dine at the *Restaurante Danubio* in Mexico City. Choose what you would like to eat. Then calculate the total price of the food items you ordered, add 7 percent in taxes, 10 percent in tips and convert the total amount from pesos into U.S. dollars. Obtain the current exchange rate from the Internet or from a newspaper.

Restaurante Danubio Cocina Internacional

Ensaladas	
Ensalada mixta	44 pesos
Ensalada especial Danubio	61 pesos
Para comer	
Mojarra	95 pesos
Calamares	99 pesos
Ostras	92 pesos
Filete con champiñones	98 pesos
Filete a la parrilla	92 pesos
Pollo frito	44 pesos
Pollo a la cacerola	53 pesos
Bebidas	
Refrescos	16 pesos
Jugo de naranja	13 pesos
Limonada	12 pesos

C Conexión con otras disciplinas: historia

Prepare a tourist guide for Mexico City. Include information about history, the main tourist attractions, museums, places to shop, places to eat and transportation in the city. Be sure to use photos or illustrations to illustrate your guide.

Notes Follow up the activities with a fiesta, allowing students to try some of the recipes they created in activity A.

Teacher Resources

p. 69

Answers

A Creative self-expression.
B Answers will vary.
C Creative self-expression.

Activities

Connections

Have students imagine they were just elected mayor *(el alcalde/la alcaldesa)* of a city in Mexico. Their first duty is to create a plan for a new park and business district to be located in the heart of the city. As good mayors, they want the new area to have a balance of business, culture and green space. How would students design one of the new neighborhoods? What would they name the streets and avenues? What would they name the buildings? What sort of transportation would service the area? Students should draw a proposed plan of their project and then write a brief paragraph giving an overview of what they included in their model.

National Standards

Communication
1.1, 1.3

Cultures
2.1, 2.2

Connections
3.1, 3.2

Teacher Resources

 *Trabalenguas*

 Episode 3, DVD 1, Track 32

Answers

Resolviendo el misterio

1. José discovered that they are going on a date.
2. No. They try to gain entrance, but are interrupted by the arrival of Don Pedro.
3. Answers will vary.

Activities

Communities

See if students can name any well-known Mexicans or celebrities of Mexican descent. Then find out how many of the following Mexican and Mexican-American figures students can identify: Frida Kahlo (painter); Diego Rivera (muralist); Octavio Paz (writer, winner of the Nobel Prize in literature); Selena Quintanilla (Grammy Award-winning singer); Emiliano Zapata (leader of the Mexican Revolution); Luis Miguel (popular singer).

Trabalenguas

Assign days when students have to recite the *Trabalenguas* as a ticket to enter or exit the classroom.

National Standards	
Communication 1.1	**Connections** 3.1
Cultures 2.2	

REPASO

Now that I have completed this chapter, I can...	Go to these pages for help:
talk about places in a city.	90
make introductions and express courtesy.	94
ask and answer questions.	97
discuss how to go somewhere.	100
say some things people do.	100
say where someone is going.	110
talk about the future.	114
order food and beverages.	116
I can also...	
identify some things to do in Mexico.	93
state personal benefits to learning Spanish.	115
use pause words in conversation.	118
talk about food and drink in Mexico.	119
recognize the importance of review.	123
read in Spanish about Mexican artists.	126
write a simple poem in Spanish.	128

Trabalenguas

Erre con erre pizarra, erre con erre barril.
Rápido corren los carros, los carros del ferrocarril.

Resolviendo el misterio

After watching Episode 3 of *El cuarto misterioso*, answer the following questions.

1. What did José discover about Francisco and Ana?
2. Do José and Francisco gain entrance to the secret room? Why or why not?
3. What will José and Francisco serve Ana and Conchita for lunch?

Notes

Loose translation of the *Trabalenguas:* R with R in blackboard, R with R in barrel. Quickly the cars are running, the cars of the train.

Explain to students that the edible part of the popular food *tamales* is baked inside corn husks. For this reason, when people eat a tamale, they must peel back the layers of corn husks and just eat the filling in the center. *Tamales* come in two major varieties—cornmeal and meat filling or a sweetened cornmeal filling.

Vocabulario

Go online EMCLanguages.net

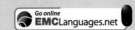

a caballo on horseback *3A*
a pie on foot *3A*
¿adónde? (to) where? *3A*
el **agua (mineral)** (mineral) water *3B*
ahora now *3B*
al to the *3A*
el **autobús** bus *3A*
la **avenida** avenue *3B*
el **avión** airplane *3A*
el **banco** bank *3A*
el **barco** boat, ship *3A*
la **bebida** drink *3B*
la **biblioteca** library *3A*
la **bicicleta** bicycle *3A*
bueno well, okay *3B*
el **caballo** horse *3A*
la **calle** street *3B*
caminar to walk *3A*
el **camión** truck *3A*
el **cantante,** la **cantante** singer *3B*
el **carro** car *3A*
el **centro** downtown, center *3B*
cerca (de) near *3A*
el **cine** movie theater *3A*
la **ciudad** city *3A*
¡claro! of course! *3A*
comer to eat *3B*
la **comida** food *3B*
¡cómo no! of course! *3B*
el **concierto** concert *3B*
¿cuándo? when? *3A*
de acuerdo agreed, okay *3B*
del of the, from the *3A*
el **dentista,** la **dentista** dentist *3A*
el **edificio** building *3B*
El gusto es mío. The pleasure is mine. *3A*
en *(means of transportation)* by *3A*
en carro by car *3A*
encantado,-a delighted, the pleasure is mine 3A
la **ensalada** salad *3B*
la **escuela** school *3A*
fantástico,-a fantastic, great *3A*
favorito,-a favorite *3B*
la **fiesta** party *3A*
los **frijoles** beans *3B*
grande big *3B*
hacer to do, to make *3B*
hacer una pregunta to ask a question *3B*
el **hotel** hotel *3A*
hoy today *3B*
ir to go *3A*
ir a *(+ infinitive)* to be going to (do something) *3B*
el **jugo** juice *3B*
le/les/te presento a let me introduce you to *3A*
leer to read *3B*
lejos (de) far (from) *3A*
el **médico, la médica** doctor *3A*
el **menú** menu *3B*
el **mesero, la mesera** food server *3B*
el **metro** subway *3A*
el **momento** moment *3B*
la **moto(cicleta)** motorcycle *3A*
el **museo** museum *3B*
la **naranja** orange *3B*
la **oficina** office *3A*
oye hey, listen *3B*
el **parque** park *3A*
para for, to, in order to *3A*
pero but *3B*
el **pescado** fish *3B*
la **plaza** plaza, public square *3B*
el **pollo** chicken *3B*
¿por qué? why? *3A*
porque because *3A*
preguntar to ask *3B*
el **problema** problem *3A*
pues thus, well, so, then (pause in speech) *3B*
¿quiénes? who? (pl.) *3A*
quiero I want, I love *3A*
el **refresco** soft drink, refreshment *3B*
el **restaurante** restaurant *3A*
saber to know *3B*
sabes you know *3A*
siempre always *3B*
simpático,-a nice, pleasant *3A*
también also, too *3A*
Tanto gusto. So glad to meet you. *3A*
el **taxi** taxi *3A*
el **teatro** theater *3B*
la **tienda** store *3B*
tomar to take; to drink; to have *3B*
el **transporte** transportation *3A*
el **tren** train *3A*
¡vamos a *(+ infinitive)***!** let's *(+ infinitive)* *3B*
¡vamos! let's go! *3A*
ver to see; to watch *3B*
¿verdad? right? *3A*

Cómo viajar
por México
gastando menos
Secretaría de Turismo

Notes Tell students that some food names vary according to the country. In Mexico, *el maíz is el elote; los tomates* would be *los jítomates.* Remind students that even in the United States there can be different names for food items. A submarine sandwich, for example, is called a sub, hoagie, dagwood, hero, poor boy or torpedo, depending on where in the United States it is served.

Teacher Resources

Ch. 1, repaso 1–3

***¡Aventureros!*, Ch. 3**

Internet Activities

i-Culture

Assessment
Test Booklet
Quizzes
ExamView Assessment Suite

Activities

Multiple Intelligences (bodily-kinesthetic)
Have students draw and label places and objects from the chapter (e.g., places, foods). Display the drawings around the room or use them to review vocabulary.

Students with Special Needs
Review some places where students could go in the downtown area of a city. Then, using transparency 25, have students create sentences saying they are going to the place named and asking other students if they are also going to the named place.

National Standards

Communication
1.1

Cultures
2.1

Comparisons
4.1

Teacher Resources

 *Capítulo 4*

 *Capítulo 4*

Episode 4, DVD 1, Track 37

Connections with Parents

Because this chapter deals with family and friends, encourage your students to spend more time interacting with their families. Challenge students to teach their families the words and expressions that they are learning in class. Create an explanation sheet that describes the activities and documents how much time students spend teaching and families spend learning Spanish.

Answers

El cuarto misterioso

1. Ana y Conchita son hermanas.
2. José es el sobrino de don Pedro. Don Pedro es el tío de José.
3. Las respuestas variarán.
4. Las respuestas variarán pero podrían incluir: comer, tomar, hablar.

Activities

Connections

Show students where Puerto Rico and the Dominican Republic are located, using the maps in the front of the book.

National Standards	
Connections	Communities
3.1	5.1

CAPÍTULO 4

Mi familia y mis amigos

El cuarto misterioso

Contesta las siguientes preguntas sobre *Episodio 4–Mi familia*.

1. ¿Cuál es la relación entre Ana y Conchita?
2. ¿Cuál es la relación entre José y don Pedro?
3. ¿Cómo son Ana, Conchita, José y don Pedro?
4. Haz una lista de verbos que describen las acciones que van a pasar en la casa de don Pedro durante esta escena.

Las muchachas Montero llegan a la casa del tío de José.

Objetivos

- talk about **family** and **relationships**
- seek and provide **personal information**
- express **possession**
- say some **things people do**
- express an **opinion**
- state **likes** and **dislikes**
- describe **people and things**

Notes

Service Learning. As you begin this chapter about family, friends and relationships, remind students they have talents and skills they can use in the community to help others. Students may wish to inquire how they may volunteer (e.g., with the bookmobile, in a senior citizen center, etc.).

Contexto cultural

Puerto Rico
Nombre oficial: Estado Libre Asociado de Puerto Rico
Población: 3.700.000
Capital: San Juan
Ciudades importantes: Ponce, Mayagüez, Bayamón
Unidad monetaria: el dólar (EE.UU.)
Gente famosa: Raúl Julia (actor); Miguel Pou (pintor); Roberto Clemente (beisbolista); Ricky Martin (cantante)

República Dominicana
Nombre oficial: República Dominicana
Población: 9.650.000
Capital: Santo Domingo
Ciudades importantes: Santiago de los Caballeros, Puerto Plata
Unidad monetaria: el peso dominicano (RD$)
Fiesta nacional: 27 de febrero, Día de la Independencia
Gente famosa: Juan Luis Guerra (cantante); Sammy Sosa (beisbolista); Óscar de la Renta (diseñador de ropa)

Activities

Prior Knowledge
Ask students to review the chapter objectives. Ask students to compare the size of their families with a partner. Ask questions such as: What are the parts of speech called that indicate possession? What pet peeves do you have? What activities do you already know how to say in Spanish? What is your favorite pastime? What is your least favorite chore? What person in the classroom do you look like the most?

Notes A checklist of these objectives, along with additional functions, appears on page 178 so students can evaluate their own progress.

National Standards
Connections 3.1

Teacher Resources

 Vocabulario I *Mi familia*

 Activities 27–28

 Activities 1–2

 Activities 1–4

 p. 68

 p. 15

 Activity 1
Activity 2

 Activity 1

Content reviewed in *Lección A*

- gender and number of adjectives
- seeking and providing personal information
- stating the time
- saying how someone is feeling

Lección A Vocabulario I

Mi familia

Puerto Rico

abuela Gloria
abuelo Pedro
abuela Carlota
abuelo Guillermo
hijos
hijos
esposos
hermanos
Rosa (mi tía)
Álvaro (mi tío)
Rodrigo (mi padre)
Carmen (mi madre)
Juan
Clara
hijos
hijos
hija única
sobrino
nietos
Julia (mi prima)
Soy yo, José.
Mónica (mi hermana)
Nancy
Enrique
Diego
mis primos

National Standards

Communication
1.1, 1.3

Connections
3.1

Notes

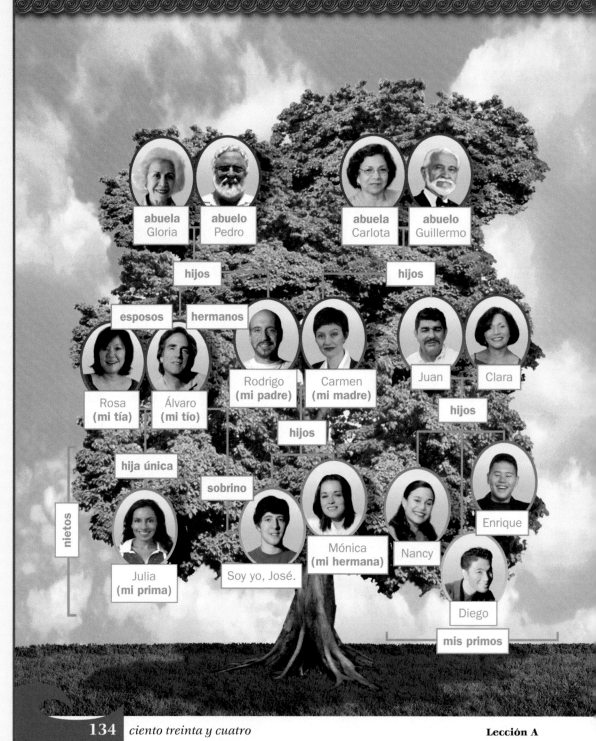

Be sure students understand that Pepe is the nickname that the family uses for José García Rojas.

Ask students what they know about Puerto Rico. Find out if they have heard recent news stories or read articles about Puerto Rican famous people, notable events, etc. Ask for student volunteers to create a bulletin board or travel brochure about this Spanish-speaking commonwealth of the United States.

Me llamo José García Rojas, pero para mi familia soy Pepe. Estoy todo el verano en Puerto Rico con unos parientes, en la casa de mi abuelo. ¡Soy su nieto favorito! Mis padres y yo vivimos en Nueva York.
la casa
Aquí está mi padre. Quiero mucho a mi padre. Él nunca está mucho tiempo en casa.
Mónica está en la playa con Enrique y Diego, ¡los primos más divertidos! Ella es muy guapa y popular.
Ésta es Julia, la hija única de mi tío Álvaro. Ella es bonita y amable. Siempre sale con sus amigos.
Esta foto es de mi abuelo, mi tío Álvaro y su esposa.

1 ¿Cierto o falso?

Di si lo que oyes es cierto o falso, según la información en el Vocabulario I. Si es falso, di lo que es cierto.

2 Pepe y su familia

Completa el párrafo sobre Pepe y su familia.

Soy José García Rojas. Mi (1) se llama Mónica. Ella es muy popular. Mi (2), Julia, es la (3) de mi (4) Álvaro y mi (5) Rosa. Ellos son divertidos. El (6) Juan es el (7) de mi (8), Carmen. Mi (9) es Rodrigo. Quiero mucho a mi padre. También quiero mucho a mi (10) Pedro. ¡Soy el (11) favorito de él!

¡Extra!

Los papás o los padres

Some people prefer to use the terms *mamá y papá* (mom and dad) instead of *madre y padre* (mother and father). Regardless of which terms you use, when referring to both parents simultaneously, use the masculine plural form: *padres* or *papás* (parents).

el padre + la madre = los padres
el papá + la mamá = los papás

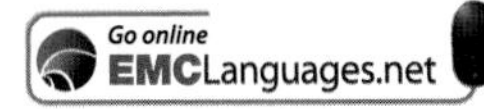

Go online EMCLanguages.net

Notes Note for your students that the word *foto* is feminine because it is short for *la fotografía.*

Comparisons. Explain to students that the false cognate *parientes* does not mean **parents**. Ask students if they can determine the meaning of *parientes:* **relatives**.

Remind students that just as they have learned with *ellos*, they should always use the masculine plural form when referring to a mixed group of both males and females: *los papas/los padres* (parents); *los hermanos* (brothers and sisters); *los tíos* (uncles and aunts); *los abuelos* (grandparents); *los primos* (cousins).

Teacher Resources

Activity 1

Answers

1 Possible answers:
1. Falso. Se llaman Rodrigo y Carmen.
2. Cierto.
3. Falso. Son Enrique, Nancy y Diego.
4. Falso. Las abuelas de Pepe se llaman Gloria y Carlota.
5. Cierto.
6. Falso. Mónica es la hermana de Pepe.

2 1. hermana; 2. prima; 3. hija (única); 4. tío; 5. tía; 6. tío; 7. hermano; 8. madre; 9. padre; 10. abuelo; 11. nieto

Activities

Prereading Strategy
Instruct students to look at the illustrations on pages 134–135. Have them look through the content quickly to find cognates and any words they recognize. Then ask students what they think the illustrations depict. Finally, ask several questions to prepare students for the new content. Whose family is shown on page 134?

TPR
Present Pepe's family tree. Then using overhead transparencies 27 and 28, ask students to come up and point to the person as you describe each relationship to José (Pepe) in Spanish.

National Standards

Communication
1.2

Connections
3.1

Comparisons
4.1

Teacher Resources

Diálogo I
En la fiesta del abuelo
Activity 3
Activity 4
Activity 5

Answers

3 1. Se llama Julia.
2. El abuelo es amable y cariñoso.
3. Es la esposa de Juan.
4. Es la hija de Juan.

4 Answers will vary.

5 1. D
2. A
3. B
4. C

Activities

Critical Listening
Play the audio version of the dialog as students cover the words and listen to develop good listening skills. Ask several individuals to state what they believe is the main theme of the dialog.

Critical Thinking
Have students look at the photographs as they imagine what the speaker is saying. Then ask if students know where the dialog takes place and what is the main theme of the dialog.

Language through Action
Ask for volunteers to come to the front of the class to act out the dialog *En la fiesta del abuelo*.

National Standards
Communication 1.2, 1.3
Cultures 2.1
Comparisons 4.1

Diálogo I En la fiesta del abuelo

JOSÉ: Hola, Javier. Te presento a mi prima, Julia.
JULIA: Mucho gusto.
JAVIER: Encantado, Julia.
JOSÉ: Ella es la nieta favorita de mi abuelo Pedro.

JAVIER: Tu abuelo es muy amable.
JULIA: Sí, y muy cariñoso. Vivimos con él en Puerto Rico todo el verano.
JOSÉ: ¡Mira, allí está el abuelo!

JAVIER: ¡Ay, sí! ¡Allí está! ¿Quiénes están con él?
JULIA: La señora de rojo es la esposa de mi tío Juan, y la chica de azul es su hija.
JAVIER: ¡Es muy guapa!

3 ¿Qué recuerdas?

1. ¿Cómo se llama la nieta favorita de Pedro?
2. ¿Quién es amable y cariñoso?
3. ¿Quién es la señora de rojo?
4. ¿Quién es la chica de azul?

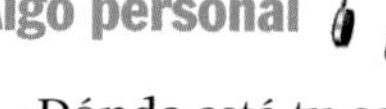

4 Algo personal

1. ¿Dónde está tu casa? ¿Estás en casa mucho?
2. En tu familia, ¿quién es amable? ¿Divertido/a? ¿Popular?
3. ¿Tienes muchos parientes? ¿Quiénes son?
4. ¿Cómo se llaman tus abuelos? ¿Y tus tíos?
5. ¿Tienes sobrinos? ¿Cómo se llama(n)?
6. ¿Cuántos primos tienes?
7. ¿Quién es tu pariente favorito? ¿Por qué?

5 ¿Quién es?

Escucha la información y, luego, escoge la letra de la respuesta correcta.

A. Es mi abuelo. **B.** Es mi tía. **C.** Es mi prima. **D.** Es mi padre.

Notes

Comparisons. Etiquette related to social gatherings offers an interesting cultural comparison. In the Spanish-speaking world, it is common to arrive later than the time stated on an invitation to a party, and a written invitation does not indicate an ending time, as sometimes occurs in the United States.

Mention to students that many Hispanics celebrate both a birthday and a saint's day. For example, a person named Juan might celebrate his birthday on October 8 and his saint's day on June 24 *(el día de San Juan)*.

Cultura   

Puerto Rico

What do you know about the enchanting Caribbean island of Puerto Rico? Did you know, for example, that English and Spanish are official languages and are required courses in school? Why? The answer lies hidden in Puerto Rico's history. After landing on a small tropical island that inhabitants called *Borinquén* (originally Boriquén) in 1493, Christopher Columbus *(Cristóbal Colón)* claimed the land for Spain. Spain then ceded the island to the United States in 1898 as a result of the Spanish-American War, beginning Puerto Rico's continuous affiliation with the United States. In 1952, the island became a Commonwealth *(Estado Libre Asociado)* of the United States, which means residents are United States citizens but the main governmental functions remain independent.

Unas casas en el Viejo San Juan.

What might you see and do on a visit to Puerto Rico? You can experience city life in the capital, San Juan; stroll along beautiful beaches (e.g., *la playa de Luquillo*); visit quaint ports like Fajardo; or travel to the mountains, all within a matter of hours. Do you like fine dining? Puerto Rico offers some of the finest cuisine in the Caribbean. Does music talk to your soul? Listen and dance to the beat of Caribbean music (*salsa* is popular in Puerto Rico). Interested in history? Be swept back in time as you admire colonial architecture in old San Juan *(el Viejo San Juan)*, such as *El Castillo de San Felipe del Morro*, a fort that was constructed in 1591 to protect the island. Does art move you? The fascinating *Museo de Arte* in Ponce will inspire you! Are you active outdoors? You can hike through the only tropical rain forest *(el Yunque)* found in the U.S. National Forest System or surf along Puerto Rico's Atlantic coast.

El Castillo de San Felipe del Morro, Puerto Rico.

6 En Puerto Rico

Imagine you are going on vacation to Puerto Rico. Describe some things you might like to see and do while you are there. List five bits of information you learned that would be helpful to know before touring the country.

7 Conexiones con otras disciplinas: historia

Complete the statements about Puerto Rico logically, using the answers shown in the column on the right.

1. Puerto Rico es...
2. Las lenguas oficiales de Puerto Rico son...
3. Cristóbal Colón llegó a la isla en...
4. San Juan es...

A. el inglés y el español.
B. 1493.
C. un Estado Libre Asociado.
D. la capital.

Notes

Inform interested students that more than 100 billion gallons of rain fall in el *Yunque* each year! Also, surfers claim the best season for surfing in Puerto Rico is October through April.

Many American firms have invested heavily in Puerto Rico. However, tourism remains one of the island's leading industries.

The names of certain cities and countries in Latin America reflect the Spanish exploration and colonization of the region that began with Columbus. *Puerto Rico* literally means **rich port**.

Teacher Resources

 Activity 3

 p. 66

 Activity 3

 Answers

6 Creative problem solving.

7 1. C
2. A
3. B
4. D

 Activities

Communities

Conduct a class discussion about Puerto Rico's status as a commonwealth. (Have your native Spanish-speaking students conducting research about the topic assist by providing information and insights.) Finally, conduct a poll about whether students think Puerto Rico should remain a commonwealth or become a state or an independent nation.

Spanish for Spanish Speakers

Have students write a short composition in Spanish summarizing what they know about Puerto Rico. Expand the activity by having students seek out additional information about Puerto Rico at the library.

Technology

Have students use the Internet to research and then compare and contrast food and eating in Puerto Rico and Mexico.

National Standards	
Communication 1.3	**Communities** 5.1
Cultures 2.2	
Connections 3.1, 3.2	

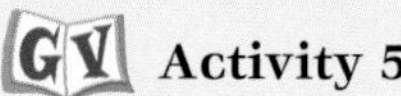

 Activity 5

Answers

8 1. favorito
2. amable
3. divertidas
4. toda
5. otra
6. simpáticas
7. cariñosa
8. bonita
9. populares
10. fantásticos

Activities

Cooperative Learning
To illustrate the use of last names in the Spanish-speaking world, divide students into groups. Each group should become a family with its corresponding members and first and last names. Students must prepare a short presentation for the class including information such as names, family roles, ages and professions. Encourage creativity.

National Standards

Cultures
2.1

Connections
3.1

Comparisons
4.1

Idioma

Repaso rápido

Adjectives

You will recall that adjectives (e.g., colors) may be masculine or feminine and singular or plural since they must match the gender and number of the noun they are describing. To make a singular adjective plural, add *-s* if the adjective ends in a vowel or *-es* if the adjective ends in a consonant. Although most adjectives usually follow the nouns they modify, adjectives of quantity, such as *cinco, mucho (mucha), otro (otra), todo (toda),* and question-asking words precede their nouns.

8 Mis parientes puertorriqueños

Completa las oraciones con la forma apropiada de las palabras en paréntesis.

MODELO Tengo __ parientes en Puerto Rico. (mucho)
Tengo muchos parientes en Puerto Rico.

1. Mi tío __, Diego, es de San Juan. (favorito)
2. ¡Qué __ es mi tío Diego! (amable)
3. También tengo dos primas __ en San Juan, Alicia y Ana. (divertido)
4. Pero no __ mi familia está en San Juan. (todo)
5. Mi __ prima, Marta, está con mi tía, Eva, en Ponce. (otro)
6. ¡Qué __ son Marta y la tía Eva! (simpático)
7. La tía Eva es __. (cariñoso)
8. Ella es muy __ también. (bonito)
9. Alicia, Ana y Marta son todas __. (popular)
10. ¡Tengo unos parientes __. (fantástico)

Exclamaciones

The word *qué* may be followed by an adjective (or other descriptive phrase) as in the second and sixth sentences of activity 8 to express strong feelings, much as you might use **How...!** in English: *¡Qué amable!* (How nice!).

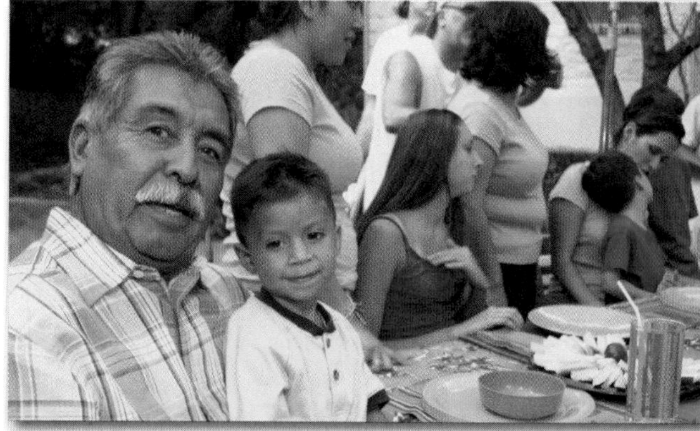

Tengo muchos parientes en Puerto Rico.

Notes For several years, Puerto Rico has been considering whether to become a U.S. state or an independent nation or remain a commonwealth.

Explain to students that Puerto Ricans are U.S. citizens, with most of the same rights and obligations. One difference is that they cannot vote in presidential elections unless they reside in one of the fifty states.

Remind students that Spanish punctuation has certain unique features, including the inverted exclamation point at the beginning of expressions such as *¡Qué interesante!*

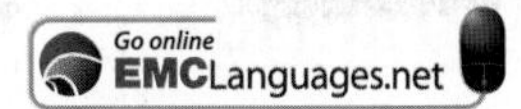

Estructura

Expressing possession: possessive adjectives

- Possessive adjectives *(adjetivos posesivos)* express possession or describe relationships between people. In Spanish, possessive adjectives precede the noun they modify and must agree in number and in gender with that noun.

mi(s)	hermano(s) hermana(s)	*my*	*brother(s)* *sister(s)*
tu(s)	tío(s) tía(s)	*your (informal)*	*uncle(s)* *aunt(s)*
su(s)	sobrino(s) sobrina(s)	*your (formal)*	*nephew(s)* *niece(s)*
su(s)	sobrino(s) sobrina(s)	*his*	*nephew(s)* *niece(s)*
su(s)	sobrino(s) sobrina(s)	*her*	*nephew(s)* *niece(s)*
nuestro(s) **nuestra(s)**	hermano(s) hermana(s)	*our*	*brother(s)* *sister(s)*
vuestro(s) **vuestra(s)**	tío(s) tía(s)	*your (informal)*	*uncle(s)* *aunt(s)*
su(s)	sobrino(s) sobrina(s)	*your (formal)*	*nephew(s)* *niece(s)*
su(s)	sobrino(s) sobrina(s)	*their*	*nephew(s)* *niece(s)*

- Possessive adjectives have both singular and plural forms. Although the masculine and feminine forms for *mi, mis, tu, tus, su* and *sus* are the same (i.e., *su abuelo* and *su abuela*), notice that *nuestro/nuestra, nuestros/nuestras* and *vuestro/vuestra, vuestros/vuestras* have recognizably different masculine and feminine forms.

*Pepe es **nuestro** primo.*	Pepe is **our** cousin.
*Teresa es **nuestra** hermana.*	Teresa is **our** sister.

- You can clarify the meaning of *su* and *sus*, and you can add emphasis to what you are saying, by replacing the possessive adjective with *de* plus a pronoun or a person's name.

*Es **su** tía.* → *Es la tía **de ella**. (Es la tía **de Teresa**.)*

Notes Inform students that the subject pronoun *tú* has a written accent mark, whereas the possessive adjective *tu* does not.

You may wish to tell students that possessive adjectives are not used with body parts as they are in English: *Me lavo **la** cara.*

Nuestro and *vuestro* are the only possessive adjectives that have four forms.

Remind students that *vuestro* is the plural of *tu* and that it is used only in Spain.

Teacher Resources

 Activities 4–6

 Activity 6

 Activity 4

 Unit 9

 Activity 2

Activities

Language through Action
Tell the class you are going to borrow certain items for a class activity. Collect objects such as a book, notebook, watch, pen and pencil. For each item ask several students the question *¿Es tu* (name the object)?" or *¿Son tus* (name the objects)?" Then ask *¿De quién es/son* (name the objects)? so that the owner identifies himself/herself. When an item has been returned to its original owner, ask *¿De quién es/son* (name the object or objects)? once more to show possession with an object plus *de* plus the owner or with the possessive adjective *su(s)*.

Students with Special Needs
Tell students to write each subject pronoun and each possessive adjective on separate slips of paper or on small index cards (including the words that follow in parentheses). Then have them mix up each set and try to match the appropriate cards. You may choose to have them work individually, in pairs or in small groups.

National Standards

Communication
1.1

Cultures
2.1

Teacher Resources

Activity 9

Answers

9 1. ¿Es ... tu hermano?/Sí, es mi hermano.
2. ¿Son ... tus primos?/Sí, son mis primos.
3. ¿Son ... tus abuelos?/Sí, son mis abuelos.
4. ¿Son ... tus tías?/Sí, son mis tías.
5. ¿Es ... tu sobrina?/Sí, es mi sobrina.
6. ¿Es ... tu tío?/Sí, es mi tío.

10 1. nuestra; 2. mi; 3. tus; 4. su; 5. sus; 6. su; 7. tu

11 Possible answers:
1. sus; 2. sus; 3. su; 4. sus; 5. su; 6. su

Activities

TPR

For this TPR activity use possessive adjectives and the *Uds.* form of commands for the whole class (*Abran sus libros; Cierren sus cuadernos; Toquen sus pupitres.*) or the *tú* form of commands for individual students (*Abre tu cuaderno; Cierra tu libro; Toca tu libro*) to ask students to do various tasks. In addition, try asking students to do something involving another student's possessions (*Cierra su cuaderno; Toca sus bolígrafos; Señala sus libros; Toca su pupitre*). Continue with *Ve a mi escritorio; Cierra mi cuaderno.*

National Standards
Communication 1.1
Comparisons 4.1
Communities 5.1

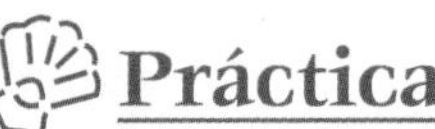

Práctica

9 ¿Quiénes son?

En parejas, alternen en preguntar y confirmar quiénes son las siguientes personas. ***(In pairs, take turns asking and confirming who the following people are.)***

MODELO Verónica / hermana
A: ¿Es Verónica tu hermana?
B: Sí, es mi hermana.

1. Pablo / hermano
2. Rodrigo y José / primos
3. doña Amalia y don Rogelio / abuelos
4. ellas / tías
5. María / sobrina
6. él / tío

10 Nuestra familia

Marta and her cousins, Elena and Diego, are discussing the digital photos Marta took with her new camera. Complete their conversation with the possessive adjectives indicated by the cues in parentheses.

MODELO **Elena:** Aquí hay una foto de nuestros abuelos en la playa. (nosotros)

Diego: Están con (1) madre en la playa de Luquillo. (nosotros)
Marta: ¿Hay dos fotos de (2) tía? (yo)
Elena: Sí. Una con doña Carmen y don Enrique, y otra es con (3) padres. (tú)
Diego: Aquí están doña Carmen y don Enrique en (4) casa nueva. (ellos)
Elena: ¿Están todos (5) nietos en la foto con ellos? (ellos)
Marta: No, yo no estoy en la foto y soy (6) prima favorita. (Uds.)
Diego: Pues, mi foto favorita está aquí con (7) hermano, Kathy, la *au pair*, y yo en El Yunque. ¡Qué día tan divertido! (tú)

¡Oportunidades!

¿Quieres ser au pair?
Are you interested in experiencing life with a Spanish-speaking family and getting to really know their lifestyle and culture? If so, you might be interested in becoming an au pair.

There are many reliable agencies in the United States that place young people with Spanish families for periods of up to a year. Au pairs live with the family and take care of the children. You would learn how the family lives day to day and you could also attend educational courses, make new friends, travel and improve your Spanish. Find out through local agencies how you might become part of a real *familia*.

11 ¿Quién va a venir a nuestra fiesta?

Use an appropriate possessive adjective to complete this guest list for a cookout at your home.

1. Julia y______ amigas, Amy y Paula
2. la Sra. y el Sr. García y______ tres hijos
3. los González y______ sobrino, Enrique
4. Juana Ruiz y______ dos hermanas
5. Amalia y Rogelio de la Torre y______ madre
6. el doctor Diego Fernández y______ familia

Notes

Explain that the number and the gender of the possessive adjective must match what is possessed, not the possessor. For example, the *s* on *tus* is not necessary unless the noun that follows is plural: *¿Es **tu tía** de Luquillo?* (Is **your aunt** from Luquillo?); *¿Son **tus primos** de Ponce?* (Are **your cousins** from Ponce?).

Comunicación

12 Mis parientes

Create your own family tree. Next, in small groups, take turns naming the people and asking and answering questions about how members of your family are related. Finally, describe the people you name and add any additional information you wish.

MODELO Soy Juana. Mateo es mi tío. Es muy amable.

Estructura

Saying what someone does: present tense of *-ir* verbs

- Form the present tense of a regular *-ir* verb, such as *vivir* (to live), by removing the *-ir* ending and attaching the endings shown. Note that except for *-imos* and *-ís*, the endings are the same as those of *-er* verbs.

vivir			
yo	viv**o**	nosotros nosotras	viv**imos**
tú	viv**es**	vosotros vosotras	viv**ís**
Ud. él ella	viv**e**	Uds. ellos ellas	viv**en**

- Another verb that ends in *-ir*, *salir* (to go out, to leave), is regular in all forms except the first-person singular: *yo* ***salgo***.

*Yo **salgo** a las dos.*	I leave at two.
*Nosotros **salimos** a las cuatro.*	We leave at four.

Notes Sometimes students are hesitant to provide personal information when doing activities. Before assigning activity 12, inform the class that it is okay to make up information for their family tree.

Point out the similarities in forming regular *-ar*, *-er* and *-ir* verbs: Remove the infinitive ending and add endings that match the subject pronouns, as indicated in the paradigm.

Teacher Resources

 Activities 7–8

 Activities 7–8

 p. 149

 Activity 5

 Activity 3

Answers

12 Creative self-expression.

Activities

Expansion
As a variation for activity 12, suggest that students create an imaginary family including several well-known Spanish-speaking people.

Multiple Intelligences (linguistic)
Have students write an original composition about their family as a follow-up to activity 12.

Prereading Strategy
Review Pepe's family tree first as an introduction to activity 12. Have students look at the family tree and identify the members of Pepe's family. Then ask students to read about his family and look at the pictures from the family photo album.

National Standards

Communication
1.1

Teacher Resources

Activity 14
Activity 15

Answers

13 1. vivimos; 2. viven; 3. viven; 4. vive; 5. viven; 6. vive; 7. viven; 8. vives

14 Possible answers:
1. ¿... vive...?/Vive en....
2. ¿... viven...?/Viven en....
3. ¿... vive...?/Vive en....
4. ¿... vive...?/Vive en....
5. ¿... viven...?/Viven en....
6. ¿... vives... ?/Vivo en....

15
1. ¿A qué hora salen...?/ Ellos salen a las once.
2. ¿A qué hora salimos...?/ Nosotros salimos a las tres y cuarto.
3. ¿A qué hora sale...?/Ella sale a las once y cuarto.
4. ¿A qué hora salen...?/Ellas salen a las dos menos cuarto.
5. ¿A qué hora sales...?/Yo salgo a las tres.

Activities

Critical Thinking

Have students find examples of several infinitives that end in *-ir* in the Spanish/English glossary at the end of *¡Aventura! 1.* Students can prepare a written list of infinitives to turn in or, as an alternative, you may want to review their lists orally in class. As an extension to this, have students find additional infinitives in magazine or newspaper articles.

National Standards

Communication
1.1

Connections
3.1

Práctica

13 Viven en...

Pepe's cousin, Julia, is contacting family and friends to invite them to her mother's birthday party. Complete this paragraph with the appropriate forms of the verb *vivir*.

Nosotros (1) aquí en San Juan. Los tíos (2) cerca de nosotros aquí en la capital, pero los abuelos (3) lejos de nosotros en Ponce. La hermana de mi madre, la tía Rosa, también (4) en San Juan. Clara y Rafael (5) en Arecibo, pero van a estar en Miami. Yoli (6) en Orlando pero va a estar en casa de sus primos, Mona y Jorge. Ellos (7) en Bayamón. Y tú, ¿dónde (8)? ¿Vienes tú a nuestra fiesta?

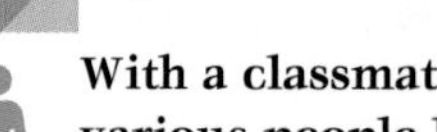

14 ¿Dónde viven?

With a classmate, take turns asking and answering questions about where various people live. Answer using the words in parentheses.

MODELO tu hermano (San Juan)
A: ¿Dónde vive tu hermano?
B: Vive en San Juan.

1. el hijo único de tu tío Alfonso (Ponce)
2. ellos (una casa grande y nueva)
3. Hernán (la casa de su tío)
4. mi tía (París)
5. tu madre y tu padre (San Juan)
6. tú (?)

15 ¿A qué hora salen?

Working in pairs, take turns asking and telling when the following people are leaving their houses to arrive on time for the birthday party.

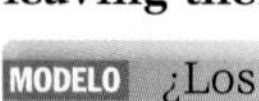

MODELO ¿Los tíos? PM 5:00

A: ¿A qué hora salen los tíos?
B: Ellos salen a las cinco.

1. ¿Los abuelos? AM 11:00

2. ¿Nosotros? PM 3:15
3. ¿La madre de una amiga? AM 11:15
4. ¿La tía Rosa y Julia? PM 1:45
5. ¿Tú? PM 3:00

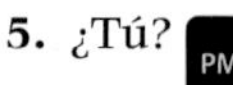
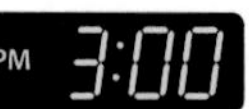

Los tíos salen a las cinco.

Notes Students may find it interesting to learn how names associated with Puerto Rico's geography changed over time. Shortly after his arrival, Columbus renamed the island of Borinquén *San Juan Bautista* (Saint John the Baptist). In 1508, Juan Ponce de León founded the first Spanish village on the island, Villa de Caparra, which the king of Spain renamed San Juan de Puerto Rico. A year later, Ponce de León was named the first governor and the city of Ponce was named after him. The island eventually became known as Puerto Rico, and its capital was called San Juan.

Review how to ask for and tell time before assigning activity 15.

Comunicación

Tu familia y la familia de Julia

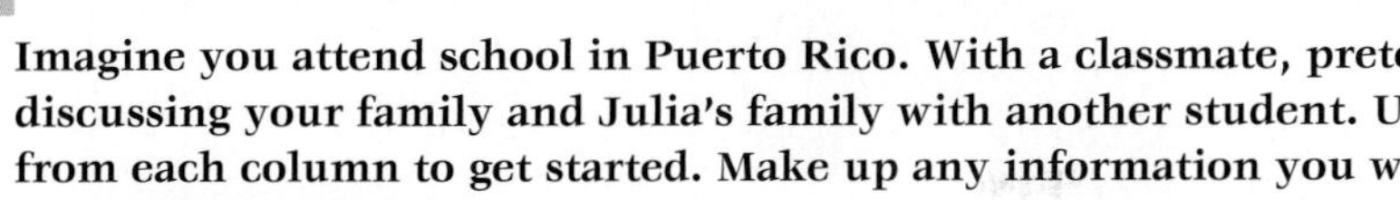

Imagine you attend school in Puerto Rico. With a classmate, pretend you are discussing your family and Julia's family with another student. Use words from each column to get started. Make up any information you would like to create logical sentences.

MODELO **A:** ¿Dónde viven los abuelos de Julia?
B: Los abuelos de Julia viven en Arecibo. Van a vivir en Ponce no lejos del Museo de Arte.

el primo	salir	de	Bayamón
los abuelos	vivir	aquí en	Mayagüez
yo		allí en	Arecibo
nosotros		en	San Juan
Uds.		lejos de	el Yunque
las hermanas		cerca de	el Morro
tú			Ponce
la madre y el padre			la Playa de Luquillo

Mi familia

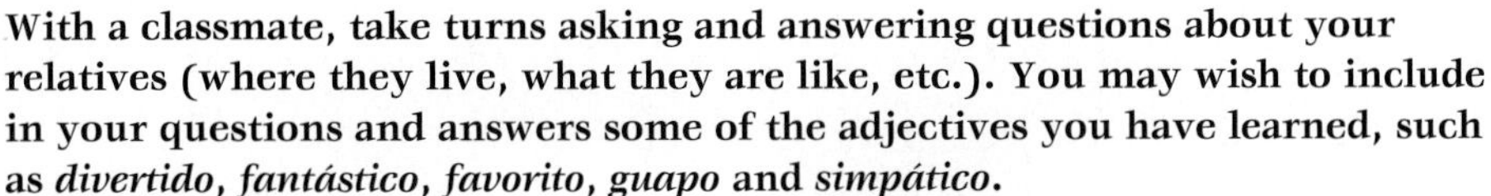

With a classmate, take turns asking and answering questions about your relatives (where they live, what they are like, etc.). You may wish to include in your questions and answers some of the adjectives you have learned, such as *divertido*, *fantástico*, *favorito*, *guapo* and *simpático*.

MODELO **A:** ¿Cómo se llama tu prima?
B: Se llama Diana. Es profesora y vive en Chicago. Es amable.

Otros miembros de la familia

el hermanastro, la hermanastra	*stepbrother, stepsister*
el hijastro, la hijastra	*stepson, stepdaughter*
el medio hermano, la media hermana	*half brother, half sister*
el padrastro, la madrastra	*stepfather, stepmother*

¿Dónde viven?

Working in small groups, talk about your families and/or friends. Discuss such things as the names of various family and/or friends, their ages and where they live, adding any other interesting information you wish.

MODELO **A:** ¿Dónde viven tus abuelos?
B: Viven en Chicago.
A: ¿Tienes familia o amigos en otro país?
B: Mis abuelos viven en Puerto Rico.
C: Mi amigo Rafael vive en Puerto Rico también, pero no es un país. Es un Estado Libre Asociado de los Estados Unidos.

Notes Activities 17 and 18 are similar. However, because activity 17 is for pairs and 18 is for groups, 17 may be used to prepare students for 18.

Answers

16 Creative self-expression.
17 Creative self-expression.
18 Creative self-expression.

Activities

Pronunciation (*la letra* h)
Review the pronunciation of the letter *h* by practicing the following: *Humberto, Hernández, Hatillo, Héctor* and *Hilda*. Point out that the consonant *h* is always silent in Spanish. You may wish to add that words beginning with *h* in Spanish are usually linked in pronunciation to the preceding word. Have students practice the following sentence: *Humberto Hernández y su hermana Hilda están en un hotel en La Habana.*

Students with Special Needs
As preparation for the *Comunicación* activities, practice verb conjugation using choral response to each form of the verbs *vivir* and *salir.* Start with the *yo* form of each verb (remind students that *salir* has an irregular *yo* form). Then ask for the *tú* form of each verb, and so on, until students have had a chance to practice all forms of each verb.

National Standards

Communication
1.1

Teacher Resources

 **Vocabulario II** *¿Cómo está?*

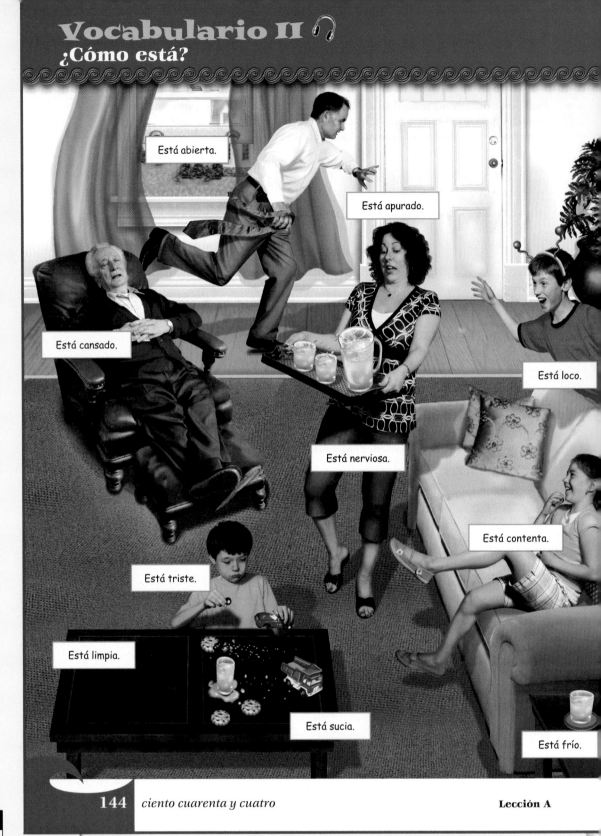

 **Activity 29**

 **Activities 9–10**

 **p. 16**

 **Activity 6**

 **Activity 4**

Activities

Prereading Strategy
Have students look at *Vocabulario II* and identify cognates and other words they recognize. Then ask students to guess what the people on pages 144 and 145 are feeling.

Students with Special Needs
After reviewing the present-tense forms of *estar*, have students practice creating sentences using *estoy, estás, está, estamos, estáis* and *están* with the adjectives on pages 144–145.

National Standards
Communication 1.1

Vocabulario II

¿Cómo está?

Está abierta.

Está apurado.

Está cansado.

Está loco.

Está nerviosa.

Está contenta.

Está triste.

Está limpia.

Está sucia.

Está frío.

Notes

Explain to the class the difference between *estar cansado* (to be tired) and *tener sueño* (to be sleepy).

Review how to conjugate the verb *estar* in the present tense.

Quickly check student comprehension of the descriptions that accompany the illustrations on these two pages.

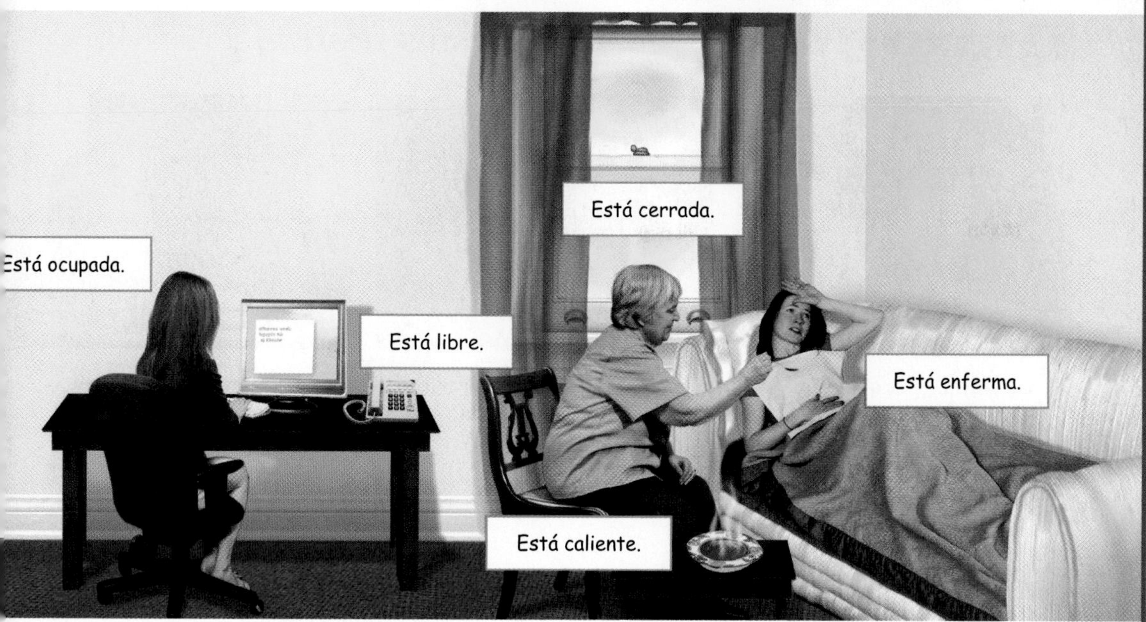

19 ¿Cómo están? 

Selecciona la letra de la ilustración que corresponde con lo que oyes.

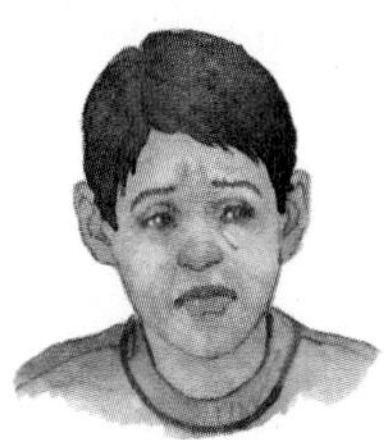

A B C D

20 A corregir

Corrige la información incorrecta, según el Vocabulario II.

MODELO Mi hermana está triste.
Mi hermana está contenta.

1. El teléfono está ocupado.
2. Mi tía está muy bien.
3. El refresco está caliente.
4. La comida está fría.
5. La ventana está cerrada.

Estamos contentos.

Notes Activity 19 has been recorded as part of the Audio Program. A reproducible answer sheet for activity 19 can be found at the end of the Audio Program Manual.

Note for students that masculine adjectives are used with forms of *estar* when describing males, and feminine adjectives are used with females.

Teacher Resources

 Activity 19

Answers

19
1. D
2. A
3. B
4. C

20
1. está libre
2. enferma
3. frío
4. caliente
5. abierta

National Standards

Communication
1.1, 1.2

Teacher Resources

Diálogo II
¿Por qué estás triste?
Activity 21
Activity 22
Activity 23

Answers

21 1. Julia está triste.
2. Está triste porque su abuelo está enfermo.
3. Se llama don Pedro García Montoya.
4. Julia está nerviosa.
5. Va a su casa.

22 Answers will vary.

23 1. B
2. F
3. D
4. A
5. E
6. C

Activities

Critical Listening
Play the audio version of the dialog. Instruct students to cover the words as they listen to the dialog to develop good listening skills. Have students look at the photographs as they imagine what the speaker is saying. Ask students to state what they believe is the main theme of the dialog.

Prereading Strategy
Instruct students to cover up the text and imagine where Javier and Julia are and how they are feeling. Ask students to identify cognates in the dialogue.

National Standards

Communication
1.2

Cultures
2.1

Diálogo II ¿Por qué estás triste?

JAVIER: Julia, ¿por qué estás triste?
JULIA: Mi abuelo está enfermo.
JAVIER: ¿Don Pedro García Montoya?

JULIA: Sí, y estoy muy nerviosa.
JAVIER: Él va a estar bien.
JULIA: Gracias. Eres muy amable.

JAVIER: Bueno, adiós. Estoy apurado.
JULIA: ¿Adónde vas?
JAVIER: Voy a casa, estoy muy cansado.

21 ¿Qué recuerdas?

1. ¿Quién está triste?
2. ¿Por qué está triste?
3. ¿Cómo se llama el abuelo?
4. ¿Quién está nervioso?
5. ¿Dónde va Javier?

22 Algo personal

1. ¿Estás triste o contento/a? Explica.
2. ¿Estás enfermo/a?

23 ¿Cómo están todos?

Listen as several people talk about how they are feeling. Then match the names with the description that fits each person.

1. Ángel
2. Esperanza
3. Benjamín
4. Natalia
5. Josefina
6. Verónica

A. Está contenta.
B. Está muy ocupado.
C. Está nerviosa.
D. Está apurado.
E. Está triste.
F. Está enferma.

Está nerviosa.

Notes Explain that it is common for Spanish-speaking people to have two last names. The first last name is the father's and the second is the mother's, as seen in this dialog, although only the father's name is used in most conversation.

Activity 23 has been recorded as part of the Audio Program. A reproducible answer sheet for the activity has been included at the end of the Audio Program Manual for your convenience.

Cultura  II 

El autor Gabriel García Márquez.

¿Cómo se llama?

Most people in Spanish-speaking countries have not one, but two last names. They use their father's family name followed by their mother's. For example, to find the phone number of a friend named José García Rodriguez, look in the phone directory under *G* for *García Rodríguez*, not *R* for *Rodríguez*. To find books by the famous author Gabriel García Márquez, look under *G* for *García Márquez*.

Traditionally, when a woman married, she would add the name of her husband, preceded by *de*, meaning "of" or "belonging to." For example, if Jennifer López married Gabriel García Márquez, she would become Jennifer López *de García*. Today, however, many women are opting to keep the same name they had before marriage.

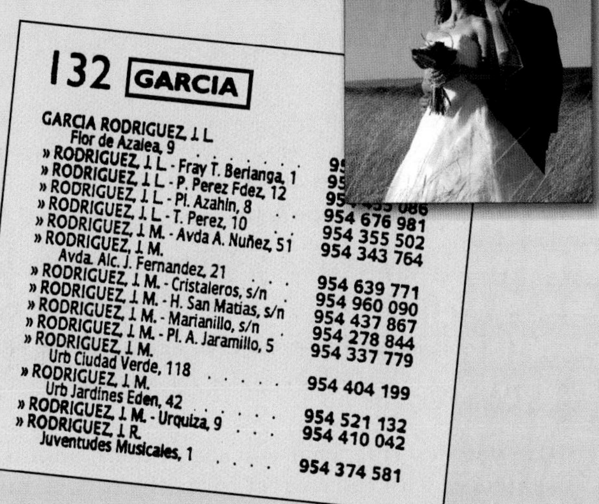

132 GARCIA

GARCIA RODRIGUEZ, J. L.
Flor de Azalea, 9 95
» RODRIGUEZ, J. L. - Fray T. Berianga, 1 95
» RODRIGUEZ, J. L. - P. Perez Fdez, 12 95
» RODRIGUEZ, J. L. - Pl. Azahin, 8 . . . 086
» RODRIGUEZ, J. L. - T. Perez, 10 . . . 954 676 981
» RODRIGUEZ, J. M. - Avda A. Nuñez, 51 954 355 502
» RODRIGUEZ, J. M. 954 343 764
Avda. Alc. J. Fernandez, 21 . . . 954 639 771
» RODRIGUEZ, J. M. - Cristaleros, s/n . 954 960 090
» RODRIGUEZ, J. M. - H. San Matias, s/n 954 437 867
» RODRIGUEZ, J. M. - Marianillo, s/n . 954 278 844
» RODRIGUEZ, J. M. - Pl. A. Jaramillo, 5 954 337 779
» RODRIGUEZ, J. M.
Urb Ciudad Verde, 118 . . . . . . 954 404 199
» RODRIGUEZ, J. M.
Urb Jardines Eden, 42 . . . . . . 954 521 132
» RODRIGUEZ, J. M. - Urquiza, 9 . . . 954 410 042
» RODRIGUEZ, J. R.
Juventudes Musicales, 1 . . . . 954 374 581

 **24** ¿Cuál es su nombre completo? 

Look at some information about students' families. Write down each person's complete name, according to what you learned in the *Cultura viva* titled *¿Cómo se llama?*

MODELO Margarita es la hija de Pablo Cruz y Josefina Miranda.
Se llama Margarita Cruz Miranda.

1. Alicia es la hija de Marta Fuentes de Bazán y Ernesto Bazán Rojas.
2. La madre de Bárbara es Carmen Prado Correa y su padre es Martín Sosa Tovar.
3. Paz es la hija de Ricardo Olmedos Acosta y Natalia Bravo de Olmedos.
4. Los padres de Jorge son Virginia Triana Gómez y Enrique Sandoval Gaviria.
5. Andrés es el hijo de Antonio Cervantes Díaz y Luisa Carrillo de Cervantes.
6. Los padres de Mercedes son Ernesto Lorente Soto y Gabriela Medina Gálvez.

Teacher Resources

 Activity 24

 Activity 11

 Activity 7

 Activity 5

Answers

24 1. ... Alicia Bazán Fuentes.
2. ... Bárbara Sosa Prado.
3. ... Paz Olmedos Bravo.
4. ... Jorge Sandoval Triana.
5. ... Andrés Cervantes Carrillo.
6. ... Mercedes Lorente Medina.

Activities

Cooperative Learning

Have students ask one another *¿Cuál es tu apellido paterno?* (for the paternal name) and *¿Cuál es tu apellido materno?* (for the maternal name) to get a feel for this cultural point.

Notes

Explain to the class that last names are made plural in Spanish by putting the plural definite article in front of the name: *los López, los Marín*, etc.

Comparisons. Have students compose their last names using the system described in the *Cultura viva* on page 147.

National Standards

Communication
1.1

Cultures
2.1

Comparisons
4.1, 4.2

Teacher Resources

 Activity 12

 Activities 9–10

 Unit 8

 Activity 6

Answers

25 Possible answers:
1. están contentos
2. está triste
3. están fríos
4. está caliente
5. está sucia
6. está ocupado

Activities

Students with Special Needs
Complete one or two sentences with students to be sure they understand what to do for activity 25.

Estructura

Describing people and things with *estar*

- You have already learned to use the verb *estar* to indicate location. *Estar* can also be used with adjectives to describe conditions that are likely to change *(caliente, cansado, frío)* or to express how someone or something is at a given moment *(bonito, nervioso, sucio).*

El agua está ***caliente****.*	The water is hot.
¿Está ella ***cansada****?*	Is she tired?
Ellos están ***nerviosos****.*	They are nervous.
¡Estás muy ***bonita*** *hoy!*	You are (look) very pretty today!
El carro está ***sucio****.*	The car is dirty.

- Note, however, that some adjectives that describe appearance or personality can be used with either *ser* or *estar*, but with a difference in meaning.

Eduardo ***está guapo*** *hoy.*	Eduardo is (looks) handsome today.
Eva ***es*** *una muchacha* ***guapa****.*	Eva is a beautiful girl.

Práctica

25 ¿Cómo están?

Can you describe what you see in these photos? Complete the following sentences with the correct form of *estar* and an appropriate adjective.

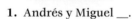

1. Andrés y Miguel __.

2. Clara __.

3. Los refrescos __.

4. La comida __.

5. La playa __.

6. El profesor Fernández __.

National Standards

Comparisons
4.1

Notes Remind students that the descriptive adjectives used in activities 25–31 must correspond with the words they describe and be either masculine or feminine and singular or plural.

Review the forms of *estar* before doing activity 25. Also, point out that answers for the activity consist of two words, a form of *estar* and an adjective.

26 Una barbacoa con los parientes

Pretend your family is having a cookout at your grandparents' house and one of your friends came with you. Take turns asking a classmate questions about some of the things you see there, using the words provided. Answer each question using the cues in parentheses.

MODELO estar abierto / la puerta de la casa de tus abuelos (ventanas)
A: ¿Está abierta la puerta de la casa de tus abuelos?
B: No, no está abierta, pero las ventanas están abiertas.

1. estar sucio / el carro de tu padre (el carro de mi tía)
2. estar apurado por ir a la playa / tus tíos de Fajardo (mis primos)
3. estar muy enfermo / tu tía (mi hermana)
4. estar cansado / tus abuelas (mi abuelo)
5. estar nervioso / tus padres (mis abuelos)
6. estar libre para ir al Yunque mañana / tú (mis primas)
7. estar triste / tus tías (la nueva esposa de mi primo)
8. estar ocupado / tus padres (tú y yo)

27 Hoy mi familia está...

Make a list of your family members (include yourself) and tell how each person is doing today. Then give a reason why the person is feeling that way. You may wish to use some of the following words in your descriptions: *apurado, contento, enfermo, loco, nervioso, triste.*

MODELO Mi hermano está contento hoy porque va a estar con sus amigos.

Mi familia está contenta.

Answers

26 1. ¿Está sucio el carro de tu padre?/No, no está sucio, pero el carro de mi tía está sucio.
2. ¿Están apurados por ir a la playa tus tíos de Fajardo?/ No, no están apurados por ir a la playa, pero mis primos están apurados por ir a la playa.
3. ¿Está muy enferma tu tía?/ No, no está muy enferma, pero mi hermana está muy enferma.
4. ¿Están cansadas tus abuelas?/No, no están cansadas, pero mi abuelo está cansado.
5. ¿Están nerviosos tus padres?/No, no están nerviosos, pero mis abuelos están nerviosos.
6. ¿Estás tú libre para ir al Yunque mañana?/No, no estoy libre, pero mis primas están libres para ir al Yunque mañana.
7. ¿Están tristes tus tías?/No, no están tristes, pero la nueva esposa de mi primo está triste.
8. ¿Están ocupados tus padres?/No, no están ocupados, pero tú y yo estamos ocupados/ ocupadas.

27 Answers will vary.

Notes For activity 27, encourage creativity and suggest students prepare a family tree that consists of celebrities and other well-known people. Students then make statements about their famous family members. Tell students they may make up any of the information for activity 27 if they prefer.

National Standards

Communication
1.1

Answers

28 Possible answers:
¿Está la puerta abierta o cerrada? La puerta está cerrada.
¿Cómo está la abuela? La abuela está muy cansada.
¿Cómo están los refrescos? Los refrescos están fríos.
¿Cómo está Félix/el gato? Félix está nervioso.
¿Cómo está María? María está enferma.
¿Cómo está Lucas/el perro? Lucas está loco.
¿Cómo está Andrea? Andrea está ocupada.
¿Cómo está Jaime? Jaime está apurado.

29 Creative self-expression.

Activities

Cooperative Learning

Working in pairs, have students describe the classroom and the people in it, as an extension and reinforcement of activity 28. For example, they might talk about how many boys and how many girls there are in the class (*¿Cuántos muchachos hay en la clase?*). Then they might comment on how others in the class are feeling today (*¿Cómo está el professor/la profesora hoy?*). Circulate around the room to be sure students are using the correct form of *estar* and the new adjectives from this lesson in their conversation.

National Standards
Communication 1.1
Connections 3.1

Comunicación

28 ¿Cómo está todo hoy?

With a classmate, discuss what you see in this illustration. Talk about who the people are and say how they feel (including the pets). You also may ask and answer questions about anything else you see.

MODELO
A: ¿Cuántas personas hay en la casa hoy?
B: Hay cinco personas y dos animales.
A: ¿Cómo está Humberto?
B: Está ocupado.

29 ¡Hola! ¿Cómo estás?

Working in groups, form two circles with six to eight students. Half of the students should be in an inside circle facing the students in an outside circle. Students who are facing one another should pretend they meet and begin a conversation about their families' health or emotional condition. Next, students in the outer circle move one to the right and begin a similar conversation with a new partner. Be sure to have a conversation with everyone in the opposing circle.

MODELO
A: Hola, Jaime. ¿Qué tal?
B: Estoy bien, pero apurado. Y tú, ¿cómo estás?
A: Yo estoy bien, gracias. ¿Cómo están tus padres?
B: Están nerviosos porque van a Vieques en avión.

Notes

As a follow-up to activity 28, conduct a class discussion about the contents of the illustration on page 150.

Ask students to find Vieques on a map. Point out that Vieques and Culebra are two islands that are part of Puerto Rico. Vieques is a small community; Culebra offers some of the world's most beautiful and secluded beaches for swimming. Students may want to find out more about what each island offers.

¡Tengo una familia famosa!

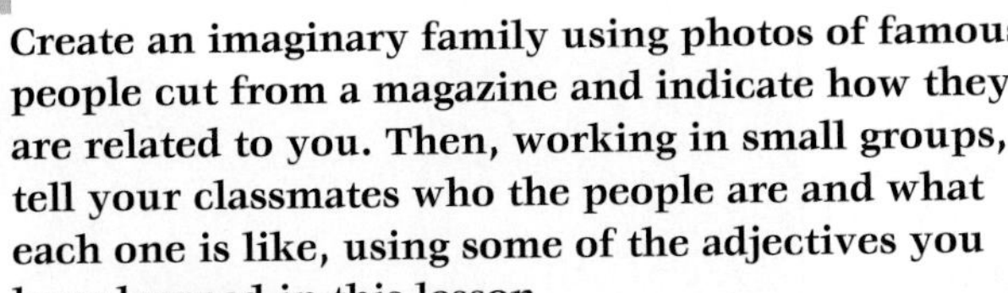

Create an imaginary family using photos of famous people cut from a magazine and indicate how they are related to you. Then, working in small groups, tell your classmates who the people are and what each one is like, using some of the adjectives you have learned in this lesson.

MODELO Es mi hermana y es muy bonita. *(Show a photo of a famous female such as Salma Hayek.)*

¿Es Salma Hayek tu hermana?

Te presento a mi familia

In small groups, pretend you are all members of the same family (decide who will play each role). Then, form concentric circles with another group so that members of your family in the circle face another group's family. Opposing family members should then alternate telling one another the names and relationships of family members in the circle, adding any relevant descriptions. When each opposing pair of students completes all introductions, the family in the inner circle rotates one person to the left and begins the activity again.

MODELO Aquí está mi primo. Es divertido.
Allí está mi abuela favorita, Ana María.

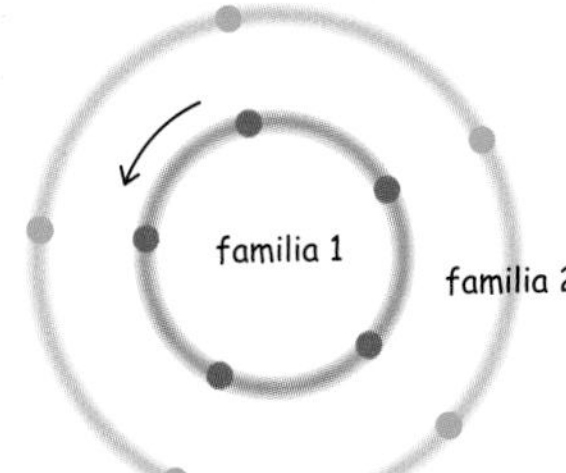

Aquí están mi mamá y mis dos hermanas.

¡Te presento a mi tío favorito!

Notes Set a time limit for activities 30–31. Then, while students are completing the activity, walk around the classroom and listen to some of the descriptions. Stop to offer help as needed and check to be sure students remain on task. While facilitating the conversations, extend the activity by selecting a few of the better descriptions for students to share with the class.

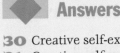

Answers

30 Creative self-expression.
31 Creative self-expression.

Activities

Language through Action
Have students walk around the classroom showing their photo albums to one another and telling one another in Spanish about the people in the photographs.

TPR
Write words and expressions such as *está triste* on separate pieces of paper. Have students select one of the pieces of paper at random. Then call on several students to act out the feelings while classmates guess what the expressions are in Spanish.

National Standards

Communication
1.1

Teacher Resources

Lectura Cultural
¿Qué es la familia?
Activity 32
Activity 33

Answers

32 1. No.
2. No.
3. No.
4. Sí.
5. Sí.

33 Answers will vary.

Activities

Communities
Conduct a class discussion about family life in your community. Use the cultural reading *¿Qué es la familia?* and the questions in *Algo personal* as your starting point. Ask students how families seem similar or different in Puerto Rico.

National Standards

Cultures
2.1

Connections
3.1

Comparisons
4.1, 4.2

Lectura cultural

¿Qué es la familia?

Una familia hispana.

¿Cómo es una familia típica de Puerto Rico? Según el censo más reciente[1], aproximadamente 3,5 personas viven en una casa y las familias tienen aproximadamente 1,9 hijos. Tres o más generaciones viven juntas[2] en solamente 7,36% de las casas.

El censo dice que las familias puertorriqueñas son pequeñas[3], pero los números no lo dicen todo. El término *familia*—en Puerto Rico y en muchos países hispanos—no solamente incluye a los padres y a los hijos sino también a los abuelos, tíos, primos y a los parientes políticos[4]. Tal vez[5] en una casa no vivan muchas personas, pero la familia sigue siendo[6] extensa y es una red de apoyo[7] importante. En toda celebración (o hasta[8] para una despedida en el aeropuerto) la familia extendida se junta[9].

El cumpleaños de la abuela.

Aunque[10] los censos muestran[11] que la familia hispana se vuelve[12] más pequeña (en México, por ejemplo, una madre tiene ahora 3 hijos, a diferencia de 6,5 hijos en 1973), la familia sigue siendo muy importante. De niños, los hispanos aprenden a ser leales[13] a su familia, a estar unidos y a ayudarse[14] siempre. La familia hispana enseña a los niños respeto, honor y cortesía. Es el grupo social más importante en la cultura hispana.

[1]most recent census [2]together [3]small [4]in-laws [5]Perhaps [6]continues to be [7]support system [8]even [9]gets together [10]Even though [11]show [12]is becoming [13]loyal [14]to help each other

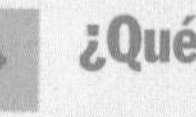

32 ¿Qué recuerdas?

¿Sí o no?

1. Las familias en Puerto Rico tienen muchos hijos.
2. En Puerto Rico, los abuelos típicamente viven con sus hijos y sus nietos.
3. Por lo general, para el hispano la palabra *familia* se refiere *(refers)* solamente a los parientes que viven en su casa.
4. Muchas familias hispanas enseñan a los niños respeto, honor y cortesía.
5. En la cultura hispana, la familia es el grupo social más importante.

33 Algo personal

1. Al describir tu familia, ¿a quiénes incluyes? ¿Es tu definición de "familia" igual *(the same)* o diferente que la definición hispana? Explica.
2. ¿Es la familia importante para ti? Explica.
3. Compara una familia típica en Puerto Rico con una familia típica en los Estados Unidos.

- **After reading the article, what generalization can you make about the size of Puerto Rican families? The importance of the family unit?**

Notes

You may wish to introduce additional family vocabulary: *cuñado* (brother-in-law), *cuñada* (sister-in-law), *suegro* (father-in-law), *suegra* (mother-in-law) and so on.

The family is the focal point of life in the Hispanic world. Almost all activities—parties, outings, etc.—include the family.

Communities. Tell students that because of Puerto Rico's political affiliation with the United States, its people are U.S. citizens and can travel freely between the island and the mainland. For this reason, there are very large Puerto Rican populations in the United States, especially in the Northeast.

Autoevaluación

As a review and self-check, respond to the following:

1. Give the names of five members of your family and say how each is related to you.
2. Describe two or three members of your family.
3. Imagine you are looking at a picture of your best friend's family. Name the people in the picture and their relationship to your friend.
4. Name three or four friends or relatives who do not live in your state and say where they live.
5. What might you ask someone in Spanish who looks happy? Sad?
6. What do you know about family life in the Spanish-speaking world?

Palabras y expresiones

How many of these words and expressions do you recognize?

Para describir
abierto,-a
amable
apurado,-a
bonito,-a
caliente
cansado,-a
cariñoso,-a
cerrado,-a
contento,-a
divertido,-a
enfermo,-a
frío,-a
guapo,-a
libre
limpio,-a
loco,-a
más
mis
nervioso,-a
nuestro,-a
ocupado,-a
otro,-a
popular
su, sus
sucio,-a
todo,-a
triste
tus
único,-a

Familia
el abuelo, la abuela
el esposo, la esposa
la familia
el hermano, la hermana
el hijo, la hija
la madre
el nieto, la nieta
el padre
los padres
el pariente, la pariente
el primo, la prima
el sobrino, la sobrina
el tío, la tía

Otras expresiones
la casa
la foto(grafía)
mucho
nunca
la playa
por
¡qué (+ *description*)!
el tiempo
el verano

Verbos
quiero
salir
vivir

Estructura

Do you remember the following grammar rules?

Expressing possession: possessive adjectives

Possessive adjectives describe relationships between people and must agree in number and gender with the noun.

singular possessive adjectives		plural possessive adjectives	
mi	nuestro, nuestra	mis	nuestros, nuestras
tu	vuestro, vuestra	tus	vuestros, vuestras
su	su	sus	sus

Regular *-ir* verbs: *vivir*

vivo	vivimos
vives	vivís
vive	viven

Describing people and things with *estar*

Estar can be used with adjectives to describe conditions that are likely to change or to express how someone or something is at a given moment.

Teacher Resources

 Activity 13

 p. 51

 Juegos

Flash Cards

Answers

Autoevaluación

Possible answers:

1. *(Name)* es mi hermano.
2. Mis padres son amables.
3. Ella es su madre. Tomás y Mario son sus hermanos.
4. Mis primos viven en (*name of city, state or country*).
5. ¿Estás contento/contenta? ¿Estás triste?
6. Answers will vary.

Activities

Cooperative Learning

Have students play the parts of various members of two families, *la familia Chávez* and *la familia Galván*, who meet for the first time while attending an event in the Grand Ballroom of the *Hotel San Juan*. Working in groups of five or six, members of each family should take turns introducing one another and offering any details they can about their families. Try to include brothers, sisters, parents, grandparents, etc.: *Tengo dos tías. Ellas son de Ponce.*

Notes **Communities.** There are many famous people of Puerto Rican descent born in the United States, such as actors Rosie Pérez and Jimmy Smits.

National Standards

Communication 1.1
Comparisons 4.1
Cultures 2.1
Connections 3.1

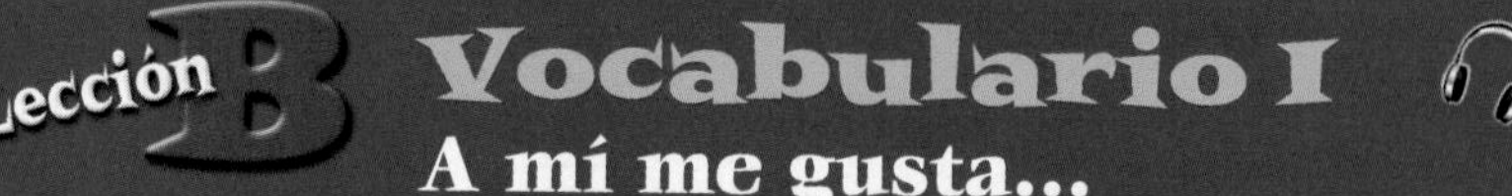

Teacher Resources

 **Vocabulario I** *A mí me gusta...*

 Activities 30–31

 Activities 1–2

 Activities 1–2

 pp. 73–74, 76

 p. 17

 Activity 1

 Activity 1

Content reviewed in *Lección B*

- everyday activities
- seeking and providing personal information
- family
- describing people
- present tense of *ser* and *estar*

Activities

Expansion

With books closed, call on one or more students to act out a word or expression for the class.

Spanish for Spanish Speakers

Have students model words and expressions in *Vocabulario I* for the class and then call on classmates to try pronouncing the new vocabulary.

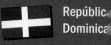

nadar

patinar (sobre ruedas)

jugar al béisbol

Tigres vs. Osos

jugar al tenis

ir a un partido de fútbol

bailar

¿Dónde vives?

Vivo en la República Dominicana.

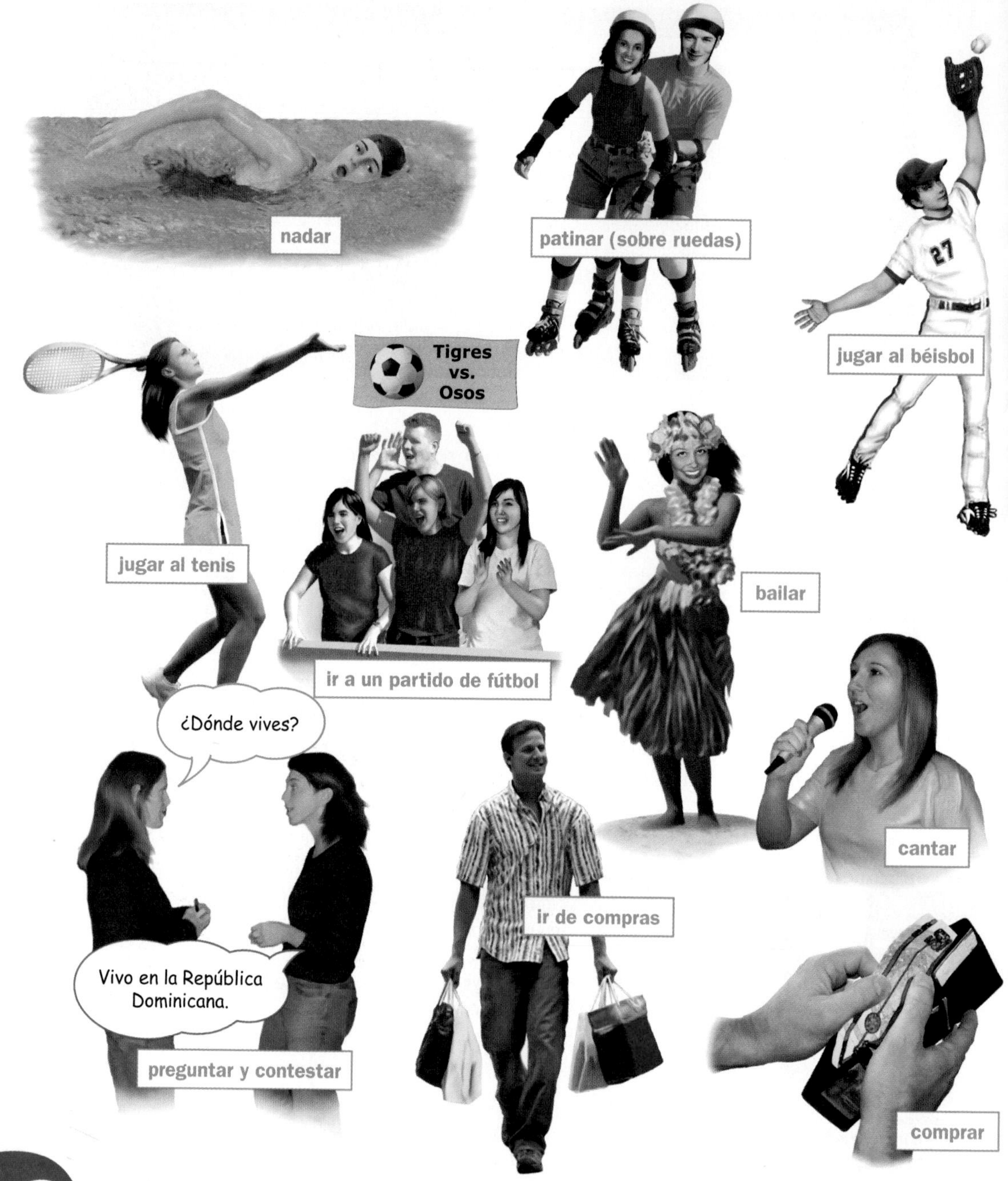

preguntar y contestar

ir de compras

cantar

comprar

National Standards
Communication 1.1, 1.2

Notes Use a variety of *¡Aventura! 1* support materials to teach and reinforce the vocabulary presented on pages 154–155. For example, the Audio Program Manual, the Listening Activities Manual, Overhead Transparencies, Workbook and Grammar and Vocabulary Exercises Manual. Quizzes support the teaching and evaluation of the content on these pages.

Consider playing the audio of *Vocabulario I* and have students practice their pronunciation before looking at the new words and expressions. Use any of the other ancillaries to tailor the content to match your teaching style.

1 ¿Qué es?

Go online EMCLanguages.net

 Selecciona la foto apropiada a lo que oyes.

A

B

C

D

E

F

2 Me gusta...

Write sentences saying five things you like to do and with whom you like to do each activity.

MODELO Me gusta ver la televisión con mi familia.

Notes

Inform students that in Spanish, *televisión* is the signal we watch; a *televisor* is the apparatus that receives a picture and audio signal. Likewise, *la radio* (short for *radiotransmisión*) is the signal; *el radio* is the apparatus that receives an audio signal.

Explain that both *mirar* (to look at) and *ver* (to see) are used to say that someone watches television.

Teacher Resources

 Activity 1

Answers

1
1. F
2. A
3. C
4. B
5. D
6. E

2 Answers will vary.

Activities

Expansion
Play the audio version of the vocabulary and have students practice repeating the expressions in Spanish before opening their books and seeing how the new words and expressions are written.

Language through Action
Use TPR and overhead transparencies 31–32 to teach and reinforce the vocabulary shown in *Vocabulario I*.

National Standards
Comparisons 4.1

Teacher Resources

Diálogo I
Me gusta mucho
Activity 3
Activity 4
Activity 5

Answers

3 1. A Andrés le gusta mucho la playa.
2. Natalia y otros amigos.
3. Hay un partido de fútbol.
4. Le gusta nadar.
5. Van al partido y a la playa.

4 Answers will vary.

5 **Natalia**
1. ir de compras
(2) ir a la playa
(3) bailar
4. tocar el piano
5. jugar al tenis

Andrés
6. jugar al béisbol
(7) ir a la playa
(8) bailar
9. patinar sobre ruedas
10. nadar

Activities

Critical Listening
Have students listen to the audio version of the dialog without referring to the text or photos.

Expansion
Additional questions *(Algo personal)*: *¿Cómo se llama tu playa favorita?; ¿Dónde está?; ¿Con quién vas a la playa?; ¿Te gusta nadar?*

National Standards	
Communication	**Comparisons**
1.1, 1.2	4.1

Diálogo I Me gusta mucho

ANDRÉS: Felipe, ¡vamos a la playa!
FELIPE: ¿A la playa? ¿Te gusta la playa?
ANDRÉS: Sí, me gusta mucho.

ANDRÉS: Natalia y otros amigos van a ir allí.
FELIPE: Bueno, yo quiero ir al partido de fútbol.
ANDRÉS: Ah, sí... pero me gusta más nadar.

FELIPE: A ti no te gusta nadar. A ti te gusta Natalia.
ANDRÉS: ¿Por qué no vamos al partido y, luego, a la playa?
FELIPE: Está bien, chico. ¡Vamos!

¿Qué recuerdas?

1. ¿A quién le gusta mucho la playa?
2. ¿Quiénes van a ir a la playa?
3. ¿De qué hay un partido?
4. ¿Qué le gusta a Andrés hacer en la playa?
5. ¿Adónde van los muchachos hoy?

Algo personal

1. ¿Te gusta ir a la playa?
2. ¿Te gusta ir a los partidos de fútbol?
3. ¿Qué te gusta hacer?

Estrategia

Using contextual cues
The context in which a word is used often determines its meaning. One example of this is *chico,* which can mean **boy** or **small.** In the dialog, however, Felipe uses *chico* as a term of friendship that Andrés does not take literally, much as you might use the words **buddy** or **pal.** Additional terms that are used include *hombre, compa* (from *compadre*), *chica, niña* and *guapa* (used among female friends). Other contextual cues include facial expressions and gestures. Looking at the context often indicates the intended meaning of words.

¿Qué les gusta?

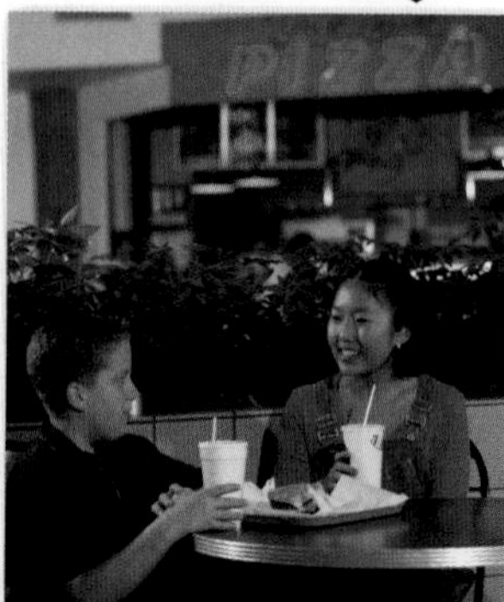

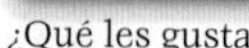
¿Qué les gusta?

Write the names Natalia and Andrés. Next, listen and list under each person's name what he or she likes to do. Then circle any item on the lists that they both like to do.

Notes

Play activities 3, 4 and 5 from the Audio Program or use the transcript that appears in the ATE Introduction if you prefer to read the activities yourself.

A reproducible answer sheet for activity 5 can be found at the end of the Audio Program Manual.

You may wish to have students use a Venn diagram to do activity 5.

Cultura viva! 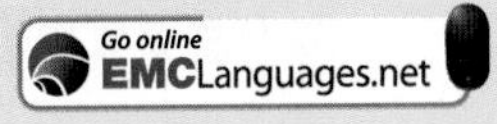

La República Dominicana

Unos amigos en la playa.

Actividades

Do you like baseball? More foreign-born U.S. professional baseball players originate from the Dominican Republic than from any other country. Do you enjoy sun-filled days on beautiful beaches, snorkeling, scuba diving or other water sports? Visitors may choose to explore beautiful beaches, such as *Boca Chica* and *El Dorado*. Does lively music make you want to get up and dance? Dominican music, particularly the *merengue*, a unique, fast-paced Caribbean music style, is popular throughout Latin America. If any of these activities appeal to you, you may want to visit *la República Dominicana*.

Geografía

The Caribbean island of Hispaniola *(La Española)* is shared by the Dominican Republic, which occupies the eastern three-fourths of this tropical island, and Haiti, which is located on the remaining western portion of the island. Christopher Columbus *(Cristóbal Colón)* claimed the Caribbean island for Spain in December 1492.

Historia

Santo Domingo, the capital of the Dominican Republic and the first capital in the Americas, was founded by Christopher Columbus' brother Bartholomew *(Bartolomé)* in 1496. You may recognize the names of other explorers who visited the Dominican Republic such as Ponce de León, Hernán Cortés, Diego de Velázquez and Vasco Núñez de Balboa.

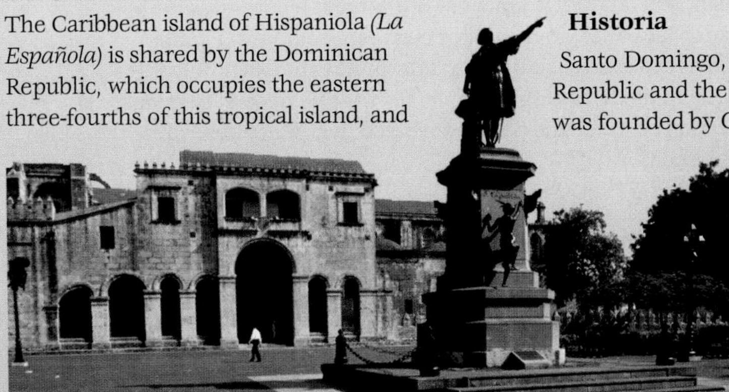
Una estátua de Cristóbal Colón en la capital, Santo Domingo.

6 Conexiones con otras disciplinas: historia y geografía

Use an encyclopedia or search the Internet for information about the Dominican Republic and list four or five interesting details about some aspect of the country's history (explorers, development as a country, native populations, important dates, etc.). Then create a map of Hispaniola, indicating the border between the two countries that make up the island and identify major cities, rivers, etc.

Notes

Conduct an information-gathering class discussion to find out what students know about the Dominican Republic. For example, ask if anyone knows of any recent news about the country, if they have read any articles about celebrities or famous people, etc. Then ask for student volunteers to gather information and create a bulletin board or travel brochure about the country.

There is controversy today about where Christopher Columbus is buried: in Santo Domingo or in Sevilla, Spain. Groups from both countries have argued about this claim for centuries.

Teacher Resources

 Activity 3

 p. 67

 Activity 2

Answers

6 Creative self-expression.

Activities

Expansion
Ask questions about the *Cultura viva: ¿Cuándo llegó Cristóbal Colón a La Española?; ¿Cómo se llama el hermano de Cristóbal Colón?; ¿Dónde está la tumba de Colón?; ¿Hay playas bonitas en la República Dominicana?; ¿Cómo se llaman?*

Multiple Intelligences (spatial/linguistic)
Using the resources of the Internet and the library, have students prepare a report about Dominican designer Óscar de la Renta. Have students illustrate their report with magazine photos, illustrations or computer graphics.

Spanish for Spanish Speakers
Have students read *In the Time of the Butterflies* by Dominican writer Julia Álvarez. Then have students write a paper in which they discuss how Rafael Leónidas Trujillo's dictatorship is depicted in the book.

National Standards
Communication 1.1
Cultures 2.1, 2.2
Connections 3.1, 3.2

Teacher Resources

 Activity 7

 Activity 4

 Activities 3–6

 p. 143

 Activity 3

 Unit 12

 Activity 2

Answers

7
1. Sí, (No, no) me gusta....
2. Sí, (No, no) me gusta....
3. Sí, (No, no) me gusta....
4. Sí, (No, no) me gustan....
5. Sí, (No, no) me gustan....

Activities

Language through Action

Use magazine pictures of items and activities found in *Vocabulario I,* glued or taped to stiff paper or cardboard. Place them individually along the chalk tray and write a number above each. Then use several commands to ask students to point out objects they like or dislike: (name), *ve (camina) a la pizarra; Toca el número...; ¿Te gusta* (item or activity pictured)? Listen for an appropriate response. Have each student touch two or three pictures, each time asking whether or not the student likes the item or activity he or she is touching.

National Standards

Communication
1.1

Comparisons
4.1

Idioma

Estructura

Using *gustar* to state likes and dislikes

- When talking about what they like or dislike, Spanish-speaking people use the verb *gustar*. Use the words *me, te, le, nos, os* or *les* before the singular *gusta* to say what someone likes when referring to an infinitive or a singular noun. Use the same *me, te, le, nos, os* or *les* before *gustan* when referring to a plural noun.

me	nos
te	(os)
le	les

gusta (followed by an infinitive or singular noun)

gustan (followed by a plural noun)

singular noun:	*¿**Te gusta** el libro?*	**Do you like** the book?
plural noun:	***Me gustan** todos los libros.*	**I like** all books.
infinitive:	***Me gusta** mucho leer.*	**I like** to read a lot.

Note: Earlier in this lesson, you learned to consider the context when determining the meaning of words like *chico* (in the dialog between Andrés and Felipe). You may need to apply this same skill when determining the meaning of *le* and *les*. For instance, in the following example, it would be necessary to hear the entire conversation or to see the people involved in order to determine the meaning of the sentence.

*¿**Le** gusta jugar al béisbol?*
- Do **you** ***(Ud.)*** like to play baseball?
- Does **he** like to play baseball?
- Does **she** like to play baseball?

- Make a sentence negative by placing *no* before *me, te, le, nos, os* or *les gusta/gustan*.

***No** me gusta hacer la tarea.*	I do not like to do homework.
*¿**No** te gustan las fotos de tu amiga?*	Don't you like your friend's pictures?
***No** nos gusta ir de compras.*	We do not like to go shopping.

Práctica

7 ¿Te gusta(n)...?

Contesta las siguientes preguntas.

1. ¿Te gusta el colegio?
2. ¿Te gusta la clase de español?
3. ¿Te gusta hacer la tarea?
4. ¿Te gustan los sábados?
5. ¿Te gustan los partidos de fútbol en la televisión?

Notes Activity 7 is appropriate for individuals or may be assigned to pairs or small groups of students, according to your individual preference and class needs.

You may wish to introduce other verbs, such as *encantar* and *molestar*, that follow a pattern similar to that of *gustar*.

8 Me gusta(n)...

En parejas, alternen en preguntar y contestar si lo que *(what)* ven en la ilustración les gusta(n) o no.

MODELO **A:** ¿Te gustan los partidos de béisbol?
B: Sí, (No, no) me gustan los partidos de béisbol.

1

2

3

4

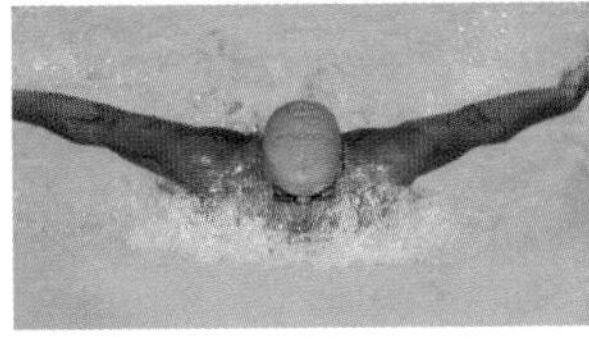

5

6

Comunicación

9 Encuesta

Working in small groups, create a survey to determine what activities your classmates enjoy. (The survey should consist of the same number of activities as there are members in your group.) Each person in your group selects one activity from the list and must then ask other students in class if they like that activity. Finally, one person from each group should give a summary *(resumen)* of the results of the survey to the class.

MODELO **A:** ¿Te gusta mirar fotos?
B: Sí, me gusta./No, no me gusta.
Resumen: A tres estudiantes les gusta mirar fotos y a un estudiante no le gusta mirar fotos.

ENCUESTA

¿Te gusta...?	Sí	No
1. mirar fotos	☑	☐
2. cantar	☐	☑
3. tocar el piano	☑	☐
4. jugar al fútbol	☑	☐

¡Extra!

¿Qué más te gusta hacer?

Me gusta jugar...	Me gusta tocar...
al básquetbol	el clarinete
a los bolos	la flauta
al fútbol americano	la guitarra
al golf	el saxofón
al hockey	el tambor

Notes

Remind students as they do activities 8 and 9 that an infinitive can follow *gusta* but not *gustan*.

Make sure students keep moving around the classroom as they complete activity 9. Circulate among them, monitoring their use of Spanish. If you wish, participate in the survey by answering their questions.

Answers

8 Possible answers:

1. ¿Te gusta escuchar la radio? Sí, (No, no) me gusta escuchar la radio.
2. ¿Te gustan las naranjas? Sí, (No, no) me gustan las naranjas.
3. ¿Te gusta patinar sobre ruedas? Sí, (No, no) me gusta patinar sobre ruedas.
4. ¿Te gustan las motocicletas? Sí, (No, no) me gustan las motocicletas.
5. ¿Te gusta nadar? Sí, (No, no) me gusta nadar.
6. ¿Te gustan los refrescos? Sí, (No, no) me gustan los refrescos.

9 Creative self-expression.

Activities

Cooperative Learning
Have students create their own surveys about pastime activities similar to the ones in activity 9. You may wish to have students work in pairs and exchange surveys. Then ask volunteers to give a summary of their partner's answers.

Language through Action
Play a game of charades in which students dramatize different sports and musical performances.

National Standards

Communication
1.1, 1.3

Connections
3.1

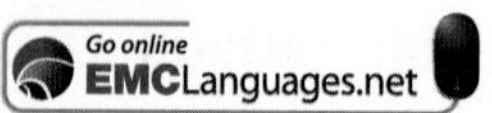

Teacher Resources

 Activities 5–6

 Activities 7–9

 p. 142

 Activity 4

 Activity 3

Answers

10 1. nos gusta
2. le gustan
3. le gusta
4. les gustan
5. les gusta
6. les gusta
7. me gustan
8. te gusta

Activities

Expansion

Use transparencies to talk about what people in activity 11 like to do: *Les gusta oír música, le gusta bailar*, etc.

Estructura

Using *a* to clarify or emphasize what you are saying

You can add *a* plus someone's name, a noun or a pronoun to clarify an otherwise confusing sentence or to emphasize what you are saying. Look at the following:

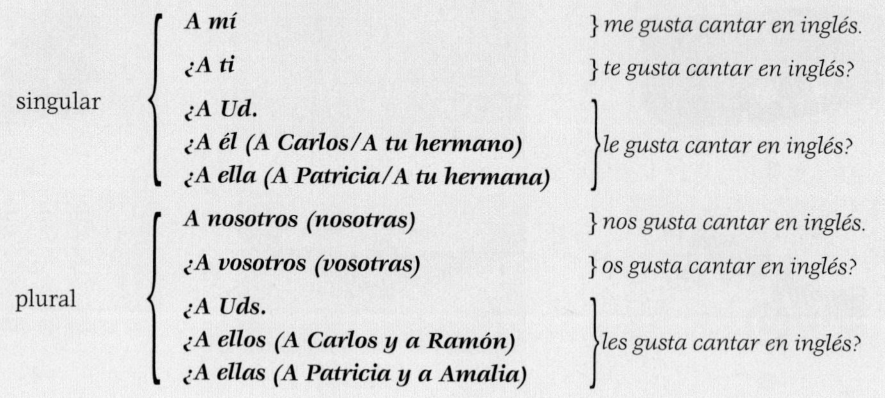

singular	***A mí***	*me gusta cantar en inglés.*
	¿A ti	*te gusta cantar en inglés?*
	¿A Ud. / ***¿A él (A Carlos/A tu hermano)*** / ***¿A ella (A Patricia/A tu hermana)***	*le gusta cantar en inglés?*
plural	***A nosotros (nosotras)***	*nos gusta cantar en inglés.*
	¿A vosotros (vosotras)	*os gusta cantar en inglés?*
	¿A Uds. / ***¿A ellos (A Carlos y a Ramón)*** / ***¿A ellas (A Patricia y a Amalia)***	*les gusta cantar en inglés?*

Práctica

¿Qué nos gusta hacer en casa?

Completa el siguiente párrafo con una palabra apropiada de cada columna.

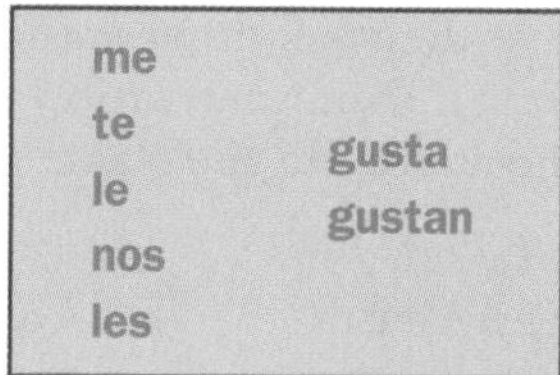

En mi casa a todos nosotros (1) mucho escuchar la radio y ver la televisión. A mi abuelo (2) todos los deportes en la televisión, como el fútbol, el béisbol y el básquetbol. A mi abuela (3) un programa de música española en la radio. A mis hermanos (4) los conciertos de rock y de música pop en la televisión pero también (5) escuchar música en la radio. A mamá y a mis hermanas siempre (6) un programa por cable donde hablan de la construcción, de la remodelación y de la decoración de las casas. ¡Es su programa favorito! Personalmente, a mí (7) los programas que le permiten a uno comprar por teléfono productos fantásticos. Y a ti, ¿qué (8) escuchar en la radio o ver en la televisión?

National Standards

Comparisons
4.1

Notes

Discuss activity 10 with students. Ask them to explain how the addition of *a* and a name, a noun or a pronoun helped them choose the correct form of *gustar* to clarify an otherwise confusing sentence.

¿Está claro?

Working in pairs, take turns reading these unclear sentences and clarify them by adding the given cues and making any other changes necessary. Follow the model.

MODELO A: Le gusta escuchar la radio y bailar. (Diana)
B: ¿A quién?
A: A Diana le gusta escuchar la radio y bailar.

B: Les gusta bailar merengue. (mis hermanas)
A: ¿A quiénes?
B: A mis hermanas les gusta bailar merengue.

1. Les gustan mucho los conciertos de música dominicana. (los Suárez)
2. Les gusta ir de compras. (mis primas)
3. Le gustan los partidos de béisbol. (Eduardo)
4. Le gusta patinar sobre ruedas. (ella)
5. Les gusta jugar al tenis. (Sara y Alberto)
6. Les gustan mucho las ciudades de Santo Domingo y Puerto Plata en la República Dominicana. (la Sra. y el Sr. García)

¿Qué les gusta?

The following people all have strong opinions about what they like and what they do not like. In pairs, take turns asking and answering questions using the cues below, clarifying each person's preference.

MODELO ella / nadar / jugar al tenis
A: ¿A ella le gusta nadar?
B: ¡No! ¡A ella no le gusta nadar! Le gusta jugar al tenis.

1. tú / ver televisión / ir al cine
2. Uds. / jugar al fútbol / jugar al béisbol
3. él / tocar el piano / bailar
4. ellas / ir de compras / escuchar música en la radio y cantar
5. los Fernández / las playas de Puerto Rico / las playas de la República Dominicana
6. los estudiantes / contestar en inglés / contestar en español

Me gustan las playas en la República Dominicana. (Las Terrenas Beach, R.D.).

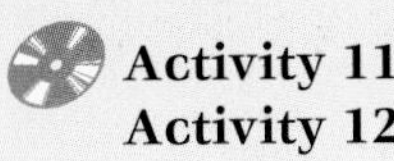

Teacher Resources

Activity 11
Activity 12

Answers

11
1. ¿A quiénes?/A los Suárez les gustan mucho los conciertos de música dominicana.
2. ¿A quiénes?/A mis primas les gusta ir de compras.
3. ¿A quién?/A Eduardo le gustan los partidos de béisbol.
4. ¿A quién?/A ella le gusta patinar sobre ruedas.
5. ¿A quiénes?/A Sara y Alberto les gusta jugar al tenis.
6. ¿A quiénes?/A la Sra. y al Sr. García les gustan mucho las ciudades de Santo Domingo y Puerto Plata en la República Dominicana.

12
1. ¿A ti te gusta...?/¡No! ¡A mí no me gusta...! Me gusta....
2. ¿A Uds. les gusta...?/¡No! ¡A nosotros no nos gusta...! Nos gusta....
3. ¿A él le gusta...?/¡No! ¡A él no le gusta...! Le gusta....
4. ¿A ellas les gusta...?/¡No! ¡A ellas no les gusta...! Les gusta....
5. ¿A los Fernández les gustan...?/¡No! ¡A ellos no les gustan...! Les gustan....
6. ¿A los estudiantes les gusta...?/¡No! ¡A ellos no les gusta...! Les gusta....

Notes

Point out that the prepositional phrases for emphasis or clarity shown on page 160 do not change to match verb phrases. For example: *A mí me gusta la playa. A mí me gustan las playas de la República Dominicana. A ellos les gusta la ciudad. A ellos les gustan las ciudades grandes.*

National Standards

Communication
1.1

Teacher Resources

 Activity 13

Answers

13 Questions follow this pattern: *¿Les gusta...?* Answers will vary but begin with *Sí, nos gusta...* or *No, no nos gusta....*
14 Creative self-expression.
15 Creative self-expression.

Activities

Critical Thinking
Ask students to express their preferences in relation to the following options: *¿Te gusta más la música rock o la música clásica? ¿Te gusta más el fútbol (americano) o el béisbol? ¿Te gusta más el golf o el tenis? ¿Te gusta más la comida mexicana o la comida italiana? ¿Te gusta más la televisión o el cine? ¿Te gusta más leer o ver la televisión? ¿Te gustan más los coches o las motos?* Have students explain each preference by posing the question *¿Por qué?*

National Standards
Communication 1.1

13 ¿Les gusta a todos en tu familia? 

Working with a classmate, take turns asking and answering questions about what everyone in your family likes to do. If there is someone who does not like an activity that follows, say who that person is.

MODELO bailar
A: ¿Les gusta bailar a todos en tu familia?
B: Sí, nos gusta bailar a todos./No, no nos gusta bailar a todos porque a mi padre no le gusta bailar.

1. ir a restaurantes
2. leer libros
3. pasear en el parque
4. vivir en los Estados Unidos
5. visitar a la familia
6. salir de casa los sábados
7. ir a conciertos de rock

Nos gusta bailar.

14 A mi familia y a mis amigos...

Name at least six people who are important in your life and say how you know each person (they are either family or friends). Then say something each person likes and at least one thing the person does not like.

MODELO A mi amigo Miguel le gustan las playas.
A Miguel no le gusta nadar.

Comunicación

15 Nos gusta(n)...

With a classmate, find out four things that both of you like. Write down your findings, using *Nos gusta(n)*.

MODELO **A:** ¿Te gusta tocar el piano?
B: No, no me gusta. ¿A ti te gusta cantar?
A: ¡Sí, claro! Me gusta mucho.
A y B: (Write Nos gusta cantar.)

A Manu Ginóbli le gusta jugar básquetbol.

Sus actividades favoritas

In small groups, discuss the activities you like most and least. Each member of the group must then compile a list of two things others in the group like and do not like to do. Finally, choose one member of your group to report the information to the class.

MODELO **A:** A mí me gusta nadar. ¿Qué les gusta hacer a Uds.?
B: A mí me gusta ir de compras.
C: A mí me gusta escuchar música en la radio.
B: A *(name of student A)* le gusta nadar, a *(name of student C)* le gusta escuchar la radio y a mí me gusta ir de compras.

¿Les gusta(n)?

Make a list of seven activities or items that are common in your daily life. Then ask your classmates if they like the activity or item. When you find someone who likes what you named, have the person sign his or her name *(Firma aquí, por favor.)* next to the appropriate activity or item. You have ten minutes to locate one person for each activity or item on your list. Next, summarize your findings in several short sentences. Finally, report the results to the class.

MODELO ver televisión
A: Ana, ¿te gusta ver la televisión?
B: Sí, me gusta ver la televisión.
A: Firma aquí, por favor.
A: *(Writes and says:* A Ana le gusta ver la televisión.*)*

A ellos les gusta leer el periódico.

¿Le gusta/Le gustan?	Sí	No	Firma
1. los partidos de tenis	X		María A.
2. jugar al béisbol			
3. ...			

Answers

16 Creative self-expression.
17 Creative self-expression.

Activities

Cooperative Learning
Have students bring in magazine pictures of four items and/or activities they like and four they do not like. They should look up any new vocabulary and learn new words, as appropriate. Ask students to work in pairs to do the following: First they should teach each other the new vocabulary; then they should take turns asking each other which activities or objects they like, asking: *¿Te gusta...?* When all students have completed their interviews, select several students to report on the likes and dislikes of the interview partner while holding up and showing the appropriate picture: *A* (name) *(no) le gusta....*

Notes You can save time and frustration when assigning activity 17 by asking students to prepare their list of activities/items and their summary at home.

Reminder: When doing paired and group activities requiring students to interact, be sure to circulate among them and monitor their use of Spanish. Encourage them to avoid using English and to stay on task asking the questions on their lists about most and least favorite activities.

National Standards

Communication
1.1, 1.3

Connections
3.1

Teacher Resources

 **Vocabulario II** *¿Cómo son?*

 **Activities 32–33**

 **Activities 7–8**

 **Activities 10–11**

 **pp. 69–70**

 **p. 18**

 **Activity 5**

 **Activity 4**

Activities

Expansion

Model the pronunciation of the words for student repetition. Then model sentences that include the new vocabulary as you act out adjectives from pages 164–165.

National Standards

Comparisons
4.1

Vocabulario II

¿Cómo son?

lenta

rápido

guapa

feo

alto

bajo

difícil

$\int f(x)dx = g(b)-g(a)$

$2+2=4$

fácil

inteligente

cómica

importante

malo

bueno

divertido

ideal

aburrido

gordo

horrible

interesante

fantástico

delgado

Notes Explain that *aburrido/aburrida* means **boring** when it is used with *ser*, but the meaning changes to **bored** when this adjective is used with *estar*: *El programa es aburrido.* (The program is boring.); *Mi hermana está aburrida.* (My sister is bored.).

Additional adjectives for describing people: *tímido* (timid), *valiente* (valiant), *estudioso* (studious), *serio* (serious) and *activo* (active).

Go online EMCLanguages.net

18 ¿Cómo es?

Mira las fotos y contesta las preguntas con sí o no, según lo que oyes.

1

2

3

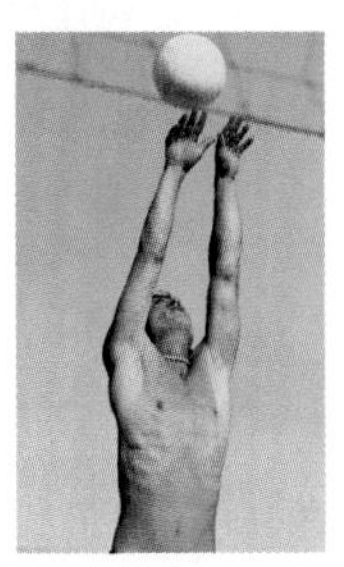

4

5

6

7

8

19 ¿Quién y cómo?

Create a list of six friends or relatives and indicate their relationship to you. Under each name write words that describe the person, categorizing the words according to whether they refer to physical traits *(características físicas)* or personality characteristics *(características de personalidad)*.

MODELO Patti Funston (hermana)

características físicas	características de personalidad
guapa y delgada	inteligente y divertida

Notes

Activity 18 is intended to offer listening comprehension practice on the adjectives on pages 164 and 165. A reproducible answer sheet for the activity is located at the end of the Audio Program Manual.

Note for students that *moreno/morena* is used to refer to skin or hair color.

Teacher Resources

 Activity 18

 p. 1

Answers

18 1. Sí.
2. No.
3. No.
4. Sí.
5. Sí.
6. No.
7. Sí.
8. No.

19 Answers will vary.

Activities

Multiple Intelligences (linguistic)

Ask students to find pairs of opposites in *Vocabulario II* (e.g., *bueno/malo*).

Spanish for Spanish Speakers

Ask students to write an essay describing their two best friends. They should include their names, ages and characteristics of personality and appearance. Also, ask them to discuss the activities they like to do and don't like to do when they are together. As an alternative, have students write a composition in Spanish about their favorite relative. They should include the relative's name, age, personality, appearance and the three things they like most about the person.

National Standards

Communication
1.2

Teacher Resources

Diálogo II
¿Cómo es ella?
Activity 20
Activity 21
Activity 22

Answers

20 1. Es morena y es muy inteligente.
2. Es de Santo Domingo.
3. A las muchachas de Santo Domingo les gusta bailar.
4. Con una chica pelirroja.

21 Answers will vary.

22 1. mala
2. alta
3. tristes
4. lento
5. fácil
6. tontos
7. guapo/bonito
8. divertido/interesante

Activities

Pronunciation
Native speakers pronounce similar sounds at the end of one word and at the beginning of another as if they were connected (*¿dónde está?/ doctor Rivera*); link dissimilar vowel sounds that occur in sequence (*a ella*); link a consonant sound that ends a word to a vowel sound that occurs at the beginning of the following word (*el esposo*). Practice this point by having students either act out the dialog from the book or create their own dialogs to be presented orally in class.

National Standards
Communication 1.2, 1.3

Diálogo II

¿Cómo es ella?

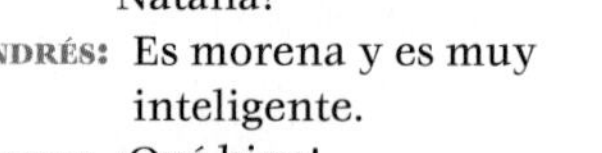

FELIPE: ¿Cómo es tu amiga Natalia?
ANDRÉS: Es morena y es muy inteligente.
FELIPE: ¡Qué bien!

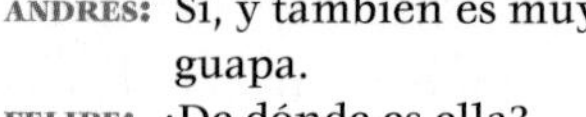

ANDRÉS: Sí, y también es muy guapa.
FELIPE: ¿De dónde es ella?
ANDRÉS: Ella es de Santo Domingo.

FELIPE: ¡A las muchachas de Santo Domingo les gusta bailar!
ANDRÉS: Sí, ella baila muy bien el merengue. ¡Mira, allí está!
FELIPE: ¡Ah, sí!, con la chica pelirroja.

20 ¿Qué recuerdas?

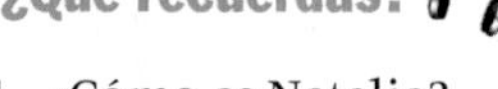

1. ¿Cómo es Natalia?
2. ¿De dónde es Natalia?
3. ¿A quiénes les gusta bailar?
4. ¿Con quién está Natalia?

21 Algo personal

1. ¿Cómo eres tú?
2. ¿Cómo es tu amigo/a favorito/a?
3. ¿Dónde estás ahora?

22 ¿Cuál es el opuesto?

You will hear some descriptions of people and objects. Give the opposite *(el opuesto)* of each adjective you hear.

MODELO gordos

Mis amigas son inteligentes.

Notes

Diálogo II contextualizes the new words and expressions that are introduced in *Vocabulario II*, allowing students to practice the new vocabulary in complete-sentence answers to activities.

Diálogo II and the activities that follow have been recorded by native Spanish speakers and can be found in the Audio Program.

Student answer sheets for activity 22 can be found in the back of the Audio Program Manual.

Have students match the gender and number of the antonyms they give for activity 22.

Cultura   Viva II

El merengue

Ellos bailan merengue.

What do you associate with the Dominican Republic? Along with baseball, this Spanish-speaking Caribbean country is known for its music and dance. One example is the folkloric dance and musical style known as the *merengue*. Although *merengue* music is varied in tempo, the dance is recognizable because the dancing couples hold one another in a waltz-like position as they move about the floor dragging one foot with each step they take. *Merengue* has existed for more than one hundred years. Although no one can be certain exactly how *merengue* evolved, most probably it has African and European roots. One interesting theory suggests the music consists of a mix of African slave songs and the sophisticated French minuet of the late eighteenth century. Regardless of how it originated, *merengue* remains the national dance of the Dominican Republic and is extremely popular throughout the Caribbean and South America as well. When you visit the country, you will more than likely see people dancing *merengue* and you will most certainly hear *merengue* music performed by a number of popular musicians such as Juan Luis Guerra.

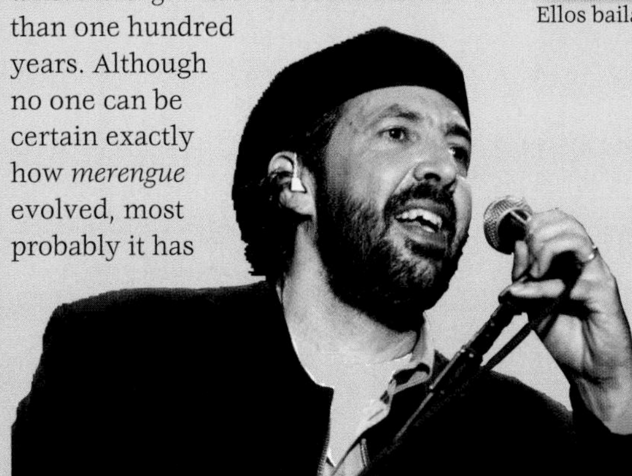
Juan Luis Guerra.

23 Conexión con otras disciplinas: música

Using an encyclopedia or the Internet, research some aspect of Dominican music that interests you (e.g., *merengue*, Juan Luis Guerra, Wilfrido Vargas). Prepare a short report on your findings. If possible, demonstrate what you found out (dance the *merengue*, play a CD with Dominican music, etc.).

24 Comparando

Compare music in the Dominican Republic with popular music you usually listen to in the United States. What seems similar? What is different? What do you like about both kinds of music?

Teacher Resources

 **Activity 6**

 **Activity 5**

Answers

23 Creative self-expression.
24 Answers will vary.

Activities

Multiple Intelligences (intrapersonal)
Ask students to keep a log for a week in which they note ways they have contact with Spanish and the Spanish-speaking world. Such contact may include people, products, classes, current events, music, etc.

Notes

Merengue was introduced into the United States through New York in the early twentieth century, and one version, the *merengue de salón*, is one of the classic Latin American dances in ballroom competitions throughout the world.

You may wish to offer some additional background information about Dominican *merengue*: Juan Luis Guerra graduated from the Dominican Conservatory and Berkley College in Boston. He and his group, 4.40, created music he calls *el merengue dual* because it makes people dance and think at the same time.

National Standards	
Cultures 2.1, 2.2	**Communities** 5.1
Connections 3.1	
Comparisons 4.1, 4.2	

Teacher Resources

 Activities 9–12

 Activities 12–13

 Activity 7

 Activity 6

Answers

25 1. C; 2. A; 3. F; 4. C; 5. D; 6. B

Activities

Critical Listening
Tell the class that they will hear several statements about two sisters, Clara and Ana. After each statement they must say whether *ser* or *estar* was used and explain why: *Clara y Ana son hermanas; Clara y Ana están en el colegio; Ana está cansada; Clara es cómica y simpática; A Ana le gusta jugar al tennis. Su partido es en el colegio; Los padres de Clara y Ana son profesores; Su madre es de España y su padre es de los EE.UU.*

Critical Thinking
Write several phrases on the board that are preceded by *ser* (*de Puerto Rico, inteligente, las 8:00*) and several that are preceded by *estar* (*bien, regular, en Santo Domingo, en la clase*). Point to a word or phrase and ask: "*¿Ser o estar?*"; after students respond, ask "*¿Por qué?*" and call on one student to support the answer. (Teach students the Spanish words: *origen, característica, condición* and *lugar.*)

National Standards
Communication 1.1
Connections 3.1
Comparisons 4.1

Idioma

Estructura

Ser vs. *estar*

Both *ser* and *estar* are equivalent to the English verb **to be**. However, the two verbs are used in very different situations.

- *Ser* may be used to express origin.
  Soy de la República Dominicana. — I am from the Dominican Republic.
- *Ser* is also used to indicate characteristics that distinguish people or objects from one another.
  Jaime es alto. — Jaime is tall.
- *Estar* is used to express a temporary condition.
  ¡Qué bonita está hoy! — How pretty she is (looks) today!
- *Estar* may also refer to where someone or something is located.
  ¿Dónde está tu casa? — Where is your house?

Note: Although *estar* is generally used to express location, ser is used to refer to the location of an event, in which case it means **to take place**.

¿Dónde es el concierto? — Where is the concert (taking place)?

Práctica

25 ¿De dónde son?

Selecciona la letra de la forma apropiada de *ser* para completar las oraciones.

1. Juan Luis Guerra __ de la República Dominicana.
2. Yo __ de los Estados Unidos.
3. Shakira y Juan Pablo Montoya __ de Colombia.
4. ¿__ Ricky Martin de Puerto Rico?
5. ¿Pues, __ tú y yo de la misma ciudad?
6. ¿De dónde __ tú?

A. soy
B. eres
C. es
D. somos
E. sois
F. son

¿De dónde es Juan Pablo Montoya?

Notes Review the present-tense forms of *ser* and *estar* with students before explaining their differences in usage.

Many Dominican baseball players in the United States originate from San Pedro de Macorís.

26 ¿Cómo son?

Describe your relatives, your friends and yourself, using the appropriate form of *ser* and one or two adjectives. You may make up any of the information you wish.

MODELO el profesor/la profesora de inglés
El profesor de inglés es calvo y muy divertido.

1. yo
2. mi madre
3. mis abuelos
4. mi dentista
5. mi amiga favorita
6. los otros estudiantes de la clase de español y yo

27 ¿Cómo están allí?

Completa las oraciones con la forma apropiada de *estar*.

1. Yo __ en mi clase favorita ahora.
2. Mi amiga favorita no __ en la clase.
3. Tres estudiantes __ enfermos hoy.
4. La profesora es simpática y hoy __ muy bonita.
5. Nosotros __ muy cansados pero contentos porque mañana es sábado.
6. ¿Cómo __ tú hoy?

28 *¿Ser o estar?*

Usa la forma correcta de *ser* o *estar* para completar las siguientes oraciones.

1. Óscar de la Renta __ de la República Dominicana.
2. Su casa __ en Santo Domingo.
3. Eduardo __ el tío de Mónica.
4. No __ cansado... ¡Estoy apurado!
5. El carro __ de Hernán y Gloria.
6. El Yunque __ en Puerto Rico.
7. ¡Qué simpática __ tú!
8. Nosotros __ contentos de estar en San Pedro de Macorís.
9. ¿Tienes calor o __ bien?
10. ¿Dónde __ el concierto de merengue?

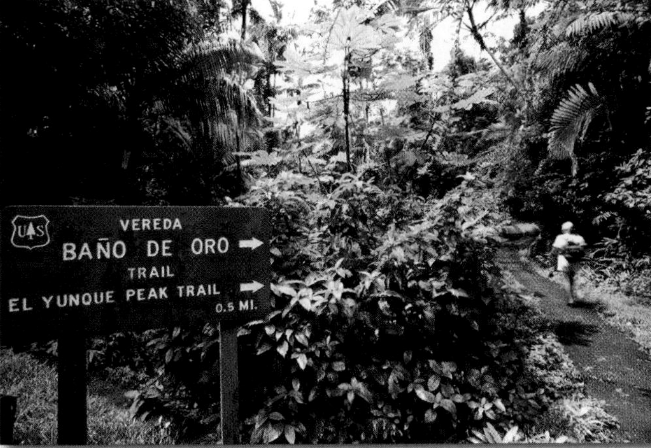

El Yunque está en Puerto Rico.

Notes In activity 28 have students give a reason for their choices of *ser* or *estar*, such as origin, location, condition, characteristic.

Point out the sign in the photograph and ask students if they recall where El Yunque is located.

Teacher Resources

 **Activity 26**

Answers

26 Creative self-expression. Students should use an adjective and the following forms of ser in their answers:
1. soy; 2. es; 3. son; 4. es; 5. es; 6. somos

27
1. estoy
2. está
3. están
4. está
5. estamos
6. estás

28
1. es
2. está
3. es
4. estoy
5. es
6. está
7. eres
8. estamos
9. estás
10. es

Activities

Critical Thinking
After completing activity 26, extend the practice by having students describe the following people: *el profesor/la profesora de español; el director/la directora de la escuela; yo; mi abuelo; mis hermanos; mi actor favorito; mi actriz favorita.*

National Standards

Communication
1.1

Connections
3.1

Answers

29 Creative self-expression. Students should use the appropriate forms of *ser* and *estar* in their descriptions.
30 Creative self-expression.
31 Creative self-expression.

Activities

Expansion
Encourage students to bring cutouts of at least one Spanish-speaking sports figure, musician or actor when completing activity 30. For closure to activity 30, have the biographer of each group summarize the information for the class.

Multiple Intelligences (linguistic/spatial)
Have students create a collage with the pictures they and their partners bring to class for activity 30. Then ask for volunteers to present the collages to the class.

National Standards

Communication
1.1, 1.3

Cultures
2.2

29 ¿Cuál es tu opinión?

En parejas, describan a las personas en las fotos.

1

2

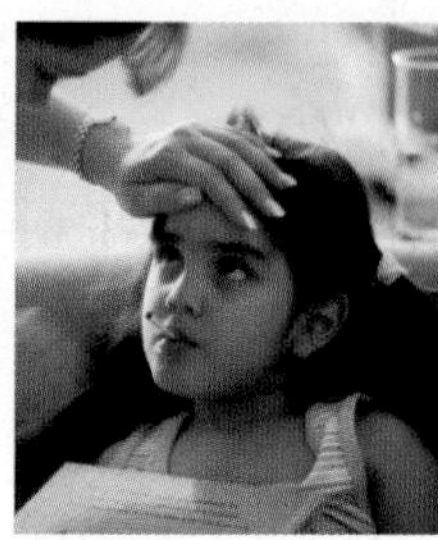

3

30 Biografía

Bring to class magazine cutouts of a famous person (e.g., singer, athlete, television/film star). Next, working in small groups, decide who will be the "biographer" and write down what others say about and how they describe each person (everyone in the group should be the biographer one time). Finally, one student holds up a picture, while the others add a sentence to describe the person shown (and the biographer writes down what everyone in the group says).

MODELO A: ¿Cómo es Jennifer López?
B: Es guapa.
C: Es una cantante popular.
(The biographer writes *Jennifer López es guapa y es una cantante popular.*)

Jennifer López es guapa y es una cantante popular.

Comunicación

31 ¿Quién es?

Write five or six sentences about a celebrity, including where the person is from, what the person is like, why the person is famous, etc. Do not name the celebrity. Then, working with a partner, describe the celebrity as your classmate draws the person's picture. The activity ends when your partner guesses the name of the person. Switch roles.

Notes As a follow-up to activity 30, ask for volunteers to read the biographers' summaries in front of the class as an assistant holds up the pictures.

After completing activity 31, play a guessing game with the class to see if students know who is being described:
1) Call on a student to read the first sentence from one of the descriptions he or she discussed with another student for activity 31; 2) ask *¿Quién es?* and see if anyone recognizes the person; 3) continue one sentence at a time, either until someone guesses who the person is or until there are no more sentences to read.

32 Juego

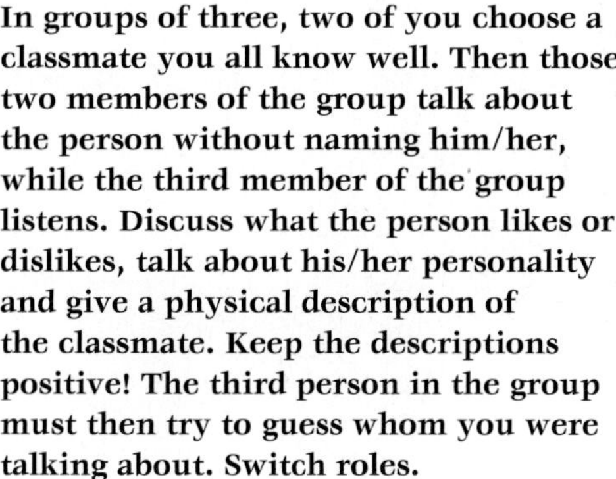

In groups of three, two of you choose a classmate you all know well. Then those two members of the group talk about the person without naming him/her, while the third member of the group listens. Discuss what the person likes or dislikes, talk about his/her personality and give a physical description of the classmate. Keep the descriptions positive! The third person in the group must then try to guess whom you were talking about. Switch roles.

Hacemos preguntas.

33 Entrevista

Write six questions you would like to ask someone in class. Include questions about how the person feels today, what the person likes and dislikes, favorite pastimes, personality, what the person's family is like, and so forth. Next, interview a classmate you do not know well and take notes. Then switch roles. Finally, write a summary describing how you are alike and different, making positive statements only. Present the results to the class.

¿Cómo es tu familia?

¿Te gusta nadar?

¿Te gusta escuchar música?

Notes Have students prepare the interview questions as homework. Pair students of varying language ability levels so that less accomplished students can work with more advanced students. Also, if you pair them up, your students will become accustomed to working with different peers instead of always choosing their friends.

Answers

32 Creative self-expression.
33 Creative self-expression.

Activities

Students with Special Needs

Provide the following for students who require a model of what to do for activity 33:

A: *¿Cómo te llamas?*
B: *Me llamo* (name of B).
A: *¿Qué te gusta hacer?*
B: *Me gusta....*
A: *¿Qué más te gusta?*
B: *Me gusta....*
A: *¿Qué no te gusta?*
B: *Pues, no me gusta....*

Resumen: Mi nuevo/nueva amigo/amiga se llama (name of B). *Le gusta...y.... A mí me gusta más.... A* (name of B) *no le gusta...y a mí no me gusta...tampoco.* (Name of B) *es generoso/generosa, alto/alta.*

National Standards

Communication
1.1, 1.3

Teacher Resources

Lectura personal
Activity 34
Activity 35

Answers

34 1. Sammy Sosa nació en la República Dominicana en San Pedro de Macorís.
2. Tiene seis hermanos.
3. Manuel admira a Sammy Sosa porque juega muy bien al béisbol y es una persona generosa y amable.
4. Anotó un nuevo récord de jonrones en 1998.
5. Va a ver la casa en donde vivió Sammy Sosa.

35 Answers will vary.

Activities

Technology
Have students do an Internet search using the words **Sammy Sosa** to find out more about this Dominican baseball player.

National Standards

Cultures
2.2

Connections
3.1, 3.2

Comparisons
4.1

Lectura personal

Dirección http://www.emcp.com/músico/aventura1/

Archivo Edición Ver Favoritos Herramientas Ayuda

página principal | miembros | e-diario

Nombre: **Manuel Andrade Blanco**
Edad: **17 años**
País natal: **Panamá**
Deporte favorito: **el béisbol**
La muchacha ideal: **alta, morena, generosa, inteligente**

Estamos ahora en la bonita isla de la República Dominicana, el país natal de mi héroe: el beisbolista Sammy Sosa. A mí me gusta mucho el béisbol y admiro mucho a Sammy Sosa. Sé todo sobre él. Samuel Peralta Sosa nació[1] el doce de noviembre de 1968. Su familia era pobre[2] y por lo tanto[3] Sammy jugaba[4] al béisbol (o a la pelota como dicen los dominicanos) con un palo[5] y un calcetín[6]. Empezó[7] a jugar profesionalmente a los dieciséis años con los Texas Rangers. En 1998, anotó[8] 64 jonrones, un nuevo récord. En mi opinión, Sammy Sosa es uno de los grandes jugadores de la historia y también es una persona generosa y amable. Él ha donado[9] millones de dólares a su país. Estoy muy, muy contento porque esta tarde voy a ir a San Pedro de Macorís para ver la casa donde vivió[10] Sammy Sosa con su madre y sus seis hermanos. Es una casa pequeña y rosada[11]. Claro, ¡voy a sacar muchas fotos!

[1]was born [2]poor [3]therefore [4]played [5]stick [6]sock [7]He began [8]he hit [9]has donated [10]lived [11]small and pink

34 ¿Qué recuerdas?

1. ¿Dónde nació Sammy Sosa?
2. ¿Cuántos hermanos tiene?
3. ¿Por qué admira Manuel a Sammy Sosa?
4. ¿En qué año anotó Sammy Sosa un nuevo récord de jonrones?
5. ¿Qué va a ver Manuel en San Pedro de Macorís?

35 Algo personal

1. ¿Te gusta el béisbol? ¿Cuántos jugadores de la República Dominicana puedes nombrar?
2. ¿Quién es tu héroe? ¿Por qué admiras a esa persona?
3. ¿Piensas *(Do you think)* que los jugadores famosos deben ayudar *(should help)* a sus países? Explica.

- **How does your hero's childhood compare with Sammy Sosa's childhood?**

Notes Sammy Sosa is one of the most famous baseball players from the Dominican Republic. He received international attention in 1998 due to his race against Mark McGwire to break the single-season home-run record.

Students interested in baseball may wish to visit the following Internet site:
Dominican Republic Baseball
www.baseball-reference.com/bio/D-R-_born.shtml

Autoevaluación

As a review and self-check, respond to the following:

1. Name two activities you enjoy.
2. Ask if your friend likes something. How would you ask your teacher the same question?
3. Your cousin tells you he likes to study. How would you respond, emphasizing that you like to play tennis?
4. Describe your best friend in Spanish.
5. How would you say in Spanish that something is interesting? Sad?
6. How would you say Marta is a good student, but she is bored today?
7. What do you know about the Dominican Republic?

Palabras y expresiones

How many of these words and expressions do you recognize?

Para describir
aburrido,-a
alto,-a
bajo,-a
bueno,-a
calvo,-a
canoso,-a
cómico,-a
delgado,-a
difícil
egoísta
fácil
feo,-a
generoso,-a
gordo,-a
horrible
ideal
importante
inteligente
interesante
lento,-a
malo,-a
moreno,-a
pelirrojo,-a
rápido,-a
rubio,-a
tonto,-a

Otras expresiones
el béisbol
la compra
el fútbol
me
mí
nos
el partido
el piano
la radio
la tarea
la televisión
el tenis
ti

Verbos
bailar
cantar
comprar
contestar
escuchar
gustar
ir de compras
jugar (ue)
jugar a (+ *sport/game*)
mirar
nadar
patinar (sobre ruedas)
tocar

Estructura

Do you remember the following grammar rules?

Using *gustar* to state likes and dislikes			
Singular – followed by an infinitive verb or singular noun		**Plural** – followed by a plural noun	
me gusta el libro	**nos gusta** bailar	**me gustan** los libros	**nos gustan** las computadoras
te gusta comer	**os gusta** la naranja	**te gustan** los frijoles	**os gustan** los zapatos
le gusta la bebida	**les gusta** hablar	**le gustan** los discos compactos	**les gustan** las camisas

Ser vs. *estar*	
When to use ***ser***	When to use ***estar***
Description – *Ella **es** alta.* Occupation – ***Soy** profesor.* Characteristic – *Él **es** bajo.* Time & Date / Event – ***Son** las ocho; La fiesta es en la casa de Antonio.* Origin – ***Soy** de Colombia.* Relationship – *Ella **es** mi madre.*	Location: – ***Estás** en Nueva York.* Condition – ***Estoy** enfermo.* Emotion – *La chica **está** muy bien.*

Notes

Although 80 percent of the island is mountainous, the Dominican Republic's valleys have lush vegetation and fertile farmland. Agriculture is the country's leading industry and provides its most important trading partner, the United States, with sugar, coffee, bananas and cocoa. Tourism is also important to the economy. In fact, the Dominican Republic is the second most visited Caribbean destination.

Model words from the list of *Palabras y expresiones* and have students repeat after you. Then call on individuals to simultaneously practice and evaluate pronunciation.

Teacher Resources

 Activity 13

 pp. 52, 86

 Juegos

Flash Cards

Answers

Autoevaluación

Possible answers:

1. Me gusta....
2. ¿Te gusta...?/¿Le gusta...?
3. A mí me gusta jugar al tenis.
4. Mi amigo/amiga es.... Le gusta....
5. Es interesante. Es triste.
6. Marta es una estudiante buena, pero está aburrida hoy.
7. Answers will vary.

Activities

Cooperative Learning

Have students work in pairs, asking one another to describe people and objects in their lives. Students should use *¿Cómo es...?* and *¿Cómo son...?* and the provided nouns. The student answering should respond with the correct form of an appropriate adjective. Have students switch roles so each has an opportunity to use all the nouns. (Nouns: *tu profesor/profesora favorito/favorita; tu amigo favorito; tu hermana; tus padres; tu casa; tu carro; tus fiestas.* Adjectives: *amable, popular, cariñoso, divertido, favorito, simpático, nuevo, fantástico.*)

National Standards

Communication
1.1

Cultures
2.2

Connections
3.1

Teacher Resources

 *El béisbol y la familia Martínez*

Answers

Preparación

1 El béisbol es muy popular en los países hispanos y muchos beisbolistas profesionales son hispanos. La familia Martínez tiene tres hijos que son lanzadores profesionales en los Estados Unidos.

2
1. D
2. J
3. B
4. H
5. C
6. G
7. A
8. E
9. F
10. I

Activities

Prereading Strategy

Note for students that it is not essential to understand every word to read in Spanish. As with most readings in *¡Aventura!*, equivalents for some unknown words have been provided and others may be understood through context and background knowledge.

National Standards

Cultures
2.2

Connections
3.1, 3.2

Tú lees

Estrategia

Skimming

Before beginning to read an article, quickly look over the contents. Skimming through the reading will give you an idea what the article is about and will tell you whether the content interests you or not. To skim the article that follows, read the title and first line or two of each paragraph, note highlighted words and look for supportive visuals such as photographs or illustrations.

Preparación

Contesta las siguientes preguntas como preparación para la lectura.

1. ¿Cuál es la idea principal de la lectura?
2. Selecciona los equipos de la columna de la derecha que van con las ciudades de la columna de la izquierda.

1. Cleveland	A. los Rancheros
2. Cincinnati	B. los Atléticos
3. Oakland	C. los Bravos
4. Boston	D. los Indios
5. Atlanta	E. los Dodgers
6. Filadelfia	F. los Gigantes
7. Texas	G. los Filis
8. Los Ángeles	H. los Medias Rojas
9. San Francisco	I. los Piratas
10. Pittsburgh	J. los Rojos

El béisbol y la familia Martínez

El béisbol no sólo es un deporte[1] muy popular en los Estados Unidos, también es muy popular en muchos de los países hispanos. A muchas personas de Puerto Rico, Cuba y la República Dominicana les gusta mucho jugar al béisbol y muchos beisbolistas profesionales son hispanos.

La familia Martínez de la República Dominicana, por ejemplo, tiene tres hijos que han sido[2] beisbolistas en las ligas profesionales de los Estados Unidos. Su hijo mayor[3], Ramón Martínez, fue[4] un lanzador[5] para los Dodgers de Los Ángeles. Pedro Martínez, que es el hermano menor[6], es* un lanzador para los Mets de Nueva York. Además, Jesús Martínez, el hijo menor de la familia, fue un lanzador en las ligas menores de los Dodgers.

Pedro Martínez.

Notes

Be sure to review the contents of the *Estrategia* on skimming before assigning this reading about Pedro Martínez.

Additional information about the Dominican Republic can be located on the Internet:

Dominican Republic News and Travel Information http://www.dr1.com

Electronic Embassy
http://www.embassy.org

Organization of American States
http://www.oas.org

General travel information
http://www.expedia.com

Ramón Martínez.

Ramón es el ídolo de sus hermanos menores, pero Pedro es el más[7] famoso de los tres porque es el primer[8] dominicano que ha ganado[9] tres veces el premio[10] Cy Young. Los tres hermanos no juegan al béisbol todo el tiempo. También les gusta nadar, escuchar música y pasar tiempo con sus padres en la República Dominicana. Los Martínez—una familia unida por el béisbol.

[1]sport [2]have been [3]older [4]was [5]pitcher [6]younger [7]the most [8]first [9]has won [10]award

A ¿Qué recuerdas?

1. ¿Dónde es popular el béisbol?
2. ¿A qué personas les gusta jugar mucho al béisbol?
3. ¿Cuántos hijos de la familia Martínez han sido beisbolistas?
4. ¿En qué posición juega* Pedro Martínez?
5. ¿Para qué equipo juega* Pedro?
6. ¿Por qué es muy famoso Pedro?
7. ¿Qué hacen los hermanos Martínez además de jugar al béisbol?

B Algo personal

1. ¿Te gusta jugar al béisbol? ¿Qué deporte te gusta jugar?
2. ¿Cuál es tu equipo de béisbol profesional favorito?
3. ¿Quién es tu beisbolista favorito?
4. ¿Ves por televisión o vas a los partidos profesionales? ¿A cuáles?
5. ¿Cuál es el deporte más popular donde vives?

*Pedro Martínez retired from baseball in 2009.

Los hermanos Ramón y Pedro Martínez.

Notes The reading *El béisbol y la familia Martínez* and the activities that follow have been recorded by native speakers and are available on the *¡Aventura! 1* Audio Program.

Teacher Resources

Activity A
Activity B

Answers

A
1. Es popular en los Estados Unidos y en muchos países hispanos.
2. A muchas personas de Puerto Rico, Cuba y la República Dominicana les gusta mucho jugar al béisbol.
3. Tres hijos han sido beisbolistas.
4. Es lanzador.
5. Pedro juega para los Mets de Nueva York.
6. Porque es el primer dominicano que ha ganado tres veces el premio Cy Young.
7. Les gusta nadar, oír música y pasar tiempo con sus padres en la República Dominicana.

B Answers will vary.

Activities

Expansion
Ask students if they know of any other Spanish-speaking baseball players. Find out what country each player is from.

National Standards

Cultures
2.2

Connections
3.1

Answers

A Creative-thinking skill development.
B Creative writing practice.

Activities

Technology
Plan an e-mail exchange in which students describe their families and ask for information about the families of their key pals. Allow students to use imaginary families if they prefer and to write to classmates if they have no key pal. Students should write about the following: biographical information, descriptions of family and friends and favorite activities. Have students make hard copies of the letters they are exchanging so you can assess vocabulary and grammar and maintain a record of their work.
Note: Search for the term **Intercultural E-mail Connections** to find Spanish teachers in the United States or English teachers in other Spanish-speaking parts of the world with whom to exchange information.

Tú escribes

Estrategia
Creating an outline
You can better organize your thoughts before beginning to write by creating an outline of your ideas on paper. This visual map of your thoughts may also allow you to discover connections about the theme that you had not considered before.

A **Make a list of everyone who is in your family, leaving space under each name to write comments. Then write related ideas in the space, creating an outline consisting of everyone's ages, their interests and your opinion about each person.**

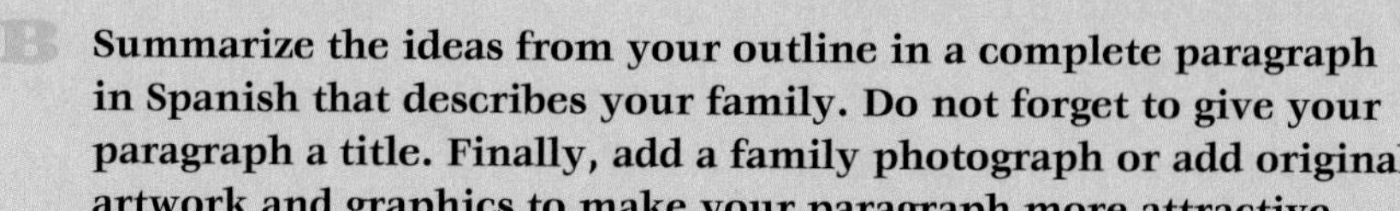

B **Summarize the ideas from your outline in a complete paragraph in Spanish that describes your family. Do not forget to give your paragraph a title. Finally, add a family photograph or add original artwork and graphics to make your paragraph more attractive.**

Mi familia.

National Standards
Communication
1.3
Communities
5.1

Notes Students sometimes are reticent to talk or write about their own families. In such cases, they should be encouraged to develop an imaginary family to complete the assignment.

Consider displaying the finished descriptions with accompanying photographs on a bulletin board in the classroom or in a display case in the building. This is especially effective to have on display when parents visit. Putting the writing projects on display around the school is also a good way to recruit students to sign up for Spanish class.

Go online EMCLanguages.net

Proyectos adicionales

A Conexión con la tecnología

Research your family's history using the resources available on the Internet. If you prefer, make up an identity or pretend to be someone famous (preferably someone Hispanic). Do you have any Spanish-speaking ancestors? Where did your ancestors come from? Investigate the life of one relative who was born and lived in another country. Find out the name of the country (and city) where the person was born, where the country (and city) is located on a map and details about the country (population, principal attractions, capital, holidays, etc.). Share your research with the class.

B Conexión con otras disciplinas: geografía/cultura

In small groups, create a travel brochure on Puerto Rico or the Dominican Republic. Include information such as: geographical location, capital city, population, main cities, major tourist attractions, events and anything else you find interesting or fun. Use the Internet or the library for your research. Present your group's travel brochure to the rest of the class as if you were a travel agent or a representative of the country's Tourist Bureau.

C Comparaciones

Give the Spanish equivalents for the baseball terms shown. You can find them on the Internet or in a dictionary. Next, draw a baseball field and identify in Spanish as many of the people and other elements as you can (e.g., infield, baseball, umpire, pitcher, etc.). Label the drawing *el campo de béisbol*. Then, compare your drawing with a classmate's to see what is similar and what is different.

los jugadores *(players)*

1. the batter
2. the catcher
3. the first baseman
4. the outfielder
5. the pitcher
6. the player
7. the second baseman
8. the shortstop
9. the third baseman
10. the umpire

el juego *(game)*

11. first/second/third base
12. out
13. strikeout
14. ball
15. bat
16. baseball glove
17. home run
18. infield
19. inning
20. outfield
21. run
22. strike

Notes The National Standards are practiced throughout the chapter. These end-of-chapter culminating projects are optional. They offer additional standards practice, opportunities for applying technology to problem-solving activities and cross-curricular learning opportunities. Pick and choose the activities that suit your style and that help you accomplish your teaching goals and curriculum requirements.

Teacher Resources

p. 70

Answers

A Creative self-expression.

B Creative self-expression.

C Possible answers:

1. the batter = *el bateador*
2. the catcher = *el receptor*
3. the first baseman = *el inicialista, el primer base*
4. the outfielder = *el jardinero, el guardabosque*
5. the pitcher = *el lanzador, el serpintero, el abridor*
6. the player = *el pelotero*
7. the second baseman = *el intermedista, el segunda base, el camarero*
8. the shortstop = *el jardinero corto*
9. the third baseman = *el antesalista, el tercera base*
10. the umpire = *el árbitro*
11. first/second/third base = *la primera/segunda/terecera base*
12. out = *out, fuera el hombre*
13. strikeout = *ponche, ponchado, ponchete*
14. ball = *la bola, la pelota*
15. bat = el *bate*
16. baseball glove = *el guante*
17. home run = *el cuadrangular, el jonrón*
18. infield = *el campo interior*
19. inning = *el inning, la entrada, el episodio*
20. outfield = *el campo exterior*
21. run = *la carrera*
22. strike = *el strike, el estrike*

National Standards

Communication
1.1, 1.3

Connections
3.1, 3.2

Comparisons
4.1

Teacher Resources

 *Trabalenguas*

 Episode 4, DVD 1, Track 37

Answers

Resolviendo el misterioso

1. Answers will vary.
2. The girls learn that don Pedro is a widower and that José has a cousin who lives in Colombia. The girls see photos of Francisco's brothers and sisters.
3. Answers will vary.

Activities

Multiple Intelligences (spatial)

Divide the class into groups of three or four. Using colored markers, have them make a drawing on half of the paper to depict the concept of using *ser* and on the other half depict the concept of *estar*. Label each side. Have each group explain the visuals.

Spanish for Spanish Speakers

Have students give a complete answer to the following question, listing pros and cons: *¿Debe Puerto Rico convertirse en un estado de los Estados Unidos, en una nación independiente o permanecer como estado libre asociado?*

Trabalenguas

Give each student a tissue. Ask them to hold it in front of their mouths as they recite the *Trabalenguas.* Ask students to say it first without making the tissue move. Then, ask students to say it loudly so that the tissue moves a lot.

National Standards

Communication
1.3

Connections
3.1, 3.2

REPASO

Now that I have completed this chapter, I can...	Go to these pages for help:
talk about family and relationships.	134
seek and provide personal information.	135
express possession.	139
say some things people do.	154
express an opinion.	154
state likes and dislikes.	158
describe people and things.	164
I can also...	
identify members of my family in Spanish.	134
talk about life in Puerto Rico and the Dominican Republic.	137, 157
talk about *merengue* dance.	167
read in Spanish about baseball in Spanish-speaking countries.	174
read and use Spanish words in context.	174
write a paragraph in Spanish.	176

Trabalenguas
Papá, pon para Pepín pan.

Resolviendo el misterio

After watching Episode 4 of *El cuarto misterioso*, answer the following questions.

1. Why is Rafael stalking Ana and Conchita?
2. What do the young people learn about one another?
3. At lunch, the girls mention that they like Mexico. Give reasons why.

Notes

Additional information about Puerto Rico can be located in many sites on the Internet:

Escape to Puerto Rico
http://escape.topuertorico.com
Welcome to Puerto Rico
http://welcome.topuertorico.org

Organization of American States
http://www.oas.org
General travel information
http://www.expedia.com

Loose translation of the *Trabalenguas*: Daddy, get some bread to Pepín.

Vocabulario

abierto,-a open *4A*
el **abuelo**, la **abuela** grandfather, grandmother *4A*
aburrido,-a bored, boring *4B*
alto,-a tall, high *4B*
amable kind, nice *4A*
apurado,-a in a hurry *4A*
bailar to dance *4B*
bajo,-a short (not tall), low *4B*
el **béisbol** baseball *4B*
bonito,-a pretty, good-looking, attractive *4A*
bueno,-a good *4B*
caliente hot *4A*
calvo,-a bald *4B*
canoso,-a white-haired *4B*
cansado,-a tired *4A*
cantar to sing *4B*
cariñoso,-a affectionate *4A*
la **casa** house *4A*
cerrado,-a closed *4A*
cómico,-a comical, funny *4B*
la **compra** purchase *4B*
comprar to buy *4B*
contento,-a happy, glad *4A*
contestar to answer *4B*
delgado,-a thin *4B*
difícil difficult, hard *4B*
divertido,-a fun *4A*
egoísta selfish *4B*
enfermo,-a sick *4A*
escuchar to listen to *4B*
el **esposo**, la **esposa** husband, wife, spouse *4A*
fácil easy *4B*
la **familia** family *4A*
feo,-a ugly *4B*
la **foto(grafía)** photo *4A*
frío,-a cold *4A*
el **fútbol** soccer *4B*
generoso,-a generous *4B*
gordo,-a fat *4B*
guapo,-a good-looking, attractive, handsome, pretty *4A*
gustar to like, to be pleasing to *4B*
el **hermano**, la **hermana** brother, sister *4A*
el **hijo**, la **hija** son, daughter *4A*
horrible horrible *4B*
ideal ideal *4B*
importante important *4B*
inteligente intelligent *4B*
interesante interesting *4B*
ir de compras to go shopping *4B*
jugar (ue) to play *4B*
jugar a *(+ sport/game)* to play *4B*
lento,-a slow *4B*
libre free *4A*
limpio,-a clean *4A*
loco,-a crazy *4A*
la **madre** mother *4A*
malo,-a bad 4B
más more, else *4A*
me (to, for) me *4B*
mí me (after a preposition) *4B*
mirar to look (at) *4B*
mis my (pl.) *4A*
moreno,-a brunette, dark-haired, dark-skinned *4B*
mucho,-a much, a lot, very, very much *4B*
nadar to swim *4B*
nervioso,-a nervous *4A*
el **nieto**, la **nieta** granddaughter, grandson *4A*
nos (to, for) us *4B*
nuestro,-a our *4A*
nunca never *4A*
ocupado,-a busy, occupied *4A*
otro,-a other, another *4A*
el **padre** father *4A*
los **padres** parents, fathers *4A*
para for, to, in order to *4A*
el **pariente**, la **pariente** relative *4A*
el **partido** game, match *4B*
patinar (sobre ruedas) to in-line skate *4B*
pelirrojo,-a red-haired *4B*
el **piano** piano *4B*
la **playa** beach *4A*
popular popular *4A*
por for *4A*
el **primo**, la **prima** cousin *4A*
¡qué *(+ description)***!** how *(+description)*! *4A*
quiero I love, I want *4A*
la **radio** radio (broadcast) *4B*
rápido,-a rapid, fast *4B*
rubio,-a blond *4B*
salir to go out *4A*
el **sobrino**, la **sobrina** nephew, niece *4A*
su, sus his, her, its, your (*Ud./Uds.*), their *4A*
sucio,-a dirty *4A*
la **tarea** homework *4B*
la **televisión** television *4B*
el **tenis** tennis *4B*
ti you (after a preposition) *4B*
el **tiempo** time *4A*
el **tío**, la **tía** uncle, aunt *4A*
tocar to play *4B*
todo,-a all, every, whole, entire *4A*
tonto,-a silly *4B*
triste sad *4A*
tus your (pl.) *4A*
único,-a only, unique *4A*
el **verano** summer *4A*
vivir to live *4A*

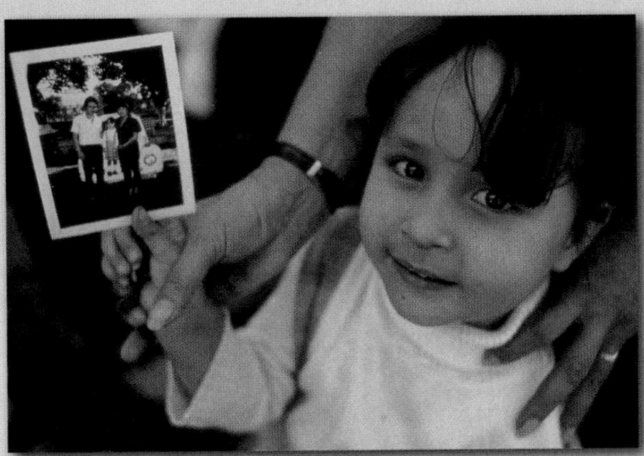

Mira la foto de mis padres y yo.

Teacher Resources

Las aventuras de la familia Miranda

Repaso

***¡Aventureros!*, Ch. 4**

Internet Activities

i-Culture

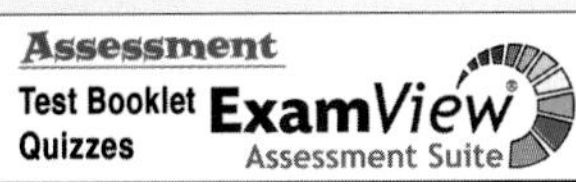

Activities

Cooperative Learning

Have students pair up for this fun activity called *¿Cómo es tu novio/novia ideal?* Students should pretend they are on a reality televisión show where they get to pick their mate (*pareja*). Working in pairs, have students discuss physical and behavioral traits for their ideal boyfriend (*novio*) or girlfriend (*novia*). They must then explain how important those qualities are in a relationship.

MODELO
A: *¿Es tu novia ideal guapa?*
B: *No, no es importante. ¿Es tu novio ideal generoso?*
A: *¡Claro! Es importante.*

Expansion

Model new words and expressions and have students repeat them after you to improve their pronunciation. Then call on individuals to use the new words and expressions in sentences.

National Standards

Communication
1.1

Notes

Point out and explain why the verb *jugar* is listed in the *Vocabulario* for the chapter with the letters *ue* in parentheses: *jugar (ue)*. Explain that the letters following the infinitive indicate the verb has a spelling change in its conjugated forms. The conjugation of verbs with the *u* → *ue* changes is taught later in *Lección 7A*.

Quizzes have been formatted to allow you to evaluate how well students are learning key content. If you did not use all quizzes where indicted in the margins of the ATE, you may choose to use those quizzes at the end of a lesson as a comprehensive test over the contents of the entire lesson.

Teacher Resources

TPRS *Capítulo 5*

 *Capítulo 5*

 **Episode 5, DVD 1, Track 48**

Connections with Parents

There are numerous benefits to increasing the involvement of parents and guardians in their children's school lives. Teachers can do many things to encourage parents and guardians to have a larger role in their children's classroom education. Some examples include parent/teacher organizations, letters, school visitations, open houses, conferences, volunteer opportunities and assignments that involve interaction between the students and their parents or guardians.

Answers

El cuarto misterioso

1. Un mariachi toca para la fiesta de cumpleaños de Conchita.
2. Voy a oír una guitarra, un violín, un guitarrón, una guitarra de golpe, una vihuela, una trompeta, y posiblemente un arpa.
3. Las respuestas variarán.

National Standards

Cultures
2.2

CAPÍTULO 5

Una semana típica

El cuarto misterioso

Contesta las siguientes preguntas sobre *Episodio 5–El cumpleaños de Conchita*.

1. ¿Qué pasa en esta escena?
2. ¿Qué tipos de instrumentos vas a oír?
3. ¿Cómo se celebran los cumpleaños los jóvenes americanos?

Un mariachi toca para la fiesta de cumpleaños de Conchita.

Objetivos

- describe everyday activities
- say what someone is going to do
- seek and provide personal information
- write about everyday life
- say what someone likes or dislikes
- express strong feelings
- talk about dates and holidays

Notes Talk with students about the contents of these pages. Students might want to compare and contrasts these celebrations: the Quinceañera, the Sweet Sixteen celebration, Bar Mitzvahs and Bat Mitzvahs.

A checklist of these objectives, along with additional functions, appears on page 222 so students can evaluate their own progress.

Activities

Prior Knowledge
Ask students to review the chapter objectives. Ask students questions such as: What is one activity that you enjoy doing every day? How long do you think it takes to get to know a person very well? Do you set daily goals? How often do you do what you say you are going to do? How often do you do something that you don't really like to do? Why do you do it? Do you keep a journal or blog? Why or why not? What holiday are the young people in the photograph celebrating?

Contexto cultural

Costa Rica
Nombre oficial: República de Costa Rica
Población: 4.576.000
Capital: San José
Ciudades importantes: Alajuela, Cartago, Puerto Limón
Unidad monetaria: el colón
Fiesta nacional: 15 de septiembre, Día de la Independencia
Gente famosa: Óscar Arias Sánchez (ex-presidente); Ana Brown-Hernández (escritora)

Nicaragua
Nombre oficial: República de Nicaragua
Población: 5.666.000
Capital: Managua
Ciudades importantes: Granada, León
Unidad monetaria: el córdoba
Fiesta nacional: 15 de septiembre, Día de la Independencia
Gente famosa: Violeta Barrios de Chamorro (ex-presidente); Rubén Darío (escritor)

National Standards

Cultures	Connections
2.2	3.1

Notes The cultural focus of this chapter combines the Central American countries of Costa Rica and Nicaragua. The Costa Rican currency is *el colón*, which is named after Christopher Columbus *(Cristóbal Colón)*, who first explored the country on his fourth voyage to the Americas in 1502.

The monetary unit of Nicaragua, *el córdoba*, is also named after an explorer, Francisco Fernández de Córdoba, who founded the major Nicaraguan cities of Granada and León.

Teacher Resources

Vocabulario I
Un sábado en la tienda de artículos electrónicos

 **Activity 5**

 **Activities 34–35**

 **Activity 1**

 **Activity 1**

 **Activity 1**

Content reviewed in *Lección A*

- schedules and daily activities
- expressing likes and dislikes
- days of the week
- family
- telling time
- making a sentence negative

Activities

Prereading Activity

Play the audio recording of the new vocabulary. Instruct students to close their books or cover the words as they listen to and repeat the new words and expressions. Call on one or two students to see if they can name the setting.

National Standards

Connections
3.1

Lección A Vocabulario I

Costa Ric

Un sábado en la tienda de artículos electrónicos

la grabadora

¡Qué lástima! Aho
tenemos el CD co
canciones de la pe
¡Loco por ti!

el reproductor de DVDs

Buscamos el CD con la canción *Loco amor*, que es de la película *¡Loco por ti!*

¿No tienen el CD? ¡Caramba! ¡Qué sorpresa!

el equipo de sonido

el quem
de CD

La chica entra a la tienda.

el dinero

el cas

el reproductor de MP3

el DVD

el reproductor de CDs

Los chicos pasan tiempo cada semana en la tienda de artículos electrónicos.

el disco compacto (CD)

Notes Use the ancillaries listed under Teacher Resources above to introduce the new vocabulary and to begin to teach elements of the lesson. The audio can be used to practice pronunciation of new words; overhead transparencies offer a visual introduction to the new vocabulary as well as spelling reinforcement; written practice is available using Listening Activity 1. Evaluate student comprehension of the new vocabulary using Quiz 1. Pick and choose materials that suit your goals.

¿Qué buscan?

Selecciona la ilustración que corresponde con lo que oyes.

En la tienda de artículos electrónicos

A

B

C

D

E

F

Lógico

Completa en forma lógica las frases de la izquierda con las frases de la derecha.

1. Buscamos el DVD...
2. Los chicos pasan...
3. ¡Qué lástima! No tenemos...
4. La chica entra...
5. ¡Caramba, no tenemos dinero...

A. ...para comprar el CD.
B. ...a la tienda de artículos electrónicos.
C. ...el CD con la canción *Loco amor*.
D. ...tiempo cada semana en la tienda de artículos electrónicos.
E. ...de la película *¡Loco por ti!*

A mí me gusta escuchar música.

Notes Tell students that *el CD* is the abbreviated form of *el disco compacto* and that the abbreviation is commonly used in conversations by Spanish-speaking people. The word *disco* in the past meant **record** (record album). Today, however, *el disco* is also a shortened form of *el disco compacto*. Similarly, *el tocadiscos*—formally "record player"—is now used colloquially as **CD player**.

Activity 1 is intended for listening comprehension practice. Play the audio of the activity that is part of the Audio Program or use the transcript that appears in the ATE Introduction if you prefer to read the activity yourself.

Teacher Resources

Activity 1

Answers

1 1. D
2. A
3. C
4. B
5. F
6. E

2 1. E
2. D
3. C
4. B
5. A

Activities

Expansion

Use overhead transparencies 34 and 35 to introduce the new words and expressions in *Vocabulario I*. Begin by showing students transparency 34. Point to one of the objects in the electronics store and identify it in Spanish. Students should repeat after you. Continue on to the next item and repeat the process. As a second step, show students transparency 35. Once again identify each item in Spanish, allowing students to see how the word is spelled.

Students with Special Needs

Using overhead transparencies 34 and 35, point to one of the objects in the electronics store as students spell out each item one by one. Then pronounce words in *Vocabulario I* and call on students to repeat after you.

National Standards

Communication
1.2

Teacher Resources

Diálogo I
Me gustan las tiendas
Activity 3
Activity 4
Activity 5

Answers

3
1. Van a ver si tienen el CD de Alejandro Sanz.
2. No, no tienen CDs de Alejandro Sanz.
3. A Marta le gustan las tiendas.
4. Answers will vary.

4 Answers will vary.

5 **Soy Marta**
1. unos DVDs
2. (circled) unos CDs
3. (circled) un reproductor de CDs
4. un quemador de CDs
5. una computadora

Soy Sofía
6. un equipo de sonido
7. un reproductor de MP3
8. unos DVDs
9. (circled) unos CDs
10. (circled) una impresora láser

Activities

Prereading Strategy
Ask students to tell what they might find in a store where they sell CDs and audio equipment. Then instruct students to open their books and to cover up the dialog with one hand and look at the photographs. Ask them to imagine where the conversation takes place and what the people are saying to one another.

National Standards	
Communication	**Connections**
1.1, 1.2	3.1

Diálogo I

Me gustan las tiendas

MARTA: Vamos a ver si tienen el CD de Alejandro Sanz en la tienda.
SOFÍA: ¿Otra tienda? No tenemos más dinero.
MARTA: Sólo quiero mirar si tienen el disco compacto.

MARTA: Buenas. Buscamos el CD de Alejandro Sanz.
SEÑOR: No, no tenemos CDs de Alejandro Sanz.
MARTA: ¡Qué lástima! Bueno, gracias.

SOFÍA: ¡Ahora sí! ¡Vamos a casa!
MARTA: No. ¿Por qué no vamos a otra tienda?
SOFÍA: ¡Caramba! ¡Qué sorpresa!

3 ¿Qué recuerdas?

1. ¿Qué van a ver Marta y Sofía si tienen en la tienda de artículos electrónicos?
2. ¿Tienen el CD de Alejandro Sanz en la tienda de artículos electrónicos?
3. ¿A quién le gustan las tiendas?
4. ¿Van a casa las chicas?

4 Algo personal

1. ¿Cuál es tu disco compacto favorito?
2. ¿Qué canción te gusta? ¿Por qué?
3. ¿Te gustan las tiendas de artículos electrónicos? Explica.
4. ¿Qué artículos electrónicos tienes en casa?

5 ¿Lo tienen?

Write the names Marta and Sofía. Next, listen and list under their names what they are looking for at an electronics store. Then circle any items on the lists that are the same.

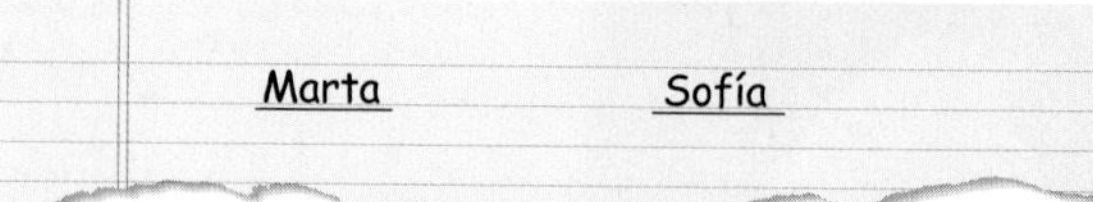

Notes Several musical instruments were introduced earlier in *¡Aventura! 1*. You may wish to share additional vocabulary with students interested in musical performance: *la guitarra, el bajo, el arpa, el violín, la viola, el violoncelo, el contrabajo (instrumentos de cuerda); la flauta, el clarinete, el oboe, la trompeta, el trombón, la tuba (instrumentos de viento); el piano, el tambor, los címbalos, el triángulo, el xilófono, el timbal (instrumentos de percusión).*

Play the audio version of activity 5 for listening comprehension practice. A reproducible student answer sheet for the activity is provided for your convenience at the end of the Audio Program Manual.

Cultura viva

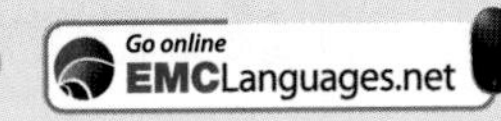

El volcán Arenal y una orquídea *(orchid)* en Costa Rica.

Costa Rica

Christopher Columbus visited Cariari (now the city of Puerto Limón) in 1502. He named the land Costa Rica (rich coast) because he thought the area offered a wealth of gold and silver. Today, this small, Spanish-speaking country has a population of about four million people, most of whom live in the capital and industrial city of San José. Situated at the center of the American continent, Costa Rica features a diverse landscape of beaches, mountains, volcanos (like the Irazú) and rain forests *(selvas tropicales or bosques lluviosos)*. In fact, Costa Rica is famous throughout the world for its ecological tourism and has dedicated over twenty-five percent of its land as protected areas, national parks and reserves, which are the seasonal home for 10 percent of the world's birds, more than 9,000 species of plants and 1,200 species of orchids. The country has a long democratic tradition, spends more money on education than many of its Latin American neighbors and has had no army for more than fifty years. It is noteworthy in this peace-loving nation that one of Costa Rica's former presidents, Óscar Arias, was awarded the Nobel Peace Prize.

Una selva tropical en Monteverde, Costa Rica

6 Conexiones con otras disciplinas: geografía y ciencias

Use an encyclopedia or search the Internet for information about Costa Rica and plan a vacation there. Find out about places to visit, things to do, what you will see or eat and so forth. Summarize your findings, adding visuals (e.g., photographs, maps), and share your plans with the class.

MODELO Voy a visitar el volcán Irazú en Cártago.

¡Oportunidades!

¿Trabajar en Costa Rica?

How would you like to be paid for traveling and having a good time? Travel-related companies throughout the world require bilingual employees and since tourism is one of the top industries in countries like Costa Rica, the job prospects are nearly limitless. Companies that offer eco-touring, hotels, cruise lines, travel agencies and airlines all need employees who can speak both Spanish and English. If you are hired by a company in a country you would like to visit for pleasure, the rewards are double. For example, during your free time in Costa Rica you might enjoy river rafting, camping on the side of a volcano *(Poás* or *Irazú)* or spending a week in a wildlife sanctuary or government-protected rain forest.

Teacher Resources

 Activity 2

P p. 77

 Activity 2

Answers

6 Creative self-expression.

Activities

Connections
Offer an opportunity to connect with language arts by having students write a journal page about an imaginary trip to Costa Rica. They should include what they saw and did.

Multiple Intelligences (visual)
Have students create a brochure or travel poster in Spanish on Costa Rica using information gathered from the Internet, the library, travel agents, etc. Encourage them to include photographs, magazine clippings or illustrations to make the brochure or travel poster more colorful.

Students with Special Needs
Read the culture section aloud to the student(s) having difficulties, or prepare a tape recording for the student(s) to listen to, allowing time to stop and repeat if needed. Pair a student requiring additional help with another student with strong reading skills and allow them to work on the *Cultura viva* reading together.

National Standards	
Communication 1.3	Communities 5.1
Cultures 2.2	
Connections 3.1, 3.2	

Notes

Encourage students to contribute any information they may have about Costa Rica, such as recent news stories, articles on the environment, etc.

Activity 6 is a cross-curricular exercise that addresses Spanish as well as geography and science.

Have students use a dictionary to find words they do not know as they complete activity 6. Decide what you would like students to do with the completed work. They might present their work to the entire class; you may want them to discuss their project in small groups; or you may choose to have students submit their work as a written assignment.

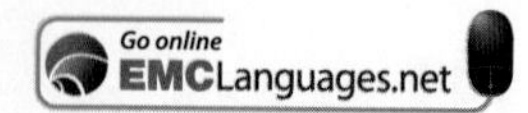

Teacher Resources

Activities 3–5

Activities 2–4

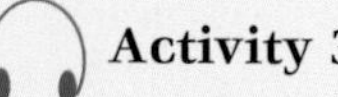

p. 145

Activity 3

Activity 2

Answers

7
1. tiene
2. tiene
3. Tienen
4. tenemos
5. tenemos
6. tenemos
7. tengo
8. tengo
9. tienes
10. tengo

Activities

Cooperative Learning

After students complete the dialog for activity 7 in writing, have them form groups of three to practice the dialog. Inform the class you will be selecting two or three groups to perform the dialog in front of the class. Encourage groups to perform the dialog.

Students with Special Needs

Practice the verb *tener* by combining it with vocabulary students have already studied: *¿Cuántos hermanos tienes?; ¿Cuántos tíos tienes?; ¿Cuántas clases tienes?; ¿Cuántos años tiene el profesor/la profesora de español?*

National Standards

Communication
1.1, 1.3

Idioma

Estructura

Saying what someone has: *tener*

The verb *tener* (to have) is an irregular verb.

tener			
yo	**tengo**	nosotros nosotras	**tenemos**
tú	**tienes**	vosotros vosotras	**tenéis**
Ud. él ella	**tiene**	Uds. ellos ellas	**tienen**

***Tengo** un equipo de sonido nuevo.*	**I have** a new sound system.
*Marisol **tiene** veinte CDs.*	Marisol **has** twenty CDs.

Note: *Tener* is sometimes used in Spanish expressions where the verb **to be** is used in English. One such expression is *tener* (+ number) *años*, which you have already used to talk about someone's age.

*¿Cuántos años **tienes**?*	How old **are you**?
***Tengo** dieciséis años.*	**I am** sixteen (years old).

Práctica

7 Un CD para Susana

Completa el diálogo con las formas apropiadas de tener.

Jorge: Quiero ver si la tienda de artículos electrónicos (1) un CD para Susana.
Pilar: ¿Qué CD buscas?
Jorge: Ella no (2) el nuevo disco compacto del grupo Presuntos Implicados.
Pilar: Bueno, vamos a preguntar.
Jorge: Hola, señor. ¿(3) Uds. el nuevo disco compacto de Presuntos Implicados?
Señor: Nosotros (4) muchos CDs, pero no (5) CDs de Presuntos Implicados.
Jorge: ¡Caramba! ¡Qué lástima! Muchas gracias.
Pilar: Son las siete, nosotros (6) una hora. ¿Vamos a otra tienda?
Jorge: Está bien, pero sabes, yo (7) un problema. No (8) dinero. ¿Cuánto (9) tú?
Pilar: Pues, Jorge, yo tampoco (10) dinero.

Notes

As with all verb paradigms in *¡Aventura! 1*, the *vosotros/vosotras* verb endings have been provided for passive reference. If you have decided to make these forms active, adapt the provided activities as necessary.

Frequently used expressions that include *tener* will be taught in *Capítulo 6*.

The indefinite article is often omitted after the verb *tener*, except when it is used with a modified noun: *Tengo una amiga de Limón, Costa Rica.*

8 Todos tienen algo

Working in pairs, take turns asking one another questions about what various people have. Answer according to what you see in the illustrations, adding any details you wish.

MODELO don Carlos
A: ¿Qué tiene don Carlos?
B: Tiene un reproductor de MP3 fantástico.

1. tú

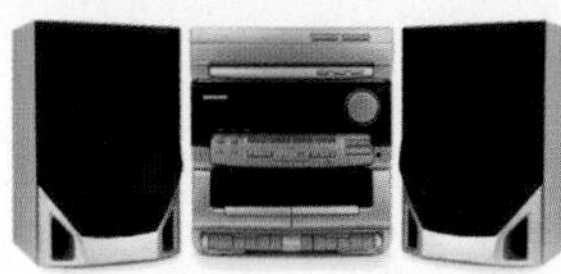

2. Silvia y su hermano

3. yo

4. Ud.

5. Elvira y Alejandra

6. nosotros

9 Conexión con otras disciplinas: matemáticas

Di cuántos años tienen las siguientes personas de acuerdo al año en que nacieron *(were born)*.

1. Kathy / 1961
2. Doña Marta / 1927
3. Daniel y Estefanía / 2002
4. Keeley / 1989
5. Rafael y Gustavo / 1976
6. el Sr. Cortés / 1956
7. yo / 1953
8. tú / ?

Comunicación

10 Tengo muchos CDs

Working in pairs, talk about your interests in entertainment. For example, find out what kind of music and films you like. You might also discuss such things as how many CDs you have of different types of music, whether or not you have DVDs, which CDs or DVDs you have and what equipment you use to play the CDs and DVDs. Try to determine what interests you have in common *(en común)* and how your interests are different. Be creative!

¡Extra!

Tipos de música

clásica	mariachi	rock
cumbia	merengue	romántica
disco	popular	salsa
flamenco	ranchera	tejana (Tex-Mex)
jazz	rap	vallenato

MODELO **A:** ¿Te gusta la música rock?
B: Sí, me gusta mucho. Tengo veinte CDs de rock.

Notes

You may want to have students write answers for oral activities (e.g., activities 8, 9, 10) to reinforce basic skills.

Other types of music include: *folklórica, samba, reggae, nueva era* and *bosanova.*

Bring a cassette player or portable CD player to class. Play different styles of Latin music for students: *salsa, merengue, nueva canción* (if available), *romance, pop* or Spanish-language rap.

Teacher Resources

Activity 9

Answers

8 Possible answers:
1. ¿Qué tienes tú?/Tengo mucho dinero.
2. ¿Qué tienen Silvia y su hermano?/Tienen un equipo de sonido.
3. ¿Qué tengo yo?/Tú tienes un quemador de CDs.
4. ¿Qué tiene Ud.?/Yo tengo un disco compacto nuevo.
5. ¿Qué tienen Elvira y Alejandra?/Tienen muchos casetes.
6. ¿Qué tenemos nosotros?/ Tenemos un reproductor de DVDs.

9 Answers will vary for ages according to the current year.
1. Kathy tiene *(number of years).*
2. Doña Marta tiene *(number of years).*
3. Daniel y Estefanía tienen *(number of years).*
4. Keeley tiene *(number of years).*
5. Rafael y Gustavo tienen *(number of years).*
6. El Sr. Cortés tiene *(number of years).*
7. Tú tienes *(number of years).*
8. Yo tengo *(number of years).*

10 Creative self-expression.

National Standards

Communication
1.1

Cultures
2.2

Connections
3.1

Teacher Resources

 Activity 6

 Activity 5

 Activity 4

 Activity 3

Answers

11 Creative self-expression.
12 Possible answers:
1. ¡Qué divertido!
2. ¡Qué frío!
3. ¡Qué sucio!
4. ¡Qué triste!
5. ¡Qué fantástico!

Activities

Critical Listening
Tell the class that you are going to read aloud several recent news headlines. For each headline, the students should provide several logical exclamations by using *¡Qué...!* with a noun or with an adjective (e.g., *¡Qué música!; ¡Qué divertido!*).

National Standards

Communication
1.1, 1.2

Comparisons
4.1

11 ¿Qué tenemos en casa?

Working in small groups, take turns talking about your families' entertainment preferences. First, find out who is in each person's family. Then discuss family members' favorite music, television and radio programs *(programas de televisión y radio)* and movies. Next, find out what kind of electronics your classmates' families have for listening to music or watching movies at home.

MODELO **A:** Tengo dos hermanos y una hermana. A mis hermanos les gusta ver partidos de fútbol en la televisión. A mi hermana le gusta escuchar música en su reproductor de MP3.
B: Yo tengo un hermano. Le gusta la música merengue y le gusta ver películas en DVD.
C: Yo no tengo hermanos, pero tengo muchos tíos. A ellos les gustan los CDs de música clásica.

Estructura

Expressing strong feelings with *¡Qué* (+ adjective/noun)*!*

There are times when you may wish to express strong feelings — both positive and negative — about something or someone. In Spanish, use *qué* followed by an adjective as the equivalent of **How...!** Similarly, when *qué* is followed by a person, place or thing, it is equivalent to **What a...!**

¡Qué (+ adjective)*!*		*¡Qué* (+ noun)*!*	
¡Qué fantástico!	How fantastic!	*¡Qué CD!*	What a CD!
¡Qué aburrido!	How boring!	*¡Qué lástima!*	What a shame!

Práctica

12 ¿Cómo reaccionas?

Using *qué* and an adjective, react to the following circumstances.

MODELO *A good friend buys you your favorite CD.*
¡Qué amable!

1. *You are watching a very funny DVD.*
2. *It is very cold outside.*
3. *You just dropped a brand new MP3 player in the mud.*
4. *Your parents tell you some really sad news.*
5. *You have just learned to use your new CD burner.*

¡Qué amable!

Notes

Activity 11 reviews family vocabulary and the numbers while offering students an open-ended opportunity to discuss their daily life at home, their family's interests and their entertainment preferences.

Model the examples in the *Estructura* for students with varying tone and intonation to show how *qué* (+ noun) can convey delight *(¡Qué película!)*, fear *(¡Qué perro!)* or sadness/disappointment *(¡Qué lástima!)*.

13 Expresando tu opinión

Write captions for the following photos, using *qué* plus a noun.

MODELO  ¡Qué equipo de sonido!

1 
2 
3 
4 
5 
6 

14 Me gusta lo que tienen

The following people have just purchased some electronic equipment. Say what they have and express how much you like each item.

MODELO Belia / una computadora rápida
Belia tiene una computadora rápida. ¡Qué computadora!

1. mis primos / equipo de sonido nuevo
2. Clara / reproductor de CDs para diez CDs
3. Sonia / dos DVDs fantásticos
4. los López / carro BMW nuevo
5. tú / CD nuevo de Alejandro Sanz

Comunicación

15 ¡Qué tienda tan estupenda!

Imagine that you and a friend are window-shopping at a fantastic home audio and video store that carries computers, DVD and CD players, CD burners, etc. With your partner, create a dialog in which you talk about some of the things you see, expressing how you feel about each one. Discuss who you know has each item you are looking at and add any other details you wish. Be creative!

MODELO **A:** Oye, Carlos. ¡Mira! ¡Qué equipo de sonido!
B: Sí, muy bonito. Rogelio tiene uno.

Notes You may want to teach the students that when they are exclaiming about something bad, the **Oh!** they might say in English is the equivalent of *¡Ay!* before the exclamation: *¡Ay, qué lástima!*; *¡Ay, qué terrible!*

Point out to students that they should use the verb *tocar* (to play) when referring to electronic equipment such as CD and DVD players.

Teacher Resources

 **Activity 14**

Answers

13 Possible answers:
1. ¡Qué música!
2. ¡Qué caballo!
3. ¡Qué piano!
4. ¡Qué sorpresa!
5. ¡Qué casa!
6. ¡Qué CD!

14
1. Mis primos tienen un equipo de sonido nuevo. ¡Qué equipo de sonido!
2. Clara tiene un reproductor de CDs para diez CDs. ¡Qué reproductor de CDs!
3. Sonia tiene dos DVDs fantásticos. ¡Qué DVDs!
4. Los López tienen un carro BMW nuevo. ¡Qué carro!
5. Tú tienes un CD nuevo de Alejandro Sanz. ¡Qué CD!

15 Creative self-expression.

Activities

Critical Thinking
Show students several visuals featuring interesting people, places and things. For each visual the students should provide several logical exclamations using *¡Qué...!*

Multiple Intelligences (interpersonal)
Have students say an exclamation in reaction to pictures that other students in class cannot see. Ask the class to guess the content of each picture based on the student's facial expression.

National Standards
Communication 1.1
Comparisons 4.1

Teacher Resources

Vocabulario II
Las actividades de Virginia la semana que viene

 **Activity 36**

 **Activity 7**

 **Activities 6–7**

 **p. 71**

 **pp. 20–21**

 **Activity 5**
Activity 6

 **Activity 4**

Activities

Cooperative Learning
Ask students to imagine that they are going to take a one-week trip to Costa Rica. In small groups they should write their itineraries for the week, including daily activities. They may include information found in the lesson or by doing additional research, etc.

Critical Thinking
Have students scan Virginia's schedule for cognates and other words they recognize.

Students with Special Needs
Have students identify the days of the week that appear in Virginia's schedule. Then have students read what Virginia has planned for each day.

National Standards
Connections 3.1

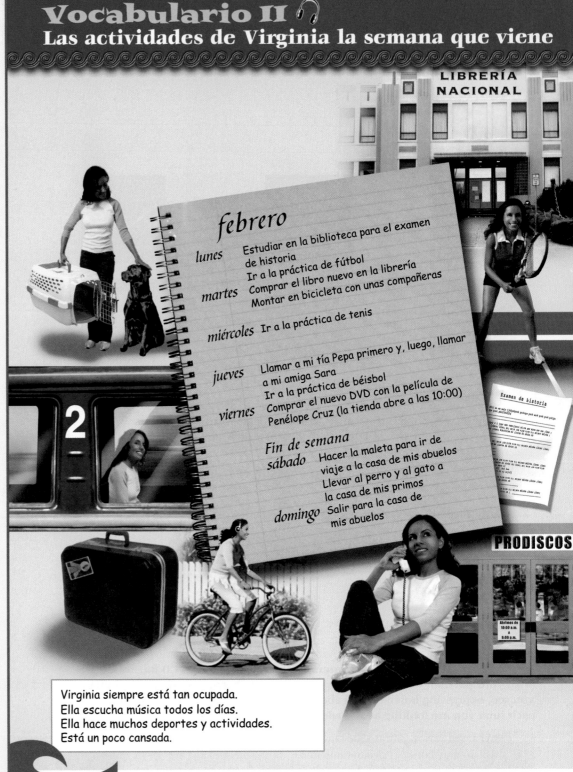

Vocabulario II
Las actividades de Virginia la semana que viene

LIBRERÍA NACIONAL

febrero

lunes Estudiar en la biblioteca para el examen de historia
Ir a la práctica de fútbol

martes Comprar el libro nuevo en la librería
Montar en bicicleta con unas compañeras

miércoles Ir a la práctica de tenis

jueves Llamar a mi tía Pepa primero y, luego, llamar a mi amiga Sara
Ir a la práctica de béisbol

viernes Comprar el nuevo DVD con la película de Penélope Cruz (la tienda abre a las 10:00)

Fin de semana

sábado Hacer la maleta para ir de viaje a la casa de mis abuelos
Llevar al perro y al gato a la casa de mis primos

domingo Salir para la casa de mis abuelos

Examen de historia

PRODISCOS

Virginia siempre está tan ocupada.
Ella escucha música todos los días.
Ella hace muchos deportes y actividades.
Está un poco cansada.

Notes Give students the phrases *salir de viaje* (to leave on a trip), *hacer un viaje* (to take a trip) and *estar de viaje* (to be on a trip), all of which recycle active verb forms.

Refer to the Teacher Resources at the top of the page for ancillaries that offer activities for expanding or reinforcing the content of the pages of the pupil's edition of the textbook.

The word for the month of February *(febrero)* appears here for passive recognition. The months will be taught in *Lección 5B* (page 208).

Las actividades de Javier la semana que viene

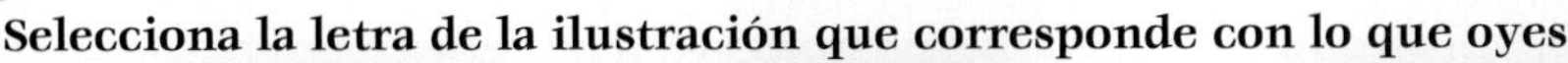

Selecciona la letra de la ilustración que corresponde con lo que oyes.

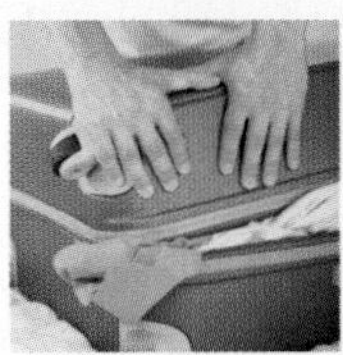

A

B

C

D

E

F

El horario de Josefina

Unscramble the following sentences to find out about a typical week in Josefina's life.

MODELO el lunes / de fútbol / práctica / tiene
El lunes tiene práctica de fútbol.

1. en bicicleta / monta / el martes / con unas compañeras
2. tiene / el miércoles / un partido de fútbol
3. el jueves / con una amiga / de compras / va / a la librería
4. un examen de historia / el viernes / tiene
5. hace / el sábado / para / la maleta / ir de viaje / a Limón
6. de la película / compra / nuevo / el DVD / el domingo / de Penélope Cruz

Una semana típica

Make a list of the activities you would normally do on each day of a typical week.

MODELO El lunes voy a la librería.
El martes tengo clase de piano.

¿Cómo son los días de la semana?

In most Spanish-speaking countries, the first day of the week is *lunes* and days of the week are not capitalized. Only *sábado* and *domingo* have different plural forms *(sábados, domingos)*. In addition, you must use *el* or *los* with the days of the week when telling when activities or events take place. Spanish does not use *en* as English uses **on:** *Josefina tiene práctica de fútbol el lunes* (Josefina has soccer practice on Monday).

Notes

Activity 16 has been recorded as part of the Audio Program. A reproducible answer sheet for the activity has been included at the end of the Audio Program Manual for your convenience.

Whereas Friday the 13th is considered bad luck in the United States, *martes 13* symbolizes bad luck in many Spanish-speaking countries.

Teacher Resources

Activity 16

Answers

16 1. D
2. B
3. F
4. E
5. C
6. A

17 Possible answers:
1. El martes monta en bicicleta con unas compañeras.
2. El miércoles tiene un partido de fútbol.
3. El jueves va de compras a la librería con una amiga.
4. El viernes tiene un examen de historia.
5. El sábado hace la maleta para ir de viaje a Limón.
6. El domingo compra el DVD nuevo de la película de Penélope Cruz.

18 Creative self-expression.

Activities

Students with Special Needs

To help students master the days of the week in Spanish, have them practice discussing daily schedules. Give them a day of the week and a time of day. Students then must say something they will do or something that will occur on that day at the time indicated.

National Standards

Communication	Comparisons
1.1, 1.2	4.1, 4.2
Cultures	
2.1	

Teacher Resources

Diálogo II
¡Qué semana!
Activity 19
Activity 20
Activity 21
Activity 22

Answers

19 1. Marta está muy ocupada.
2. Primero tiene que estudiar para el examen de biología.
3. Tomás está un poco cansado.
4. A Marta le gustan el tenis y el fútbol.
5. Tiene que ir de viaje a Puntarenas.

20 Answers will vary.

21 1. B; 2. F; 3. A; 4. C; 5. B

22 Check for correct spelling.

Activities

Expansion

Additional questions (*¿Qué recuerdas?*): *¿Cuándo va a estudiar Marta? ¿Por qué?; ¿Cuándo va Marta a la librería?; ¿A quién llama Marta?*

Additional questions *(Algo personal): ¿Te gusta el tenis?; Los sábados, ¿te gusta jugar al fútbol o te gusta estudiar?; ¿Estás muy ocupado/ocupada? Explica.*

Language through Action

Ask for volunteers to come to the front of the class to act out the dialog *¡Qué semana!*

National Standards
Communication 1.1, 1.2, 1.3
Connections 3.1

Diálogo II ¡Qué semana!

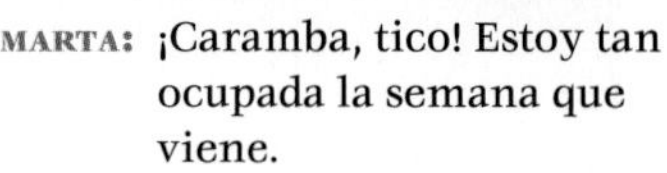

MARTA: ¡Caramba, tico! Estoy tan ocupada la semana que viene.
TOMÁS: ¿Por qué? ¿Qué vas a hacer?
MARTA: El lunes voy a estudiar para el examen de biología.
TOMÁS: Yo también, pero estoy un poco cansado.
MARTA: El martes tengo práctica de tenis y, luego, de fútbol.
TOMÁS: ¡Pues, Marta, te gusta hacer muchos deportes!
MARTA: El miércoles voy a la librería y el sábado voy a hacer un viaje.
TOMÁS: ¿Adónde vas?
MARTA: A casa de mi tía en Puntarenas. ¡Ay! La voy a llamar. Adiós.
TOMÁS: ¡Adiós! ¡Qué semana!

19 ¿Qué recuerdas?

1. ¿Quién está muy ocupada la semana que viene?
2. ¿Qué va a hacer Marta primero?
3. ¿Quién está un poco cansado?
4. ¿Qué deportes le gusta hacer a Marta?
5. ¿Adónde tiene que ir de viaje Marta?

20 Algo personal

1. ¿Estás un poco cansado/a hoy? Explica.
2. ¿Te gustan los deportes? ¿Cuáles?
3. ¿Qué haces primero los fines de semana? ¿Y luego?

¿Te gustan los deportes?

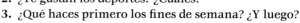

21 ¿Cuándo?

Marta dice lo que tiene que hacer. Indica el día en que va a hacerlo, según el diálogo.

A. lunes
B. martes
C. miércoles
D. jueves
E. viernes
F. sábado

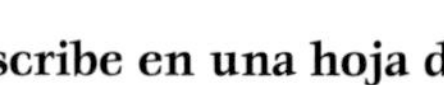

22 Las actividades de Tomás

Escribe en una hoja de papel lo que vas a escuchar.

Notes

Point out Marta's use of the *tico* the first time she talks. The term is explained in the *Cultura viva* on page 193.

Activities 19–22 have been recorded for listening comprehension practice. They are included in the Audio Program. In addition, reproducible student answer sheets for activities 21–22 are provided for your convenience at the end of the Audio Program Manual.

Using a wall map or the *¡Aventura! 1* transparencies, point out where Puntarenas is located.

Cultura viva II

Go online EMCLanguages.net

¡Pura vida!

Costa Ricans have their own regional words and expressions that give their Spanish its own special flavor. For example, they refer to themselves as *ticos* or *ticas*, which is a typical ending they add to everyday words (*chico—chiqui**tico***). *Ticos* and *ticas* are courteous and respectful terms and they do not use *tú* as freely as people from other Spanish-speaking countries. When you are visiting the country, you may hear the phrase *pura vida* (pure life), which is very popular as a positive response or reaction to almost any situation. Other popular expressions in Costa Rica include the following:

expresión	***equivalente***
¡Buena nota!	Okay!
el chunche	thing (or whatchamacallit)
macho, macha	refers to anyone with blond hair
maje	buddy, pal (among friends)

Una tica macha.

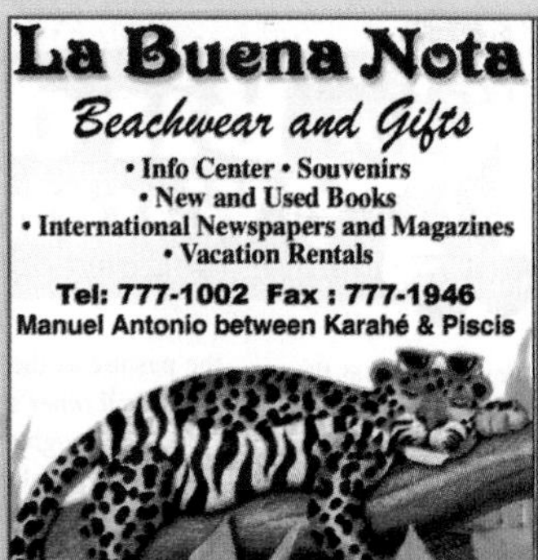

23 ¡Dilo en tico!

Answer the questions on the left with the most appropriate response on the right.

1. ¿Cómo estás, tico?	**A.** La rubia es la tica nueva.
2. ¿Vamos a comer?	**B.** Es un reproductor de CDs.
3. Oye, ¿quién es la macha?	**C.** No, amigo, hoy estoy un poco cansado.
4. Maje, ¿vamos a la práctica de tenis?	**D.** Pura vida.
5. ¿Qué es ese chunche?	**E.** ¡Buena nota!

Notes Ask students if they would be interested in a school trip to Costa Rica or to another Spanish-speaking country. Such travel experiences are a great way to immerse your students in the language and culture they are studying.

Based upon the *Cultura viva*, ask students to guess what the photo caption *Una tica macha* would mean to a Costa Rican. Answer: a blond girl from Costa Rica.

Teacher Resources

 **p. 81**

 **Activity 5**

Answers

23 1. D
2. E or C
3. A
4. C or E
5. B

Activities

Communities

The *Cultura viva* presents several colloquial expressions typical of Costa Rica. If possible in your school or community, ask students to interview Spanish speakers from several other countries to find out some other typical expressions. Ask students to share their findings with the class.

Critical Thinking

Ask students to imagine that they have been asked to visit an English class while studying abroad in Costa Rica. What five popular colloquial expressions used by young people in English would they share with the class?

National Standards	
Communication 1.3	**Communities** 5.1
Cultures 2.1	
Comparisons 4.1	

Teacher Resources

 Activities 8–13

 Activities 8–11

 p. 150

 p. 19

 Activity 7

 Unit 10

 Activities 6–7

Activities

Expansion
Provide further basic practice with direct object pronouns by asking students simple questions about various classroom objects. They may make up their answers: *¿Tienes la regla? (Sí, la tengo./No, no la tengo.)*

National Standards

Communication
1.1

Comparisons
4.1

Idioma

Estructura

Direct object pronouns

A direct object is the person or thing in a sentence that receives the action of the verb directly and answers the question **what?** or **whom?** Add the word *a* (called the *a personal*) before any direct object that refers to a person. Note, however, that you should not use the *a personal* with the verb *tener*.

Veo el reproductor de DVDs.	(I see **what?**)	I see the DVD player.
*Veo **a** la profesora y **a** Sandra.*	(I see **whom?**)	I see the teacher and Sandra.
*Tomás **tiene** dos hermanas en San José.*	(He has **what?**)	Tomás has two sisters in San José.

Sometimes the following direct object pronouns *(pronombres de complemento directo)* replace a direct object.

los pronombres de complemento directo			
me	*me*	**nos**	*us*
te	*you* (tú)	**os**	*you* (vosotros,-as)
lo	*him, it, you* (Ud.)	**los**	*them, you* (Uds.)
la	*her, it, you* (Ud.)	**las**	*them, you* (Uds.)

Notice in the following examples that direct object pronouns usually precede the conjugated form of the verb and any negative expressions (such as *no* or *nunca*) are placed before the object pronouns. In addition, the direct object pronouns *lo, la, los* and *las* can refer to either people or objects.

*No **la** veo.*	I do not see **her** *(Blanca)*. I do not see **it** *(la biblioteca)*.
*Nunca **lo** veo.*	I never see **him** *(Rubén)*. I never see **it** *(el libro)*.

Sometimes the direct object pronoun *lo* is used to refer to a nonspecific direct object or a direct object that is expressed as an idea or a phrase (instead of a person or object).

¿Sabes dónde está el gato?	Do you know where the cat is?
*Sí, **lo** sé.*	Yes, I do (know it).

Note: Some people place an *a* in front of a direct object that refers to a pet they consider part of the family: *Veo **al** perro* (I see the dog).

Notes

Extend the explanation if students ask about the use and meaning of the direct object pronoun *la* in a sentence *(No la veo)* by pointing out that English words sometimes appear alike but have different meanings when they are used in different contexts.

Remind students that they have already learned to recognize *la* as the definite article that accompanies a feminine singular noun (***la*** *regla*, **the** ruler). Now they are learning that *la* may also be a direct object pronoun that replaces a feminine singular noun or pronoun (*No **la** veo*; I do not see **her**).

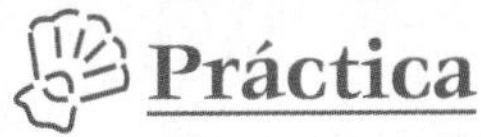

Práctica

La *a* personal

Completa las siguientes oraciones con la *a* personal cuando sea necesario.

1. El sábado voy a ver __ una película en mi nuevo reproductor de DVD.
2. Veo __ mis abuelos cada semana.
3. Sí, quiero __ mi mamá.
4. Busco __ un quemador de CDs.
5. ¿Te gusta escuchar __ música en un reproductor de MP3?
6. ¿Tienes __ tres hermanos?
7. Voy a llamar __ mi primo el lunes.
8. Llevo __ mi gato a casa de mis padres.

Unas preguntas

Alterna con un(a) compañero/a de clase en hacer y contestar las siguientes preguntas.

1. ¿A quién ves ahora?
2. ¿Buscas a tus amigos los fines de semana para escuchar CDs?
3. ¿A quién llamas hoy por teléfono?
4. ¿A quién escribes un correo electrónico hoy?
5. ¿Comprendes a tu profesor(a) de español?
6. ¿Ves a tus amigos todos los días?

Veo a mi perro.

¿Ves a tus amigos todos los días?

Notes Tell students that the personal *a* has no equivalent in English. Stress how essential its use is in Spanish.

Explain to students that *no lo veo* should be used when they do not see an object named by a masculine noun; *no la veo* is used when they do not see an object named by a feminine noun.

Teacher Resources

Activity 25

Answers

24 The sentences 2, 3, 7 and perhaps 8 require the *a* personal.

25 Answers will vary.

Activities

Pronunciation *(las letras* r y rr*)*
Explain that the sound of (intervocalic) *r* usually is soft, consisting of a single vibration that is produced when the tip of the tongue briefly touches the roof of the mouth just behind the teeth. The sound is similar to the **dd** in the English word **ladder**. The sound is modified slightly when *r* ends a word. When the letter *r* begins a word, when *r* follows the consonants *l, n* or *s*, and for *rr*, the tongue flaps softly against the palate two, three or even four times. Review and contrast the sound of *r* and *rr* by practicing the following words: *comer, comprar, ahora, estar, entran, caramba, sorpresa, amor, popular, otros, gracias, dinero* (these words require a single tap on the alveolar ridge); *Ricardo, República Dominicana, Costa Rica, rápido, rápidamente, carro, guitarra, pizarra* (these words are trilled).

Spanish for Spanish Speakers
Pair bilingual and nonbilingual students for activity 25.

National Standards
Communication 1.1
Comparisons 4.1

Teacher Resources

Activity 26
Activity 28

Answers

26 1. Sí, (No, no) la veo.
2. Sí, (No, no) lo veo.
3. Sí, (No, no) los veo.
4. Sí, (No, no) la veo.
5. Sí, (No, no) lo veo.
6. Sí, (No, no) lo veo.
7. Sí, (No, no) los veo.
8. Sí, (No, no) te veo.

27 1. los; 2. nos; 3. me; 4. la; 5. las; 6. los; 7. Lo

28 1. ...lo llevo.
2. ...la monto.
3. ...las leo.
4. ...los escucho.
5. ...los llamo.
6. ...las canto.
7. ...las veo.

Activities

Critical Listening
Using overhead transparencies, ask students in Spanish about objects that may or may not appear in the screen. Students must look at the illustration and, using a direct object pronoun, answer in Spanish whether or not they see the items you name: *¿Ves el perro? (Sí, lo veo.); ¿Ves el caballo? (No, no lo veo.)*.

Expansion
As an alternative to activity 28, have students turn in their sentences as written homework.

National Standards

Communication
1.1

Comparisons
4.1

26 ¡Lo veo!

With a classmate, take turns asking and answering whether or not you can see the following from where you are sitting.

MODELO A: ¿Ves la puerta?
B: Sí, (No, no) la veo.
A: ¿Ves el reproductor de CDs?
B: Sí, (No, no) lo veo.

1. ¿Ves la pizarra?
2. ¿Ves el pupitre?
3. ¿Ves los discos compactos?
4. ¿Ves la computadora?
5. ¿Ves el libro de español?
6. ¿Ves el reloj?
7. ¿Ves los casetes?
8. ¿Me ves?

Estrategia

Avoiding interference with English
Try to avoid letting English interfere with new structures and vocabulary that you are learning in Spanish. For example, the pronouns *lo* and *la* are the Spanish equivalents of the English pronoun **it** only when **it** functions as a direct object of the verb. When **it** is the subject of a sentence, the Spanish subject pronoun is omitted.

*¿**Lo** ves?*	Do you see **it**?
*No, no **lo** veo.*	No, I do not see **it**.
but:	
No está aquí.	**It** is not here.
Es bonito.	**It** is pretty.

27 Un fin de semana con mis abuelos

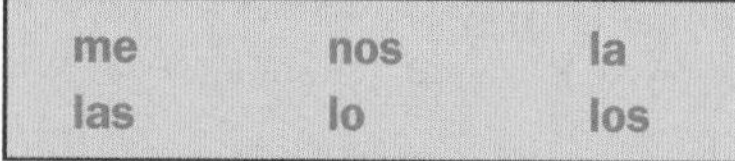

Completa el párrafo, escogiendo de las siguientes palabras.

me	nos	la
las	lo	los

Este fin de semana voy a ir a Puntarenas para estar con mis abuelos. No (1) veo mucho porque mi familia y yo vivimos en San José. Pero ellos (2) ven en el verano porque les gusta ir a la capital. A mí me gusta pasar tiempo en Puntarenas porque mi abuelo Raúl (3) comprende. A él le gusta mucho la música y (4) toca también en el piano. Las canciones de amor son sus canciones favoritas. Siempre (5) canta. También compra muchos CDs y (6) escucha todos los días. Mi abuelo Raúl es muy cariñoso. ¡(7) quiero mucho!

28 ¿Qué haces todos los días?

Trabajando con un compañero o una compañera, contesta las siguientes preguntas. Usa *lo*, *los*, *la* o *las* para las respuestas.

MODELO A: ¿Practicas tenis todos los días?
B: Sí, (No, no) lo practico.

1. ¿Llevas a tu perro a caminar todos los días?
2. ¿Montas en bicicleta todos los días?
3. ¿Lees revistas en español todos los días?
4. ¿Escuchas discos compactos de tu cantante favorito/a todos los días?
5. ¿Llamas a tus parientes todos los días?
6. ¿Cantas canciones de amor todos los días?
7. ¿Ves películas en DVD todos los días?

Llevo a mi perro a caminar todos los días.

Notes

After reading the *Estrategia*, write additional examples on the board of object pronouns that cause interference with English. Discuss the sentences with the class.

Have students write answers to activities 26 and 28 in addition to completing the activities orally with a classmate in order to reinforce basic writing skills.

29 Visita Puntarenas

Pretend you and a classmate are members of a tour that is going to visit Puntarenas, Costa Rica. Ask your partner questions using the cues given to find out if members of the group have the indicated items. Your partner should answer each question affirmatively or negatively, using a direct object pronoun.

MODELO la Sra. Ordóñez / tener / mapa de Puntarenas
A: ¿Tiene la Sra. Ordóñez el mapa de Puntarenas?
B: Sí, (No, no) lo tiene.

1. nosotros / tener / maletas
2. tú / tener / discos compactos para el viaje
3. yo / tener / reproductor de CDs
4. Gabriel / tener / reproductor de MP3 para el viaje
5. tú / tener / número de la oficina de turismo de Puntarenas
6. Néstor y Lina / tener / dinero para el viaje

La Playa Coco en Costa Rica.

Comunicación

30 Adivina, adivinador

Try this guessing game *(juego de adivinanzas)* with a classmate. First, one partner writes on a piece of paper the name of another classmate. Then the other partner asks questions about people in class until he or she can guess the person's name. It may be helpful to use the verbs *ver, mirar* and *buscar* as you play the game. Switch roles.

MODELO **A:** ¿A quién ves?
B: Veo a un muchacho moreno y delgado.
A: ¿Ves a Raúl?
B: Sí. Veo a Raúl.

31 Un viaje a Costa Rica

Imagine that you and a friend are planning to go to Costa Rica. Discuss what you are going to do to prepare for the trip. Then ask and answer questions about when and how you are going to do each activity.

MODELO **A:** ¿Cuándo compramos el libro sobre Costa Rica en la librería?
B: Lo compramos el martes. ¿Cuándo vas a hacer las maletas?
A: Las hago mañana, hoy estoy un poco cansado. ¿Vas a llevar tus CDs de Presuntos Implicados?
B: Sí, los llevo.

Answers

29 1. ¿Tenemos las maletas?/Sí, (No, no) las tenemos.
2. ¿Tienes discos compactos para el viaje?/Sí, (No, no) los tengo.
3. ¿Tengo el reproductor de CDs?/Sí, (No, no) lo tienes.
4. ¿Tiene Gabriel el reproductor de MP3 para el viaje?/Sí, (No, no) lo tiene.
5. ¿Tienes el número de la oficina de turismo de Puntarenas?/Sí, (No, no) lo tengo.
6. ¿Tienen Néstor y Lina el dinero para el viaje?/Sí, (No, no) lo tienen.

30 Creative self-expression.

31 Creative self-expression.

Activities

Students with Special Needs

Write on the board these examples of how to find a direct object and explain them for the class: They see **the library**. (They see **what?**); Rúben sees **Blanca**. (Rúben sees **whom?**). Extend the activity with additional sentences as needed.

Notes

If you have not already done so, you may wish to tell students about the places of interest in and around San José: *el Museo Nacional, la Catedral de San José* and *el Tren Histórico*, which takes passengers on a guided excursion through the rain forest. Also of interest are the day trips to visit *el Parque Nacional del Volcán Irazú.*

Sarchí, a small town near San José, is famous for its handicrafts, especially for the traditional multicolored ox carts for which Costa Rica is known.

Extend activity 31 by having students develop an itinerary for their trip to Costa Rica.

National Standards
Communication 1.1
Cultures 2.2
Connections 3.1

Teacher Resources

Lectura cultural
Los chicos ticos
Activity 32
Activity 33

Answers

32
1. Susana va a la escuela a las 8:00 A.M.
2. Va a la casa de una amiga o habla por teléfono.
3. Van a un parque, a la casa de una amiga, al estadio, al cine o a bailar en un club para jóvenes. Regresan a casa a las 11:00 P.M.
4. Escuchan rock en español, rave, pop, vallenato. Les gusta ver el fútbol.
5. No, no trabajan cuando hay escuela.

33 Answers will vary.

Activities

Critical Thinking
Have students create a Venn diagram depicting similarities and differences between teenagers in Costa Rica and teenagers in the United States.

Spanish for Spanish Speakers
Have students write a short composition in Spanish summarizing what they know about Costa Rica. Expand the activity by having students seek out additional information about Costa Rica at the library. As an alternative, have students write a report about Costa Rica's ecological reserves.

National Standards	
Communication 1.3	**Comparisons** 4.1, 4.2
Cultures 2.1	
Connections 3.1	

Lectura cultural

Los chicos ticos

¿Cómo es la vida diaria[1] de los chicos costarricenses[2]? La revista *SOMOS* entrevistó[3] a Susana Paniagua Vargas, de dieciséis años, que vive en San Rafael de Heredia, Costa Rica, con esa misma[4] pregunta.

Somos: ¿Cómo es un día típico?
Susana: Voy a la escuela de las 8:00 a.m. hasta las 2:20 p.m. Luego, llego[5] a mi casa y tomo un refresco. Cuando no puedo[6] ir a casa de alguna amiga, por lo general, paso toda la tarde en el teléfono.
Somos: ¿Qué hacen tú y tus amigos los fines de semana?
Susana: Nos reunimos[7] en un parque o en casa de una amiga. Cuando hay partidos de fútbol vamos al estadio. O, vamos al cine y después pasamos a algún[8] club de jóvenes[9] a bailar.
Somos: ¿Qué tipo de música escuchan?
Susana: Rock en español, rave, pop, vallenato[10].
Somos: ¿A qué hora tienen que regresar[11] a casa?
Susana: Entre semana[12] a las 9:00 p.m. pero los fines de semana a las 11:00 p.m.
Somos: Cuando salen, ¿qué medio[13] de transporte usan?
Susana: Generalmente[14] el bus, pero prefiero el taxi. (Para manejar[15] carro se necesita tener 18 años.)
Somos: ¿Algunos trabajan medio tiempo?
Susana: No es común que los jóvenes de mi edad trabajen en Costa Rica cuando hay clases; sin embargo[16], cuando hay vacaciones muchos trabajan en tiendas de ropa.

[1]daily life [2]Costa Ricans [3]interviewed [4]same [5]I arrive [6]not able to [7]We get together [8]any [9]youth [10]a combination of African, European and Colombian folkloric sounds [11]return [12]Weekdays [13]means [14]Generally [15]drive [16]however

32 ¿Qué recuerdas?

- How are teenagers in Costa Rica similar to teenagers in the U.S.? What are some differences?

1. ¿A qué hora va Susana a la escuela?
2. ¿Qué hace por las tardes?
3. ¿Adónde van Susana y sus amigos los fines de semana? ¿A qué hora regresan a casa?
4. ¿Qué música escuchan los jóvenes en Costa Rica? ¿Qué deporte les gusta ver?
5. ¿Trabajan los estudiantes en Costa Rica cuando hay escuela?

33 Algo personal

1. ¿A qué hora vas tú a la escuela? ¿Qué haces después? ¿Tienes un trabajo?
2. ¿Adónde van tú y tus amigos los fines de semana? ¿En qué van?
3. ¿Qué música escuchan tus amigos? ¿Qué deporte ven tus amigos?
4. ¿A qué hora tienes que estar en casa entre semana? ¿Y los fines de semana?

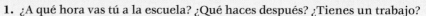

Notes Costa Rica was one of the first countries in the world to be concerned with ecological issues. People in Costa Rica and in the United States are working together to try to find ways to preserve the rain forests and their rich animal life, such as buying some of the land away from developers. Encourage students to learn more about this beautiful country and this issue that is so critical to the health of the entire planet.

¿Qué aprendí?

Autoevaluación

As a review and self-check, respond to the following:

1. Name one item you have in your house from an electronics store. Then name one thing you want to buy there.
2. Name an activity you usually do at least once a week and say what day you do the activity.
3. What activity are you going take part in during the coming weekend?
4. What might you say in Spanish as a reaction in the following situations: you are watching a funny DVD; you heard some bad news about a family member.
5. Ask if a friend sees the following: the new compact discs, the teacher.
6. How would you answer the questions you asked in number 5?
7. What is your schedule for this week? Name two of your activities for next week.
8. Say two things you have learned about Costa Rica.

Palabras y expresiones

How many of these words and expressions do you recognize?

Artículos electrónicos
el casete
el DVD
el equipo de sonido
la grabadora
el quemador de CDs
el reproductor de CDs/DVDs/MP3

Actividades
la actividad
el deporte
la librería
la película
la práctica
el viaje

Pronombres
la
las
lo
los
me
nos
te

Otras expresiones
el amor
cada
la canción
¡caramba!
el compañero, la compañera
el dinero
el fin (de semana)
el gato, la gata
la lástima
la maleta
el perro, la perra
un poco
primero
que
¡qué (+ *noun*)!
que viene
la semana
si
La sopresa tan
tener (+ *number*) años
todos los días
hacer un viaje

Verbos
abrir
buscar
entrar
llamar
montar
pasar
tener

Estructura

Do you remember the following grammar rules?

tener	
tengo	tenemos
tienes	tenéis
tiene	tienen

Expressing strong feelings with *¡Qué* + (adjective/noun)!

In Spanish, To express strong feelings about something or someone use the construction ***¡Qué*** + (adjective/noun)!

¡Qué bueno! How great! ***¡Qué camisa!*** What a shirt!

Direct object pronouns

Direct object pronouns can be used to substitute the person, event, or thing affected by the verb.

singular	plural
me	nos
te	os
lo	los
la	las

Notes

The Costa Rican government provides small plots of land for the citizens of San José so they can plant flowers and vegetables.

Many Central and South American countries are known for their production of coffee. Some coffee connoisseurs consider Costa Rican coffee to be among the best in the world.

Teacher Resources

Activity 14

pp. 53, 87

Juegos

Flash Cards

Answers

Autoevaluación

Possible answers:

1. Tengo un reproductor de CDs. Quiero comprar un DVD.
2. Miro una película en DVD los sábados.
3. Voy a buscar una computadora en la tienda de artículos electrónicos.
4. ¡Qué divertido!; ¡Qué lástima!
5. ¿Ves los CDs nuevos? ¿Ves al/a la profesor(a)?
6. Sí, (No, no) los veo. Sí, (No, no) lo/la veo.
7. Answers will vary.
8. Answers will vary.

Activities

Cooperative Learning

Have students work in pairs by asking and answering questions using *tener* and possessive adjectives. Provide models: *¿Tienes tu cuaderno?; ¿Tiene él/ella su libro?*

Multiple Intelligences (logical-mathematical)

Have students find out the value in dollars for the *colón* (Costa Rican currency) and for the *córdoba* (Nicaraguan currency).

National Standards

Communication
1.1

Connections
3.1

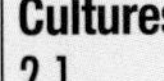

Cultures
2.1

Teacher Resources

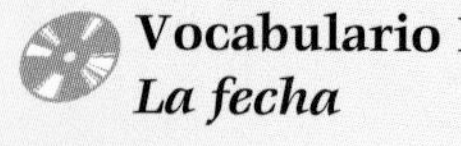

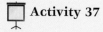

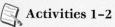

Vocabulario I
La fecha

Activity 37

Activities 1–2

Activities 1–2

p. 78

Activity 1

Activity 1

Content reviewed in *Lección B*

- days of the week
- asking for and stating age
- present tense to indicate future
- transportation

Activities

Critical Thinking
Have students scan Virginia's schedule for cognates and other words they recognize. Ask if they can guess what month *febrero* is. Ask if they remember having seen any other months in Spanish. (They saw *febrero* in the schedule on page 190.)

National Standards

Connections
3.1

Lección B

Vocabulario I

La fecha

Nicar

DICIEMBRE

LUNES	MARTES	MIERCOLES	JUEVES	VIERNES	SABA
1 anteayer	2 ayer	3 hoy	4 mañana	5 pasado mañana	6
8	9	10	11	12	13
15	16	17	18	19	20
22	23	24	25 Navidad	26	27
29	30	31	Luna Nueva 4	C. Creciente 11	Luna Llena 19

C. Men

Ayer, dos de diciembre, fue mi cumpleaños. Me gusta mucho celebrar mi cumpleaños.

Aquí estoy con mi hermana menor, mi hermano mayor y mi tía. Mi tía siempre viene para mi cumpleaños.

Feliz Anõ Nuevo

El cumpleaños de mi tía es el primero de enero, el Día de Año Nuevo.

Mi tía y yo vamos mañana temprano a hacer compras.

Voy a escribir en el periódico de mi colegio sobre mi fiesta de cumpleaños.

Notes The preterite tense form *fue* appears here as a lexical item so students can refer to the past as well as the present and the future when talking about days. All forms of the preterite tense of *ser* appear in the *¡Extra!* on page 201 should you decide to expand the presentation and explain the conjugation of this past tense, which is practiced in activity 3.

The end-of-book Appendices provide a comprehensive overview of the preterite forms that you can use for expanding the presentation to other commonly used verbs.

¿Qué día es?

Escoge una respuesta correcta a cada pregunta que escuchas.

1. A. Navidad B. Año Nuevo C. mi cumpleaños
2. A. sábado B. lunes C. viernes
3. A. sábado B. martes C. jueves
4. A. miércoles B. sábado C. domingo
5. A. 24 de diciembre B. 25 de diciembre C. 31 de diciembre

2 Un e-mail

Gonzalo escribe un e-mail a su amiga Rosario. Completa el e-mail de una manera lógica.

Enviar | Guardar ahora | Descartar

Para: Rosario

Añadir Cc | Añadir CCO

Asunto: Mi cumpleaños

Adjuntar un archivo Insertar: Invitación

« Texto Corrector ortográfico ▾

(1), Rosario. ¿Cómo estás? Yo estoy muy (2). Ayer viernes fue mi cumpleaños. ¡17 años!
Fue un día (3). Ahora estoy en Managua con mis tías y mis dos hermanos. Mañana, (4), voy de compras muy (5) con mi tía y mi hermano (6) de 12 años, Jorge. A mi hermano (7), Ernesto, no le gusta ir de compras. El martes voy a un partido de fútbol.
Y tú, ¿cuándo vienes? ¿En (8), para Navidad?
Ahora no voy a (9) más porque mi tía necesita la computadora.
Adiós,
Gonzalo

Enviar | Guardar ahora | Descartar

¡Extra!

El pretérito de *ser*

You already have learned how to form and use present tense of some verbs in Spanish. Here are the past-tense (preterite) forms of the verb *ser*.

	ser		
yo	**fui**	nosotros nosotras	**fuimos**
tú	**fuiste**	vosotros vosotras	**fuisteis**
Ud. él ella	**fue**	Uds. ellos ellas	**fueron**

3 Las fechas

Contesta las siguientes preguntas.

1. Si hoy es jueves, ¿qué día es mañana?
2. Si hoy es jueves, ¿qué día es pasado mañana?
3. Si hoy es jueves, ¿qué día fue ayer?
4. Si hoy es jueves, ¿qué día fue anteayer?
5. Si ayer fue domingo, ¿qué día es hoy?
6. Si mañana es martes, ¿qué día fue ayer?
7. Si hoy es miércoles, ¿qué día es mañana?
8. ¿Qué día es hoy?
9. ¿Cuál es la fecha?
10. ¿En qué mes estamos?

Teacher Resources

Activity 1
Activity 3

Answers

1
1. B
2. C
3. A
4. C
5. B

2 Possible answers:
1. Hola
2. bien
3. fantástico
4. domingo
5. temprano
6. menor
7. mayor
8. diciembre
9. escribir

3
1. Mañana es viernes.
2. Pasado mañana es sábado.
3. Ayer fue miércoles.
4. Anteayer fue martes.
5. Hoy es lunes.
6. Ayer fue domingo.
7. Mañana es jueves.
8. Hoy es....
9. Hoy es el *(today's day, month and year)*.
10. Estamos en....

Activity

Pronunciation
Model the pronunciation of several words and phrases from *Vocabulario I* for students to repeat.

National Standards

Communication
1.2

Notes

Explain to the class that the verb forms that appear in the *¡Extra!* are preterite, or past-tense, forms (referred to as the *pretérito* in Spanish) of the verb *ser*. The chart has been provided for reference purposes only in this *¡Extra!*

The preterite tense will be presented and applied beginning in *Capítulo 8*.

You may decide to mention that the past-tense *(pretérito)* forms of the verbs *ser* and *ir* are identical. Context will make clear which verb is being used.

Teacher Resources

Diálogo I
¿Cuándo es tu cumpleaños?
Activity 4
Activity 5
Activity 6

Answers

4 1. Es pasado mañana.
2. Va a tener una fiesta.
3. Su hermano mayor viene de Arizona.
4. Viene mañana temprano.
5. Está en la Florida.

5 Answers will vary.

6 1. B
2. A
3. B
4. B
5. A
6. A

Activities

Critical Listening
Play the audio version of the dialog. Tell students to listen for the main ideas and two specific events of importance.

Expansion
Additional questions *(Algo personal): ¿Tienes una fiesta de cumpleaños?; ¿Tienes fiestas de cumpleaños con los amigos? ¿con la familia?; ¿Te gusta la Navidad?*

Prereading Strategy
Ask students how they like to celebrate their birthday. Also ask them what special things other family members do for them on their birthday.

National Standards
Communication 1.1, 1.2
Cultures 2.1

Diálogo I ¿Cuándo es tu cumpleaños?

ISABEL: Oye, Sergio, ¿cuándo es tu cumpleaños?
SERGIO: ¡Chica! ¡Mi cumpleaños es pasado mañana!
ISABEL: ¡Ay, sí!

DARÍO: Y, ¿cómo lo vas a celebrar?
SERGIO: Voy a tener una fiesta. Mi hermano mayor viene de Arizona. Mis primos van a estar aquí también.
ISABEL: ¡Fantástico!

DARÍO: ¿Y cuándo viene tu hermano Jaime?
SERGIO: Viene mañana temprano.
ISABEL: ¿Y tu hermana menor?
SERGIO: Ella está en la Florida, pero viene para la Navidad.

4 ¿Qué recuerdas?

1. ¿Cuándo es el cumpleaños de Sergio?
2. ¿Cómo va a celebrar su cumpleaños?
3. ¿Quién viene de Arizona?
4. ¿Cuándo viene Jaime?
5. ¿Dónde está la hermana menor de Sergio?

5 Algo personal

1. ¿Cuándo es tu cumpleaños?
2. ¿Celebras los cumpleaños con tu familia?
3. ¿Tienes un(a) hermano/a mayor? ¿Menor? ¿Cómo se llama?

6 ¿Cuál es la respuesta?

Escoge una respuesta correcta a lo que escuchas.

1. **A.** mi hermano mayor **B.** mi hermano menor
2. **A.** el jueves **B.** el domingo
3. **A.** el 25 de diciembre **B.** el 31 de diciembre
4. **A.** su hermano mayor **B.** su hermano menor
5. **A.** el viernes **B.** el sábado
6. **A.** el día de la Navidad **B.** el Día de Año Nuevo

Notes Point out to students that many Spanish speakers celebrate their birthday and also their saint's day. For example, the saint's day for someone named Juan is June 24 *(el Día de San Juan).*

For students who may celebrate a holiday other than Christmas, offer the following alternatives: *el Janucá* (Hanukkah), *el Kwanzaa* (Kwanzaa).

Cultura viva

Managua, Nicaragua.

El Lago Nicaragua es muy grande.

Granada, Nicaragua.

Nicaragua

Costa Rica's Spanish-speaking neighbor to the north is the largest country of Central America, Nicaragua. This beautiful country of lakes, mountains, volcanoes, forests and friendly people suffered through a long civil war, and a U.S. trade embargo during the 1980s hurt the economy. Many roads are damaged or unpaved and communication systems do not extend to the rural areas. However, improvements are being made and the capital, Managua, is a large and growing commercial center with a population of one million. It is located on the shores of Lake Managua and is connected by the river Tipitapa to Lake Nicaragua, which was once an ocean bay and today is one of the largest lakes in the world. In fact, it is the only freshwater lake in the world to have swordfish and sharks *(tiburones)*.

7 Nicaragua

¿Cierto o falso?

1. Costa Rica está muy lejos de Nicaragua.
2. La capital de Nicaragua es Managua.
3. Un millón de personas viven en la capital.
4. Managua no está cerca del Lago Managua.
5. El Lago Nicaragua tiene tiburones.

8 Conexión con otras disciplinas: geografía

Find out more about Nicaragua on the Internet or at the library. Then create a map in Spanish showing major cities, lakes, rivers, mountains, surrounding countries and oceans.

Notes Whereas Spanish is clearly the predominant language of Nicaragua, it is interesting that English is commonly used in the Bluefields area on the eastern coast. Also, although Spanish speaking today, the lowlands (known as *Costa de los Mosquitos*) on the western shore were occupied by the British for almost 100 years.

El lago de Managua is called *la Cocibolca* by natives.

Your students may find it interesting that education in Nicaragua is free and mandatory, although students must pay for their own supplies, uniforms and expenses.

Teacher Resources

 Activity 7

 Activity 3

 Activity 2

Answers

7 1. Falso.
2. Cierto.
3. Cierto.
4. Falso.
5. Cierto.

8 Answers will vary.

Activities

Connections

Show students where Nicaragua is located, using the maps in the front of the book or the overhead transparencies that are part of this program.

Critical Thinking

Have students create a Venn diagram depicting how Nicaragua and the United States are similar or different.

National Standards

Cultures
2.1

Connections
3.1, 3.2

Teacher Resources

 Activities 4–6

 Activities 3–5

 Activity 3

 Activity 2

Answers

9 1. vienen
2. vienen
3. viene
4. vengo
5. viene
6. vienen
7. viene
8. vienes

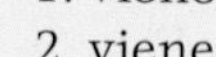

Activities

Critical Thinking

Show the infinitive and conjugations of *tener* and *venir* on the board or on an overhead transparency. Then ask students to point out similarities and differences in the infinitive and conjugations.

National Standards

Comparisons
4.1

Idioma

Estructura

Telling where someone is coming from: *venir*

The present tense of *venir* (to come) is very similar to that of the irregular verb *tener*.

¿Viene Ud. para la Navidad?

venir			
yo	**vengo**	nosotros nosotras	**venimos**
tú	**vienes**	vosotros vosotras	**venís**
Ud. él ella	**viene**	Uds. ellos ellas	**vienen**

*¿**Vienes** tú para la Navidad?* — **Are you coming** for Christmas?

*No, pero **vengo** para el Año Nuevo.* — No, but **I am coming** for New Year's Day.

Práctica

9 El cumpleaños de la abuela

Completa el párrafo que sigue con las formas apropiadas de *venir*.

Pasado mañana es el cumpleaños de la abuela. Va a cumplir ochenta años y hay una fiesta grande en un hotel de Managua. Pero, ¿cómo (1) todos a la fiesta? Pues, mis tíos y mis primos (2) en carro de León. ¡Mi tío siempre (3) a celebrar el cumpleaños de la abuela! Claro, yo (4) a pie porque el hotel está cerca de mi casa. Francisca, la nieta favorita de la abuela, (5) en avión de Costa Rica. Doris y Leonardo (6) de Granada el día de la fiesta. El tío Ricardo (7) en bicicleta porque también vive muy, muy cerca. Y tú, ¿cómo (8)?

Notes

The *vosotros/vosotras* verb endings are included for passive recognition. If you have decided to make these forms active, adapt the provided activities as necessary.

You can teach other verbs in the present tense anytime you would like using the Appendices, a handy reference at the end of *¡Aventura! 1*.

La fiesta de Año Nuevo 

Sergio's parents are having a New Year's party. Working in pairs, take turns asking and answering how each of the guests will arrive. Include an appropriate means of transportation (a pie, en autobús, bicicleta, carro, metro, taxi) in your answers.

MODELO **A:** ¿Cómo vienen tus abuelos a la fiesta?
B: Mis abuelos vienen en taxi.

1. los tíos
2. Isabel y tu hermana
3. Darío
4. el primo de Sergio
5. los padres de Sergio
6. mis abuelos
7. yo
8. tú

Tú vienes en metro.

Repaso rápido

Present tense to indicate the future

You have learned to use the present tense of a verb to say what people are doing now or what they do frequently. The present tense of a verb can also be used to refer to the not-too-distant future as long as a future time expression is used.

*Ella **viene** a mi casa el fin de semana.*	She **is coming** to my house on the weekend.
*Mañana **celebro** mi cumpleaños.*	Tomorrow I **will celebrate** my birthday.
*¿Uds. **están** en casa el domingo?*	**Will you be** home on Sunday?
*Laura **va** a la fiesta el sábado.*	Laura **is going** to the party on Saturday.

Mañana celebro mi cumpleaños.

Teacher Resources

 Activity 10

 Activity 6

 p. 144

Answers

10 Answers will vary.

Activities

Expansion

To practice the use of the present tense in expressing the not-too-distant future, ask students to explain their plans for later today and tomorrow. Summarize their activities on an overhead transparency or on the board and then review the future by asking students to restate their plans with *ir a* (followed by an infinitive).

Notes

As you review the contents of the *Repaso rápido*, remind students that a definite article followed by a day (or days) of the week can convey the message that something happens on that/those given day(s): *Los martes tengo que trabajar; No voy a la fiesta el sábado.* Unlike in English, in Spanish there is no need for a preposition.

National Standards

Communication
1.1

Comparisons
4.1

Answers

11 1. Viene el domingo.
2. Viene el sábado.
3. Vienen el domingo.
4. Vienen el sábado.
5. Vengo el sábado y el domingo.
6. Viene el sábado.
7. Vienes el sábado y el domingo.
8. Venimos el sábado y el domingo.

Activities

Expansion

Use pictures of places and methods of transportation such as those shown in *Lección 3A* (overhead transparencies 23–24). Choose one of each and ask the question *¿Vienes a...en...?* according to the pictures. You may have one student ask the question and call on another for the response. If the response is not logical, a follow-up question is *Entonces, ¿cómo vienes a...?*. Be sure to choose illogical methods of transportation for a little humor *(¿Vienes a Puerto Rico en tren? Entonces, ¿cómo vienes a Puerto Rico? ¿Vienes al concierto a caballo?)*. To emphasize the context for the use of *venir* in contrast to *ir*, have students stand next to, point to or hold the pictures.

National Standards

Communication
1.1

El concierto de Navidad

Pretend that you and your partner are in charge of the invitations for the Christmas holiday concert at your school. Using this incomplete invitation list, take turns asking and answering questions about who is attending on Saturday night and who is attending on Sunday night.

MODELO **A:** ¿Mis padres?
B: Vienen el domingo.

Lista de invitaciones

sábado	domingo
Marta y su prima	Srta. López y su hermano
Gabriel	Sr. Robles
yo	mis padres
tú	yo
la madre de Fernando Peña	tú

1. ¿El Sr. Robles?
2. ¿Gabriel?
3. ¿La Srta. López y su hermano?
4. ¿Marta y su prima?
5. ¿Tú?
6. ¿La madre de Fernando Peña?
7. ¿Yo?
8. ¿Tú y yo?

Notes You have several options when assigning activity 11. Consider having students write out the answers before assigning students to work with a partner. Alternatively, you may wish to pair students requiring additional help with stronger students and have them do the activity orally in class. As a third alternative, follow up the in-class oral activity by telling students they must write the answers for homework, informing them that you now want to see that they understand and can retain what they practiced.

Comunicación

12 Los planes del mes

Pretend today is *el miércoles 8* and you are talking with a friend about activities that happened or will happen this month. Among the activities that will happen, include a birthday celebration that you are having for someone you know and say who is coming to the celebration. Use the calendar as a guide.

MODELO
A: ¿Cuándo es la fiesta para celebrar el cumpleaños de Julia?
B: La fiesta es pasado mañana, el viernes diez.
A: ¿Y quién viene a la fiesta?
B: Vienen muchos amigos.

L	M	M	J	V	S	D
		1	2	3	4	5
6	7	(8)	9	10	11	12
13	14	15	16	17	18	19

13 Año nuevo, vida nueva

Imagine today is December 26th and you are writing an e-mail to your best friend to tell him/her about the New Year's party your family is having for your relatives and special friends. Tell them who is invited and how and when each person is coming. Include as many details as you can.

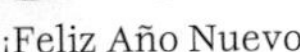

¡Feliz Año Nuevo!

Answers

12 Creative self-expression.
13 Creative written expression.

Activities

Cooperative Learning
Ask students to bring in magazine pictures of a site they have learned to name in Spanish (beach, city, school, etc.). Then ask them to talk about where they are now and if they are coming back, using the cutouts. For example: *Estamos en la playa ahora. Vengo a la playa mañana también. ¿Vienes a la playa mañana?*

National Standards

Communication
1.1

Notes Offer these helpful expressions for completing activities 12 and 13: *¿Qué día es hoy?* (What day is today?); *Hoy es lunes.* (Today is Monday.); *Ayer fue domingo.* (Yesterday was Sunday.); *Mañana es martes.* (Tomorrow is Tuesday.); *Los sábados no tengo clases.* (I don't have classes on Saturday.); *Voy el viernes que viene.* (I am going next/this coming Friday.).

Stress the use of cardinal numbers when expressing the date, noting *el primero* as the only exception.

Teacher Resources

 **Vocabulario II**
Los meses

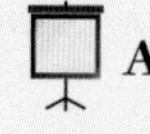 **Activities 38–39**

 **Activity 7**

 **Activities 7–9**

 **p. 22**

 **Activity 4**

 **Activity 3**

Activities

Expansion
Use overhead transparencies 38 and 39 to introduce the new words and expressions in *Vocabulario II*. Begin by showing students transparency 38 and say the months one at a time in Spanish. Students should repeat after you. Continue with overhead transparency 39 and practice the numbers in Spanish, allowing students to see how the word is spelled.

Students with Special Needs
Say a month of the year and have students tell you the months that follow in order. Repeat this activity several times starting with a different month.

National Standards

Connections
3.1

Vocabulario II
Los meses

marzo, abril, mayo

junio, julio, agosto

diciembre, enero, febrero

septiembre, octubre, noviembre

Notes In relation to the twelve months, you may wish to introduce the four seasons of the year at this time: *la primavera, el verano, el otoño, el invierno.*

Activity 14 is intended for listening comprehension practice. Play the audio of the activity that is part of the Audio Program or use the transcript that appears in the ATE introduction if you prefer to read the activity yourself.

A veces los años pasan rápidamente.
¿Cuál es la fecha?
¿De veras? ¡Feliz cumpleaños!
Es el cinco de octubre. ¡El día de mi cumpleaños!
¿Cuántos años cumples?
¿Veinte? La idea no me gusta ni un poquito.
Luis es un chico muy joven. Él no es viejo.
Cumplo dieciséis años, pero quiero tener veinte.

Los números del 101 al 999.999

101	ciento uno
122	ciento veintidós
200	doscientos, -as
201	doscientos uno
300	trescientos, -as
400	cuatrocientos, -as
500	quinientos, -as
600	seiscientos, -as
700	setecientos, -as
800	ochocientos, -as
900	novecientos, -as
1.000	mil
1.001	mil uno
1.999	mil novecientos noventa y nueve
2.000	dos mil
100.000	cien mil

14 ¿Cuándo cumplen años?

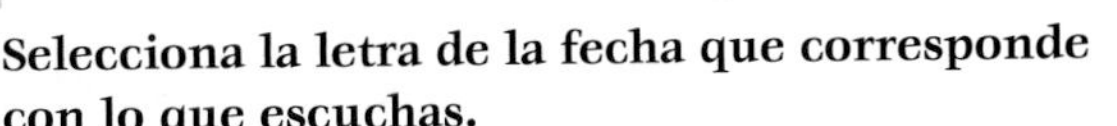

Go online EMCLanguages.net

Selecciona la letra de la fecha que corresponde con lo que escuchas.

A. 16.06 **C.** 20.05 **E.** 12.11
B. 02.03 **D.** 30.08 **F.** 23.01

15 ¡Me gusta!

Say how much you like or dislike the following situations, using *gustar* and any expressions you have learned.

MODELO El mes que viene es diciembre. ¡Es Navidad!
¡Qué bueno! Me gusta mucho./No me gusta ni un poquito.

1. Las horas de clase no pasan rápidamente.
2. Mi cumpleaños es en enero.
3. Un día vamos a ser viejos.
4. Soy muy joven.
5. Hoy es el día de mi cumpleaños.
6. Tengo una fiesta y vienen todos mis amigos.
7. A veces celebro mi cumpleaños con mis abuelos.
8. No tengo CDs ni reproductor de CDs.

16 Conexión con otras disciplinas: matemáticas

Continue the pattern up to the number shown in parentheses.

1. ciento cincuenta, trescientos, cuatrocientos cincuenta... (1.050)
2. cuatrocientos, seiscientos, ochocientos... (2.000)
3. nueve mil, ocho mil, siete mil... (1.000)
4. treinta y cinco mil seiscientos, treinta mil quinientos, veinticinco mil cuatrocientos... (5.000)
5. cien mil, noventa mil, ochenta mil... (10.000)

Notes Before beginning activity 14, point out to students that the day precedes the month. The day and the month are often separated by a period. (*8.10* would be *el ocho de octubre*.) Given that this order differs from what they are used to in English, remind students to pay special attention when completing any form in Spanish that requires birthdates or other dates of importance.

Teacher Resources

Activity 14
Activity 15

Activities 8–9

Answers

14 1. E
2. B
3. F
4. C
5. A
6. D

15 Creative self-expression.

16 1. seiscientos, setecientos cincuenta, novecientos, mil cincuenta
2. mil, mil doscientos, mil cuatrocientos, mil seiscientos, mil ochocientos, dos mil
3. seis mil, cinco mil, cuatro mil, tres mil, dos mil, mil
4. veinte mil trescientos, quince mil doscientos, diez mil cien, cinco mil
5. setenta mil, sesenta mil, cincuenta mil, cuarenta mil, treinta mil, veinte mil, diez mil

Activities

Critical Thinking

Ask students if they notice anything different about the numbers 1.000, 1.001, 1.999, etc. Point out that a period (or sometimes a space) is used in numbers in Spanish where a comma is used in English.

National Standards

Communication 1.2
Comparisons 4.1
Connections 3.1

Teacher Resources

Diálogo II
¡Feliz cumpleaños!
Activity 17
Activity 18
Activity 19

p. 80

Answers

17 1. Es el veinticinco de octubre.
2. Cumple diecisiete años.
3. Los años pasan rápidamente.
4. No le gusta la idea ni un poquito.

18 Answers will vary.

19 1. Cierto.
2. Cierto.
3. Falso. / ...es joven.
4. Falso. / ...diecisiete años.
5. Cierto.
6. Cierto.

Activities

Prereading Strategy
Instruct students to cover up the dialog with one hand and look at the photographs. Ask them to imagine where the conversation takes place and what the people are saying to one another. Finally, have students look through the dialog quickly to find cognates and words they recognize.

National Standards

Communication
1.1, 1.2

Diálogo II

¡Feliz cumpleaños!

ISABEL: ¿Cuál es la fecha de hoy?
DARÍO: Hoy es el veinticinco de octubre.
ISABEL: ¡Hoy es el cumpleaños de Sergio!
DARÍO: ¡Pues vamos a su casa!

ISABEL: ¡Feliz cumpleaños, Sergio!
DARÍO: ¿Cuántos años cumples? ¿Veinticinco? ¿Treinta?
SERGIO: ¡Oye, no! Yo soy joven. Cumplo diecisiete años.
DARÍO: Ja, ja. Pero los años pasan rápidamente.

SERGIO: ¡Los años y el tiempo pasan rápidamente!
ISABEL: Sí, en dos meses estamos en Navidad.
SERGIO: ¡Qué bueno!
DARÍO: ¿Bueno? No me gusta la idea ni un poquito.

17 ¿Qué recuerdas?

1. ¿Cuándo es el cumpleaños de Sergio?
2. ¿Cuántos años cumple Sergio?
3. ¿Qué pasan rápidamente?
4. ¿Le gusta la idea de la Navidad a Darío?

¿Te gusta la Navidad?

18 Algo personal

1. ¿Cuándo es la fecha de tu cumpleaños?
2. ¿Cuántos años vas a cumplir?
3. En tu opinión, ¿pasan los años rápidamente?

19 ¡Feliz cumpleaños, Sergio!

Di si lo que oyes es cierto o falso, según el Diálogo II. Si es falso, corrige la información.

Notes Activities 17–19 have been recorded for listening comprehension practice. They are included in the Audio Program. A reproducible student answer sheet for activity 19 is provided for your convenience at the end of the Audio Program Manual.

Cultura viva II

Go online EMCLanguages.net

Celebramos el Día de los Reyes Magos.

Los días de fiesta

Family life in Nicaragua, Costa Rica and throughout the Spanish-speaking world reflects Catholic traditions such as baptisms, communions and weddings. Holidays honoring local patron saints, as well as other Catholic holidays, are important events throughout the country. In addition, the Nicaraguan people are very sociable and on *días especiales* they enjoy being with their family and friends and perhaps listening to music, dancing and sharing good food. Here are some important holidays *(días especiales)* celebrated throughout the Spanish-speaking world:

1. el Día de Año Nuevo *(New Year's Day)* el primero de enero
2. el Día de los Reyes Magos *(Epiphany)* el 6 de enero
3. el Día de San Valentín *(Valentine's Day)* el 14 de febrero
4. la Semana Santa *(Holy Week)* variable date, usually April
5. el Domingo de Ramos *(Palm Sunday)* variable date, usually April
6. el Viernes Santo *(Good Friday)* variable date, usually April
7. el Domingo de Resurrección *(Easter Sunday)* variable date, usually April
8. el Día del Trabajo *(Labor Day)* el primero de mayo
9. el Día de la Raza/de la Hispanidad *(Columbus Day)* el 12 de octubre
10. el Día de Todos los Santos *(All Saints' Day)* el primero de noviembre
11. la Nochebuena *(Christmas Eve)* el 24 de diciembre
12. la Navidad *(Christmas)* el 25 de diciembre
13. el Día de los Santos Inocentes *(Fools' Day)* el 28 de diciembre
14. la Noche Vieja *(New Year's Eve)* el 31 de diciembre

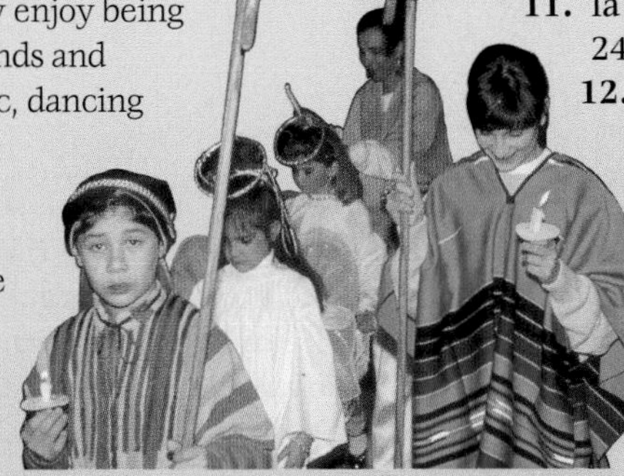
La Nochebuena es el 24 de diciembre.

20 Los días de fiesta

Create a list of at least ten holidays or events in Spanish. Then, working with a partner, take turns asking and answering in what month the holidays or events take place.

MODELO el Día de San Valentín
A: ¿En qué mes es el Día de San Valentín?
B: Es en febrero.

21 Comparando

Compare the holidays in the *Cultura viva* with holidays where you live. For example, say which holidays you celebrate that are not listed and which holidays are celebrated on the same date or different dates.

Notes Let students know that November 1st *(el primero de noviembre)* can be also referred to as *Día de los muertos* or *Día de los difuntos*.

Another way to say **holidays** in Spanish is *días festivos*.

El Día de la Raza is referred to as *el Día de la Hispanidad* in some countries, such as Costa Rica. Similarly, some people use *el Día de los Enamorados* instead of *el Día de San Valentín*.

Teacher Resources

Cultura viva II
Los días de fiesta

Activity 10

Activity 5

Activity 4

Answers

20 Answers will vary.
21 Creative self-expression.

Activities

Expansion
Ask students to find the name of a holiday that is not listed in *Cultura viva* and that is celebrated by Spanish-speaking people where you live. Have students investigate and report on the significance of the holiday in your state.

Multiple Intelligences (intrapersonal)
As a follow-up to *Los días de fiesta*, ask students which of the days listed they celebrate with family or friends. For each day listed they should briefly describe their typical activities.

Spanish for Spanish Speakers
Ask students to write a dialog between two friends who are in charge of preparations for a party to celebrate any of *Los días de fiesta* listed on page 211. You may also instruct them to perform the completed dialog with another student in front of the class.

National Standards

Communication
1.1, 1.3

Cultures
2.1, 2.2

Comparisons
4.1, 4.2

Teacher Resources

 Activity 11

 Activity 10

 Activity 6

 Activity 5

Answers

22 1. la camiseta: quinientos ochenta y dos córdobas
2. el libro: doscientos noventa y un córdobas
3. la computadora: once mil seiscientos cuarenta córdobas
4. el equipo de sonido: siete mil doscientos setenta y cinco córdobas
5. el reproductor de MP3s: dos mil novecientos diez córdobas
6. los zapatos: ochocientos setenta y tres córdobas

Activities

Multiple Intelligences (logical-mathematical)
Have students convert the prices from *córdobas* to dollars.

Students with Special Needs
You may wish to refer to the Appendices at the end of the book to review numbers 1–100.

TPR
Using an overhead transparency, have students come up and touch each number you say in Spanish.

National Standards

Connections
3.1

Comparisons
4.1

Idioma

Estructura

Using the numbers 101 – 999,999

You have already learned to use *cien* (100) before a noun. Use *ciento* in place of *cien* for the numbers 101 to 199: *Tengo* **cien** *casetes y* ***ciento*** *veinte discos compactos*. The numbers from 200 to 999 have masculine and feminine forms that agree with the noun they describe: *Hay quinient**os** ochenta chic**os** y seiscient**as** cincuenta chic**as** en el colegio*. *Mil* (1,000) has only one form. Numbers beginning with *mil* are written with a period in Spanish instead of a comma: *1.000*.

4.000	=	*cuatro mil*
105.800	=	*ciento cinco mil ochocientos*
999.999	=	*novecientos noventa y nueve mil, novecientos noventa y nueve*

When the year is written in Spanish, it has no period. When it is spoken, it is read like any other four-digit number, **not** grouped two numbers at a time, as is done in English.

1562	=	*mil quinientos sesenta y dos*

Práctica

22 Un regalo de cumpleaños

Imagine you are shopping for a birthday gift while visiting friends in Managua and you see the items that follow. Make a list of each article along with the price written out as you would write out numbers on a check. Remember that the prices are given in *córdobas nicaragüenses (NIO)*.

MODELO
El reproductor de CDs
1164
Fecha 23 diciembre
Pagar a
C 4.256
cuatro mil doscientos cincuenta y seis
Córdobas
BANCO NACIONAL
NIO 4.256

1. NIO 582

2. NIO 291

3. NIO 11.640

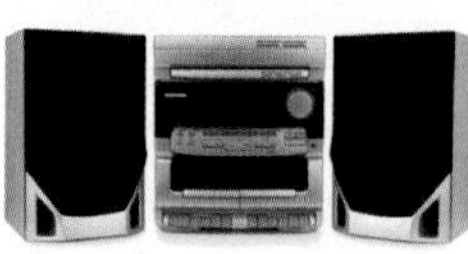
4. NIO 7.275

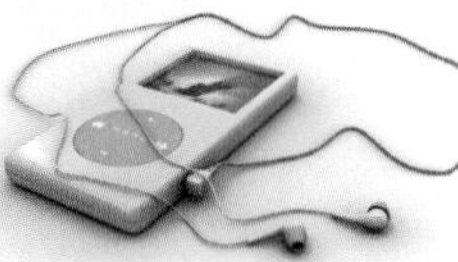
5. NIO 2.910

6. NIO 873

Notes

Explain to the class that in countries where the period is used in place of the comma, the comma is used to separate the decimal figures from the number. In other words, the period and comma are switched around: *NIO 1.459,75* (to refer to *córdobas*).

Be sure students understand the abbreviation *NIO* in activities 22 and 24: *córdobas nicaragüenses*.

23 Conexión con otras disciplinas: matemáticas

Imagine that Nicaragua is hosting a world youth meeting *(reunión juvenil mundial)* and you are in charge of recording how many boys and girls are attending the event and where they are from. Write out how many people are coming from each of the following countries.

MODELO 2.800 / Ecuador
Vienen dos mil ochocientos muchachos de Ecuador.

¿Cuántos muchachos vienen del Ecuador?

1. 153 / El Salvador
2. 721 / Bolivia
3. 2.199 / Argentina
4. 362 / Venezuela
5. 586 / Colombia
6. 93.537 / México
7. 3.738 / Chile
8. ¿Cuántos muchachos vienen en total?

24 ¿Cuánto dinero tienen?

Trabajando en parejas, alternen en preguntar y contestar cuánto dinero tienen las personas indicadas y qué van a comprar.

MODELO tú / NIO 200
A: ¿Cuánto dinero tienes tú?
B: Tengo doscientos córdobas.
A: ¿Qué vas a comprar?
B: Voy a comprar unos calcetines.

1. tus padres / NIO 4.500

2. Gloria / NIO 950

3. Antonio / NIO 5.700

4. los hermanos Ruiz / NIO 18.000

5. la profesora / NIO 820

6. yo / NIO 250

Notes

Activity 23 makes the cross-curricular connection to mathematics.

Using maps at the front of *¡Aventura! 1*, overhead transparencies or a wall map, show students where the countries mentioned in activity 23 are located.

Teacher Resources

Activity 23

Answers

23
1. ...ciento cincuenta y tres muchachos de....
2. ...setecientos veintiún muchachos....
3. ...dos mil ciento noventa y nueve muchachos de....
4. ...trescientos sesenta y dos muchachos de....
5. ...quinientos ochenta y seis muchachos de....
6. ...noventa y tres mil quinientos treinta y siete muchachos de....
7. ...tres mil setecientos treinta y ocho muchachos de....
8. ...ciento cuatro mil noventa y seis muchachos.

24
1. ¿...tienen...?/Tienen cuatro mil quinientos..../¿...van...?/ Van...una impresora.
2. ¿...tiene...?/Tiene novecientos cincuenta..../ ¿...va...?/Va...una blusa.
3. ¿...tiene...?/Tiene cinco mil setecientos..../ ¿...va...?/Va...un equipo de sonido.
4. ¿...tienen...?/Tienen dieciocho mil..../¿...van...?/ Van...una computadora.
5. ¿...tiene...?/Tiene ochocientos veinte..../¿... va...?/Va...unos jeans.
6. ¿...tengo...?/Tienes doscientos cincuenta..../ ¿...voy...?/Vas...un disco compacto.

National Standards

Communication
1.1

Connections
3.1

Teacher Resources

 Activity 12

 Activities 11–13

 Activity 7

 Activity 6

Answers

25 Creative self-expression.

Activities

Critical Thinking
Do several number series puzzles or brain teasers for the numbers 1–999,999. For example, say aloud in Spanish the series: 111, 222, 999, 333, 444, 888, 555. Then ask what the next two numbers should be if the sequence were to continue: 666, 777.

Technology
If you are collaborating with a classroom in another country, encourage your students to share cultural information regarding birthdays to compare and contrast traditions in both cultures.

National Standards	
Communication 1.1	**Communities** 5.1
Connections 3.1	
Comparisons 4.1	

Comunicación

25 La fiesta de fin de año

Imagine you and a friend are in charge of organizing a party for 200 people to celebrate the end of the year at your school. The school has allocated a budget of $5,000 *(dólares)* for the party. Working in pairs, prepare a list of the things you would need for the party and discuss how much money you would need to allocate for each item. Be creative!

MODELO **A:** Bueno, necesitamos mil quinientos dólares para comida.
B: Mil quinientos es mucho. Para comida necesitamos setecientos.
A: Está bien. ¿Y para refrescos?
B: Para los refrescos necesitamos trescientos cincuenta dólares.

Fiesta de fin de año
- *comida*
- *refrescos*
- *música*

Estructura

Asking for and giving the date

Use *¿Cuál es la fecha de hoy?* to ask for the date in Spanish. The answer follows this pattern:

form of *ser* + *el* + number for day of month (or *primero*) + *de* + month + *de* + year

Note: The word *primero* (abbreviated *1º*) is used for the first day of a month instead of *uno.*

Es el ocho de marzo.	It is March eighth.
Es el primero de enero.	It is January first.

In written form the date may appear as follows:

8 de marzo de 2006 or *8.3.06 (or 8/3/06)*

The following expressions may be helpful when talking about days and dates:

¿Qué día es hoy?	*Hoy es viernes.*
¿En qué mes estamos?	*Estamos en mayo.*
¿En qué año?	*En 2006.*

When you want to express **on** in Spanish, use the definite article *el* or *los.*

No voy el sábado. I am not going on Saturday.

Notes

Note that *de* is used with years beginning with **19** *(el veinticinco de diciembre **de 1999**)*, as well as with years beginning with **20** *(el cuatro de julio **de 2002**)*.

Explain to the class that although *primero* (*1º*) is used for the first day of a month instead of *uno*, students may encounter native speakers who use *uno (el uno de marzo)*, following the pattern of using cardinal numbers when stating dates.

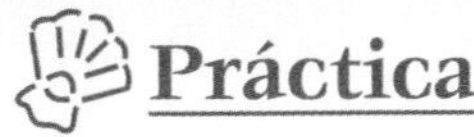

Práctica

26 Fechas memorables

Give the following dates, first in numbers and then in words.

1. *(day, month and year you were born)*
2. *(date you obtained or plan to obtain your driver's license)*
3. *(year you plan to buy a car)*
4. *(year you will be able to vote)*
5. *(year of your high school graduation)*
6. *(date of some other important future event in your life)*

¿Cuál es la fecha de tu graduación?

27 Conexión con otras disciplinas: historia

In pairs, take turns asking and answering questions about several important dates in Nicaragua's history. Follow the model.

MODELO Nicaragua / tener / su fiesta nacional de independencia: septiembre
A: ¿En qué mes tiene Nicaragua su fiesta nacional de independencia?
B: Nicaragua tiene su fiesta nacional de independencia en septiembre.

1. los nicaragüenses / celebrar / 200 años de independencia: 2021
2. en Nicaragua / el Día del Trabajo / ser: 1º mayo
3. los nicaragüenses / celebrar / el Día de la Liberación: 19 de julio
4. Nicaragua / declarar / la independencia de España: 1821

Comunicación

28 Días especiales

With another student, talk about events or special occasions you celebrate during the year. Discuss when these special days occur (name the day of the week, if possible), say what you do to make the day(s) special and mention what you do or do not like about each occasion. If possible, bring a photo that depicts how you celebrate or observe the special event.

MODELO ¿Qué celebras en mayo?
Celebro el Día del Trabajo.

Notes Because students do not know how to form the past tense yet, allow them to use the historical present tense for activity 27.

Activity 27 makes the cross-curricular connection to history.

Answers

26 Answers will vary.

27 Possible answers:

1. ¿Cuándo celebran...?/...en el año dos mil veintiuno.
2. ¿Cuándo es...?/...el primero de mayo.
3. ¿Cuándo celebran...?/...el diecinueve de julio.
4. ¿Cuándo declara...?/...en mil ochocientos veintiuno.

28 Creative self-expression.

Activities

Connections
Have students find out more about the dates and holidays mentioned in activity 27.

Critical Thinking
Have students prepare a calendar of special events that typically occur during the year and that have a significant impact on students. Ask them to try to include at least one event per month. Then have students write two or three paragraphs to describe the year. They may include dates, events, activities, people involved and what they like or dislike.

Expansion
Have students write the names of the months and several holidays on index cards. The two sets of cards should be shuffled. Then have students work in pairs, matching the holidays to the months: *¿Cuándo es...?* and *¿En qué mes es...?*

National Standards

Communication
1.1

Connections
3.1

Teacher Resources

Lectura personal
Activity 29
Activity 30

Answers

29 1. Nicaragua es el único país que celebra La Gritería.
2. Es el siete de diciembre.
3. Empieza a las 6:00 P.M.
4. Hay cohetes y grupos de personas que van de casa en casa. Cantan canciones a la Virgen María y, luego, comen frutas y dulces.
5. Esta celebración es en honor a la Virgen María.

30 Answers will vary.

Activities

Spanish for Spanish Speakers
Have students write a short composition in Spanish summarizing what they know about Nicaragua. Expand the activity by having students seek out additional information about Nicaragua at the library.

National Standards	
Communication 1.3	**Comparisons** 4.1, 4.2
Cultures 2.2	
Connections 3.2	

Lectura personal

Dirección http://www.emcp.com/músico/aventura1/

Archivo Edición Ver Favoritos Herramientas Ayuda

página principal | miembros | e-diario

Les da dulces a la gente en la Gritería.

Queridos amigos, estamos ahora en Nicaragua. Ayer fue el concierto en Managua... ¡Fue fantástico! Me gustan mucho los nicaragüenses porque son muy alegres. Esta noche estamos en casa de un pariente de Manuel que vive en Managua. Es el siete de diciembre y ¡qué noche! Desde las 6:00 P.M. se escuchan cohetes[1]. Hay grupos de niños y adultos que van de casa en casa gritando[2], "¿Quién causa tanta alegría? ¡La concepción de María!"[3] Luego, cantan canciones especiales a la Virgen María y las personas de las casas les dan[4] frutas y dulces[5]. ¡Novecientas personas han venido[6] a esta casa! ¿Qué celebración es? Se llama La Gritería, una fiesta católica muy popular que solamente se celebra en Nicaragua. Interesante, ¿verdad?

[1]firecrackers [2]shouting [3]Who causes so much joy? The Conception of the Virgin Mary! [4]they give them [5]candy [6]have come

29 ¿Qué recuerdas?

1. ¿Cuál es el único país que celebra La Gritería?
2. ¿En qué fecha es la fiesta de La Gritería?
3. ¿A qué hora empieza la fiesta?
4. ¿Cómo celebran La Gritería en Nicaragua?
5. ¿En honor a quién es esta celebración?

- What holiday does La Gritería remind you of? Compare and contrast the two holidays.

30 Algo personal

1. ¿Cuál es una fiesta popular en tu comunidad? ¿Es una fiesta religiosa o no?
2. ¿Qué fiestas religiosas conoces? ¿En qué fecha se celebran?
3. ¿Hay una fiesta que solamente se celebra en los Estados Unidos? ¿Cuál(es)?

Notes Be sure students understand that *La Gritería* is unusual because, as Ceci points out, although it is a Catholic celebration, it is celebrated only in Nicaragua.

Encourage students to find out more about Nicaragua by going to the following Web sites:

Nicaraguan Institute of Tourism
http://www.intur.gob.ni/
Electronic Embassy
http://www.embassy.org
Organization of American States
http://www.oas.org
General travel information
http://www.expedia.com

Autoevaluación

As a review and self-check, respond to the following:

1. How would you say in Spanish that your birthday was yesterday?
2. Imagine your birthday is today. In Spanish, say who is coming to the party.
3. What do you say to wish someone a happy birthday in Spanish? How would you ask how old the person is?
4. Write an e-mail to a friend describing your plans for next week.
5. What day is today? What was yesterday?
6. What is today's date?
7. Name two common holidays/celebrations in Spanish-speaking countries.
8. Say two things you have learned about Nicaragua.

Palabras y expresiones

How many of these words and expressions do you recognize?

Para describir
feliz
joven
mayor
menor
pasado,-a
poquito
primero,-a
rápidamente
viejo,-a

Números
ciento
doscientos,-as
trescientos,-as
cuatrocientos,-as
quinientos,-as
seiscientos,-as
setecientos,-as
ochocientos,-as
novecientos,-as
mil

Fechas
abril
agosto
el año
el Año Nuevo
anteayer
ayer
el cumpleaños
diciembre
enero
febrero
la fecha
julio
junio
marzo
mayo
el mes
la Navidad
noviembre
octubre
pasado mañana
septiembre

Verbos
celebrar
cumplir (años)
fue
venir

Otras expresiones
a veces
¿de veras?
¡Feliz cumpleaños!
la idea
ni
temprano
la vez (*pl.* veces)

Estructura

Do you remember the following grammar rules?

venir	
vengo	venimos
vienes	venís
viene	vienen

Asking for and giving the date	
Question: ***¿Cuál es la fecha de hoy?***	What is the date today?
Answer: form of ***ser*** + ***el*** + the date + ***de*** + month + ***de*** + year	
Es el cinco de mayo de dos mil trece	It is May 5, 2013.

Notes

Nicaragua shares the same date for the *fiesta nacional* as Costa Rica.

Note that in many Spanish-speaking homes throughout the world, gifts are traditionally given on January 6, *el Día de los Reyes Magos*. Children look forward to the arrival of the three Wise Men, who often arrive the afternoon or evening the night before.

In the hot climate of Nicaragua and Costa Rica, Hispanic men often wear an embroidered dress shirt, called a *guayabera*, instead of a coat and tie. It fits loosely, is open at the neck, and is cut straight across the bottom so it can be worn outside the trousers.

Teacher Resources

Activity 13

pp. 54, 88

Juegos

Flash Cards

Answers

Autoevaluación
Possible answers:

1. Mi cumpleaños fue ayer.
2. Mi amiga viene. Vienen mis primos.
3. ¡Feliz cumpleaños! ¿Cuántos años cumples?
4. The e-mails should include the phrase *El fin de semana que viene voy a...*
5. Answers will vary.
6. Answers will vary.
7. Answers will vary.
8. Answers will vary.

Activities

Critical Listening
To practice recognition of larger numbers, divide students into groups of ten and tape a number (zero through nine) on the back of each student. In turn, as you state different numbers, the groups compete by seeing who can line up first in the appropriate order. (**Note:** If the class does not divide evenly into groups of ten, certain digits may be repeated in a group or the remaining students may serve as number readers and judges.)

National Standards

Communication
1.2

Cultures
2.1

Connections
3.1

Teacher Resources

 *Viaje por Costa Rica*

Answers

Preparación

1. Costa Rica.
2. Aves tropicales, monos, iguanas y cocodrilos.

Activities

Critical Listening
Play the audio version of the reading. Tell students to listen for the main ideas the speaker is addressing. Finally, have several individuals state what they believe is the main theme of the reading.

Expansion
Ask if students can identify other popular ecotourism destinations.

Prereading Strategy
Tell students they do not need to understand every word in order to read in Spanish. Equivalents for most unknown words have been provided to help students enjoy the contents of the readings without having to look up important but passive vocabulary. Be sure to cover the *Preparación* and *Estrategia* prior to beginning *Tú lees.*

National Standards
Cultures 2.2
Connections 3.1

Tú lees

Estrategia

Scanning for details before reading
Quickly look over what you are about to read and search for specific details. For example, imagine you want to buy something and are hoping to find a sale in the newspaper. You would not read every advertisement you find. Instead, you would look very quickly for the item and prices. The same holds true when you scan any article you are about to read: Instead of trying to understand every word, just look for specific details that stand out and that help you understand the main idea of a reading.

Preparación

Busca estos detalles como preparación para la lectura.

1. ¿En qué país hace viajes Safaris Corobicí?
2. En los viajes, ¿qué observan los turistas?

Viaje por Costa Rica

Safaris Corobicí

Viajes en bote por Costa Rica

- Especializado en tours escénicos en el Río[1] Corobicí para naturalistas y observadores de aves[2]
- Viajes en bote diarios–desde las 7 A.M. hasta las 4 P.M.
- Viajes desde 2 horas hasta medio día de duración

Los viajes pueden ser arreglados para su comodidad[3]–familias con niños[4] o personas con requerimientos especiales. Organizamos viajes para grupos grandes (21 hasta 100 personas) o grupos pequeños (1 hasta 20 personas). Nuestros guías reman[5] el bote y Uds. sólo disfrutan[6] del río. Excepto por algunas[7] pequeñas partes, este río no tiene aguas turbulentas. En el Río Corobicí, hay varias zonas para nadar. Este es un paraíso donde los turistas pueden observar muchas aves tropicales, monos con caras blancas[8], tres especies de iguanas y cocodrilos en las orillas[9] del Río Corobicí. Uds. sólo necesitan traer un traje de baño[10], un sombrero[11], una cámara, unos binoculares y loción de protección solar.[12]

[1]river [2]birds [3]comfort [4]children [5]row [6]enjoy [7]some [8]white faced monkeys [9]riverbank [10]bathing suit [11]hat [12]sun-protection lotion

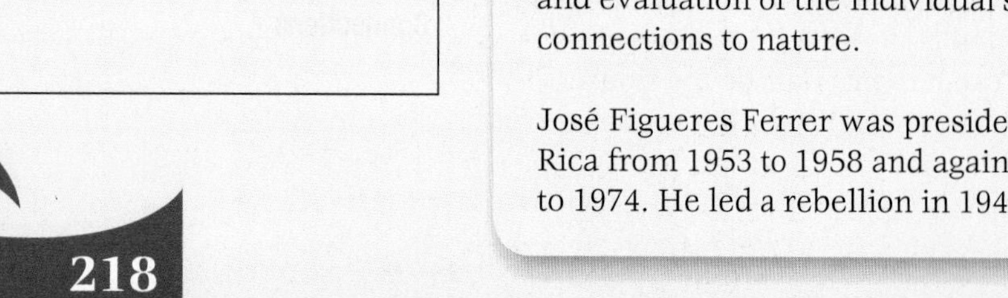

Notes

Costa Rica has evolved into a popular destination for ecotourism, a style of tourism focused on environmental issues and evaluation of the individual's own connections to nature.

José Figueres Ferrer was president of Costa Rica from 1953 to 1958 and again from 1970 to 1974. He led a rebellion in 1948 to abolish the army and devote the military budget to education. Today Costa Rica has one of the highest literacy rates in Latin America.

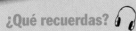

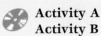

A ¿Qué recuerdas?

1. ¿Para cuántas personas son los viajes?
2. ¿Por cuánto tiempo es el viaje más corto?
3. ¿A qué hora son los viajes?
4. ¿De cuántas personas es un grupo grande?
5. ¿Qué necesitan traer los turistas?

B Algo personal

1. ¿Te gusta hacer viajes en bote? ¿Dónde?
2. ¿Te gusta observar animales? ¿Cuáles?
3. ¿Qué te gusta de los safaris Corobicí?

Vamos a hacer un viaje por Costa Rica.

El tucán es un ave tropical que vive en Costa Rica.

Unos monos con caras blancas.

Notes Encourage students to find out more about Costa Rica by going to the following Web sites:

Costa Rica Tourism Board
http://www.tourism-costarica.com
Electronic Embassy
http://www.embassy.org
Organization of American States
http://www.oas.org
General travel information
http://www.expedia.com

Teacher Resources

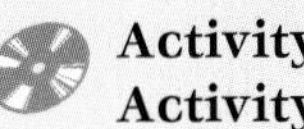

Activity A
Activity B

Answers

A 1. Son para grupos grandes y para grupos pequeños.
2. Es por dos horas.
3. Son desde las siete de la mañana hasta las cuatro de la tarde.
4. De 21 hasta 100 personas.
5. Necesitan traer un traje de baño, un sombrero, una cámara, unos binoculares y loción de protección solar.

B Answers will vary.

Activities

Expansion

Additional questions (*¿Qué recuerdas?*): *¿De cuántas personas es un grupo pequeño?; ¿Quiénes disfrutan del río?; ¿Tiene el río aguas turbulentas?; ¿Puedes nadar en el río Corobicí?*

Additional questions (*Algo personal*): *¿Te gusta la naturaleza?; Te gusta nadar?; ¿Dónde te gusta nadar más, en un río, en un lago o en una piscina?*

Technology

Ask students to search the Internet for ecotours in Costa Rica. Have them summarize their findings in a written report or orally with the class.

National Standards	
Communication 1.1, 1.3	**Connections** 3.1, 3.2
Cultures 2.2	

Answers

A Creative-thinking skill development.

B Creative writing practice.

Activities

Multiple Intelligences (linguistic)

For additional writing practice, ask students to imagine they have plans for the upcoming weekend that include three or four outdoor activities. Unfortunately, the weather does not cooperate, and it is a rainy, cold Saturday. In one paragraph (3–4 sentences) have them describe the original plans, using the present tense to tell what they plan to do *el sábado que viene*. In a second paragraph, have them tell what they are doing indoors instead *(Hoy es sábado y estoy en casa...)*. Students should say whether or not they like the indoor activities and use a variety of verbs and new vocabulary from the lesson.

National Standards

Communication
1.3

Tú escribes

Estrategia

Brainstorming

Brainstorming consists of setting your mind free to think about everything that relates to a certain topic. Concentrating on one or two of the main ideas and jotting down what comes to mind will provide information you need to organize and express your ideas about a topic.

A Brainstorm about your favorite and least favorite holidays of the year. Think about as many ideas as you can relate to both of them—where you are, people you are with, activities and so on. Finally, list what you like or do not like about each holiday.

B Write at least two short paragraphs in Spanish that contrast the two holidays you have chosen. In one paragraph write about the holiday that you like and in the other write about the one you do not like. Develop each contrasting theme of your paper with information such as when the holiday occurs, whom you are with, what activities go on, where you are, how you feel about the holiday and anything else you wish to include. Finally, add graphics or artwork to make the composition attractive and interesting.

¿Te gusta el Día de los Reyes Magos?

Notes The teaching strategy of modeling the desired writing outcome is especially useful (e.g., you may want to write your own contrasting paragraphs to read or show to students as a sample of the desired product). After students finish the assignment, it is a good idea to save some of the best ones to use as models for future classes. Be sure to ask the students' permission or remove their names from the samples.

Proyectos adicionales

A Conexión con la tecnología

Imagine you are about to take a vacation to Costa Rica. Locate information from the Internet or at the library to help you plan your trip (e.g., cities you wish to visit, weather, food, things to do, important events, geography, means of transportation, where you can stay and cost). Finally, create an itinerary for every day of the trip and present it to the class.

B Comparaciones

Choose a Spanish-speaking country and find out how the people there celebrate a special holiday of your choosing. You can do your research at the library, on the Internet or, if you prefer, you can use e-mail and write to a key pal who lives in the selected country. Find out about traditions that make the holiday special, if there are certain foods that people eat and any other information you might consider interesting. Then compare how the holiday is similar or different in that country and where you live.

Bailamos merengue todos los fines de semana.

C Conexión con otras disciplinas: música

Working in pairs, complete a survey *(encuesta)* identifying what kind of music your peers enjoy. Ask if they are familiar with Latin American music *(vallenato, merengue, salsa, etc.)* or Spanish music *(flamenco)*. Then find out if someone watches musical performances in Spanish on television and, if so, when. Share your findings with the class.

MODELO A cinco estudiantes les gusta la música rock. A mí me gusta la música popular y a diez estudiantes les gusta el rap. Tres estudiantes ven cantantes famosos que cantan en español los sábados en Univisión.

Nombre	Tipo de música	Música latina o española que conocen	Ven cantantes que cantan en español
yo	popular	flamenco	no
Carlos	rock	salsa	no
Stephanie	rap	no	sí, sábados en Univisión
David	rap	merengue	no

Teacher Resources

p. 71

Answers

A Creative self-expression.
B Creative self-expression.
C Answers will vary.

Activities

Connections
Have students do a report about Lake Nicaragua. They may want to search the Internet and/or write to the Nicaraguan embassy.

Multiple Intelligences (artistic)
Have students design their own birthday card in Spanish.

Technology
Have each student choose a Spanish-speaking country that he or she would like to visit. Each student may search the Internet for a list of its holidays, or *días festivos*. Students can then compare the number and type of the country's holidays with those in U.S. culture.

Notes

Activity C offers cross-curricular connections to music.

You may wish to have students create a Venn diagram to help them visualize the similarities and differences when doing activity B of the *Proyectos adicionales*.

Display the more interesting projects around the room or arrange to display the better projects in a public place in the school if one is available. (You may want to ask students first if they would mind having their work displayed for others to see.)

National Standards

Communication
1.3

Cultures
2.2

Connections
3.1, 3.2

Comparisons
4.1, 4.2

Teacher Resources

 *Trabalenguas*

 **Episode 5, DVD 1, Track 48**

Answers

Resolviendo el misterio

1. Answers will vary but could include: extended family members are present, mariachi music, and dancing.
2. Answers will vary.
3. Answers will vary.

Activities

Expansion

Ask students to obtain the populations of the following cities: León, Granada, Matagalpa, Bluefields (Nicaragua); Limón, Cartago, Puntarenas (Costa Rica). Provide the populations on a visual. Ask students to correctly state the numbers in Spanish.

Multiple Intelligences (musical)

Call on students to say what kind of music they like. Play excerpts of various types of the music listed in the *¡Extra!* section on page 187. Have students try to identify the type of music being played. Then have students look for examples of music from Spanish-speaking countries and bring them to class. As an alternative to this activity, borrow from the school band some percussion instruments that are used in Latin American music (bongos, tambourines, maracas, etc.). Students should take turns playing the instruments to accompany examples of Latin American music.

Trabalenguas

Ask students to sing the *Trabalenguas* or say it as a cheerleader or a rap singer would.

National Standards
Cultures 2.1, 2.2
Connections 3.1

REPASO

Now that I have completed this chapter, I can...	Go to these pages for help:
describe everyday activities.	182
say what someone is going to do.	190
seek and provide personal information.	200
write about everyday life.	200
say what someone likes or dislikes.	209
express strong feelings.	209
talk about dates and holidays.	209

I can also...	
identify some objects in an electronics store.	182
identify opportunities to use Spanish for work or leisure travel.	185
talk about life in Costa Rica and Nicaragua.	185, 203
describe music you like.	187
talk about the days of the week.	190
recognize how my English can interfere with learning Spanish.	196
read in Spanish about things to do in Costa Rica.	198
talk about the months.	200
state when something happened or will happen.	200
use the numbers 101– 999,999.	209
use some weather expressions.	209
identify and discuss special days.	211
write in Spanish about special times of the year.	211

Trabalenguas

Hoy ya es ayer y ayer ya es hoy,
ya llegó el día y hoy es hoy.

Resolviendo el misterio

After watching Episode 5 of *El cuarto misterioso*, answer the following questions.

1. How does Conchita's birthday party differ from the typical birthday celebration of a typical American teenager?
2. Does José have a right to be jealous when he sees Conchita dancing with Rafael?
3. What do you think is the relationship between don Pedro and Fernando Medina?

Notes

Loose translation of the *Trabalenguas:* Today is already yesterday and yesterday is today, the day has arrived and today is today.

Note for your students that some holidays may have more than one name. *El Domingo de Pascua* is also called *el Domingo de Resurrección* and *la Víspera del Día de Todos los Santos* is also called *la Noche de Brujas.* Additionally, *el Día del Trabajo* can be *el Día de los Trabajadores; el Día de los Muertos* sometimes is *el Día de los Fieles Difuntos; el Día de Fin de Año* can be *la Noche Vieja. El Día del Padre* could be *el Día de los Padres* and *el Día del Año Nuevo* could be *el Año Nuevo,* depending upon the country.

Vocabulario

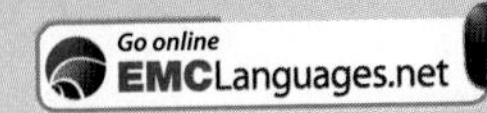

a veces sometimes, at times *5B*
abril April *5B*
abrir to open *5A*
la **actividad** activity, exercise *5A*
agosto August *5B*
el **amor** love *5A*
anteayer the day before yesterday *5B*
el **año** year *5B*
el **Año Nuevo** New Year's Day *5B*
el **artículo** article, item *5A*
ayer yesterday *5B*
buscar to look for *5A*
cada each, every *5A*
la **canción** song *5A*
¡caramba! wow! *5A*
el **casete** casette *5A*
celebrar to celebrate *5B*
ciento one hundred *5B*
el **compañero**, la **compañera** classmate, partner *5A*
cuatrocientos,-as four hundred *5B*
el **cumpleaños** birthday *5B*
cumplir *(+ años)* to become *(+ number of years)*, to reach *5B*
¿de veras? really? *5B*
el **deporte** sport *5A*
diciembre December *5B*
el **dinero** money *5A*
doscientos,-as two hundred *5B*
el **DVD** DVD, digital videodisc *5A*
electrónico,-a electronic *5A*
enero January *5B*
entrar to go in, to come in *5A*
el **equipo de sonido** sound system *5A*
febrero February *5B*
la **fecha** date *5B*
feliz happy *5B*

Tengo una maleta vieja.

¡Feliz cumpleaños! Happy Birthday! *5B*
el **fin (de semana)** weekend *5A*
el **gato, la gata** the cat *5A*
la **grabadora** tape recorder *5A*
hacer un viaje to take a trip *5A*
la **idea** idea *5B*
joven young *5B*
julio July *5B*
junio June *5B*
la her, it, you *(d.o.)* *5A*
las them, you *(d.o.)* *5A*
la **lástima** shame *5A*
la **librería** bookstore *5A*
llamar to call, to telephone *5A*
lo him, it, you *(d.o.)* *5A*
los them, you *(d.o.)* *5A*
la **maleta** suitcase *5A*
marzo March *5B*
mayo May *5B*
mayor older, oldest *5B*
me me *(d.o.)* *5A*
menor younger, youngest *5B*
el **mes** month *5B*
mil thousand *5B*
montar to ride *5A*
la **Navidad** Christmas *5B*
ni not even *5B*
nos us *(d.o.)* *5A*
novecientos,-as nine hundred *5B*
noviembre November *5B*
ochocientos,-as eight hundred *5B*
octubre October *5B*
pasado,-a past *5B*
pasado mañana the day after tomorrow *5B*
pasar to pass, to spend *(time)* *5A*
la **película** movie, film *5A*
el **perro**, la **perra** dog *5A*
poquito a very little *(bit)* *5B*
la **práctica** practice *5A*
primero first *(adverb)* *5A*
primero,-a first *5B*

¡qué *(+ noun)*! what a *(+ noun)*! *5A*
que that, which *5A*
el **quemador de CDs** CD burner *5A*
que viene upcoming, next *5A*
quinientos,-as five hundred *5B*
rápidamente rapidly *5B*
el **reproductor de CDs/DVDs/MP3** CD/DVD/MP3 player *5A*
seiscientos,-as six hundred *5B*
la **semana** week *5A*
septiembre September *5B*
setecientos,-as seven hundred *5B*
si if *5A*
la **sorpresa** surprise *5A*
tan so *5A*
te you *(d.o.)* *5A*
temprano early *5B*
tener *(+ number)* **años** to be *(+ number)* years old *5A*
tener to have *5A*
todos los días every day *5A*
trescientos,-as three hundred *5B*
un poco a little *(bit)* *5A*
venir to come *5B*
la **vez** *(pl.* veces) time *5B*
el **viaje** trip *5A*
viejo,-a old *5B*

¿Es el cumpleaños del perro?

Teacher Resources

Las aventuras de la familia Miranda

Repaso

¡Aventureros!, Ch. 5

Internet Activities

i-Culture

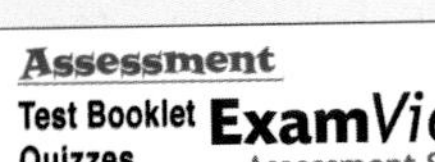

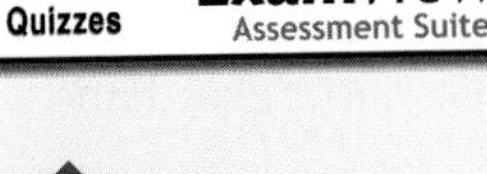

Activities

Communities

Ask students to listen to a local radio station or visit a music store to find out the names of some of the top-rated Spanish-speaking singing groups and/or songs. Students should bring a sample of the music to share with the class.

Expansion

Bring in (or have students bring in) samples of music styles and discuss the following: Salsa is an Afro-Latin musical rhythm that originated in New York City among Caribbean immigrants. Flamenco (música flamenca) is music from southern Spain that is usually played on the guitar and that is characterized by a syncopated and varied rhythm. Merengue is a fast tropical rhythm from the Dominican Republic. Mariachi is a very popular type of music from Jalisco, Mexico, that is played by a small group of musicians who use a large guitar (guitarrón), smaller guitars, trumpets and violins.

Notes Remind students that the words and expressions listed on page 223 are provided as a handy reference list of vocabulary they are required to know from *Capítulo 5*. Students should review and test themselves on the content of the *Vocabulario* in preparation for the chapter test and for future chapters in *¡Aventura! 1*.

Model words from the list by having students repeat after you. Then call on individuals to repeat words to simultaneously practice and evaluate pronunciation.

National Standards

Communication
1.3

Cultures
2.2

Communities
5.1

Teacher Resources

 *Capítulo 6*

TPRS *Capítulo 6*

Episode 6, DVD 1, Track 65

Connections with Parents

Involve more parents and guardians in their children's school lives. Ask for volunteers to assist in class and assign activities that require students and their parents or guardians to interact.

Answers

El cuarto misterioso

1. José está en "el cuarto misterioso."
2. Las respuestas variarán.
3. Las respuestas variarán.

Activity

Prior Knowledge

To review the chapter objectives, ask students: What do you do in Spanish class every day? How does the house pictured differ from your home? Instead of pointing, what words help you be specific about something you want? What words and expressions help you express your opinions? When is gossip positive?

National Standards

Cultures
2.2

CAPÍTULO 6

En casa

El cuarto misterioso

Contesta las siguientes preguntas sobre *Episodio 6–La llave.*

1. ¿Dónde está José en esta escena?
2. Describe este cuarto. ¿Tienes un cuarto similar en tu casa?
3. ¿Qué va a encontrar José?

José entra en "el cuarto misterioso" después de encontrar una llave en un libro de su tío.

Objetivos

- identify **items in the kitchen**
- express **obligations, wishes and preferences**
- talk about **everyday activities**
- state an **opinion**
- discuss **food** and **table items**
- point out **people** and **things**
- describe a **household**
- tell what **someone says**
- say **how someone is doing**

Notes

A checklist of these objectives, along with additional functions, appears on page 266 so students can evaluate their own progress.

Activities

Connections
Ask students to name some cities in Venezuela and Colombia. Then ask if anyone in class has visited or knows someone who has visited either country. Ask if students can tell the class any interesting information about these countries.

Contexto cultural

Venezuela
Nombre oficial: República Bolivariana de Venezuela
Población: 27.635.000
Capital: Caracas
Ciudades importantes: Maracaibo, Valencia, Barquisimeto
Unidad monetaria: el bolívar
Fiesta nacional: 5 de julio, Día de la Independencia
Gente famosa: Simón Bolívar ("El Libertador"); Rómulo Gallegos (escritor)

Colombia
Nombre oficial: República de Colombia
Población: 44.725.000
Capital: Bogotá
Ciudades importantes: Medellín, Cali, Cartagena
Unidad monetaria: el peso
Fiesta nacional: 20 de julio, Día de la Independencia
Gente famosa: Fernando Botero (pintor); Gabriel García Márquez (escritor); Shakira (cantante)

Notes The cultural focus of this chapter combines the South American countries of Venezuela and Colombia. The two countries have had many connections over the years. They remain connected today due in part to the disputes about oil reserves located between the two countries. Students will find it interesting that Venezuela is named after Venice due to its extensive waterways; Colombia is named for Christopher Columbus.

National Standards

Cultures
2.2

Connections
3.1

Teacher Resources

 **Vocabulario I**
¿Qué tenemos que hacer en la cocina?

 **Activities 40–41**

 **pp. 90–11**

 **Activity 1**

 **Activity 1**

Content reviewed in *Lección A*
- family
- express courtesy
- discuss food
- the verb tener

 **Activities**

Expansion
Use overhead transparencies 40 and 41 to introduce the new words and expressions in *Vocabulario I.* Begin by showing students transparency 40. Point to one of the objects in the kitchen and identify it in Spanish. Students should repeat after you. Continue on to the next item and repeat the process. As a second step, show students transparency 41. Once again identify the objects in Spanish, allowing students to see how each word is spelled.

Prereading Strategy
Play the audio recording of the vocabulary and have students repeat the words while showing them overhead transparency 40.

National Standards
Connections
3.1

Lección A

Vocabulario I

¿Qué tenemos que hacer en la cocina?

Vene

¿Qué cosas tene
que hacer?

el horno microondas

la estufa

el refrigerador

Él enciende las luces.

¿La pongo con los platos
de todos los días?

¡Ah, sí! ¡Ya los veo!

Para empezar, Santiago,
debes cerrar la puerta
del refrigerador.

Después, pienso que
tienes que hacer más
arepas. Y, Daniela, tú
debes poner la mesa.

el plato

No. Prefiero los
platos especiales.

el lavaplatos

el fregadero

los cubiertos

Los chicos quieren ayudar en la cocina.
Mañana ellos viajan otra vez a Colombia.

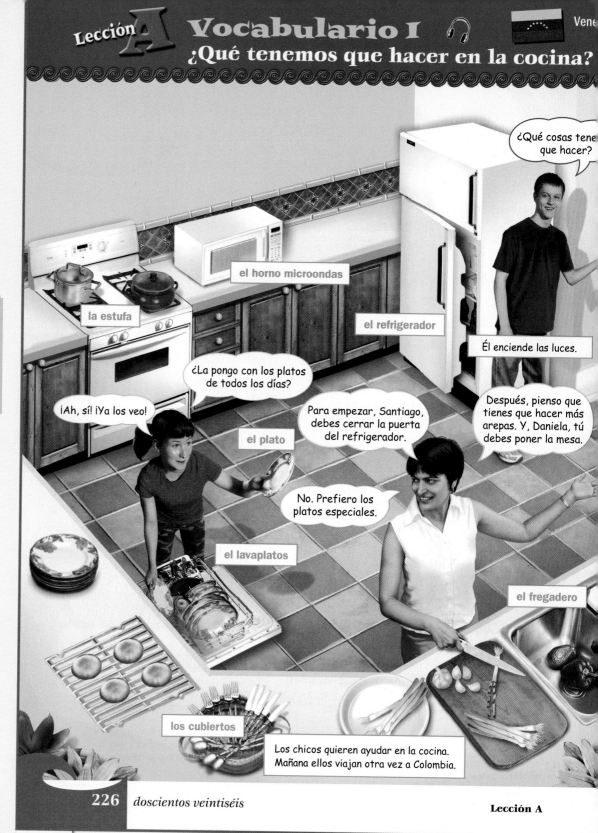

Notes The verb *poner* is presented here as new vocabulary in the expression *poner la mesa*. Students will not learn all forms of *poner* until *Lección 7B*. For the time being, however, they are able to use all present-tense forms of this new verb except for the first-person singular form *pongo*. Page 424 of the Appendices contains a chart with the present-tense forms.

Tell students that *poner* is also used with appliances to mean **to turn on**: *poner la televisión*.

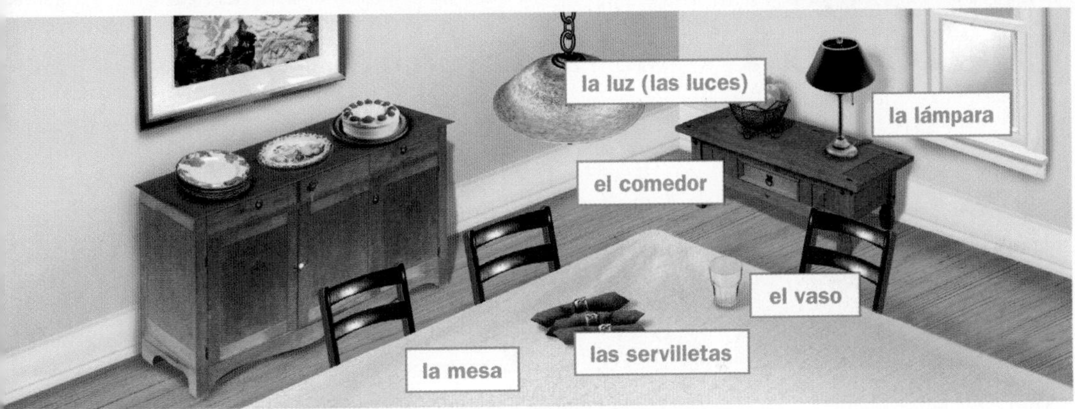

1 ¿Qué tenemos que hacer en la cocina? 

Selecciona la ilustración que corresponde con lo que oyes.

A

B

C

D

E

F

2 ¿Adónde llamo? 

Imagine you live in Caracas, Venezuela, and several appliances in your home are broken. Decide whom you would call to come and have them fixed.

A

ELÉCTRICOS GALAXIA

¡Los mejores técnicos en reparación de electrodomésticos en Caracas!

Todas las marcas: estufas, lavaplatos, fregaderos y triturador de desperdicios, lavadoras, secadoras, aspiradoras, planchas. Garantía total, domicilios, Av. Junín, llámenos hoy: 614-22-64.

B

CENTRALES

Somos especialistas en la reparación de microondas, refrigeradores, lavaplatos, licuadoras, tostadoras, procesadores de comida. Servicio a domicilio. Venta de repuestos. 40 años sirviendo a Caracas. Servicio las 24 horas del día. Línea directa: 215-58-78.

1

2

3

4

5

Teacher Resources

 Activity 1

 Activity 1

 Activity 1

Answers

1
1. E
2. F
3. B
4. A
5. D
6. C

2
1. A
2. B
3. A, B
4. B
5. A

Activities

Prereading Strategy
Have students look at *Vocabulario I* and identify cognates and other words they recognize. Then ask students to summarize what each box on page 226 says.

Pronunciation
Model the pronunciation of several words and phrases from *Vocabulario I* for students to repeat.

Students with Special Needs
Help students with the two advertisements on page 227. Then give a model for activity 2.

Notes Select ancillaries listed under Teacher Resources at the top of pages 226 or 227 for introducing and reinforcing the new content on these pages. For example, you may wish to introduce vocabulary using overhead transparencies 40 and 41 or you may prefer to use the audio. Written activities for practicing the new vocabulary are available in the Workbook and in the Grammar and Vocabulary Exercises Manual. Choose support items that help you accomplish your goals.

National Standards

Communication
1.2

Connections
3.1

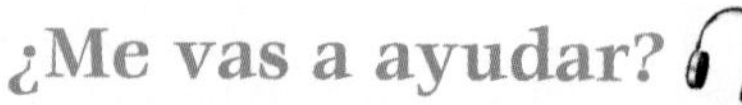

Diálogo I ¿Me vas a ayudar?

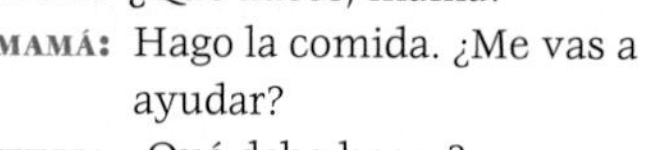

JULIO: ¿Qué haces, mamá?
MAMÁ: Hago la comida. ¿Me vas a ayudar?
JULIO: ¿Qué debo hacer?

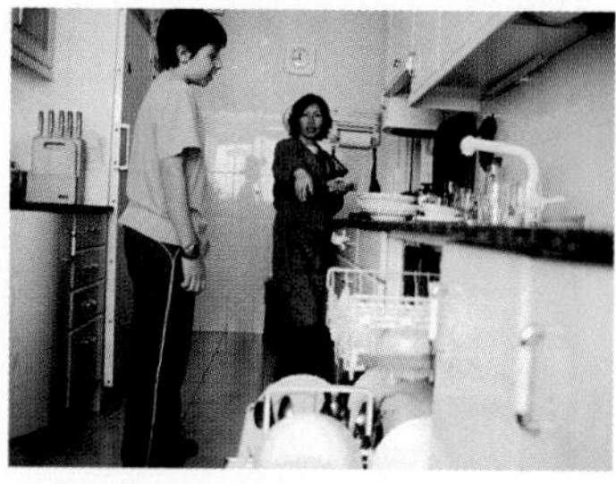

MAMÁ: ¿Por qué no enciendes el lavaplatos?
JULIO: ¿Qué más?
MAMÁ: ¿Por qué no limpias el refrigerador?

JULIO: No, ¡el refrigerador no! Prefiero otra cosa mamá.
MAMÁ: Bueno, ¿por qué no pones la mesa?
JULIO: ¡Sí, cómo no!

3 ¿Qué recuerdas?

1. ¿Qué hace la mamá de Julio?
2. ¿Va a ayudar Julio a su mamá?
3. ¿Qué hace Julio primero?
4. ¿Julio va a limpiar el refrigerador o prefiere hacer otra cosa?

4 Algo personal

1. ¿Ayudas en la cocina en tu casa?
2. ¿Qué cosas haces para ayudar en la cocina?
3. ¿Qué cosas hay en la cocina de tu casa?

5 ¿Qué hacen para ayudar?

Mira las palabras de la lista. Di la que corresponde con lo que oyes.

el refrigerador	la lámpara	la estufa
el vaso	la mesa	el fregadero

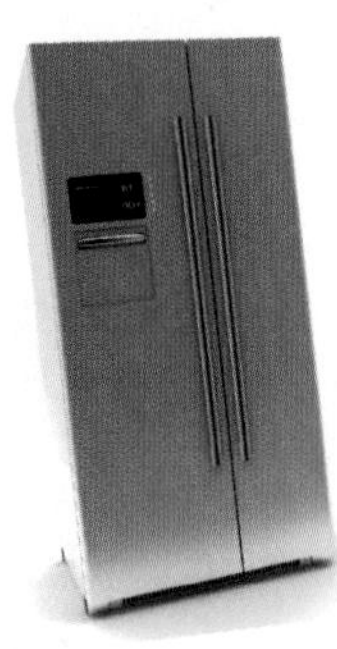

Teacher Resources

Diálogo I
¿Me vas a ayudar?
Activity 3
Activity 4
Activity 5

Answers

3 1. Hace la comida.
2. Sí, la va a ayudar.
3. Enciende el lavaplatos.
4. Prefiere hacer otra cosa.

4 Answers will vary.

5 1. la lámpara; 2. el refrigerador; 3. la estufa; 4. el fregadero; 5. la mesa; 6. el vaso

Activities

Cooperative Learning

After completing the presentation of the dialog (playing the audio, modeling words and phrases for student repetition, covering the activity items), have students work in pairs practicing the dialog. Circulate and assist with pronunciation and intonation.

Expansion

Additional questions (*Algo personal*): *¿Te gusta estar en la cocina? ¿Por qué?; ¿En qué piensas cuando estás en la cocina?; ¿Te gusta poner la mesa?*

Students with Special Needs

In order to better remember the spelling change *z* → *c*, it may help some students to rhyme the spelling rule. Say, for example, "change the *z* to *c* in front of an *e*."

National Standards

Communication
1.1, 1.2

Notes

Remind students that words ending in *-z* require a spelling change when they become plural: *la luz* → *los luces; el lápiz* → *los lápices.*

Play the audio version of activity 5 for listening comprehension practice. As an alternative, remember you can read the activity using the transcript that appears in the ATE Introduction. A reproducible student answer sheet for the activity can be found at the end of the Audio Program Manual.

Ask students to review the vocabulary from the previous page and then scan the dialog for familiar words or phrases.

Cultura viva

Go online EMCLanguages.net

Explorando Venezuela

When European explorers came to the shores of Lake Maracaibo, they named the area Venezuela (meaning "Little Venice") because the homes that were located along the shores of the lake reminded them of Venice, Italy. Venezuela is a land of varied geography, with wonderful beaches *(Playa Medina, Playa Colorada)*, mountains *(Andes)*, plains and deserts *(Médanos de Coro)*. One of the most sensational natural attractions found in the country is Angel Falls *(el Salto del Ángel)*, the highest waterfall in the world. Venezuela also has big industrialized cities, such as Caracas, the capital and economic and political center of the nation. Other large cities include Maracaibo, known for its petroleum production, Mérida, a cultural and intellectual center, and Puerto Cruz, a very popular destination for tourists from all over the world.

El Salto del Ángel.

At one time Venezuela had one of the highest standards of living in South America due to its many natural resources, especially the vast abundance of oil *(el petróleo)* found near Lake Maracaibo. The country is one of the world's principal producers of oil and an important member of OPEC (in Spanish, *OPEP*, or *Organización de Países Exportadores de Petróleo*). Venezuela is also known for its pearl industry. In addition to exporting big quantities of oil and pearls *(las perlas)*, the country is one of the world's largest exporters of cocoa beans *(el cacao)*, the basic ingredient for chocolate.

When Venezuelans gather, they enjoy talking, laughing and sharing good food, such as *arepas*, *ropa vieja* and *cachapas*. Investigate this fascinating South American country. You may be surprised by what you find!

Venezuela exporta petróleo, perlas y cacao.

6 Explorando Venezuela

Completa las siguientes oraciones Venezuela.

1. *Venezuela* quiere decir...
2. Dos playas famosas en Venezuela son...
3. Una de las atracciones más importantes de Venezuela es...
4. La capital de Venezuela es...
5. Tres productos de exportación de Venezuela son...
6. Tres comidas famosas de Venezuela son ropa vieja, cachapas y...

Teacher Resources

 **Activity 3**

 **p. 82**

 **Activity 2**

Answers

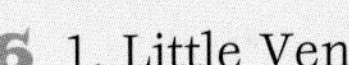

6 1. Little Venice.
2. Playa Medina y Playa Colorada.
3. el Salto del Ángel.
4. Caracas.
5. petróleo, perlas y cacao.
6. arepas.

Activities

Expansion

Ask students to use the Internet and/or library to learn more about a topic they find interesting in the *Cultura viva.* They should then list in Spanish three or four interesting facts they found and share the information with the class.

Technology

Have students search the Internet for Web pages advertising trips to Venezuela. Are any of the sites written in Spanish? Students should print information from a Spanish-language site, skim it for phrases that they recognize and then share it with the class.

National Standards

Communication
1.3

Cultures
2.2

Connections
3.1, 3.2

Notes

Ropa vieja, literally **old clothes**, is a hearty stew-like dish of shredded meat and vegetables that is served over rice or in a warm flour tortilla. *Cachapas* are similar to corn cakes. They can be eaten with cheese, whipped cream or butter.

The acronym OPEC stands for the Organization of Petroleum Exporting Countries.

New words that students may not recognize include the following: *exportadores* (exporters); *petróleo* (oil).

Teacher Resources

 Activity 8

 Activity 4

 Activities 2–3

 p. 153

 Activity 3

 Activity 2

Answers

7 Possible answers:
1. Debo
2. Tengo que
3. Debo
4. debo
5. Tengo que
6. Tengo que

8
1. Ellos deben ayudar a su madre
2. Mi hermana debe llamar....
3. Tengo que poner....
4. Debes cerrar siempre....

Activities

Cooperative Learning

Have students write three sentences stating they have to do something when they should be doing something else. Then have students work in small groups correcting one another's sentences and making appropriate changes. Inform students that groups have five minutes to make any necessary corrections, after which time you will select students from each group to read aloud their sentences.

National Standards
Communication 1.1

Idioma

Estructura

Expressing obligations with *tener que* and *deber*

Use the expressions ***tener que*** **(+ infinitive)** and ***deber*** **(+ infinitive)** when you wish to express what someone is obligated to do. Whereas *tener que* (+ infinitive) indicates what someone **has to do**, *deber* (+ infinitive) implies more of a moral obligation or what someone **should do**.

Tengo que *poner la mesa.*	**I have to** set the table.
Debo *ayudar a mi madre.*	**I should (ought to)** help my mother.

Práctica

7 ¿Debo o tengo que?

Complete the following sentences with the correct form of *deber* or *tener que* as appropriate.

1. Mi padre tiene mucho que hacer en la cocina. __ ayudarlo.
2. __ comer todos los días para vivir.
3. Los refrescos están calientes y me gustan fríos. __ ponerlos en el refrigerador.
4. Para comer la comida caliente rápidamente __ usar el horno microondas y no la estufa.
5. Mañana hay un examen de historia. __ estudiar mucho hoy.
6. El fin de semana viajo a Colombia. __ tener un pasaporte.

8 ¿Deben hacerlo o tienen que hacerlo?

Create sentences using the following cues and adding the appropriate form of either *deber* or *tener que*, according to what fits logically.

MODELO lavar los platos mañana (Pedro)
Pedro tiene que lavar los platos mañana.

estudiar primero y hacer deportes después (los estudiantes)
Los estudiantes deben estudiar primero y hacer deportes después.

1. ayudar a su madre (ellos)
2. llamar a nuestra abuela (mi hermana)
3. poner los platos sucios en el lavaplatos (yo)
4. cerrar siempre la puerta del refrigerador (tú)

Los estudiantes deben estudiar.

Notes

Point out that *deber* is a regular *-er* verb.

Students have already learned the various forms of *tener* in *Capítulo 5*. Do a quick review of the forms of tener at this time. Explain that the verbs *tener* and *venir* have this same stem change *e* → *ie*, except for the yo irregular forms of these two verbs (*tener: tengo; venir: vengo*).

Remind students that when two verbs appear together (e.g., *tener que* + verb), the first is conjugated and the second must remain an infinitive.

Comunicación

9 Nuestras obligaciones

First, create a list of at least two things you must do and two things you should do this week. Then, in small groups, talk about your schedules and obligations.

MODELO **A:** El jueves tengo que ir de compras.
B: Por las tardes yo debo estudiar.

Go online EMCLanguages.net

Estructura

Stem-changing verbs: *e* → *ie*

The verb *pensar* (to think) requires the spelling change *e* → *ie* in all forms of the present-tense stem except for *nosotros* and *vosotros*. Note, however, that this stem change does not affect the regular verb endings *(o, as, a, amos, áis, an)*.

pensar (ie)	
p**ie**nso	pensamos
p**ie**nsas	pensáis
p**ie**nsa	p**ie**nsan

When combined with other words, *pensar* has several different uses:

- When followed immediately by an infinitive, *pensar* indicates what someone plans or intends to do.

Pienso ir *a Venezuela.*	I plan to go to Venezuela.
¿Cuándo ***piensas ir?***	When do you intend to go?

- When combined with *de*, *pensar* is used to ask for an opinion. Use *pensar* followed by *que* to express your opinion or thoughts.

¿Qué ***piensas de*** *los platos nuevos?*	What do you think of the new plates?
Pienso que *son bonitos.*	I think they are pretty.

- *Pensar* may be combined with *en* to indicate whom or what someone is thinking about.

¿En *qué* ***piensas?***	What are you thinking about?
Pienso en *mi tarea de español.*	I am thinking about my spanish homework.

Pensar (ie) is just one of many *e* → *ie* stem-changing verbs. (The letters in parentheses after the infinitive are to help you identify these verbs and to indicate the change that occurs in the stem.) Others include the following: *cerrar (ie), empezar (ie), encender (ie), preferir (ie), querer (ie)* and *sentir (ie).*

Note: The verb *empezar* is used with *a* when an infinitive follows, as in *Empiezo a estudiar* (I am beginning to study).

Teacher Resources

 Activities 5–8

 Activities 4–9

 Activity 4

Activity 3

Answers

9 Creative self-expression.

Activities

Expansion
After completing activity 9, have a member of each group summarize the information for the class as a way of practicing the plural forms. *Dos personas en nuestro grupo tienen que hacer....; Todos nosotros debemos estudiar*, etc.

Students with Special Needs
Review the conjugation of *-ar* verbs before introducing the stem change *e* → *ie.*

Notes Explain to students that the letters *ie* shown in parentheses after infinitives listed in *¡Aventura!* serve as a help for students to remember how these verbs are formed: *cerrar (ie).*

Note for students that the verbs *tener* and *venir* have this same stem change *e* → *ie* except for the *yo* irregular forms.

Comparisons. Note the distinction between *pensar* (to think) and *creer* (to believe). Tell students that the equivalent in Spanish for **I think so** is *Creo que sí* (I believe so). Likewise, to say **I don't think so**, they should use *Creo que no* (I don't believe so).

National Standards

Communication
1.1, 1.3

Comparisons
4.1

 Activity 12

 p. 23

Answers

10 Answers will vary.

11 1. piensan; 2. piensa; 3. quiere; 4. empiezan; 5. piensan; 6. viene; 7. piensan; 8. siente; 9. viene; 10. debe; 11. prefiere; 12. quiere; 13. piensas; 14. Vienes

12
1. ...queremos...quieren
2. ...pensamos...piensan....
3. ...encendemos... encienden....
4. ...tenemos que...tienen que....
5. ...queremos...quieren....
6. ...cerramos...abren....
7. ... preferimos... prefieren...
8. ...empezamos... empiezan....

Activities

Multiple Intelligences (spatial)
Make memory models to assist in learning the concept of the stem-changing verb. (For example, draw a line around the forms that change, and you can see the shape of a boot; then call it a **boot verb**.)

Students with Special Needs
Have students write out the conjugation of several *e* → *ie* verbs.

National Standards

Communication
1.2

Práctica

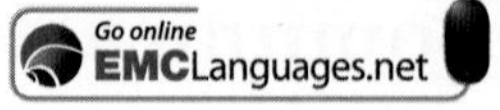

10 ¿Qué piensan hacer?

Tell what these people are planning to do, using words from each column and the appropriate form of *pensar*. Verb forms may be repeated.

A	B	C
Juan y Raúl	pienso	hacer un almuerzo especial
unos amigos y yo	piensas	hacer arepas
yo	piensa	comer en el comedor
una amiga	pensamos	buscar los platos de todos los días
Ana y Eva	piensan	poner la mesa
tú		ayudar en la cocina

11 Un almuerzo especial

Completa el siguiente párrafo con la forma correcta de los verbos indicados entre paréntesis.

Paco y Aurora 1. *(pensar)* hacer un almuerzo especial para su amiga María. Ella va a estudiar a Colombia por un año. Aurora 2. *(pensar)* hacer unas arepas y Paco 3. *(querer)* hacer un pollo con mole y una ensalada. Ellos 4. *(empezar)* a hacer la comida muy temprano. Otros amigos 5. *(pensar)* venir al almuerzo. Rafael 6. *(venir)* y Carmen y José 7. *(pensar)* venir también. Graciela lo 8. *(sentir)* mucho, pero no 9. *(venir)* al almuerzo porque tiene que estudiar. Pedro 10. *(deber)* ayudar a sus padres en la casa y 11. *(preferir)* venir después del almuerzo. Él 12. *(querer)* decirle "adiós" a María. Y tú, ¿qué 13. *(pensar)*? ¿14. *(venir)* al almuerzo?

12 ¡Somos diferentes!

Use the cues that follow to create sentences that compare and contrast how different Sara and Julio are from their parents.

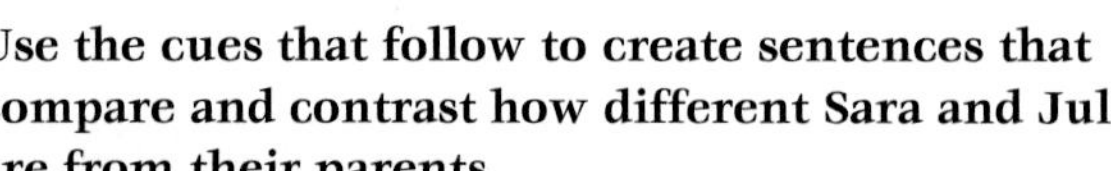

MODELO empezar a escuchar música / empezar a leer
Si nosotros empezamos a escuchar música, ellos empiezan a leer.

1. querer nadar en la playa / querer caminar en la playa
2. pensar ir al parque / pensar ir a un museo
3. encender el reproductor de CDs / encender el televisor
4. tener que hacer la tarea / tener que lavar los platos
5. querer comer en un restaurante / querer hacer arepas y comer en casa otra vez
6. cerrar la puerta / abrir las ventanas
7. preferir ir al cine / preferir ver un DVD en casa
8. empezar a mirar la televisión / empezar a escuchar la radio

¿Prefieres nadar o caminar en la playa? (Los Roques, Venezuela.)

Notes

Although students have already seen the expression *lo siento*, in this chapter they are learning how to conjugate the entire present-tense conjugation of *sentir* and other stem-changing verbs.

Remind students that when a verb like *pensar* is followed by another verb, the second verb must be an infinitive.

13 Una fiesta

In pairs, take turns asking and answering questions about what your family and friends are thinking about, according to the illustrations, as you all prepare for a holiday dinner.

MODELO tu madre
A: ¿En qué piensa tu madre?
B: Mi madre piensa en la comida.

1. yo

2. Gloria

3. tus hermanos

4. Andrés y Camila

5. nosotros

6. tú

Comunicación

14 Pensamos hacer mucho

In small groups, talk about some things you are planning to do next summer or at some time during your life. Be creative. You might also discuss what you think of each person's aspirations. Then decide what your remarks have in common. One student should report the results of your discussion to the class.

MODELO
A: Pienso viajar a otro país. Quiero ir a Venezuela el verano que viene.
B: En el verano yo pienso ayudar a mis padres en casa y leer cien libros.
C: Pienso cantar con JLo en un concierto.

¡Oportunidades!

¿Piensas viajar a otro país?
Do you enjoy travel? Have you ever wondered what it might be like to live in another country? What if you were transferred to Venezuela to work? Do you think you would enjoy the experience? Do any members of your family live in another country? Would you like to visit them if they did? Can you think of any benefits your language skills might afford you while traveling?

Answers

13 1. ¿En qué pienso?/Piensas en los platos sucios.
2. ¿En qué piensa...?/Piensa en los amigos que vienen a la fiesta.
3. ¿En qué piensan...?/ Piensan en la música.
4. ¿En qué piensan...?/ Piensan en los vasos.
5. ¿En qué pensamos...?/ Pensamos (Piensan) en la mesa y las sillas.
6. ¿En qué piensas?/Pienso en....

14 Creative self-expression.

Activities

Expansion
Ask students the following personalized questions to further practice the verbs: *¿A qué hora empiezan las clases?; ¿A qué hora empieza la clase de español?; ¿Cuántas clases tienes en un día típico?; ¿Prefieres las clases de ciencia o las clases de humanidades?; ¿Qué quieres estudiar en el futuro?; ¿Piensas estudiar más español?; ¿Dónde quieres estudiar o trabajar en el futuro?; ¿Dónde quieres vivir?; ¿Prefieres las ciudades grandes o los pueblos pequeños?*

Multiple Intelligences (linguistic)
If students are maintaining a writer's journal, have them use the theme **travel** as a journal entry: *Pienso que me gustaría viajar a Venezuela.*

National Standards

Communication
1.1, 1.3

Communities
5.1

Notes

Spot-check student conversations for activities 13 and 14 for the appropriate forms of *pensar* and *querer*.

Note for students that the verb *querer* may mean **to want** or **to love**. Context will help make an intended message clear. Also, remind students to use the *a personal* when using *querer* to refer to people: *Quiero **a** mis abuelos.*

Have students make a list of verbs with the stem change *e* → *ie*.

Teacher Resources

 **Vocabulario II** ***En la mesa***

 **Activities 42–43**

 **Activities 9–11**

 **Activities 10–12**

 **p. 24**

 **Activity 5**

 **Activity 4**

Activities

Expansion
Use overhead transparencies 42 and 43 to introduce the new words and expressions in *Vocabulario II.* First, using transparency 42, point to the objects on the table and identify them in Spanish one at a time. Ask students to repeat after you. Then, using transparency 43, identify each vocabulary item in Spanish, allowing students to see how each object is spelled. As an alternative, use an actual table setting to introduce the new dinner-table vocabulary (*el plato, la taza, el tenedor,* etc.).

National Standards
Connections 3.1

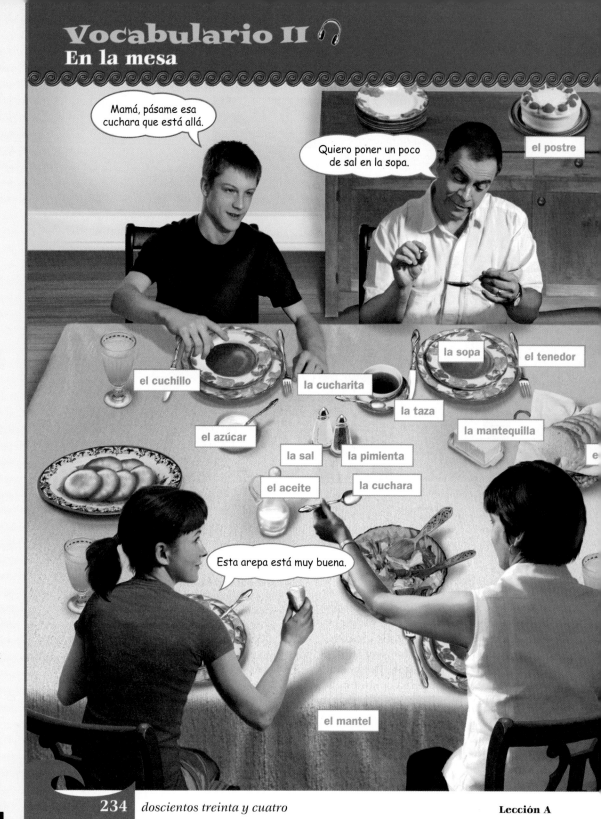

Vocabulario II
En la mesa

Mamá, pásame esa cuchara que está allá.

Quiero poner un poco de sal en la sopa.

el postre

la sopa

el tenedor

el cuchillo

la cucharita

la taza

el azúcar

la mantequilla

la sal

la pimienta

el aceite

la cuchara

Esta arepa está muy buena.

el mantel

Notes Introduce the new vocabulary and reinforce the content of pages 234 and 235 by using overhead transparencies 42 and 43, the audio recording of *En la mesa* and other ancillaries listed under Teacher Resources at the top of these two pages. You can evaluate student progress using Quiz 4.

¿Qué necesitas?

Di lo que necesitas para hacer lo que oyes. ***(Say what you need in order to do what you hear.)***

MODELO Necesito una cuchara.

16 A la hora de comer

Completa las siguientes oraciones, según las ilustraciones.

MODELO Pásame un tenedor, por favor.

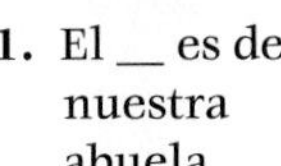

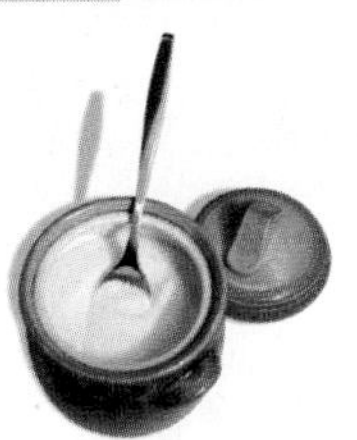

1. El __ es de nuestra abuela.
2. Pásame la __, por favor.
3. Necesito la __.
4. Pásame el __, por favor.
5. Me gusta la __ bien caliente.

6. Quiero más __ para la ensalada.
7. Necesitan unas __ para el postre.
8. Son las __ de los días especiales.
9. Quiero un __ de agua fría.
10. Los __ son muy bonitos.

¿Qué vemos en el comedor?

Working in pairs, take turns asking what your partner needs while you point to an item shown in the illustration *En la mesa*. Your partner then must ask you to pass the item to him or her.

MODELO **A:** ¿Qué necesitas? ¿Qué quieres?
B: Pásame el pan, por favor.

¿Qué buscamos?

Create a drawing similar to the one in the illustration *En la mesa*, but with three items missing. Then, in pairs, take turns asking each other questions about which objects are missing (or not) from your illustration. List in Spanish the objects missing from your partner's illustration. Check to see if you guessed which objects were missing.

Teacher Resources

Activity 15

Answers

15 Possible answers:
1. Necesito un cuchillo.
2. Necesito un vaso.
3. Necesito una cucharita/ un tenedor.
4. Necesito una taza.
5. Necesito un tenedor.
6. Necesito un vaso.

16
1. mantel
2. mantequilla
3. sal
4. azúcar
5. sopa
6. aceite
7. cucharitas
8. tazas
9. vaso
10. cubiertos

17 Check for correct pronunciation.

18 Check for correct pronunciation and spelling.

Activities

TPR

Choose a theme, such as things in a kitchen or popular activities. Then inform students that they are to raise their right hand (*la mano derecha*) if the named item is usually found in the kitchen, for example. They must raise their left hand (*la mano izquierda*) if the item is normally not found in the kitchen. Then say several words in Spanish to teach and test student comprehension of vocabulary: *la sal* (right hand), *la computadora* (left hand), etc.

National Standards

Communication
1.1, 1.2

Connections
3.1

Notes

Point out that *azúcar* is feminine although it requires the masculine definite article for pronunciation reasons similar to the word *agua*, which students have already learned.

For additional listening comprehension practice, play the recorded version of the activity that is available in the Audio Program or read the activity using the transcript that appears in the ATE Introduction. A reproducible student answer sheet for the activity can be found at the end of the Audio Program Manual if you choose to use it.

Teacher Resources

Diálogo II
¿Te gusta la sopa?
Activity 19
Activity 20
Activity 21

Answers

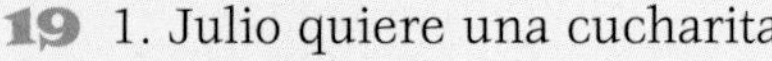

19 1. Julio quiere una cucharita.
2. Sí, le gusta.
3. La sopa necesita un poco más de sal.
4. No tiene una cuchara.
5. Le gusta la arepa.

20 Answers will vary.

21 1. C; 2. G; 3. A; 4. E; 5. D; 6. F; 7. B; 8. H

Activities

Expansion

Additional questions (*¿Qué recuerdas?*): *¿Dónde están Julio, Sara y sus padres?; ¿Quién es Sara?*

Additional questions (*Algo personal*): *¿Come tu familia mucho en el comedor?; Si no comen en el comedor, ¿dónde comen Uds.?*

Prereading Strategy

Ask students to list things typically found in a kitchen and at the dinner table. Then instruct them to cover up the dialog with one hand and look at the photographs. Ask them to imagine where the conversation takes place and what the people are saying to one another. Finally, have students look through the dialog quickly to find cognates.

National Standards
Communication 1.1, 1.2
Comparisons 4.1

Diálogo II ¿Te gusta la sopa?

JULIO: Mamá, pásame esa cucharita, por favor.
MAMÁ: ¿Cuál? ¿Esta cucharita?
JULIO: Sí, esa cucharita, mamá.

PAPÁ: Sara, ¿cómo está la sopa?
SARA: Me gusta, pero necesita un poco más de sal.
JULIO: Mira, aquí está la sal.

MAMÁ: ¿Y tú, amor? ¿Te gusta la sopa?
PAPÁ: No sé. No tengo cuchara.
MAMÁ: Lo siento. Aquí está.
PAPÁ: Esta arepa está buena.

19 ¿Qué recuerdas?

1. ¿Qué quiere Julio?
2. ¿Le gusta a Sara la sopa?
3. ¿Qué necesita un poco más de sal?
4. ¿Qué no tiene el papá?
5. ¿Qué le gusta al papá?

Esta casa tiene un comedor elegante.

20 Algo personal

1. ¿Tiene comedor tu casa?
2. ¿Cómo es la mesa del comedor de tu casa?
3. ¿Qué sopa te gusta? Explica.

21 Yo necesito...

Selecciona la letra de la frase que completa lógicamente cada oración que oyes. ***(Select the letter of the phrase that logically completes each sentence you hear.)***

A. de agua mineral
B. sal
C. tenedor
D. el lavaplatos
E. arepas
F. sobre el pan caliente
G. una cuchara y un plato
H. mantel

¿Te gustan estos platos?

Notes Point out to students the lack of articles in Spanish when using negative phrases: *No tengo cuchara.; No quiero postre.; Nunca como pan.*

Provide some of the following expressions as students discuss quantities at the table: *más* (more), *menos* (less), *mucho* (a lot), *poco* (a little), *un poco de sal* (a little salt), *un poquito* (very little), *un poco más/menos* (a little more/less).

Whereas *uno, mucho* and *poco* have masculine, feminine, singular and plural forms, *más, menos, un poco (de)* and *(ni) un poquito* require no additional changes in their forms.

Ask students to review the vocabulary from the previous page and then scan the dialog for familiar words or phrases.

Cultura viva II

Go online EMCLanguages.net

Las arepas venezolanas

Arepas are perhaps the most common food in Venezuela. Originally they were made from corn that was ground to make corn meal. As with many everyday foods in the United States, however, today *arepas* are usually prepared using packaged, precooked white corn flour, salt and water. The resulting easy-to-make buns can be eaten alone or as a kind of bread to accompany a meal. *Arepas* can also be stuffed with meat, cheese, scrambled eggs or other fillings, much like *tortillas* or *empanadas*. Another very popular Venezuelan dish is *hallaca*, which is served in nearly every Venezuelan home at Christmas. This typical food consists of a corn-flour pie filled with pork, chicken, vegetables and spices. It is cooked in plantain leaves from a variety of bananas called *plátano*.

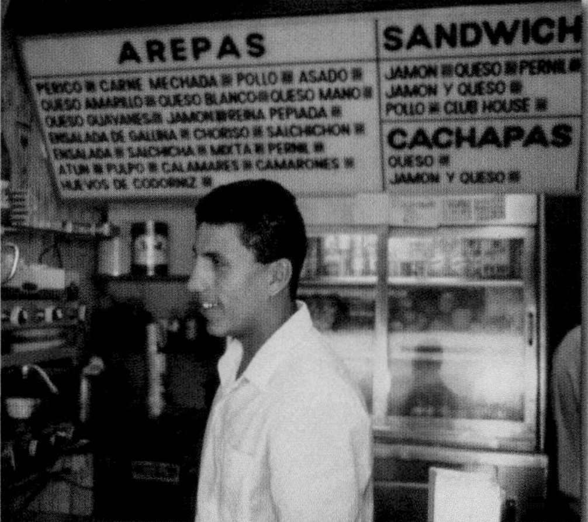

Las arepas son populares en Venezuela.

De la cocina de ______

Las arepas
2 tazas de harina de maíz
2 cucharitas de sal
2 tazas de agua caliente

Preparación

Para empezar, poner la harina de maíz[1] en una taza grande y poco a poco poner el agua con sal. Luego, mezclar[2] el agua con la harina hasta que se convierta en masa. Después, dejar[3] la masa en reposo[4] por cinco minutos. Hacer con la masa unos rollos[5] de tres pulgadas[6] de diámetro y de una pulgada a dos pulgadas de ancho[7]. En una sartén[8] con un poco de aceite, freír[9] las arepas hasta ver los rollos dorados[10]. Después, poner las arepas en el horno a 350 grados para cocinar por aproximadamente treinta minutos, hasta tener arepas crujientes[11].

Preparando arepas.

[1]corn flour [2]mix [3]leave [4]rest [5]rolls [6]inches [7]thick [8]frying pan [9]fry [10]golden [11]crunchy

22 Conexión con otras disciplinas: habilidades para la vida diaria

You can easily prepare the recipe at home for a taste of this typical Venezuelan bread. Look at the recipe for *arepas* and answer these questions.

1. ¿Cuáles son los ingredientes para hacer arepas?
2. ¿Qué debes hacer para empezar?
3. ¿Qué diámetro deben tener los rollos?
4. Después de hacer rollos con la masa, ¿qué debes hacer?
5. ¿A qué temperatura tiene que estar el horno?
6. ¿Cuánto tiempo deben estar las arepas en el horno?

Teacher Resources

Cultural viva
Las arepas venezolanas
Activity 22

pp. 89, 92

Activity 5

Answers

22
1. Los ingredientes son sal, harina de maíz y agua.
2. Para empezar, debo poner la harina de maíz en una taza grande y poco a poco poner el agua con sal.
3. Los rollos deben tener tres pulgadas de diámetro.
4. Debo poner un poco de aceite en una sartén para cocinar las arepas hasta ver los rollos dorados.
5. El horno tiene que estar a 350 grados.
6. Deben estar en el horno aproximadamente treinta minutos.

Activities

Multiple Intelligences (bodily-kinesthetic)
Have students prepare *arepas* using the recipe found in *Cultura viva.* Then they may share the *arepas* with the rest of the class.

Spanish for Spanish Speakers
Ask students to explain to the class (in Spanish) how to prepare their favorite dish. Make sure they give a detailed explanation.

National Standards	
Communication 1.3	**Comparisons** 4.2
Cultures 2.2	
Connections 3.1, 3.2	

Notes

The special flour made from ground corn is not cornmeal and is not available everywhere. Suggest students look for ground corn in a specialty foods store or a store that specializes in Hispanic foods.

Tell students the meaning of *habilidades para la vida diaria* (life skills).

Before students attempt to make *arepas* at home, point out that the shapes should not look like pancakes. The *arepas* should look more like small hamburger buns.

Activity 22 is a cross-curricular activity that addresses Spanish as well as cooking.

Teacher Resources

 Activities 12–15

 Activity 13

 Activity 6

 Activity 6

 Activities

Critical Thinking

You can practice both demonstrative and possessive adjectives by providing several models and then cuing students with words to which they may respond: *Este libro es mi libro. Ese libro es tu libro. Aquel libro es su libro* (pointing to another student). Cue students with a variety of nouns that are masculine, feminine, singular and plural.

Estructura

Pointing out someone or something: demonstrative adjectives

Use a demonstrative adjective *(adjetivo demostrativo)* before a noun to point out or draw attention to where someone or something is located in relation to yourself ("this house," "that car," etc.).

Los adjetivos demostrativos			
singular		plural	
masculino	**femenino**	**masculino**	**femenino**
este vaso *(this glass)*	esta taza *(this cup)*	estos vasos *(these glasses)*	estas tazas *(these cups)*
ese vaso *(that glass)*	esa taza *(that cup)*	esos vasos *(those glasses)*	esas tazas *(those cups)*
aquel vaso *(that glass over there)*	aquella taza *(that cup over there)*	aquellos vasos *(those glasses over there)*	aquellas tazas *(those cups over there)*

When pointing out people or objects that are nearby, use *este, esta, estos* or *estas* (this/these). Use *ese, esa, esos* or *esas* (that/those) to draw attention to people or objects that are farther away. Call attention to people or objects that are even farther away ("over there") by using *aquel, aquella, aquellos* or *aquellas* (that/those over there).

near speaker *(aquí)*	*Me gusta **este** refrigerador.*	I like **this** refrigerator.
away from speaker *(allí)*	*¿Te gustan **esos** refrigeradores?*	Do you like **those** refrigerators?
far away from speaker *(allá)*	*Prefiero **aquel** refrigerador.*	I prefer **that** refrigerator **(over there)**.

National Standards

Communication
1.1

Notes

Emphasize that *este, esta, estas* and *estos* in English mean **this/these**. *Ese, esa, esos* and *esas* mean **that/those** and *aquel, aquella, aquellos* and *aquellas* mean **that/those over there**.

The demonstrative pronouns will be taught in the *¡Aventura! 2* textbook.

Tell students that demonstrative adjectives always precede the noun they modify.

Práctica

23 ¡Otra cocina!

Completa las oraciones con la forma apropiada de *este*.

Quiero otra cocina para mi casa porque (1) cocina es muy fea. (2) paredes tienen un color muy triste. La puerta de (3) horno microondas no cierra. (4) fregadero es muy pequeño, necesito un fregadero doble. (5) refrigerador está muy viejo y (6) lavaplatos es muy malo. (7) luces no encienden y (8) lámpara es muy fea. No me gusta (9) mesa y (10) sillas son horribles.

24 ¿Qué vamos a poner en la mesa?

With a classmate, pretend you are discussing whether or not you need the following items as you are preparing the table for dinner. Answer each question negatively as shown in the model.

MODELO las servilletas verdes
A: ¿Quieres estas servilletas verdes?
B: No, no quiero esas servilletas verdes.

1. los cubiertos
2. el mantel
3. la mantequilla
4. el aceite
5. los platos de sopa
6. las tazas
7. el cuchillo
8. los vasos nuevos
9. la silla

25 ¿Qué prefieres?

Imagine you are in a department store buying kitchenware for your new house. Use the appropriate form of *este*, *ese* or *aquel* to say what items you prefer, based upon the cues shown in the illustration.

MODELO ¿Qué platos prefieres?
Prefiero esos platos.

1. ¿Qué mantel prefieres?

2. ¿Qué cubiertos prefieres?

3. ¿Qué servilletas prefieres?

4. ¿Qué lámpara prefieres?

5. ¿Qué taza prefieres?

6. ¿Qué vasos prefieres?

Notes Point out that the distinction among the demonstratives that many Spanish speakers make is to use forms of *este* for items near the speaker, forms of *ese* for items near the person spoken to and forms of *aquel* for items that are far from both.

Teacher Resources

Activity 24

Answers

23 1. esta; 2. Estas; 3. este; 4. Este; 5. Este; 6. este; 7. Estas; 8. esta; 9. esta; 10. estas

24
1. ¿Quieres estos cubiertos?/No, no quiero esos cubiertos.
2. ¿Quieres este mantel?/No, no quiero ese mantel.
3. ¿Quieres esta mantequilla?/ No, no quiero esa mantequilla.
4. ¿Quieres este aceite?/No, no quiero ese aceite.
5. ¿Quieres estos platos de sopa?/No, no quiero esos platos de sopa.
6. ¿Quieres estas tazas?/No, no quiero esas tazas.
7. ¿Quieres este cuchillo?/ No, no quiero ese cuchillo.
8. ¿Quieres estos vasos nuevos?/No, no quiero esos vasos nuevos.
9. ¿Quieres esta silla?/No, no quiero esa silla.

25
1. Prefiero este mantel.
2. Prefiero aquellos cubiertos.
3. Prefiero esas servilletas.
4. Prefiero aquella lámpara.
5. Prefiero esta taza.
6. Prefiero esos vasos.

Activities

Language through Action
Assemble several common kitchen items. Have students work in small groups to act out activity 24.

National Standards
Communication 1.1
Connections 3.1

Answers

26 Creative self-expression.
27 Creative self-expression.

Activities

Multiple Intelligences (spatial)
Locate and bring to class a map of your state. Then ask students to imagine that they are in an airplane flying over the state as they look at the map. Working in pairs, have students identify geographical sites (rivers, cities, etc.) they might see from the air and, then, say where they intend to go (*pensar ir*) at some point in their future.

Comunicación

26 Para la nueva casa de mi familia

Imagine you are with a friend in the store shown in the illustration. With a classmate, discuss which items you are thinking about buying. Express your preferences, ask each other's opinion and try to decide which things you want to, have to or ought to buy.

MODELO **A:** ¿Qué piensas de estos cubiertos?
B: Prefiero aquellos cubiertos porque son más bonitos.

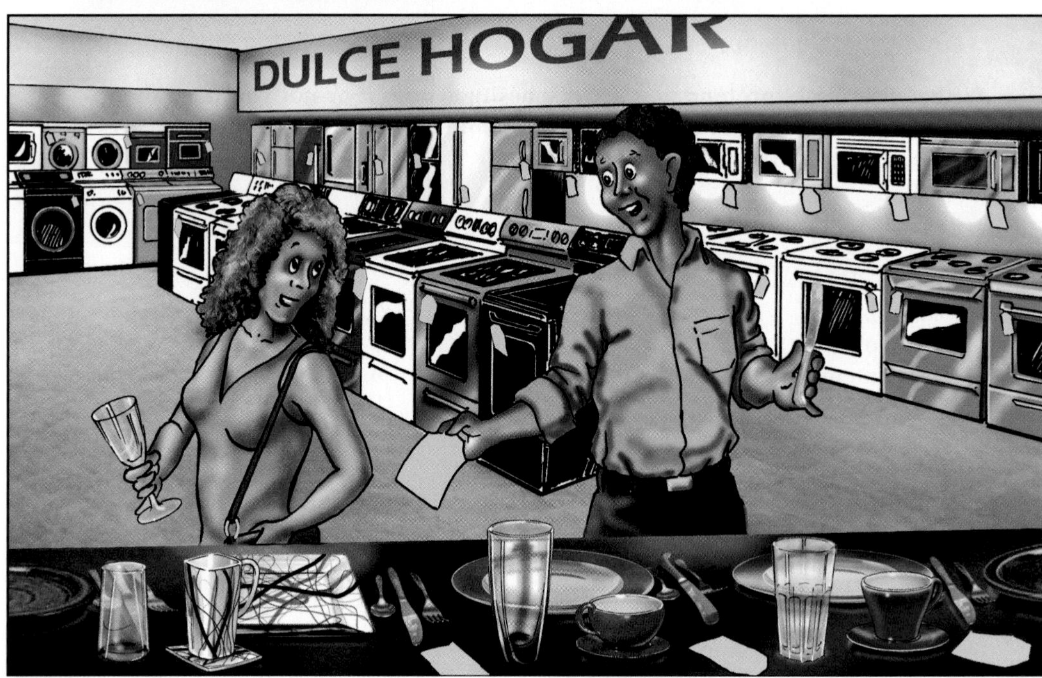

27 En un restaurante en Caracas

During lunch with a friend in Caracas, you discuss your plans for the week. Talk about some things you want to do, ought to do, have to do or prefer to do each day this week. Make the conversation realistic by politely interrupting one another, asking for things to be passed to you and commenting on things and people you see.

MODELO **A:** El lunes tengo que ir con mi mamá a la tienda a mirar unas estufas nuevas.
B: ¿Unas estufas?... ¡Ay, qué aburrido! Por favor, pásame esa cucharita.
A: Sí, cómo no.

National Standards

Communication
1.1

Connections
3.1

Comparisons
4.1

Notes

For simple activities, have students write out the answers before assigning students to work with a partner; for more difficult activities, pair students requiring additional help with stronger students. Follow up some oral activities (e.g., activity 27) by assigning a variation of the exercise as written homework.

Comparisons. You may wish to explain to students that demonstrative adjectives are also used to indicate time in relation to the present moment: ***esta*** *tarde* (**this** afternoon); ***esa*** *tarde* (**that** afternoon); ***aquella*** *tarde* (**that** afternoon **farther off in the past**).

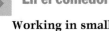

En el comedor

Working in small groups, pretend you are having dinner together in your dining room in Venezuela. Each member of the group should make at least four questions or statements including some of the following: requests for items at the table, questions about what your friends think and need, comments about the food, questions about what your friends are going to do during the week, and so on. Be polite (use *por favor* and *gracias*).

MODELO A: Pásame ese cuchillo y la mantequilla, por favor.
B: Aquí tienes. ¿Qué piensan de las arepas?
C: Están muy buenas, pero la ensalada necesita un poco de aceite.

Más comida

el flan	*caramel custard*
el panecillo	*bread roll*
la papa	*potato*
el pastel (la torta)	*cake*
las verduras	*vegetables*

La comida está muy buena.

El plato con arepas.

El aceite.

Notes Ask for volunteers or select several groups to present their dining-room conversations for the entire class. Consider bringing utensils and table items to class that students can use for role-playing.

If you or your students prepared *arepas* using the recipe in the *Cultura viva* on page 237, this would be a good time to share the recipe with the class.

Answers

28 Creative self-expression.

Activities

Cooperative Learning
Ask small groups of students to prepare a dinner menu featuring items from several Spanish-speaking countries. Possible sources of information include *¡Aventura!*, personal experiences, ethnic cookbooks and foreign exchange students in your school. Each group should share its menu with the class. As a follow-up activity, you may wish to identify a day or event when the students prepare and then bring sample menu items for tasting.

National Standards

Communication
1.1, 1.3

Connections
3.1, 3.2

Teacher Resources

Lectura cultural
Una deliciosa tradición
Activity 30

Answers

29 1. la hallaca.
2. un plato indígena llamado Hayaco Iritari.
3. tamal grande.
4. elaborada.
5. Amigos y parientes

30 Answers will vary.

National Standards

Cultures
2.1, 2.2

Connections
3.1, 3.2

Comparisons
4.1, 4.2

Lectura cultural

Una deliciosa tradición

Es diciembre y, por toda Venezuela, muchas familias hacen las tradicionales hallacas. Es una vieja tradición y es el plato representativo de la Navidad venezolana. El origen de las hallacas viene de un plato de los indígenas llamado[1] Hayaco Iritari. La hallaca es similar a un tamal grande envuelto[2] en una hoja de plátano[3].

La mayoría de las familias hacen una fiesta de la preparación de las hallacas. En las cocinas, se reúnen[4] parientes y amigos para participar en este animado proceso. Mientras que[5] escuchan la gaita — ritmo típico venezolano — todos en la cocina ayudan en la labor, desde lavar[6] las hojas donde se pone la masa[7] hasta amarrar[8] las hallacas.

El proceso es laborioso[9] porque la preparación es elaborada y porque se preparan muchas para almacenar[10] en el refrigerador y comer durante todo el mes de diciembre.

Cuando los venezolanos piensan en la Navidad, piensan en hallacas.

Cuando comes hallaca, tienes que abrir la hoja de plátano. Comes la masa con un tenedor. No debes comer la hoja. Muchas personas prefieren comer las hallacas con pan.

[1]called [2]wrapped [3]plantain/banana leaf [4]get together [5]While [6]from washing [7]dough [8]tie [9]tedious [10]to store

29 ¿Qué recuerdas?

Completa las siguientes oraciones.

1. En Venezuela, el plato típico de la Navidad es...
2. El nombre *hallaca* viene de...
3. La hallaca es como un...
4. La preparación de hallacas es...
5. . . . se reúnen en la cocina para ayudar a hacer hallacas.

30 Algo personal

1. ¿Cuál es un plato representativo de la Navidad en los Estados Unidos? Compara ese plato con las hallacas de Venezuela.
2. ¿Se reúnen tu familia o tus amigos en la cocina? ¿Qué hacen?
3. ¿Preparan en tu casa un plato que tiene un proceso laborioso? ¿Cómo dividen la labor?

- How do Venezuelans make the preparation of *hallacas* fun? Describe something your family or your acquaintances do that is also hard work yet fun.

Notes

Encourage students to find out more about Venezuela by going to the following Web sites:

The Venezuela Online Tour
http://www.ve.net/travel/
Electronic Embassy
http://www.embassy.org
Organization of American States
http://www.oas.org
General travel information
http://www.expedia.com

¿Qué aprendí?

Autoevaluación

As a review and self-check, respond to the following:

1. Name three items you might see on the table while having dinner with a Venezuelan family in Caracas.
2. You are in charge of preparing dinner. Tell the people helping you three things they have to do or should do to help you.
3. What might you say to ask a friend what he or she is thinking about?
4. Ask two friends what they are thinking about doing this Saturday.
5. Say that you like arepas but that you prefer bread with butter.
6. Imagine you are seated at the dining-room table and the glass and silverware you need are far away from you, near your friend. How can you ask your friend politely to pass you that glass and that silverware?
7. Name two typical Venezuelan dishes.

Palabras y expresiones

How many of these words and expressions do you recognize?

En la cocina
el aceite
el azúcar
la cocina
los cubiertos
la cuchara
la cucharita
el cuchillo
la estufa
el fregadero
el horno microondas
el lavaplatos
la luz
el mantel
la mantequilla
la mesa
el pan
la pimienta
el plato
el postre
el refrigerador
la sal
la servilleta
la sopa
la taza
el tenedor
el vaso

Otras expresiones
allá
aquel, aquella (aquellos, aquellas)
el comedor
la cosa
de todos los días
después
entonces
ese, esa (esos, esas)
especial
este, esta (estos, estas)
la lámpara
otra vez
pensar de/en/que
un poco de
poner la mesa
ya

Verbos
ayudar
cerrar (ie)
deber
empezar (ie)
encender (ie)
pásame
pensar (ie)
poner
preferir (ie)
querer (ie)
sentir (ie)
tener que
viajar

Estructura

Do you remember the following grammar rules?

Expressing obligations: *tener que* and *deber*

tener que **+ infinitive**	
Tengo que estudiar para el examen.	***I have to*** *study for the test.*
deber **+ infinitive**	
Debo que ayudar a mi hermano.	***I should*** *help my brother.*

Stem-changing verbs: e → ie

When conjugating stem changing verbs the endings change as well as the stem

pensar (ie)	
pienso	pensamos
piensas	pensáis
piensa	piensan

Demonstrative adjectives

Demonstrative adjectives are used before a noun to point out where someone or something is located.

		this/these	that/those	that/those (over there)
masculine	singular	este	ese	aquel
masculine	plural	estos	eses	aquellos
feminine	singular	esta	esa	aquella
feminine	plural	estas	esas	aquellas

Notes Talk with the class about Venezuela's national hero, Simón Bolívar (1783–1830). This diplomat and military leader was born in Caracas. He was a PanAmerican and helped liberate Bolivia, Ecuador, Colombia, Perú and Venezuela from Spain. Bolivia was named after him.

The monetary unit of Venezuela, *el bolívar*, is named after the national hero Simón Bolívar.

Teacher Resources

 **Activity 16**

 **pp. 55, 89**

 **Juegos**

Flash Cards

Answers

Autoevaluación

Possible answers:

1. Hay un mantel, unas servilletas y unos vasos.
2. Deben encender las luces. Tienen que poner la mesa. Tienen que ayudar con la comida.
3. ¿En qué piensas?
4. ¿Qué piensan hacer este sábado?
5. Me gustan las arepas, pero prefiero el pan con mantequilla.
6. Pásame ese vaso y esos cubiertos, por favor.
7. arepas, hallacas, ropa vieja, cachapas

Activities

Communities

Ask small groups of students to identify interesting professions involving Spanish. In turn, they should discuss the requirements and obligations of this job by using the expressions *tener que* (+ infinitive) and *deber* (+ infinitive). Have students share their conclusions with the class.

National Standards

Cultures
2.2

Connections
3.1

Communities
5.1

Teacher Resources

Vocabulario I
La casa de Julián

Activities 44–45

Activities 1–3

Activities 1–4

pp. 84–87, 93–94

Activity 1

Activity 1

Content reviewed in *Lección B*

- noun/adjective agreement
- present tense of regular verbs
- the verbs deber and querer
- family

Activities

Critical Listening
Play the audio of the letter. Tell students to listen for the main ideas the speaker is addressing. Finally, have several individuals state what they believe is the main theme of the reading.

Expansion
You may want to ask some of the following questions about the letter: *¿Cuál es la fecha de la carta?; ¿Dónde está Cartagena?; ¿De dónde son Daniela y Santiago?; ¿Qué no le gusta a Daniela?; ¿Adónde van a viajar Daniela y Santiago con su tío?; ¿Cuándo va a llamar Daniela a sus padres?*

National Standards
Communication 1.1
Cultures 2.1
Connections 3.1

Lección B

Vocabulario I
La casa de Julián

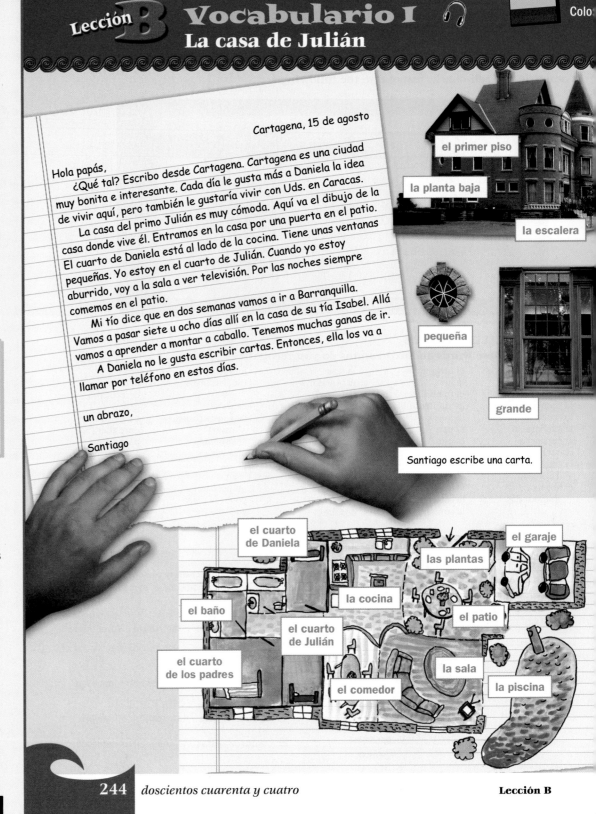

Cartagena, 15 de agosto

Hola papás,

¿Qué tal? Escribo desde Cartagena. Cartagena es una ciudad muy bonita e interesante. Cada día le gusta más a Daniela la idea de vivir aquí, pero también le gustaría vivir con Uds. en Caracas.

La casa del primo Julián es muy cómoda. Aquí va el dibujo de la casa donde vive él. Entramos en la casa por una puerta en el patio. El cuarto de Daniela está al lado de la cocina. Tiene unas ventanas pequeñas. Yo estoy en el cuarto de Julián. Cuando yo estoy aburrido, voy a la sala a ver televisión. Por las noches siempre comemos en el patio.

Mi tío dice que en dos semanas vamos a ir a Barranquilla. Vamos a pasar siete u ocho días allí en la casa de su tía Isabel. Allá vamos a aprender a montar a caballo. Tenemos muchas ganas de ir.

A Daniela no le gusta escribir cartas. Entonces, ella los va a llamar por teléfono en estos días.

un abrazo,

Santiago

el primer piso
la planta baja
la escalera
pequeña
grande

Santiago escribe una carta.

el cuarto de Daniela
el garaje
las plantas
la cocina
el baño
el patio
el cuarto de Julián
el cuarto de los padres
la sala
el comedor
la piscina

Notes

Remind students that when two verbs are combined in one sentence, the first verb is conjugated and the second verb is usually an infinitive.

Cultures. Note that Daniela and Santiago are visiting a cousin in Colombia. In the Spanish-speaking world it is common to spend vacation time with extended family members.

Point out several characteristics of informal letter writing in Spanish. The month is not capitalized; the most popular salutation is *Querido(s)* or *Querida(s)* plus one or more names; common farewells include un *abrazo; un fuerte abrazo; besos.*

Dictado

Escucha la información y escribe lo que oyes.

¿Dónde están?

Look at these illustrations and tell what Santiago and Daniela's relatives are doing somewhere in their house in Cartagena.

MODELO su abuela
Su abuela come en el patio.

¡Extra!

Altos y bajos

Some people refer to *la planta baja* as *los bajos* (downstairs). The expression *los altos* is roughly equivalent to the English **upstairs** or **upper floor(s).** The term *el primer piso* (the first floor) often identifies the second floor of a building, although many people also use the term to refer to the main floor.

1. su prima pequeña
2. su abuelo
3. su primo Julián
4. su tío
5. su tía

¿Adónde deben ir?

Read the statements and say where the people should go.

MODELO Quiero un vaso de agua.
Debes ir a la cocina.

1. Mi hermana quiere buscar una naranja y un refresco.
2. Mis padres necesitan usar el carro.
3. Yo tengo ganas de ver televisión.
4. Mis abuelos están aquí para comer con la familia.
5. Mi hermana viene de jugar al fútbol.
6. Voy a leer y escuchar CDs.

Conexión con otras disciplinas: dibujo

Create a blueprint (or make a pop-up) of the floor plan of your home and label the rooms in Spanish. Make up the information if you wish. Then write at least five sentences in Spanish that describe your blueprint. For example, state if the blueprint is of a house *(casa)* or an apartment *(apartamento)*, how large it is, the number and type of rooms, etc.

Notes

Comparisons. Note that the concept of *casa* may vary among cultures and even among Spanish speakers. For example, a home for a family in an urban area may be an apartment or a condominium in a multiresidence building. In other cases, a home may be a freestanding structure with a yard and a garage.

Additional words students might want to use when talking about their home: *el ático/el desván* (attic), *el apartamento* (apartment), *el jardín* (garden, yard), *el sótano* (basement), *el techo* (ceiling), *el tejado* (roof).

Teacher Resources

Activity 1
Activity 3

p. 26

Answers

1 Play a portion of the recorded letter and have students write what they hear. As an alternative, you may choose to read the selection yourself. Check the accuracy of student spelling.

2 Possible answers:
1. Su prima pequeña juega en el garaje.
2. Su abuelo lee el periódico en el comedor.
3. Su primo Julián juega en el cuarto con la computadora.
4. Su tío lee un libro en la sala.
5. Su tía ve televisión en la cocina.

3 Possible answers:
1. Debe ir a la cocina.
2. Deben ir al garaje.
3. Debes ir a la sala.
4. Deben ir al comedor.
5. Debe ir al baño.
6. Debes ir al patio/a tu cuarto.

4 Creative writing practice.

Activities

Critical Thinking

Ask students to think of typical activities in different parts of a house. Mention various rooms/areas and ask the students to explain what they do there.

National Standards	
Communication 1.1, 1.2, 1.3	**Comparisons** 4.1, 4.2
Cultures 2.1	
Connections 3.1	

Teacher Resources

Diálogo I
La casa de Elisa
Activity 5
Activity 6
Activity 7

Answers

5 1. Juan dice que la casa de Elisa es grande.
2. Rosa tiene ganas de ir a la casa de Elisa.
3. A Javier le gustaría mucho verla.
4. La casa de Elisa es grande e interesante.
5. Tiene tres pisos.
6. Tiene siete u ocho cuartos.

6 Answers will vary.

7 1. Está en la casa.
2. Está en el colegio.
3. Está en la casa.
4. Está en el parque.
5. Está en la casa.
6. Está en la casa.
7. Está en el colegio.
8. Está en la casa.

Activities

Critical Listening

Play the audio version of the dialog. Tell students to listen for the main ideas. They should then summarize them for the class.

Multiple Intelligences (spatial/linguistic)

Have students draw a plan of their dream house and label all the rooms and items in it.

National Standards

Communication
1.1, 1.2

Diálogo I La casa de Elisa

JAVIER: Juan dice que la casa de Elisa es muy grande.
ROSA: Sí, yo tengo ganas de ir a su casa.
JAVIER: A mí también me gustaría mucho verla.
ROSA: ¡Vamos mañana!

JAVIER: Mira, allí está Juan.
ROSA: Oye, Juan, ¿cómo es la casa de Elisa?
JUAN: Es una casa grande e interesante. Tiene tres pisos.

ROSA: ¡Qué grande!
JUAN: Sí, tiene siete u ocho cuartos, dos salas y una piscina.
JAVIER: ¡Es la casa ideal!
ROSA: ¿Ideal? No pienso eso, prefiero casas pequeñas.

5 ¿Qué recuerdas?

1. ¿Quién dice que la casa de Elisa es grande?
2. ¿Quién tiene ganas de ir a la casa de Elisa?
3. ¿A quién le gustaría mucho ver la casa de Elisa?
4. ¿Cómo es la casa de Elisa?
5. ¿Cuántos pisos tiene la casa de Elisa?
6. ¿Y cuántos cuartos tiene?

¡Extra!

Las palabras *e* y *u*

Before words that begin with *i* or *hi*, the word *y* becomes *e*. Similarly, the word *o* changes to *u* before words that begin with *o* or *ho*.

*Marcos **e** Inés viven en Cartagena. Dicen que van a montar a caballo mañana **u** otro día.*

6 Algo personal

1. ¿Cómo es tu casa ideal?
2. ¿Te gustan las casas grandes o pequeñas? Explica.

7 ¿Está en la casa, en el colegio o en el parque?

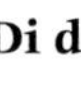
Di dónde están las siguientes personas según lo que oyes.

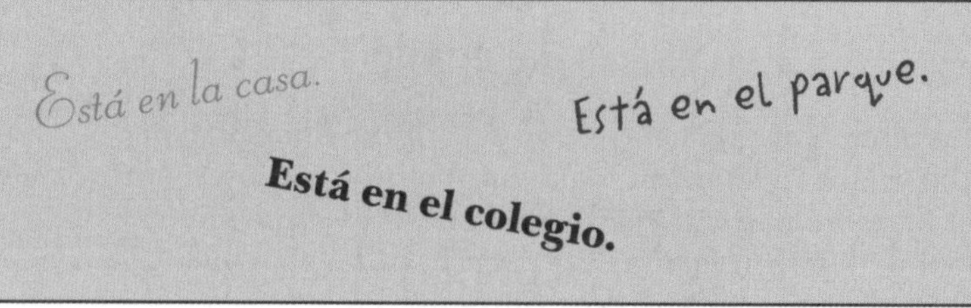
Está en la casa.
Está en el parque.
Está en el colegio.

Notes

Point out that *gustaría* is the conditional tense of the verb *gustar*. (The conditional tense will not be taught until level 2.) Tell students they can use this form of the verb with the indirect object pronouns (*me, te, le, nos, les*) to say what people would or would not like, as Javier does in the dialog.

Students have already learned to use the indirect object pronouns with *gusta* and *gustan*. Give them examples of indirect object pronouns used with gustaría: *¿Te gustaría ir a Venezuela?; A mi hermana le gustaría hacer un viaje.*

Ask students to review the vocabulary from the previous page and then scan the dialog for familiar words or phrases.

Cultura viva

Bogotá, Colombia.

Cartagena, Colombia.

Colombia

The Spaniards founded *Cartagena de Indias* on the northwest coast of Colombia in 1533. Pirates frequently attacked the port seeking gold and other valuables, so a wall was constructed around the city as a means of defense. The wall *(la muralla)* remains today, one of the symbols of colonial times in Colombia. The capital, *Bogotá*, was founded in 1538. The city is vibrant and modern today, but you can catch a glimpse of the country's extensive history if you visit the exceptional *Museo del Oro* (Gold Museum), which holds more than 30,000 pieces of pre-Columbian gold.

Colombia has a varied terrain, consisting of mountains, tropical jungles, plains, lowlands and a lengthy coastline that touches on two oceans. The country's climate does not change with the seasons but rather is determined by Colombia's elevations. Whereas the lowlands and the coastal areas offer a tropical climate, such as you might experience when visiting the beautiful city of *Cartagena*, the temperature in the capital ranges between fifty and seventy degrees all year long.

Máscara de oro en el Museo del Oro, Bogotá.

Most people know that Colombia is famous for producing large quantities of excellent coffee, but not everyone knows it is a major exporter of emeralds. The country is also famous for its music, including the distinctive dance rhythms of *la cumbia, el porro, el merecumbé* and the accordion accompaniment of songs known as *vallenatos*. Visit Colombia sometime and experience this South American jewel!

8 ¿Qué sabes de Colombia? 

Tell whether the statements are *cierto* or *falso*.

1. Colombia está en América Central.
2. Cartagena es una ciudad muy nueva.
3. El clima en Colombia es determinado por la elevación.
4. Cartagena es un símbolo del período colonial.
5. Cali es la capital del país.
6. Colombia es famosa por el café, las esmeraldas y la música.

9 Conexiones con otras disciplinas: geografía

Create a map of Colombia that shows major cities and rivers, mountains and surrounding countries.

Notes Explain that in Colombia, coffee is the primary agricultural export product. Point out that many people are employed in this important industry. Also note that Colombian exports include many other important products such as coal, minerals, flowers and 95 percent of the world's emeralds.

The majority of the people in Colombia live in large cities, such as *Santa Fe de Bogotá, Medellín, Cali, Barranquilla, Cartagena* and *Bucaramanga*. Other towns with interesting names are *Anapoima, Facatativá, Tocaima, Cúcuta, Armenia* and *Popayán*.

Teacher Resources

 Activity 8

 Activity 4

 p. 83

 Activity 2

Answers

8
1. Falso.
2. Falso.
3. Cierto.
4. Cierto.
5. Falso.
6. Cierto.

9 Answers will vary.

Activities

Communities
Show students where Colombia is located, using the maps in the front of the book or the transparencies that are part of this program.

Multiple Intelligences (spatial)
Ask students to create a map of Colombia. They should add cities, rivers, mountains and any other features of their choosing.

National Standards

Cultures
2.1, 2.2

Connections
3.1

Teacher Resources

 Activity 10

 Activities 5–7

 Activity 5

 p. 25

 Activity 3
Activity 4

 Activity 2

Answers

10 Possible answers:

1. Yo digo "¡Lo siento!"
2. Nosotros decimos "¡Feliz cumpleaños!"
3. Uds. dicen "¡Qué problema!"
4. Tú dices "¡Qué bonitas!"
5. Ellas dicen "¡Qué bueno!"
6. Daniela dice "Sí, habla con ella."

Activities

Critical Listening

Tell the class that you are going to share with them several interesting news headlines and pieces of personal information. Some statements will be true and others will be false. The students should listen to each statement and then decide: *Dice la verdad* or *No dice la verdad/Dice una mentira.* As an extension, ask pairs of students to prepare a list of recent headlines to present to the class.

National Standards

Communication
1.1

Idioma

Estructura

Telling what someone says: *decir*

The present tense of *decir* (to say, to tell) has an irregular *yo* form and requires a stem change for all forms except *nosotros/as* and *vosotros/as.* Use *decir* to tell what someone says.

decir	
digo	decimos
dices	decís
dice	dicen

When you are summarizing what someone says, use *que* between *decir* and the expression or phrase that follows:

¿Qué ***dice*** *Javier?* — What does Javier **say**?
Dice que *la casa de Elisa es muy grande.* — He **says** (**that**) Elisa's house is very big.

Práctica

10 ¿Qué dicen? 

What might the response be to what the following people say?

MODELO ¿Cómo te llamas? (Ramiro)
Ramiro dice "Me llamo Ramiro."

1. Estoy enfermo. (yo)
2. Hoy es mi cumpleaños. (nosotros)
3. No hay luz en mi casa. (Uds.)
4. ¿Te gustan mis plantas? (tú)
5. Voy a comprar una casa con una piscina muy grande. (ellas)
6. ¡Aló¡ ¿Puedo hablar con Daniela? (Daniela)

Yo digo, "Me llamo Elisa."

Notes

Review the following verbs with students, which also can be used with *que* to connect two thoughts: *pensar, sentir, escribir, comprender, contestar, saber, leer, ver.* Example: *¿Qué escribe Ana en su carta? Escribe que a ella le gusta Colombia.*

Point out the difference between *decir* (to say, to tell) and *hablar* (to speak, to talk).

Check for correct conjugation of the verb *decir*.

Una encuesta

Results of a poll show who would like to spend the summer in Colombia as part of an exchange program with a high school in Cartagena. Summarize whether the indicated people say they would like to participate or not.

MODELO Julia
Julia dice que no.

1. Ud.
2. Raúl y la señorita García
3. el señor Gaviria y César
4. Sara
5. la señora Sosa y Eva
6. Ernesto y yo

Viaje de Intercambio
Sí No
☑ ☐ Sara
☑ ☐ yo
☑ ☐ Ernesto
☑ ☐ la señorita García
☑ ☐ Raúl
☐ ☑ Julia
☑ ☐ Enrique
☐ ☑ Eva
☐ ☑ Ud.
☐ ☑ el señor Gaviria
☐ ☑ la señora Sosa
☐ ☑ César

Comunicación

En tu casa

In groups, discuss your homes (*casa* or *apartamento*) and weekly activities. What is similar and what is different about the homes, your routines and your lives in general? You may wish to include some of the following activities in your discussion: *comer*, *escribir cartas*, *leer* and *ver televisión*. Make up any information you would like. Take notes as you talk and report what you discuss to the class.

MODELO
A: ¿Dónde come tu familia?
B: Comemos en la cocina. ¿Y Uds.?
A: Nosotros comemos mucho en restaurantes. En casa comemos en la sala y vemos televisión.
C: En mi casa comemos en la sala, pero no los domingos. Los domingos comemos en el comedor.
A: **B** dice que su familia come en la cocina. **C** dice que en su casa comen en la sala, pero no los domingos. Mi familia come mucho en restaurantes, pero en casa comemos en la sala y vemos televisión.

Nosotros comemos en el comedor.

Answers

11
1. Ud. dice que no.
2. Raúl y la señorita García dicen que sí.
3. El señor Gaviria y César dicen que no.
4. Sara dice que sí.
5. La señora Sosa y Eva dicen que no.
6. Ernesto y yo decimos que sí.

12 Creative self-expression.

Activities

Critical Listening
Ask pairs of students to prepare a list in Spanish of recent headlines, quotes that are common knowledge or other bits of information someone has said. (The information should be public knowledge.) The students should also make up some headlines that are not true. In front of the class, one student reads the headline or statement aloud: *El presidente va a Colombia en dos semanas.* The partner says whether he or she thinks the statement is true or not (*...dice que....*) and then calls on a classmate to agree or disagree. The classmate must say whether the statement is true or not, and then responds with *Dice la verdad* or *No dice la verdad/Dice una mentira.*

Notes

Students may choose to elect one person from their group to take notes for activity 12 or have one person from each group present to the class a summary of what members of the group discussed.

Comparisons. Although the Spanish word *que* must always be used when joining two phrases, the word **that** may be eliminated from an English sentence: They say (**that**) we are going to Colombia.

National Standards

Communication
1.1, 1.3

Comparisons
4.1

Teacher Resources

 Activity 6

Activity 3

Answers

13
1. Yo quiero tener una piscina.
2. A ti te gustaría tener un cuarto en la planta baja.
3. Mi hermano quiere una cocina con un lavaplatos.
4. A mis padres les gustaría tener un garaje para dos carros.
5. A nosotros nos gustaría tener un comedor cómodo.
6. A mí me gustaría tener plantas en el patio.
7. Mis hermanas quieren tener cuartos en el primer piso.

14 Creative self-expression.

Activities

Cooperative Learning

Working in groups of three or four, have students discuss what they wrote for activity 14.

Multiple Intelligences (intrapersonal)

Ask several questions to further practice the expression of wishes: *¿Qué quieres ser/hacer en el futuro?; ¿Dónde te gustaría estudiar o trabajar?; ¿Dónde quieres vivir?; ¿Te gustaría ser famoso/famosa?; ¿Adónde te gustaría viajar?; ¿Qué países quieres visitar?*

National Standards

Communication
1.1

Comparisons
4.1

Estructura

Expressing wishes with *querer* or *gustaría*

You have learned to express someone's wishes by using a form of *querer* and an infinitive. You can also express wishes by combining *me, te, le, nos, os* or *les* with the more polite but less emphatic *gustaría* and an infinitive.

Quiero viajar *a Colombia.*	**I want to travel** to Colombia.
Me gustaría viajar *a Colombia.*	**I would like to travel** to Colombia.
Quieren comprar *una estufa nueva.*	They **want to buy** a new stove.
Les gustaría comprar *una estufa nueva.*	They **would like to buy** a new stove.

Práctica

13 Una casa nueva

Choose a word or expression from each column and create complete sentences telling what members of the Martínez family want when they buy a new house.

MODELO Nosotros queremos comprar una casa grande.

A	B
yo	quieren tener cuartos en el primer piso
a ti	te gustaría tener un cuarto en la planta baja
mi hermano	les gustaría tener un garaje para dos carros
a mis padres	queremos comprar una casa grande ✓
a nosotros	me gustaría tener plantas en el patio
a mí	quiero tener una piscina
mis hermanas	nos gustaría tener un comedor cómodo
nosotros ✓	quiere una cocina con un lavaplatos

14 ¿Qué te gustaría?

Completa las oraciones de una manera original.

MODELO Me gustaría tener...
Me gustaría tener una casa grande.

1. No me gustaría vivir....
2. Me gustaría viajar....
3. No me gustaría ir....
4. Me gustaría vivir....
5. Me gustaría comprar....
6. Me gustaría ir....

Me gustaría tener una casa grande.

Notes

Remind students that they may need to add *a* (plus a person's name or a pronoun) or *a mí, a ti, a él, a ella, a Ud., a nosotros, a nosotras, a vosotros, a vosotras, a ellos, a ellas, a Uds.* to clarify the meaning of *gustaría: A mis padres les gustaría comprar un refrigerador nuevo.*

Encourage students to make up funny or out-of-the-ordinary sentences for activity 14.

15 Comparaciones

Write a paragraph of four or five sentences describing the wishes, intentions and obligations of people you know well, using *gustaría*, *pensar*, *preferir* and *querer*. Then exchange your paper with a partner and take turns asking and answering questions about what each of you wrote.

MODELO **A:** ¿Adónde les gustaría ir a tus padres?
B: A mis padres les gustaría ir a Bogotá para ver a mis abuelos.

Mis padres quieren viajar a Colombia en julio. Les gustaría ver a mis abuelos en Bogotá. Un día pienso vivir en Bogotá, pero tengo que terminar las clases en el colegio.

Comunicación

16 Encuesta

Complete a survey about what rooms and furnishings your classmates would like to have in their ideal house *(casa ideal)*. Talk with at least two other people and, then, compare the information you obtained with a partner. Finally, one of you should report your survey results to the class.

MODELO **A:** ¿Cómo es tu casa ideal?
B: Me gustaría tener una casa grande de dos pisos.
C: Yo prefiero una casa cómoda de un piso y también quiero tener una piscina.
A: **B** dice que le gustaría tener una casa grande con dos pisos, pero **C** dice que prefiere una casa cómoda de un piso y tener una piscina.

17 ¿Cómo es tu casa?

In Spanish, write several statements describing your home, what you or someone in your family would like to buy for the house and where you would like to live in the future *(el futuro)*. Then, based on what you have written in small groups, talk about the homes. Try to use some of the alternative words suggested in the *Estrategia* during the discussion. You might talk about such things as the number of rooms, what you like or do not like, where the home is located and whether or not there is something you would like to buy for the house. Add details making up any of the information you wish.

MODELO **A:** ¿Cómo es tu casa?
B: Es muy grande. Tiene cinco piezas y cada pieza tiene un cuarto de baño. También tiene dos salas y un comedor grande. A mis padres les gustaría comprar una mesa grande para el comedor.
C: Pues, mi casa es pequeña. Tiene seis cuartos: dos alcobas, un baño, una sala, un comedor y una cocina.

Estrategia

Recognizing words in context
Words and expressions you read and hear in Spanish vary from speaker to speaker and from one country to another. You may hear *cuarto, habitación* and *pieza* are all used to refer to a **room.** For the word **bedroom** you may see the words *alcoba, dormitorio, habitación, pieza, recámara* and *cuarto de dormir* (literally, a **room for sleeping**), which is sometimes shortened to *cuarto.* However, you should not confuse this shortened form of *cuarto* for the expression *cuarto de baño* (bathroom), which is usually shortened to *baño.* Knowing that these differences exist will help you in your goal of becoming fluent in Spanish. Always keep in mind that your goal is communication.

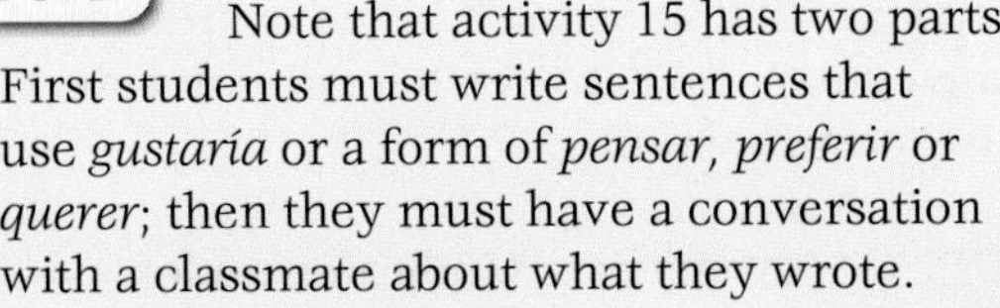

Notes

Note that activity 15 has two parts. First students must write sentences that use *gustaría* or a form of *pensar, preferir* or *querer*; then they must have a conversation with a classmate about what they wrote.

Read and discuss the *Estrategia* with students before assigning activities 16 and 17. Encourage students to use context to determine meaning as they converse.

Answers

15 Creative self-expression.
16 Answers will vary.
17 Creative self-expression.

Activities

Spanish for Spanish Speakers
Have students write an essay describing the house of their dreams. They should prepare a floor plan to accompany the description.

National Standards

Communication
1.1, 1.3

Connections
3.1

Comparisons
4.1

Vocabulario II
Un día en casa

 Activity 46

 Activity 8

 Activities 7–8

 Activity 5

 Activity 4

Activities

Prereading Strategy

Have students look at the illustration and determine what the people are doing. Inform them that what the people are saying matches their actions. Next, ask students to look at each speech bubble and look for cognates and other words they recognize. Finally, ask students to guess what each person is saying.

TPR

Write the expressions from the illustration *Un día en casa* on separate pieces of paper. Have students select one of the pieces of paper at random. Call on several students to act out the expressions while classmates guess what the expressions are.

Vocabulario II

Un día en casa

National Standards
Communication 1.1
Comparisons 4.1

Notes

Review the forms of the verb *tener* prior to introducing the *tener* expressions.

Comparisons. Compare the expressions using *tener* (+ noun) and meaning **to be** (+ adjective) with English equivalents. Examples: *tengo hambre* = **I am hungry**; *tengo miedo* = **I am afraid**. Then remind students that in Spanish, some expressions use *estar* (+ adjective) whereas others may use *tener* (+ noun).

Use support materials indicated under Teacher Resources at the top of the page to introduce and practice words and expressions in *Vocabulario II.*

Tengo dieciséis años.
Yo tengo quince años.
Eso es mentira. Debes pedir perdón.
Sí, lo siento. Es una mentira. Tengo treinta años.
Clara dice la verdad.
Guillermo quiere decir que prefiere ser joven.

Lo siento. Eres muy pequeño.
"Lo siento. Eres muy pequeño."
El chico pide prestado el carro de su hermano.
La chica repite lo que dice su hermano.

18 ¿Cierto o falso?

Di si lo que oyes es cierto o falso, según la información en el Vocabulario II. Si es falso, di lo que es cierto.

19 Un día en casa

With a classmate, take turns asking and answering the following questions, according to the illustration.

MODELO A: ¿Qué tiene Cristina?
B: Cristina tiene prisa.

1. ¿Qué tiene Nicolás?
2. ¿Qué tiene Rogelio?
3. ¿Quién tiene mucha sed?
4. ¿Quién tiene frío?
5. ¿Qué tiene Mateo?
6. ¿Quién tiene mucha hambre?
7. ¿Quiénes tienen mucho calor?
8. ¿Qué tienes tú?

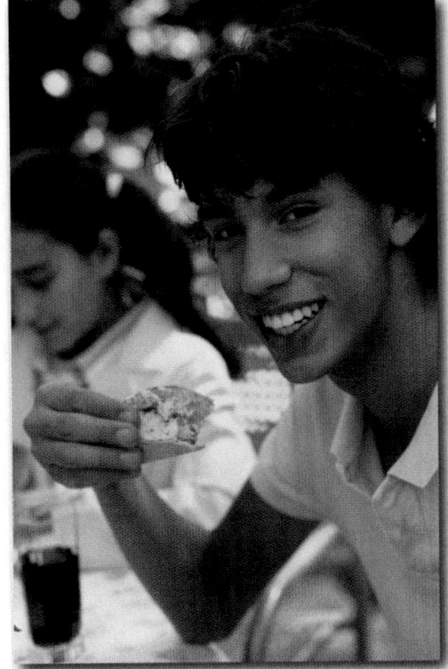

Paco tiene hambre.

Notes Play the audio version of activity 18 for listening comprehension practice or read the activity using the transcript that appears in the ATE introduction.

Teacher Resources

Activity 18
Activity 19

Activities 9–10

Answers

18 Possible answers:
1. Falso. Nicolás tiene sueño.
2. Cierto.
3. Falso. El abuelo dice que tiene frío.
4. Falso. Los tíos tienen calor.
5. Cierto.
6. Cierto.

19
1. Nicolás tiene sueño.
2. Rogelio tiene poca hambre.
3. La abuela tiene mucha sed.
4. El abuelo tiene frío.
5. Mateo tiene ganas de correr.
6. Verónica tiene mucha hambre.
7. Los tíos tienen mucho calor.
8. Tengo....

Activities

Critical Thinking

See if students can use an appropriate *tener* expression to make a statement about the following situations: *1) Carlitos tiene nueve años. Está en casa solo y son las 11:00 de la noche. 2) Son las 2:30 de la mañana pero Juan no va a su cuarto. Tiene mucho trabajo y está cansado. 3) Don Pedro está en el desierto del Sahara y es el mediodía. 4) El señor Vega está en Alaska en febrero. 5) Marisol busca algo de comer pero no hay nada en la casa.*

National Standards

Communication
1.1, 1.2

Teacher Resources

Diálogo II
Tengo mucho calor
Activity 20
Activity 21
Activity 22

Answers

20 1. Javier tiene mucho calor.
2. Javier tiene mucha sed.
3. Es de Elisa.
4. No, es mentira.
5. Quiere ir a la playa.

21 Answers will vary.

22 1. F
2. A
3. D
4. B
5. E
6. C

Activities

Critical Listening
Play the audio recording of the dialog. Instruct students to cover the words as they listen to the conversation to develop good listening skills before concentrating on reading Spanish. Have students look at the photographs and imagine what the people are doing. Ask several individuals to state what they believe is the main theme of the conversation. Finally, ask if students know where the conversation takes place.

National Standards

Communication
1.1, 1.2

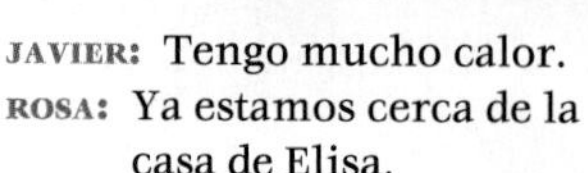

Diálogo II Tengo mucho calor

JAVIER: Tengo mucho calor.
ROSA: Ya estamos cerca de la casa de Elisa.
JAVIER: También tengo mucha sed.
ROSA: ¡Allí está la casa de Elisa!

ROSA: ¡Qué grande y bonita es tu casa!
ELISA: Muchas gracias. Es tu casa también.
JAVIER: A Rosa no le gusta tu casa.
ROSA: Mentira, Elisa. No es verdad.

JAVIER: Pero dices que te gustan las casas pequeñas.
ROSA: Lo que digo es que prefiero una casa pequeña.
ELISA: Está bien. Yo comprendo. ¡Vamos a la playa!
JAVIER: Buena idea. Tengo mucho calor.

20 ¿Qué recuerdas?

1. ¿Quién tiene mucho calor?
2. ¿Quién tiene mucha sed?
3. ¿De quién es la casa grande y bonita?
4. ¿Es verdad que a Rosa no le gusta la casa de Elisa?
5. ¿Adónde quiere ir Elisa?

21 Algo personal

1. ¿Tienes calor? ¿Y sed?
2. ¿Dices mentiras? Explica.
3. ¿Adónde vas cuando hace mucho calor?

22 ¿Qué tienen?

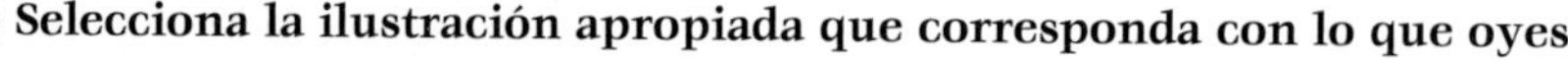

Selecciona la ilustración apropiada que corresponda con lo que oyes.

A

B

C

D

E

F

Notes

Explain that Elisa's statement *Es tu casa también* is an expression of courtesy to make Rosa feel at home.

The activities that follow the dialog are recorded and can be found in the Audio Program. Student answer sheets for activity 22 are located in the back of the Audio Program Manual.

Ask students to review the vocabulary from the previous page and then scan the dialog for familiar words or phrases.

Cultura viva II

¡Hogar, dulce hogar!

Una casa grande en Cartagena.

Homes in Spanish-speaking parts of the world are like castles in sentiment, if not in actual size. They offer a private refuge from the outside world and vary in their styles to reflect individual tastes, customs and availability of construction materials. Homes in rural areas are often small and simple, whereas homes in large cities and suburbs can be large and impressive. Interestingly, many Hispanic families in metropolitan areas live in apartment buildings or condos, which they may own instead of renting. These homes can have as many as four or five bedrooms, a balcony, two bathrooms, a kitchen and a living room. In some older Hispanic neighborhoods, homes often adjoin the sidewalk, leaving little or no room for a front yard. These homes traditionally have a patio at the back or the center of the residence that offers privacy and a place to relax among plants, birds and, sometimes, even small trees and beautiful fountains. In addition, older homes often have a flat roof (*la azotea*), which may be accessible by stairs, usually from the patio or a room near the back of the home. The *azotea* is sometimes used for hanging the laundry to dry or growing flowers and herbs, and even some vegetables, in pots. Today, *chalets* (e.g., houses with yards that resemble homes in the United States) are becoming popular, especially on the outskirts of some cities in part because city apartments and condos are becoming prohibitively expensive for most middle class families.

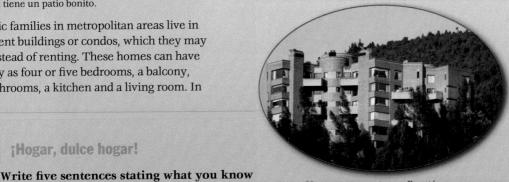

Esta casa tiene un patio bonito.

Unos apartamentos en Bogatá.

23 ¡Hogar, dulce hogar!

Write five sentences stating what you know about homes in the Spanish-speaking world.

24 Nuestras casas

Compare housing in the United States with what you know about homes in the Spanish-speaking world.

Notes Inform the class that houses in the Spanish-speaking world may be large or small, made from concrete, brick, wood or adobe, or have one or more floors. There is no one model that fits the variety of sizes and shapes.

Many homes in Spanish-speaking cities are apartments or condominiums and do not have a yard. These buildings are commonly made out of concrete and steel. The inhabitants probably park their vehicles in a parking garage tucked under the apartments or condominiums.

Teacher Resources

Activity 5

Answers

23 Possible answers:

1. Home is a private place reserved for family and close friends.
2. Rural homes are often smaller and simpler than city homes.
3. Many Hispanic families in metropolitan areas live in apartment buildings or condos.
4. A patio offers a private place where families can relax amongst plants, birds and fountains.
5. Houses on the outskirts of town are becoming popular in part due to their lower cost.

24 Answers will vary.

Activities

Cooperative Learning
Working in pairs, have students take turns naming the rooms of a house as the partner makes a sketch of what he or she hears. Students may choose to describe the house more fully if they wish.

National Standards	
Communication 1.1	**Comparisons** 4.1, 4.2
Cultures 2.2	
Connections 3.1	

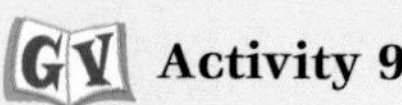

 Activity 9

Answers

25 1. vivimos; 2. tenemos; 3. tiene; 4. prefiero; 5. quiere; 6. gustan; 7. estudio; 8. dice; 9. tenemos; 10. escribe; 11. escriben; 12. pienso; 13. Quiero

Activities

Cooperative Learning

Have students work in pairs to practice asking and answering questions using the *tú* and *yo* forms of several verbs (make sure they use the rising intonation of questions). Student A could ask *¿Comes ...?; ¿Corres ...?; ¿Comprendes ...?*; etc. Student B would then respond affirmatively to each question (*Sí, como ...*). After all verbs have been covered, Student A again asks the questions and Student B responds negatively (*No, no corro ...*). Then have students change roles.

Critical Thinking

For additional practice with *-ar*, *-er* and *-ir* verbs, have students prepare a list of seven or eight things they do during the week. They may use the following verbs and any other verbs they have learned: *caminar, cantar, comer, correr, estudiar, hablar, hacer, ir, leer, nadar* and *ver*. Then, working in pairs, have students talk about their lists of activities and take turns asking and answering when they do each activity listed.

National Standards

Communication
1.1

Repaso rápido

Regular present-tense verbs

You are already familiar with how to conjugate regular verbs:

hablar		comer		vivir	
hablo	hablamos	como	comemos	vivo	vivimos
hablas	habláis	comes	coméis	vives	vivís
habla	hablan	come	comen	vive	viven

 La familia de Elisa

Completa el siguiente párrafo con las formas apropiadas de los verbos entre paréntesis.

Me llamo Elisa y soy la amiga de Javier y Rosa. Mis padres y yo 1. *(vivir)* en Cartagena, Colombia. Nosotros 2. *(tener)* una casa muy grande. La casa 3. *(tener)* cinco cuartos y cuatro baños. Yo 4. *(preferir)* tener una casa más pequeña. Mi madre también 5. *(querer)* una casa un poco más pequeña. Mi padre es de San José, California, y le 6. *(gustar)* las casas grandes y cómodas. Ahora yo 7. *(estudiar)* inglés en el colegio. Mi padre 8. *(decir)* que yo hablo muy bien el inglés. Mis hermanos y yo 9. *(tener)* ganas de ir a Estados Unidos. Mi papá tiene mucha familia en California—sus padres, seis hermanos, tres tíos y quince primos. Él les 10. *(escribir)* muchos mensajes por correo electrónico a ellos, pero ellos 11. *(escribir)* muy poco. Yo 12. *(pensar)* que para Navidad vamos a California. 13. *(Querer)* conocer a la familia de mi padre.

¿Tienes ganas de ir a Cartagena, Colombia?

Notes

Skip the *Repaso rápido* and activity 25 if you feel students have a good grasp of the present tense.

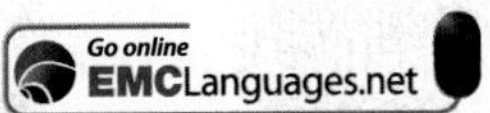

Estructura

Stem-changing verbs: e → i

You have already learned to use verbs like *pensar (ie)* that require the spelling change *e → ie: yo pienso, nosotros pensamos*. The verb *pedir (i, i)* requires the spelling change *e → i* in all forms of their present-tense stem except for *nosotros* and *vosotros*.

pedir	
pido	pedimos
pides	pedís
pide	piden

Pedir is the English equivalent of "to ask for, to request, to order (in a restaurant)." Take care to avoid using *pedir* instead of *preguntar* or *hacer una pregunta*, which are both used for "to ask a question." Other expressions with *pedir*:

- ***Pedir permiso (para)*** is "to ask for permission (to do something)."
- ***Pedir perdón*** can be used to excuse yourself and to ask for forgiveness for having done something wrong.
- ***Pedir prestado/a*** is "to ask for a loan" or "to borrow something."

The verbs *repetir* and *decir* follow the same pattern as *pedir*, with the exception of the irregular *yo* form or *decir*: *digo*.

Con permiso y Perdón

Although they may be used with the verb *pedir*, *Con permiso* and *Perdón* can also be used alone for "Excuse me" or "Pardon me."

Práctica

26 Mi amigo Javier

Completa este párrafo con la forma apropiada del verbo *pedir* o *repetir*.

Hola, soy Juan. Javier y yo somos amigos. Javier siempre (1) prestado muchas cosas. Un día (2) prestado unos cubiertos; otro día (3) azúcar. A veces tiene que (4) prestado dinero para comer más porque siempre tiene hambre. Cuando va a un restaurante, él y su hermana (5) muchas bebidas porque siempre tienen sed, y cuando están en el colegio siempre (6) ropa prestada a sus amigos porque siempre tienen frío. Yo nunca (7) prestado nada, y lo (8), nada. A mí no me gusta cuando los estudiantes (9) cosas prestadas. ¡Es muy malo! Yo siempre le debo (10) a Javier una y otra vez, "No debes pedir más cosas prestadas" pero él dice que yo soy egoísta. Mmm, ¿qué opinas si nosotros le (11) prestadas cosas a Javier todos los días? ¿Qué va a pensar?

Teacher Resources

 Activities 11–14

 Activities 10–12

 Activity 6
Activity 7

 Activity 6

Answers

26
1. pide
2. pide
3. pide
4. pedir
5. piden
6. piden
7. pido
8. repito
9. piden
10. repetir
11. pedimos

Activities

Expansion

Have a class discussion about how to use the expressions *pedir permiso (para), perdir perdón and pedir prestado/prestada.* Then call on students to use the *pedir* expressions in sentences as a volunteer writes each on the board.

Students with Special Needs

Review the *e → ie* stem-changing verbs before introducing the change *e → i*.

National Standards
Comparisons 4.1

Notes

Explain that while the *e → ie* spelling change can occur in *-ar, -er* or *-ir* verbs, only *-ir* verbs make the *e → i* stem change. This change is indicated in *¡Aventura!* by the first *i* shown in parentheses after listed infinitives.

You may wish to let students know that the second *i* in parentheses after the verbs *pedir (i, i)* and *repetir (i, i)* will be explained in *Capítulo 7*.

The *vosotros/vosotras* verb endings are included for passive recognition. If you have decided to make these forms active, adapt the provided activities as needed.

Teacher Resources

 Activity 29

Answers

27 1. Pide
2. preguntamos
3. pedir
4. pide
5. pregunta
6. Pides
7. preguntan
8. pide

28 1. E
2. A
3. D
4. B
5. C, E
6. B, D
7. D

29 Possible answers:
1. Pido perdón.
2. Digo: "Perdón. Con permiso."
3. Pido permiso.
4. Digo "Muchas gracias, mamá."
5. Pido prestado una camisa a mi hermano.

Activities

Critical Thinking

Check your students' ability to write what they hear, using the following dictation: *Julio pide la cucharita a su mamá. Sara piensa que la sopa necesita sal. Julio le pasa la sal a Sara. Papá necesita una cuchara también. Al papá de Julio y Sara le gustan las arepas. La mamá de Julio y Sara cocina todos los días. Todos pedimos permiso para salir.*

National Standards
Communication 1.2
Comparisons 4.1

27 ¿Pedir o preguntar?

Completa las siguientes oraciones con la forma apropiada de *pedir* o *preguntar*.

1. ¿__ Ud. ayuda con su tarea a sus amigos?
2. Mi hermana y yo nos __ ¿cuándo vamos a vivir en una casa nueva?
3. A veces Rocío tiene que __ blusas prestadas a su mamá.
4. Javier siempre __ perdón cuando no comprende lo que dice la profesora.
5. Claudia siempre __ mucho en la clase de historia.
6. ¿__ siempre tú permiso para hablar por teléfono en tu casa?
7. Mis padres siempre me __ adónde voy.
8. Mi abuela siempre __ ayuda para subir la escalera.

Pedimos ayuda de nuestro profesor.

28 ¿Qué haces o dices?

Match the circumstances in the column on the left with the most appropriate response in the column on the right.

1. Tienes que poner una mesa para diez amigos.
2. Necesitas con qué escribir.
3. Dices lo que no debes decir a tu madre.
4. Quieres salir del comedor.
5. No comprendes nada en clase de matemáticas.
6. Caminas en la calle y tienes prisa.
7. Dices una mentira a tu padre y él lo sabe.

A. Pido prestado un lápiz.
B. Digo "con permiso".
C. Hago preguntas al profesor.
D. Pido perdón.
E. Pido ayuda.

29 En familia

¿Qué dices o haces en estas situaciones? Sigue el modelo.

> MODELO **Situación:** Tu madre te pide hacer muchos quehaceres antes de poder ver la televisión.
> Pido ayuda a mis hermanos menores.

1. **Situación:** Estás en el comedor y tu madre dice que debes hablar poco y comer más.
2. **Situación:** Eres el primero/la primera en terminar de comer y quieres ir a tu cuarto porque tienes mucho sueño.
3. **Situación:** Quieres ir con tus amigos a una fiesta por la noche.
4. **Situación:** Tú dices que tienes mucha sed y tu madre te pasa un refresco.
5. **Situación:** Vas a salir para ir al colegio y ves que no tienes una camisa limpia.

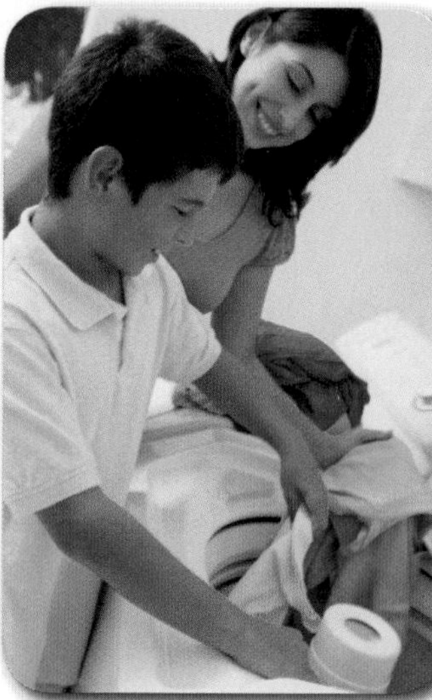

Mi madre me pide hacer muchos quehaceres.

Notes

Note that *pedir* doesn't require the preposition **for** because it is already included in the verb.

Comunicación

30 ¿Cuándo pides perdón?

In large groups, choose one person to be the moderator. Then conduct a discussion about circumstances in which you must ask someone to forgive you for what you have done. Make up any of the information you wish.

MODELO **A:** Margarita, ¿cuándo pides perdón?
B: Pido perdón cuando digo lo que no debo decir.

31 Para su cumpleaños

In groups of two or three talk first about a relative, and then say what he or she always asks for his/her birthday but never gets.

MODELO **A:** Tienes un hermano, ¿verdad?
B: Sí. Se llama Miguel. Tiene dieciocho años.
C: ¿Qué pide siempre tu hermano para su cumpleaños?
B: Mi hermano siempre pide un carro nuevo.

Mi hermano pide un carro nuevo para su cumpleaños.

32 ¿Qué piden prestado?

Working in pairs, each of you must create two columns on a piece of paper. In the first column, list five or six family members or friends you know very well. Leave the other column blank for your partner to fill in as you talk. Exchange lists and discuss what the people listed always ask to borrow (e.g., *un bolígrafo, dinero*). As your partner talks, list next to the person's name in the second column what your partner says each person borrows. See if the people on the lists seem to borrow some objects more than others.

MODELO **A:** ¿Qué pide siempre prestado tu prima?
B: Siempre pide prestado dinero.

mi prima — dinero
mi hermano — ______
mi amigo Julio — ______
Ana y Diego — ______
yo — ______

Answers

30 Creative self-expression.
31 Creative self-expression.
32 Creative self-expression.

Activities

Expansion

After completing activity 30, call on students to read some of the sentences they came up with for the activity and share them with the rest of the class.

Spanish for Spanish Speakers

Pair bilingual and nonbilingual students for activities 30 and 31.

Notes See which students can create funny circumstances for activity 30. Then have several pairs or small groups of students present the situations in front of the class.

Walk around the room as students are doing activities 30 and 31 and listen in on conversations. Offer help when needed.

Call on several students to summarize the lists they created for activity 32 with the class.

National Standards

Communication
1.1, 1.3

Teacher Resources

Lectura personal
Activity 33
Activity 34

Answers

33 Possible answers:
1. Están en Pereira, en la región cafetera de Colombia.
2. Practican agroturismo.
3. Villa María es una finca cafetera. La casa tiene cinco cuartos, cuatro baños, una cocina y una sala.
4. Hay una piscina para nadar, caballos y senderos donde caminar.
5. Tiene ganas de continuar los conciertos.

34 Answers will vary.

Activities

Connections
As a connection to language arts, have students imagine they are travel writers for a local newspaper. Have them write a one-page article about a Colombian city of their choice. They should include what to see and do, where to stay and where to eat.

Technology
Have students search the Internet for sites that advertise vacations in Colombia.

National Standards

Communication	Comparisons
1.1, 1.3	4.1, 4.2
Cultures	
2.2	
Connections	
3.1, 3.2	

Lectura personal

Dirección http://www.emcp.com/músico/aventura1/

Archivo Edición Ver Favoritos Herramientas Ayuda

página principal | miembros | e-diario

Nombre: **Chantal Morales Rivera**
Edad: **16 años**
País natal: **República Dominicana**
Actividad favorita: **correr por la playa**

Una plantación de café en Colombia.

¡Otro gran concierto en Cali, Colombia! Ya son diez conciertos y la verdad es que estamos un poco cansados. Por eso[1] desde el viernes estamos en la región cafetera[2] de Colombia, disfrutando[3] de una forma de turismo relativamente nueva: el agroturismo. En los años noventa, los caficultores[4] decidieron que sus plantaciones de café no solamente servían[5] para exportar "*the richest coffee in the world*" sino también para importar turistas y generar ingresos[6] complementarios. Así fue como[7] cientos de fincas[8] han sido[9] adaptadas para invitar al turista. La finca en que estamos se llama Villa María y está a veinte minutos de Pereira. La casa tiene cinco cuartos, cuatro baños, una cocina y una sala. También hay piscina, caballos y muchos senderos[10]. De aquí me gustan mucho el olor[11] del café, el silencio del campo[12] y los diferentes verdes de las montañas. Ya comprendo por qué miles de personas se dedican al agroturismo en la tierra[13] del café. Ahora estoy descansada[14] y tengo ganas de continuar los conciertos. ¡Gracias, Colombia!

[1]That is why [2]coffee growing [3]enjoying [4]coffee growers [5]served [6]income [7]That is how [8]plantations [9]have been [10]pathways [11]smell [12]countryside [13]land [14]rested

33 ¿Qué recuerdas?

1. ¿Dónde están los miembros del grupo musical La Ola?
2. ¿Qué tipo de turismo practican?
3. ¿Qué es Villa María? ¿Cómo es la casa?
4. ¿Qué hay para hacer en Villa María?
5. Al final, ¿qué tiene ganas de hacer Chantal?

- Make several comparisons between the coffee-growing region of Colombia and the region in the United States in which you live. Which one emphasizes rural life more?

34 Algo personal

1. ¿Adónde te gusta ir de vacaciones? ¿Qué haces allí?
2. Describe tu hotel ideal.
3. ¿Te gustaría hacer agroturismo? ¿Por qué sí o por qué no?

Notes

Students may write to the Colombian embassy or the Organization of American States (OAS) in Washington, D.C., for information regarding tourism in Cali and other Colombian cities. They also may search the Internet, where they will find a number of different sites with information about travel in Colombia. (Give students the addresses listed in the ATE margin on page 261 or refer to the *¡Aventura! 1* ATE Introduction for help with using the Internet.)

Autoevaluación

As a review and self-check, respond to the following:

1. Describe your house.
2. Tell a friend what two different people say, including yourself.
3. Say where you would like to live.
4. Tell how you feel in these situations: it is hot and your mouth is dry, it is noon and you have not eaten, you stayed up too late and it is the next morning.
5. Imagine a classmate needs to borrow a pen and paper. How can you tell the person he or she should borrow the items from someone else because you do not have them?
6. What two things have you learned about Colombia?

Palabras y expresiones

How many of these words and expressions do you recognize?

La casa
el baño
el cuarto
la escalera
el garaje
el patio
la piscina
el piso
la planta
la planta baja
el primer piso
la sala

Para describir
al lado de
cómodo,-a
cuando
desde
donde
el lado
pequeño,-a
poco, -a
por
por la noche
primer

¿Cómo estás?
el calor
el frío
la gana
el hambre *(f.)*
el miedo
la prisa
¿Qué (+ tener)?
la sed
el sueño
tener (calor, frío, ganas de, hambre, miedo de, prisa, sed, sueño)

Otras expresiones
el abrazo
la carta
el dibujo
lo que
me/te/le/nos/les gustaría
la mentira
pedir (perdón, permiso, prestado,-a)
por teléfono
querer decir
querido,-a
la verdad

Verbos
aprender a
correr
decir (+ que)
escribir
gustaría
pedir (i, i)
repetir (i, i)

Estructura

Do you remember the following grammar rules?

Telling what someone says: *decir (i)*

The verb *decir* is irregular in the *yo* form and is a stem-changing verb

decir	
digo	decimos
dices	decís
dice	dicen

Expressing wishes: *querer* and *gustaría*

	querer	+	infinitive	**Quiero** bailar en la fiesta.
me *te* *le* *nos* *os* *les*	*gustaría*	+	infinitive	**Me gustaría** bailar en la fiesta.

Stem-changing verbs: e → i

The verb *pedir* is a stem changing verb except in the *nosotros* and *vosotros* forms

pedir	
pido	pedimos
pides	pedís
pide	piden

Teacher Resources

 Activity 15

 pp. 56, 90

 Juegos

Flash Cards

 **Answers**

Autoevaluación
Possible answers:

1. Mi casa es azul. Tiene dos pisos. Mi cuarto está al lado del baño en el primer piso.
2. Mi mamá dice que debo estudiar más. Yo digo que Colombia es un país interesante.
3. Me gustaría vivir en Cartagena.
4. Tengo sed. Tengo hambre. Tengo sueño.
5. Debes pedir prestados un bolígrafo y papel de otro/otra estudiante porque yo no los tengo.
6. Answers will vary.

 **Activities**

Spanish for Spanish Speakers
Have students write a short composition in Spanish summarizing what they know about Colombia. Expand the activity by having students seek additional information about Colombia at the library or via the Internet.

National Standards

Communication
1.3

Connections
3.2

Notes

Encourage students to find out more about Colombia by going to the following Web sites:

Lonely Planet World Guide
http://www.lonelyplanet.com/destinations/south_america/colombia/
Electronic Embassy
http://www.embassy.org
Organization of American States
http://www.oas.org
General travel information
http://www.expedia.com

Teacher Resources

 *La casa de mis sueños*

Answers

Preparación

1. El dibujo es de una casa.
2. Hay tres cuartos.
3. Hay un piano.
4. Answers will vary.

Activities

Pronunciation (*las letras* g y j)
Review the sound of *g* with students by explaining that when *g* is followed by *a, o* or *u* or by a consonant, the sound is similar to the sound of *g* in the English word **goat**: *ganas, tengo, gustar*. In addition, be sure to point out that students should pronounce both vowels in the letter combinations *ua* and *uo* (*ambiguo, guapo*), whereas the letter combinations *ue* and *ui* should be pronounced as one sound (*Miguel, guitarra*). The letters *j* and *g* sound similar when the *g* is followed by *e* or *i*. The sound is similar to the sound of *wh* in the English word **who** (*baja, relojes, jirafa, dibujo, jueves, Cartagena, página*). **Note:** It may be necessary to explain the meaning of the two example words *ambiguo* (ambiguous) and *jirafa* (giraffe).

National Standards

Connections
3.1

Comparisons
4.1

Tú lees

Estrategia

Using graphics to understand a reading
Look at graphics, artwork, photographs and so forth that accompany what you are reading. The visual support will help you predict what the reading is about.

Preparación

Mira el dibujo para contestar las siguientes preguntas como preparación para la lectura.

1. ¿De qué es el dibujo?
2. ¿Cuántos cuartos hay en el dibujo?
3. ¿Qué hay en la sala?
4. ¿Qué piensas que vas a leer?

La casa de mis sueños

Me llamo Santiago y soy de Caracas. Aquí hay un dibujo de la casa de mis sueños[1]. Claro que[2] el dibujo no es perfecto. En la casa de mis sueños hay tres cuartos y todos son grandes. En la sala hay un piano para tocar música clásica y una biblioteca con todos los libros que me gustan. Al lado de la sala hay un cuarto para ver la televisión y películas en DVD. También hay una computadora con quemador de CDs y muchos videojuegos. Mi cuarto es grande, con una cama también grande, muchos pósters en la pared y un equipo de sonido. El cuarto de mis padres tiene una puerta que abre al patio y al jardín. El patio y el jardín son bonitos, con muchas flores. La flor favorita de mi mamá es el jazmín. Nuestro jardín está rodeado[3] de jazmines. En el jardín hay también una piscina olímpica con un trampolín donde puedo nadar todos los días.

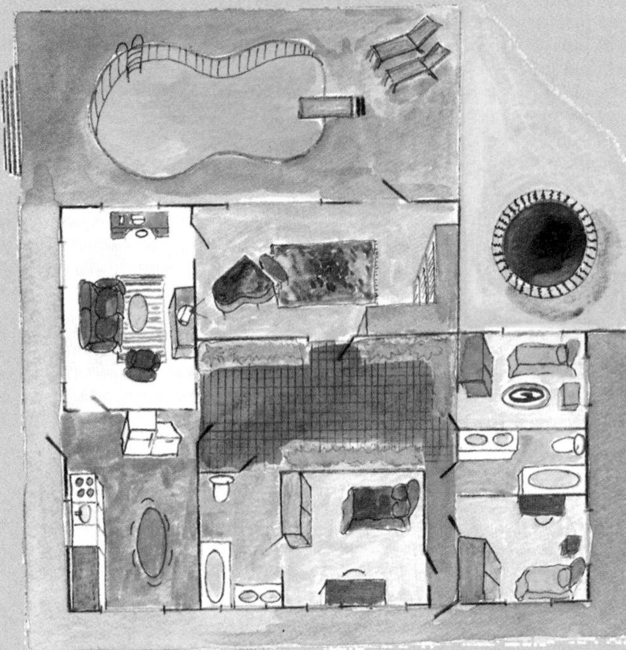

Notes

Complete the *Preparación* with the class. Ask what students think the reading is about.

The reading *La casa de mis sueños* is recorded and available in the Audio Program. You may wish to play the audio to allow students to hear Santiago's description of his dream home.

En la casa de mis sueños, el lugar favorito de mis papás es la cocina. En la cocina papá y mamá preparan comidas exquisitas para cenar. Mi comida favorita es el ajiaco, ¡esa sopa de Colombia tan rica de papas, pollo, maíz, aguacate y crema de leche[4]! Como la cocina es tan grande[5], ellos siempre tienen muchos invitados[6]. La casa tiene muchas ventanas y mucha luz. ¡Quiero algún día construir[7] la casa de mis sueños!

[1]dreams [2]Of course [3]surrounded by [4]potatoes, chicken, corn, avocado and whipping cream [5]so big [6]guests [7]some day build

A ¿Qué recuerdas?

1. ¿De quién es el dibujo de la casa?
2. ¿Cómo son los cuartos de la casa?
3. ¿Qué hay en la biblioteca?
4. ¿Dónde están la computadora y los videojuegos?
5. ¿Qué hay en el cuarto de Santiago?
6. ¿Cuál es el lugar favorito de los padres de Santiago?
7. ¿Qué hacen los padres en la cocina?
8. ¿Qué flores hay en el jardín?
9. ¿Qué es el ajiaco y de dónde es?

B Algo personal

1. ¿Cómo es la casa de tus sueños?
2. ¿En qué son diferentes la casa de los sueños de Santiago y tu casa de los sueños? ¿En qué son similares?
3. ¿Cómo es tu cuarto en la casa de tus sueños? ¿Qué hay en él?
4. ¿Cuál es tu lugar favorito en la casa de tus sueños?

¿Cómo es la casa de tus sueños?

Muchos escalones.

Notes In Spanish-speaking countries a patio is an outdoor area that may have plants and a place where people might sit and chat. However, when talking about homes in the United States, the word *patio* in Spanish can mean **yard**.

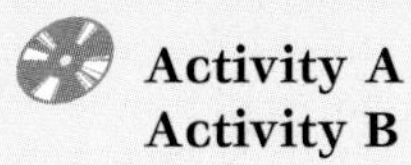

Teacher Resources

Activity A
Activity B

Answers

A 1. Es de Santiago.
2. Son grandes.
3. Los libros que le gustan a Santiago.
4. Están en un cuarto al lado de la sala.
5. Hay una cama grande, muchos pósters en la pared y un equipo de sonido.
6. Su lugar favorito es la cocina.
7. Preparan comidas exquisitas.
8. Hay muchos jazmines.
9. Es una sopa de Colombia.

B Answers will vary.

Activities

Multiple Intelligences (spatial)
Ask for volunteers to create a pop-up version of the home and present it to the class.

Prereading Strategy
Remind students they should not feel they must understand every word to read in Spanish.

Technology
Search the Internet for free floor plans to get ideas for completing a project titled *La casa de mis sueños.*

National Standards	
Communication 1.3	**Comparisons** 4.1, 4.2
Cultures 2.1	
Connections 3.1, 3.2	

Activities

Technology
Locate a Spanish teacher in another school and arrange to have students at each school write e-mail to one another about their homes. As an alternative, try to locate key pals in Colombia or Venezuela and have students in the two countries write to one another about their homes.

Tú escribes

Estrategia

Connecting phrases
Your writing style may seem choppy in Spanish unless you connect your thoughts using transition words like *a causa de* (because of), *como* (since, like, as), *después* (later), *entonces* (then), *pero* (but), *por eso* (therefore), *sin embargo* (however), *también* (also), *y* (and). These words can act like adhesive to bind together the ideas in a paragraph as a connected unit.

First, write several sentences that describe your *casa de tus sueños*. Include information such as what the house looks like, where it is located, what rooms it has, how many windows and doors it has, where rooms are located and any other details you wish to include. Then add transition words to make your sentences flow more smoothly and put the sentences together, one after another in paragraph form, to create a composition. Finally, create a colorful drawing of the house, including details that match your description.

MODELO La casa de mis sueños está en una playa en América del Sur. Es muy grande. Tiene muchos cuartos y jardines....

La casa de mis sueños está en la playa.

National Standards

Communication
1.3

Communities
5.1

Notes

Review the contents of the *Estrategia* with the class. Then give several examples of sentences that contain connecting words before assigning the writing.

Consider having students pair up to review one another's sentences before having them finalize their compositions.

Ask individuals if it is all right to display their composition for others in the class to read.

Proyectos adicionales

A Conexión con la tecnología

Write a short e-mail in Spanish to someone you know about your home and family. Use Santiago's letter (see p. 244) as a model, if necessary.

B Conexión cultural

Imagine you are traveling with your family to Venezuela and Colombia on vacation and your parents have asked you to make suggestions about what to see and do. Use the library or the Internet to investigate cities you might visit. Then create a travel itinerary offering suggestions for the trip to both countries. Consider including the following in your list of recommendations: cities to visit, tourist attractions, your recommendation for the best time to visit South America and any other information you can find that may be of use during the trip.

Castillo de San Felipe, Cartagena.

C Comparando

Working in pairs, talk about what you know about housing and home life in the United States and in Spanish-speaking parts of the world such as Venezuela, Colombia, Puerto Rico and the Dominican Republic. Then make a side-by-side comparison listing at least five similarities or differences.

D ¡A escribir!

Help Santiago's parents write back to him (see p. 244). Include the following information: They are happy to hear from their dear son; they know that he is far from home in Caracas, but not far from his family; they want to see the photos of the trip to Cartagena. Include any other details you wish. Remember to include the city and the date and use appropriate greetings and farewells.

Notes

Cultures. Note for students that in Latin America, many middle- and upper-class families traditionally employ a maid to assist with household chores.

Two well-known literary figures from Venezuela are Rómulo Gallegos, author of *Doña Bárbara* and former president of Venezuela, and Arturo Uslar Pietri, critic, short-story writer and novelist. Pietri's best-known work is *Las lanzas coloradas*. In 1990 he received the *Príncipe de Asturias* prize, one of the most important literary prizes in the Hispanic world.

One of Colombia's most famous citizens is Gabriel García Márquez, winner of the Nobel Prize in Literature.

Teacher Resources

p. 72

Answers

A Creative self-expression.
B Creative problem solving.
C Creative self-expression.
D Creative self-expression.

Activities

Critical Thinking

One of the many fascinating results of European exploration was the food exchange that brought new foods and animals to the Americas and took others to Europe. For example, the Spaniards brought cattle and spices to the Americas and returned with many foods new to Europe, such as tomatoes and potatoes. Ask students to research this food exchange and consider its impact on the diets of people around the world.

Multiple Intelligences (spatial)

Invite students to make a collage in which they profile a Spanish-speaking country of special interest. Good sources of information include sites on the Internet and materials provided by national tourism offices.

National Standards	
Communication 1.1	**Comparisons** 4.1, 4.2
Cultures 2.1, 2.2	
Connections 3.1, 3.2	

Teacher Resources

 *Trabalenguas*

 Episode 6, DVD 1, Track 65

Answers

Resolviendo el misterio

1. José finds letters and a woman's photograph.
2. Answers will vary.
3. Answers will vary.

Activities

Connections

In groups of four, have students research the life of Simón Bolívar. Then have them write a simple dialog, design a piece of art or prepare some other artistic reflection of his life and present it to the class.

Language through Action

Bring in table place settings and food items (or magazine pictures of these items). Then use the *tú* and *Uds.* commands of *pasar, comer, tomar* and other verbs, along with the food and table vocabulary from this lesson.

Spanish for Spanish Speakers

Have students research and write about Rómulo Gallegos, Arturo Uslar Pietri or Gabriel García Márquez.

Trabalenguas

An artist drew one picture to illustrate the *Trabalenguas*. Ask students to draw the *Trabalenguas* using an individual image for each piece of the poem. Students should recite the poem using only their drawings as a prompt.

National Standards
Communication 1.3
Cultures 2.2
Connections 3.1

Now that I have completed this chapter, I can...	Go to these pages for help:
identify items in the kitchen and at the dinner table.	226
express obligations, wishes and preferences.	230
talk about everyday activities.	230
state an opinion.	231
discuss food and table items.	234
point out people and things.	238
describe a household.	244
tell what someone says.	248
say how someone is doing.	252
I can also...	
talk about products and foods from Venezuela and Colombia.	229, 247
discuss home life in Venezuela and Colombia.	237, 255
describe my home.	244
recognize words in context.	251
recognize when to use *pedir* or *preguntar*.	257
plan a trip to Venezuela or Colombia.	265

Trabalenguas

La casa está en la plaza, en la casa hay un cuarto, dentro del cuarto hay un piso, encima del piso hay una mesa, encima de la mesa hay una jaula, dentro de la jaula hay un loro que canta y dice: de loro en jaula, jaula en mesa, mesa en piso, piso en cuarto, cuarto en casa, casa en la plaza.

Resolviendo el misterio

After watching Episode 6 of *El cuarto misterioso*, answer the following questions.

1. What surprised José in this episode?
2. Do you think that it was a good idea for Conchita to get into the car with Rafael?
3. Why do you think Rafael is interested in Conchita?

Notes

Loose translation of the *Trabalenguas*: The house is on the square, in the house there is a room, in the room there is a floor, on the floor there is a table, on the table there is a bird cage, in the bird cage there is a parrot who sings and says: from parrot to bird cage, bird cage to table, table to floor, floor to room, room to house, house to the square.

Although large earthquakes (*terremotos*) are not common in Colombia, they do sometimes occur. In January of 1999, an earthquake that measured 6.0 on the Richter scale destroyed the cities of Pereira and Armenia and several villages in the coffee-producing region of Colombia. The earthquake killed nearly 1,000 people.

Vocabulario

Go online EMCLanguages.net

el **abrazo** hug *6B*
el **aceite** oil *6A*
al lado de next to, beside *6B*
allá over there *6A*
aprender to learn *6B*
aquel, aquella (aquellos, aquellas) that, (those) far away *6A*
ayudar to help *6A*
el **azúcar** sugar *6A*
el **baño** bathroom *6B*
el **calor** heat *6B*
la **carta** letter *6B*
cerrar (ie) to close *6A*
la **cocina** kitchen *6A*
el **comedor** dining room *6A*
cómodo,-a comfortable *6B*
correr to run *6B*
la **cosa** thing *6A*
cuando when *6B*
el **cuarto** room, bedroom *6B*
los **cubiertos** silverware *6A*
la **cuchara** spoon *6A*
la **cucharita** teaspoon *6A*
el **cuchillo** knife *6A*
de todos los días everyday *6A*
deber should, to have to, must, ought *6A*
decir *(+ que)* to tell, to say *6B*
desde since, from *6B*
después afterwards, later, then *6A*
el **dibujo** drawing, sketch *6B*
dónde where *6B*
e and *(used before a word beginning with* i *or* hi*)* *6B*
empezar (ie) to begin, to start *6A*
encender (ie) to light, to turn on *(a light)* *6A*
entonces then *6A*
la **escalera** stairway, stairs *6B*
escribir to write *6B*
ese, esa (esos, esas) that (those) *6A*
especial special *6A*
este, esta (estos, estas) this (these) *6A*
la **estufa** stove *6A*
el **fregadero** sink *6A*
el **frío** cold *6B*
la **gana** desire *6B*
el **garaje** garage 6B
gustaría would like 6B
el **hambre** *(f.)* hunger *6B*
el **horno microondas** microwave oven *6A*
el **lado** side *6B*
la **lámpara** lamp *6A*
el **lavaplatos** dishwasher *6A*
lo que what, that which *6B*
la **luz** light *6A*
el **mantel** tablecloth *6A*
la **mantequilla** butter *6A*
me/te/le/nos/les gustaría I/you/he/she/it/we/they would like *6B*
la **mentira** lie *6B*
la **mesa** table *6A*
el **miedo** fear *6B*
otra vez again, another time *6A*
el **pan** bread *6A*
pásame pass me *6A*
el **patio** courtyard, patio, yard *6B*
pedir (i, i) to ask for, to order, to request; *pedir perdón* to say you are sorry; *pedir permiso (para)* to ask for permission (to do something); *pedir prestado,-a* to borrow *6B*
pensar (ie) to think, to intend, to plan *6A*
pensar de/en/que to think about *6A*
pequeño,-a small *6B*
el **permiso** permission, permit *6B*
la **pimienta** pepper (seasoning) *6A*
la **piscina** swimming pool *6B*
el **piso** floor *6B*
la **planta** plant *6B*
la **planta baja** ground floor *6B*
el **plato** dish, plate *6A*
el **plato de sopa** soup bowl *6A*
poco,-a not very, little *6B*
poner to put, to place *6A*
poner la mesa to set the table *6A*
por through, by *6B*
por la noche at night *6B*
por teléfono by phone *6B*
el **postre** dessert *6A*
preferir (ie) to prefer *6A*
primer first *6B*
el **primer piso** first floor *6B*
la **prisa** rush, hurry, haste *6B*
¿Qué *(+ tener)?* What is wrong (with someone) *6B*
querer (ie) to love, to want, to like *6A*
querer decir to mean *6B*
querido,-a dear *6B*
el **refrigerador** refrigerator *6A*
repetir (i, i) to repeat *6B*
la **sal** salt *6A*
la **sala** living room *6B*
la **sed** thirst *6B*
sentir (ie) to be sorry, to feel sorry, to regret *6A*
la **servilleta** napkin *6A*
la **sopa** soup *6A*
el **sueño** sleep *6B*
la **taza** cup *6A*
el **tenedor** fork *6A*
tener (calor, frío, hambre, miedo de, prisa, sed, sueño) to be (hot, cold, hungry, afraid, in a hurry, thirsty, sleepy) *6B*
tener ganas de to feel like *6B*
tener que to have to *6A*
u or *(used before a word that starts with* o *or* ho*)* *6B*
un poco (de) a little (bit) *6A*
el **vaso** glass *6A*
la **verdad** truth *6B*
viajar to travel *6A*
ya already *6A*

Notes

Other ways to say *la estufa* include *la hornilla* and *el fogón*. In some countries people refer to the stove as *la cocina.*

El refrigerador is also called *el frigorífico*, although some people prefer to use the term *la nevera,* which is equivalent to icebox.

Teacher Resources

Las aventuras de la familia Miranda

Repaso

¡*Aventureros!*, Ch. 6

Internet Activities

i-Culture

Activities

Critical Listening

Pronounce the following carefully, having students say the sentence several times before writing what they hear: *Zoraida, Susana y yo vamos a hacer un mapa de Venezuela con la tiza en la pizarra.* Ask students if they understand the meaning of the sentence. Pronunciation (*las letras c, s* y *z*) Review the pronunciation of the letters *c, s* and *z* with students by explaining that the letter *c* (followed by *e* or *i*), the letter *s* and the letter *z* are pronounced like the **s** in the English word Sally, except in most of Spain, where *c* and *z* followed by *e* or *i* are pronounced like **th** in the English word **thin**. Your students may find it interesting to hear you model this difference in pronunciation.

National Standards

Communication
1.2

Comparisons
4.1

Teacher Resources

 *Capítulo 7*

TPRS *Capítulo 7*

 Episode 7, DVD 2, Track 7

Answers

El cuarto misterioso

1. Ana está en un gimnasio.
2. Las respuestas variarán pero podrían incluir comer bien, tomar mucho agua, descansar y hacer ejercicios.
3. Probablemente el fútbol, el básquetbol y el béisbol son deportes populares en la escuela de José.

Activities

Prior Knowledge

Ask students to review the chapter objectives. Ask students questions such as: When was the last time you participated in a race? In what place did you finish? What can you do that no one else can do? What is your favorite leisure-time activity? How much time do you spend playing video games every day? What is your favorite sport? What is your favorite season? Why?

Expansion

At the end of the unit, make a chart that summarizes the favorite activities, sports and seasons of class members.

National Standards
Cultures 2.2
Connections 3.1
Communities 5.1

CAPÍTULO 7

El tiempo libre

El cuarto misterioso

Contesta las siguientes preguntas sobre *Episodio 7–Deportes*.

1. ¿Dónde está Ana?
2. ¿Qué pueden hacer los jóvenes para estar en buena condición física?
3. ¿Qué deportes son populares en la escuela de José?

Francisco ve que Ana es muy fuerte mientras ella hace ejercicios en el gimnasio.

Objetivos

- talk about **leisure time activities**
- discuss **sports**
- say what **someone can do**
- discuss **length of time**
- describe **what is happening**
- talk about the **seasons** and **weather**
- indicate **order**

Notes A checklist of these objectives, along with additional functions, appears on page 314 so students can evaluate their own progress.

Activities

Expansion
Ask students what they know about Argentina and Chile. Ask for two volunteers to go to the board. One student should list what students know about Argentina and the other student should write down what classmates say about Chile. After five or six points are listed for each country, have students decide how the countries are similar and how they are different. (Start the list by stating that both are countries in South America.)

Contexto cultural

Argentina
Nombre oficial: República Argentina
Población: 41.769.000
Capital: Buenos Aires
Ciudades importantes: Córdoba, Mendoza, San Juan
Unidad monetaria: el peso
Fiesta nacional: 9 de julio, Proclamación de la Independencia
Gente famosa: Jorge Luis Borges (escritor); Evita Perón (líder popular)

Chile
Nombre oficial: República de Chile
Población: 16.888.000
Capital: Santiago de Chile
Ciudades importantes: Valparaíso, Viña del Mar
Unidad monetaria: el peso
Fiesta nacional: 18 de septiembre, Día de la Independencia
Gente famosa: Pablo Neruda, Isabel Allende, Gabriela Mistral (escritores)

Notes The cultural focus of this chapter is on the South American countries of Argentina and Chile. Students will be learning to discuss what people do in their free time, in particular what people in Argentina and Chile do during their free time.

National Standards
Cultures 2.1
Connections 3.1
Comparisons 4.1

Teacher Resources

 Vocabulario I
Los pasatiempos

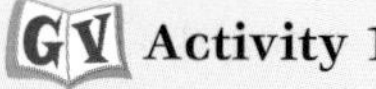

 Activity 1

Content reviewed in *Lección A*

- telling time
- days of the week
- direct object pronouns
- the verb estar

Activities

Critical Thinking

Before playing the audio for *Vocabulario I*, ask students if they can guess who the people are. Then ask what they think the boy wants to watch and what the girl wants to watch. Finally, ask students if they have ever been in a similar situation.

National Standards

Connections
3.1

Comparisons
4.1

Lección A Vocabulario I
Los pasatiempos

Arge

¿Cuándo vas a hacer las tareas?

Todavía no. Esta noche, después del partido.

¿No recuerdas que quiero ver mi programa favorito? Vuelvo en cinco minutos.

Sí, sí, está bien.

el televisor

A Graciela le gusta ver la telenovela *Toda Una Vida* y ahora no puede. A Graciela le gustaría tener un televisor en su cuarto pero cuestan mucho. El papá de Graciela le va a dar un televisor para su cumpleaños.

Notes The word *dar* is presented in *Lección A* in its infinitive form only. The present tense of *dar* is taught in *Lección B*.

Explain to the class that the word *televisor* refers specifically to the television set. Thus, native Spanish speakers say *poner el televisor* but *ver televisión*.

Point out that students may hear *encender* or *prender* used as they travel in some countries instead of *poner* to mean to turn on a light or appliance.

Telenovelas are very popular in Hispanic countries.

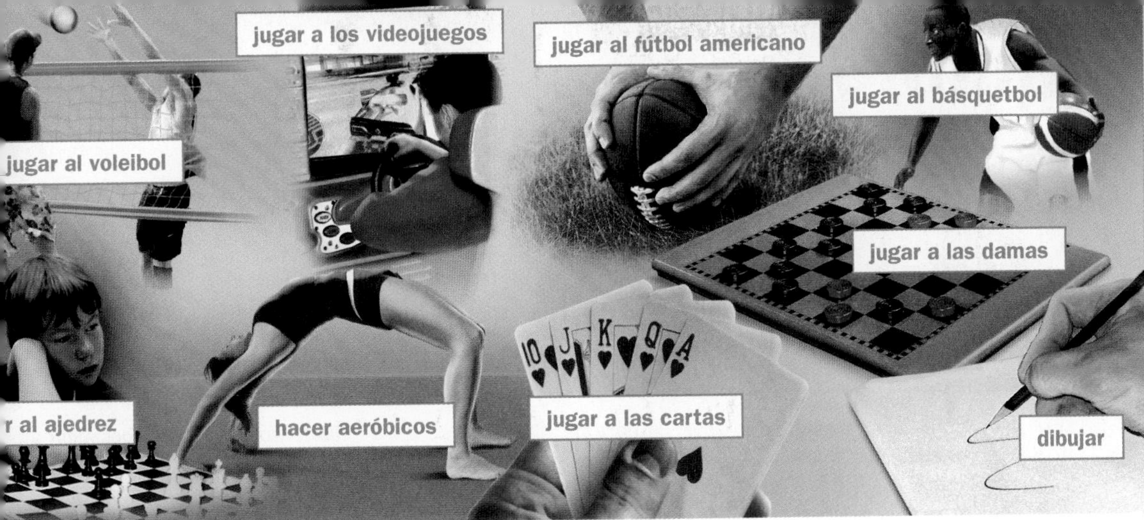

1 ¿Qué actividad es?

Identifica la actividad que oyes.

A

B

C

D

E

F

2 ¡Yo sé lo que vas a hacer!

Create a list of at least ten leisure activities. Then, working in small groups, take turns playing charades to act out activities on your list. The winner is the person who first says ¡*Yo sé lo que vas a hacer!*

Notes Point out for students that the word **volleyball** has several variations in Spanish, the most common being *voleibol* and *volibol*.

Ask your students if they have ever seen a soap opera in Spanish. Spanish-language television channels in the United States present soap operas primarily from Mexico and Venezuela.

Teacher Resources

 Activity 1

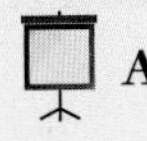 Activities 47–48

 Activities 1–2

 Activities 2–3

 p. 102

 p. 27

 Activity 1

 Activity 1

Answers

1 1. C
2. A
3. B
4. D
5. E
6. F

2 Creative self-expression.

Activities

TPR

In advance, write on separate pieces of paper the Spanish terms for the pastimes shown on page 271. Then have students select one of the pieces of paper at random. Call on several students to act out the expressions while classmates guess what the expressions are in Spanish.

Communication
1.1, 1.2

Connections
3.1

Communities
5.1

Teacher Resources

Diálogo I
¿No quieres jugar al ajedrez?
Activity 3
Activity 4
Activity 5

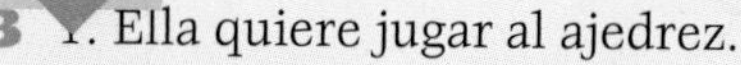

Answers

3 1. Ella quiere jugar al ajedrez.
2. Ve su telenovela favorita.
3. Va a jugar el equipo de Argentina.
4. Va a ver fútbol.
5. Su vida ahora es ver televisión y jugar al fútbol.

4 Answers will vary.

5 1. Falso.; 2. Cierto.; 3. Cierto.; 4. Falso.; 5. Falso.

Activities

Expansion
Additional questions *(Algo personal): ¿Hay telenovelas en español en tu ciudad? ¿Cómo se llaman?; ¿Cómo se llama tu programa favorito? ¿A qué hora es el programa?; ¿Te gusta ver deportes en la televisión?*

Prereading Strategy
Prepare students for the reading by having them cover up the dialog with one hand and look at the photographs. Then ask them to imagine where the conversation takes place and what the people are saying to one another. Finally, have students scan the dialog to find cognates and other words they recognize.

National Standards
Communication 1.1, 1.2
Cultures 2.1
Connections 3.1

Diálogo I ¿No quieres jugar al ajedrez?

LUZ: ¿No quieres jugar al ajedrez?
HUGO: Sí, pero después de este programa.
LUZ: ¿Qué programa es?
HUGO: Es mi telenovela favorita.

LUZ: ¿Ahora sí?
HUGO: ¿Por qué no vienes en dos horas?
LUZ: ¿Cómo? ¿No vamos a jugar al ajedrez?
HUGO: Es que el equipo de Argentina va a jugar ahora.

LUZ: ¡Veo que ya no sabes jugar al ajedrez!
HUGO: Sí, ya no recuerdo cómo jugar.
LUZ: ¡Claro! Tu vida ahora es ver televisión.
HUGO: No. ¡Mi vida ahora es ver televisión y jugar al fútbol!

3 ¿Qué recuerdas?

1. ¿A qué quiere jugar Luz?
2. ¿Qué programa ve Hugo?
3. ¿Qué equipo va a jugar?
4. ¿Qué va a ver Hugo?
5. ¿Cómo es ahora la vida de Hugo?

4 Algo personal

1. ¿Sabes jugar al fútbol?
2. ¿Te gusta jugar al ajedrez?
3. ¿Qué vas a hacer esta noche?
4. ¿Te gusta ver televisión?

5 ¿Qué comprendiste?

Di si los que oyes es cierto o falso, según el diálogo *¿No quieres jugar al ajedrez?*

¡Extra!

La fiebre del gol

It is easy to understand why Hugo is distracted as he talks with Luz. For many people, soccer *(el fútbol)* is more than just a simple pastime in Argentina and throughout the Spanish-speaking world. During the World Cup *(la Copa Mundial)* fans of all ages follow the action and nearly everyone has *la fiebre del gol* (goal fever).

¿Sabes jugar al ajedrez?

Notes

La fiebre del gol is at its peak during *la Copa Mundial de Fútbol* (World Cup), which is held every four years. Ask if students are able to name recent World Cup winners or host countries.

The *¡Aventura! 1* Video/DVD Program uses a soap opera format and was filmed on location by professional actors. Episodes were written to reflect the content of corresponding chapters in the textbook. Students will enjoy meeting the characters and following them through the challenges they face in everyday life.

Cultura viva

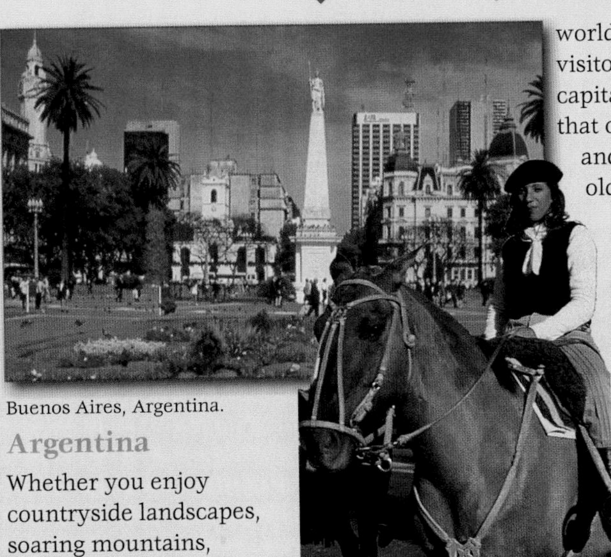

Buenos Aires, Argentina.

Una gaucha.

Argentina

Whether you enjoy countryside landscapes, soaring mountains, beautiful beaches or the hustle and bustle of modern city life, Argentina has it all. As the largest Spanish-speaking country in the world, the southernmost tip of Argentina begins near the frigid South Pole and extends north to the tropics of central South America. The plains of Patagonia in the south are the heart of the sheep-raising industry. In the central plains *(las pampas)*, cowboys known as *gauchos* tend herds of cattle on large ranches called *estancias*. (Argentina produces beef that is sold and shipped throughout the world.) In addition, world-class ski resorts, such as Bariloche, draw visitors from many countries. Argentina's capital, Buenos Aires, is a vibrant, modern city that combines skyscrapers *(rascacielos)*, plazas and parks, outstanding food and interesting old buildings into what has been called the "Paris of the Spanish-speaking world."

While visiting Argentina, you may find yourself alone atop a mountain *(Aconcagua)* or in a crowded cafe. Argentina's population includes descendants from large numbers of people from Spain, Italy, Poland, Germany, Great Britain and Japan. Wondering what to do? Ski the famous slopes of the *Andes*, dance the tango in the colorful neighborhood called *La Boca*, participate in the national sport—*el fútbol* or sit back and gaze at the breathtaking *Iguazú* waterfalls. And before you leave, try grilled beef *(carne a la parrilla)* in one of the capital's many fine restaurants or have a seat and sip a wonderful tea-like hot drink called *mate*.

Las cascadas de Iguazú.

6 Argentina

¿Cierto o falso?

1. Hay playas bonitas en la Argentina.
2. El país más grande de habla hispana es Ecuador.
3. Los gauchos viven en grandes estancias de las pampas.
4. Bariloche es la capital de la Argentina.
5. Hay muchas personas en la Argentina de Italia y Polonia.
6. El baile más famoso de la Argentina es el tango.
7. *Mate* es una ciudad en la Argentina.
8. El deporte nacional de la Argentina es el fútbol.

Teacher Resources

 Activity 6

 Activity 3

 p. 95

 Activity 2

Answers

6
1. Cierto.
2. Falso.
3. Cierto.
4. Falso.
5. Cierto.
6. Cierto.
7. Falso.
8. Cierto.

Activities

Critical Listening

Explain to the class that the term *rascacielos* (skyscraper) comes from a combination of the words *rascar* and *cielos*. Other such combinations exist in both Spanish and English. Ask students to listen to the following words and try to identify their English equivalents: *telenovela, aeropuerto, paraguas, parabrisas, quitasol, quitanieves.*

Cultures
2.1, 2.2

Connections
3.1

Comparisons
4.2

Notes

The *gauchos* of Argentina have a rich and colorful history and can be compared in many ways to the cowboys of the United States. Their main tool is the *bola*, a type of sling consisting of heavy weights tied to the ends of a leather cord. It is thrown to entangle the legs of cattle or game.

Argentina produces a lot of beef, much of which is exported.

Aconcagua is the highest mountain peak in the Western Hemisphere.

The *tango* is discussed in greater detail later in this lesson.

Teacher Resources

 Activity 7

 Activities 4–7

 Activities 4–6

 Activity 3

 Activity 2

Answers

7 1. Papá puede comprar....
2. Yo puedo buscar....
3. Mi mamá puede hacer....
4. Tú puedes poner....
5. Nosotros podemos preparar....
6. Mis hermanos pueden poner....

8 1. recuerdo; 2. juega; 3. puede; 4. podemos; 5. cuestan; 6. vuelve; 7. puede; 8. juego

Activities

Language through Action
Ask students to write out the conjugation of the present tense of either *poder* or *jugar*. Then have them draw a line around the forms that change and they will see the shape of a boot. Remind the class that they learned other verbs that follow a similar shoe pattern in *Capítulo 6* (*pensar, cerrar, empezar, preferir, querer, sentir*).

Students with Special Needs
Give a second model sentence for activity 7.

National Standards
Connections 3.1
Comparisons 4.1

Idioma

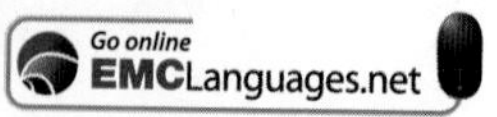

Estructura

Stem-changing verbs: *o* → *ue* and *u* → *ue*

Some verbs require the change *o* → *ue (poder)* or *u* → *ue (jugar)* in all forms of their present-tense stem except for *nosotros* and *vosotros*. These stem changes do not interfere with regular verb endings.

poder	
puedo	podemos
puedes	podéis
puede	**pue**den

jugar	
juego	jugamos
juegas	jugáis
juega	**jue**gan

Other *o* → *ue* stem-changing verbs include *costar (ue)*, *recordar (ue)* and *volver (ue)*.

Práctica

7 Todos quieren ayudar 

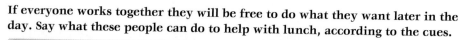

If everyone works together they will be free to do what they want later in the day. Say what these people can do to help with lunch, according to the cues.

MODELO Marta (buscar los platos)
Marta puede buscar los platos.

1. papá (comprar leche y pan)
2. yo (buscar los cubiertos)
3. mi mamá (hacer el almuerzo)
4. tú (poner la mesa)
5. nosotros (preparar un postre)
6. mis hermanos (poner los platos sucios en el lavaplatos)

¿Quién puede buscar los platos?

8 El televisor

Completa el siguiente párrafo con la forma apropiada de uno de los siguientes verbos: *poder, costar, volver, jugar, recordar*.

Yo siempre (1) cuando (2) el equipo de Argentina. Mi papá y yo vemos el partido por televisión. A mi hermana no le gusta el fútbol pero ella (3) leer o salir con sus amigos. No (4) tener otro televisor porque (5) mucho y nuestra casa no es grande. Mi hermana (6) a las cuatro, ella (7) ver su telenovela y entonces yo (8) al fútbol con mis amigos en el parque.

Notes The verbs *poder* and *recordar* can be followed by an infinitive in double-verb constructions: *puedo ir con ella a la tienda; recuerda comprar un vestido azul.*

The preposition *a* typically follows the verb *jugar* and precedes the name of a sport or game: *jugar al fútbol* and *jugar a las cartas.*

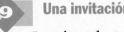

9 Una invitación

In pairs, take turns inviting one another to do the indicated activities. Answer by either refusing or accepting the invitation, giving an excuse if you refuse or changing the suggested time if you accept.

MODELO jugar al básquetbol
A: ¿Puedes jugar al básquetbol hoy?
B: Lo siento, pero no puedo. Es muy tarde.

1. jugar a los videojuegos esta tarde
2. ver mis fotos de Chile ahora
3. ir al cine pasado mañana
4. jugar al fútbol americano el sábado
5. jugar al voleibol a las 6:30
6. hacer aeróbicos mañana

10 ¿Cuándo vuelven?

In pairs, talk about when these people will be returning from the places mentioned.

MODELO Eva / la casa de Gloria PM 7:00
A: ¿A qué hora vuelve Eva de la casa de Gloria?
B: Eva vuelve de la casa de Gloria a las siete.

1. Ana y Luz / la piscina 

2. tú y yo / la tienda 

3. tú / el cine 

4. Esteban / el partido 

Comunicación

11 ¿A qué juegan?

With a classmate, talk about what these people are doing.

1 

2 

3 

4 

12 Los pasatiempos

In small groups, ask one another about your favorite pastimes *(pasatiempos)*. Start with the activities shown in *Vocabulario I*, taking notes as you talk. Then choose one member of the group to report the information to the class.

MODELO **A:** ¿Juegas al fútbol?
B: Sí, (No, no) juego al fútbol. Es mi pasatiempo favorito. ¿Y tú?

Teacher Resources

Activity 9

Answers

9 Answers will vary.

10 1. ¿...vuelven ... de la piscina...?/...vuelven ... a las siete menos veinte.
2. ¿...volvemos ... de la tienda?/...volvemos ... a la una y veinticinco.
3. ¿...vuelves ... del colegio?/... vuelvo ... a las dos menos diez.
4. ¿...vuelve...?/...vuelve ... a las nueve y media.

11 Possible answers:
1. Los chicos juegan al fútbol americano.
2. Ellas juegan a las cartas.
3. Ella juega al básquetbol.
4. Ellos juegan al ajedrez.

12 Creative self-expression.

Activities

Expansion
Practice the stem-changing verbs by asking the following personalized questions: *¿Quién es tu atleta favorito/a y qué deporte juega?; ¿Cuánto cuesta un televisor nuevo? ¿Lo puedes comprar?; ¿Cuánto cuesta una bicicleta nueva? ¿La puedes comprar?; En un día normal, ¿a qué hora vuelves a casa (después del colegio)?; ¿Cuándo vuelves tarde a casa?*

Communication
1.1, 1.3

Notes Tell students that many Spanish-speaking natives drop the *al, a la, a las* and *a los* after *jugar* when naming a sport or game they play: *juego fútbol.* This practice is becoming common in speech.

Jugar is the only verb in Spanish that changes *u* to *ue* as part of a regular pattern.

Inform students whether you will be selecting the person to present the information to the class for activity 12 or whether students may choose their own group representative.

Teacher Resources

 **Vocabulario II**
El tiempo libre

 **Activity 49**

 **Activities 8–9**

 **Activities 7–8**

 **p. 74**

 **Activity 4**

 **Activity 3**

Activities

Critical Thinking
Before playing the audio for *Vocabulario II*, ask students questions about the scene: Who are the people? What do students think the boy is doing? What is the man saying? What are the girls doing? What do they want to do in the afternoon?

National Standards

Communication
1.1

Vocabulario II
El tiempo libre

Es casi mediodía. ¿Cuánto tiempo hace que estás viendo televisión?

Natalia tiene una lista de películas nuevas. Ella no quiere ver las mism películas del mes pasado.

Bueno, parece casi un siglo. Debes apagar el televisor ahora.

¿Cuándo vamos a alquilar la película?

Estupendo. ¿Cuándo jugamos a las damas?

Por la tarde.

Ahora mismo.

Hace una hora.

Sí, sí, en un segundo lo voy a apagar.

Pascual

el control remoto

Pascual está durmiendo.
Mario le permite a Pascual dormir a su lad

Notes

As you review *Vocabulario I*, explain that centuries are expressed with cardinal numbers in Spanish and that years cannot be abbreviated in spoken Spanish as they are in English. For example, the **21st century** would be *el siglo veintiuno* and **2005** would be *dos mil cinco*.

Help students with the meaning of the sentences in the speech bubbles and in the boxes.

Note the pause word *Bueno* when the father talks. Ask students if they remember any other pause words he could have used.

El tiempo libre

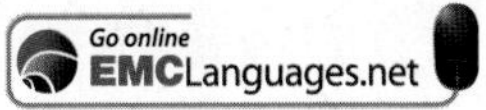

Selecciona la ilustración que corresponde con lo que oyes.

A

B

Tienda de video ABC
Nuevas películas:
· Historia de amor
· El hombre araña V
· El cuarto misterioso

C

D

14 ¿Cuánto tiempo hay en...?

Contesta las siguientes preguntas.

1. ¿Cuántas semanas hay en un año?
2. ¿Cuántos años hay en un siglo?
3. ¿Cuántas horas hay en un día?
4. ¿Cuántos cuartos de hora hay en una hora?
5. ¿Cuántos segundos hay en un minuto?
6. ¿Cuántos minutos hay en una hora?
7. ¿Cuántos segundos hay en una hora?
8. ¿Cuántas horas hay en una semana?

¿Cuántos minutos hay en una hora?

Notes

Activity 13 is intended for listening comprehension practice. Play the audio of the activity or use the transcript that appears in the ATE Introduction if you prefer to read the activity yourself.

Before assigning activity 13, point out the symbols AM and PM in the two clocks.

You may want to have students complete activity 14 working in pairs.

Teacher Resources

Activity 13
Activity 14

Answers

13
1. D
2. A
3. B
4. C

14
1. Hay cincuenta y dos semanas en un año.
2. Hay cien años en un siglo.
3. Hay veinticuatro horas en un día.
4. Hay cuatro cuartos de hora en una hora.
5. Hay sesenta segundos en un minuto.
6. Hay sesenta minutos en una hora.
7. Hay 3.600 segundos en una hora.
8. Hay ciento sesenta y ocho horas en una semana.

Activities

Critical Thinking

Additional questions: *¿Cuántos minutos hay en un cuarto de hora?; ¿Cuántos días hay en una semana? ¿en tres semanas?; ¿Cuántos minutos hay en cuatro horas y media?; ¿Cuántos segundos hay en cuarenta y siete minutos?; ¿Cuántos meses hay en siete años?; ¿Cuántos meses hay en dos siglos?; ¿Cuántos meses hay en siete siglos?*

National Standards

Communication
1.1, 1.2

Connections
3.1

Teacher Resources

 Diálogo II
Quiero alquilar una película
Activity 15
Activity 16
Activity 17

Answers

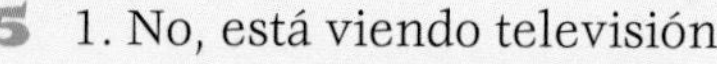

15 1. No, está viendo televisión.
2. Hugo quiere ir a alquilar una película.
3. Quiere ir ahora mismo. Antes de comer.
4. Hace mucho tiempo. Casi dos meses.

16 Answers will vary.

17 Play a portion of the recorded dialog as students write what they hear. As an alternative, you may choose to read the selection yourself. Check the accuracy of student dictations.

Activities

Critical Listening

Use a newspaper published in Spanish or Internet resources to obtain the Spanish titles of popular films made in the United States. Read the titles to the class and ask them to identify the name of each film in English.

Expansion

Additional questions *(Algo personal): ¿Te gusta ver películas por la tarde o por la noche en casa?; ¿Vas al cine también? ¿Cuándo vas?; ¿Te gustan más las películas nuevas o las películas viejas?*

National Standards

Communication
1.1, 1.2

Connections
3.1, 3.2

Diálogo II Quiero alquilar una película

HUGO: ¿Estás durmiendo?
LUZ: No. Estoy viendo televisión. ¿Por qué?
HUGO: Porque quiero ir a alquilar una película.

LUZ: ¿Ahora mismo?
HUGO: Sí, quiero ir antes de comer. ¿Quieres ir?
LUZ: Un segundo.... Ya voy.

LUZ: No quiero ver las mismas películas otra vez.
HUGO: ¿Cuánto tiempo hace que no ves una película?
LUZ: ¡Uy! Hace mucho tiempo. Casi dos meses.
HUGO: ¡Entonces no vas a ver las mismas películas!

15 ¿Qué recuerdas?

1. ¿Está Luz durmiendo?
2. ¿Qué quiere hacer Hugo?
3. ¿Cuándo quiere ir Hugo?
4. ¿Cuánto tiempo hace que Luz no ve una película?

16 Algo personal

1. ¿Cuánto tiempo hace que no alquilas una película?
2. ¿Haces una lista de películas antes de ir a alquilar una?
3. ¿Cuánto tiempo hace que no ves una película?
4. ¿Por cuánto tiempo ves televisión en una semana?
5. ¿Cuánto tiempo libre tienes en una semana? ¿Qué haces?

17 Dictado

Escucha la información y escribe lo que oyes.

¿Cuánto tiempo hace que no alquilas una película?

Notes Vary how you assign the *¿Qué recuerdas?* and *Algo personal* activities. For example, you may wish to have students listen to the audio of the activity and answer orally; you may decide to have students listen to the audio and then write their answers; or you may choose to have students write their answers and then do the activities in class orally.

Connections. Activity 18 makes the cross-curricular connection to the arts.

Cultura viva II

Che, bailá conmigo...

In the world of dance and music, *tango* is synonymous with Argentina, and especially Buenos Aires. This well-known song was born a century ago near the docks of the capital in the neighborhood known as *La Boca*. While there, if you look carefully, you will see a street sign with the name *Caminito* that denotes the short dead-end street *(callejuela)*. This street's name has its origins in one of Carlos Gardel's most famous tangos. Carlos Gardel is considered the father of the tango and he is revered in Argentina still today, decades after his death. From the docks in *La Boca*, the *tango* spread throughout the Americas to Europe and, today, is popular in ballrooms throughout the world.

Bailamos el tango.

El Caminito, una callejuela en La Boca, Buenos Aires.

El tango es de la Argentina.

18 Conexiones con otras disciplinas: baile y música

Prepare a project on the tango, choosing from one of the following options or making up your own:

- Search the word *tango* on the Internet or by looking up the words *Argentina* and *tango* in an encyclopedia at the library and write a summary of your findings.
- Locate someone who teaches the tango and invite the person to speak or demonstrate the tango for the class.
- Attend tango classes at a local community center or at a local dance studio and demonstrate the dance for the class.
- Play a tango for the class, comparing it to another musical style.

Teacher Resources

Activity 4

Answers

18 Creative self-expression.

Activities

Multiple Intelligences (bodily-kinesthetic)
Invite guests to demonstrate to students how to dance the tango. As an alternative, have students investigate how to dance the tango and then ask them to show some of the steps they learned to the class.

Notes

Remind students that language changes as people travel, as demonstrated in the title of this *Cultura viva*. For example, in Argentina, the word *che* is equivalent to **buddy** or **friend** and is used in informal conversations. Costa Ricans would probably use the term *maje* in the same circumstances. Similarly, *vos bailás* is used in Argentina to say **you dance**, whereas in most other Spanish-speaking countries people would probably say *tú bailas*.

The title of this *Cultura viva* is derived from the combination of *che* (explained above) with the informal command *bailá* (formed by dropping *tú* and the final *-s*) and adding the word *conmigo* (meaning **with me**) to complete the invitation.

National Standards	
Communication 1.3	**Comparisons** 4.1, 4.2
Cultures 2.1, 2.2	
Connections 3.1	

Teacher Resources

 Activity 19

 Activities 10–11

 Activities 9–10

 Activity 5

Answers

19 1. Hace más de un siglo que juegan al béisbol en los Estados Unidos.
2. Hace un año que jugamos al voleibol.
3. Hace quince años que vivo aquí.
4. Hace veinte minutos que Uds. juegan a los videojuegos.
5. Hace un cuarto de hora que mi sobrina dibuja una casa.
6. Hace treinta segundos que jugamos al ajedrez.

Activities

Students with Special Needs
Give a second model sentence for activity 19.

National Standards
Comparisons 4.1

Idioma

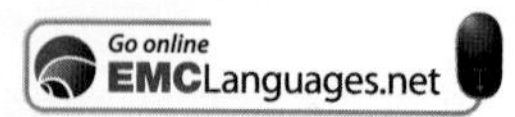

Estructura

Expressions with *hace*

You can describe an action that began in the past and has continued into the present using ***hace*** **+ a time expression +** ***que*** **+ the present tense of a verb.**

Hace diez minutos que veo televisión.	I have been watching television for ten minutes. (Ten minutes ago I started watching television.)

Reverse the order of *hace* and the time expression if a form of *¿cuánto?* introduces the question.

¿Cuánto tiempo hace que ves televisión?	How long have you been watching television?

Práctica

19 ¿Cuánto tiempo hace?

Say how long the following activities have been taking place.

MODELO haces aeróbicos / una hora
Hace una hora que haces aeróbicos.

1. juegan al béisbol en los Estados Unidos / más de un siglo
2. jugamos al voleibol / un año
3. vivo aquí / quince años
4. Uds. juegan a los videojuegos / veinte minutos
5. mi sobrina dibuja una casa / un cuarto de hora
6. jugamos al ajedrez / treinta segundos

Hace una hora que hacen aeróbicos.

Notes Note for your students the difference between the use of *hace* as a form of the verb *hacer* and *hace* as it is used here to indicate an amount of time that has elapsed.

Point out to students the possible confusion between *¿Cuánto tiempo hace que...?* and *¿Qué tiempo hace?*

¿Qué haces?

In pairs, take turns asking and answering the following questions. Then summarize your partner's answers for each question.

MODELO A: ¿Juegas a los videojuegos?
B: Sí, juego a los videojuegos.
A: (*Write:* **B** juega a los videojuegos.)

Jugamos a los videojuegos.

1. ¿Cuánto tiempo hace que no juegas al ajedrez? ¿Y a las damas?
2. ¿Sabes jugar al ajedrez o a las damas?
3. ¿Cuánto tiempo hace que no lees una revista?
4. ¿Qué revistas lees?
5. ¿Cuánto tiempo hace que dibujas?
6. ¿Sabes dibujar?
7. ¿Cuánto tiempo hace que no ves una telenovela?
8. ¿Te gusta ver televisión? ¿Te gustan las telenovelas?
9. ¿Cuánto tiempo hace que estudias español?
10. ¿Cuánto tiempo hace que no escribes una carta?

Comunicación

21 Mis pasatiempos

Prepare a list of your pastimes. Include at least six or seven activities. Then, with a partner, ask and answer questions about your favorite pastimes.

Nuestro pasatiempo favorito es el ajedrez.

¡Extra!

¿Damas en los baños?

The games *ajedrez* (chess) and *damas* (checkers) are two of the world's oldest pastimes. However, if you see the word *Damas* (Ladies) on the door of a public restroom not very far from another door labeled *Caballeros* (Gentlemen), do not assume you are going in to play checkers. Remember what you have learned: The meaning of any word may vary according to the context in which the word is used.

¿Te gusta dibujar?

Teacher Resources

Activity 20

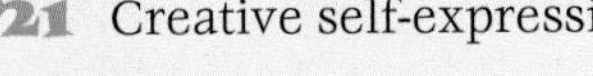

Answers

20 Answers will vary.
21 Creative self-expression.

Activities

Multiple Intelligences (interpersonal)
First, have students make a list in Spanish consisting of their relatives' and friends' favorite pastimes. For each person or activity identified, they should write a logical statement with *hace* (+ time + *que* + the present tense of a verb). For example, *Hace cinco años que mi amigo Marco juega al golf.* Then have students talk about their sentences with a partner or with the class.

Spanish for Spanish Speakers
Have students write a composition of at least 100 words describing their favorite *pasatiempos*.

National Standards

Communication
1.1

Cultures
2.1

Notes

Vary the way you assign oral activities. For example, pair students requiring additional help with stronger students for activity 21. You might even consider asking several volunteers to share with the class some of the pastimes from their discussions in pairs.

In addition to *Damas* and *Caballeros*, students may see *Señoras* and *Señores* or *Mujeres* and *Hombres* to indicate women's and men's bathrooms.

Teacher Resources

 Activity 22

 Activity 12

 Activities 11–13

 p. 29

 Activity 6
Activity 7

 Activity 5

Answers

22
1. Mi padre y mi madre están saliendo....
2. Mi hermano está buscando....
3. Esteban está alquilando....
4. Tú estás pensando....
5. Uds. están apagando....
6. María está poniendo....

Activities

Critical Thinking
As follow-up to activity 22, ask students to name several well-known people in your state, and then explain what they think each person is doing right now.

Students with Special Needs
With their books closed, give students several verbs that have irregular present participles and have them form the present progressive tense.

National Standards

Communication
1.1

Comparisons
4.1

Estructura

Saying what is happening: present progressive

You can say what is happening right now using the *presente progresivo*, which consists of the present tense of *estar* plus a present participle *(gerundio)*.

*¿Qué **están haciendo** Uds.?*	What **are** (all of) you **doing?**
*Marta **está dibujando**, Enrique **está comiendo** y yo **estoy saliendo**.*	Marta **is drawing**, Enrique **is eating** and I **am leaving**.

Form the present participle of most verbs by changing the infinitive endings (*-ar, -er, -ir*) to *-ando* for *-ar* verbs or to *-iendo* for *-er* and *-ir* verbs.

-ar	-er	-ir
alquil**ar** → alquil**ando**	hac**er** → hac**iendo**	permit**ir** → permit**iendo**

Some *-ir* verbs with a stem change in the present tense require a different stem change in the present participle. This second change is shown in parentheses after infinitives in this book. Three verbs that follow this pattern are *dormir (ue, **u**)*, *preferir (ie, **i**)* and *sentir (ie, **i**)*.

verbo	presente	gerundio
dormir **(ue, u)**	d**ue**rmo	d**u**rmiendo
preferir **(ie, i)**	pref**ie**ren	pref**i**riendo
sentir **(ie, i)**	s**ie**nto	s**i**ntiendo

Some verbs have minor irregularities in their present participles. For example, the *i* in *-iendo* changes to *y* after most verb stems that end in a vowel and for the verb *ir*: *leer* (stem: *le*) → *le**y**endo*; *oír* (stem: *o*) → *o**y**endo*; *ir* → ***y**endo*. The present participle for the irregular verb *venir* requires a change in the stem from *e* to *i*: venir → v**i**niendo. Finally, the present participle for poder involves a stem change from *o* to *u*: *p**u**diendo*.

Práctica

22 Todos están haciendo algo

Using the *presente progresivo* and the provided cues, say what these people are doing right now.

MODELO nosotros / leer el periódico
Nosotros estamos leyendo el periódico.

1. mi padre y mi madre / salir de casa
2. mi hermano / buscar el control remoto
3. Esteban / alquilar una película estupenda
4. tú / pensar en tus pasatiempos
5. Uds. / apagar la luz de la cocina
6. María / poner la mesa

Ellas están leyendo el periódico.

Notes

Comparisons. It may help some students to know that the present participle (*gerundio*) is equivalent to **-ing** in English.

Review the forms of the verb *estar* with students.

¿Qué estás haciendo?

In pairs, take turns asking and answering what you are doing right now, according to the illustrations.

MODELO A: ¿Qué estás haciendo?
B: Estoy alquilando una película.

1

2

3

4

5

24 Tomando un mate

Pretend you are sitting in an outdoor café in Buenos Aires. Using the *presente progresivo*, describe what you see from your table.

MODELO una chica / escribir una carta
Una chica está escribiendo una carta.

1. otra chica / dibujar
2. el mesero / poner una mesa
3. un muchacho / hablar por el celular
4. el niño / mirar a sus padres
5. un padre y una madre / comer con sus hijos
6. unos señores / jugar al ajedrez
7. tú / salir

Answers

23 Possible answers:
1. ¿...haciendo?/...escuchando música/cantando.
2. ¿...haciendo?/...apagando/poniendo el televisor.
3. ¿...haciendo?/...comiendo una ensalada.
4. ¿...haciendo?/...jugando al fútbol.
5. ¿...haciendo?/...durmiendo.

24
1. Otra chica está dibujando.
2. El mesero está poniendo una mesa.
3. Un muchacho está hablando por el celular.
4. El niño está mirando a sus padres.
5. Un padre y una madre están comiendo con sus hijos.
6. Unos señores están jugando al ajedrez.
7. Tú estás saliendo.

Activities

Cooperative Learning
Working in pairs or in small groups, have students take turns asking and answering the questions for activity 24.

TPR
Write the expressions from the answers for activity 23 on separate pieces of paper. Have students select one of the pieces of paper at random. Call on several students to act out the expressions while classmates guess what the expressions are in Spanish.

National Standards

Communication
1.1

Comparisons
4.1

Notes

Comparisons. Explain to students that in Spanish, the present progressive is not used as frequently as it is in English. Rather, the present tense is normally used. The present progressive is reserved for stating more emphatically that the action is currently going on.

Comparisons. You may wish to note for students that in Spanish, present participles cannot be used as nouns as they are in English (Learning is fun). In Spanish, the noun form of the verb is the infinitive. This point will be explained later in the lesson.

Answers

25 Creative self-expression.
26 Creative self-expression.

Activities

Spanish for Spanish Speakers
Pair native Spanish-speaking students with Spanish-language learners for activity 25.

Students with Special Needs
Write on the board several sentences that use the present progressive and a direct object: *Estoy leyendo el libro; Está escuchando su MP3; Están viendo la telenovela.* Call on students to replace the direct object with a pronoun and then restate the sentence, placing the direct object pronoun correctly in the new sentence.

Comunicación

25 Estoy...

Working in pairs, imagine you are in the following places: *una cafetería, Buenos Aires, una tienda de videos, una fiesta para tu cumpleaños, una clase de español, la sala de la casa, el museo, la calle, el parque.* Pretend you are talking on the phone with a friend and discuss what you are doing right now. Add to the conversation by asking such things as who you are with, where each place is located, etc.

MODELO **A:** ¿Qué estás haciendo?
B: Estoy tomando café en una cafetería.
A: ¿Dónde está la cafetería?
B: Está en La Boca.

26 Están ocupados

With a classmate, pretend you are calling one another trying to reach various people on the phone. The person answering must apologize and say the person you are trying to reach is not home and, then, say what the person is doing. Be creative!

MODELO **A:** Hola. ¿Puedo hablar con Eduardo por favor?
B: Lo siento. Eduardo está paseando por la calle ahora mismo.

Estrategia

Clarifying meaning by asking questions
If you hear a new word in a conversation but do not understand what it means, do not be afraid to ask someone to fill you in. Many words in Spanish have different uses depending on the region or country where they are used. So the next time you hear a word or expression you are unsure of, do not be embarrassed; ask someone to explain it to you.

Repaso rápido

Direct object pronouns

You have already learned to use direct objects to show the person or thing in a sentence that receives the action of the verb. Do you remember the direct object pronouns?

los pronombres de complemento directo

me	*me*	**nos**	*us*
te	*you (tú)*	**os**	*you (vosotros,-as)*
lo	*him, it, you (Ud.)*	**los**	*them, you (Uds.)*
la	*her, it, you (Ud.)*	**las**	*them, you (Uds.)*

*No **la** veo.* — I do not see **her**. / I do not see **it**. (*la lista de las películas nuevas*)
*Nunca **lo** veo.* — I never see **him**. / I never see **it**. (*el programa*)

National Standards
Communication
1.1

Notes

Tell students that the present participle is sometimes used without a form of *estar*: *Caminando por el parque, veo a muchos amigos.*

Before assigning activity 25, tell students that local phone rates in many Spanish-speaking parts of the world are much higher than rates in the United States. Instead of chatting on the telephone, people tend to meet in an outdoor café or in a restaurant to talk and catch up on what is happening in each other's lives.

Encourage students to apply the content of the *Estrategia* to everyday conversation, asking questions to clarify what someone tells them.

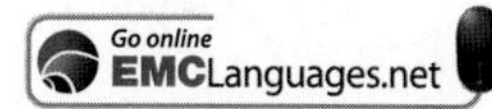

Estructura

Using the present progressive with direct object pronouns

You have already seen that direct object pronouns usually precede conjugated verbs. However, direct object pronouns may be attached to an infinitive.

***Lo** voy a alquilar.* *Voy a alquilar**lo**.*	I am going to rent **it**. (*el DVD*)

Similarly, you may choose to attach an object pronoun to the end of a present participle. When doing so, however, you must add an accent mark to the present participle in order to maintain the original pronunciation of the present participle without the pronoun.

***La** estamos leyendo.* *Estamos leyéndo**la**.*	We are reading **it**. (*la revista*)

Práctica

27 Lo estamos haciendo

Tell what the following people are doing right now, using direct object pronouns.

1. la señora Herrera / empezar / un viaje a Venezuela
2. Uds. / escribir / la lista de películas nuevas
3. nosotros / leer / un libro sobre Buenos Aires ahora
4. yo / escuchar / la radio ahora
5. Pilar / buscar / el control remoto

Estoy tomando mate.

28 Haciéndolo

Imagine you and your friend are watching television and commenting on various characters and programs. Working in pairs, take turns asking and answering questions using the provided cues. Follow the model, attaching direct object pronouns to the verbs in each sentence.

MODELO los hermanos / leer el diario de la hermana
A: ¿Están leyendo los hermanos el diario de la hermana?
B: Sí, están leyéndolo.

1. tú / buscar el programa servilleta
2. el cantante / cantar una canción de amor
3. Julia / escuchar la radio
4. nosotros / ver esta telenovelaen la
5. Mónica / dibujar un mapa
6. mi equipo favorito / jugar un partido importante

Notes

Write on the board several sentences that demonstrate the use of the present progressive tense with direct object pronouns. Remind students that the direct object answers the question (subject + verb +) **who?** or **what?**

Mate (shown in the photograph) is a hot beverage similar to tea. It is very popular in Argentina. It is customarily served in a wooden cup called a *mate* and sipped through a metal straw (the best of which are silver) called a *bombilla*.

Refer to the list of Teacher Resources at the top of the page to find ancillaries for practicing the present progressive with direct object pronouns.

Teacher Resources

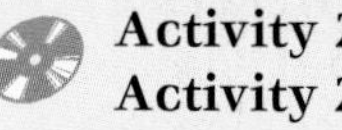

Activity 27
Activity 28

Activity 13

Activity 14

Activity 6

Answers

27
1. La señora Herrera lo está empezando.
2. Uds. la están escribiendo.
3. Nosotros lo estamos leyendo.
4. Yo la estoy escuchando.
5. Pilar lo está buscando.

28
1. ¿Estás buscando...?/...estoy buscándolo.
2. ¿Está cantando...?/...está cantándola.
3. ¿Está escuchando...?/...está escuchándola.
4. ¿Estamos viendo...?/...estamos viéndola.
5. ¿Está dibujando...?/...está dibujándolo.
6. ¿Está jugando...?/...está jugándolo.

Activities

Expansion

The present progressive tense can be made negative by placing a negative expression such as *no* before the conjugated form of *estar*: *estoy dibujando (no estoy dibujando).*

National Standards
Communication 1.1
Cultures 2.2
Comparisons 4.1

Answers

29 1. La señora Herrera está empezándolo.
2. Uds. están escribiéndola.
3. Nosotros estamos leyéndolo.
4. Yo estoy escuchándola.
5. Pilar está buscándolo.

30 Creative self-expression.

31 Answers will depend on where students complete the assignment (i.e., in school or at home): *pensando, ayudando, buscando, caminando, comiendo, empezando, haciendo, leyendo, escuchando, pensando, terminando, viendo.*

Activities

Critical Thinking

Ask students to imagine it is 7:30 on a typical Friday night. What are they doing? What are their family and friends doing? Students should write a composition of at least six sentences describing what people they know are doing at this imaginary moment. Give students a model for the first lines of the composition: *Es viernes y son las siete y media de la noche y estoy alquilando una película. Mi amiga y yo la estamos buscando en una tienda de videos.*

Multiple Intelligences (spatial)

Have students make a bar graph depicting their findings for activity 31.

National Standards

Communication
1.1, 1.3

Connections
3.1

Comparisons
4.1

29 Otra vez

Redo activity 27 by attaching the direct object pronouns to the end of the present participle. Make any other appropriate changes.

30 Conexión con otras disciplinas: estadística

Prepare a list of at least eight pastimes in Spanish *(ir al cine, jugar al voleibol).* Then ask five people to rank the pastimes, with *1* being their favorite and *8* being their least favorite activity. Prepare a written summary of your findings in Spanish. Follow the model.

MODELO ¿Qué pasatiempos de mi lista son tus favoritos, en una escala del uno al ocho?

¿Qué pasatiempos de mi lista son tus favoritos, en una escala del uno al ocho?

1. Me gusta leer revistas. 1 2 3 4 5 6 7 8
2. Me gusta escuchar la radio. 1 2 3 4 5 6 7 8

31 Mirando y haciendo

Mira a cuatro o cinco personas desde donde tú estás ahora. ¿Qué están haciendo?

MODELO El profesor está ayudando a un estudiante.

¡Extra!

Comparando inglés y español

You have learned to combine the present tense of *estar* with a present participle *(gerundio)* of a verb in Spanish to describe what is going on right now. This verb form is comparable to the *-ing* form of a verb in English. Notice, however, that words ending in *-ing* in English may require an infinitive in Spanish if the English word functions as a noun instead of a verb. Compare the following:

*Me gusta **jugar** al voleibol.*	I like **playing** volleyball. *(noun)*
***Nadar** es divertido.*	**Swimming** is fun. *(noun)*

but:

*Estoy **jugando** al voleibol.*	I am **playing** volleyball. *(verb)*
*¿Estás **nadando**?*	Are you **swimming**? *(verb)*

Notes Activity 30 offers a cross-curricular connection to mathematics (specifically, statistics).

Have students share the results of their surveys with the class. Ask a volunteer to write each new activity on the board.

Follow up activity 31 with a class discussion reviewing everyone's activities in the classroom.

Comunicación

32 Los pasatiempos

Write the names in Spanish of at least five or six of your favorite pastimes. Next to the list, add columns telling where you participate in the activity, how long you have done the activity and with whom you do the activity. Then, working with a partner, take turns asking and answering questions about each other's pastimes.

Juego al voleibol en la playa.

MODELO
A: ¿Cuál es tu pasatiempo favorito?
B: Mi pasatiempo favorito es jugar al voleibol.
A: ¿Dónde juegas al voleibol?
B: Juego en la playa.
A: ¿Cuánto tiempo hace que tienes este pasatiempo?
B: Hace dos años que tengo este pasatiempo.

33 El tiempo libre

In small groups, talk about the activities and pastimes you enjoy during school breaks and vacation. Make sure each of you describes at least two activities/pastimes. Have a group member make a list of all the activities and pastimes you talk about and share the information with the class.

¡Nuestro pasatiempo favorito es el fútbol!

Answers

32 Creative self-expression.
33 Answers will vary.

Activities

Expansion

Ask students to find magazines containing pictures of different places where students would like to go. Working in pairs or small groups, each student should teach classmates any new vocabulary required for describing the pictures or naming the locations shown. Then have students try the following. Student A shows a picture and Student B asks: *¿Dónde estás?*. Student A responds as if he or she were at the place shown: *Estoy en un playa en Argentina.* After the response, Student B asks: *¿Qué estás haciendo?*. Student A responds with what he or she is doing, according to the picture: *Estoy nadando.*

National Standards
Communication 1.1, 1.3
Connections 3.1, 3.2

Teacher Resources

Lectura cultural
El juego del pato
Activity 34
Activity 35

Answers

34 1. El fútbol es el deporte más popular de Argentina./El juego del pato es el deporte nacional de Argentina.
2. Hace más de 400 años que se originó el juego del pato.
3. Originalmente, los gauchos jugaban al pato con un pato vivo.
4. En 1822 fue prohibido el juego del pato.
5. Hoy, el juego del pato se juega entre ocho jinetes.

35 Answers will vary.

Activities

Multiple Intelligences (linguistic)
Ask individuals to research Argentina and then report their findings to the class. Possible topics: compare and contrast the Argentine *gaucho* with the American cowboy; discuss the Argentinean economy; compare what Evita Perón was really like to the image presented in the movie *Evita*.

Spanish for Spanish Speakers
Students write a short composition in Spanish in which they discuss something they know about Argentina. Expand the activity by having students seek out additional information about Argentina at the library or on the Internet.

National Standards
Cultures 2.1
Connections 3.1, 3.2
Comparisons 4.1, 4.2

Lectura cultural

El juego del pato

En Argentina, el deporte más popular es el fútbol, pero el deporte nacional es el juego del pato[1]. Éste es un deporte hípico[2] similar al polo que se originó hace más de 4 siglos entre los gauchos[3] de Argentina.

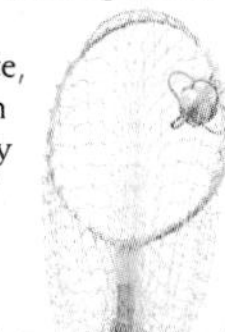

Originalmente, el juego del pato se jugaba con un pato vivo[4] que se arrojaba hacia arriba[5] y dos grupos de jinetes[6] se atropellaban[7] para capturarlo y pasarlo unos a otros. Había tantos resultados trágicos que fue prohibido en 1822.

Pasando la pelota por el aro.

En 1937, el juego del pato volvió, reglamentado[8] y modernizado. Ya no se juega con un pato sino con una pelota blanca con seis asas[9]. Dos equipos de cuatro jugadores cada uno juegan en un campo de 220 metros por 90 metros. El objetivo del juego es pasar la pelota—a la que se llama pato—por un aro[10] que tiene un metro de diámetro. Los jugadores, a caballo, deben recoger[11] el pato y lanzarlo con la mano derecha. Es un deporte de fuerza[12] y habilidad, y aunque no es muy popular, es el deporte más tradicional de Argentina.

El juego del pato, el deporte nacional de la Argentina.

[1]the duck game [2]equine [3]Argentinian cowboys [4]live duck [5]thrown into the air [6]horsemen [7]would trample each other [8]regulated [9]handles [10]hoop [11]pick up [12]strength

34 ¿Qué recuerdas?

Correct these false statements.

1. El juego del pato es el deporte más popular de Argentina.
2. Hace más de 40 años que se originó el juego del pato.
3. Originalmente, los gauchos jugaban al pato con una pelota.
4. En 1953 fue prohibido el juego del pato.
5. Hoy, el juego del pato se juega entre dos jinetes.

- **Why do you think *el juego del pato* is not very popular today among Argentines? Do you think it could become popular in the United States if it were introduced here? Explain.**

35 Algo personal

1. ¿Cuál crees que es el deporte nacional de Estados Unidos?
2. ¿Qué deporte practican los *cowboys* de Estados Unidos?
3. ¿A qué deporte es el juego del pato similar? Explica.
4. ¿Te gustaría aprender a jugar al pato? ¿Por qué sí o por qué no?

Notes The *Lectura cultural* has been recorded and is available in the Audio Program along with activities 34 and 35. You may wish to help students with the reading and then assign the reading and the questions as homework. After reviewing the contents of the *Lectura cultural*, play the recording and allow students to read along silently. Then play the audio of the activities, pausing after each question and calling on students to provide an answer.

Autoevaluación

As a review and self-check, respond to the following:

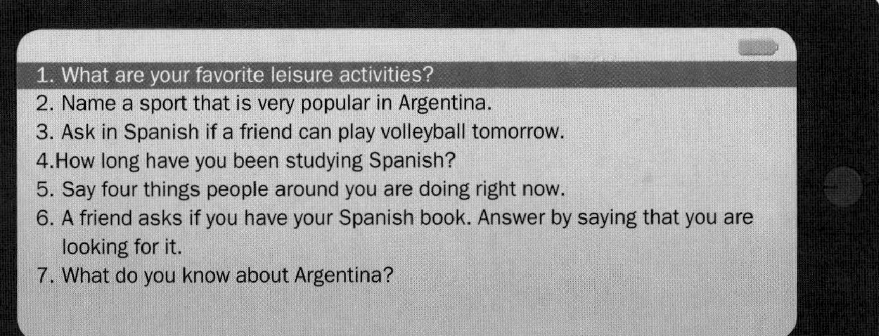

1. What are your favorite leisure activities?
2. Name a sport that is very popular in Argentina.
3. Ask in Spanish if a friend can play volleyball tomorrow.
4.How long have you been studying Spanish?
5. Say four things people around you are doing right now.
6. A friend asks if you have your Spanish book. Answer by saying that you are looking for it.
7. What do you know about Argentina?

Palabras y expresiones

How many of these words and expressions do you know?

Pasatiempos
los aeróbicos
el ajedrez
el básquetbol
las cartas
las damas
el equipo
el fútbol americano
hacer aeróbicos
el pasatiempo
el programa
la telenovela
el videojuego
el voleibol

Otras expresiones
ahora mismo
antes de
¿Cuánto (+ *time expression*) hace que (+ *present tense of verb*). . . ?
después de
esta noche
hace (+ *time expression*) que
el minuto
mismo
por la (mañana, tarde, noche)
el segundo
el siglo
todavía

Verbos
alquilar
apagar
costar (ue)
dar
dibujar
dormir (ue, u)
jugar (ue)
permitir
poder (ue, u)
recordar (ue)
volver (ue)

Expresiones y otras palabras
americano,-a
casi
el control remoto
estupendo,-a
la lista
mismo,-a
remoto,-a
el televisor
la vida

Estructura

Do you remember the following grammar rules?

Stem-changing verbs: *o* → *ue* and *u* → *ue*

The verbs *poder (ue)* and *jugar (ue)* are stem changing verbs except in the *nosotros* and *vosotros* forms.

poder (ue)		jugar (ue)	
p**ue**do	podemos	j**ue**go	jugamos
p**ue**des	podéis	j**ue**gas	jugáis
p**ue**de	p**ue**den	j**ue**ga	j**ue**gan

Expressions with *hace*

Question: ¿***Cuánto tiempo hace que*** *ves television?*

Answer: ***hace*** + expression of time + ***que*** + conjugated verb in the present tense.

Saying what is happening: present progressive

Use the present tense of ***estar*** **+ present participle (*gerundio*)**

-ar verbs	-er verbs	-ir verbs
hablar → **ando** habl**ando**	comer → **iendo** com**iendo**	escribir → **iendo** escrib**iendo**

**¡Ojo!* Some verbs require a spelling change or stem change in the present participle.

Using the present progressive with direct object pronouns

Direct object pronouns can precede a conjugated verb or can be attached to the end of an infinitive.

Lo leo en el parque.	*I see **it** in the park.*
Voy a leer**lo** en el parque.	*I am going to see **it** in the park.*
La estamos alquilando.	*We are renting **it**.*
Estamos alquilándo**la**.	*We are renting **it**.*

Notes **Comparisons.** Remind students that in Spanish, present participles cannot be used as gerunds as they are in English (Learning is fun). In Spanish the noun form of the verb is the infinitive: *Me gusta cantar* (I like singing); *Bailar es divertido* (Dancing is fun).

Teacher Resources

 **Activity 14**

 **pp. 57, 91**

 **Juegos**

Answers

Autoevaluación

Possible answers:

1. Answers will vary.
2. El fútbol es muy popular en (la) Argentina.
3. ¿Puedes jugar al voleibol mañana?
4. Hace un año que estudio español.
5. Mi amigo está escribiendo ahora...
6. Estoy buscándolo.
7. Large cattle ranches there are called *estancias*.

Activities

Multiple Intelligences (bodily-kinesthetic/linguistic)

Assign students to read *The House of the Spirits* by Isabel Allende. Then have them write their own copy for a book jacket. They should include pictures, line drawings, type design, a blurb about the book and a sketch of the author.

Technology

Check with your media center or ask your students if they have access to a Spanish-speaking station on their cable network or from a satellite dish. Have them record a segment of a Sunday afternoon soccer match and bring it in to share with the rest of the class.

National Standards

Connections
3.1, 3.2

Comparisons
4.1

Teacher Resources

 Vocabulario I
Las estaciones en Chile

 Activity 50

 Activities 1–3

 Activities 1–2

 pp. 97–101

 Activity 1

 Activity 1

Content reviewed in *Lección B*

- months and seasons of the year
- expressing likes and dislikes
- present progressive tense
- sports

Activities

Prereading Strategy
Conduct a discussion about the activities students enjoy during each of the four seasons. Then have students look through the scenes quickly to find cognates and words they recognize.

Spanish for Spanish Speakers
Call on students to state in Spanish activities people like to do during different seasons in their country of origin.

National Standards
Cultures 2.1
Connections 3.1
Comparisons 4.1

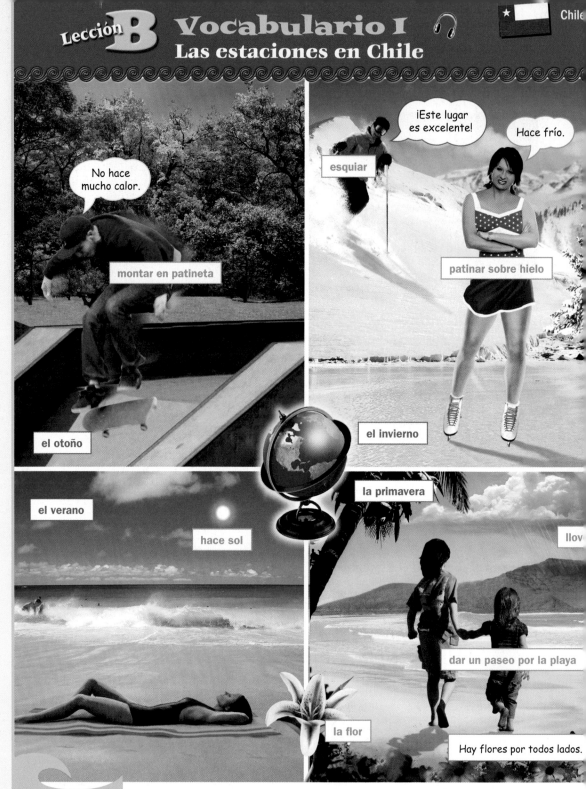

Vocabulario I
Las estaciones en Chile

Chile

No hace mucho calor.
montar en patineta
el otoño
¡Este lugar es excelente!
Hace frío.
esquiar
patinar sobre hielo
el invierno
el verano
hace sol
la primavera
llov
dar un paseo por la playa
la flor
Hay flores por todos lados.

Notes When speaking informally, native Spanish speakers occasionally abbreviate words. For example, *la bicicleta* may be referred to as *la bici* and *la televisión* may be called *la tele*. Ask students to think of similar abbreviations in English or Spanish.

Remind students that an infinitive can act as a noun in Spanish: *Esquiar es mi deporte favorito.*

No me gusta esquiar, pero en cambio me gusta ver televisión.
Sí, pero ya estoy lista.
¿Todavía continúas en la computadora?
La chica envía un correo electrónico a Juan. Ella copia la dirección de Juan en su cuaderno. Ella pone los papeles en su lugar.

1 Las estaciones

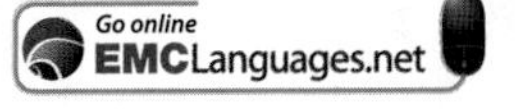

Escoge la estación correcta, según lo que oyes.

el otoño
la primavera
el verano
el invierno

2 Las estaciones en Chile

Contesta las siguientes preguntas.

1. ¿En qué estación pueden patinar sobre hielo en Chile?
2. ¿En qué meses hay flores en Chile?
3. ¿En qué meses están esquiando en Chile?
4. ¿Qué estación es en abril y mayo en Chile?
5. ¿Qué estación es en enero y febrero en Chile?
6. ¿Qué estación es en junio y julio en Chile?

¡Extra!

¿Cuándo es verano?

In the Southern Hemisphere, the seasons are the reverse of the seasons in the Northern Hemisphere. For this reason, people ski in Chile from June to August because it is winter there. Similarly, the summer months in Chile are December, January and February.

Notes Tell students that although the infinitives *poner* and *dar* were introduced earlier, the present-tense forms of these verbs are taught in *Capítulo 7, Lección B.*

Your students may find it interesting that the school year in many South American countries begins in February or March.

Activity 1 is intended for listening comprehension practice. Play the audio of the activity that is part of the Audio Program or use the transcript that appears in the ATE Introduction if you prefer to read the activity yourself.

Teacher Resources

Activity 1
Activity 2

Answers

1 1. el invierno; 2. la primavera; 3. el verano; 4. el otoño

2 1. Pueden patinar sobre hielo en el invierno.
2. Hay flores en los meses de septiembre, octubre y noviembre.
3. Están esquiando en junio, julio y agosto.
4. Es otoño.
5. Es verano.
6. Es invierno.

Activities

Pronunciation (*las letras* m, n, ñ)
Review the sound of *m* (*mucho, tiempo, minutos, menos, primavera, mes*), *n* (*cuestan, cuánto, verano, nuevas, tengo, poner*) and *ñ* (*año, cumpleaños, mañana, niño, otoño, cariñosa*). Then pronounce the following carefully, having students say the sentence several times before writing what they hear: *Mañana es el primer día del invierno, que nos gusta mucho en Chile, pero que al señor Núñez no le gusta.* Ask students if they understand the meaning of the sentence.

TPR
Using TPR, introduce or review expressions that name various pastimes: *dar un paseo, montar en bicicleta, nadar, ver televisión, jugar al fútbol, jugar al tenis, esquiar, patinar.*

National Standards

Communication
1.2

Connections
3.1

Comparisons
4.1

Teacher Resources

Diálogo I
¡Vamos a esquiar!
Activity 3
Activity 4
Activity 5

Answers

3 1. Diego quiere dar un paseo por la playa.
2. Porque hace mucho calor.
3. Prefiere montar en patineta.
4. Quiere ir a esquiar.
5. A Pablo le gusta el invierno.

4 Answers will vary.

5 All answers begin with *Puedo* and end with an appropriate activity for the indicated season.

Activities

Critical Listening
Play the audio recording of the dialog as students cover the words and listen to the conversation. Then ask several individuals to state what they believe the conversation is about.

Expansion
Additional questions (*Algo personal*): *¿Qué tiempo hace en tu ciudad en primavera/verano/otoño/invierno?; ¿Qué te gusta hacer en la primavera/el verano/el otoño/el invierno?*

Prereading Strategy
Instruct students to cover up the dialog with one hand and look at the photographs. Ask them to look through the dialog quickly to find cognates and words they recognize.

National Standards

Communication
1.1, 1.2

Connections
3.1

Diálogo I ¡Vamos a esquiar!

DIEGO: ¿Vamos a dar un paseo por la playa?
PABLO: No, gracias. Hace mucho calor.
ELENA: Yo prefiero montar en patineta.

PABLO: ¡Vamos a esquiar!
ELENA: ¡En enero no podemos esquiar en Chile!
PABLO: No, aquí, no. ¡Vamos a Colorado!

ELENA: ¡Qué tonto eres!
PABLO: Me gusta el invierno.
ELENA: ¡Ya está bien! Vamos a tomar un refresco.

3 ¿Qué recuerdas?

1. ¿Quién quiere dar un paseo por la playa?
2. ¿Por qué no quiere Pablo ir a la playa?
3. ¿Qué prefiere hacer Elena?
4. ¿Qué quiere hacer Pablo?
5. ¿A quién le gusta el invierno?

4 Algo personal

1. ¿Cuál es tu estación favorita? Explica.
2. ¿Qué te gusta hacer en tu estación favorita?
3. ¿Qué deportes practicas donde tú vives en la primavera? ¿Y en el verano? ¿Y en el otoño? ¿Y en el invierno?

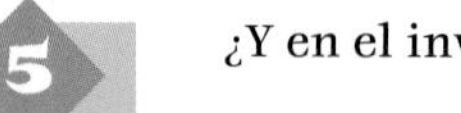

5 ¿Qué actividades puedes hacer?

Escucha la información y di qué actividad o actividades puedes hacer.

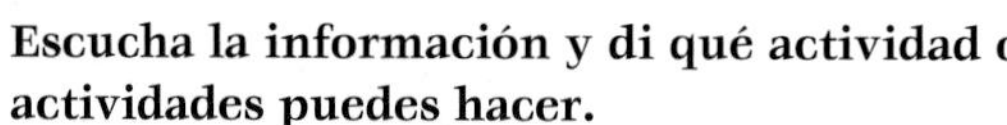

MODELO Puedo montar en patineta en el parque.

Monto en patineta.

Notes Explain that the articles *el* and *la* may be omitted after *en* and after forms of the verb *ser*: *hace sol en (el) verano; mi estación favorita es (la) primavera.*

This dialog and activities 3, 4 and 5 have been recorded by native speakers and are included in the *¡Aventura!* Audio Program. Have students cover up the dialog on page 292 and look at the photographs as you play the dialog. Then discuss the contents of the dialog to evaluate what students have understood.

Cultura viva

Go online EMCLanguages.net

La Isla de Pascua.

La región de los lagos (southern lakes region), Chile.

Chile

Mainland Chile is located along the western coast of South America between the Andes Mountains and the Pacific Ocean. The country also has many interesting islands, including the *Juan Fernández Islands*, where Robinson Crusoe lived for four years, and Easter Island *(Isla de Pascua)*, an island with a mysterious past which is inhabited by people of Polynesian ancestry. Most Chileans live in urban areas, like the capital, Santiago. The population is well educated and the country has a strong literary tradition: Chileans are very proud of their two Nobel Prize-winning poets, Gabriela Mistral and Pablo Neruda. Since much of Chile's population has European origins, it is not uncommon to encounter people of Italian, English, German, Irish or Polish ancestry, or to see street signs with names that are obviously not of Spanish origin. Indeed, the southern city of Puerto Montt was for many years a German colony and the liberator and first ruler of Chile was Bernardo O'Higgins.

When you visit, you will discover that Chile is a country of magnificent contrasts offering everything, from large cosmopolitan cities with the latest in modern-day conveniences and skyscrapers *(rascacielos)* that reach to the sky to the beautiful rustic countryside of the southern lakes region. Just a short distance away from cosmopolitan Santiago, ski resorts like Portillo or Farellones in the Andes Mountains and resort beaches near Viña del Mar offer an escape from the pressures of modern life.

Los rascacielos de Santiago.

6 Chile

Contesta las siguientes preguntas sobre Chile.

1. ¿Está Chile en América del Sur o en América del Norte?
2. ¿Qué montañas están en Chile?
3. ¿Qué océano está al oeste de Chile?
4. ¿En qué isla vive gente de ancestro polinesio?
5. ¿Cuál es la capital del país?
6. ¿Quién es una persona famosa de Chile?
7. ¿Adónde puede uno ir a esquiar? ¿Y a nadar en la playa?

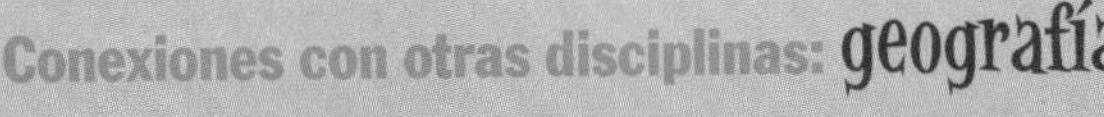

7 Conexiones con otras disciplinas: geografía

Use an encyclopedia or search the Internet for information about Chile. Then list four or five interesting details about places mentioned in the *Cultura viva* (e.g., Juan Fernández Islands, Isla de Pascua, Viña del Mar, etc.).

Teacher Resources

 Activity 6

 Activity 4

 p. 96

 Activity 2

Answers

6
1. Está en América del Sur.
2. Los Andes están en Chile.
3. El océano Pacífico está al oeste de Chile.
4. En la Isla de Pascua vive gente de ancestro polinesio.
5. Santiago es la capital del país.
6. Gabriela Mistral (Pablo Neruda, Bernardo O'Higgins) es una persona famosa de Chile.
7. Uno puede ir a esquiar a Portillo o a Farellones. Uno puede nadar en la playa de Viña del Mar.

7 Answers will vary.

Activities

Connections

Ask students to find Chile on a world map. Then locate some of the sites mentioned in *Cultura viva*.

Spanish for Spanish Speakers

Suggest that students read several poems by Gabriela Mistral or Pablo Neruda and summarize the themes presented (either orally or in writing).

National Standards

Cultures
2.1, 2.2

Connections
3.1, 3.2

Notes

Your students will find it interesting that a person with an Irish name, Bernardo O'Higgins, is the national hero of Chile.

Easter Island lies in isolation about 2,300 miles west of the Chilean coast in the Pacific Ocean. Its nearest neighbor, Pitcairn Island, is 1,200 miles away. The first Polynesian settlement took place around A.D. 400.

Before beginning activity 7, point out on a Chilean map where the sites named in the *Cultura viva* are located.

Teacher Resources

 Activities 5–6

 Activity 3

 Activity 2

Answers

8 1. esquían
2. copia
3. continúas
4. envían
5. esquiamos
6. continúo
7. ve
8. patina
9. envía

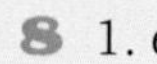

Activities

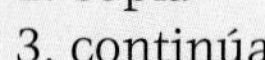

Students with Special Needs
Model a second sentence for activity 8.

Idioma

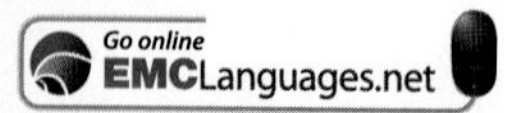

Estructura

Verbs that require special accentuation

Sometimes verbs that end in *-uar* or *-iar* (*esquiar*, *enviar* and *continuar*, for example) require a written accent mark to indicate that a vowel should be stressed for all present-tense forms except for *nosotros*. You will have to learn which verbs follow this pattern since some verbs that end in *-uar* or *-iar* may not follow this pattern (such as the verb *copiar*).

esquiar: esquío, esquías, esquía, esquiamos, esquiáis, esquían
enviar: envío, envías, envía, enviamos, enviáis, envían
continuar: continúo, continúas, continúa, continuamos, continuáis, continúan

but:

copiar: copio, copias, copia, copiamos, copiáis, copian

Práctica

8 Todos hacen algo

Indica qué hacen estas personas cuando tienen tiempo libre.

MODELO Yo (esquiar) con mis padres.
Yo esquío con mis padres.

1. Eva y Luis (esquiar) en Portillo.
2. Claudia (copiar) canciones de la Internet.
3. Tú (continuar) dando paseos por el parque.
4. Sara y Paz (enviar) correos electrónicos a sus amigos.
5. Nosotros (esquiar) en Farillones.
6. Yo (continuar) montando en patineta, mi actividad favorita.
7. Alberto (ver) DVDs.
8. Victoria (patinar) sobre hielo.
9. Mamá (enviar) cartas a mis abuelos.

Yo esquío con mi madre y mi hermano.

National Standards

Connections
3.1

Notes You may wish to mention that *mandar* is a synonym for *enviar*.

Syllabification and accentuation are explained in the Appendices.

Some other verbs that require an accent when conjugated are *criar* (to raise, breed); *fiar* (to confide); *guiar* (to lead); *telegrafiar* (to telegraph); *desafiar* (to challenge); *extraviar* (to lose).

9 ¿Qué pasa?

Read the following statements and indicate where there are missing accent marks. Then identify the letter of the illustration that best matches each statement.

1. Hace calor y están en la playa.
2. Esquiamos todos los días.
3. Ellos continuan esquiando en la nieve.
4. Ella copia el número de teléfono.
5. Continua haciendo sol.
6. Él envia una carta.
7. Está nublado.
8. Ellos esquian ahora mismo.

A

B

Comunicación

10 Un correo electrónico

Imagine you have a key pal in Chile. Write an e-mail telling him or her about your home and school life. You may want to say, for example, that you like to ski during the winter, that you and your family ski once a month, that you would like to go to Portillo, that you continue studying Spanish at school and that you are sending pictures of you and your family with the e-mail. Add any other details you would like.

Yo envío un correo electrónico a Chile.

Notes Inform students that a key pal (or pen pal) in Spanish is *amigo/amiga por correspondencia*.

Have students apply strategies they have already learned in previous chapters as they complete activity 10.

Answers

9
1. B
2. A
3. A/Ellos continúan esquiando en la nieve.
4. B
5. B/Continúa haciendo sol.
6. B/Él envía una carta.
7. A
8. A/Ellos esquían ahora mismo.

10 Creative self-expression.

Activities

Multiple Intelligences (interpersonal/linguistic)
There are companies that can arrange penpal contacts if your students are interested. A friendship with a teacher or student abroad is another good way to initiate an e-mail exchange between students.

Students with Special Needs
Have students do activity 10 in pairs or in small groups.

National Standards

Communication
1.1

Connections
3.1

Communities
5.1

Teacher Resources

 Activity 11

 Activities 7–8

 Activities 4–5

 Activity 3

 Activity 3

Answers

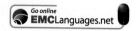

11 Answers may vary for the means of transportation; verb forms are as follows:
1. ...doy....
2. ...das....
3. ...damos....
4. ...dan....
5. ...da....
6. ...dan....

12
1. pone
2. pongo
3. ponen
4. pone
5. pones
6. ponemos

Activities

Expansion
Ask students to create sentences using the verbs *dar, hacer, poner, saber, salir* and *ver*, making sure that they use the first-person singular forms.

National Standards

Comparisons
4.1

Estructura

Present tense of *dar* and *poner*

The verbs *dar* and *poner* have irregular present-tense *yo* forms. In addition, the verb *dar* has an irregular *vosotros, -as* form. Other verbs that are regular in the present tense except for the *yo* form of the verbs: *hacer (yo hago), saber (yo sé), ver (yo veo), salir (yo salgo)*.

dar	
doy	damos
das	**dais**
da	dan

poner	
pongo	ponemos
pones	ponéis
pone	ponen

Práctica

11 ¿Dan un paseo a pie o en carro? 

Create logical sentences using the expression *dar un paseo* and either *a pie* or *en carro*, according to what makes the most sense.

MODELO Enrique / por el parque
Enrique da un paseo por el parque a pie.

1. yo / por la playa
2. tú / por la ciudad
3. nosotros / por el centro
4. Marta y Esperanza / por la calle
5. mi amigo / por la Avenida de la Independencia
6. mis padres / por la plaza

Ellos dan un paseo a pie.

12 ¡Ponen todo en su lugar!

Completa las oraciones con la forma apropiada del verbo *poner*.

MODELO Elena pone la patineta en su cuarto.

1. Paz __ las flores en la mesa del comedor.
2. Yo __ los papeles en el escritorio.
3. Carlos y Paula __ sus bicicletas en el garaje.
4. Mi padre __ el televisor en la sala.
5. Tú __ la leche en el refrigerador.
6. Todos nosotros __ los cubiertos sucios en el lavaplatos.

Notes

The verb *poner* is sometimes used in place of *encender* when you are talking about turning on an appliance: *Voy a encender (poner) el televisor.*

Review the various uses of *poner*: *poner* (to put), *poner el televisor* (to turn on), *poner la mesa* (to set the table).

13 ¡Me gusta la primavera!

Completa el siguiente párrafo con la forma apropiada de *comer*, *poner*, *dar*, *salir* y *ver* para saber por qué Sara dice que le gusta la primavera.

En la primavera yo siempre (1) con mi madre los domingos por la mañana a buscar flores. Yo (2) flores por toda la casa. Casi todas las mañanas yo (3) paseos por el parque con mi hermana y por la tarde alquilamos películas en una tienda cerca de la casa para verlas por la noche. Mi padre siempre me (4) dinero para alquilarlas. Claro, a veces, nosotros no las (5) porque (6) a dar un paseo por la noche y entonces no hay tiempo para verlas. Ahora mis hermanos y yo (7) la mesa para la comida. Hoy vamos a (8) en el patio porque no hace calor y no llueve. ¡Me gusta la primavera!

Pongo flores por toda la casa.

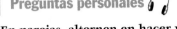

Comunicación

14 Preguntas personales

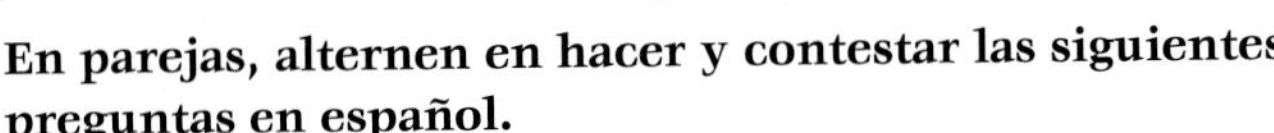

En parejas, alternen en hacer y contestar las siguientes preguntas en español.

1. ¿Qué haces cuando tienes tiempo libre?
2. ¿Te gusta dar paseos? ¿Dónde?
3. ¿Dan tu familia y tú paseos en carro los fines de semana? ¿Adónde van?
4. ¿Cómo das paseos en el verano? ¿En carro? ¿A pie? ¿En bicicleta?
5. ¿Dan tus amigos y tú paseos en el verano? ¿Adónde?
6. ¿En qué estación del año te gusta más dar paseos? ¿Por qué?
7. ¿Adónde vas de viaje con tu familia en el verano? ¿En la primavera? ¿En el otoño? ¿En el invierno?
8. ¿Quién pone las maletas en el carro cuando vas de viaje con tu familia?
9. ¿Pones flores en tu casa en la primavera? ¿Quién las pone?
10. ¿Dónde pones tu mochila en las vacaciones, cuando no hay clases?

15 ¿Qué actividades haces?

Working in small groups, talk about the activities you enjoy during different times of the year according to the season. Include activities such as going for a walk, taking rides, skiing, ice-skating, watching television or any other favorite pastimes. Include details such as when and with whom you do an activity, what the weather is like at that time of year and why you like or dislike the activity.

MODELO **A:** ¿Qué actividades haces en el verano?
B: En el verano doy paseos por las playas de Viña del Mar todos los fines de semana. Siempre voy con mi padre y caminamos por una hora.

Notes

Complete one or two answers as a class before assigning activity 13.

You may wish to have students write out the answers for activity 14 before pairing up with a classmate. As an alternative, after doing the activity orally in pairs, have students write their answers to be sure they understand and can retain what they practiced.

Teacher Resources

Activity 14

Answers

13 1. salgo
2. pongo
3. doy
4. da
5. vemos
6. salimos
7. ponemos
8. comer

14 Answers will vary.

15 Creative self-expression.

Activities

Expansion

After completing activity 15, have a member of each group summarize what members of their group discussed.

Students with Special Needs

Provide a model for activities 13 and 14.

National Standards

Communication
1.1, 1.3

Teacher Resources

 **Vocabulario II** *El tiempo*

 **Activity 51**

 **Activities 9–11**

 **Activities 6–9**

 **p. 30**

 **Activity 4**

 **Activity 4**

Activities

Critical Thinking

Play the audio CD of *Vocabulario II* as students observe and consider the following: what is happening in each scene; where and when each scene takes place; what the people are saying. Finally, have students guess what they believe is the main theme of each scene.

Language through Action

Using overhead transparency 51, have students come to the front of the class and point to the different scenes as you describe them randomly in Spanish.

National Standards

Connections
3.1, 3.2

Vocabulario II
El tiempo

¿Qué temperatura hace?

Hace 15° grados. Estamos en otoño.

el tenista

Hace fresco.
Hay neblina.
Hace viento.

la lluvia

Hace mal tiemp

la futbolista/
la jugadora de fútbol

No está soleado.
Está nublado.
Llueve.

los deportistas

Ahora nieva.

la patinadora

el esquiador

la nieve

La temperatura mínima de hoy es 2 grados.

Hace buen tiempo.

el basquetbolista

La temperatura máxima de hoy es 34 grados.

Notes

Encourage students to obtain current weather information in Spanish via the Internet:

The Weather Channel
http://espanol.weather.com/

It may help some students to know that it is also possible to ask for the temperature using the expressions *¿Cuál es la temperatura?* or *¿A cuánto está la temperatura?* The answers could be *Es de* (number) *grados* or *Está a* (number) *grados.*

CORREDOR No
PRIMERO 1º 208
SEGUNDO 2º 103
TERCERO 3º 501
CUARTO 4º 931
QUINTO 5º 002
SEXTO 6º 321
SEPTIMO 7º 711
OCTAVO 8º 600
NOVENO 9º 820
DECIMO 10º 030
208
el corredor

16 ¿Quién es?

Go online EMCLanguages.net

Selecciona la foto de la persona apropiada.

A B C D E F

17 El tiempo

Contesta las siguientes preguntas en español.

1. ¿En qué estación hace mucho frío?
2. ¿En qué estación llueve mucho?
3. ¿Cuándo hace mucho calor?
4. Cuando va a llover, ¿cómo está el día?
5. ¿Qué tiempo hace en primavera? ¿Y en verano? ¿Y en otoño? ¿Y en invierno?

18 ¿Qué tiempo hace?

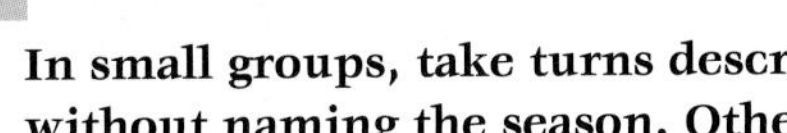

In small groups, take turns describing the weather during one of the seasons without naming the season. Others then try to guess which season you are describing.

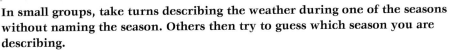

Notes Using overhead transparencies 51 and 52, present and practice the vocabulary on pages 298 and 299.

Expand the presentation of weather-related vocabulary by providing the class with the following words and phrases: *huracán, ciclón, relámpago, trueno; hace fresco; hay neblina.*

Expand activity 18 by extending the discussion to the entire class.

Teacher Resources

Activity 16
Activity 17

Activity 52

Answers

16
1. C
2. E or F
3. A
4. D
5. B
6. E

17 Possible answers:
1. Hace frío en el invierno.
2. Llueve mucho en la primavera.
3. Hace mucho calor en el verano.
4. Está nublado.
5. Answers will vary.

18 Creative self-expression.

Activities

Expansion

Have students answer the following questions in relation to the weather where they live: *¿Qué tiempo hace en el invierno?; ¿Cuándo hace mucho frío y nieva?; ¿Cuándo hace mucho calor?; ¿Cuándo hace un poco de frío y viento?; ¿Cuándo hay muchas flores?; ¿Nieva en tu ciudad? ¿Hay mucha nieve o poca?; ¿Cuándo hay mucha nieve?; Cuando hace sol, ¿qué te gusta hacer?; ¿Cómo sabes cuando va a llover?; ¿Te gusta caminar o correr en la lluvia?; ¿Qué haces cuando llueve?*

National Standards
Communication 1.1, 1.2

Teacher Resources

Diálogo II
¿Qué temperatura hace?
Activity 19
Activity 20
Activity 21

Answers

19 1. Dice que hace calor. Hace treinta y cinco grados.
2. Quiere jugar al básquetbol.
3. Pablo es un buen esquiador.
4. Pueden ir a Portillo.
5. Pablo va a ser el primero en terminar el refresco.

20 Answers will vary.

21 1. F; 2. C; 3. D; 4. A; 5. B; 6. E

Activities

Critical Thinking

Remind students that in the Southern Hemisphere the seasons are the reverse of the seasons in the Northern Hemisphere. Check student understanding of weather expressions by asking several questions. For example, ask questions about the weather north and south of the equator: *En los Estados Unidos es invierno, ¿qué tiempo hace en Chicago? ¿Qué tiempo hace en Santiago? ¿Hace mucho frío en el sur de Chile?; En los Estados Unidos es primavera, ¿qué tiempo hace en Virginia? ¿Qué tiempo hace en Buenos Aires? ¿Hace mucho viento en Chile?; En los Estados Unidos es verano, ¿qué tiempo hace en Missouri? ¿Está nevando en el sur de Chile? ¿Hace calor en Buenos Aires?*

National Standards

Communication
1.2

Connections
3.1

Comparisons
4.1

Diálogo II ¿Qué temperatura hace?

DIEGO: ¡Qué buen refresco!
PABLO: ¿Qué temperatura hace?
ELENA: Hace calor. Hace treinta y cinco grados.

DIEGO: ¡Vamos a jugar al básquetbol!
PABLO: Soy mal jugador de básquetbol.
ELENA: Eres un buen basquetbolista.
PABLO: No, soy un buen esquiador.

ELENA: En julio podemos ir a esquiar a Portillo.
DIEGO: ¿Quién va a ser el primero en terminar el refresco?
PABLO: ¡Yo! Y el segundo vas a ser tú.

19 ¿Qué recuerdas?

1. ¿Dice Elena que hace calor o hace frío?
2. ¿A qué quiere jugar Diego?
3. ¿Quién es un buen esquiador?
4. ¿Adónde pueden ir a esquiar en julio?
5. ¿Quién va a ser el primero en terminar el refresco?

20 Algo personal

1. ¿Qué temperatura hace ahora?
2. ¿Qué tiempo hace?
3. ¿Te gusta cuando hace mucho calor? ¿Y cuando hace frío?

21 ¿Qué tiempo hace?

Selecciona la ilustración que corresponde con lo que oyes.

A 

B 

C 

D  

E 

F 

Notes

Using the recorded version of the dialog, ask students to cover the words and try to figure out what Diego, Pablo and Elena are saying to one another.

You may choose whether to have students do activities 19 and 20 orally or in writing since they are recorded and included in the *¡Aventura!* Audio Program.

Activity 21 has been provided for listening comprehension practice. A recorded version of the activity is included in the Audio Program. A reproducible answer sheet for the activity has been provided at the end of the Audio Program Manual should you wish to have students use it.

Cultura viva II

¿Fahrenheit o centígrados?

Whereas in the United States most people generally refer to the temperature in degrees Fahrenheit *(grados Fahrenheit)*, throughout most of the world the temperature is given in degrees centigrade, also referred to as degrees Celsius *(grados centígrados o grados Celsius)*. To ask for and understand the temperature in Spanish, you must know more than just the words that tell the temperature. You must be able to use degrees centigrade. For example, the temperature at which water freezes is 0 in degrees centigrade and 32 in degrees Fahrenheit. You can make conversions using the following formula:

$$\frac{°C}{5} \times 9 + 32 = °F$$

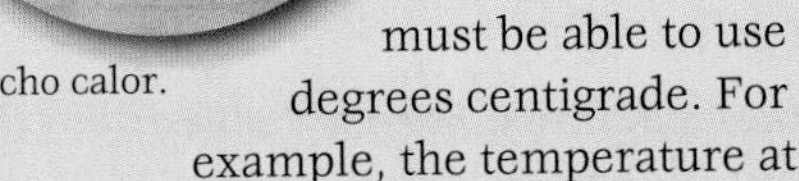

Hace mucho calor.

Hace -5 grados centígrados.

22 Conexión con otras disciplinas: matemáticas

Cambia las temperaturas de grados centígrados a grados Fahrenheit para las siguientes ciudades en Chile.

MODELO La Serena 12°C
Hace 53.6°F.

1. Iquique	28°C
2. Arica	25°C
3. Concepción	20°C
4. Santiago	35°C
5. Balmaceda	30°C
6. Puerto Montt	18°C
7. Temuco	15°C
8. Punta Arenas	9°C

¿Qué temperatura hace en Santiago?

23 Pronóstico del tiempo

Present a weather forecast to your class in Spanish using any props, charts and maps you wish or ones that you create. Make believe you are an actual meteorologist reporting for the ten o'clock news.

Notes

When converting Fahrenheit to Celcius, you may wish to use the following formula:

$$\frac{5(°F - 32)}{9} = °C$$

Note that metric measurements are commonly used in the Spanish-speaking world. For example, distances are measured in *kilómetros* and weight is given in *kilogramos* or simply *kilos*.

Select several students each day to present weather forecasts.

Teacher Resources

Activity 5

Answers

22
1. Hace 82,3 grados.
2. Hace 77 grados.
3. Hace 68 grados.
4. Hace 95 grados.
5. Hace 86 grados.
6. Hace 64,4 grados.
7. Hace 59 grados.
8. Hace 48,2 grados.

23 Creative self-expression.

Activities

Cooperative Learning
Divide the class into small groups and ask each group to choose one of the countries featured in *¡Aventura!*. The groups should each prepare a country-specific weather report to share with the class.

Technology
Have students do an Internet search for the five-day forecast for Santiago, Chile. They should then print out a copy of the report to share with the class.

National Standards

Communication
1.3

Cultures
2.1

Connections
3.1, 3.2

Teacher Resources

 Activity 24

 Activity 12

 Activity 10

 Activity 5

 Activity 6

Answers

24
1. Es futbolista.
2. Es patinadora.
3. Somos deportistas.
4. Es tenista.
5. Son esquiadores.
6. Soy basquetbolista.
7. Eres beisbolista.
8. Soy corredor(a).

Activities

Communities

Have students name several well-known athletes (past or present) from your state. They should then call on a classmate who must describe the person as a *corredor, corredora,* etc.

Students with Special Needs

Model a second sentence for activity 24.

National Standards

Connections
3.1

Idioma

Estructura

Describing people using *-dor* and *-ista*

You can identify someone who participates in a particular sport or activity by changing the ending on the sport to *-dor (-dora)* in some cases or *-ista* in others (which remains the same for males or females).

patinar	– el patina**dor** /la patina**dora**	el tenis	– el/la ten**ista**
esquiar	– el esquia**dor**/la esquia**dora**	el básquetbol	– el/la basquetbol**ista**
correr	– el corre**dor**/la corre**dora**	el fútbol	– el/la futbol**ista**
jugar	– el juga**dor**/ la juga**dora**		

Note: The accent mark is not used on the newly formed word when these endings are added.

Práctica

24 ¿Qué son?

Describe a estas personas usando las siguientes palabras: *basquetbolista, beisbolista, corredor(a), deportista, esquiador(a), futbolista, nadador(a), patinador(a), tenista.*

MODELO Mis primas nadan en la piscina.
Son nadadoras.

1. Juan está jugando al fútbol.
2. Beatriz está patinando sobre hielo.
3. Nosotros tenemos práctica de deportes.
4. Marta está jugando al tenis.
5. Jorge e Iván esquían muy bien.
6. Estoy jugando al básquetbol.
7. Tú estás listo para jugar al béisbol.
8. Estoy corriendo en el parque.

Juan es fútbolista.

Notes Take a few minutes to review the meaning of the new terms created by adding the endings *-dor* and *-ista*. Ask students, for example, if they can figure out the meaning of *patinador/patinadora, esquiador/esquiadora, corredor/corredora, tenista, basquetbolista* and *futbolista*. Finally, ask if students can guess what a *deportista* is.

25 ¿Qué deportes practican?

Di qué tipo de deportistas son las personas de las fotografías.

MODELO 

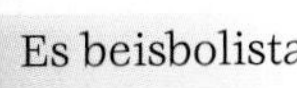
Es beisbolista.

1

2

3

4

5

6

Comunicación

26 Mis deportistas favoritos

In small groups, talk about your favorite athletes. Try to include the names of one or two Spanish-speaking athletes, if possible. Say the person's name, sport and where the person is from (if you know). If the person plays with a team, name the team. Be as specific and detailed as you can, and add any information you can to your classmates' descriptions.

MODELO
A: Mi deportista favorito es Albert Pujols. Es beisbolista y es de la República Dominicana.
B: Juega con San Luis, ¿verdad?
A: Sí. Juega con San Luis.
C: Pues, mi deportista favorito es un basquetbolista. Se llama Pau Gasol.

¡Oportunidades!

El español y los deportes

You probably are familiar with a number of Spanish-speaking sports figures who learned English either before becoming famous or while traveling internationally as they participated in their sport. Knowing another language has helped them communicate with people they have met in their travels. What opportunities do you think might occur for you if you participate in sports and become really good? How might knowing Spanish help you if you are an athlete? Can you think of ways Spanish might help if you were a member of a sports team that competes internationally?

Answers

25
1. Es futbolista.
2. Es basquetbolista.
3. Es corredora.
4. Es tenista.
5. Es patinadora.
6. Es esquiador.

26 Creative self-expression.

Activities

Critical Listening

Describe a well-known athlete without stating his/her name and ask the students to identify the person described. As a follow-up activity, have students work in pairs to prepare and present similar descriptions.

Notes

Sports are important in countries throughout the world, the Spanish-speaking world included. In addition to baseball, soccer, bicycling and boxing, several other sports are very popular.

A popular sport in some Spanish-speaking countries is *jai alai,* a form of handball for singles or doubles competition played on a court with one or three walls. Players use a curved wicker basket (*cesta*) for returning the ball. The sport originated in the Basque region of Spain.

National Standards	
Communication 1.1	**Communities** 5.1
Cultures 2.1, 2.2	
Connections 3.1	

Teacher Resources

 Activity 27

 Activities 13–15

 Activities 11–12

 Activity 6

Answers

27
1. sexto
2. séptima
3. noveno
4. octava
5. tercer
6. primera
7. segundo
8. cuarta
9. quinto
10. décima

Activities

Language through Action
Make several correct and incorrect statements about the order of finish shown in the *Competencia Anual* that accompanies activity 27. Students should raise their hands if what you say matches the information shown.

National Standards

Connections
3.1

Comparisons
4.1

Go online EMCLanguages.net

Estructura

Using ordinal numbers

You use ordinal numbers to place things in order (first, second, third, etc.). In Spanish, only the first ten ordinal numbers are used often. They generally follow definite articles and precede nouns. Like other adjectives in Spanish, the ordinal numbers agree in gender (masculine/feminine) and number (singular/plural) with the noun they modify.

*¿Cuáles son los **primeros** corredores en terminar?*

When *primero* and *tercero* appear before a masculine singular noun, they are shortened to *primer* and *tercer*.

*Francisco es el **primer** corredor en terminar.*
*Lorenzo es el **tercer** corredor en terminar.*

You can abbreviate ordinal numbers ending in *-o*, *-a*, *-os*, *-as* or *-er* by placing those letters at the upper right-hand side of the number: *primero* → *1º*, *primera* → *1ª*, *primeros* → 1os, *primeras* → 1as, *primer* → 1er, *tercer* → 3er.

Práctica

27 La competencia anual del colegio 

El Colegio San Ignacio de Santiago tiene una competencia de esquí en Portillo todos los años. Completa los resultados de la competencia de este año con el número ordinal apropiado.

MODELO Ingrid fue la décima esquiadora en terminar.

Competencia Anual

1ª	Olga	6º	Javier
2º	Edgar	7ª	Paula
3º	Hugo	8ª	Paz
4ª	Natalia	9º	Alfonso
5º	Enrique	10ª	Ingrid

1. Javier fue el __ esquiador en terminar.
2. Paula fue la __ esquiadora en terminar.
3. Alfonso fue el __ esquiador en terminar.
4. Paz fue la __ esquiadora en terminar.
5. Hugo fue el __ esquiador en terminar.
6. Olga fue la __ esquiadora en terminar.
7. Edgar fue el __ esquiador en terminar.
8. Natalia fue la __ esquiadora en terminar.
9. Enrique fue el __ esquiador en terminar.
10. Ingrid fue la __ esquiadora en terminar.

Ingrid fue la décima esquiadora en terminar.

Notes

Inform students that ordinal numbers are usually placed before a noun.

Point out the similarity in the spelling of the words *cuatro* (number four) and *cuarto* (fourth, room).

Note for students that the noun sometimes is omitted when using ordinal numbers:

Nosotros somos los primeros (corredores) en terminar.

Tell students that it is common to use the abbreviated forms of the ordinal numbers. For example, such abbreviations are very common in addresses (street and avenue names, floor numbers, etc.).

¡El pasatiempo nacional!

Irene loves soccer and would like to find out the standings for her favorite Chilean teams. Use the information provided in the chart to update her.

Tabla de posiciones

Equipos	PJ	PG	PE	PP	Pts.
1. Palestino	38	32	2	4	66
2. Everton	38	30	4	4	64
3. Colo Colo	38	27	5	3	59
4. Cobresal	38	24	3	11	51
5. Concepción	38	23	2	13	48
6. La Española	38	20	5	13	45
7. O'Higgins	38	18	6	14	42
8. La Católica	38	15	10	13	40
9. Cobreloa	38	12	5	21	29
10. La Serena	38	9	7	22	25

PJ: Partidos jugados; PG: Partidos ganados; PE: Partidos empatados; PP: Partidos perdidos; Pts.: Puntos

1. El Cobresal es el __ equipo.
2. El O'Higgins es el __ equipo.
3. El Colo Colo todavía es el __ equipo.
4. El Concepción es el __ equipo.
5. La Serena es el __ equipo.
6. La Católica es el __ equipo.
7. El Everton es el __ equipo.
8. El Palestino es el __ equipo.
9. El Cobreloa es el __ equipo.
10. La Española es el __ equipo.

Comunicación

¿Quién fue el primero en terminar la carrera?

Working in pairs, talk about the final results of the girls' and boys' cross-country race.

MODELO **A:** ¿Quién fue el octavo en terminar?
B: Gerardo fue el octavo en terminar.

muchachos	muchachas
1º Jorge	1ª Ana
2º Pedro	2ª Marta
3º Carlos	3ª Susana
4º Ramiro	4ª Paula
5º Juan	5ª Julia
6º Javier	6ª Luisa
7º Alejandro	7ª Yolanda
8º Gerardo	8ª Raquel
9º Rogelio	9ª Carlota
10º Víctor	10ª Paz

¿Quién va a ser el primero en terminar?

Answers

28
1. cuarto
2. séptimo
3. tercer
4. quinto
5. décimo
6. octavo
7. segundo
8. primer
9. noveno
10. sexto

29 All questions are similar: *¿Quién fue el/la* (position) *en terminar?* Answers will vary.

Activities

Critical Thinking
Have students write the ordinal numbers on a set of cards. They should write the numerals one to ten on another set of cards and the first ten months in Spanish on a third set. The three sets should be shuffled separately. Then, working in pairs, students should place the cards in numerical order with the appropriate ordinal number, numeral and month (e.g., *primero, 1, enero*).

Expansion
Have students redo activity 29 using the standings for their favorite sport.

National Standards

Communication
1.1

Connections
3.1

Notes

Before beginning activity 29, check to be sure that students know the meaning of the preterite-tense form *fue*, which they learned in *Capítulo 5*.

Follow up activity 29 by asking students to write out their answers.

Point out that in everyday language only cardinal numbers are used after *décimo*. Therefore, Alfonso the Thirteenth is *Alfonso XIII (trece).*

Answers

30 Creative self-expression.

Activities

Expansion
Ask questions pertaining to students' class schedules: *¿Cuál es tu primera clase del día?; ¿Cuál es tu segunda clase del día?; ¿Cuál es tu tercera clase del día?;* etc.

National Standards
Communication 1.1
Cultures 2.2
Connections 3.1

30 Los deportes en familia

Members of the Spanish Club participate in different sports throughout the year. Working in pairs, talk about the information provided here depicting their activities during different seasons. You may want to talk about what each person is doing, what the season is, what the weather is like or anything else you can say in Spanish. Correct any information your partner says that you think is wrong.

Pedro

1

Ana

Esteban

2

Rosa

Alejandro

3

Carmen

MODELO
A: En el primer dibujo es otoño.
B: No, no es otoño, es primavera. Hace viento. Pedro está jugando al básquetbol.
A: Sí, y Ana está jugando al tenis.

Notes Chile offers many impressive ski resorts in addition to Portillo and Farellones (see page 293). Valle Nevado near Santiago is the largest ski resort in South America. It has 50 ski lifts and 22,000 acres of Andean ski slopes. Some runs are 10 miles long and 17,908 feet high.

En el verano

In groups of three, each of you should list five summer activities in order from most to least favorite, using ordinal numbers. Then discuss your preferences.

1º ir a la playa
2º dar paseos por el parque
3º jugar al fútbol

MODELO A: Primero, me gusta ir a la playa en el verano. Hace sol y es muy divertido. Segundo, me gusta dar paseos por el parque.
B: Bueno, primero me gusta dormir.
C: A mí, primero, me gusta montar en patineta.

Una playa en Chile.

Answers

31 Creative self-expression.

Activities

Multiple Intelligences (bodily-kinesthetic)
Borrow a soccer ball from the physical education department. Call out one of the ordinal numbers and throw the ball to a student, who must call out the next ordinal number in the sequence before catching the ball. You may vary the drill by having the students say the previous ordinal number to the one you call out before catching the ball.

Notes Spanish-speaking countries have won medals in several popular sports in the Olympics, including boxing (*boxeo*), swimming and diving (*natación y clavado*), weight lifting (*levantamiento de pesas*) and equestrian sports (*equitación*).

Your students may find it interesting to learn that Chile was the first Spanish-speaking country to participate in the Olympics in 1896.

Just as *Estados Unidos* is abbreviated *EE.UU.*, the abbreviation for *Juegos Olímpicos* is *JJ.OO.*

National Standards

Communication
1.1

Cultures
2.1

Connections
3.1

Teacher Resources

Lectura personal
Activity 32
Activity 33

Answers

32 1. Carlos es de Chile. Él practica el andinismo.
2. Desde Santiago de Chile se puede ver la Cordillera Sur de los Andes.
3. El Monumento Natural de El Morado es una montaña en un parque a hora y media de Santiago. Está cerrado en el invierno porque hay mucha nieve.
4. El primer día, Carlos va a dar un paseo por la laguna El Morado.
5. El segundo día, va a hacer mucho frío.

33 Answers will vary.

Activities

Spanish for Spanish Speakers
Have students write a short composition in Spanish, summarizing what they know about Chile. Expand the activity by having students seek additional information about Chile in the library or via the Internet.

National Standards
Cultures 2.2
Connections 3.1, 3.2
Comparisons 4.1

Lectura personal

Dirección http://www.emcp.com/músico/aventura1/

Archivo Edición Ver Favoritos Herramientas Ayuda

página principal | miembros | e-diario

Nombre: **Carlos Cubillas Lorca**
Edad: **19 años**
País natal: **Chile**
Su estación favorita: **verano**

¡Otro excelente concierto en Santiago de Chile! Saben amigos, estoy muy contento de estar en mi país después de tantos meses. Eché de menos[1] mis montañas. Chile tiene 4.200 kilómetros (2.260 millas) de cordillera[2]. Desde casi cualquier[3] lugar de la capital se puede ver la majestuosa Cordillera Sur de los Andes. Cuando no toco la guitarra con el grupo La Ola, practico el andinismo: deporte de escalar[4] montañas, específicamente los Andes. ¡Me gusta mucho el andinismo! Después de enviar este mensaje, voy a ir al Monumento Natural de El Morado con un buen amigo (y excelente esquiador). El Morado está a sólo hora y media de Santiago. El parque está cerrado entre[5] los meses de mayo y septiembre porque hay mucha nieve, pero estamos en otoño, entonces está bien. El primer día vamos a dar un paseo por la laguna[6] El Morado. Probablemente va a hacer fresco. El segundo día, en cambio, va a hacer mucho frío. Ese día pensamos escalar en hielo por el glaciar de San Francisco. A pesar de las bajas temperaturas, la falta[7] de oxígeno y el viento, vale la pena[8] visitar este lugar para poder presenciar[9] la magia de las montañas, mis montañas chilenas.

[1]I missed [2]mountain chain [3]any [4]climb [5]between [6]lagoon [7]lack [8]it is worthwhile [9]to witness

32 ¿Qué recuerdas?

1. ¿De dónde es Carlos? ¿Qué deporte practica?
2. ¿Qué se puede ver desde Santiago de Chile?
3. ¿Qué es el Monumento Natural de El Morado? ¿En qué estación está cerrado? ¿Por qué?
4. ¿Adónde va a dar un paseo Carlos el primer día?
5. ¿Qué tiempo va a hacer el segundo día?

- From what you can infer from the reading, what is Chile's geography and climate like? Compare it with the geography and climate of the state in which you live.

33 Algo personal

1. ¿Hay montañas donde vives? ¿Cómo se llaman?
2. ¿Te gustaría escalar El Morado? ¿Por qué sí o por qué no?
3. ¿Qué estación es buena para practicar el andinismo?

Notes Encourage students to find out more about Chile by going to the following Web sites:

Chile http://www.chile.com/
LanChile http://www.lanchile.com
General travel information
http://www.expedia.com

Autoevaluación

As a review and self-check, respond to the following:

1. Name a favorite activity during each of the seasons.
2. What is the weather like where you live in the spring? Summer? Fall? Winter?
3. How would you ask what the temperature is today in Santiago, Chile?
4. Ask a friend how to send an e-mail letter and where you should put the address.
5. Imagine you are recording finishing times at a school track meet and it is your job to rank the runners as they finish. Using the ordinal numbers, count the first ten runners to cross the line in order to tell each runner where they are ranked.
6. What do you know about Chile?

Palabras y expresiones

How many of these words and expressions do you know?

El tiempo
el cambio
está nublado,-a /soleado,-a
la estación
el fresco
el grado
hace (+ *weather expression)*
hay neblina/sol
el hielo
el invierno
la lluvia
máximo,-a
mínimo,-a
la neblina
la nieve
nublado,-a
el otoño
la primavera
¿Qué tiempo/ temperatura hace?
el sol
soleado,-a
la temperatura
el tiempo
el viento

Para describir
buen
cuarto,-a
décimo,-a
excelente
listo,-a
mal
noveno,-a
octavo,-a
quinto,-a
segundo,-a
séptimo,-a
sexto,-a
tercero (tercer),-a
todavía

Deportistas
el basquetbolista, la basquetbolista
el corredor, la corredora
el deportista, la deportista
el esquiador, la esquiadora
el futbolista, la futbolista
el jugador, la jugadora
el patinador, la patinadora
el tenista, la tenista

Verbos
continuar
copiar
enviar
esquiar
llover (ue)
montar en patineta
nevar (ie)
patinar sobre hielo

Expresiones y otras palabras
dar un paseo
en cambio
la flor
el lugar
el paseo
la patineta
por
por todos lados

Estructura

Do you remember the following grammar rules?

Present tense of *dar* and *poner*

The verbs *dar* and *poner* are irregular in the present tense *yo* form.

dar		poner	
doy	damos	**pongo**	ponemos
das	**dais**	pones	ponéis
da	dan	pone	ponen

Using ordinal numbers

Use ordinal numbers 1 to 10 which are placed between the definite article and noun. Ordinal numbers match the noun in gender and number.

El **primer** día de clase. *The **first** day of class.*
*Las **segundas** páginas son mejores.* *The **second** pages are better.*

Verbs that require special accentuation

When conjugating some verbs that end in *-uar* or *-iar* require a written accent mark in the present tense, **except** for in the *nosotros* form.

continuar		esquiar	
continúo	continuamos	esquío	esquiamos
continúas	continuáis	esquías	esquiáis
continúa	continúan	esquía	esquían

Describing people using *-dor* and *-ista*

You can identify someone who participates in a particular sport or activity by changing the ending of the verb to *-dor* and the noun to *-ista*.

patinar → el patina**dor**/ la patina**dora**
el fútbol → el/la futbol**ista**

Notes

The name Chile comes from the indigenous word *Tchili* meaning **the deepest point of the earth.**

In 1980, Chile initiated an intensive literacy campaign. The rate of adult literacy rose from 89 percent in 1980 to 93.4 percent in 1990.

Chile is a country of young people, with over half of the population under the age of twenty. The country has one of the lowest rates of population growth in South America, roughly 1.5 percent per year.

Teacher Resources

Activity 16

pp. 58, 92

Juegos

Flash Cards

Answers

Autoevaluación
Possible answers:

1. Me gusta montar en patineta en la primavera....
2. En la primavera hace viento....
3. ¿Qué temperatura hace hoy en Santiago de Chile?
4. ¿Cómo envío mi carta por correo electrónico y dónde pongo la dirección?
5. Primero, segundo, tercero, cuarto, etc.
6. Two writers from Chile, Gabriela Mistral and Pablo Neruda, have won Nobel Prizes in Literature.

Activities

Multiple Intelligences (logical-mathematical)
Ask students to give the Fahrenheit equivalent of several temperatures: 39°C (102.2°F), 100°C (212°F) and so on.

Spanish for Spanish Speakers
As an alternative to one of the *Autoevaluación* activities, ask students to read one or two poems by Pablo Neruda and summarize the themes presented (either orally or in writing).

National Standards

Communication
1.3

Cultures
2.1

Connections
3.1

Teacher Resources

 *El mundo de los deportes*

Answers

Preparación

1. El tema principal de esta lectura es los deportes en el mundo hispano.
2. El deporte más popular del mundo hispano es el fútbol.
3. Answers will vary.

Activities

Expansion

Talk with students about the Olympics (see the Notes below and on page 307). Then ask students to search the following key words for information on the Olympics: *deportes, deportes olímpicos, Comité Olímpico Internacional.* Have students list five facts they learned during their search and share the information with the class.

National Standards

Communication
1.3

Cultures
2.1

Connections
3.1

¡Viento en popa!

Tú lees

Estrategia

Previewing

Before starting to read, try various activities that will help you preview what the reading is about. For example, you will understand more and enjoy what you are about to read on this page if you quickly skim the first and last paragraph of the following reading.

Preparación

Contesta las siguientes preguntas como preparación para la lectura.

1. ¿Cuál es el tema principal de esta lectura?
2. ¿Cuál es el deporte más popular del mundo hispano?
3. Identifica cinco cognados en la lectura *El mundo de los deportes*.

Previewing Activities

Read the title.
Look for cognates.
Skim the first paragraph.
Skim the last paragraph.
Look at information in accompanying charts.
Ask yourself what the main points are.

El mundo de los deportes

Los deportes son populares e importantes en el mundo hispano, y el fútbol es sin duda alguna[1] el deporte favorito de todos. Miles de personas ven los partidos de fútbol todas las semanas y la Copa Mundial[2] de fútbol es el evento más importante del mundo deportivo. Millones de personas en todo el mundo miran los partidos de la Copa Mundial y se contagian de la fiebre del "¡Gol!"[3]. La Copa Mundial sólo se juega una vez cada cuatro años y países de todo el mundo participan en este gran espectáculo del deporte.

Futbolistas de Inglaterra y Argentina.

El béisbol es otro deporte muy popular en el Caribe, especialmente en Cuba, la República Dominicana y Puerto Rico. También es muy popular en algunas

Notes The first Hispanic Olympic medal winner was Ramón Fonst, from Cuba, in 1900. The first Olympic Games to be held in a Spanish-speaking country took place in Mexico in 1968. The most recent Spanish-speaking nation to host the Olympics was Spain (Barcelona, 1992). The Spanish-speaking country with most gold medal winners for one sport is Uruguay, which has eight athletes with two medals each in soccer. Cuba is the Spanish-speaking country that has won the most gold medals.

Many of most famous soccer players in the world have come from Argentina and Uruguay.

Estos chicos juegan al jai alai.

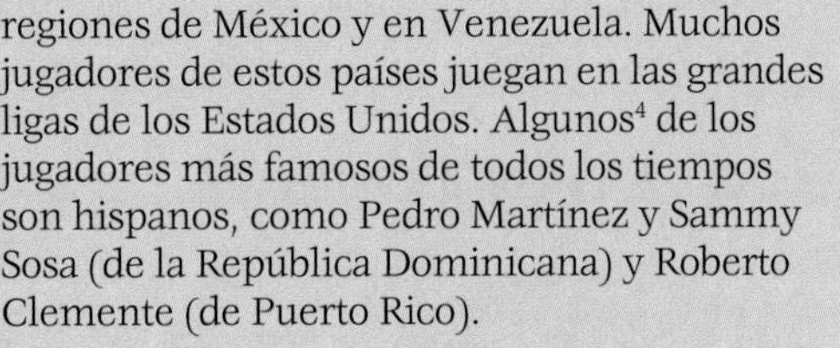

regiones de México y en Venezuela. Muchos jugadores de estos países juegan en las grandes ligas de los Estados Unidos. Algunos[4] de los jugadores más famosos de todos los tiempos son hispanos, como Pedro Martínez y Sammy Sosa (de la República Dominicana) y Roberto Clemente (de Puerto Rico).

El boxeo (también llamado[5] el deporte de las narices chatas[6]), el frontón[7], el jai alai y el ciclismo son también deportes populares en los países hispanos. Estos dos últimos también son muy populares en España, junto con[8] el básquetbol (también llamado baloncesto).

El ciclismo es popular en los países hispanos.

En el mundo hispano se practican muchos otros deportes y desde hace décadas los hispanos, al igual que[9] el resto del mundo, practican deportes no sólo como pasatiempo, sino también para mantener buena salud[10] y una vida activa.

[1]Without a doubt [2]World Cup [3]they all catch "goal" fever [4]Some [5]called [6]flat noses [7]a sport similar to squash or handball [8]along with [9]just as [10]good health

A ¿Qué recuerdas?

1. ¿Cómo son los deportes en el mundo hispano?
2. ¿Qué ven miles de personas cada semana?
3. ¿Cuál es el evento más importante en el fútbol?
4. ¿Qué deporte es muy popular en la región del Caribe?
5. ¿Qué otros deportes son populares en el mundo hispano?

B Algo personal

1. ¿Haces alguno de estos deportes? ¿Cuál? ¿Dónde? ¿Con quién?
2. ¿Cuál es tu deporte favorito?
3. ¿Cuánto tiempo hace que haces ese deporte?
4. ¿Sabes algo de los deportes en el mundo hispano? ¿Qué sabes?
5. ¿Ves muchos deportes en la televisión? ¿Cuáles?

Nuestro deporte favorito es el béisbol.

Notes Discuss with the class what students know about some of the people mentioned in the reading. Pedro Martínez was one of the best pitchers in baseball. Sammy Sosa received international attention in 1998 during his race with Mark McGwire to break the single season home-run record. Roberto Clemente was a batting champion four times during his career playing right field for the Pittsburgh Pirates. His career ended with his untimely death in a plane crash on his way from Puerto Rico to Managua, Nicaragua, to help victims of a devastating earthquake on New Year's Eve of 1972.

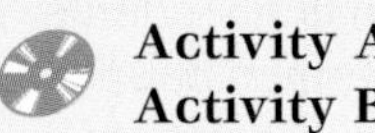

Teacher Resources

Activity A
Activity B

Answers

A 1. Los deportes en el mundo hispano son populares e importantes.
2. Ven los partidos de fútbol.
3. El evento más importante es la Copa Mundial de Fútbol.
4. El béisbol es muy popular en la región del Caribe.
5. Otros deportes populares son el boxeo, el frontón, el ciclismo, el básquetbol, el jai alai.

B Answers will vary.

Activities

Critical Listening
Describe a celebrity without stating his/her name and ask the students to identify the person described. As a follow-up activity, have students work in pairs to prepare and present similar descriptions.

National Standards

Communication	Comparisons
1.1	4.2
Cultures	
2.1	
Connections	
3.1	

Answers

Answers will vary. When students have finished their compositions, have them divide into groups to peer edit each other's work and correct any errors they may find. After editing and correcting their compositions, encourage them to add artwork or graphics to add more interest to the finished product. You may want to display them around the room on the walls or bulletin boards.

Activities

Multiple Intelligences (linguistic)
Students can improve their writing by comparing their style to classic writers from the past. Ask for volunteers to read two or three poems by Gabriela Mistral in translation and compare them to the poetry of Emily Dickinson.

Spanish for Spanish Speakers
To improve their reading and writing skills, and to expand their knowledge of Latin writers, ask students to read Ernesto Sábato's *El túnel* and write a two-page paper about the relationship between the main character, Juan Pablo Castel, and his mother.

National Standards

Communication
1.2

Connections
3.1

Tú escribes

Estrategia

Questioning

The steps you are learning to take to improve a composition are sometimes referred to as the writing process. For example, after selecting a topic, coming up with ideas to include in the composition can be challenging. However, you have learned one technique to overcome this difficulty: brainstorming for ideas. Another way to get started involves answering questions that will guide you in considering your theme from different points of view.

Answer the questions that follow in order to generate ideas for writing on the theme *Mi tiempo libre*. Then select some of the ideas that you like and write a paragraph about your free time. Remember to incorporate some transition words *(en cambio, entonces, pero)* to tie your ideas together and make your composition flow smoothly.

1. ¿Cuáles de estas actividades te gustan?

montar en patineta	practicar deportes
ver la tele	escuchar música
leer revistas	esquiar
ir a un concierto	ir a partidos de béisbol, fútbol, etc.
hacer ejercicios	montar a caballo
montar en bicicleta	hacer un picnic
ir al cine	trabajar con la computadora
ir de compras	tocar un instrumento musical
patinar sobre hielo	ir a fiestas con amigos
dar un paseo	hablar por teléfono

2. ¿Qué otras actividades te gusta hacer?
3. Completa estas frases pensando en lo que te gusta hacer.
   - **A.** En el verano, me gusta....
   - **B.** En el invierno, me gusta....
   - **C.** Cuando hace mal tiempo, yo....
   - **D.** Cuando estoy enfermo/a, prefiero....
   - **E.** Si estoy aburrido/a, yo....
   - **F.** Cuando estoy solo/a, me gusta....
   - **G.** Cuando estoy con mi familia, prefiero....
   - **H.** Cuando estoy con mis amigos....
   - **I.** Si tengo dinero, me gusta....
   - **J.** Cuando no tengo dinero, prefiero....

Notes

Review. The use of transition words was taught in the *Tú escribes* section of *Capítulo 6*.

Tú escribes provides a formal opportunity for students to improve their ability to write in Spanish. The *Estrategia* provides helpful tips that students must practice in the activities provided.

Proyectos adicionales

A Conexión con la tecnología

Using the Internet, visit a Web site that gives weather information for different cities around the world. Find the current weather conditions for several Spanish-speaking countries. Then write several paragraphs in Spanish to summarize what you find. Be sure to include the following information: identify the different symbols used to represent weather conditions, describe today's weather in several cities, give the current temperature, tell what season it is and predict what people are doing now due to the weather.

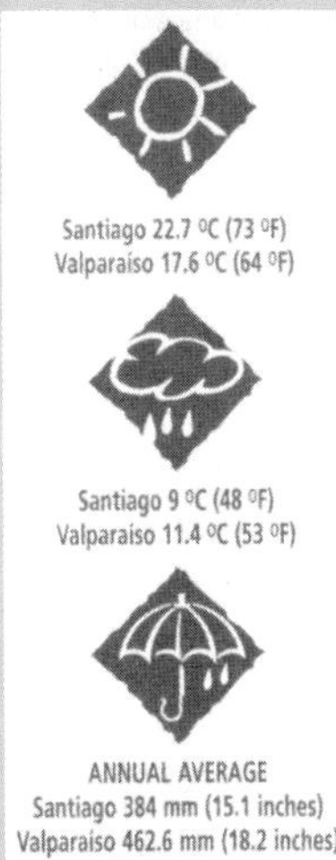

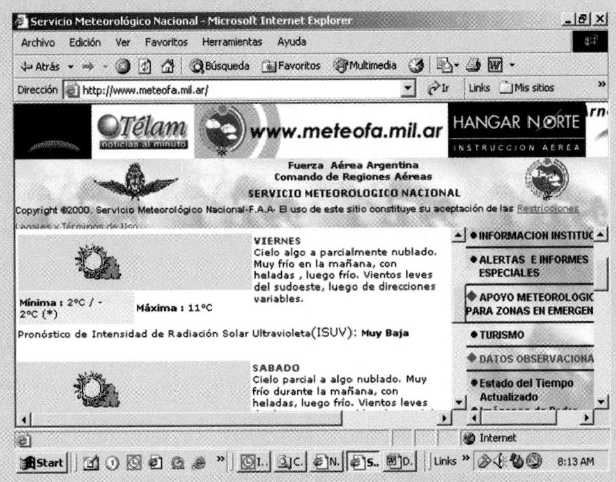

B Comunidades

Using the Internet, the newspaper, information from family and friends, etc., find out what you can about five well-known athletes in your local community or state (try to find at least one person who speaks Spanish). Try to find out where they are from, where they live, whether they speak Spanish, what they do when they have free time or anything else that interests you. Then write two or three statements describing each person.

C Comparisons

Compare sports where you live with what you know about sports in Spanish-speaking countries. Are the same sports popular? Does the weather have an effect on the sports being practiced? Are the sports played at the same time of the year? During the same season?

Notes Encourage students to find out more about Argentina by going to the following Web sites:

Lonely Planet World Guide
http://www.lonelyplanet.com/destinations/south_america/argentina/
La Nación http://www.lanacion.com.ar
Electronic Embassy
http://www.embassy.org
Organization of American States
http://www.oas.org
General travel information
http://www.expedia.com

Teacher Resources

p. 73

Answers

A Creative self-expression.
B Creative-thinking skill development.
C Answers will vary.

Activities

Language through Action
Prepare cards with a variety of statements in the *presente progresivo,* such as *él/ella está bailando.* Pass the cards to different students and ask them to dramatize the actions. As a student performs an action, the class must say what he/she is doing.

Multiple Intelligences (linguistic)
Have students research and then summarize some similarities and differences in the lives of Bernardo O'Higgins and George Washington.

Technology
Have students search the Internet for ecotours to view Iguazú Falls or vacation packages to ski on the slopes in Argentina. They should print out some of the Web pages advertising these trips and report their findings to the class.

National Standards	
Communication 1.3	**Communities** 5.1
Connections 3.1, 3.2	
Comparisons 4.1, 4.2	

Teacher Resources

 *Trabalenguas*

 Episode 7, DVD 2, Track 7

Answers

Resolviendo el misterio

1. Answers will vary.
2. Answers will vary.
3. Answers will vary.

Activities

Connections

Have students draw a map of Argentina that shows major cities, rivers, mountains and surrounding countries. They may add any other geographical features they wish.

Spanish for Spanish Speakers

Assign the book *El jardín de senderos que se bifurcan* by Jorge Luis Borges. Next, students must write a 50–100-word summary of the contents printed on colored paper. Then have students design a poster to promote the story by combining the summary with illustrations and appropriate lettering to create a visually attractive poster.

Trabalenguas

Using the same format as the *Trabalenguas*, ask students to write a tongue twister or poem about summer, fall, and winter.

National Standards
Communication 1.3
Cultures 2.2
Connections 3.1

Now that I have completed this chapter, I can...	Go to these pages for help:
talk about leisure time activities.	270
discuss sports.	271
say what someone can do.	274
discuss length of time.	280
describe what is happening.	282
talk about the seasons and weather.	290, 298
indicate order.	304
I can also...	
talk about life in Argentina and Chile.	273, 293
talk about television and renting movies.	276
convert temperatures from centigrade to Fahrenheit.	301
understand a weather forecast in Spanish.	313

Trabalenguas

Es primavera: ¡Cuántas flores florean en el florido campo!

Resolviendo el misterio

After watching Episode 7 of *El cuarto misterioso*, answer the following questions.

1. Why did José agree to invite Rafael to his uncle's house for lunch?
2. Why is Conchita hanging around Rafael?
3. What has been revealed about Rafael's character so far?

Notes

Chile is the only Spanish-speaking Latin American country with two Nobel Prize winners in literature. Gabriela Mistral received the prize in 1945 and Pablo Neruda in 1971.

Argentina has long been noted for the high quality of its intellectual life and for its many artistic influences. Among its modern literary figures of international reputation are Jorge Luis Borges, Julio Cortázar, Ernesto Sábato and Manuel Puig.

Loose translation of the *Trabalenguas*: It is spring. How many flowers blooming in the flowery field!

Vocabulario

Go online EMCLanguages.net

los **aeróbicos** aerobics *7A*
ahora mismo right now *7A*
el **ajedrez** chess *7A*
alquilar to rent *7A*
americano,-a American *7A*
antes de before *7A*
apagar to turn off *7A*
el **básquetbol** basketball *7A*
el **basquetbolista**, la **basquetbolista** basketball player *7B*
buen good *7B*
el **cambio** change *7B*
las **cartas** playing cards *7A*
casi almost *7A*
continuar to continue *7B*
el **control remoto** remote control *7A*
copiar to copy *7B*
el **corredor**, la **corredora** runner *7B*
costar (ue) to cost *7A*
¿Cuánto *(+ time expression)* **hace que** *(+ present tense of verb) ... ?* How long ... ? *7A*
cuarto,-a fourth *7B*
las **damas** checkers *7A*
dar un paseo to go for a walk, to go for a ride *7B*
dar to give *7A*
décimo,-a tenth *7B*
el **deportista**, la **deportista** athlete *7B*
después de after *7A*
dibujar to draw, to sketch *7A*
dormir (ue, u) to sleep *7A*
en cambio on the other hand *7B*
enviar to send *7B*
el **equipo** team *7A*
el **esquiador**, la **esquiadora** skier *7B*
esquiar to ski *7B*
esta noche tonight *7A*
está nublado,-a/soleado,-a it's cloudy, it's sunny *7B*
la **estación** season *7B*
estupendo,-a wonderful, marvelous *7A*
excelente excellent *7B*
la **flor** flower *7B*
el **fresco** cool *7B*
el **fútbol americano** football *7A*
el **futbolista**, la **futbolista** soccer player *7B*
el **grado** degree *7B*
hace *(+ time expression)* **que** *(time expression +)* ago *7A*
hace *(+ weather expression)* it is *(+weather expression) 7B*
hacer aeróbicos to do aerobics *7A*
hay neblina/sol it is misting/it is sunny *7B*
el **hielo** ice *7B*
el **invierno** winter *7B*
el **jugador**, la **jugadora** player *7B*
jugar (ue) to play *7A*
la **lista** list *7A*
listo,-a ready *7B*
llover (ue) to rain *7B*
la **lluvia** rain *7B*
el **lugar** place *7B*
mal bad *7B*
la **maquinita** little machine, video game *7A*
máximo,-a maximum *7B*
mínimo,-a minimum *7B*
el **minuto** minute *7A*
mismo,-a same *7A*
montar en patineta to skateboard *7B*
la **neblina** mist *7B*
nevar (ie) to snow *7B*
la **nieve** snow *7B*
noveno,-a ninth *7B*
nublado,-a cloudy *7B*
octavo,-a eighth *7B*
el **otoño** autumn *7B*
el **pasatiempo** pastime, leisure activity *7A*
el **paseo** walk, ride, trip *7B*
el **patinador**, la **patinadora** skater *7B*
patinar sobre hielo to ice-skate *7B*
la **patineta** skateboard *7B*
permitir to permit *7A*
poder (ue, u) to be able to *7A*
por la mañana in the morning *7A*
por la noche at night *7A*
por la tarde in the afternoon *7A*
por todos lados everywhere *7B*
por by *7B*
la **primavera** spring *7B*
el **programa** program *7A*
¿Qué temperatura hace? What is the temperature? *7B*
¿Qué tiempo hace? How is the weather? *7B*
quinto,-a fifth *7B*
recordar (ue) to remember *7A*
remoto,-a remote *7A*
el **segundo** second *7A*
segundo,-a second *7B*
séptimo,-a seventh *7B*
sexto,-a sixth *7B*
el **siglo** century *7A*
el **sol** sun *7B*
soleado,-a sunny *7B*
la **telenovela** soap opera *7A*
el **televisor** television *7A*
la **temperatura** temperature *7B*
el **tenista**, la **tenista** tennis player *7B*
tercero (tercer),-a third *7B*
el **tiempo** weather *7B*
todavía yet *7A*
todavía still *7B*
la **vida** life *7A*
el **viento** wind *7B*
el **voleibol** volleyball *7A*
volver (ue) to return, to go back, to come back *7A*

Teacher Resources

Las aventuras de la familia Miranda

Repaso

***¡Aventureros!*, Ch. 7**

Internet Activities

i-Culture

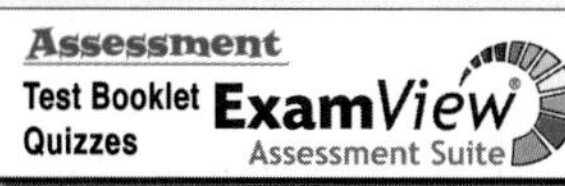

Activities

Critical Thinking

See if students can guess the meaning of the words *bilingüe* (bilingual), *antigüedad* (antiquity) and *pingüino* (penguin). For practice, have students say some sentences that combine words that focus on the pronunciation of *u* in Spanish: *Querido Miguel: ¿Por qué no quieres ir a aquel parque en Mayagüez para ver los pingüinos?; ¿Qué película quieres alquilar?* Be sure to model the sentence several times before asking them to write what they hear. Finally, ask students if they understand the meaning of the sentences.

Pronunciation (*la letra u*)

Review the sound of *u*, pointing out that the sound is similar to the **u** sound in the English word **shoot**, but the sound is shorter: *octubre, gusta, mucho, muy, nunca, lugar*. Then note that the letter *u* is silent in the syllables *gue, gui, que* and *qui*: *Guillermo, guitarra, aquel, equipo*. Exceptions to this rule are indicated with two dots (*diéresis*) over the *u*: *bilingüe, antigüedad, pingüino*.

Notes

Remind students that the *ue* or *u* shown in parentheses after infinitives listed in *¡Aventura!* help students remember how these verbs are formed, for example, *costar (ue)* and *jugar (ue)*.

Spanish is the official language of Argentina. However, it is a distinctly Argentine Spanish, characterized by special words, expressions and pronunciation. A dialect called Spanish Lunfardo, which developed in Buenos Aires before 1900, with many borrowed words from Italian and Portuguese, has had a significant impact on the Spanish that is spoken in the capital.

National Standards
Cultures 2.2
Comparisons 4.1

Teacher Resources

Capítulo 8

TPRS *Capítulo 8*

Episode 8, DVD 2, Track 11

Connections with Parents

Try to encourage parents and guardians to have a larger role in their child's classroom education. In *Capítulo 8*, students will be learning vocabulary associated with chores and helping around the house. As you begin the new chapter, encourage students to talk with their parents or guardians about what they are learning in class. Consider having students ask if they may prepare a dish at home using a recipe from a Spanish-speaking country. A recipe for *paella* appears on page 341.

Answers

El cuarto misterioso

1. Las respuestas variarán.
2. Las respuestas variarán.
3. Mole, (MOH-lay) viene de la palabra Nahuatl *molli* que significa "mezcla". Generalmente, mole es una salsa mezclada con cebolla, ajo, chiles y un poco de chocolate.

National Standards

Connections
3.1, 3.2

CAPÍTULO 8

Mis quehaceres

El cuarto misterioso

Contesta las siguientes preguntas sobre *Episodio 8–En casa.*

1. ¿Qué quehaceres probablemente tienen que hacer José y don Pedro para preparar el almuerzo para Ana, Conchita y Rafael?
2. A los jóvenes, les gusta comer juntos. ¿Por qué piensas que es divertido y popular comer con los amigos?
3. ¿Qué es mole?

Mientras José y su tío preparan la casa para la visita de Ana, Conchita y Rafael, José le pregunta a su tío sobre "el cuarto misterioso."

Objetivos

- talk about **household chores**
- say **what just happened**
- **ask for and offer help**
- talk about **the past**
- identify and describe **foods**
- discuss **food preparation**
- make **comparisons**

Notes A checklist of these objectives, along with additional functions, appears on page 360 so students can evaluate their own progress.

Activities

Prior Knowledge
Review the chapter objectives. Ask questions such as: What chores do you do at home? What is the time difference between describing "What happened?" and "What just happened?" What categories of adjectives describe foods (for example, taste, smell, color, size)? What vocabulary do we use in English to compare things (for example, words that end in *–er*, *-est*, the expressions "as" and "than")? What dishes do you and your family like to prepare? Does your family hang its laundry outside to to dry? Why or why not?

Critical Thinking
Have students look at the photos at the start of the chapter. Ask students to guess which country they will be studying in this chapter and what else they think they will be learning about in this chapter.

Contexto cultural

España
Nombre oficial: Reino de España
Población: 46.754.000
Capital: Madrid

Ciudades importantes: Barcelona, Valencia, Sevilla
Unidad monetaria: el euro
Fiesta nacional: 12 de octubre, Día de la Hispanidad

Gente famosa: Antonio Banderas (actor), Pablo Picasso (pintor), Enrique Iglesias (cantante), Penélope Cruz (actriz)

Notes The cultural focus of this chapter is Spain. Spain is the only Spanish-speaking country with a monarchy. *Juan Carlos de Borbón* has been king and his wife, *Sofía*, queen since 1975.

National Standards

Cultures
2.1, 2.2

Connections
3.1

Teacher Resources

 Vocabulario I
Los quehaceres

 Activities 53–54

 Activity 1

 Activities 1–2

 pp. 104, 111

 p. 3

 Activity 1

 Activity 1

Content reviewed in *Lección A*

- rooms in a house
- family
- direct object pronouns
- present progressive
- objects in a kitchen

Activities

Prereading Strategy
Ask students to identify cognates and any known vocabulary in *Vocabulario I.*

Connections
3.1

Lección A Vocabulario I
Los quehaceres

Quizás debo sólo adornar esta pared.

Ramón sube algo al primer piso.
Él le sube una cami
a su hermano.

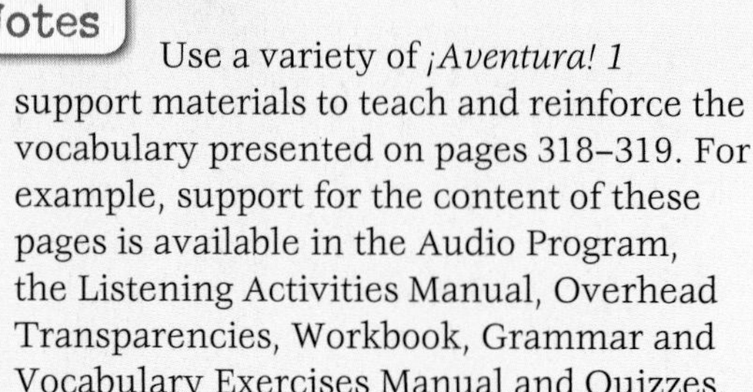

Notes Use a variety of *¡Aventura! 1* support materials to teach and reinforce the vocabulary presented on pages 318–319. For example, support for the content of these pages is available in the Audio Program, the Listening Activities Manual, Overhead Transparencies, Workbook, Grammar and Vocabulary Exercises Manual and Quizzes.

Tell students that another common way of saying **to cook** is *hacer la comida.*

1 ¿Qué tienen que hacer? 

Write the names Julia and Enrique. Next, listen and list under each of their names what chores *(quehaceres)* each of them has to do. Then circle any items on the lists that they both have to do. The first one has been done for you.

MODELO Julia — Enrique
adornar la sala

2 La familia García 

Contesta las siguientes preguntas, según la información en el Vocabulario I.

1. ¿Quién acaba de llegar?
2. ¿Dónde deja el abrigo el abuelo?
3. ¿Qué le sube Ramón a su hermano?
4. ¿Hay mucha gente en la familia García? ¿Cuántas personas son?
5. ¿Hacen juntos los quehaceres?

3 Tu familia

Haz una lista de los quehaceres que hacen en tu casa según lo que aprendiste en el Vocabulario I. Luego, di quién hace cada uno de esos quehaceres en tu familia.

MODELO	
hacer las camas	mi hermana
limpiar la sala	yo
limpiar la cocina	mi padre y mi madre

Estrategia

Increasing your vocabulary

When reading or learning new vocabulary in Spanish, you can figure out the meaning of a new word by relating it to your knowledge of other words that are spelled similarly. Such groups of similar words are called "word families." All the "members" of a word family share a common, easily recognizable root. Can you see how the verb *cocinar* (to cook) and the noun *cocina* (kitchen) are related in this way since people cook in a kitchen? Recognizing word families can help you expand your Spanish vocabulary and can make learning new words easier.

Notes Remind students they have already learned that cognates *(cognados)* are words that are similar in English and Spanish. Words that appear the same but that are not cognates are considered false cognates *(cognados falsos)* because their meaning or usage is different in the two languages. Have students give the meaning for the cognate that appears on page 318, *preparar*, and the false cognates *sacar*, *ropa* and *aprender*, all of which students have already seen in previous chapters.

Teacher Resources

 **Activities 1–2**

 **p. 32**

Answers

1 **Julia**
(1.) adornar la sala
2. cocinar el pollo
3. trabajar en el jardín
(4.) hacer la cama
(5.) limpiar la cocina

Enrique
(6.) adornar la sala
7. preparar la ensalada
8. doblar la ropa
(9.) hacer la cama
(10.) limpiar la cocina

2 Possible answers:
1. El abuelo acaba de llegar.
2. Deja el abrigo en la sala.
3. Ramón le sube un abrigo a su hermano.
4. Sí, hay mucha gente en la familia García. Son nueve personas.
5. Sí, hacen juntos los quehaceres.

3 Answers will vary.

Activities

Prereading Strategy
Ask students to discuss the chores they are expected to do at home. Then instruct students to cover up the words in *Vocabulario I* with their hands and look only at the illustrations. Ask them to imagine what is taking place. Finally, have students look through the text bubbles and boxes quickly to find cognates and words they recognize.

National Standards
Communication 1.2
Connections 3.1

Teacher Resources

Diálogo I
¿Me ayudas?
Activity 4
Activity 5
Activity 6

Answers

4 1. Hace unos quehaceres.
2. Ella quiere ir al cine.
3. Tiene que terminar de limpiar la casa.
4. Limpia la cocina.
5. Dice, ¡Qué casa tan limpia!

5 Answers will vary.

6 1. ...la tercera foto.
2. ...la primera foto.
3. ...la segunda foto.
4. ...la tercera foto.
5. ...la segunda foto.

Activities

Critical Listening
Play the audio CD recording of the dialog. Instruct students to cover up the words as they listen to the conversation. Have students look at the photographs and imagine what the people are saying to one another.

Expansion
Additional questions (*¿Qué recuerdas?*): *¿Qué deben limpiar?; ¿Van a trabajar juntos en los quehaceres?*

Prereading Strategy
Ask students to discuss the chores they are expected to do at home. Then instruct students to look through the dialog quickly to find cognates and words they recognize.

Communication
1.1, 1.2

Diálogo I ¿Me ayudas?

INÉS: Víctor, ¿qué haces?
VÍCTOR: Hago unos quehaceres.

INÉS: ¡Qué aburrido! ¿Por qué no vamos al cine?
VÍCTOR: Tengo que terminar de limpiar la casa. ¿Me ayudas?
INÉS: Sí, dejo mi abrigo aquí y te voy a limpiar la cocina.

INÉS: Bueno, la cocina ya está limpia. Hola, señora Zea.
SRA. ZEA: Hola, Inés. Hola, Víctor. ¡Qué casa tan limpia!
VÍCTOR: Gracias, mamá. Ahora voy al cine con Inés.

4 ¿Qué recuerdas?

1. ¿Qué hace Víctor?
2. ¿Adónde quiere ir Inés?
3. ¿Qué tiene que terminar Víctor primero?
4. ¿Qué limpia Inés?
5. ¿Qué dice la Sra. Zea?

5 Algo personal

1. ¿Cómo ayudas con los quehaceres en casa?
2. ¿Piensas que hacer los quehaceres es aburrido? Explica.
3. ¿Te gusta ir al cine?

6 ¿Me ayudas?

Mira las tres fotos que van con el diálogo y di si lo que oyes va con la primera, la segunda o la tercera foto.

MODELO Va con la tercera foto.

Todos ayudan en la cocina.

Notes This dialog and activities 4, 5 and 6 have been recorded by native speakers and are included in the *¡Aventura!* Audio Program. Have students cover up the words of the dialog and look at the photographs as you play the audio.

A reproducible student answer sheet for activity 6 has been provided for your convenience.

Cultura viva

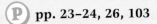

España: país multicultural

Spain's culture and diverse population today reflect the influence of people from many different ethnic groups and races over thousands of years. For example, cave paintings indicate people lived in an area *(Altamira)* of northern Spain between 25,000 and 10,000 B.C. Over 4,000 years ago the Iberians *(íberos)* invaded the area

Granada, España.

that would later be named the Iberian Peninsula *(Península Ibérica)* and that is shared today by Spain and Portugal. In 1100 B.C., the Phoenicians *(fenicios)* from present day Lebanon founded cities where Cádiz and Málaga are located. Blue-eyed, blond Celts *(celtas)* traveled from northern Europe south to Spain between 800 and 700 B.C., which explains why many Spaniards have those features today. The Greeks *(griegos)*, who arrived between 800 and 700 B.C., along with the Phoenicians, brought with them olive trees and grapevines. As a result, both olives *(aceitunas)* and grapes *(uvas)* are important products in Spain's economy today. Many other people

Córdoba es una ciudad bonita.

arrived later: the Carthaginians *(cartagineses)* from the area known today as Tunisia; the Romans *(romanos)*, who introduced Latin, which evolved into Spanish; the Visigoths *(visigodos)* from Germany; and the Arabs from northern Africa, also called Moors *(moros)*, who introduced the cultivation of rice *(arroz)* and oranges *(naranjas)* and turned Córdoba and Granada into important and prestigious cities. By the time the Moors were defeated in Granada and removed from power in 1492 by the Catholic monarchs Ferdinand *(Fernando)* and Isabella *(Isabel)*, many elements in contemporary Spain had taken root and are still evident today.

Los Reyes Católicos, Isabel y Fernando.

7 Conexiones con otras disciplinas: historia y ciencias sociales

Conecta la información de las dos columnas de una manera lógica.

1. los griegos y los fenicios
2. los moros
3. los celtas
4. los romanos
5. los fenicios
6. 25,000–10,000 B.C.

A. el latín
B. Altamira
C. el arroz y las naranjas
D. Cádiz y Málaga
E. las aceitunas y las uvas
F. rubios

Notes As another indication of Moorish influence in Spain, inform students that approximately 25 percent of Spanish words come from Arabic. Examples include *alcalde*, *alfombra* and *ojalá*.

Encourage students to find out more about Spain by going to the following Web sites:

All about Spain
http://www.red2000.com/spain/1index.html
Traveling to Spain
http://www.sispain.org/english/otherweb

Teacher Resources

 Activity 2

 pp. 23–24, 26, 103

 Activity 2

Answers

7
1. E
2. C
3. F
4. A
5. D
6. B

Activities

Connections

Have students research one of the groups that inhabited Spain. Then have them list any influences or products they brought with them to Spain.

Expansion

Using transparencies 1, 2, 7 and 8, show students where Spain is located and identify some of the country's larger cities.

Multiple Intelligences (linguistic/spatial)

Ask students to draw a time line indicating some of the various cultures that have existed in Spain. Then have students divide into small groups and use the media center and the Internet to research contributions these cultures made to the development of contemporary Spain. Include the contributions of the various cultures on the time line.

National Standards

Cultures
2.1, 2.2

Connections
3.1, 3.2

Teacher Resources

 Activity 8

 Activity 3

 Activity 3

 p. 31

Answers

8
1. Alfredo las está buscando./ Alfredo está buscándolas.
2. María y Fernando la están preparando./Están preparándola.
3. Lo estamos adornando./ Estamos adornándolo.
4. Carlos la está limpiando./ Está limpiándola.
5. Mis hermanos las están haciendo./Mis hermanos están haciéndolas.
6. Yo los estoy colgando./Yo estoy colgándolos.
7. Los estamos haciendo juntos./ Estamos haciéndolos juntos.

Activities

Multiple Intelligences (linguistic/spatial)
Divide students into groups of three or four and assign one-third of the groups to make a visual image of the direct object pronoun located to the left of the conjugated verb. Another third of the groups must make a visual image of the direct object pronoun attached to the infinitive. The final third must make a visual image of the direct object pronoun attached to the present participle.

National Standards

Communication
1.3

Idioma

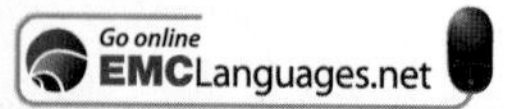

Repaso rápido

Direct object pronouns

You have already learned that direct object pronouns can precede conjugated verbs, attach to the end of an infinitive or attach to the end of a present participle.

me	nos
te	os
lo/la	los/las

Remember to add an accent mark to the present participle in order to maintain the original pronunciation of the present participle without the pronoun.

Marta está limpiando la cocina.
Marta ***está limpiándola****.*
Marta ***la está limpiando****.*

8 Todos están haciendo quehaceres

Sigue el modelo para decir la misma oración de forma diferente, usando un pronombre de complemento directo.

MODELO Yo estoy doblando *la ropa.*
Yo la estoy doblando./Yo estoy doblándola.

1. Alfredo está buscando *las tazas.*
2. María y Fernando están preparando *la comida.*
3. Estamos adornando *el cuarto.*
4. Carlos está limpiando *la cocina.*
5. Mis hermanos están haciendo *las camas.*
6. Yo estoy colgando *los abrigos.*
7. Estamos haciendo juntos *los trabajos de la casa.*

El verbo *colgar*

The present tense of *colgar* (to hang) follows the pattern of other verbs that require the change *o → ue*: *cuelgo, cuelgas, cuelga, colgamos, colgáis, cuelgan.*

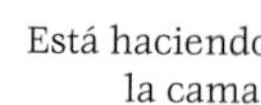

Está haciendo la cama.

Notes Remind students that they can find the direct object in a sentence by answering the question (subject + verb +) **who?** or **what?**

Use the following examples as you review direct object pronouns: ***La*** *voy a terminar* (before a conjugated verb); *Voy a terminar**la*** (attached to the end of an infinitive); *Estoy terminándo**la*** (attached to the end of a present participle).

See if students can remember any other verbs with the *o → ue* change: *poder, dormir,* etc.

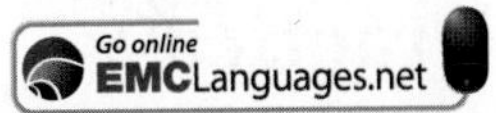

Estructura

Indirect object pronouns

An indirect object indicates **to whom** or **for whom** something is said or done. An indirect object pronoun *(pronombre de complemento indirecto)* may replace an indirect object. You have already learned to use indirect object pronouns with the verb *gustar*. They look the same as direct object pronouns except for *le* and *les*.

los pronombres de complemento indirecto			
me	to me, for me	**nos**	to us, for us
te	to you, for you (tú)	**os**	to you, for you (vosotros,-as)
le	to you, for you (Ud.) to him, for him to her, for her	**les**	to you, for you (Uds.) to them, for them

Indirect object pronouns follow the same rules for placement in a sentence that you learned for the direct object pronouns:

- They usually precede the conjugated form of the verb, but they also may follow and attach to an infinitive or a present participle. (Add an accent mark to the present participle in order to maintain the original pronunciation of the present participle.)

*Pilar **me** va a preparar una ensalada.*
*Pilar va a prepara**rme** una ensalada.* — Pilar is going make a salad **for me.**

***Te** estoy escuchando.*
*Estoy escuchándo**te**.* — I am listening **to you.**

- Place negative expressions (e.g., *nunca*) before the indirect object pronouns.

***Nunca nos** hacen la cama.* — They **never** make the bed **for us.**

Add the word *a* plus a pronoun or noun to a sentence in order to clarify the meaning of *le* and *les*, or in order to add emphasis.

Le** escribo* ***a ella. / a María. / a mi hermana.

Les** escribo* ***a ellas. / a María y a Mario. / a mis primos.

Le escribo a María.

Teacher Resources

 Activities 4–6

 Activities 4–7

 Activity 3
Activity 4

 Unit 11

 Activity 2

Activities

Expansion
Ask the class for sample sentences using direct object pronouns.

Language through Action
Expand the discussion of the indirect object pronouns using gestures as you walk around the room and give objects to students. Tell students what you are giving them as you hand the object to a person: *Te estoy dando un libro; Le doy un lápiz a Jorge.* You can vary the verb forms, but use indirect object pronouns in your sentences. As a second step in this activity, have students repeat your sentences after you. Finally, call on a few volunteers to demonstrate the transfer of knowledge, asking several students to make a statement using an indirect object pronoun while performing an action.

Multiple Intelligences (musical)
Play music from Spain as you explain to your students the use of *vosotros/vosotras* to give students an auditory connection to help them remember that this subject pronoun is used in Spain.

National Standards

Communication
1.3

Connections
3.1

Comparisons
4.1

Notes

Show the class they can locate the indirect object in a sentence by asking themselves the following question: (subject + verb +) **to whom** or **for whom?**

Point out that in English sentences using an indirect object or indirect object pronoun, the word **to** is commonly understood: I'm writing **(to)** him.

Teacher Resources

Activity 10
Activity 11

Answers

9 1. me
2. le
3. les
4. le
5. nos

10 1. ...puede limpiarle....
2. ...puede ponerte....
3. ¿...quieres prepararme...?
4. ...debo escribirte....
5. Estamos colgándoles....
6. ¿...está Ud. adornándonos...?

11 1. ¿Me limpias...?/...te limpio....
2. ¿Me doblas...?/...te doblo....
3. ¿Me limpias...?/...te limpio....
4. ¿Me buscas...?/...te busco....
5. ¿Me enciendes...?/...te enciendo....
6. ¿Me haces...?/...te hago....
7. ¿Me pones...?/...te pongo....
8. ¿Me subes...?/...te subo....

Activities

Critical Thinking
Ask students for an alternative way of saying the sentences for activity 9, placing the object pronouns after the infinitives.

Students with Special Needs
Provide a second model for activity 11.

National Standards

Communication
1.1

Práctica

¡Extra!

El uso de *vosotros*

It is common to use the direct and indirect object pronoun *os* in Spain in the same circumstances in which you have learned to use *vosotros:* when talking informally with two or more people.

9 Antes de ir de vacaciones

Pablo y su familia van de vacaciones y unos amigos van a ayudar a la familia a prepararse para el viaje. Completa tus oraciones con *me, te, le, nos* o *les*, diciendo qué van a hacer.

MODELO Marta nos va a limpiar las ventanas (a nosotros).

1. Raúl __ va a buscar las maletas (a mí).
2. Marta __ va a doblar la ropa (a mi madre).
3. La Sra. Martínez __ va a preparar la comida (a mis padres).
4. El Sr. Martínez __ va a colgar los abrigos (a mi padre).
5. Raúl y Marta __ van a hacer las camas (a nosotros).

10 De otra manera

Estás hablando de los quehaceres de la casa con unos amigos. ¿Cómo puedes decir la misma oración de otra manera *(another way)*?

MODELO ¿*Me* estás colgando la ropa?
¿Estás colgándo*me* la ropa?

1. Él nunca *le* puede limpiar la casa.
2. Quizás Carlos *te* puede poner la mesa.
3. ¿No *me* quieres preparar la comida?
4. Quizás *te* debo escribir una lista de quehaceres.
5. *Les* estamos colgando la ropa.
6. ¿No *nos* está Ud. adornando el cuarto?

11 ¿Me ayudas?

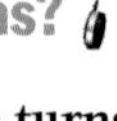

In pairs, take turns asking one another for help with the indicated tasks. The person responding may agree or refuse to help.

MODELO colgar los abrigos
A: ¿Me cuelgas los abrigos?
B: Sí, (No, no) te cuelgo los abrigos.

1. limpiar el patio
2. doblar las servilletas
3. limpiar la mesa del comedor
4. buscar la sal
5. encender las luces del comedor
6. hacer las camas
7. poner la mesa
8. subir la ropa a mi cuarto

¿Me estás colgando la ropa?

Notes You may wish to remind students that in the fifth sentence of activity 11, the verb *encender* requires the stem change *e* → *ie*.

If you are teaching *vosotros/vosotras*, give students several sentences that practice the direct and indirect object pronoun *os*. You can easily accomplish this by modifying one or two of the sentences for each activity.

Ayudando en casa

Las personas de la ilustración están ayudándote en las tareas de la casa. Describe lo que hace cada una de las personas.

MODELO Marta  Marta me está limpiando la mesa./Marta está limpiándome la mesa.

1. Antonio y Carlota

2. Ernesto

3. Cristóbal

4. Julia

Comunicación

¿Qué haces?

Make a list of your household chores and another list of what you do to help specific members of your family. Then talk with a classmate about what you do to help around the house and who you help with the household duties.

MODELO **A:** ¿Qué haces para ayudar en tu casa?
B: Doblo mi ropa y la subo a mi cuarto. ¿Y tú? ¿Ayudas a tus padres?
A: Sí. Le pongo la mesa a mi madre.

¿Me ayudas?

A group of exchange students from Spain will be staying with families in your community. With a classmate, take turns asking one another when each of you will be able to help with various chores to prepare for their visit. Answers should indicate if and when the person answering will be able to help with the indicated tasks.

MODELO **A:** ¿Cuándo me puedes limpiar la cocina?
B: Quizás te puedo limpiar la cocina por la tarde./Quizás puedo limpiarte la cocina por la tarde.

Notes Before beginning activity 12, remind students that the direct and indirect object pronouns may be used before the form of *estar* (or other verb helper) or after and attached to the present participle.

Answers

12 Possible answers:
1. ...me están haciendo la cama./...están haciéndome la cama.
2. ...me está poniendo la mesa./...está poniéndome la mesa.
3. ...me está adornando/...está adornándome la sala.
4. ...me está preparando la comida./...está preparándome la comida.

13 Creative self-expression.

14 Creative self-expression.

Activities

Expansion

Conduct a class discussion about household chores using the information students discussed in activities 13 and 14.

National Standards

Communication
1.1

Teacher Resources

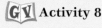

 Activity 16

 Activity 7

 Activity 8

 Activity 5

 Activity 3

Answers

15 Creative self-expression.

16
1. Ana acaba de doblarlas.
2. Pedro y Pablo acaban de hacerlas ahora mismo.
3. Alejandro y yo acabamos de limpiarlo juntos.
4. Elena acaba de adornarla.
5. Yo acabo de colgarlos.
6. Ángel acaba de limpiarlas hace media hora.

Activities

Language through Action
Expand on this presentation of *acabar de* by walking around the room and performing tasks as you describe what you have just done: *Acabo de cerrar la puerta; Acabo de abrir el libro.* Vary the verb forms, but use *acabar de* plus an infinitive for each sentence. As a second step in this activity, have students repeat your sentences after you. Finally, call on volunteers to demonstrate the transfer of knowledge, asking them to make a statement using *acabar de* plus an infinitive after performing an action.

National Standards

Communication
1.1, 1.3

Comparisons
4.1

15 ¿Qué les gusta hacer?

In small groups, discuss your most favorite and least favorite household chores. Each person should make a list of at least three chores you all like to do and a second list of three chores that you do not like to do. Each member of your group should then talk with members of other groups to find out how your lists compare. Finally, one person from each group should summarize the findings for the class.

MODELO **A:** ¿Les gusta cocinar la comida?
B: Sí, nos gusta cocinarla.
A: A nosotros también nos gusta.

Nos gusta	No nos gusta
cocinar	poner la mesa

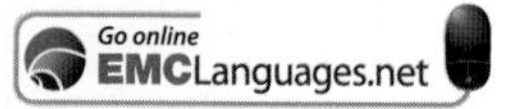

Estructura

Saying what just happened with *acabar de*

You can say what has just happened using a form of the verb *acabar* (to finish, to complete, to terminate) followed by *de* and an infinitive.

acabar de + infinitive

Acabo de llegar.	I just arrived.
Mi padre ***acaba de poner la mesa.***	My father just set the table.

Práctica

16 ¡Gracias por la ayuda!

Francisco tiene muchos quehaceres y muchos buenos amigos. A sus amigos les gusta ayudar con sus quehaceres. Contesta las preguntas para decir quién acaba de hacer cada quehacer, usando las pistas entre paréntesis.

MODELO ¿Los platos? (Alicia / limpiar)
Alicia acaba de limpiarlos.

1. ¿Las camisas? (Ana / doblar)
2. ¿Las camas? (Pedro y Pablo / hacer / ahora mismo)
3. ¿El cuarto? (Alejandro y yo / limpiar / juntos)
4. ¿La sala? (Elena / adornar)
5. ¿Los abrigos? (yo / colgar)
6. ¿Las ventanas? (Ángel / limpiar / hace media hora)

Alicia acaba de limpiar los platos.

Notes The verb *acabar* is always followed by the preposition *de* before an infinitive because it refers to actions that have already happened or that are coming to an end.

Other verbs like *acabar* are *alegrarse, arrepentirse, dejar* and *terminar*.

La fiesta de despedida 

You and a friend are organizing the farewell party for the Spanish exchange students who just spent the last week with families in your community. Take turns asking and answering questions to find out what everyone has just done to help out.

MODELO Uds. / limpiar la cocina
A: ¿Qué acaban de hacer Uds.?
B: Acabamos de limpiar la cocina.

1. Ana / poner la mesa
2. Andrés y Rosa / adornar las paredes
3. tú / limpiar las ventanas
4. Jaime y Cristina / preparar la comida
5. Mercedes / llegar con la comida
6. yo / leer la lista de quehaceres

¡Oportunidades!

Estudiante de intercambio

It is becoming more and more popular for language students to spend time overseas as exchange students. After you have studied Spanish for a couple of years, it would be a great opportunity for you to become an exchange student in Spain or in another Spanish-speaking country. What you learn at school will be very valuable to you. Living within the culture in a different country, practicing the language you have learned with native speakers, developing life long friendships, and gathering firsthand experience will be very rewarding and exciting.

Comunicación

¿Qué acabas de hacer?

Imagine it is Saturday at noon and you are talking on the phone with a friend. Discuss some things each of you did just recently and what you are going to do later in the day. You may want to include in your conversation something interesting that someone in your family or a friend did recently, too.

MODELO **A:** ¿Qué haces?
B: Bueno, yo acabo de poner la mesa. ¿Y tú?
A: Pues, yo acabo de terminar mi tarea. Mis padres dicen que puedo salir. ¿Quieres hacer algo?

Acabo de poner la mesa.

Teacher Resources

 Activity 17

Answers

17 1. ¿...acaba de...?/Acaba de....
2. ¿...acaban de...?/Acaban de....
3. ¿...acabas de...?/Acabo de....
4. ¿...acaban de...?/Acaban de....
5. ¿...acaba de...?/Acaba de....
6. ¿...acabo de...?Acabas de....

18 Creative self-expression.

Activities

Critical Listening

Tell students that they will hear several statements that give impressions of recent travels in the Spanish-speaking world. They should listen to each statement and use *acabar de* to say where the speaker has recently traveled or visited. Possible statements include: *Madrid es una ciudad muy bonita; Me gusta mucho el Parque de Chapultepec; Caracas es grande y moderna; En San Juan y toda la isla el béisbol es muy popular; Me encantan las playas de Viña del Mar pero también me gusta esquiar en las montañas.* As closure, review what students have learned about different countries in *¡Aventura! 1*.

National Standards

Communication
1.1

Connections
3.1

Communities
5.1

Teacher Resources

 Vocabulario II
Más quehaceres

 Activities 55–56

 Activity 8

 Activities 9–10

 p. 79

 Activity 6

 Activity 4

Activities

Language through Action
In advance, write the expressions from *Vocabulario II* and other household chores students have learned on separate pieces of paper. Have each student select one of the pieces of paper at random. Then call on them to act out the expressions while classmates guess what the expressions are in Spanish.

National Standards
Communication 1.1, 1.3

Vocabulario II

Más quehaceres

lavar las ollas

barrer

dar de comer al pe

recoger la mesa

arreglar el comedor

¡Pedro, Pedro! ¿No me oyes? ¡Qué listo eres!

poner las cosas en su lugar

pasar la aspiradora

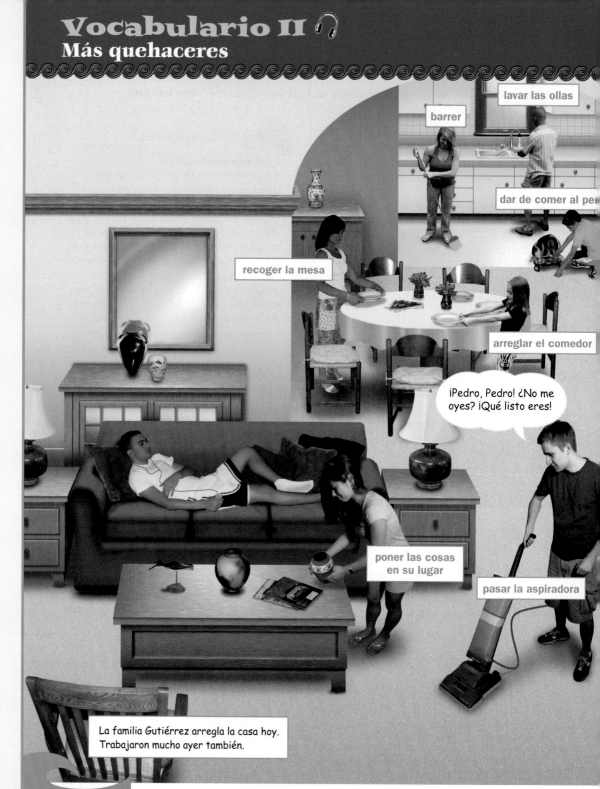

La familia Gutiérrez arregla la casa hoy. Trabajaron mucho ayer también.

Notes Other *¡Aventura! 1* components that practice and reinforce the vocabulary presented on pages 328 and 329 include the Audio Program, the Listening Activities Manual, Overhead Transparencies, Workbook, Grammar and Vocabulary Exercises Manual and Quizzes. The Teacher Resources listed at the top of the page indicate the specific numbered activities coordinated to the content of these pages for your convenience. Use any of the other ancillaries you feel will help you tailor the content to your teaching style.

Yo traigo el pan
y la leche.
sacar la basura
Él va a buscar leche y pan a la tienda.

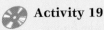

19 Los quehaceres

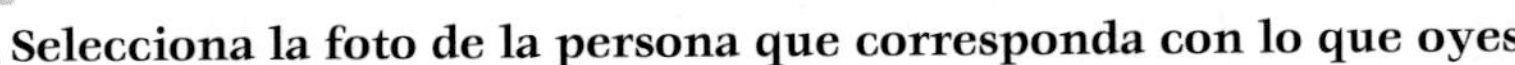

Selecciona la foto de la persona que corresponda con lo que oyes.

A

B

C

D

20 ¡Más quehaceres!

Di qué quehaceres debes hacer, según las ilustraciones.

Debo poner la mesa.

1

2

3

4

5

6

Notes

Play the audio of *Vocabulario I* to provide students with pronunciation practice before they try to figure out the meaning of the new words and expressions on pages 328 and 329.

Activity 19 is intended for listening comprehension practice. Play the audio of the activity or use the transcript that appears in the ATE Introduction if you prefer to read the activity yourself.

Teacher Resources

Activity 19

Answers

19 1. C
2. A
3. D
4. B

20 1. ...pasar la aspiradora.
2. ...lavar las ollas.
3. ...dar de comer al perro.
4. ...sacar la basura.
5. ...lavar la ropa.
6. ...preparar la comida.

Activities

Cooperative Learning

Have students bring in pictures from magazines or newspapers of people performing household chores that were taught in the lesson. They should also bring in a picture of a household chore not taught in this lesson, learn the term and teach it to a classmate. Then have students work in pairs or small groups, pretending they are doing the chore shown in each picture. Use Spanish sentences as models, if necessary: *¿Arreglas el cuarto?/Sí (No, no) arreglo el cuarto.* You can extend the activity by having students review the present progressive with the same pictures: *¿Qué estás haciendo ahora?/Estoy arreglando el cuarto.*

National Standards

Communication
1.1, 1.2

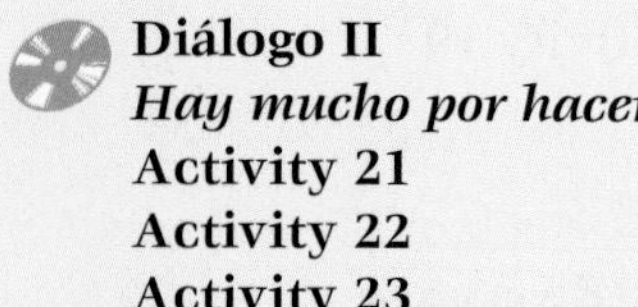

Teacher Resources

Diálogo II
Hay mucho por hacer
Activity 21
Activity 22
Activity 23

Answers

21 1. Los hijos de la Sra. Zea trabajaron mucho ayer.
2. Va a recoger la mesa y lavar las ollas.
3. David pasa la aspiradora.
4. David es listo.
5. No quiere ir a buscar leche a la tienda.

22 Answers will vary.

23 1. Es un deporte.
2. Es un quehacer.
3. Es un quehacer.
4. Es un deporte.
5. Es un quehacer.

Activities

Expansion

Additional questions *(Algo personal): ¿Prefieres recoger la mesa o lavar las ollas?; ¿Quién pone la mesa en tu casa?; ¿Quién recoge la mesa en tu casa?*

Pronunciation *(la letra g)*

Demonstrate how the consonant *g* changes its pronunciation with all five vowels. Write *ga, ge, gi, go, gu* on the board and practice the sounds. Explain that the *g* has the harder consonant sound with the vowels that open the mouth *(a, o, u)* and the softer *h* sound with the vowels that close the mouth *(e, i)*.

National Standards
Communication 1.1, 1.2
Cultures 2.1

Diálogo II Hay mucho por hacer

SRA. ZEA: Ayer trabajasteis mucho, pero hoy hay quehaceres también.
VÍCTOR: Pues, yo voy a recoger la mesa y lavar las ollas.
SRA. ZEA: Entonces, David puede pasar la aspiradora.

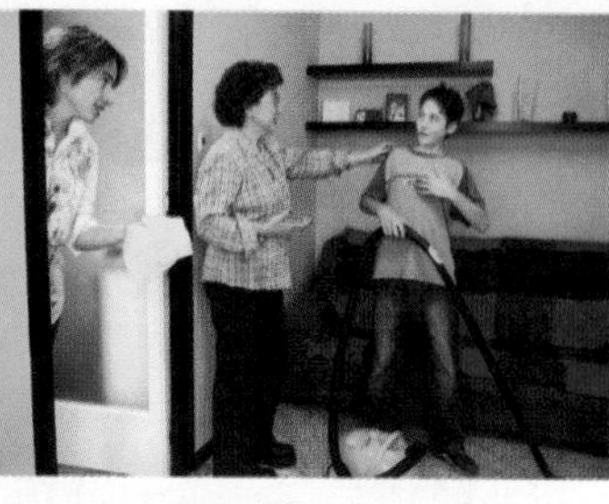

SRA. ZEA: ¿Quién va a la tienda a buscar leche?
DAVID: ¿Qué?
SRA. ZEA: ¿No me oyes? ¡Qué listo!

SRA. ZEA: ¿Puedes ir a buscar leche a la tienda?
DAVID: ¿Y por qué yo? ¿Por qué no va Víctor?
SRA. ZEA: Porque él va a lavar las ollas. ¿Quieres hacer eso?

21 ¿Qué recuerdas?

1. ¿Quiénes trabajaron mucho ayer?
2. ¿Qué va a hacer Víctor?
3. ¿Quién pasa la aspiradora?
4. ¿Quién es listo?
5. ¿Qué no quiere hacer David?

¡Extra!

El cambio de *g* → *j*

You have learned to use several verbs that are regular in the present tense except for a minor stem change *(poder, jugar)* or a spelling change. These changes do not affect the verb's present-tense endings. For verbs that end in *-ger* (such as *recoger*) the letter *g* changes to *j* before the letters *a* and *o* to maintain pronunciation: *Yo recojo la mesa muchas veces.*

22 Algo personal

1. ¿Qué quehaceres haces en casa?
2. ¿Eres listo/a?
3. ¿Te gusta ir a la tienda a buscar leche o pan? Explica.
4. ¿Quién saca la basura en tu casa? ¿Quién pasa la aspiradora?

23 ¿Vais a hacer un quehacer o a hacer un deporte?

Las siguientes personas van a hablar de sus actividades de hoy. Di si lo que oyes es *un quehacer* o *un deporte*.

Notes

Ask students if they recognize the verb form *trabajasteis*, which appears in the dialog. Then ask what the infinitive form of the verb is *(trabajar)*. This would be a good time to review this cultural and linguistic point with students. Remind them that many Spaniards (especially in the south) use this plural informal form of the verb. Note that the verb form may be accompanied by the subject pronouns *vosotros* or *vosotras* when the subject is not clear. Finally, practice conjugating several verbs using *vosotros* and *vosotras*.

Tell the class that they will remember the spelling change for *-ger* and *-gir* verbs if they think of them as the *yo-jo* verbs *(recojo)*.

Cultura viva II

Los quehaceres en una casa española

Do you like doing chores? Helping with the household chores is a long-standing tradition in many homes throughout the world. In Spain, young people generally help with chores starting at an early age, and everyone helps out with the cleaning *(la limpieza)* and upkeep of the home. Spanish houses do not, as a general rule, have wall-to-wall carpeting *(alfombra, moqueta)*. Instead, floors often consist of uncovered tile *(losa)*, marble *(mármol)* or wood *(madera)* and they are usually washed every day. If there are teenagers in the house, they usually are the ones chosen to perform this chore. The laundry is another household task that must be performed nearly every day. Dryers *(secadoras de ropa)* are not common in Spanish homes because of the high cost of energy, so laundry *(lavado de ropa or colada)* in many instances must be washed daily or every other day, and clothes are left to hang from lines to dry *(tender la ropa en el tendedero)*. Both girls and boys often have to hang the laundry, take it down and fold it. In addition, boys are often required to run errands *(hacer recados)* for their parents, while girls, traditionally, help with cooking.

Limpiando el suelo.

Ropa en el tendedero (Almería, España).

How do you help with the cleaning and maintenance of your home? Regardless of your answer, one thing you have in common with young people in Spain and throughout the world: Although you may accept that they are an integral part of living together as a family, nobody seems to like doing chores!

24 Los quehaceres en una casa española 

¿Es cierto o falso? Si es falso, di lo que es cierto.

1. Es tradicional empezar a ayudar con los quehaceres de casa cuando uno es joven en España.
2. Sólo los padres hacen la limpieza en las casas españolas.
3. Muchas casas tienen alfombra o moqueta en los pisos.
4. Hay muchas secadoras porque la energía no cuesta mucho en España.
5. Las muchachas y los muchachos cuelgan la ropa y la doblan.

25 Comparando

Make two lists of chores, one with what you and your friends do and another one with the chores you know young people in Spain do. Do you see any differences? Are there similarities? In what other ways do you think young people in Spain help around the home?

Notes Have students use a Venn diagram to complete activity 25.

As a review, make a list of chores in Spanish, including the ones given on this page. Encourage students to use this non-required vocabulary for enrichment as they do activity 25.

Teacher Resources

 **Activity 24**

 **Activity 5**

Answers

24 1. Cierto.
2. Falso. Toda la familia ayuda con la limpieza.
3. Falso. Pocas casas tienen alfombras moquetas en los pisos.
4. Falso. Hay pocas secadoras porque la energía cuesta mucho en España.
5. Cierto.

25 Answers will vary.

Activities

Connections
Have students use a Venn diagram to compare chores in a Spanish household and in their own homes.

Spanish for Spanish Speakers
Ask students to write an essay describing the chores they are expected to do at home. Then have them tell which ones they like to do most, and why, and which ones they like to do least, and why.

National Standards
Communication 1.3
Cultures 2.1
Comparisons 4.1, 4.2

Teacher Resources

 Activities 9–10

 Activities 11–12

 p. 155

 Activity 7

Activity 6

Answers

26 1. oyen
2. oye
3. oye
4. oyen
5. oímos
6. oigo
7. oyendo
8. oyes

Activities

Critical Thinking
Inquire whether students remember other verbs that have -go in the yo form *(vengo, tengo, pongo, salgo, hago).*

Expansion
Practice these two new irregular verbs by asking the following questions: *¿Qué traes a la escuela en un día típico?; ¿Qué traes a la clase de español?; ¿Qué trae el maestro/la maestra a la clase?; ¿Oyen Uds. anuncios en la escuela? ¿Cuándo?*

National Standards
Communication 1.1
Cultures 2.1

Idioma

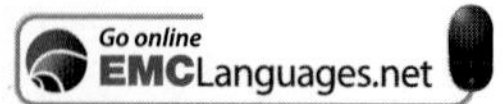

Estructura

Present tense of *oír* and *traer*

The verbs *oír* (to hear, to listen) and *traer* (to bring) are irregular.

oír	
oigo	oímos
oyes	oís
oye	oyen
gerundio: oyendo	

traer	
traigo	traemos
traes	traéis
trae	traen
gerundio: trayendo	

Práctica

26 A todos nos gusta oír la radio

Completa el siguiente párrafo con las formas correctas del verbo *oír*.

A toda mi familia le gusta oír la radio. Mis primos (1) las noticias todas las noches. Son muy listos. Mi tía (2) un programa de música española por las tardes. Mi hermano (3) los deportes, cuando no puede verlos en la televisión. Si mi abuelo y mi padre están trabajando en el garaje, (4) música popular y cantan. Mamá y yo siempre (5) el pronóstico del tiempo para saber si va a llover. Yo (6) la radio cuando escribo e-mails y también siempre estoy (7) música cuando hago la tarea. Y tú, ¿cuándo (8) la radio?

A mis hermanos les gusta oír la radio.

Notes Remind students that *vosotros/vosotras* is used in Spain, the country featured in *Capítulo 8*. If you are requiring students to learn the *vosotros/vosotras* form of verbs, be sure to practice the verbs *oír* and *traer* in sentences that contain either *vosotros* or *vosotras*.

¿Qué trae cada uno?

Unos amigos vienen a una fiesta en tu casa y cada persona tiene que traer algo diferente. Trabajando en parejas, alterna con tu compañero/a preguntando y contestando qué trae cada persona.

MODELO 
el Sr. y la Sra. Lorenzo
A: ¿Qué traen el Sr. y la Sra. Lorenzo?
B: El Sr. y la Sra. Lorenzo traen el pollo.

1. Paloma

2. Enrique y Tomás

3. mi amiga y yo

4. Alberto

5. Blanca y Graciela

6. Pedro

Comunicación

En mi casa

Working in pairs, talk about how your families and friends balance fun and work, describing some of your families' and your friends' favorite pastimes and telling how everyone helps when organizing activities or when doing chores. Mention which of the activities people like a lot or do not like. You may wish to use some of these activities to get started.

oír la radio	cocinar	buscar la leche y el pan
mirar la televisión	lavar las ollas	limpiar la cocina
tener una fiesta	traer CDs	arreglar el cuarto

MODELO **A:** En mi familia nos gusta hacer quehaceres los sábados y, luego, algunas veces tenemos una fiesta con los amigos y la familia. Mis primos siempre traen la música para bailar.
B: Yo siempre oigo música y arreglo mi cuarto los fines de semana.

Answers

27 1. ¿...trae...?/Paloma trae su guitarra.
2. ¿...traen...?/Enrique y Tomás traen su equipo de sonido.
3. ¿...traen Uds....?/Mi amiga y yo traemos los refrescos.
4. ¿...trae...?/Alberto trae la ensalada.
5. ¿...traen...?/Blanca y Graciela traen los CDs.
6. ¿...trae...?/Pedro trae el postre.

28 Creative self-expression.

Activities

Cooperative Learning

Working in pairs, students pretend it is Saturday night and everyone in their family has been doing chores all day. Even a couple of friends came over to the house to help out, so everyone has decided to go home, change clothes and return for a little party with music, food and fun to celebrate all the hard work. Students should describe the party, including the music they are listening to, what everyone brings to eat or to do at the party, etc.

Students with Special Needs

Try this brainstorming activity with students before assigning activity 27: Ask students to identify in Spanish each of the illustrated items; then do the first mini-dialog as a second model.

National Standards

Communication
1.1, 1.3

Cultures
2.1

Notes

Students will find it interesting that in addition to the use of *vosotros*, the pronunciation of certain letters and words heard in Spain has certain unique features. For example, most Spaniards pronounce the soft *c* and the letter *z* with a sound that is similar to the English sound *th*, as in the words *gracias* and *feliz*.

Walk around the room as students are doing activity 28 and listen in on conversations. Offer help when needed.

Teacher Resources

 Activity 11

 Activity 13

 p. 151

 Activity 8

 Activity 7

Answers

29
1. llegaron
2. cociné
3. limpió
4. ayudó
5. pasó
6. sacaste
7. trabajaron
8. hablaron
9. lavó
10. bailamos

Activities

Students with Special Needs
Practice conjugating several verbs with students using *vosotros/vosotras.* First, try several verbs in the present tense. Then, after presenting the preterite tense of regular *-ar* verbs, practice conjugating some verbs in the preterite tense. Verb charts present forms throughout the book and the Appendices offer examples for reference.

TPR
Give students the commands: *Cierra la puerta* and *Abre la puerta.* Then have them restate the action: *Él/Ella cerró la puerta y luego la abrió.*

National Standards

Communication
1.1

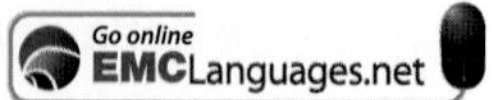

Estructura

Talking about the past: preterite tense of *-ar* verbs

Use the preterite tense when you are talking about actions or events that were completed in the past. Form the preterite tense of a regular *-ar* verb by removing the last two letters from the infinitive and attaching the endings shown.

lavar					
yo	lav**é**	I washed	nosotros nosotras	lav**amos**	we washed
tú	lav**aste**	you washed	vosotros vosotras	lav**asteis**	you washed
Ud. él ella	lav**ó**	you washed he washed she washed	Uds. ellos ellas	lav**aron**	you washed they washed they washed

Note: Regular verbs that end in *-car (buscar, explicar, sacar, tocar), -gar (apagar, colgar, jugar, llegar)* and *-zar (empezar)* require a spelling change in the *yo* form of the preterite in order to maintain the original sound of the infinitive.

infinitivo				pretérito
bus**car**	*c*	→	*qu*	yo bus**qué**
apa**gar**	*g*	→	*gu*	yo apa**gué**
empe**zar**	*z*	→	*c*	yo empe**cé**

Práctica

29 Ayer en la casa de Pilar

Completa las siguientes oraciones con la forma correcta del pretérito de los verbos entre paréntesis para decir lo que pasó ayer en la casa de Pilar.

1. Mis amigos *(llegar)* temprano.
2. Yo *(cocinar)* desde las nueve.
3. Daniel *(limpiar)* el piso del comedor.
4. Ángela me *(ayudar)* mucho también.
5. Ella *(pasar)* la aspiradora por la sala.
6. Tú *(sacar)* la basura antes de comer.
7. Uds. *(trabajar)* todo el día ayudándome.
8. Todos *(hablar)* bien de la comida.
9. Después de comer, Paco me *(lavar)* los platos.
10. Luego, nosotros *(bailar)* en la sala.

Notes Review some of the handy time expressions students can add to a sentence when they are talking about the past: *ayer, anoche, la semana pasada, el año pasado.* Ask students if they can add any other expressions to the list.

Do the first sentence of activity 29 as a class.

30 ¿Qué cocinaste?

Completa el siguiente párrafo con la forma apropiada del pretérito de los verbos entre paréntesis.

Yo *(1. cocinar)* una sopa ayer en mi casa para toda la familia. Mi hermana me *(2. ayudar)*. Yo *(3. empezar)* a preparar todo muy temprano. Primero yo *(4. buscar)* los ingredientes. Luego *(5. lavar)* la olla grande y *(6. sacar)* los cubiertos. Después *(7. preparar)* unos refrescos. Al terminar de cocinar, *(8. apagar)* la estufa y *(9. arreglar)* los cubiertos en la mesa. Entonces, *(10. llamar)* a todos a comer.

31 ¿Qué hiciste?

In pairs, take turns asking whether your classmate has completed the indicated chores. Your partner should say that he or she did not do each task because someone else already did it.

MODELO comprar el pan / Roberto
A: ¿Compraste el pan?
B: No, yo no compré el pan porque Roberto ya lo compró.

1. buscar los platos / Ernesto
2. apagar la estufa / Miguel
3. sacar la basura / Pedro
4. colgar los abrigos / Alfonso y Ana
5. preparar la comida / Jorge y Luisa
6. lavar la olla grande / Isabel

Comunicación

32 Mini-diálogos

Working in pairs, discuss some of the things that needed to be done around the home recently and whether or not either of you has done any of them. Some suggested chores and activities are provided to get you started.

A: ¿Preparaste la comida?
B: Sí, (No, no) la preparé.

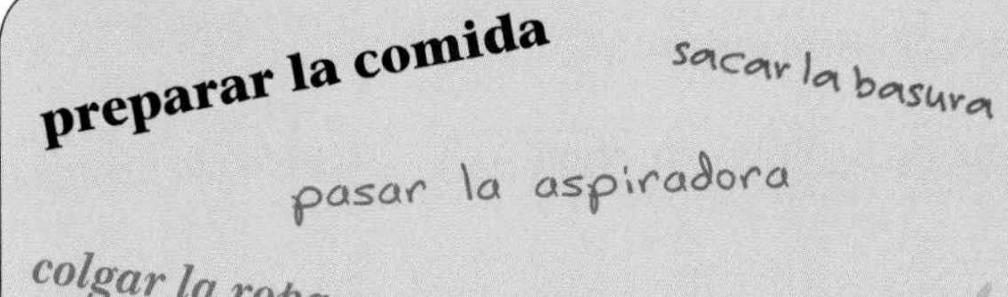

preparar la comida
sacar la basura
arreglar el cuarto
pasar la aspiradora
colgar la ropa en tu cuarto
comprar la leche
lavar las ollas

33 Todos en mi familia ayudaron

Talk about what everyone in your family did last week to help around the house.

Notes Set a time limit for activities 31, 32 and 33.

To extend activities 32 and 33, have students write out a summary of what they discussed. As an alternative, have students make a list of the chores they will be discussing before assigning students to work with a partner.

Hold students accountable for their work and provide additional practice speaking by calling on several individuals to summarize the results of their discussions for activities 32 and 33.

Teacher Resources

Activity 31

Answers

30 1. cociné; 2. ayudó; 3. empecé; 4. busqué; 5. lavé; 6. saqué; 7. preparé; 8. apagué; 9. arreglé; 10. llamé

31
1. ¿Buscaste...?/No, yo no busqué los platos porque Ernesto ya los buscó.
2. ¿Apagaste...?/No, yo no apagué la estufa porque Miguel ya la apagó.
3. ¿Sacaste...?/No, yo no saqué la basura porque Pedro ya la sacó.
4. ¿Colgaste...?/No, yo no colgué los abrigos porque Alfonso y Ana ya los colgaron.
5. ¿Preparaste...?/No, yo no preparé la comida porque Jorge y Luisa ya la prepararon.
6. ¿Lavaste...?/No, yo no lavé la olla grande porque Isabel ya la lavó.

32 Possible answers:
1. ¿Lavaste las ollas?/Sí, (No, no) las lavé.
2. ¿Pasaste la aspiradora?/Sí, (No, no) la pasé.
3. ¿Colgaste la ropa en tu cuarto?/Sí, (No, no) la colgué.
4. ¿Sacaste la basura?/Sí, (No, no) no la saqué.
5. ¿Compraste la leche?/Sí, (No, no) la compré.
6. ¿Arreglaste el cuarto?/Sí, (No, no) no lo arreglé.

33 Creative self-expression.

National Standards

Communication
1.1, 1.3

Teacher Resources

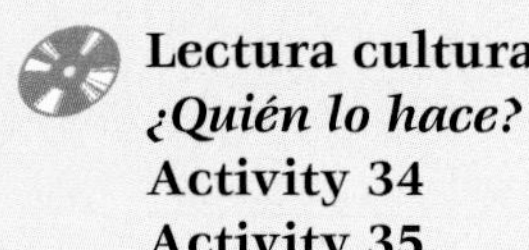

Lectura cultural
¿Quién lo hace?
Activity 34
Activity 35

Answers

34 1. No.
2. Sí.
3. No.
4. Sí.
5. Sí.

35 Answers will vary.

Activities

Expansion
The *Lectura cultural* offers a good opportunity for you to conduct a class discussion or have a debate about who does what around the house. Be sure to review the conjugation of *deber* and *tener que* before starting the activity.

National Standards

Communication	Comparisons
1.1	4.1, 4.2
Cultures	
2.1	
Connections	
3.1, 3.2	

Lectura cultural

¿Quién lo hace?

En España, mientras la participación de las mujeres[1] en el mercado laboral incrementa cada día (40% de mujeres trabajan), la desigualdad[2] entre los sexos todavía existe en las tareas domésticas. Las mujeres dedican siete horas y veintidós minutos cada día a los quehaceres. Los hombres, en cambio, dedican tres horas y diez minutos. Si nos referimos a quehaceres específicos de la casa (lavar, planchar, barrer, etc.), las mujeres dedican cinco veces más tiempo que los hombres.

Entre los jóvenes de 15–17 años, son las mujeres, otra vez, las que hacen más labores domésticas.

	Mujeres	Hombres
Total	7 h 22'	3 h 10'
Trabajo de la casa	3 h 58'	0 h 44'
Mantenimiento	0 h 27'	0 h 55'
Cuidado de la familia	1 h 51'	0 h 51'
Compras	0 h 53'	0 h 26'
Servicio	0 h 13'	0 h 14'

Fuente: Encuesta sobre "Usos del tiempo", Instituto de la Mujer, 2001.

Porcentaje de jóvenes que no hacen nunca o sólo en ocasiones los siguientes quehaceres

	Mujeres 15–17años	Hombres 15–17años
Cuidar a los niños	57,1%	65,7%
Limpiar la casa	50,6%	75,8%
Hacer la cama	32,2%	49,5%

Fuente: INJUVE, Informe Juventud en España, 2000.

En el año 2000, la Unión Europea recomendó a los estados miembros (España es uno) la inclusión en la escuela de una asignatura de trabajo doméstico. Quizás, esta nueva asignatura ayude a establecer la igualdad[3] en los quehaceres. Después de todo, la democracia empieza en casa.

[1]women [2]inequality [3]equality

34 ¿Qué recuerdas?

¿Sí o no?

1. 40% de las mujeres en España trabajan en casa.
2. Las mujeres españolas pasan siete horas y veintidós minutos todos los días en los quehaceres de la casa.
3. En España, 75,8% de los hombres entre quince y diecisiete años limpian la casa.
4. En España, 67,8% de las mujeres entre quince y diecisiete años hacen las camas.
5. La Unión Europea quiere que las escuelas enseñen trabajo doméstico.

- **Complete a survey of your classmates like the one in the article. Find out the percentage of girls and boys that never or only occasionally take care of younger siblings, clean the house and make their beds. Compare yourselves with the fifteen- to seventeen-year-old Spaniards surveyed. In your group, is there more or less equality among who does the chores?**

35 Algo personal

1. ¿Qué tareas domésticas tienes que hacer en casa?
2. ¿Crees que las mujeres y los hombres deben compartir *(share)* todos los quehaceres? Explica.
3. ¿Piensas que todos los estudiantes deben tomar una asignatura de trabajo doméstico? ¿Por qué sí o por qué no?

Notes Remind students that when talking about numbers, a comma is used in Spanish where a period would be used in English (e.g., 75,8%).

Help students with reading the tables that accompany the *Lectura cultural*.

Autoevaluación

As a review and self-check, respond to the following:

1. What do you do to help around the house?
2. Name two things you have just done in the last week.
3. Your family is having a party at your house and you are in charge of getting the house ready for guests. Ask your sister or brother to do three or four things to help with preparations.
4. List three or four things you did to help your parents.
5. State something you learned in this lesson about Spain.

Palabras y expresiones

How many of these words and expressions do you know?

En casa
el abrigo
la aspiradora
la basura
la cama
la gente
el jardín
la leche
la olla
pasar la aspiradora
la persona
el quehacer
recoger la mesa

Verbos
acabar
adornar
arreglar
barrer
cocinar
colgar (ue)
doblar
dejar
lavar
limpiar
llegar
oír
preparar
recoger
sacar
subir
trabajar
traer

Expresiones y otras palabras
acabar de (+ infinitive)
algo
dar de comer
junto,-a
listo,-a
quizás
sólo
el trabajo

Estructura

Do you remember the following grammar rules?

Indirect object pronouns

Indirect object pronouns indicate **to whom** or **for whom.**

singular		plural	
me	*to me, for me*	nos	*to us, for us*
te	*to you, for me (tú)*	os	*to you, for you (vosotros, as)*
le	*to you, for me (Ud.) to him, for him to her, for her*	les	*to you, for you (Uds.) to them, for them*

Saying what just happened with *acabar de*

The verb *acabar de* means to finish, to complete or to terminate

***acabar de* + infinitive**

***Acabo de** llegar.* I just arrived.

Irregular verbs: Present tense of *oír* and *traer*

oír		traer	
oigo	oímos	traigo	traemos
oyes	oís	traes	traéis
oye	oyen	trae	traen
gerundio: **oyendo**		gerundio: **trayendo**	

Preterite tense of regular *-ar* verbs

cocinar	
cociné	cocin**amos**
cocin**aste**	cocin**asteis**
cocinó	cocin**aron**

Notes Tell the class that in Spain the Spanish language is commonly called *castellano* (the language of Castilla). Other regional languages include *gallego, catalán* and *vasco/euskera.*

Spain occupies most of the Iberian Peninsula, which is at the southwestern corner of the European continent. Mainland Spain is divided into autonomous regions that make up 98 percent of the national territory. Other *autonomías* include the Balearic Islands, in the Mediterranean Sea, and the Canary Islands, 650 miles southwest of the mainland, off the coast of Africa.

Teacher Resources

 Activity 12

 pp. 59, 93

 Juegos

Flash Cards

Answers

Autoevaluación

Possible answers:

1. Arreglo mi cuarto.
2. Acabo de preparar la comida y trabajar en el jardín.
3. ¿Me puedes colgar la ropa? ¿Puedes ayudarme a preparar la comida? ¿Puedes sacarme la basura?
4. Saqué la basura todos los días la semana pasada. Preparé la comida, barrí, y colgué la ropa.
5. Spain's population is diverse and its history consists of a variety of ethnic groups and races, including the Iberians (los íberos), the Phoenicians (los fenicios) and the Moors (los moros).

Activities

Multiple Intelligences (interpersonal)

Ask students to work in small groups discussing how they feel about doing various household chores. They should use *gustar, molestar* and other verbs to discuss their likes and dislikes. Each group should then select one member to summarize the results of this informal discussion in front of the class.

National Standards

Communication
1.1, 1.3

Cultures
2.1

Connections
3.1

Teacher Resources

 **Vocabulario I**
El supermercado

 **Activities 57–58**

 **Activities 1–2**

 **Activities 1–5**

 **pp. 107–109**

 **Activity 1**

 **Activity 1**

Content reviewed in *Lección B*

- jobs around the house
- numbers
- preterite tense of regular *-ar* verbs
- celebrations

Activities

Critical Thinking

Before playing the audio for *Vocabulario I*, ask students if they can guess where the people are. Then ask what they are probably discussing.

Prereading Strategy

Have students find cognates and other words they know in *Vocabulario I*.

National Standards

Connections
3.1

Comparisons
4.1

Lección B Vocabulario I
El supermercado

Espa

¿Me prestas la receta de la paella?

Sí, claro.

De esta receta nos hace falta el ingrediente más importante, el arroz.

¡Ay, olvidamo añadirlo! La pae arroz no es pa

Verduras

la cebolla

el guisante

el ajo

los peores tomates

el tomate

el pimiento

los mejores tomates

el aguacate

el arroz

la lata

la lechuga

No todos los tomates están frescos.
Algunos parecen muy maduros.
Los chicos van a escoger los mejores tomates.
A ellos les importa llevar tomates maduros.

Notes

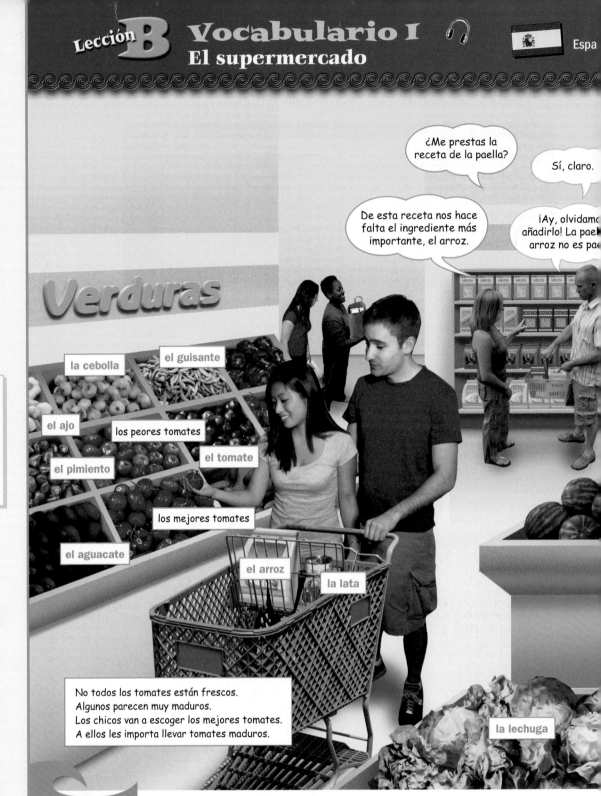

The word *receta* has two primary uses in Spanish: It may refer to a **recipe** for cooking or a **medical prescription** *(una receta médica)*. Context will make the meaning clear.

Explain to students that the verb *escoger* is conjugated like the verb *recoger*, which students learned to use in *Lección A* of this chapter.

1 En el supermercado

Selecciona la ilustración que corresponde con lo que oyes.

A

B

C

D

E

F

2 De compras en el supermercado

Di lo que *le(s) gusta*, *le(s) hace falta*, *le(s) parece* o *le(s) importa* a estas personas, usando las pistas y las ilustraciones y añadiendo los artículos indefinidos apropiados.

MODELO a mí / parecer bien / llevar unos
A mí me parece bien llevar unos tomates.

Hacer falta, importar y parecer

The expressions *hacer falta* (to need), *importar* (to matter) and *parecer* (to seem) often require an indirect object pronoun and follow a pattern like the one you learned for the verb *gustar: Me gusta el ajo; Me hace falta un aguacate; No me importa si el tomate no es maduro; Me parece buena la receta.*

1. a Uds. / hacer falta / llevar una

2. a los chicos / hacer falta / llevar un

3. a la Sra. Herrera / gustar / los

4. a Pedro y a Julio / importar / comprar las mejores

5. a Rodrigo / hacer falta / comprar el

6. a Santiago / gustar / comprar mucho

7. a mí / importar / llevar los mejores

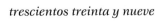

8. a Elena / no importar / llevar una

Notes It is common for Spaniards to shop either at a supermarket *(supermercado)* or at small specialty shops, such as a *panadería*. Shopping patterns vary from one country to another. Many Spaniards tend to shop for produce, meat and fish on a daily basis to have the freshest food possible for each meal.

Teacher Resources

Activity 1

Answers

1 1. E; 2. D; 3. A; 4. C; 5. F; 6. B

2
1. A Uds. les hace falta llevar una lata de guisantes.
2. A los chicos les hace falta llevar un pollo.
3. A la Sra. Herrera le gustan los aguacates.
4. A Pedro y a Julio les importa comprar las mejores cebollas.
5. A Rodrigo le hace falta comprar el arroz.
6. A Santiago le gusta comprar mucho pescado en lata.
7. A mí me importa llevar los mejores pimientos.
8. A Elena no le importa llevar una lechuga.

Activities

Cooperative Learning
Inform students that it is acceptable to use *no me importa* followed by a phrase, but that they usually should not use *no me importa* alone as a response to a choice. Responding to the question *¿Quieres estudiar o bailar?* with the phrase *no me importa* connotes **I don't give a darn!** Suggest *me es igual* or *me da igual* (it's the same to me) as more polite ways of stating **it doesn't matter to me**. Have students practice mini-dialogs in which one person makes a statement and the other answers with one of these new expressions.

National Standards

Communication
1.1, 1.2

Cultures
2.1

Teacher Resources

Diálogo I
¿Qué nos hace falta comprar?
Activity 3
Activity 4
Activity 5

 **p. 33**

Answers

3 1. Víctor la tiene.
2. Les hace falta comprar arroz, tomates y pimientos.
3. Ayer compraron el pollo.
4. No parecen frescos.
5. Víctor busca los pimientos.
6. Lo llaman el Sr. Pimiento.

4 Answers will vary.

5 1. D; 2. F; 3. B; 4. A, E; 5. C

Activities

Cooperative Learning
After discussing the content of the dialog, have students practice it in pairs. Circulate and assist with pronunciation and intonation.

Critical Listening
Play the audio recording of the dialog as students cover the words and listen. Ask several individuals to state what they believe the main theme of the conversation is.

Expansion
Additional questions *(¿Qué recuerdas?): ¿Necesitan más pollo?; ¿Los tomates son para la paella?*
Additional questions *(Algo personal): ¿Te gusta el pollo?; ¿Te gusta el arroz?*

National Standards
Communication 1.1, 1.2
Cultures 2.1, 2.2
Connections 3.1, 3.2

Diálogo I ¿Qué nos hace falta comprar? 

INÉS: ¿Tienes la receta de la paella?
VÍCTOR: Sí, aquí la tengo.
INÉS: ¿Qué nos hace falta comprar?

VÍCTOR: Ayer compramos el pollo. Todavía necesitamos arroz, tomates y pimientos.
INÉS: Vamos primero a las verduras.
VÍCTOR: ¡Ah, mira! ¿Qué te parecen estos tomates?
INÉS: No parecen muy frescos.

VÍCTOR: ¿Y estos? ¿Qué te parecen?
INÉS: Algunos parecen muy maduros.
VÍCTOR: ¿Por qué no escoges los tomates y yo escojo los pimientos? Me llaman el Sr. Pimiento.
INÉS: ¡Qué loco!

3 ¿Qué recuerdas? 

1. ¿Quién tiene la receta de la paella?
2. ¿Qué les hace falta comprar?
3. ¿Cuándo compraron el pollo?
4. ¿Cómo parecen los tomates?
5. ¿Qué busca Víctor?
6. ¿Cómo se llaman a Víctor?

4 Algo personal 

1. ¿Te gusta ir de compras al supermercado? Explica.
2. ¿Qué verduras te gustan?
3. ¿Cuáles son los ingredientes de tu receta favorita?

5 ¿Qué les hace falta? 

Di la letra de la ilustración que identifica lo que les hace falta comprar a las siguientes personas, según lo que oyes.

A

B

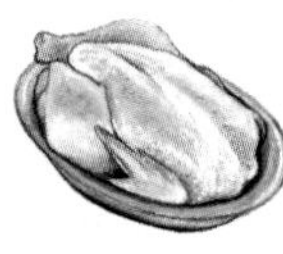
C

D

E

F

Notes

The word *paella* is related to the pan in which the food is prepared—a *paellera*—which comes from the Latin word for **pan**. The *paellera* is a round, wide, shallow receptacle made of metal with two or more handles and a depth varying from 1 1/2 to 3 inches. This utensil remains a legacy of the combined influence of the Romans and the Moors. The Romans introduced this type of pan, and the Arabs are credited with first having brought rice to Spain.

Activity 5 has been recorded as part of the Audio Program.

Cultura viva

Go online EMCLanguages.net

La paella (ingredientes para seis personas)

1 pollo en pedazos[1]	1 cebolla, troceada[6]	1 taza de guisantes
1/2 kg. de gambas[2]	2 dientes[7] de ajo, troceados	
1/2 kg. de langostinos[3]	2 zanahorias, limpias y cortadas[8]	5 hilos de azafrán[9]
1/4 kg. de mejillones[4]	2 tomates grandes	4 tazas de agua
1 lata de almejas[5] (200 gramos)	1 pimiento verde, troceado	5 cucharadas de aceite de oliva
2 tazas de arroz	1 lata de pimientos rojos, troceados	sal y pimienta

En una sartén[10] grande o paellera (sartén especial para la paella), poner el aceite y añadir el pollo, la cebolla troceada, el ajo y el pimiento verde; freír[11] hasta que se empiece a dorar—diez minutos. Luego, añadir el tomate, la zanahoria y media taza de guisantes. Cubrir[12] y dejar freír durante diez minutos. Después, añadir el arroz y el agua, los pimientos, el azafrán, sal y pimienta, y cocinar por otros quince minutos. Luego, añadir las gambas, los langostinos, los mejillones y las almejas y cocinar, con la sartén cubierta[13] otros diez minutos. Para terminar, adornar con la otra mitad de los guisantes, otra lata de pimientos (opcional) y un poco de perejil. Dejar que repose la paella durante quince minutos antes de servirla.

[1]pieces [2]shrimp [3]prawns [4]mussels [5]clams [6]diced [7]cloves [8]cut [9]saffron strings [10]frying pan [11]fry [12]cover [13]covered

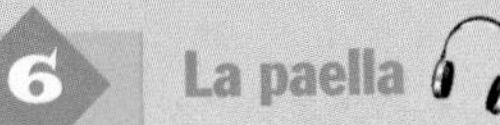

6 La paella

Contesta las siguientes preguntas.

1. ¿Cuánto langostino tiene esta paella?
2. ¿Cuáles de los ingredientes en esta receta no son frescos?
3. ¿Qué verduras tiene la paella?
4. ¿Con qué puedes adornar la paella?
5. ¿Te gustaría preparar una paella? ¿Por qué?
6. ¿Hay un restaurante en tu ciudad con paella en el menú? ¿Cuál?

7 Conexión con otras disciplinas: matemáticas

Cambia los pesos *(weights)* a libras u onzas, según la pista entre paréntesis.

1. 2 kilos de aguacates (libras)
2. 200 gramos de pollo (onzas)
3. 1,5 kilos de tomates (libras)
4. 750 gramos de judías (libras)
5. 1/2 kilo de pimientos (onzas)
6. 1/4 kilo de arroz (onzas)

¡Extra!

¿Cuánto pesa?

1 kilogram, kg. *(kilo, kg.)*	=	2.2 pounds, lbs. *(libras, lbs.)*
1 kilogram	=	1000 grams, gr. *(gramos, gr.)*
1 ounce, oz. *(onza, oz.)*	=	28.35 grams

8 ¿Puedes preparar una paella?

Prepara una paella en tu casa y cuéntale la experiencia a la clase.

Notes The word for **shrimp** in Spain is *la gamba.*

As an alternative to or extension of activity 8, ask students to bring the ingredients from home and arrange with the Family and Consumer Science Department in your school to prepare and serve the dish in class.

Activity 7 offers a cross-curricular connection to mathematics in which students must perform calculations to convert the weights and measurements indicated to ounces or pounds. This is good preparation for actually having to perform the same conversions when traveling in Spain.

Teacher Resources

Cultura viva
La paella
Activity 6

 **pp. 112–114**

 **pp. 30, 34**

 **Activity 2**

Answers

6
1. Tiene medio kilo.
2. Los pimientos rojos y las almejas no son frescos.
3. Tiene pimientos, cebolla, ajo, guisantes, zanahorias y tomates.
4. Puedo adornar la paella con guisantes, pimientos y perejil.
5. Answers will vary.
6. Answers will vary.

7
1. 4.4 lbs. de aguacates
2. 7.05 oz. de pollo
3. 3.3 lbs. de tomates
4. 1.65 lbs. de judías
5. 17.6 oz. de pimientos
6. 8.8 oz. de arroz

8 Creative self-expression.

Activities

Multiple Intelligences (bodily-kinesthetic)

Have students find a simple recipe in a cookbook of Spanish cuisine, prepare it and share it with the class. Students should also explain the recipe and its history.

National Standards

Communication	Connections
1.3	3.1, 3.2
Cultures	**Communities**
2.1, 2.2	5.1

Activities 3–6

Activities 6–10

Activity 3
Activity 4
Activity 5

Activity 2

Activities

Expansion

Review the terms used to name classroom objects. Then have students compare the sizes of objects as you or other students hold up the items in the air: *El libro es más grande que el lápiz.*

National Standards

Communication
1.1

Comparisons
4.1

Idioma

Estructura

Making comparisons

You can use the following patterns when making comparisons in Spanish:

más/menos **+ noun/adjective/adverb +** ***que***

*Hay **más/menos ajo que** sal.* There is **more/less (fewer)** garlic **than salt.**

tanto, -a, -os, -as **+ noun +** ***como***

*Hay **tanto** pescado **como** verduras en esa paella.* There is **as much** fish **as** vegetables in that paella.

tan **+ adjective/adverb +** ***como***

*Estos aguacates no están **tan maduros como** esos aguacates.* These avocados are not **as ripe as** those avocados.

verb + ***tanto como***

*Pedro **cocina tanto como** Pilar.* Pedro **cooks as much as** Pilar.

verb + más que/menos que

*Pedro **cocina más que** Tomás.* Pedro **cooks more than** Tomás.

You can also make comparisons by singling out a person, group, object or attribute as the best, most or least by using the following patterns:

definite article (+ noun) + ***más/menos*** **+ adjective**

*El ajo es **el ingrediente más importante**.* Garlic is **the most important ingredient**.

verb + ***lo*** **+** ***más/menos*** **+ adverb +** ***posible***

*Debes lavarla **lo más** pronto posible.* You should wash it **as** early **as possible**.

Use *más de* or *menos de* and a number for stating there are "more than" or "fewer than" the number of items or people indicated.

*Veo **más de/menos de** cinco cebollas.* I see **more than/fewer than** five onions.

Notes

Point out that *mayor, menor, mejor* and *peor* are usually placed in front of the word they modify: *Es el/la mejor (peor) estudiante...*

Explain that the adjectives in comparisons must agree in gender and number with the items they describe: *El tomate es más fresco que la lechuga. La cebolla es más madura que el aguacate.*

The following adjectives and adverbs have irregular comparative forms:

better	–	*mejor*
worse	–	*peor*
older	–	*mayor*
younger	–	*menor*

Esos aguacates son ***buenos****, pero aquellos aguacates son* ***mejores*** *y estos aguacates son* ***los mejores de todos****.*

Those avocados are **good**, but those avocados over there are **better** and these avocados **are the best of all**.

Note: When referring to quantity, the comparative forms of *pequeño* and *grande* are *menor* (lesser, smaller, fewer) and *mayor* (greater, larger).

Hay un ***menor (mayor)*** *número de pimientos en lata que de pimientos frescos.*

There are **fewer (more)** canned bell peppers than fresh bell peppers.

Práctica

9 En el supermercado

Estás haciendo compras en el supermercado. Completa estas comparaciones.

MODELO Estas cebollas son más grandes que esas cebollas. (grande)

1. Estos tomates están __ que esos tomates. (fresco)
2. Este pollo es __ que el otro. (pequeño)
3. Ese aguacate está __ que este aguacate. (maduro)
4. Estas lechugas son __ que esas lechugas. (pequeño)
5. Aquellos pimientos están __ que esos pimientos. (maduro)

¡Estos tomates son los mejores de todos!

Answers

9 Possible answers:
1. más/menos frescos
2. más/menos pequeño
3. más/menos maduro
4. más/menos pequeñas
5. más/menos maduros

Activities

Expansion

Talking about the quality of tomatoes works as a good review of the uses of *ser* and *estar*. Compare and contrast for students: *Los tomates son buenos* (they are of good quality; they taste good); *Los tomates son malos* (they are of poor quality; they taste bad); *Los tomates no están buenos* (they are not ripe yet); *Los tomates están verdes* (they're not ripe yet); *Los tomates están buenos* (they are ripe); *Los tomates están malos* (they are rotten). Contrast especially *son malos* (the tomatoes could be ripe but they are definitely of poor quality) with *están malos* (they could be good quality tomatoes that are rotten). Ask students to create sentences about the quality of various foods to check their understanding of this linguistic point.

National Standards

Communication
1.1

Comparisons
4.1

Teacher Resources

Activity 10
Activity 12

Answers

10 Possible answers:
1. Javier (Clara) tiene tanto arroz como Clara (Javier).
2. Las lechugas del supermercado Día no son tan grandes como las lechugas del supermercado Hypercor.
3. Ana (Alberto) va al supermercado tanto como Alberto (Ana).
4. No hay tantos guisantes como pescado en una paella valenciana./Hay menos guisantes que pescado en una paella valenciana./Hay más pescado que guisantes en una paella valenciana.
5. Teresa y Armando compran tantas latas de tomates como de guisantes.
6. Alfonso no tiene tantas recetas como Belén.

11 1. tantas/como; 2. menos/que; 3. tantos/como; 4. más/que; 5. tantas/como

12 1. ...lo mejor posible.
2. ...lo más pronto posible.
3. ...lo más rápidamente posible.
4. ...lo mejor posible.
5. ...lo mejor posible.
6. ...lo más pronto posible.
7. ...lo más tarde posible.

National Standards

Cultures
2.2

Connections
3.1

Comparisons
4.1

10 Comparando

Use the information provided to make as many comparisons as you can.

MODELO **Información:** Ana puede ir de compras al supermercado en una hora pero yo necesito dos horas para ir de compras al supermercado.
Comparación 1: No puedo ir de compras al supermercado tan rápidamente como Ana.
Comparación 2: Ana puede ir de compras al supermercado más rápidamente que yo.
Comparación 3: Yo puedo ir de compras al supermercado menos rápidamente que Ana.

1. Javier tiene dos kilos de arroz y Clara tiene dos kilos de arroz.
2. Las lechugas del supermercado Día son pequeñas pero las lechugas del supermercado Hypercor son grandes.
3. Alberto va al supermercado tres veces al mes y Ana va al supermercado tres veces al mes.
4. Hay mucho pescado en una paella valenciana pero no hay muchos guisantes.
5. Teresa y Armando compran dos latas de tomates y dos latas de guisantes.
6. Belén tiene cincuenta recetas y Alfonso tiene sólo cinco recetas.

11 ¿Cuánto necesitas?

You are preparing a paella valenciana, using the recipe in the *Cultura viva*. Complete these sentences, saying what you will need and compare whether you will need more, less or the same amount of each of the listed ingredients.

MODELO Necesito tanto pimiento verde como cebolla.

1. Necesito __ latas de almejas __ latas de pimientos rojos.
2. Necesito __ mejillones __ gambas.
3. Necesito __ tomates __ zanahorias.
4. Necesito __ agua __ aceite de oliva.
5. Necesito __ gambas __ langostinos.

¿Qué necesitas para hacer una paella?

12 ¡Deben hacer lo siguiente!

If you were the owner of a restaurant, what instructions might you give your employees during the week?

MODELO abrir el restaurante / temprano
Debes abrir el restaurante lo más temprano posible.

1. preparar las recetas / bien
2. hacer las comidas / pronto
3. recoger las mesas / rápidamente
4. barrer el suelo / bien
5. limpiar la cocina / bien
6. sacar la basura / pronto
7. cerrar el restaurante / tarde

Notes

Discuss activity 10 with the class to be sure students know what to do. Offer a second model if students have trouble.

Tell students they will need to look at the *Cultura viva* on page 341 for the recipe for paella to complete activity 11.

13 ¡Dos supermercados!

Compara lo que ves en las ilustraciones de estos dos supermercados, según las pistas.

> **MODELO** aguacates / ser grande
> Los aguacates del supermercado Día son más grandes que los aguacates del supermercado Hypercor.

1. lechugas / ser pequeñas
2. tomates / ser mejores
3. los ajos / costar menos
4. las cebollas / ser grandes
5. los guisantes / costar más
6. los pimientos / ser peores
7. el señor / ser joven
8. la señora / ser vieja

Answers

13 Possible answers:

1. Las lechugas del Hypercor supermercado son más pequeñas que las lechugas del supermercado Día.
2. Los tomates del supermercado Día son mejores que los tomates del supermercado Hypercor.
3. Los ajos del supermercado Hypercor cuestan menos que los ajos del supermercado Día.
4. Las cebollas del supermercado Día son más grandes que las cebollas del supermercado Hypercor.
5. Los guisantes del supermercado Hypercor cuestan más que los guisantes del supermercado Día.
6. Los pimientos del supermercado Día son peores que los pimientos del supermercado Hypercor.
7. El señor del supermercado Día es más joven que el señor del supermercado Hypercor.
8. La señora del supermercado Día es más vieja que la señora del supermercado Hypercor.

Notes This exercise uses metric measurements and the currency used by most European Union countries (the euro).

National Standards

Connections
3.1

Comparisons
4.1

Teacher Resources

 Activity 15

Answers

14 1. que; 2. de; 3. que; 4. de; 5. como

15 Although all answers vary, sentences should use *tanto como, más que* or *menos que.*

16
1. ¿Cuál es el supermercado más grande de la ciudad donde vives?/El supermercado más grande de la ciudad donde vivo es....
2. ¿Cuál es el supermercado más pequeño de la ciudad donde vives?/El supermercado más pequeño de la ciudad donde vivo es....
3. ¿Cuál es el supermercado más nuevo de la ciudad donde vives?/El supermercado más nuevo de la ciudad donde vivo es....
4. ¿Cuál es el supermercado más viejo de la ciudad donde vives?/El supermercado más viejo de la ciudad donde vivo es....
5. ¿Cuál es el ingrediente más importante de tu receta favorita?/El ingrediente más importante de mi receta favorita es....
6. ¿Cuál es la mejor receta de tu mamá/papá?/La mejor receta de mi mamá/papá es....

National Standards

Communication
1.1

Comparisons
4.1

14 ¡Más comparaciones!

Mira las ilustraciones de la actividad 13 y completa estas comparaciones con la palabra apropiada.

MODELO Hay más <u>de</u> una persona en los dos supermercados.

1. El supermercado Hypercor tiene más tomates __ el supermercado Día.
2. Hay menos __ cinco lechugas en el supermercado Hypercor.
3. Hay menos cebollas en el supermercado Hypercor __ en el supermercado Día.
4. El supermercado Día tiene más __ tres pimientos.
5. Los aguacates en el supermercado Hypercor cuestan tanto __ los aguacates en el supermercado Día.

15 ¿Lo hacen tanto como tú?

Compare how much you help doing chores with how much your friends and family help around the house. You may make up any of the names you wish.

MODELO pasar la aspiradora
Mi hermano pasa la aspiradora tanto como yo.
Yo paso la aspiradora más que Julio.

1. cocinar
2. hacer las camas
3. trabajar en el jardín
4. limpiar la cocina
5. poner la mesa
6. ayudar en casa

¿Pasas la aspiradora tanto como yo?

16 En tu opinión

Trabajando en parejas, alterna con tu compañero/a preguntando y contestando según las pistas.

MODELO el mejor supermercado de la ciudad donde vives
A: ¿Cuál es el mejor supermercado de la ciudad donde vives?
B: El mejor supermercado de la ciudad donde vivo es. . . .

1. el supermercado más grande de la ciudad donde vives
2. el supermercado más pequeño de la ciudad donde vives
3. el supermercado más nuevo de la ciudad donde vives
4. el supermercado más viejo de la ciudad donde vives
5. el ingrediente más importante de tu receta favorita
6. la mejor receta de tu mamá/papá

Notes When doing activity 15, point out that students should use the word *yo* when referring to themselves after *tanto como, más que* or *menos que: Ella cocina tanto como yo* (She cooks as much as I do).

Comunicación

17 Me gusta la comida

Trabajando en parejas, hagan preguntas para comparar comidas diferentes y saber cuál les gusta más.

MODELO A: ¿Te gusta la lechuga tanto como el tomate?
B: Sí, (No, no) me gusta la lechuga tanto como el tomate.

18 Lo que más comes

Working in pairs, talk about what you eat and drink. Include in your conversation what you eat or drink, and tell which are your most and least favorite foods and beverages.

MODELO A: ¿Qué te gusta comer?
B: Como más pollo que pescado, pero la paella es la mejor comida.

19 En el supermercado

Imagine you are at a supermarket in Spain shopping for ingredients to make paella. Working with a partner, take turns playing the roles of two clients. Remember to make comparisons of quality, size and price for items in the store.

El señor compra ingredientes para hacer una paella.

Notes Set a time limit for activities 17, 18 and 19.

After completing activity 18 orally in pairs, have students write out the list of foods and beverages that they included as their most and least favorite.

You may wish to have students make a list of their most and least favorite foods and beverages before asking them to work orally in pairs.

Hold students accountable for their work by calling on several pairs to present their dialogs in front of the class for activity 19.

Answers

17 Creative self-expression.
18 Creative self-expression.
19 Creative self-expression.

Activities

Expansion

As a follow-up to activity 16, have students ask and answer questions to identify the following items: *el deporte más interesante, la clase más difícil, el mejor/el peor programa de televisión, el estado más bonito, el país hispanohablante más interesante.* After working in pairs, the students should share their opinions with the class.

Pronunciation (*la letra* o)

The sound of *o* in Spanish is similar to the sound of **o** in English, but shorter. It is usually pronounced much like the **o** in the word **row**. Model several words for students: *yo, como, cocinar, cómodo, jamón, colgar, loco.* In addition, the letter *o* is a strong vowel, just like *a* and *e*. When a strong vowel joins a weak vowel (*i* or *u*), the strong vowel is normally stressed: *Mario, rubio, voy, hoy, nervioso, gimnasio, novio, limpio.* If the weak vowel is stressed, it bears an accent mark: *frío, tío, Eloísa, envío.* Many words end in *-ión*. Note for students that the *o* bears an accent mark because last syllables are not normally stressed in Spanish: *lección, canción, pronunciación, opinión, conversación.*

National Standards

Communication 1.1, 1.3
Comparisons 4.1, 4.2
Cultures 2.1, 2.2
Connections 3.1

Teacher Resources

 **Vocabulario II**
El mercado

 **Activities 59–60**

 **Activities 7–8**

 **Activities 11–13**

 **Activity 6**

 **Activity 3**

 **Activities**

Expansion
Model each word or expression and have students repeat. Then call on students to use the words or expressions in sentences.

Spanish for Spanish Speakers
Ask students to tell the class some foods that are common in their country of origin that cannot be found in the United States, and vice versa.

National Standards
Communication 1.3
Cultures 2.1
Connections 3.1

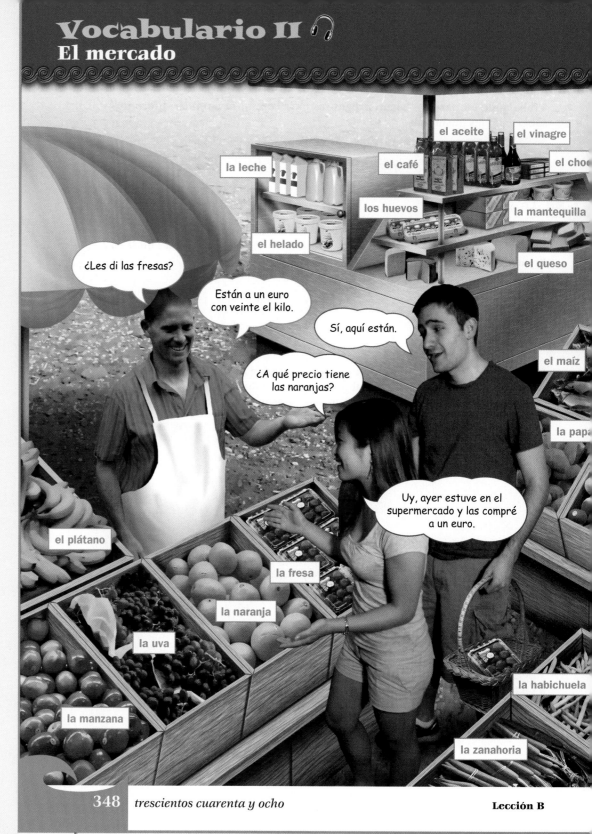

Vocabulario II
El mercado

el aceite
el vinagre
el cho
la leche
el café
los huevos
la mantequilla
el helado
el queso
¿Les di las fresas?
Están a un euro con veinte el kilo.
Sí, aquí están.
¿A qué precio tiene las naranjas?
el maíz
la papa
Uy, ayer estuve en el supermercado y las compré a un euro.
el plátano
la fresa
la naranja
la uva
la habichuela
la manzana
la zanahoria

Notes Tell students that the words *papa* and *patata* both mean **potato**. In Spain, both terms are commonly heard; in other Spanish-speaking countries, the preferred word is *papa*.

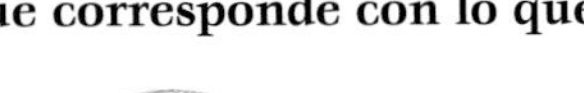

En el mercado

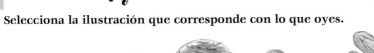

Selecciona la ilustración que corresponde con lo que oyes.

A B C D E F

21 Fuera de lugar

Say which food item does not belong in each of the following groups.

1. maíz	habichuela	zanahoria	chocolate
2. queso	mantequilla	jamón	leche
3. huevo	manzana	fresa	naranja
4. café	cebolla	pimiento	zanahoria
5. carne	pescado	pollo	papa
6. fresa	maíz	uva	plátano

22 Una dieta equilibrada

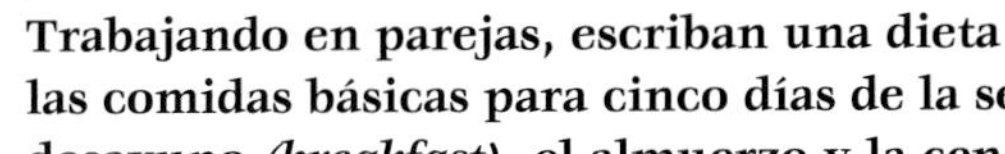

Trabajando en parejas, escriban una dieta equilibrada *(balanced)* con todas las comidas básicas para cinco días de la semana. La dieta debe incluir el desayuno *(breakfast)*, el almuerzo y la cena *(dinner)*.

Notes

Conduct a discussion about what items should be included in a healthy diet. If you are knowledgeable, talk with the class about good nutrition. As an alternative, you may want to ask the family and consumer science teacher in your building or district to spend a few minutes talking with the class about what items students should be eating.

Many fast-food restaurants have interesting and informative reading materials in Spanish that list the ingredients of the foods they serve. Some even offer tips about nutrition and a healthy diet.

Teacher Resources

Activity 20
Activity 21

Answers

20 1. B
2. C
3. F
4. A
5. D
6. E

21 1. chocolate
2. jamón
3. huevo
4. café
5. papa
6. maíz

22 Answers will vary.

Activities

Cooperative Learning

Have students prepare a shopping list of six or seven foods they like and six or seven items they dislike. Then have them work in pairs or small groups to talk about their lists.

Expansion

Ask the following questions pertaining to the new vocabulary: *¿Prefieres tomar chocolate o café?; ¿Cuál es tu fruta favorita?; ¿Te gusta la carne?; ¿Prefieres comer carne, pollo o pescado?; ¿Comes muchos huevos?; ¿Te importa el colesterol?; ¿Te hacen falta vitaminas en tu dieta?*

National Standards

Communication
1.1, 1.2

Connections
3.1

Teacher Resources

Diálogo II
Comprando chorizo
Activity 23
Activity 24
Activity 25

Answers

23
1. Compró los ingredientes para hacer paella.
2. Quiere comprar chorizo.
3. Sí, es el mejor mercado de la ciudad.
4. El kilo de chorizo está a cuatro euros.
5. Sí, lo compra.

24 Answers will vary.

25
1. Cierto.
2. Falso. Compramos los ingredientes para hacer una paella.
3. Falso. Quiero comprar chorizo.
4. Cierto.
5. Falso. Este mercado es el mejor mercado de la ciudad.
6. Cierto.

Activities

Cooperative Learning
Have students work in pairs to practice the dialog while you circulate and help with pronunciation and intonation.

Expansion
Additional questions (*Algo personal*): *¿Te gustan los chorizos americanos?; ¿Te gustan los chorizos italianos en las pizzas?*

National Standards

Communication
1.1, 1.2

Connections
3.1, 3.2

Diálogo II Comprando chorizo

INÉS: Ayer estuve con Víctor en el supermercado.
EVA: ¿Y qué compraste?
INÉS: Compramos los ingredientes para hacer paella.

EVA: Entonces, ¿qué venimos a hacer al mercado?
INÉS: Quiero comprar chorizo. El chorizo del supermercado no me gusta.
EVA: Bueno, este mercado es el mejor mercado de la ciudad.

INÉS: Señora, ¿a qué precio tiene el kilo de chorizo?
SEÑORA: El chorizo está a € 4,00 el kilo.
INÉS: De acuerdo, llevo un kilo por favor.

23 ¿Qué recuerdas?

1. ¿Qué compró Inés ayer en el supermercado?
2. ¿Qué quiere comprar Inés en el mercado?
3. ¿Es bueno el mercado donde están las chicas?
4. ¿A qué precio está el kilo de chorizo?
5. ¿Compra Inés el chorizo?

24 Algo personal

1. ¿Hay un mercado en tu ciudad? ¿Dónde está?
2. ¿Prefieres ir al mercado o al supermercado? Explica.
3. ¿Cuál es el mercado o supermercado más grande de tu ciudad?

El euro

The symbol for the European euro is €, which became the common currency of most European Union countries in 2002. Spain is a member of the European Union and adopted the euro as its currency, making the Spanish currency, *la peseta*, obsolete.

25 ¿Qué comprendiste?

Escucha lo que dicen las personas del diálogo *Comprando chorizo* y di si lo que oyes es cierto o falso. Corrige lo que no es cierto.

Notes

Additional recipes may be obtained at the following Web sites:

La Paella
http://www.lapaella.net/paella.html
Las Recetas de Marita
http://www.acocinar.com/paella.htm

The value of the euro against the dollar fluctuates daily. Many newspapers provide a chart in their business section with the current value of a euro compared to other world currencies, including the dollar.

Cultura  

¡Cómo se come en España!

Spain's cuisine is as diverse as its people are. Learning about the different regional cuisines will allow you to choose what you would like to try during a trip there. For example, *paella valenciana*, which you learned about earlier in the chapter, is a popular rice dish originally from the Mediterranean coast in the region of Valencia. It combines seafood, meat, chicken or pork. On the northern coast of Spain, in the region called Galicia, you might want to try *pulpo a la gallega*, a cooked and marinated octopus dish. In the north central and northeastern regions of Spain that border the Pyrenees, you might try the hearty Basque cuisine by ordering cod prepared the "Basque way" *(bacalao al pilpil)*, or Catalán cuisine, which is known for its delicious oxtail in *diabla* sauce and *butifarra con alubias* (beans with sausage).

Bacalao al pilpil.

Madrid, the capital, is famous for its *callos* (beef tripe). The area around Madrid is also famous for its sheep and goat cheeses, like *manchego*, and its many and delicious varieties of pork or blood sausages called *chorizos* and *morcillas*.

Gazpacho.

The southern part of Spain is well known for its vegetables and fish. Vegetables are used in the preparation of a cold soup called *gazpacho*. Gazpacho is popular in part because of its thirst-quenching qualities on hot summer days in sunny *Andalucía*. The region is also known for its ham *(jamón serrano)* and marvelous fresh sardines and smelt, fished right out of the Mediterranean Sea.

As you can see, Spaniards have plenty to choose from when it comes to meals!

Callos a la madrileña.

26 ¿Cómo se come en España?

Make a list of dishes mentioned in the *Cultura viva*. Then choose one that you would like to try, and find the recipe for it, using sources such as the Internet, cookbooks, etc.

Teacher Resources

 Activity 9

 Activity 4

Answers

26 Answers will vary.

Activities

Critical Thinking

Ask small groups of students to develop logical comparisons involving the following items: *la comida española/la comida mexicana; la comida italiana/ la comida china; los restaurantes/ las cafeterías; los supermercados/ los mercados.* Other possibilities not related to food include comparisons of classes, sports and music. The results should be shared with the class.

Expansion

As an additional activity, have students draw a map of Spain, separating the country into provinces and/or regions and placing the names of dishes given in the text in the corresponding regions.

Spanish for Spanish Speakers

Have students prepare a report in Spanish about the foods that the New World gave to Spain and how those were integrated into Spanish cuisine (e.g., the potato).

National Standards

Communication 1.1, 1.3	Comparisons 4.1, 4.2
Cultures 2.1, 2.2	
Connections 3.1, 3.2	

Notes

Using a map, point out where the places mentioned in *Cultura viva* are located.

Tell the class that many people in the United States have a mistaken impression about what food is like in Spanish-speaking countries. For example, although some people may think of *tacos* and *tortillas* when they are talking about Spanish foods, *tacos* are considered Mexican fast food and *tortillas* are corn- or flour-based pancake-like shells that are filled with other ingredients or that serve as a substitute for bread in Mexico. Point out that if students ask for a *tortilla* in Spain, they will be served a Spanish omelet.

Idioma

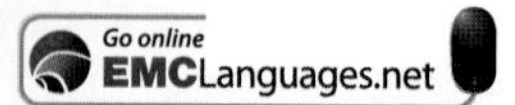

Repaso rápido

Preterite tense of regular -*ar* verbs

Do you remember how to form the preterite tense of a regular -*ar* verb? Remove the last two letters from the infinitive and add the indicated endings.

hablar	
habl**é**	habl**amos**
habl**aste**	habl**asteis**
habl**ó**	habl**aron**

Note: Regular verbs that end in -*car (buscar, explicar, sacar, tocar)*, -*gar (apagar, colgar, jugar, llegar, pagar)* and -*zar (empezar)* require a spelling change in the *yo* form of the preterite.

27 El diario de Marta

Marta siempre escribe en su diario por la noche. Haz oraciones completas con las pistas que se dan para saber lo que escribe esta noche.

1. nosotros / comprar zanahorias
2. mi madre / buscar el pollo
3. yo / buscar mi receta favorita
4. mi padre / trabajar todo el día

Estructura

Preterite tense of *dar* and *estar*

The verbs *dar* and *estar* are irregular in the preterite tense.

dar	
di	dimos
diste	disteis
dio	dieron

estar	
estuve	estuvimos
estuviste	estuvisteis
estuvo	estuvieron

28 Estuvieron en el mercado

Di cuándo las siguientes personas estuvieron en el mercado.

MODELO Enrique / el martes pasado
Enrique estuvo el martes pasado.

1. Daniel y Gloria / esta mañana
2. mi tía / el mes pasado
3. los chicos / el fin de semana pasado
4. mis primas / anteayer
5. Ud. / el viernes
6. yo / el sábado pasado
7. Uds. / ayer
8. tú / el jueves

Teacher Resources

 Activity 27
Activity 28

 Activities 10–12

 Activities 14–15

 Activity 7

 Activity 5

Answers

27 1. ...compramos....
2. ...buscó....
3. ...busqué....
4. ...trabajó....

28 1. Daniel y Gloria estuvieron esta mañana.
2. Mi tía estuvo el mes pasado.
3. Los chicos estuvieron el fin de semana pasado.
4. Mis primas estuvieron anteayer.
5. Ud. estuvo el viernes.
6. Yo estuve el sábado pasado.
7. Uds. estuvieron ayer.
8. Tú estuviste el jueves.

National Standards

Communication
1.1

Notes Review the spelling changes that are required in the first-person preterite tense for verbs that end in -*car* (change *c* to *qu*), -*gar* (change *g* to *gu*), -*zar* (change *z* to *c*). Then practice conjugating some of the verbs listed in the *Repaso rápido* before assigning activity 27.

Práctica

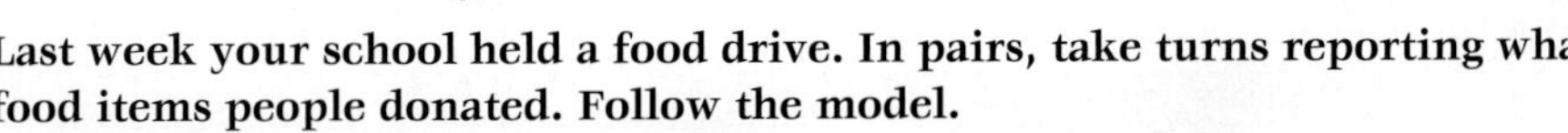

29 Todos ayudaron

Last week your school held a food drive. In pairs, take turns reporting what food items people donated. Follow the model.

MODELO tú
A: ¿Qué diste tú?
B: Yo di unas frutas.

1. yo

2. el Sr. y la Sra. García

3. tú y yo

4. la profesora

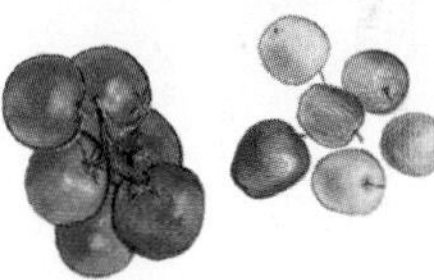

5. Pedro

6. los hermanos Jiménez

30 Mi fiesta de cumpleaños

Completa el siguiente párrafo con la forma apropiada del pretérito de los verbos entre paréntesis.

El sábado pasado mi hermano mayor *(1. dar)* una fiesta para mi cumpleaños. Muchos de mis amigos *(2. estar)* allí. Mi amigo Pedro no *(3. estar)* y mis mejores amigas, Clara y Elvira, tampoco *(4. estar)*. Nosotros *(5. estar)* muy contentos. Mi hermano me *(6. dar)* un regalo que me *(7. gustar)* mucho. Luego, mis amigos Carlos y Gabriel *(8. dar)* un concierto muy bueno. Carlos *(9. cantar)* cinco canciones y Gabriel las *(10. tocar)* en su guitarra. Yo *(11. estar)* muy contento porque mis amigos *(12. estar)* muy contentos. Todos le *(13. dar)* las gracias a mi hermano por la fiesta tan buena.

Comunicación

31 ¿Dónde estuvieron?

Working in pairs, discuss where you and people you know were last weekend, adding any details you wish.

MODELO **A:** ¿Dónde estuviste el fin de semana pasado?
B: Estuve con mi madre en el mercado.

32 ¿Qué dieron?

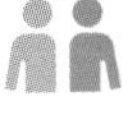

In pairs, talk about your last birthday celebration. Discuss, among other things, when your birthday was, where it took place, what kind of food was served and the gifts that were given to you. Make up any information you want.

Notes After completing activities 31 and 32 orally in pairs, consider asking students to summarize their work for either one or both activities.

Teacher Resources

Activity 29

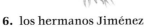

Answers

29
1. ¿... diste...?/...di tres kilos de papas y un kilo de pimientos.
2. ¿...dieron...?/...dieron una lata de pescado.
3. ¿...dimos...?/...dimos unas latas de verduras.
4. ¿...dio...?/...dio dos kilos de arroz.
5. ¿...dio...?/...dio tomates y manzanas.
6. ¿...dieron...?/...dieron zanahorias y aguacates.

30 1. dio; 2. estuvieron; 3. estuvo; 4. estuvieron; 5. estuvimos; 6. dio; 7. gustó; 8. dieron; 9. cantó; 10. tocó; 11. estuve; 12. estuvieron; 13. dieron

31 Answers will vary.

32 Answers will vary.

Activities

Communities

Extend the thought behind activity 29 by asking students to talk with their parents about how they might use their Spanish language skills and their knowledge about the Spanish-speaking community in a nursing home, in a community center or with a local organization that helps disadvantaged citizens in your city or town.

National Standards
Communication 1.1, 1.3
Communities 5.1

Teacher Resources

Lectura personal
Activity 33
Activity 34

Answers

33
1. La Tomatina.
2. En Buñol, un pueblo de Valencia, el último miércoles de cada agosto.
3. Participan aproximadamente treinta mil personas y se tiran 68.000 kilos de tomates.
4. Se tiran tomates en las calles.
5. Todos paran de tirar tomates y los residentes limpian las calles.
6. El agua la traen de un acueducto romano que está cerca.

34 Answers will vary.

Activities

Spanish for Spanish Speakers
Have students prepare a report on the Tomatina.

National Standards
Communication 1.1, 1.3
Cultures 2.1, 2.2
Comparisons 4.1

Lectura personal

Dirección http://www.emcp.com/músico/aventura1/

Archivo Edición Ver Favoritos Herramientas Ayuda

página principal | miembros | e-diario

Nombre: **Yadira Torres Ortega**
Edad: **15 años**
País natal: **México**
Verdura favorita: **lechuga**
Postre favorito: **helado de arroz**

Ayer miércoles fue un día que nunca voy a olvidar. Acabábamos[1] de dar un concierto en Madrid, la capital de España, y estábamos[2] en ruta a Valencia para otro concierto. Al mediodía, paramos en un pueblo llamado Buñol. Al bajar del camión, miles de personas en las calles estaban tirándose[3] tomates maduros los unos a los otros. ¡Fue la pelea[4] de comida más grande del mundo! Parece que lo hacen todos los años. Se llama la Tomatina, un festival popular, divertido y—debo añadir—para personas a las que no les importa estar sucios[5]. El último miércoles de cada agosto, entre las 11:00 de la mañana y la 1:00 de la tarde, treinta mil personas se tiran[6] tomates: 68.000 kilos de tomates, para ser exacta. ¡Imaginen el desastre! Las calles parecen ríos de sopa de tomate. Cuando suena[7] una sirena, todos paran[8] y los residentes empiezan a barrer las calles y lavarlas con enormes mangueras[9]. (El agua la traen de un acueducto romano que está cerca.) En unas pocas horas, las calles de Buñol están limpias, sin evidencia de que hubo[10] más tomates que en ninguna otra parte del mundo.

[1]we just finished [2]we were [3]were throwing at each other [4]fight [5]dirty [6]they throw at each other [7]blows [8]stop [9]hoses [10]there we

33 ¿Qué recuerdas?

1. ¿Cuál es la pelea de comida *(food fight)* más grande del mundo?
2. ¿Dónde y cuándo es?
3. ¿Aproximadamente cuántas personas participan? ¿Cuántos tomates usan?
4. ¿Qué hacen los participantes entre las 11 A.M. y la 1 P.M.?
5. ¿Qué hacen los residentes cuando suena una sirena *(a siren blows)*?
6. ¿De dónde traen el agua?

- **Although people know that the Tomatina began in the 1940s, nobody knows for sure how it started. How do you think it all started? Compare your theory with those of your classmates.**

34 Algo personal

1. ¿Has participado alguna vez en una pelea de comida?
2. En lugar de tomates, ¿qué otra fruta crees que es buena para una pelea de comida?
3. Imagina que vas a ir a la Tomatina. ¿Qué ropa llevas? ¿Por qué?

Notes

The *Lectura personal* and activities 33–34 are recorded and available as part of the Audio Program.

Have students pair up and take turns asking the questions for activities 33–34. Then have students write the answers to the two activities to turn in for a grade.

Autoevaluación

As a review and self-check, respond to the following:

1. Name some foods found in a supermarket. Which ones might you also find at an outdoor market (mercado al aire libre)?
2. Name some of the ingredients and how much of each is needed in a recipe to make paella valenciana for six people.
3. Compare several foods you like and dislike.
4. Name two or three things that are the most, the best or the worst possible.
5. Imagine you keep a journal and every day you write where you went, where you were and other interesting information about what you did during the day. Make a brief list of five things that you would write about today in your journal.
6. What are two things you have learned about Spain in this lesson?

Palabras y expresiones

How many of these words and expressions do you know?

En el mercado
el aguacate
el ajo
el arroz
el café
la carne
la cebolla
el chocolate
el chorizo
la fresa
la fruta
el guisante
la habichuela
el helado
el huevo
el ingrediente
el jamón
el kilo
la lata
la lechuga
el maíz
la manzana
el mercado
la papa
el pimiento
el plátano
el precio
el queso
el supermercado
el tomate
la uva
la verdura
el vinagre
la zanahoria

Para describir
fresco,-a
maduro,-a
mayor
mejor
menor
peor

Verbos
añadir
escoger
importar
olvidar
parecer
prestar

Expresiones y otras palabras
el/la/los/las (+ *noun*) más/menos (+ *adjective*)
el/la/los/las mejor/mejores/peor/peores (+ *noun*)
hacer falta
lo más/menos (+ *adverb*) posible
más/menos (+ *noun/adjective/adverb*) que
la paella
la receta
sin
tan (+ *adjective/adverb*) como
tanto como
tanto,-a (+ *noun*) como

Estructura

Do you remember the following grammar rules?

Making comparisons
más/menos + *noun/adjective/adver* + **que**
tanto, -a, -os, -as + *noun* + **como**
tan + *adjective/adverb* + **como**
verb + **tanto como**
verb + **más que/menos que**
definite article with noun + **más/menos** + *adjective*
verb + **lo** + **más/menos** + *adverb* + **posible**

Irregular verbs: Preterite tense of *dar* and *estar*			
dar		estar	
di	dimos	estuve	estuvimos
diste	disteis	estuviste	estuvisteis
dio	dieron	estuvo	estuvieron

Notes

Mention to students that the authentic *paella valenciana* was cooked outdoors over a wood fire. The classic way of eating *paella* is for everyone to sit in a circle and eat directly from the pan. Each person would have an intricately carved boxwood spoon for eating, and exact triangles would be marked out as portions for each person.

One interesting aspect of preparing *paella* is that in Valencia the dish has traditionally been prepared by males in the family. This may be due in part to the fact that making *paella* is a social event that takes place in the open air, away from the kitchen.

Teacher Resources

Activity 13

pp. 60, 94

Juegos

Flash Cards

Answers

Autoevaluación

Possible answers:

1. En un supermercado puedo comprar una cebolla, unos tomates y una lata de guisantes. En un mercado al aire libre puedo comprar una cebolla y unos tomates.
2. un pollo, medio kilo de gambas, medio kilo de langostinos, una taza de guisantes, dos tazas de arroz
3. Me gustan los tomates más que los aguacates.
4. Aprender el español es lo más importante para mí.
5. Fui al colegio esta mañana. Estuve allí todo el día. Hablé con mis amigos para hacer planes para el sábado.
6. Answers will vary.

Activities

Cooperative Learning

Have students imagine they are at an outdoor market doing grocery shopping for different foods. Then, working in pairs, they should take turns playing the roles of the vendor and the client.

National Standards

Communication
1.1

Cultures
2.1

Comparisons
4.2

Teacher Resources

 *Ir de tapas y a merendar*

Answers

Preparación

1. D
2. A

Activities

Critical Thinking

The reading presents a very different meal schedule and work schedule from what is common in the United States. Ask students their opinion of the schedules in each country and to consider the advantages and disadvantages of each.

National Standards

Cultures
2.1, 2.2

Connections
3.1

Comparisons
4.1, 4.2

¡Viento en popa!

Tú lees

Estrategia

Gathering meaning from context

When reading in another language, you will often encounter words you do not know. Before looking in a dictionary, look for clues that tell you what a word means. For example, you have already learned to recognize some unknown words because they are cognates (e.g., *familia*) or because they are related to words you have already learned (e.g., *baile/bailar*). At other times it may be necessary to look at the words before and after an unknown word (the context) in order to guess its meaning. Looking for these contextual clues will help improve your reading skills and will also make reading more enjoyable because you will spend less time looking up words in a dictionary.

Preparación

¿Qué quieren decir las palabras *tertulia* y *tapas* en las siguientes oraciones?

1. Un pasatiempo español es la **tertulia** con amigos en un café o un restaurante.
   A. comer empanadas
   B. ir de compras
   C. tomar café
   D. reunirse y conversar con amigos
2. A los españoles les gusta comer **tapas** con sus amigos antes de ir a casa para comer.
   A. comida pequeña antes de una comida principal
   B. pan con mantequilla
   C. frutas y verduras
   D. comida grande con carne y pescado

Ir de tapas y a merendar

Hay un par de pasatiempos que son muy populares entre la gente en España: ir de tapas e ir a merendar.[1] Ir de tapas es reunirse[2] con amigos o parientes para conversar y tomar aperitivos[3] antes de ir a casa para comer con la familia. Durante la conversación (o tertulia) las personas hablan de todo y comen tapas muy diversas (aceitunas, jamón serrano, patatas bravas[4], diferentes quesos, empanadas[5], etc.). Hay restaurantes y bares que sólo tienen tapas. Los grupos de amigos o familia pueden ir a tres o cuatro lugares diferentes para comer las tapas típicas de ese lugar. Hay dos

Aquí sirven tapas.

Notes

One style of *tapa* called *banderillas* (named after the colorful darts used in bullfights) consists of skewering various ingredients onto toothpicks. They should be eaten by putting the entire contents of each *banderilla* into the mouth at once so that the tastes of the various ingredients blend together.

razones para comer tapas en España: la primera es que los españoles toman el almuerzo muy tarde (a las 2:00 o a las 3:00 de la tarde) y también cenan[6] muy tarde (a las 9:00 o a las 10:00 de la noche), y la segunda, la verdadera[7] razón, es que a los españoles les gusta mucho hablar y pasar tiempo con sus amigos y familia.

Unas tapas ricas.

Merendar es otra forma de pasar tiempo con amigos y familia en donde los españoles salen para hablar y comer. En España la gente puede merendar en cafeterías, en merenderos[8] o en casa. Merendar, o la merienda, consiste de café para los adultos y de leche o chocolate para los jóvenes, además de[9] pasteles[10] y dulces. La merienda se come entre las cinco y las seis de la tarde, tres o cuatro horas antes de la cena[11], o ¡una hora antes de las tapas!

[1]to have an afternoon snack [2]to get together [3]appetizers [4]spicy potatoes [5]bread dough filled with meat or fish [6]eat dinner [7]real [8]places to have *merienda* [9]in addition to [10]pastries and cakes [11]supper

A ¿Qué recuerdas?

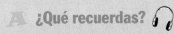

1. ¿Qué es ir de tapas?
2. ¿Qué es merendar?
3. ¿Qué tapas comen los españoles?
4. ¿Adónde puede ir la gente para merendar?
5. ¿Por qué salen los españoles de tapas y meriendas?

B Algo personal

1. ¿Te gustan los aperitivos? ¿Cuáles te gustan?
2. ¿Qué te gustaría más, ir de tapas o ir a merendar?
3. ¿Qué te gustaría comer de tapas?
4. ¿Qué te gustaría comer de merienda?

Ellas meriendan.

Notes How to prepare *banderillas:* Your students can prepare *banderillas* by skewering four or five of the following ingredients on a toothpick: pitted green Spanish olives, pitted ripe black olives, pearl onions, small marinated mushrooms, pieces of canned pimento, chunks of solid white tuna, boiled shrimp, hard-boiled egg, marinated artichoke heart and pieces of bell pepper.

Teacher Resources

Activity A
Activity B

Answers

A
1. Ir de tapas es reunirse con amigos o parientes para conversar y tomar aperitivos antes de ir a casa para comer.
2. Merendar es salir con amigos y familia para hablar y comer.
3. Comen aceitunas, jamón serrano, patatas bravas, diferentes quesos y empanadas.
4. La gente puede ir para merendar en cafeterías, merenderos o en casa.
5. Salen de tapas y meriendas porque toman el almuerzo y cenan muy tarde porque les gusta salir con amigos y familia.

B Answers will vary.

Activities

Language through Action
Have your students prepare some *tapas* from home to bring to school and share with the class. As an alternative, arrange with the consumer science department to prepare *banderillas* as a fun class project.

National Standards	
Cultures 2.1, 2.2	**Communities** 5.1
Connections 3.1	
Comparisons 4.2	

Answers

A Creative-thinking skill development.

B Creative writing practice.

Activities

Critical Thinking

Have students write a short composition of one or two paragraphs about chores in their home. Ask them to be as specific as they can, including who does the chores and when. Encourage students to try to use as much new vocabulary and grammar from this lesson as possible.

Tú escribes

Estrategia

Using graphic organizers

It is useful to brainstorm ideas about your topic before actually beginning to write. If the subjects you are going to write about are related in some way, a graphic organizer such as a Venn diagram will help you visualize different aspects of your theme.

A Venn diagram, consisting of two intersecting circles, is especially good when your writing includes a comparison of what two subjects (such as people, places or events) have in common.

A **Imagine you are going to celebrate a special event by having a special dinner with friends. First, write the name of the event you are celebrating (e.g., *cumpleaños de mi amigo Julio*, *viaje de mi amiga Elena*), and the date and the time the dinner will begin. Next, draw two intersecting circles (a Venn diagram). In one circle, list in Spanish the things you plan to do. In the second circle, list the things your friends plan to do. In the shared space, list the activities that the two of you plan to do together. Place each activity you think of in the appropriate area of the graphic. Be sure to include the *quehaceres* that must be completed both before and after the dinner.**

B **Underneath the circles of the Venn diagram you prepared, write a paragraph in Spanish describing the dinner you are planning, who is invited and who is responsible for carrying out the preparations.**

National Standards

Communication
1.3

Cultures
2.1

Comparisons
4.1, 4.2

Notes

Note for students that eating in Spain may be unlike anything they are accustomed to. Meals and snacks are planned throughout the day and offer coveted opportunities for socialization. With regard to the meal times mentioned in the reading *Ir de tapas y a merendar* (pages 356–357), note that typical business hours in Spain are 9:00–2:00 and 5:00–8:00.

Inform students whether you want them to work individually or in pairs to do activities A and B.

Proyectos adicionales

A Conexión con la tecnología

La comida española.

Search the Web for sites about Spanish cuisine using key words (cuisine, food, Spanish, paella, etc.). How many different recipes *(recetas)* can you find? For example, how many ways can *paella* be prepared? How are the recipes different? List the ingredients. Can you locate any restaurants that serve *paella*? How much does it cost? Share your findings with the class.

B Comparaciones

Working with three or four classmates, compare your food habits. For example, ask your classmates if they eat more often at home or in restaurants; talk about the location and names of restaurants where members of the group eat; find out what foods your classmates think are the best at home and in each of the restaurants they name; and find out what foods each person prepares at home (and ask whether it is better or worse than the same food at a restaurant or when someone else prepares it.) Take notes and report your findings to the class.

MODELO **A:** ¿Comes más en restaurantes que en tu casa?
B: No, como más en mi casa que en restaurantes.

C Conexión cultural

What comes to mind when you think about Spain? Prepare a list of at least ten Spanish words that convey what you associate with Spain. Try to include words that relate to Spain's history as well as to modern Spain. Then, based on the words in your list, create a poster using pictures, art and other graphics to depict the images you have of Spain. Finally, display the poster and tell the class about your project. Be creative!

La Feria de abril (Sevilla, España).

Notes The Spaniards heard about Aztec chocolate and took it to Spain in 1520. They added sugar, an important contribution, and later, cinnamon and vanilla. Spain zealously guarded the secret of chocolate production as long as it could and maintained a monopoly on the supply of cocoa, which came from its American colonies. *Chocolate a la española* is the thickest hot chocolate possible.

Teacher Resources

p. 74

Answers

A Creative self-expression.
B Creative self-expression.
C Creative self-expression.

Activities

Communities
Have students visit the school or city library and prepare a report on any Spaniards who explored your state. Students should report what influences those visits have had on life in your state today.

Critical Thinking
Discuss with students the images they associate with Spain. Then ask what images they think of in relation to the United States. Do any of the responses overlap?

Multiple Intelligences (musical)
Play flamenco music for students and have them compare it to the rhythms of rap.

Spanish for Spanish Speakers
Have students prepare a report on the origins of flamenco music and dancing.

National Standards	
Communication 1.1, 1.3	**Comparisons** 4.1, 4.2
Cultures 2.1, 2.2	**Communities** 5.1
Connections 3.1, 3.2	

Teacher Resources

 *Trabalenguas*

 Episode 8, DVD 2, Track 11

Answers

Resolviendo el misterio

1. Answers will vary.
2. Answers will vary.
3. Answers will vary.

Activities

Connections

Give students a recipe for preparing *churros con chocolate a la española* in Spanish. Read it in class, and using TPR, have students demonstrate how to prepare these fun snacks. You may ask students to prepare them at home and then bring them to class to share.

Critical Thinking

Ask students to name ten foods and compare them: *Me gustan las zanahorias tanto como las manzanas; no me gusta el chorizo tanto como el pollo.*

Trabalenguas

Ask students to answer the following questions about the *Trabalenguas* in complete sentences. *¿Quién pica? ¿Qué pica Pepe Picas? ¿Con qué pica papas Pepe? ¿Por qué piensas que Pepe Picas pica papas?*

National Standards
Cultures 2.1, 2.2
Connections 3.1
Comparisons 4.1

REPASO

Now that I have completed this chapter, I can...	Go to these pages for help:
talk about household chores.	318
ask for and offer help.	323
say what just happened.	326
talk about the past.	334
identify and describe foods.	338
discuss food preparation.	338
make comparisons.	342
I can also...	
talk about Spain's past.	321
talk about life in Spain today.	331
talk about paella.	341
name foods from different regions of Spain.	351

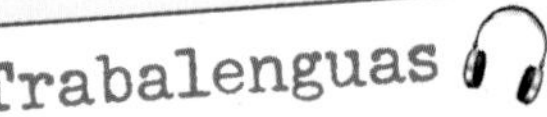

Trabalenguas

Pepe Pecas pica papas con un pico, con un pico pica papas Pepe Pecas.

Resolviendo el misterio

After watching Episode 8 of *El cuarto misterioso*, answer the following questions.

1. What chores do you perform in your house?
2. Do you enjoy cooking with family and friends? Why or why not?
3. How could Rafael possibly know anything about the mysterious room?

Notes

A custom that coincides with the tradition of *tapas* is the *paseo*, an afternoon or evening stroll with family or friends. The *paseo* provides a bit of exercise but is primarily a social activity.

Through the *Repaso*, students can measure their own progress in learning the main elements of the chapter.

Loose translation of the *Trabalenguas:* Pepe Pecas chops potatoes with a pickax, with a pickax chops Pepe Pecas potatoes.

A popular breakfast in Spain is *churros con chocolate. Churros* consist of a fried batter of flour and water. It is also customary to end the evening by eating *churros con chocolate* at a *churrería*.

Vocabulario

Go online EMCLanguages.net

el **abrigo** coat *8A*
acabar to finish, *8A*
acabar de *(+ infinitive)* to have just *8A*
adornar to decorate *8A*
el **aguacate** avocado *8B*
el **ajo** garlic *8B*
algo something, anything *8A*
añadir to add *8B*
arreglar to arrange, to straighten, to fix *8A*
el **arroz** rice *8B*
la **aspiradora** vacuum cleaner *8A*
barrer to sweep *8A*
la **basura** garbage *8A*
el **café** coffee *8B*
la **cama** bed *8A*
la **carne** meat *8B*
la **cebolla** onion *8B*
el **chocolate** chocolate *8B*
el **chorizo** sausage *(seasoned with red peppers) 8B*
cocinar to cook *8A*
colgar (ue) to hang *8A*
dar de comer to feed *8A*
dejar to leave *8A*
doblar to fold *8A*
escoger to choose *8B*
la **fresa** strawberry *8B*
fresco,-a fresh, chilly *8B*
la **fruta** fruit *8B*
la **gente** people *8A*
el **guisante** pea *8B*
la **habichuela** green bean *8B*
hacer falta to be necessary, to be lacking *8B*
el **helado** ice cream *8B*
el **huevo** egg *8B*
importar to be important, to matter *8B*
el **ingrediente** ingredient *8B*
el **jamón** ham *8B*
el **jardín** garden *8A*
junto,-a together *8A*
el **kilo (kg.)** kilogram *8B*
la **lata** can *8B*
lavar to wash *8A*
la **leche** milk *8A*
la **lechuga** lettuce *8B*
limpiar to clean *8A*
listo,-a smart *8A*
llegar to arrive *8A*
llevar to take, to carry *8A*
maduro,-a ripe *8B*
el **maíz** corn *8B*
la **manzana** apple *8B*
más *(+ noun/adjective/adverb)* **que** more *(+noun/adjective/adverb) 8B*
mayor older, oldest *8B*
mejor better, *8B*
menor lesser, least *8B*
menos *(+ noun/adjective/adverb)* **que** less *(+noun/adjective/adverb) 8B*
el **mercado** market *8B*
la **olla** pot, saucepan *8A*
olvidar to forget *8B*
oír to hear, to listen *8A*
la **paella** paella *(traditional Spanish dish with rice) 8B*
la **papa** potato *8B*
parecer to seem *8B*
pasar la aspiradora to vacuum *8A*
peor worse *8B*
peor/peores *(+ noun)* the worst *(+noun) 8B*
la **persona** person *8A*
el **pimiento** bell pepper *8B*
el **plátano** banana *8B*
el **precio** price *8B*
preparar to prepare *8A*
prestar to lend *8B*
el **quehacer** chore *8A*
el **queso** cheese *8B*
quizás perhaps *8A*
la **receta** recipe *8B*
recoger to pick up *8A*
recoger la mesa to clear the table *8A*
sacar to take out *8A*
sin without *8B*
sólo only, just *8A*
subir to climb, to go up, to go upstairs, to take up, to bring up, to carry up *8A*
el **supermercado** supermarket *8B*
tan *(+ adjective/adverb)* **como** *(person/item)* as *(+person/item)* as *8B*
tanto como as much as *8B*
tanto,-a *(+ noun)* **como** *(person/item)* as many/much *(+noun)* as *8B*
el **tomate** tomato *8B*
trabajar to work *8A*
el **trabajo** work *8A*
traer to bring *8A*
la **uva** grape *8B*
la **verdura** greens, vegetables *8B*
el **vinagre** vinegar *8B*
la **zanahoria** carrot *8B*

El jamón.

¡Hay buen chorizo! ¿Cuántos kilos quiere?

Teacher Resources

Las aventuras de la familia Miranda

Repaso

¡Aventureros!, Ch. 8

Internet Activities

i-Culture

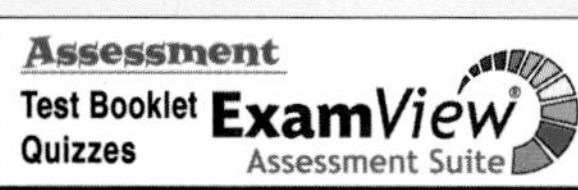
Assessment
Test Booklet
Quizzes
ExamView Assessment Suite

Activities

Multiple Intelligences (spatial/linguistic)
Have students create a map of Spain, detailing the locations and names of important cities, rivers, mountains, regions, etc. As an alternative, have students write a short composition about an aspect of Spain that interests them.

Spanish for Spanish Speakers
Have students write a composition in Spanish summarizing what they know about Spain. Expand the activity by having students seek out additional information about Spain at the library or via the Internet.

Notes Remind students that the words and expressions listed here are provided for easy reference and consist of all vocabulary they must know from *Capítulo 8*. Students should review and test themselves over the content of the *Vocabulario* in preparation for the chapter test and for future chapters in *¡Aventura!*

National Standards
Communication 1.3
Cultures 2.1, 2.2
Connections 3.1, 3.2

Teacher Resources

 *Capítulo 9*

TPRS *Capítulo 9*

 Episode 9, DVD 2, Track 27

Answers

El cuarto misterioso

1. Las respuestas variarán.
2. Las respuestas variarán.
3. Las respuestas variarán.

Activities

Connections
Have students name some cities in Ecuador and Panama. Then ask if anyone in class has visited or knows someone who has visited either country. Ask what students know about these countries.

Prior Knowledge
Ask students to review the chapter objectives. Ask questions such as: What are the differences between U.S. and European sizing of clothing and shoes? Do you prefer to shop with cash or credit cards? What words or expressions besides "no" indicate disagreement? What words and expressions signal use of the past tense (for example, yesterday, last week)? How many fabrics and design patterns can you name?

National Standards
Connections 3.1
Comparisons 4.1

CAPÍTULO 9

La ropa

El cuarto misterioso

Contesta las siguientes preguntas sobre *Episodio 9–El maletín*.

1. Para José, ¿es difícil o fácil entrar en "el cuarto misterioso"?
2. ¿Qué cosas hay en "el cuarto misterioso"?
3. ¿Qué piensas que José va a descubrir sobre "el cuarto misterioso" en este episodio?

José usa la llave para entrar en "el cuarto misterioso". Él quiere saber lo que hay adentro del maletín.

Objetivos

- describe **clothing**
- identify **parts of the body**
- express **disagreement**
- talk about **the past**
- discuss **size** and **fit**
- discuss **price** and **payment**

Notes A checklist of these objectives, along with additional functions, appears on page 408 so students can evaluate their own progress.

Contexto cultural

Panamá
Nombre oficial: República de Panamá
Población: 3.460.000
Capital: Ciudad de Panamá
Ciudades importantes: San Miguelito, Colón, David
Unidad monetaria: el balboa
Fiesta nacional: 3 de noviembre, Separación de Panamá de Colombia
Gente famosa: Rubén Blades (cantante, actor), Ómar Torrijos (ex-presidente)

Ecuador
Nombre oficial: República del Ecuador
Población: 15.000.000
Capital: Quito
Ciudades importantes: Guayaquil, Cuenca, Machala
Unidad monetaria: el sucre
Fiesta nacional: 10 de agosto, Primer Grito de la Independencia de Quito
Gente famosa: Jorge Enrique Adum (escritor), Oswaldo Guayasamin (pintor)

Notes In this chapter students will be learning how to use Spanish when shopping for clothing and gifts. They will also learn to evaluate their own shopping tastes. Finally, students will learn what it is like to go shopping in Panama and in Ecuador and what they might find in stores and markets if they travel to one of these Spanish-speaking countries in Central and South America.

National Standards

Connections
3.1

Teacher Resources

Vocabulario I
En la tienda por departamentos

 **Activities 61–62**

 **Activities 1–3**

 **Activities 1–4**

 **pp. 117–119, 122, 124**

 **pp. 35, 39**

 **Activity 1**

 **Activity 1**

Content reviewed in *Lección A*
- colors
- preterite tense of regular *-ar* verbs
- preterite tense of *ser*
- negation

Activities

Prereading Strategy
Using overhead transparencies 61 and 62, introduce the lesson vocabulary. Say the words and have students repeat after you to practice individual words and to begin to become familiar with the new words. Be sure to include both the articles of clothing and colors. Then follow up by asking students to identify and spell the words you indicate.

National Standards
Communication 1.3
Connections 3.1

Vocabulario I
En la tienda por departamentos

Departamento de ropa para hombres
la corbata
el traje de baño
el traje
la camisa de algodón
el pijama
la ropa interior
Departamento de ropa para mujeres
el pijama
morada
el vestido
la blusa de seda
marrón
el traje de baño
la ropa inter
rosada
anaranjada
el cuerpo
la cabeza
la bota
las medias
el brazo
la mano
el zapato bajo
la pierna
el pie
el dedo
el zapato de tacón

Notes Ask students what they know about Panama. Most students are familiar with the Panama Canal, which is discussed on page 367. Ask for student volunteers to create a bulletin board or travel brochure about this Spanish-speaking Central American country.

Have students find cognates and words they already know in *Vocabulario I*. Quickly check student comprehension of the descriptions that accompany the illustrations on these two pages.

¿Prefieres la camisa roja o la verde?
Prefiero la roja. Yo les pedí una roja a mis padres para mi cumpleaños, pero me dieron una azul.

Comprando ropa

Selecciona la ilustración que corresponde con lo que oyes.

A B C D E F

2 ¿De qué color son?

Describe la ropa de la actividad anterior, usando los colores.

1. el vestido
2. las botas
3. el pijama
4. la corbata
5. la blusa
6. el traje de baño

3 El cuerpo

Nombra *(name)* las partes del cuerpo.

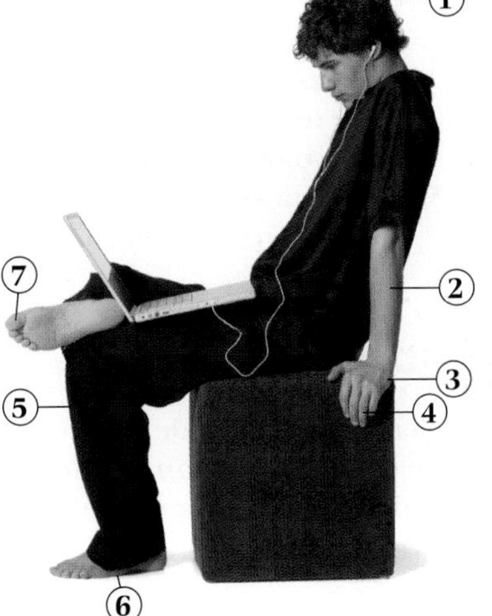

Notes Activity 1 is intended for listening comprehension practice. Play the audio of the activity or use the transcript that appears in the ATE Introduction if you prefer to read the activity yourself. A reproducible answer sheet for the activity can be found at the end of the Audio Program Manual.

You may want to have students write answers for activities 2 and 3.

Use overhead transparencies 61 and 62 to present and practice the new words and expressions in *Vocabulario I*.

Teacher Resources

Activity 1

pp. 120–121

Answers

1
1. B
2. F
3. D
4. E
5. A
6. C

2
1. El vestido es verde.
2. Las botas son marrones.
3. El pijama es azul.
4. La corbata es morada.
5. La blusa es rosada.
6. El traje de baño es anaranjado.

3
1. la cabeza
2. el brazo
3. la mano
4. el dedo
5. la pierna
6. el pie
7. el dedo

Activities

Critical Thinking

Ask individuals about the *Vocabulario I* illustration using simple questions with **yes** or **no** for answers: *¿Es roja la corbata?* Then gradually begin to ask questions that require more elaborate answers: *¿De qué color es el vestido?* Finally, personalize the questions: *¿De qué color son tus zapatos?*

Communication
1.1, 1.2

Teacher Resources

Diálogo I
¿Cuál prefieres?
Activity 4
Activity 5
Activity 6

Answers

4 1. Busca un vestido de seda.
2. Prefiere el vestido rosado.
3. No, no cuesta mucho.
4. No le gusta ni un poquito.
5. Prefiere el vestido morado.
6. Lo puede llevar con unas medias verdes.

5 Answers will vary.

6 1. B
2. A
3. B
4. B
5. A
6. A
7. A
8. B

Activities

Multiple Intelligences (bodily-kinesthetic/spatial)
Review colors by playing the game Scattergories: Divide the class into teams of four or five students. Name a color; allow one to two minutes for the groups to find and name classroom objects they see that are that color. One student in each group (the recorder) should write down the list of descriptions (remind students the color adjectives must agree with the nouns they describe).

National Standards

Communication
1.1, 1.2

Cultures
2.1

Diálogo I ¿Cuál prefieres?

ROCÍO: ¿Dónde está el departamento de ropa para mujeres?
PEDRO: ¿Qué buscas?
ROCÍO: Busco un vestido de seda para la fiesta del sábado.

ROCÍO: Aquí hay unos vestidos. ¿Cuál prefieres?
PEDRO: Prefiero el vestido rosado. Y no cuesta mucho.
ROCÍO: ¿El rosado? No me gusta ni un poquito. Prefiero el morado.

PEDRO: Con el rosado puedes llevar unas medias verdes.
ROCÍO: ¿Una medias verdes? ¡Estás loco!
PEDRO: Sí, te vas a ver muy bonita, como una flor.

4 ¿Qué recuerdas?

1. ¿Qué busca Rocío?
2. ¿Qué vestido prefiere Pedro?
3. ¿Cuesta mucho el vestido rosado?
4. ¿Le gusta el vestido rosado a Rocío?
5. ¿Qué vestido prefiere Rocío?
6. Según Pedro, ¿con qué puede llevar Rocío el vestido rosado?

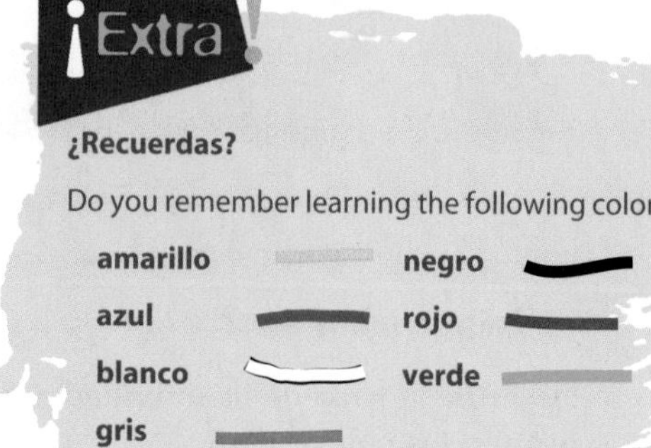

¡Extra!

¿Recuerdas?

Do you remember learning the following colors?

amarillo, negro, azul, rojo, blanco, verde, gris

5 Algo personal

1. ¿Cuál es tu color favorito?
2. ¿Tienes un color favorito para la ropa?
3. ¿Qué ropa te gustaría comprar?
4. ¿Qué colores te gusta llevar juntos?
5. ¿Te gusta ayudar a tus amigos/as a comprar ropa? Explica.

6 ¿Cuál prefieres?

Selecciona la letra de la ilustración que corresponde con lo que las siguientes personas prefieren.

A

B

Notes

This dialog and activities 4, 5 and 6 have been recorded by native speakers and are included in the *¡Aventura!* Audio Program.

Teenagers are often fairly fashion conscious, but they also recognize that how they dress represents only one aspect of who they are. With that in mind, your students may enjoy learning a proverb in Spanish that says it is not the clothes you wear that are important, but rather who you are: *Aunque la mona se vista de seda, mona se queda* (Even though it may be wearing silk, the monkey is still a monkey).

Ask students to review the vocabulary from the previous page and then scan the dialog for familiar words or phrases.

Cultura viva

La ciudad de Panamá.

Panamá, el cruce del mundo

Although small by comparison with many Spanish-speaking countries, Panama serves as an important crossroads for the world due to its geographic location and physical features. You are probably familiar with the canal *(el Canal de Panamá)* that divides the country in two. This valuable international travel route took years to build and many people died during its construction. Today the canal serves a critical function connecting the Atlantic and the Pacific oceans, shortening the time and energy required to transport goods from one part of the world to another.

Panama's people *(los panameños)* have a varied background. When Rodrigo de Bastidas, Juan de la Cosa and Vasco Nuñez de Balboa arrived in Panama in 1501, followed by Columbus in 1502, the land was inhabited primarily by natives of two indigenous groups; the *kuna* and the *chocó*. Panama's citizens today are descendants of these and other indigenous groups, Spanish conquistadors, African slaves and workers from China (who were involved in constructing the railroad in the mid-1800s), among others. Direct descendants of the *kuna* and *chocó* people still inhabit the San Blas archipelago.

Most Panamanians prefer to live in cities along the canal. For example, Panama City *(la Ciudad de Panamá)*, the capital and largest city, is located along the canal. Panama City has become an important financial center, with more than ninety banks from throughout the world registered to do business.

El canal de Panamá.

7 Panamá, el cruce del mundo 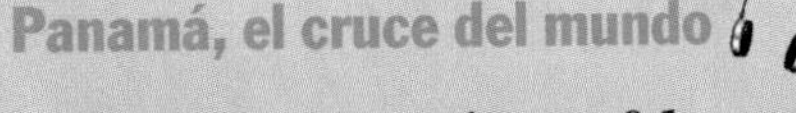

Di si lo siguiente es *cierto* o *falso*.

1. Panamá es un país pequeño.
2. La capital de Panamá es San José.
3. El Canal de Panamá va del Océano Pacífico al Atlántico.
4. La capital es la ciudad más grande del país.
5. Bastidas, de la Cosa y Balboa llegaron a Panamá en 1905.
6. Descendientes de los kuna y los chocó viven en el archipiélago de San Blas.

8 Conexión con otras disciplinas: arquitectura e historia

Working in small groups, research the history of the Panama Canal. Try to find information regarding its construction, how long the project took, etc. Share your findings with the class.

Notes The Kuna Indians who live on the San Blas archipelago are famous for their *molas*—colorful reverse appliqués—made of several layers of colorful cotton fabric.

Connections. Activity 8 makes the cross-curricular connection to architecture and history.

Teacher Resources

 **Activity 7**

 **Activity 4**

 **pp. 115, 123**

 **Activity 2**

Answers

7 1. Cierto.
2. Falso.
3. Cierto.
4. Cierto.
5. Falso.
6. Cierto.

8 Creative self-expression.

Activities

Connections (Social Studies)
Have students prepare a report about President Theodore Roosevelt's involvement in Panama's independence from Colombia.

Spanish for Spanish Speakers
Encourage interested students to study the development and operation of the Panama Canal, using the Internet and library resources. Then have students prepare a report about the canal and explain its construction to the class.

National Standards
Communication 1.1, 1.3
Cultures 2.1, 2.2
Connections 3.1, 3.2

Teacher Resources

 Activity 5

 Activity 5

 p. 36

 Activity 3

 Activity 2

Answers

9 Answers will vary.
10 1. el
2. el
3. –
4. los
5. –
6. –
7. la
8. El

Activities

Students with Special Needs
Remind students that for agreement in gender and number, color words and other adjectives ending in *-o* have four forms; those ending in *-e* or a consonant have two forms. Practice the point by choosing a color such as *negro* or *rosado* and then say several nouns to which students may respond individually when you call on them or in chorus. Do the same with *verde* and then with an adjective ending in a consonant such as *gris* or *azul*.

National Standards
Communication 1.2
Comparisons 4.1

Idioma

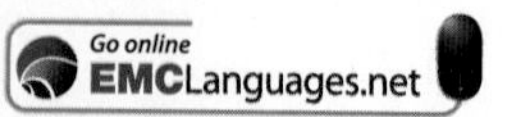

Estructura

Adjectives as nouns

Although a definite article is not usually needed when a color describes an object (because the color is an adjective), a definite article is required when naming colors in Spanish (because they are considered nouns).

Pedí un pantalón negro de cumpleaños. I asked for black pants for my birthday.

but:

Prefiero ***el*** *(color) rojo.* I prefer red.

In addition, sometimes a word being described may be omitted in order to avoid repeating a noun. In such cases the article remains and the adjective must agree with the noun that was omitted.

¿Te gusta el vestido azul o ***el*** *(vestido)* ***gris****?* Do you like the blue dress or **the grey one?**
Compré la camisa blanca, no ***la verde****.* I bought the white shirt, not **the green one.**

Práctica

9 Los colores de mi ropa

Completa las oraciones con el adjetivo apropiado para describir algunos artículos de ropa en tu cuarto.

MODELO Tengo un pantalón rojo.

1. Tengo mucha ropa __.
2. Tengo unas botas __.
3. Tengo unos zapatos __.
4. Tengo un pijama __.
5. Tengo una camisa __.
6. Tengo un traje de baño __.

Tengo un pantalón rojo.

10 Los gustos personales

Completa las siguientes oraciones con un artículo definido si lo necesitan.

1. A Marta le gusta __ color verde.
2. El color favorito de Enrique es __ morado.
3. A mi prima le gustaría comprar un impermeable __ amarillo.
4. ¿Elena prefiere los calcetines verdes o __ rojos?
5. Mi madre tiene una blusa de seda __ rosada porque es su color favorito.
6. A Pedro le gustan sus botas __ negras.
7. Esperanza compró la ropa interior azul ayer, no __ blanca.
8. __ anaranjado es mi color favorito.

Notes You may want to share with students the following additional color names: *el violeta* (violet), *el azul marino* (navy blue), *el verde claro* (light green), *el rojo vivo* (bright red).

Practice using color names as nouns before assigning activity 10.

¡Vamos de compras!

Imagina que tienes $300. Haz una lista de la ropa que te gustaría comprar este sábado, añadiendo los colores y los materiales que te gustan.

Comunicación

¿Cuánto cuesta?

Trabajando en parejas, un estudiante hace de cliente *(customer)* y el otro de vendedor(a) *(salesperson)*. Alternen en regatear los precios de los artículos en las ilustraciones.

MODELO

A: ¿Cuánto cuestan las botas?
B: Las botas cuestan $80.
A: Le doy $70.
B: No puedo. Se las doy por $75.

Estrategia

Developing language survival skills: *regatear*
Most shops and stores in Spanish-speaking parts of the world have a fixed price *(precio fijo)*, and trying to negotiate a lower price would be inappropriate. However, in some instances negotiating *(regatear)* the price for an item is a common and accepted practice. For example, street vendors selling clothing, baskets, jewelry, etc. in Panama City would expect you to negotiate with them on prices.

How might knowing Spanish help you negotiate a price while visiting a Spanish-speaking country? Do you feel confident enough with your Spanish skills to be able to negotiate a price?

1

2

3

4

5

6

¡Oportunidades!

Regatear
Is there a flea market where you live? Go there and practice bargaining for items. Learning how to bargain will be beneficial if you travel to a Spanish-speaking country where you can combine your ability to bargain with your ability to speak Spanish.

Answers

11 Creative self-expression.
12 Creative self-expression.

Activities

Expansion
Ask additional personalized questions: *¿Te gusta usar corbata?; ¿Prefieres la ropa formal o la ropa informal? ¿Qué ropa llevas a una fiesta formal? ¿Qué ropa llevas a la playa? ¿Qué ropa llevas en un día típico?; ¿Prefieres las botas o los zapatos de tacón?; Para la piscina o la playa, ¿llevas bikini o traje de baño de una pieza?*

Multiple Intelligences (bodily-kinesthetic)
Have students divide into groups to write and perform a skit demonstrating how to barter as in activity 12. Have them bring in items for their vendor to sell and base the prices on the current value of the *balboa*. (Students can locate the current price of a *balboa* in the newspaper, on the Internet or by calling a local bank.)

Notes For activity 11, ask students to assign a price (they may make up the price or check a newspaper advertisement) to each item on their list. Then follow up the activity by having students pair up and ask one another about their lists.

Follow up activity 12 by asking students to write down several lines as they role-play. Then select several pairs of students or ask for volunteers to present their dialog in front of the class.

National Standards	
Communication 1.1, 1.3	Comparisons 4.1, 4.2
Cultures 2.1, 2.2	Communities 5.1
Connections 3.1	

Teacher Resources

 Activities 6–8

 Activities 6–8

 Activity 4

 Activity 3

Answers

13 Creative self-expression.
14 Answers will vary.

Activities

Expansion
Review the present-tense forms of these verbs with students before teaching the preterite tense. Then compare the present-tense stem changes with the preterite-tense stem changes.

National Standards
Communication 1.1
Comparisons 4.1

13 ¿Qué ropa ves?

Trabajando en parejas, habla con tu compañero/a sobre la ropa de la tienda del Vocabulario I. Miren el dibujo y señalen *(point out)* con el dedo los artículos de ropa.

MODELO **A:** ¿Qué te gustaría comprar en la tienda?
B: Me gustaría comprar los zapatos negros, los marrones no me gustan.

14 ¿Qué ropa llevan?

Discuss what clothing people around you are wearing. Begin by saying who is wearing the article of clothing. Your partner then must describe the material or color. Each student must name and describe at least five articles of clothing.

MODELO **A:** Estoy mirando el pantalón de Julia.
B: Su pantalón es azul y es de algodón.

Estructura

Talking about the past: preterite tense of *-er* and *-ir* verbs

Form the preterite tense of regular *-er* and *-ir* verbs by removing the last two letters from the infinitive and adding the same set of endings for either type of verb.

correr	
corrí	corrimos
corriste	corristeis
corrió	corrieron

escribir	
escribí	escribimos
escribiste	escribisteis
escribió	escribieron

*¿Quién **corrió** a la tienda?* — Who **ran** to the store?
*¿Le **escribió** Julia una carta a su prima?* — **Did** Julia **write** a letter to her cousin?

Note: Stem changes that occur in the present tense for *-ar* and *-er* verbs do not occur in the preterite tense. However, *-ir* verbs that have a stem change in the present tense require a different stem change in the preterite tense for *Ud., él, ella, Uds., ellos* and *ellas*. This second change is shown in parentheses after infinitives in this book. Some verbs that follow this pattern include *dormir (ue, **u**), mentir (ie, **i**), pedir (i, **i**), preferir (ie, **i**), repetir (i, **i**)* and *sentir (ie, **i**)*. The stem changes do not interfere with the verb endings.

dormir	
dormí	dormimos
dormiste	dormisteis
durmió	durmieron

pedir	
pedí	pedimos
pediste	pedisteis
pidió	pidieron

preferir	
preferí	preferimos
preferiste	preferisteis
prefirió	prefirieron

Notes Review the preterite tense of *-ar* verbs before beginning the *Estructura* on *-er* and *-ir* verbs.

Be sure to practice conjugating several *-er* and *-ir* verbs so students are clear about what they need to do for the activities that follow.

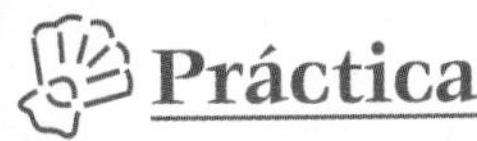

Práctica

15 ¿Lo hiciste ayer o no?

Use each of the verbs shown to state ten things you did or did not do yesterday.

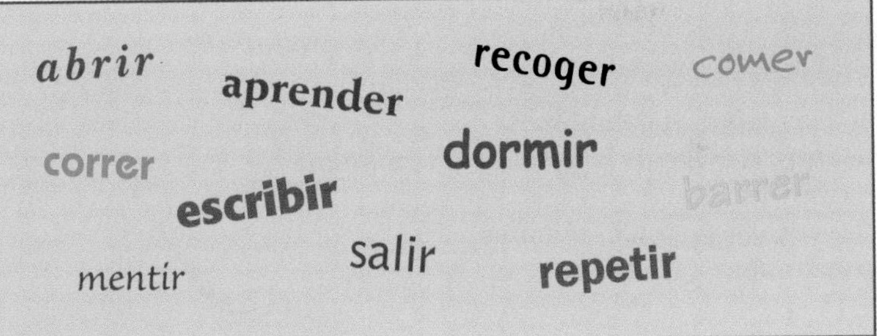

MODELO recoger
Recogí unas fotos ayer.

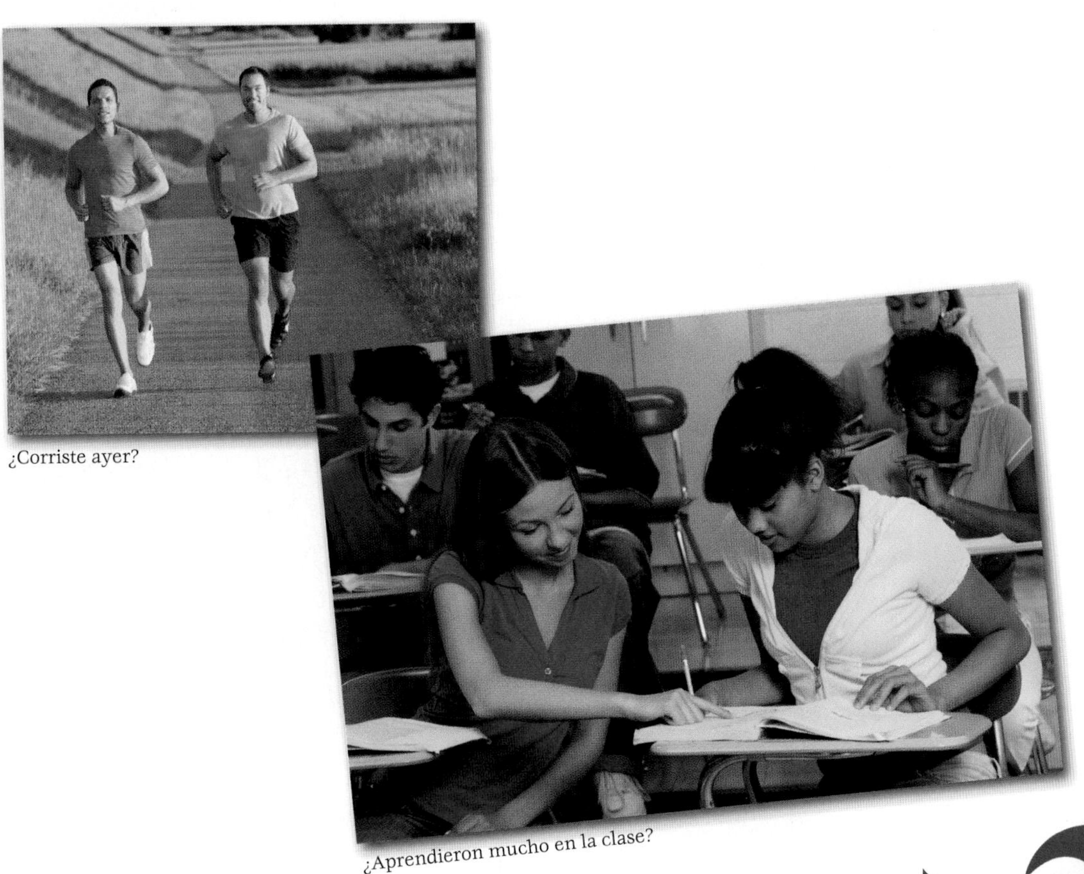

¿Corriste ayer?

¿Aprendieron mucho en la clase?

Notes Other *-ir* stem-changing verbs in the preterite tense include *morir, seguir* and *conseguir.*

Tell the class that the stem change in the third-person forms for these verbs is the same as the change in the present participle, which they have already learned.

Remind students of the difference between *pedir* (to order, to ask for) and *preguntar* (to ask a question).

Answers

15 Answers will vary.

Activities

Cooperative Learning
Give each student an index card to use in a verb drill practice. Have them choose three different verbs ending in *-ar* and three different verbs ending in *-er* or *-ir*. They should vary the subjects for each verb and write the preterite tense of each infinitive to agree with the corresponding subject: *comprar (tú)* = *compraste*, etc. When finished, have students exchange cards to look for errors and make corrections. Then divide them into pairs to drill each other with the verb cards. Collect the cards, double-check for errors and save them to use later on for a quick review before a quiz or when there are a few minutes left in the class period.

National Standards

Communication
1.1

Comparisons
4.1

Teacher Resources

 Activity 16

Answers

16 1. ¿Aprendiste...?/...los aprendí a arreglar (...aprendí a arreglarlos).
2. ¿Barriste...?/...lo barrí....
3. ¿Pediste...?/...las pedí.
4. ¿Escogiste...?/...las escogí.
5. ¿Subiste...?/...la subí.

17 Answers will vary.

Activities

Cooperative Learning

After completing activity 17, students can work in pairs, talking about what other people did yesterday. Possible subjects include classmates, friends and family members.

National Standards

Communication
1.1

16 En la tienda de ropa

Working in pairs, one person plays the part of the owner of a clothing store who has returned from vacation and one person plays the part of an employee who has been managing the store during the owner's absence. What might the conversation sound like, based upon the provided cues?

MODELO recoger las corbatas nuevas
A: ¿Recogiste las corbatas nuevas?
B: Sí, (No, no) las recogí.

1. aprender a arreglar los pantalones
2. barrer siempre el suelo de la tienda por la mañana
3. pedir las camisas
4. escoger las corbatas para los clientes
5. subir la ropa nueva a la oficina

17 ¿Qué hicieron ayer?

Usa elementos de cada columna para hacer siete oraciones completas y decir lo que pasó ayer.

MODELO Yo pedí tres corbatas.

I	II	III
tú y yo	pedir	al departamento de ropa para hombres
Uds.	estar	comprarte unas botas nuevas
la profesora	dormir	toda la tarde
Ud.	correr	ropa interior blanca
los chicos	preferir	en la tienda por departamentos
tú	repetir	tres corbatas
yo		los trajes de baño
		el precio dos veces

Estuvimos en el centro comercial ayer.

Notes

Review direct object pronouns and their position in sentences before beginning activity 16.

Consider completing one or two of the sentences in activity 17 with students to be sure they understand what they have to do.

En la tienda por departamentos

En parejas, hablen de lo que pasó en la tienda por departamentos ayer, según las pistas y las ilustraciones.

MODELO Belén/pedir ver
A: ¿Qué pidió ver Belén?
B: Belén pidió ver unas botas marrones.

1. Jorge y Edgar/ pedir ver

2. Manuel/escoger

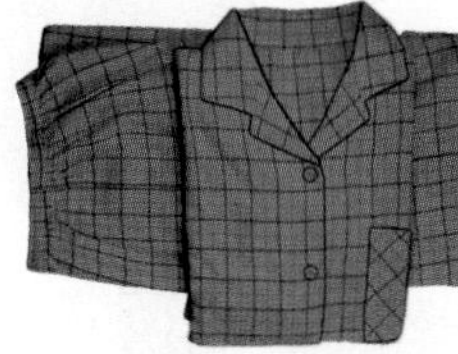

3. Alfonso y su hermano/ volver para comprar

4. la amiga de Ernesto/ correr a comprar

5. Carmen y su mamá/escoger

6. Pedro/preferir comprar

Comunicación

La semana pasada

Make a list of some things you did in the past week. Then, in small groups, talk about the activities on everyone's list. One person starts by mentioning something he or she did. Then others in the group ask questions such as when and with whom you did each activity. You may wish to include some of the following activities: *escribir un correo electrónico, dormir tarde, comer en un restaurante, salir con amigos*, etc.

MODELO **A:** Escribí un correo electrónico.
B: ¿A quién lo escribiste?
A: Lo escribí a un amigo en Panamá.
C: ¿Cuándo escribiste el correo?
A: Lo escribí anteayer.

Answers

18 1. ¿...pidieron ver...?/ ...pidieron ver unos trajes de baño.
2. ¿...escogió...?/...escogió una corbata roja y una camisa azul.
3. ¿...volvieron para comprar...?/...volvieron para comprar un pijama morado.
4. ¿...corrió a comprar...?/ ...corrió a comprar un vestido anaranjado.
5. ¿...escogieron...?/ ...escogieron unas blusas de seda.
6. ¿...prefirió comprar...?/ ...prefirió comprar unas camisetas.

19 Creative self-expression.

Activities

Pronunciation *(las letras* p y f)
The English sound of the letter *p* is "explosive": that is, if you hold your hand over your mouth when you pronounce it, you will feel a slight puff of air. In Spanish this does not happen. Try saying: *Pepe (pepepepepepe...)*. Have students practice the sound by saying the following words: *compra, impermeable, palabra, pantalón, pijama, pedir, Pilar, ropa, zapato*. Remember that the English combination *ph* does not exist in Spanish. That sound is usually represented by an *f*. Have students practice the sound by saying the following words: *café, diferente, difícil, falda, famoso, frío, fue, prefiero, Rafael*.

National Standards

Communication
1.1, 1.3

Comparisons
4.1

Notes Before beginning activity 18, call on students to identify the illustrated objects.

Follow up activity 18 by asking students to write out their answers for each question.

You may wish to assign one person in each group to take notes as people talk. Then have the person summarize the results of the group's discussion.

Teacher Resources

 **Vocabulario II**
Artículos para todos

 **Activity 63**

 **Activity 9**

 **Activity 9**

 **Activity 5**

 **Activity 4**

Activities

Critical Thinking

Students create a survey chart with items of clothing across the top *(camisas, pantalones, blusas, faldas, vestidos,* etc.*)* and colors listed down the side. They should then interview classmates asking *¿Qué ropa llevaste ayer?* and *¿de qué color?* You may have interviewers report student names in relation to clothing and colors or the total number of students who wore each of the different items.

National Standards
Communication 1.1, 1.3
Comparisons 4.1

Vocabulario II
Artículos para todos

¿Te conté que ayer fui al centro comercial Plaza Paitilla?

No. ¿Compraste algo?

Nada, pero fue fantástico.

el impermeable

el guante

el sombrero

¿Venden abrigos rosados?

Sí, pero ahora no nos queda ninguno. ¿No le gusta alguno de estos?

No, ninguno.

Puede comprar una chaqueta o un impermeable rosado.

Muchas gracias. No busco ni una chaqueta ni un impermeable.

el abrigo de lan

el suéter

Gracias, mamá. Este suéter me queda bien y lo puedo combinar con mi pantalón nuevo.

Como te prometí, te compro este suéter para tus vacaciones en Colorado.

Notes Have students find cognates and words they already know in *Vocabulario II*. Quickly check student comprehension of the text boxes and bubbles that accompany the illustrations on these two pages.

An *abrigo* is called a *gabán* in Argentina and a *tapado* in Uruguay.

Use overhead transparency 63 to present and practice the new words and expressions in *Vocabulario II*.

la chaqueta
¿Te gusta alguna chaqueta?
No, ninguna. ¿Hay alguien a quién preguntar si tienen más?
No, no veo a nadie.

20 ¿Qué es?

Go online EMCLanguages.net

Escribe el artículo de ropa que oyes.

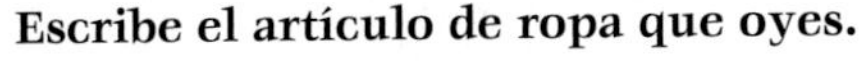

MODELO el sombrero

1. los __ 2. un __ 3. una __ 4. un __ 5. tu __ 6. el __

21 ¿Qué llevo?

Escoge la palabra apropiada para completar lógicamente las siguientes oraciones.

MODELO Si hace frío llevo un (ropa interior, abrigo, blusa).

1. Ay, está nevando y no tengo (corbata, amarillo, botas).
2. Hace sol y calor. Debo llevar mi (suéter, traje de baño, falda) a la playa.
3. Me gusta caminar por la playa sin (zapatos, seda, gris).
4. No quiero llevar una (chaqueta, corbata, camisa) porque no hace frío.
5. Hace mucho viento y no debo llevar el (sombrero, camisa, suéter).
6. El pantalón del (rosado, traje, falda) está sucio.

22 La ropa que usas

Haz una lista de la ropa que necesitas para esquiar en la nieve y otra lista para pasar un día en la playa.

Notes Activity 20 is intended for listening comprehension practice. Play the audio of the activity or use the transcript that appears in the ATE Introduction if you prefer to read the activity yourself. A reproducible answer sheet for the activity can be found at the end of the Audio Program Manual.

Consider allowing students to do activity 22 in pairs. For example, students might ask one another what they need to ski (*¿Qué necesitas par esquiar en la nieve?*) or what they need to spend a day at the beach (*¿Qué necesitas para pasar un día en la playa?*). Follow up by having students list on paper the clothing they need for each activity.

Teacher Resources

Activity 20

Answers

20 1. guantes
2. abrigo
3. chaqueta
4. impermeable
5. suéter
6. pantalón

21 1. botas
2. traje de baño
3. zapatos
4. chaqueta
5. sombrero
6. traje

22 Answers will vary.

Activities

Critical Listening
As an extension of activity 22, select and read aloud the names of articles of clothing from both lists, having students raise their left hand if the item is worn on the beach or their right hand if the item is used when snow skiing.

Expansion
As a follow-up to activity 22, ask students what items besides clothing they would take on a ski trip or to the beach.

National Standards

Communication
1.1, 1.2

Teacher Resources

Diálogo II
Un vestido de seda
Activity 23
Activity 24
Activity 25

Answers

23 1. Sí, hay una señora.
2. No, no le gusta ninguno.
3. No le gustan los vestidos de lana.
4. Puede ver guantes, abrigos o faldas.

24 Answers will vary.

25 1. pretérito
2. presente
3. presente
4. pretérito
5. pretérito
6. presente
7. presente

Activities

Critical Listening
Play the audio version of the dialog as students cover the words and listen to develop good listening skills. Ask several individuals to state what they believe is the main theme of the dialog.

Critical Thinking
Have students look at the photographs as they imagine what the speakers are saying. Then ask if students know where the dialog takes place and what is the main theme of the dialog.

National Standards
Communication 1.2, 1.3

Diálogo II Un vestido de seda

ROCÍO: ¿Hay alguien a quien preguntar por otros vestidos?
PEDRO: Sí, allí. Señora, ¿nos puede ayudar?
SEÑORA: Sí, cómo no.

ROCÍO: Busco un vestido de seda.
SEÑORA: ¿No le gusta ninguno de aquí?
ROCÍO: No, ninguno. Bueno, este azul, pero no me queda bien.

SEÑORA: Bueno, aquí hay otros pero son de lana.
ROCÍO: No, los vestidos de lana no me gustan nada.
SEÑORA: Le gustaría ver algo más, ¿guantes, abrigos, faldas?

23 ¿Qué recuerdas?

1. ¿Hay alguien a quien preguntar por otros vestidos?
2. ¿Le gustan los vestidos de seda a Rocío?
3. ¿Qué vestidos no le gustan a Rocío?
4. ¿Qué más puede ver Rocío?

24 Algo personal

1. ¿Prefieres los vestidos de lana o los de seda?
2. ¿Qué color de ropa te queda bien?
3. ¿Qué ropa compras cuando vas de vacaciones?

¿Qué vestido prefieres?

25 ¿Cuándo?

Listen carefully to statements made by several people. Indicate whether each sentence you hear is in the past *(pretérito)* or in the present *(presente)*.

Notes

This dialog and activities 23, 24 and 25 have been recorded by native speakers and are included in the *¡Aventura!* Audio Program.

You may choose to use the recorded version of activity 25 or you may wish to read the transcript of the activity, which can be found in the ATE Introduction. A reproducible answer sheet for activity 25 has been included at the end of the Audio Program Manual for your convenience.

Ask students to review the vocabulary from the previous page and then scan the dialog for familiar words or phrases.

Cultura viva II

También se dice

As you have seen many times now, words that are used to name items in Spanish often vary a great deal as you travel from one country or region to the next. Even common articles of clothing are referred to in many different ways. For example, the item you know as a *falda* may be called a *saya* in the Caribbean or a *pollera* in parts of South America. However, in Panama the term *pollera* refers to the national dress, which consists of a brightly colored blouse that is connected to a full skirt. In the Caribbean, *zapatos de tacón* are sometimes called simply *tacones*. In addition, an *abrigo* may be called a *sobretodo* in Chile, and many people use *almacén* instead of *tienda de ropa* to refer to the place where they shop for clothing.

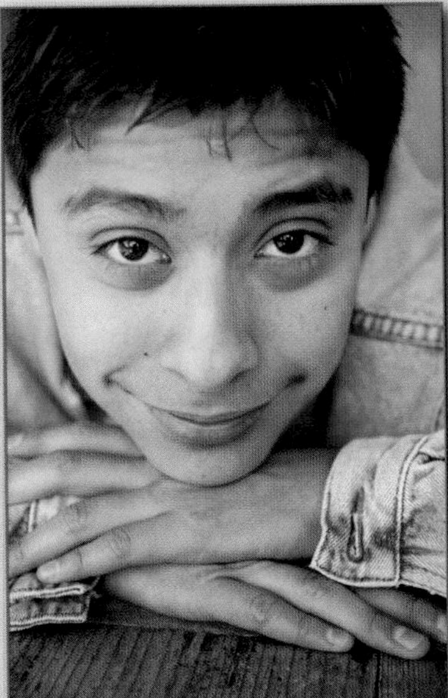

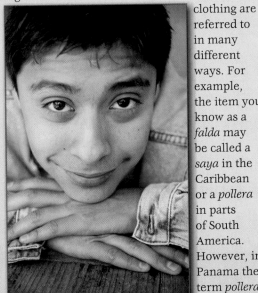

Tiene ojos castaños.

Words used to refer to some colors vary, too, as you travel from one Spanish-speaking part of the world to another. For instance, there are many different words to refer to the color brown. In countries that have been influenced by the French many people favor the word *marrón* for **brown**. In the Caribbean, *carmelita* and the expressions *color café* or *color tabaco* are used. In some countries the word for brown varies according to what is being described. For example, the word *castaño* describes brown hair or brown eyes.

Un tacón de color café.

26 Juego: ¿Quién es?

In small groups, play this game: Take turns describing what someone in the class is wearing, one article of clothing at a time, without looking directly at the person; next, ask *¿Quién es?* and have one member of the group answer after the piece of clothing has been described. If the person does not guess correctly who the person is, describe another article of clothing and continue. The winner is the person that correctly identifies the classmate who is wearing the clothing being described.

MODELO A: Lleva una camisa blanca. ¿Quién es?
B: Es Carlos.

Lleva un abrigo rosado. ¿Quién es?

Teacher Resources

Activity 5

Answers

26 Creative self-expression.

Activities

Spanish for Spanish Speakers
Pair bilingual and nonbilingual students for activity 26.

Technology
Have students search the Internet using the word *pollera*. (See the ATE Introduction for suggestions on using the Internet for searches.) Students will find many different Web pages that discuss *polleras*. Ask students to find Web pages that discuss *polleras* in Panama. Follow up and ask students if they found any sites written in Spanish. Students should print pages from a Spanish-language site, skim it for phrases that they recognize and then share it with the class. You may also want students to summarize what they found on any English-language sites as additional support for a class discussion.

National Standards	
Communication 1.1, 1.3	**Comparisons** 4.1
Cultures 2.1	
Connections 3.2	

Teacher Resources

 Activities 10–11

 Activities 10–12

 Activity 6

 Activity 6

Activities

Multiple Intelligences (linguistic/spatial)

Have students think of a memory device and make a visual representation to depict the forms of *ser* and *ir* in the preterite. Share their ideas with the rest of the class and display the best ones on a bulletin board.

National Standards

Comparisons
4.1

Estructura

Preterite tense of *ir* and *ser*

You have already seen forms of the preterite tense of *ser*. The irregular preterite-tense forms of *ir* (to go) and *ser* (to be) are identical.

ir/ser	
fui	fuimos
fuiste	fuisteis
fue	fueron

*¿Quién **fue** al centro comercial ayer?*	Who **went** to the mall yesterday?
***¿Fueron** ellos al centro comercial?*	**Did** they **go** to the mall?

but:

*¿Qué día **fue** ayer?*	What day **was** yesterday?
*Esos días **fueron** fantásticos.*	Those days **were** fantastic.

¿Fueron ellas al centro comercial?

Notes The preterite tense of *ser* was introduced briefly in *Capítulo 5* so students could talk about the days of the week.

Remember to select from the Teacher Resources indicated at the top of the page to find support materials for teaching from the pages of the textbook. For example, you will find activities that practice and reinforce the preterite tense of *ir* and *ser* in the Listening Activities Manual, Workbook and Grammar and Vocabulary Exercises Manual.

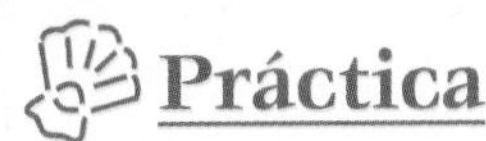

Práctica

27 ¿Adónde fueron ayer? 

Indica adónde fueron estas personas, según las ilustraciones.

MODELO 

Ana y Pablo
Ana y Pablo fueron al cine ayer.

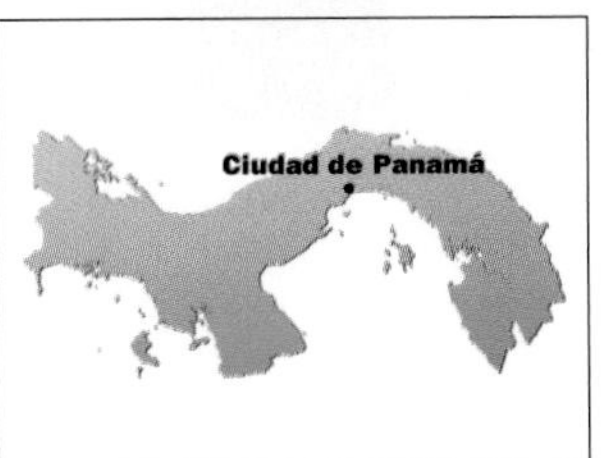

1. yo

2. tú

3. Julia

4. mis padres

5. mi amigo y yo

6. Raúl e Inés

28 Haciendo compras en la isla Contadora

Completa el siguiente párrafo con el pretérito de los verbos indicados para decir qué ropa compraron Juanita y sus dos hermanas en la isla Contadora.

Primero yo *(1. escoger)* un traje de baño porque el que tengo no me queda bien. Lo *(2. comprar)* por poco dinero. Mis hermanas también *(3. comprar)* en la misma tienda unos vestidos de algodón muy bonitos. Cuando nosotras *(4. volver)* al centro comercial, yo *(5. ir)* a buscar otro traje de baño para mí. Ese día en la tienda, los dependientes *(6. vender)* todos los trajes de baño rápidamente. Nosotras *(7. comprar)* el último. Me gustaría tener dos. Luego, mi tía Julia *(8. ir)* con nosotras de compras. Ella *(9. prometer)* comprarme ropa para mi cumpleaños y yo le *(10. pedir)* unos zapatos bajos, de color marrón. ¡Qué bonitos son! Nosotras *(11. estar)* comprando todo el día y *(12. llegar)* tarde al hotel, ¡cansadas pero contentas!

Notes Note for students that Contadora Island (mentioned in activity 28) is part of Panama.

You can use the Appendices that begin on page 430 to offer a comprehensive overview of how to conjugate verbs in the tenses that are taught in *¡Aventura! 1*.

Teacher Resources

 Activity 27

Answers

27 Possible answers:
1. Yo fui a la Ciudad de Panamá ayer.
2. Tú fuiste al parque ayer.
3. Julia fue al centro comercial ayer.
4. Mis padres fueron a la playa ayer.
5. Mi amigo y yo fuimos a un restaurante ayer.
6. Raúl e Inés fueron al concierto ayer.

28
1. escogí
2. compré
3. compraron
4. volvimos
5. fui
6. vendieron
7. compramos
8. fue
9. prometió
10. pedí
11. estuvimos
12. llegamos

Activities

Students with Special Needs
Before assigning activity 27, have students identify the sites in the illustrations.

National Standards

Communication
1.1

Connections
3.1

Answers

29 1. Marta fue a comprar una blusa amarilla.
2. Lola y Rita fueron a comprar unos zapatos (de tacón) azules.
3. Tú fuiste a comprar un pantalón marrón.
4. Nosotros fuimos a comprar una camisa anaranjada.
5. Yo fui a comprar un abrigo negro.

30 Creative self-expression.

31 Creative self-expression.

Activities

Cooperative Learning

Have students pair up and discuss a favorite vacation. The following questions can guide their discussion: *¿Adónde fuiste? ¿Con quién(es) fuiste?; ¿Qué lugares visitaste? ¿Cuál fue tu lugar favorito?; ¿Qué compraste?; ¿Escribiste un diario o cartas a tus amigos?; ¿Fuiste a un restaurante especial? ¿Qué comiste?*

Expansion

As a follow-up to the previous activity, assign a short composition in which the students summarize a favorite vacation.

National Standards

Communication
1.1, 1.3

Connections
3.1

29 Fueron y compraron lo siguiente

Imagina que tus amigos y tú fueron de compras al centro comercial el sábado pasado. Di lo que las siguientes personas fueron a comprar. Sigue el modelo.

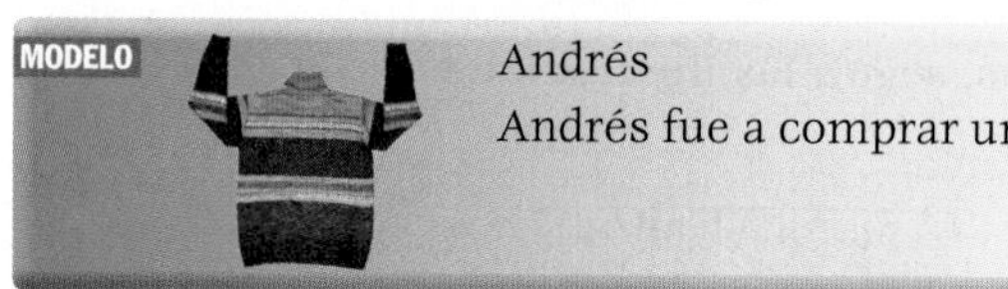

Andrés
Andrés fue a comprar un suéter verde.

1. Marta

2. Lola y Rita

3. tú

4. nosotros

5. yo

Comunicación

30 Haciendo cosas

With a partner, talk about where family and friends went yesterday, last week, last month or last year. Include in your discussion how the people named went to each place, whom they went with and what they did. Take notes as you talk. Then share the most interesting bit of information you learned with the class.

MODELO
A: ¿Fueron tú y tu familia a un buen restaurante la semana pasada?
B: Sí. Fuimos a un restaurante nuevo en el centro comercial.
A: ¿Te gustó?
B: Sí, me gustó mucho.

31 Una encuesta

Haz una investigación sobre las actividades que hacen tus compañeros/as de clase. Prepara una lista de actividades (quehaceres, deportes, pasatiempos, etc.) y trata de encontrar una persona que haya hecho *(has done)* cada actividad y pregúntale cuándo la hizo durante la semana pasada. Puedes usar las siguientes frases para completar la investigación: *dormir tarde, escribir un correo electrónico, ir al centro comercial, ir a un buen restaurante, ir al cine, ir a la playa, ir al parque.*

MODELO
A: ¿Dormiste tarde la semana pasada?
B: Sí, dormí tarde el jueves.

Actividad	Nombre	Día
dormir tarde		jueves
escribir un correo electrónico		

Notes

Inform students that they can determine whether the verb that someone is using is the preterite tense of *ir* or the preterite tense of *ser* by the context in which the verb is used. Give one or two examples in Spanish with English equivalents to support this point.

Before beginning activity 29, have students identify the article of clothing.

Have students take notes and write a summary of what each person says for activity 30.

Ask for volunteers to tell the class the results of the survey they did for activity 31.

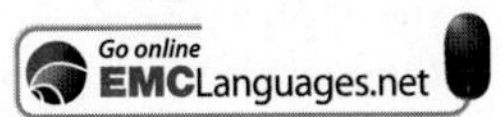

Estructura

Affirmative and negative words

You have learned to make a sentence negative by placing *no* before a verb.

No veo la chaqueta. — I do **not** see the jacket.

Unlike English, in Spanish it is sometimes possible to use two negative expressions in the same sentence. The following chart contains a list of common negative expressions along with their affirmative counterparts.

Expresiones afirmativas	Expresiones negativas
• **sí *(yes)*** **Sí,** ella habla español. Él dice que **sí.**	• **no *(no)*** **No,** él **no** habla español. Ella dice que **no.**
• **algo *(something, anything)*** ¿Quieres comprar **algo**? ¿Compraste **algo** ayer?	• **nada *(nothing, anything)*** **No** quiero comprar **nada.** **Nada** me gustó.
• **alguien *(somebody, anybody)*** ¿Lo sabe **alguien?** **Alguien** debe saberlo.	• **nadie *(nobody, anybody)*** **No** lo sabe **nadie.** **Nadie** lo sabe.
• **algún, alguna, -os, -as *(some, any)*** ¿Le gusta **algún** abrigo? ¿Le gusta **alguna** blusa? ¿Compras **algunos** calcetines? ¿Buscas **algunas** corbatas?	• **ningún, ninguna, -os, -as *(none, not any)*** No, **ningún** abrigo me gusta. No, **ninguna** me gusta. No, **no** compro **ningunos** calcetines. No, **no** busco **ningunas** corbatas.
• **o...o *(either... or)*** Puedes comprar **o** un abrigo **o** un sombrero.	• **ni... ni *(neither... nor)*** **No** voy a comprar **ni** un abrigo **ni** un sombrero.
• **siempre *(always)*** Él **siempre** lleva botas.	• **nunca *(never)*** Ella **no** lleva botas **nunca.** Ella **nunca** lleva botas.
• **también *(also, too)*** Ella viene hoy **también.** Ella **también** viene hoy.	• **tampoco *(neither, either)*** Él **no** viene mañana **tampoco.** Él **tampoco** viene mañana.

Note: The words *alguno,-a* (some, any) and *ninguno,-a* (none, not any) sometimes are used as pronouns.

*¿Va **alguno** o **alguna** de Uds. al centro comercial ahora?* — *No, **ninguno** de nosotros va al centro comercial ahora.*

Teacher Resources

 Activities 12–13

 Activities 13–14

 p. 141

 Activity 7
Activity 8

 Activity 7

Activities

Expansion
Call on several students to give examples of sentences that use these affirmative and negative expressions.

Students with Special Needs
Return to previously studied dialogs and readings and ask students to find examples of affirmative and negative expressions.

Notes Tell the class that the plural negative words *ningunos* and *ningunas* are used very little. In most cases, the singular words *ningún* and *ninguna* are preferred.

Inform students that *algún* and *ningún* are shortened forms of *alguno* and *ninguno*.

National Standards

Communication
1.3

Comparisons
4.1

Teacher Resources

Activity 33

Answers

32 1. Alguien, nadie
2. Alguien, algo
3. alguien, algo
4. alguien, nadie
5. algo, nada

33 Possible answers:
1. Tampoco voy a la tienda de ropa./No voy a la tienda de ropa tampoco.
2. No fuimos de compras con nadie ayer.
3. No prefiero ni las botas anaranjadas ni las verdes.
4. No, no vi ninguna falda de algodón.
5. No, no veo a ningún amigo del colegio.
6. No compramos ni el suéter rojo ni el suéter azul.
7. No, nuestros padres nunca nos dan..../No, nuestros padres no nos dan nunca....
8. No me gustaría vender ni ropa interior ni carros.
9. Nunca vamos de compras al centro./No vamos de compras nunca al centro.
10. Ninguno de nosotros somos de Panamá.

National Standards

Communication
1.1

Comparisons
4.1

When combining negative expressions in one sentence in Spanish, it is often possible to use one of the negative expressions before the verb and another negative expression (and sometimes even more than one) after the verb. However, *no, nada, nadie, nunca, tampoco* and forms of *ninguno* may be used alone, before the verb, without the word *no.*

No *voy* ***nunca*** *al centro.* ***Nunca*** *voy al centro.*	I **never** go downtown.
No *estoy comprando* ***nada tampoco.*** ***Tampoco*** *estoy comprando* ***nada.***	I am **not** buying **anything either**.

When *nadie* or a form of *ninguno* are direct objects referring to people they require the personal *a.*

No *veo* ***a nadie*** *aquí.*	I don't see **anyone** here.
No *veo* ***a ningún*** *amigo aquí.*	I don't see **any** friends here.

Práctica

32 A completar

Completa estos mini-diálogos lógicamente, usando una de las siguientes palabras: *algo, alguien, nada* o *nadie*.

1. __ debe ir con Uds.
   No queremos ir con __.
2. __ te llama por teléfono.
   Marta te quiere decir __.
3. ¿Va __ con Uds.?
   Sí, Isabel va con nosotras porque quiere comprar __.
4. ¿Ves a __ en esa tienda de ropa?
   No, no veo a __.
5. ¿Quieres comprar ___?
   No, no me gusta __.

33 ¡No!

Contesta las preguntas en forma negativa.

MODELO ¿Qué quieres mirar?
No quiero mirar nada.

1. Yo no voy a la tienda de ropa. ¿Y tú?
2. ¿Con quién fueron Uds. de compras ayer?
3. ¿Prefieres las botas anaranjadas o las verdes?
4. ¿Viste alguna falda de algodón?
5. ¿Ves a algún amigo del colegio?
6. ¿Compraron Uds. el suéter rojo o el suéter azul?
7. ¿Sus padres siempre les dan dinero para ir de compras?
8. ¿Te gustaría vender ropa interior o carros?
9. ¿Siempre van Uds. de compras al centro?
10. ¿Quiénes de Uds. son de Panamá?

¿Compró el suéter rojo?

Notes Model several sentences that use the negative expressions before assigning the activities on pages 382 and 383.

Ask students to pair up before starting activity 33. Follow up by having students write their answers.

¡Estoy enfermo/a y no quiero hacer nada!

Estás de mal humor porque estás enfermo/a y tus padres te hacen muchas preguntas. Trabajando en parejas, alternen en hacer las siguientes preguntas y en dar respuestas negativas a cada una.

MODELO **A:** ¿Piensas ir de compras o vas a estudiar?
B: No, no pienso ni ir de compras ni estudiar.

1. ¿Qué vas a hacer hoy?
2. ¿Quién te va a visitar en casa?
3. ¿Siempre juegas con el perro cuando estás enfermo/a?
4. ¿Quieres comer algo?
5. ¿Vas a hablar con alguien por teléfono?
6. ¿Quieres ver alguna película en DVD?
7. ¿Te puedo comprar algo?

Comunicación

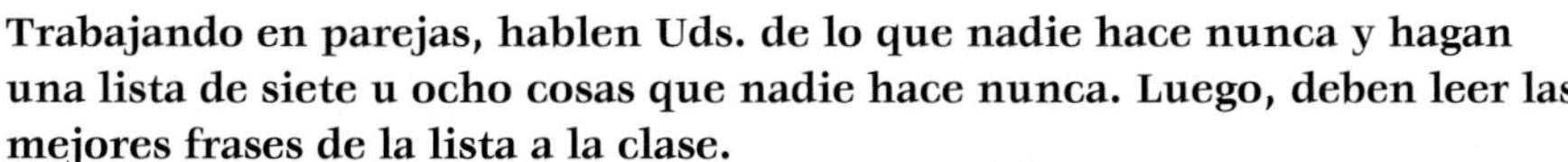

35 No se hace

Trabajando en parejas, hablen Uds. de lo que nadie hace nunca y hagan una lista de siete u ocho cosas que nadie hace nunca. Luego, deben leer las mejores frases de la lista a la clase.

MODELO Nadie va al centro comercial sin zapatos.

36 ¿Qué llevas mucho?

Talk with a classmate about the clothing you like to wear and when. Include in your discussion how often you wear various articles of clothing, the colors you prefer, when and where you went shopping and whether or not you purchased something, which articles of clothing each of you purchased last week/month/year (naming a specific time) and anything else you wish.

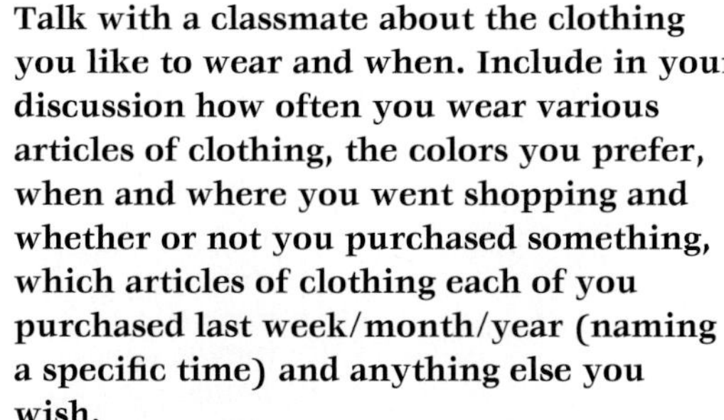

MODELO **A:** ¿Qué ropa te gusta llevar mucho?
B: Me gusta llevar este suéter anaranjado casi todos los días.
A: ¿Dónde lo compraste?
B: No lo compré, me lo regaló mi hermano.

Me gusta llevar mi vestido rojo y azul.

Notes

Activities 34, 35 and 36 can be repeated. Have students work on each activity with one partner. Then have them switch partners and try the activity again.

Set time limits for the paired activities on page 383 and keep a brisk pace.

Remember to circulate around the room as students complete these activities to keep students on task and to offer help as needed.

Activity 36 serves as a good starting point for a composition on a favorite teen topic: clothing.

Teacher Resources

Activity 34

Answers

34 Possible answers:
1. No voy a hacer nada hoy.
2. Nadie me va a visitar en casa.
3. No, nunca juego con el perro cuando estoy enfermo/a.
4. No, no quiero comer nada.
5. No, no voy a hablar con nadie por teléfono.
6. No, no quiero ver ninguna película en DVD.
7. No, no me puedes comprar nada.

35 Creative self-expression.
36 Creative self-expression.

Activities

Critical Listening

Tell students that they will hear a series of erroneous statements with affirmative or negative words. For each statement given, the students should state the opposite to provide the correct information. Possible statements: *La clase de español siempre empieza tarde; Tenemos clase el sábado y el domingo también; En esta clase no tenemos ningún examen; El profesor/la profesora no conoce a nadie en (país); Para mañana no tenemos que hacer nada.*

National Standards

Communication
1.1, 1.3

Teacher Resources

Lectura cultural
Las molas: símbolo de la cultura kuna
Activity 37

Answers

37 1. Los kunas viven en el archipiélago de San Blas a 200 millas de la costa de Panamá.
2. El traje tradicional de las mujeres kunas consiste en faldas coloridas, blusas decoradas con molas y anillos de oro en las narices.
3. Las molas se hacen con telas de diferentes colores.
4. Usan las molas para decorar las blusas.

38 Answers will vary.

Activities

Multiple Intelligences (spatial)
Have students make *molas* out of construction paper.

National Standards

Cultures
2.1, 2.2

Connections
3.1

Comparisons
4.1, 4.2

Lectura cultural

Las molas: símbolo de la cultura kuna

En el mar[1] Caribe, a 200 millas de la costa de Panamá, está el archipiélago de San Blas *(Kuna Yala)*. En estas islas tropicales viven los indios kuna. Uno de los elementos más conocidos de los indios kuna es su vestimenta tradicional[2] que es espectacular: las mujeres llevan anillos de oro[3] en la nariz, faldas coloridas y blusas decoradas con las famosas molas. Las molas son paneles de intricados diseños[4] cosidos a mano[5]. Las mujeres kuna observan, transforman y representan el mundo que ven y su medio ambiente y los convierten en estas obras de arte usando aguja, hilos y telas de colores vivos[6].

Los paneles adornan la parte delantera y trasera de las blusas y los diseños pueden ser muy antiguos, con piezas geométricas y animales sagrados, relativos a la vida diaria de las mujeres. Las molas son apreciadas piezas de arte indígena y pueden encontrarse en museos y colecciones privadas. Las molas pueden alcanzar un precio muy elevado, dependiendo del número de capas, los detalles y el mérito artístico del diseño.

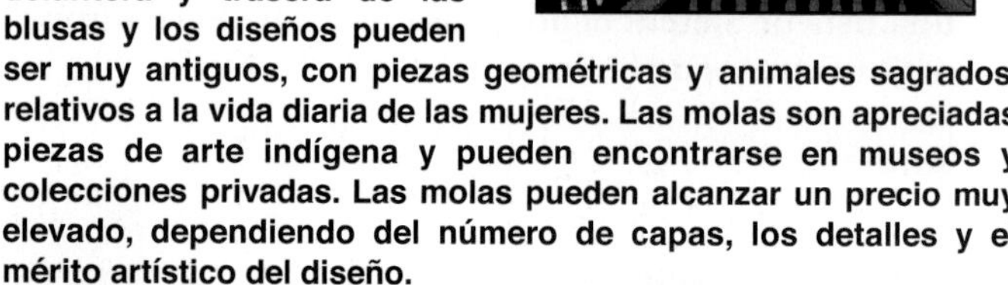

[1]sea [2]traditional clothing [3]gold [4]designs [5]hand-sewn [6]threads and fabrics of bright coloring

¿Qué recuerdas?

1. ¿Dónde viven los kunas?
2. ¿Cómo es el traje tradicional de las mujeres kunas?
3. ¿Cómo se hacen las molas?
4. ¿Para qué usan las molas?

Algo personal

1. En tu opinión, ¿son las molas ropa, arte o los dos? Explica.
2. Imagina que vas a crear una mola. Describe el diseño y los colores de tu mola.

- **Compare and contrast the molas of the Kuna Indians with a traditional piece of clothing of another culture. Are they worn just by women? Are they sold as art pieces? Are they made of cotton? Do they have colorful designs?**

Notes

The *mola* designs come from the body paintings of Kuna ancestors who didn't wear clothes until French Huguenot settlers introduced clothing in the mid-nineteenth century. The Kuna simply transposed the body paintings onto cotton fabrics.

Connections. This *Lectura cultural* makes the cross-curricular connections to art, history and geography.

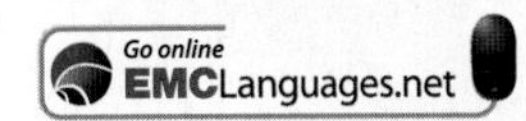

Autoevaluación

As a review and self-check, respond to the following:

1. Describe three of your favorite clothing items, saying what color they are and what they are made of.
2. Imagine you are deciding either to take a vacation to Panama to enjoy warm weather or go to Chile for a winter ski trip. List at least three articles of clothing you will need to take with you for each vacation choice.
3. State three things you did yesterday.
4. Name two places you went yesterday.
5. Make two affirmative and two negative statements about something that happened yesterday.
6. Name two things you have learned about Panama.

Palabras y expresiones

How many of these words and expressions do you recognize?

Para describir
algún, alguna
anaranjado,-a
marrón
morado,-a
ningún, ninguna
rosado,-a

Pronombres
algo
alguien
alguno,-a
nada
nadie
ninguno,-a

La ropa
la bota
la chaqueta
la corbata
el guante
el impermeable
las medias
el pijama
la ropa interior
el sombrero
el suéter
el traje (de baño)
el vestido
el zapato (bajo/de tacón)

Partes del cuerpo
el brazo
la cabeza
el cuerpo
el dedo
la mano
el pie
la pierna

Verbos
combinar
contar (ue)
prometer
quedar
vender

Expresiones y otras palabras
el algodón
el centro comercial
el departamento
el hombre
la lana
la mujer
ni... ni
o... o
quedarle bien a uno
la seda
las vacaciones

Estructura

Do you remember the following grammar rules?

Adjectives as nouns

The definite article is necessary with the adjective when it becomes a noun.

¿Te gusta la camisa roja?	Do you like the red shirt?
Sí, me gusta ***la*** *roja.*	Yes, I **like the red one.**

Preterite tense of regular *-er* and *-ir* verbs

correr	
corrí	corrimos
corriste	corristeis
corrió	corrieron

Note: *-ir* verbs that have stem changes in the present tense will also have a stem change in the preterite tense indicated by the second vowel in parenthesis after the infinitive. For example: ***dormir (ue, u)*** or ***pedir (i, i).***

Preterite tense of *ir* and *ser*

ir/ser	
fui	fuimos
fuiste	fuisteis
fue	fueron

Affirmative and negative expressions

Expresiones afirmativas	Expresiones negativas
Sí	no
Algo	nada
Alguien	nadie
algún, alguena, -os, -as	ningún, ninguna, -os, -as
o...o	ni...ni
siempre	nunca
también	tampoco

Notes

Communities. Panama wasn't established as a nation until November 3, 1903. Before that date, Panama was part of Colombia.

Students may find it interesting that although the monetary unit in Panama is the *balboa*, the U.S. dollar is also widely used in larger cities.

Tell students that the Panama Canal is not only important to Panama, it is also vital to international trade, because it allows ships to pass from one ocean to another in a matter of hours.

Teacher Resources

Activity 14

pp. 61, 95

Juegos

Flash Cards

Answers

Autoevaluación

Possible answers:

1. Answers will vary.
2. Necesito llevar una chaqueta y mis botas./Necesito llevar un traje de baño y una camisa de algodón.
3. Compré unas botas nuevas....
4. Fui al centro comercial.
5. Escribí algunas cartas./ Nunca salí con mis amigos.
6. La capital es la Ciudad de Panamá....

Activities

Cooperative Learning

Have students work in pairs to play guessing games. Students take turns describing an object in the classroom (being certain to use the colors) while the partner guesses what the object is.

National Standards

Communication
1.1

Connections
3.1

Teacher Resources

 **Vocabulario I**
Regalos

 **Activities 64–65**

 **Activity 1**

 **Activities 1–3**

 **p. 37**

 **Activity 1**

 **Activity 1**

Content reviewed in *Lección B*
- clothing
- family
- adjective-noun agreement
- talking about the past
- prepositions
- places in a city

Activities

Prereading Strategy
Play the audio recording of the vocabulary and have students repeat the words while showing them overhead transparency 64.

National Standards

Communication
1.3

Connections
3.1

Lección B Vocabulario I
Regalos

Ecua

la bufanda

el cinturón de cuero

Esta bufanda es demasiado larga.

Mi mamá me dijo que le gustaría recibir un bolso de regalo.

Esta bufanda es bastante corta.

el bolso de material sintético

¡Qué lindo bolsito! Es perfecto y está barato. Lo puede usar todos los días.

el pañuel

la billetera

el collar de perlas

la pulsera de oro

el arete de

el perfume

el anillo

las joyas

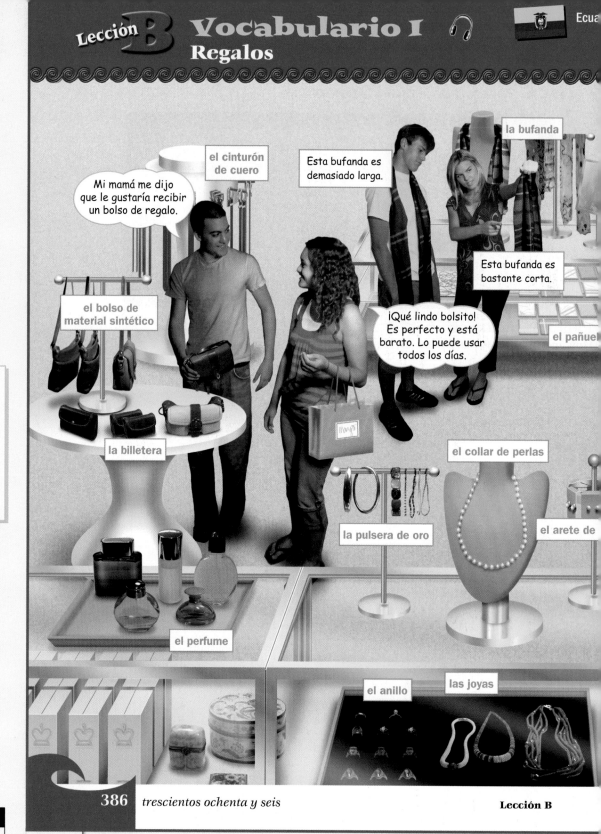

Notes Have students find cognates and words they already know in *Vocabulario I.* Quickly check student comprehension of the descriptions that accompany the illustrations on these two pages.

Ask students what they know about Ecuador. Most students are probably familiar with the Galapagos Islands, which are discussed on page 389. Ask for student volunteers to create a bulletin board or travel brochure about this Spanish-speaking South American country.

Inform students that they are about to study the country that was named for the equator: *Ecuador*.

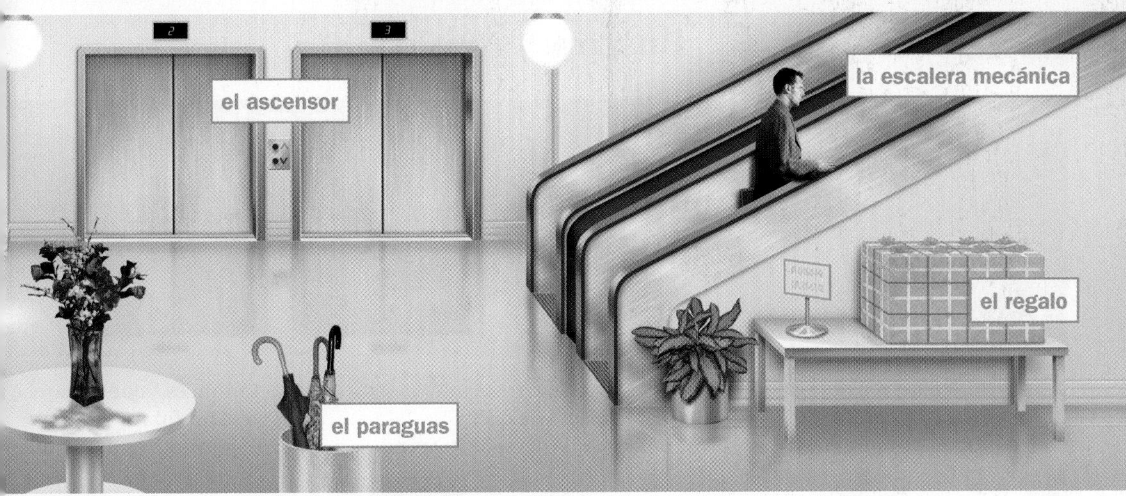

1 ¿Qué les gustaría recibir de regalo?

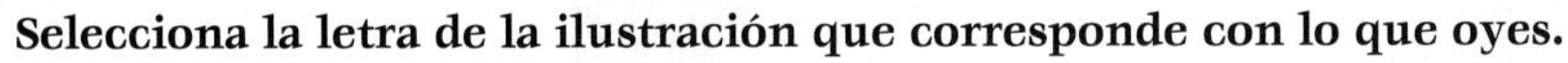

Selecciona la letra de la ilustración que corresponde con lo que oyes.

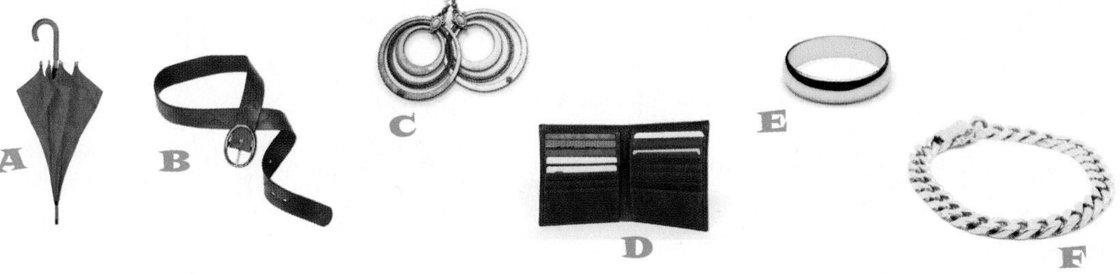

2 Hablando de los artículos de la tienda

Contesta las siguientes preguntas en español.

1. ¿Qué puede ser de cuero?
2. ¿Qué puede ser de plata?
3. ¿Qué puede ser de perlas?
4. ¿Te gusta usar perfume? Explica.
5. ¿Cuándo llevas pañuelo?
6. ¿Cuándo llevas bufanda?
7. ¿De qué materiales puede ser un bolso?
8. ¿Qué joyas te gusta llevar?

3 Regalos para todos

Trabajando en parejas, preparen tres listas de regalos, una para hombres, otra para mujeres y otra para hombres y mujeres. Cada lista debe tener tres o cuatro regalos en cada columna.

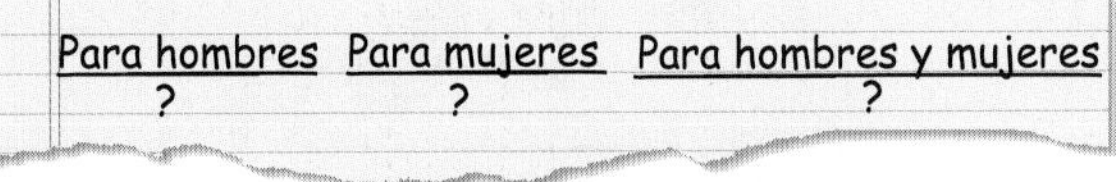

Para hombres	Para mujeres	Para hombres y mujeres
?	?	?

Notes Use overhead transparencies 64 and 65 to present and practice the new words and expressions in *Vocabulario I*.

Activity 1 is intended for listening comprehension practice. Play the audio of the activity that is included in the Audio Program or use the transcript that appears in the ATE introduction if you prefer to read the activity yourself.

A reproducible answer sheet for the activity can be found at the end of the Audio Program Manual.

Teacher Resources

Activity 1

Activities 2–3

Answers

1 1. D; 2. F; 3. A; 4. C; 5. B; 6. E

2 Possible answers:
1. Pueden ser de cuero un cinturón, un bolso o una billetera.
2. Pueden ser de plata unos aretes, una pulsera, un collar o un anillo.
3. Pueden ser de perlas un collar, una pulsera o unos aretes.
4. Answers will vary.
5. Answers will vary.
6. Llevo bufanda cuando hace frío.
7. Un bolso puede ser de material sintético o de cuero.
8. Answers will vary.

3 Answers will vary.

Activities

Expansion

Use overhead transparencies 64 and 65 to introduce the new words and expressions in *Vocabulario I*. Begin by showing students transparency 64 and point to one of the items in the store and identify it in Spanish. Students should repeat after you. Continue with the next item and repeat the process. As a second step, show students transparency 65. Once again identify the objects in Spanish, allowing students to see how each word is spelled.

National Standards

Communication
1.1, 1.2

Teacher Resources

Diálogo I
Busco un regalo
Activity 4
Activity 5
Activity 6

Answers

4 1. Busca un regalo.
2. Busca un regalo bueno, bonito y barato.
3. Busca algo para una mujer.
4. No.
5. Le parece perfecto el perfume.

5 Answers will vary.

6 1. A; 2. A; 3. B; 4. A; 5. B; 6. B

Activities

Critical Listening
Play the audio recording of the dialog. Instruct students to cover up the words as they listen to the conversation. Have students look at the photographs and ask several individuals to state what they believe is the main theme of the conversation.

Expansion
Additional questions *(Algo personal)*: *¿Te gusta comprar regalos?; ¿Prefieres comprar regalos en el centro comercial o en las tiendas?; ¿Para quién compras regalos más caros, para la familia o para los amigos?*

Prereading Strategy
Instruct students to cover up the dialog with one hand and to look at the photographs. Ask them to imagine where the conversation takes place and what the people are saying to one another.

National Standards
Communication 1.1, 1.2

Diálogo I Busco un regalo

DANIEL: Busco un regalo, bueno, bonito y barato.
SEÑORA: ¿Para hombre o para mujer?
DANIEL: Para mujer.

SEÑORA: ¿Qué le parece una pulsera de oro?
DANIEL: No. Ella dijo que joyas no.

SEÑORA: Entonces, ¿qué le parece este perfume?
DANIEL: El perfume es perfecto.

4 ¿Qué recuerdas?

1. ¿Qué busca Daniel?
2. ¿Qué tipo de regalo busca?
3. ¿Para quién busca algo Daniel?
4. ¿Va a comprar Daniel una pulsera de oro?
5. ¿Qué le parece perfecto?

¡Extra!

En otras palabras

el anillo	*la argolla, la sortija*
los aretes	*los zarcillos, los aros, los pendientes*
el bolso	*la cartera, la bolsa, el monedero*
el material sintético	*el plástico, el acrílico*
el paraguas	*la sombrilla*
el pijama	*el payama/el piyama*
la pulsera	*el brazalete*

5 Algo personal

1. Cuando buscas un regalo, ¿lo buscas bueno, bonito y barato? Explica.
2. ¿Piensas que es más fácil comprar un regalo para un hombre o una mujer?
3. En tu opinión, ¿qué regalos piensas son para hombres? ¿Y para mujeres?

6 Bueno, bonito y barato

Selecciona la letra de la ilustración que corresponde con lo que las siguientes personas buscan.

A

B

Notes This dialog and activities 4, 5 and 6 have been recorded by native speakers and are included in the *¡Aventura!* Audio Program. A reproducible student answer sheet for activity 6 is available at the end of the Audio Program Manual.

Ask students to review the vocabulary from the previous page and then scan the dialog for familiar words or phrases.

Cultura viva!

Ecuador, país de maravillas naturales

Soy de las Islas Galápagos.

Quito, Ecuador.

Ecuador is located southwest of Colombia and north of Peru. The equator (*ecuador*), which is located high in the Andes Mountains, cuts through the country just a few miles north of the nation's capital, Quito. A monument here marks the dividing point between the Northern and the Southern Hemisphere.

Ecuador was once part of the Incan Empire. When he died in the sixteenth century, the Incan emperor Huayna Cápac divided the empire between two sons: Atahualpa ruled the portion that was based in Quito, and Huáscar ruled the portion that was based in Cuzco, Peru. Huayna Cápac did not know, however, that the division would weaken the empire and lead to its rapid conquest by the Spanish conquistadors. Ecuador remained under Spanish control until becoming the first South American nation to declare its independence in 1809.

GALAPAGOS ISLANDS
PINTA I. MARCHENA I. GENOVESA I.
ISABELA I. SANTIAGO I. SEYMOUR I. BALTRA I.
PINZON I. SANTA CRUZ I. Pto. Ayora SAN CRISTOBAL I. El Progreso
Tomás de Berlanga SANTA FE I. Pto. Baquerizo Moreno
Pto. Villamil
FLOREANA I. ESPAÑOLA I.

Remains of Ecuador's colorful past are still evident throughout the nation today. Along with historical reminders of the past, Ecuador offers visitors compelling natural wonders, as well. One of these, the *Archipiélago de Colón*, also known as the Galapagos Islands (*Islas Galápagos*), is located off the coast of Ecuador in the Pacific Ocean. The islands were formed by volcanic eruptions. Today they have become a national park (*parque nacional*) consisting of more than 600 miles of coastline, where an interesting mix of tropical and cold-climate animals (*animales*) and plants (*plantas*) live that cannot be found in any other part of the world.

7 Conexión con otras disciplinas: geografía

Completa las frases de la izquierda con una de las frases de la derecha, según la información en Cultura viva.

1. El ecuador divide...
2. La capital del Ecuador...
3. El Ecuador formó parte...
4. El Ecuador declaró su independencia...
5. Al Archipiélago de Colón se le llama también...
6. Las Islas Galápagos están...
7. En las Galápagos hay...

A. ...en el Océano Pacífico.
B. ...en 1809.
C. ...el mundo en norte y sur.
D. ...un parque nacional con plantas y animales.
E. ...es Quito.
F. ...las Islas Galápagos.
G. ...del imperio inca.

Notes

Connections. Activity 7 makes the cross-curricular connection to geography.

It is noteworthy that the word *galápagos* is a Spanish term that refers to the large tortoises that live on the islands.

Connections. The six Galapagos Islands are also called *Las Islas Encantadas*. Charles Darwin's observations of life on the islands led to his theory of evolution, which he explained in his book *On the Origin of Species*.

Teacher Resources

 Activity 4

 p. 116

 Activity 2

Answers

7
1. C
2. E
3. G
4. B
5. F
6. A
7. D

Activities

Connections

Show students where Ecuador is located, using the maps in the book or the transparencies that are part of this program.

Expansion

Have a class discussion about Ecuador. You may choose to ask the following questions to stimulate other student questions: *¿Cómo se llama el inca que dividió el imperio entre sus dos hijos?; ¿Cómo se llaman los dos hijos?; ¿Existen los incas hoy?; ¿Existe la cultura india en Ecuador hoy?*

National Standards

Communication
1.1

Cultures
2.2

Connections
3.1

Teacher Resources

 Activity 8
Activity 9

 Activity 5

 Activity 4

 Activity 3

 Activity 2

Answers

8 1. el bolsito
2. la billeterita
3. el cinturoncito
4. el pañuelito
5. la bufandita
6. el collarcito
7. las botitas
8. los guantecitos
9. el suétercito

9 1. la chaqueta
2. el zapato
3. las joyas
4. el traje
5. la puerta
6. el sombrero
7. la corbata
8. el jardín
9. el hijo

10 Creative self-expression.

Activities

Critical Thinking

Ask students to give the original form of several words: *chiquita (chica), Sarita (Sara)*. Then see if students can give diminutive forms for several words: *casa (casita), regalo (regalito)*.

National Standards
Communication 1.1

Idioma

Estructura

Diminutives

Indicate affection or convey the idea that something is small by replacing the final vowel of a noun with the endings *-ito, -ita, -itos* and *-itas: Ana (Anita)*. For nouns that end in a consonant, add the endings *-cito, -cita, -citos* or *-citas* to the complete word: *collar (collarcito)*. Additional diminutive endings you may encounter include *-illo, -illa, -uelo, -uela, -ico* and *-ica*. Other words may require a spelling change: *poquito (poco)*.

Although many exceptions exist for the diminutive forms, most are easily recognized: *hotelito (hotel), Daniel (Danielito)*. It is best to learn the variations as you encounter them since they can vary from country to country and even from one person to another within countries.

Práctica

8 Todo es pequeñito

Cambia las siguientes palabras al diminutivo.

1. el bolso
2. la billetera
3. el cinturón
4. el pañuelo
5. la bufanda
6. el collar
7. las botas
8. los guantes
9. el suéter

9 ¿De dónde vienen?

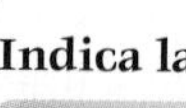

Indica la palabra original.

MODELO el regalillo → el regalo

1. la chaquetilla
2. el zapatico
3. las joyitas
4. el trajecillo
5. la portezuela
6. el sombrerito
7. la corbatica
8. el jardincito
9. el hijuelo

Los guantes.

Comunicación

10 Comprando un regalo con mucho cariño

Imagine you and a close friend are in a department store shopping for a birthday gift for someone you like a lot. Create a conversation using the diminutive to refer to the objects you are considering buying and to convey your affection for the person for whom you are shopping.

MODELO
A: Mira estas joyitas tan lindas para tu mamita. Me gustan mucho.
B: No me gustan mucho. Me gusta más este bolsito.
A: El bolsito no está mal, pero prefiero aquel collarcito de perlitas.

Notes

Explain that the diminutive of *poco* is *poquito*. This spelling change occurs to maintain the original sound of the *c* in *poco*. Ask if students recall any other words that change their spelling from *c* to *qu: buscar → busqué*.

Some adverbs that use the diminutive form include the following: *ahora (ahorita), despacio (despacito)*.

Estructura

Preterite tense of *leer, oír, ver, decir, hacer* and *tener*

The verbs *leer, oír, ver, decir, hacer* and *tener* all have irregularities in the preterite tense. For example, for *leer* and *oír*, an *i* between two vowels changes to a *y*. Both *leer* and *oír* require additional accent marks to separate vowel sounds and to indicate how these words are pronounced. The preterite tense of the verb *ver* uses the regular *-er* verb endings, but without any accent marks.

leer	
leí	leímos
leíste	leísteis
leyó	leyeron

oír	
oí	oímos
oíste	oísteis
oyó	oyeron

ver	
vi	vimos
viste	visteis
vio	vieron

Learning the irregular preterite-tense stem of *decir (dij), hacer (hic)* and *tener (tuv)* and the endings *-e, -iste, -o, -imos, -isteis* and *-ieron* will help you when you wish to use the preterite tense of these three irregular verbs.

Note: The *c* in the preterite-tense stem for *hacer* changes to *z* in *hizo*; *dijeron* is also an exception to the above because no *i* is required for the preterite ending.

decir	
dije	dijimos
dijiste	dijisteis
dijo	dijeron

hacer	
hice	hicimos
hiciste	hicisteis
hizo	hicieron

tener	
tuve	tuvimos
tuviste	tuvisteis
tuvo	tuvieron

Práctica

11 **¡No oí!**

Imagina que estás en una tienda comprando ropa con tu familia y todos te dicen algo al mismo tiempo y no oyes algunos de los comentarios. ¿Qué debes decir?

MODELO mi mamá
¿Qué dijo mi madre? No la oí.

1. tú
2. la Sra. de la tienda
3. mis hermanos
4. mi padre
5. mis hermanas
6. mi prima y mi tío

¿Qué dijo mi madre?

Teacher Resources

 Activities 6–10

 Activities 5–8

 Activity 4

 Activity 3

Answers

11
1. ¿...dijiste...? ...te....
2. ¿...dijo...? ...la....
3. ¿...dijeron...? ...los....
4. ¿...dijo...? ...lo....
5. ¿...dijeron...? ...las....
6. ¿...dijeron...? ...los....

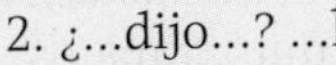

Activities

Cooperative Learning
Give each student an index card to use in a verb drill. Have them choose five different verbs that are irregular in the preterite tense. Include *ser* and *ir* if you want to recycle them as well. Vary the subjects for each verb and write the correct preterite form of each infinitive to agree with its subject: *leer (tú)* = *leíste* (you read), *hacer (nosotros)* = *hicimos* (we did; we made), etc. When finished, students may exchange cards to look for errors and make corrections. Then pair students to drill each other with their verb cards. Collect the cards, double-check for errors and save them to use another time for a quick review before a quiz or when there are a few minutes left in the class period.

National Standards

Communication
1.1

Notes Review the regular preterite tense forms for *-ar*, *-er* and *-ir* verbs and the preterite tense of *ir* and *ser*. Model and ask for students to give several examples of verbs they already know how to conjugate in the preterite tense before introducing the new irregular preterite tense verbs that appear here.

Review the use of the direct object pronouns before assigning activity 11.

Activity 12
Activity 13

Answers

12
1. (Yo) Dije que...guantes.
2. ...dijeron que...cinturones de cuero.
3. ...dijo que...bolso.
4. ...dijo que...joyas.
5. ...dijo que...paraguas.
6. ...dijimos que...billeteras.
7. (Tú) Dijiste que...suéter.
8. ...dijeron que...zapatos.

13
1. Sí, (No, no) tuve que ir....
2. Sí (No, no) oí....
3. Sí (No, no) vi....
4. Sí (No, no) hice....
5. Sí (No, no) dije....
6. Sí (No, no) compré....
7. Sí, (No, no) tuve....
8. Sí, (No, no) leí....

14
1. ¿...hicieron Uds.?/Nosotros (Nosotras) tuvimos que comprar un regalo y lo hicimos por la internet.
2. ¿...hicieron tus amigos?/ Mis amigos hicieron la tarea y fueron a jugar al fútbol con sus amigos.
3. ¿...hizo tu hermana?/Mi hermana tuvo que comprar unos zapatos cómodos e hizo unos quehaceres.
4. ¿...hiciste tú?/Yo leí un libro muy interesante y vi una película divertida en DVD.
5. ¿...hizo tu madre?/Mi madre tuvo que ir a trabajar y, luego, volvió a casa a hacer la comida.
6. ¿...hicieron tus tías?/Mis tías hicieron un viaje a las Islas Galápagos pero olvidaron llevar sus trajes de baño.

National Standards

Communication
1.1

12 ¿Qué le(s) gustaría recibir?

Di qué dijeron las siguientes personas que les gustaría recibir de regalo para su cumpleaños, según las ilustraciones.

MODELO mi padre
Mi padre dijo que le gustaría recibir unos pañuelos.

1. yo

2. mis primos

3. mi tía

4. mi mamá

5. mi hermano

6. nosotros

7. tú

8. Uds.

13 ¿Qué hice?

Di cuáles de las siguientes cosas hiciste o no hiciste ayer.

MODELO leer un libro
Sí, leí un libro ayer./No, no leí un libro ayer.

1. tener que ir a la tienda para comprar pan y leche
2. oír un CD de mi cantante favorito
3. ver televisión
4. hacer la tarea de español
5. decir una mentira
6. comprar un regalo para alguien
7. tener un examen
8. leer una revista

14 Todos hicieron algo

En parejas, hablen de lo que hicieron las siguientes personas, usando las pistas que se dan.

MODELO tu amigo: leer un libro / y / oír un disco compacto
A: ¿Qué hizo tu amigo?
B: Mi amigo leyó un libro y oyó un disco compacto.

1. Uds.: tener que comprar un regalo / y / hacerlo por la Internet
2. tus amigos: hacer la tarea / y / ir a jugar al fútbol con sus amigos
3. tu hermana: tener que comprar unos zapatos cómodos / e / hacer unos quehaceres
4. tú: leer un libro muy interesante / y / ver una película divertida en DVD
5. tu madre: tener que ir a trabajar / y luego / volver a casa a hacer la comida
6. tus tías: hacer un viaje a las Islas Galápagos / pero / olvidar llevar sus trajes de baño

Notes

Before doing activity 12, ask students to identify the articles that people would like to receive as gifts. Also, remind students how to use *gustaría*: they should not change the verb form, only the indirect object pronoun that precedes *gustaría*.

Follow up activity 13 with a class discussion of what members of the class did or did not do yesterday.

15 En la tienda por departamentos

Di lo que hicieron algunas personas el fin de semana en la tienda, según las ilustraciones y los verbos indicados.

MODELO comprar
Algunas personas compraron paraguas.

1. oír

2. hacer

3. tener

4. arreglar

5. ver

6. leer

Comunicación

16 ¿Qué hicimos?

Trabajando con un(a) compañero/a de clase, hablen de lo que hicieron el fin de semana pasado.

MODELO **A:** ¿Qué hiciste el sábado?
B: Leí un libro fascinante.
A: ¿Y qué más hiciste?
B: El sábado oí música por la mañana, luego tuve que .... Y tú, ¿qué hiciste?

17 ¿Qué tuviste que hacer?

Imagine you and a classmate work at a department store. Yesterday was a very busy day at the store and you each had to do too many things. Make up activities and talk with your classmate about all the things each of you had to do.

MODELO **A:** Ayer tuve muchas cosas que hacer en la tienda.
B: ¿Qué tuviste que hacer?
A: Para empezar, tuve que llegar muy temprano. Luego, otra persona y yo tuvimos que arreglar las billeteras, los cinturones y las bufandas en la sección de regalos antes de abrir. Luego, tuve que....

Answers

15 Possible answers:
1. Algunas personas oyeron música.
2. Algunas personas hicieron muchas compras.
3. Algunas personas tuvieron que limpiar la tienda.
4. Algunas personas arreglaron las escaleras mecánicas.
5. Algunas personas vieron bufandas.
6. Algunas personas leyeron revistas.

16 Creative self-expression.

17 Creative self-expression.

Activities

Cooperative Learning

In small groups, extend activities 16 and 17 by asking students to discuss some of the things they did last week. Afterward, each student should tell the rest of the class at least two things that one of his or her classmates did the previous week.

Students with Special Needs

Before assigning activity 15, identify the objects in the illustrations.

National Standards

Communication
1.1, 1.3

Teacher Resources

Vocabulario II
En la caja

Activity 66

Activities 11–12

Activities 9–10

p. 38

Activity 5
Activity 6

Activity 4

Activities

Prereading Strategy
Have students look through *Vocabulario II* quickly to find cognates and other words they recognize.

TPR
Ask students to do things with clothing and colors. For example, say *Toca algo azul (rojo, verde,* etc.*)* and observe to see that students respond appropriately. You may choose to bring in a bag of old clothing, especially items that are out of style, awful colors or unusual sizes as a humorous way to allow students to find and point out colors and items of clothing that you name or describe. As an alternative, you may use paper doll clothing and have students merely touch the item to show comprehension. Use commands such as *toca, ponte, quítate, guarda.*

National Standards
Communication 1.1

Vocabulario II
En la caja

CAJA

Gracias por venir conmigo.

Siempr
gusta salir

¿Cómo va a pagar? ¿En efectivo o a crédito?

la dependienta

Voy a pagar con tarjeta de crédito porque no tengo bastante efectivo.

Aquí tiene su cambio y su recibo. Lo va a necesitar si quiere cambiar algo.

el dependiente

Me gusta la calidad y el tamaño del bolso.

Sí, y no e
caro porqu
en ofe

Vamos a ahorrar dinero.

Notes

Quickly check student comprehension of the text bubbles and boxes that accompany the illustrations on these two pages.

Note the pronunciation of *ahorrar* in *Vocabulario II* by reminding students that the *h* is silent and the *rr* is trilled.

¿Cuál es la respuesta correcta? 

Escoge la letra de la respuesta correcta a lo que oyes.

A
Sí, es una seda muy buena.

B
Necesita el recibo.

C
Pago con tarjeta de crédito.

D
No, está en oferta.

E
Son tres dólares con cincuenta.

F
Sí, voy contigo.

Lo opuesto

Completa las siguientes oraciones para decir lo opuesto de las palabras indicadas.

MODELO No compré el anillo *caro*, preferí el anillo barato.

1. No compré ningún perfume *de mala calidad*, compré un perfume __.
2. No pagué *a crédito*, pagué __ en una de las cajas.
3. No me gustó el bolso *de tamaño pequeño*, me gustó el bolso __.
4. No vi los aretes *caros*, vi los aretes __.
5. No vi cinturones *cortos*, sólo vi cinturones demasiado __.
6. No le pagué *al dependiente*, le pagué __.
7. No me gusta ir de compras *contigo*, porque a ti no te gusta ir de compras __.

Notes Activity 18 is intended for listening comprehension practice. Play the audio of the activity that is included in the Audio Program or use the transcript that appears in the ATE Introduction if you prefer to read the activity yourself.

A reproducible answer sheet for the activity can be found at the end of the Audio Program Manual.

Teacher Resources

Activity 18

Answers

18
1. C
2. F
3. B
4. E
5. A
6. D

19
1. de buena calidad
2. en efectivo
3. de tamaño grande
4. baratos
5. largos
6. a la dependienta
7. conmigo

Activities

Expansion
Use overhead transparency 66 to introduce and practice the new words and expressions in *Vocabulario II*.

Prereading Strategy
Play the audio recording of the vocabulary and have students repeat the words while showing them overhead transparency 66.

Spanish for Spanish Speakers
Ask students to write a dialog between two friends who want to go shopping in a mall. Make sure they include a variety of stores they want to go to and the things they want to buy.

Students with Special Needs
Model a second sentence for students in activity 19.

National Standards

Communication
1.1, 1.2

Teacher Resources

Diálogo II
¿Cómo va a pagar?
Activity 20
Activity 21
Activity 22

Answers

20 1. El perfume está en oferta.
2. Cuesta treinta dólares.
3. Va a pagar en efectivo.
4. El cambio es de diez dólares.
5. Le da el recibo.

21 Answers will vary.

22 1. Sí.
2. No. ...barato.
3. No. ...tarjeta de crédito/en efectivo.
4. No. Muchas gracias.
5. Sí.

Activities

Cooperative Learning
Pair bilingual and nonbilingual students to invent a dialog in which they discuss things they would like to buy at the mall.

Expansion
Additional questions: *¿Qué está haciendo Daniel?; ¿Con una oferta especial el precio es más barato o más caro que el precio normal?; ¿Compras algo en oferta especial si no te gusta?; ¿Te gusta ir de compras solo/sola o con los amigos o la familia?; ¿Tienes una tarjeta de crédito?*

National Standards

Communication
1.1, 1.2

Diálogo II ¿Cómo va a pagar?

DANIEL: ¿Cuánto cuesta el perfume?
SEÑORA: Está en oferta. Cuesta treinta dólares.
DANIEL: Sí, no está caro. Lo llevo.

SEÑORA: ¿Cómo va a pagar? ¿En efectivo o a crédito?
DANIEL: Voy a pagar en efectivo.

SEÑORA: Aquí tiene diez dólares de cambio y su recibo.
DANIEL: Muchas gracias.

20 ¿Qué recuerdas?

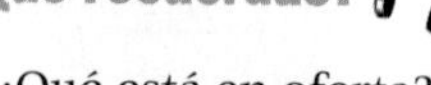

1. ¿Qué está en oferta?
2. ¿Cuánto cuesta el perfume?
3. ¿Cómo va a pagar Daniel?
4. ¿Cuánto es el cambio?
5. ¿Qué más le da la señora a Daniel?

¿Cuánto cuesta los perfumes?

21 Algo personal

1. ¿Qué compras en oferta?
2. ¿Prefieres pagar a crédito o en efectivo? Explica.
3. ¿Te gusta dar regalos caros o baratos? Explica.
4. ¿Qué haces con el dinero que recibes de cambio?

Compro camisetas en oferta.

22 ¿Sí o no?

¿Son lógicos los diálogos? Corrige lo que no es lógico.

Notes

This dialog and activities 20, 21 and 22 have been recorded by native speakers and are included in the *¡Aventura!* Audio Program. A reproducible answer sheet for activity 22 is available for your convenience at the end of the Audio Program Manual.

Tell students that the adjective *caro* normally is used with the verb *ser*. Here Daniel uses the verb *estar* to emphasize a special sale price.

Ask students to review the vocabulary from the previous page and then scan the dialog for familiar words or phrases.

Cultura viva II

De compras en Guayaquil

Unos chicos ecuatorianos en el mall.

Una artesana vendiendo su arte.

Para hacer compras en Ecuador, debes ir a Guayaquil. Para las compras modernas está en Guayaquil el Mall del Sol, el centro comercial más grande del Ecuador con más de 187 tiendas, veinticinco restaurantes de comida rápida, cinco bancos, un supermercado grande (Megamaxi), nueve cines, cibercafés, discotecas, tiendas de souvenirs, parques y estacionamiento *(parking)* para más de 2.000 carros. Es un centro comercial supergigante y muy divertido.

Si te gustan las compras menos modernas y más de artesanía, y no te gustan los centros comerciales, puedes ir al Mercado Artesano de Guayaquil. En el Mercado Artesano hay 280 exhibiciones y puestos de venta *(sales stands)* donde trabajan sólo artesanos (las personas que hacen artesanía) creando y vendiendo su arte. Al dar un paseo por las exhibiciones puedes escuchar música ecuatoriana a la vez que admiras los diferentes estilos de los artistas del país.

Unos chalecos *(vests)* en el Mercado Artesano.

Como puedes ver, tanto si te gusta la compra moderna y dinámica, como la más tranquila y tradicional, Guayaquil te ofrece infinitas posibilidades.

23 Comparando

Compara el centro comercial Mall del Sol en Guayaquil con un centro comercial de tu ciudad.

Centro comercial Mall del Sol	Centro comercial de tu ciudad
1. 187 tiendas	1. 150 tiendas
2.	2.
3.	3.

Teacher Resources

Cultura viva
De compras en Guayaquil

Activity 5

Answers

23 Answers will vary.

Activities

Expansion

As a follow-up to this reading and to activity 23, tell students that you recently bought a present for a friend and their task is to find out what it is. They may ask a maximum of twelve yes/no questions in trying to identify the mystery gift. The first student to correctly name the gift should then think of another present and the activity is repeated.

Notes You may wish to have students create Venn diagrams for activity 23. See the section *Tú escribes* (page 358) at the end of *Capítulo 8*.

Note that this *Cultura viva* is written in Spanish. Unknown words have been translated and the content has been edited to be interesting and of an appropriate reading level so students will find it enjoyable. All the *Cultura viva* readings in *¡Aventura! 1* are in Spanish.

National Standards

Communication 1.1

Comparisons 4.2

Cultures 2.2

Connections 3.1

Teacher Resources

 Activity 13

 Activities 11–13

 pp. 152, 154

 Activity 7

 Activity 6

Answers

24 1. en, sobre
2. de
3. con
4. en
5. para
6. desde
7. sin
8. por

Activities

Critical Thinking
Review the prepositions by asking students to generate original sentences about their school and city (e.g., *Uds. estudian en la biblioteca con amigos; La biblioteca está cerca de/lejos de la cafetería*).

Multiple Intelligences (linguistic/spatial)
Have students think of a memory device and make a visual representation to depict the meanings of the prepositions. For example, a drawing of a male stick figure standing beside a house with the words "There is a lad beside the house" could represent *al lado de*.

National Standards

Communication
1.3

Repaso rápido

Prepositions

How many of the following prepositions *(preposiciones)* in Spanish do you remember?

preposiciones

a	de	para	con	desde
por	en	sin	hasta	sobre

24 Unos aretes para mi mamá

Completa las siguientes oraciones, escogiendo una palabra apropiada de la lista.

con	de	desde	en
para	por	sin	sobre

1. ¿Cuánto cuestan los aretes que están (1) aquella mesa?
2. Los aretes son (2) plata y cuestan veinte dólares.
3. ¿Va a pagarlos (3) tarjeta de crédito?
4. No, voy a pagarlos (4) efectivo.
5. Los aretes son (5) mi mamá.
6. Mi madre usa aretes (6) pequeña.
7. Ella nunca sale a la calle (7) aretes.
8. Muchas gracias (8) su compra.

Estructura

Using prepositions

You have already learned to use prepositions with prepositional pronouns. For example, prepositional pronouns are sometimes used in combination with the preposition *a* to add emphasis or to clarify the meaning of a sentence: *A mí me gusta comprar todo lo que está en oferta.* The following prepositional pronouns also may be used with the other prepositions you have learned.

los pronombres después de las preposiciones			
sin mí	*without me*	sin nosotros,-as	*without us*
sin ti	*without you*	sin vosotros,-as	*without you*
sin Ud.	*without you*	sin Uds.	*without you*
sin él	*without him*	sin ellos	*without them*
sin ella	*without her*	sin ellas	*without them*

Notes

Remind students that prepositions connect verbs, nouns and adjectives with their complements. English, like Spanish, uses prepositions as linking words. However, the two languages do not always use the same preposition to convey the same meaning.

Explain that prepositional pronouns are the same as subject pronouns with the exception of *yo* and *tú*, which become *mí* and *ti* after most prepositions. Let students know that *mí* has an accent to distinguish it from the possessive *mi* (my). The pronoun *ti*, however, does not need a written accent.

Two exceptions are the words *conmigo* (with me), which is used instead of *con* followed by *mí*, and *contigo* (with you), which is used instead of con followed by *ti*.

¿Quieres ir de compras ***conmigo****?*	Do you want to go shopping **with me**?
Sí, me gusta ir de compras ***contigo****.*	Yes, I like to go shopping **with you**.

Práctica

25 Un regalo para mi tío

Completa este correo electrónico con palabras de la lista. Puedes usar las palabras más de una vez.

conmigo	contigo	ella	él	mí	nosotros	ti

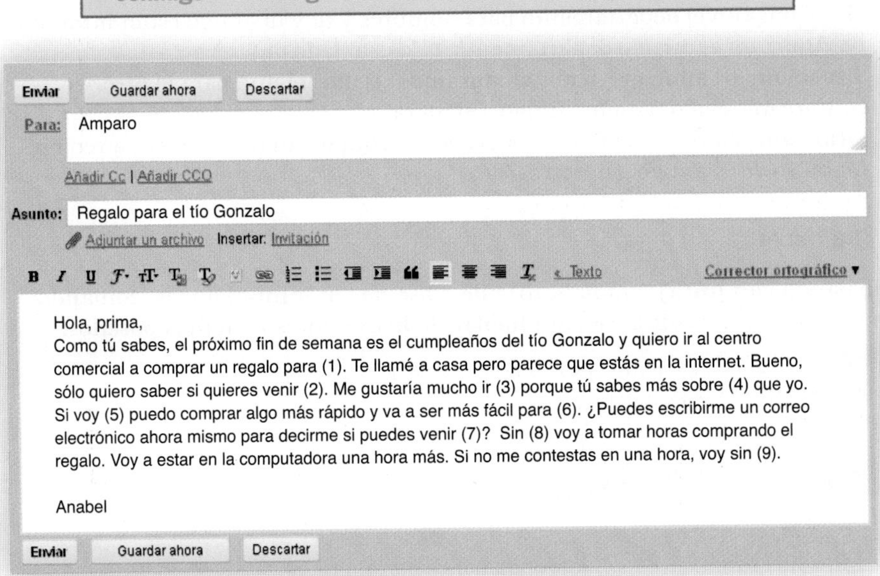

Enviar | Guardar ahora | Descartar

Para: Amparo

Añadir Cc | Añadir CCO

Asunto: Regalo para el tío Gonzalo

Adjuntar un archivo Insertar: Invitación

« Texto Corrector ortográfico

Hola, prima,

Como tú sabes, el próximo fin de semana es el cumpleaños del tío Gonzalo y quiero ir al centro comercial a comprar un regalo para (1). Te llamé a casa pero parece que estás en la internet. Bueno, sólo quiero saber si quieres venir (2). Me gustaría mucho ir (3) porque tú sabes más sobre (4) que yo. Si voy (5) puedo comprar algo más rápido y va a ser más fácil para (6). ¿Puedes escribirme un correo electrónico ahora mismo para decirme si puedes venir (7)? Sin (8) voy a tomar horas comprando el regalo. Voy a estar en la computadora una hora más. Si no me contestas en una hora, voy sin (9).

Anabel

Enviar | Guardar ahora | Descartar

26 ¿Puedes venir conmigo?

Trabajando con un(a) compañero/a de clase, alternen en hacer las invitaciones indicadas y en dar excusas para cada invitación.

MODELO al cine
A: ¿Puedes venir conmigo al cine?
B: No, no puedo ir contigo porque no tengo dinero.

1. el banco
2. a comprar unos zapatos que están en oferta
3. la tienda de artículos electrónicos
4. la tienda por departamentos
5. el centro comercial
6. a cambiar un cinturón que compré y ahora no me gusta

Notes Ask students to guess what the terms at the top of the e-mail page mean: *archivo* (file), *ver* (view), *mensajes* (messages), *ayuda* (help), *a* (to), *cc* (copy), *asunto* (subject).

Use the e-mail message in activity 25 as an opportunity to reinforce reading skills in Spanish.

Teacher Resources

Activity 26

Answers

25
1. él
2. conmigo
3. contigo
4. él
5. contigo
6. mí
7. conmigo
8. ti
9. ti

26
1. ¿...al banco?/No, no puedo ir contigo....
2. ¿...a comprar unos zapatos que están en oferta?/No, no puedo ir contigo....
3. ¿...a la tienda de artículos electrónicos?/No, no puedo ir contigo....
4. ¿...a la tienda por departamentos?/No, no puedo ir contigo....
5. ¿...al centro comercial?/No, no puedo ir contigo....
6. ¿...a cambiar un cinturón que compré y ahora no me gusta?/No, no puedo ir contigo....

Activities

Students with Special Needs

As a class activity, return to previously studied dialogs and readings and ask students to find examples of prepositions. Then, for activity 25, complete the first blank space with the appropriate pronoun *(él)* as a model.

National Standards

Communication
1.1, 1.2

Comparisons
4.1

Answers

27 1. (Yo) vivo lejos de ti.
2. (Él) vive cerca de nosotros.
3. Uds. están al lado de nosotros.
4. (Él) compró un regalo para mí.
5. (Nosotras) vamos a recibir unos bolsos de ellos.

28 Answers will vary.

Activities

Multiple Intelligences (kinesthetic/visual)

Allow for creativity by letting students work in groups of four or five to present a fashion show to the class. Have each group select a narrator to read descriptions of the clothing while the other group members act as models.

National Standards

Communication
1.1, 1.3

27 En la tienda por departamentos

Da conclusiones apropiadas para las siguientes situaciones, usando las preposiciones y pronombres apropiados. Sigue las indicaciones entre paréntesis.

MODELO **Situación:** Yo llegué a la tienda a las cuatro de la tarde, tu amigo llegó a las cuatro menos diez y tú llegaste allí a las tres y media. (yo/después de)
Conclusión: (Yo) llegué después de Uds.

1. **Situación:** Tú llegaste primero porque vives más cerca de la tienda que yo. (yo/lejos de)
2. **Situación:** Tu amigo me dijo que vive en la Calle 128, N° 171, y mi familia y yo vivimos en la Calle 128, N° 173. (él/cerca de)
3. **Situación:** Son las cinco de la tarde y mi amigo y yo estamos mirando cinturones en el departamento para hombres y tú y tu amigo están mirando perfumes en el mismo departamento. (Uds./al lado de)
4. **Situación:** Mi amigo y yo nos compramos regalos el uno para el otro. Yo compré un regalo para mi amigo. (él/para)
5. **Situación:** Yo voy a recibir un bolso de mi amigo y tú también vas a recibir un bolso de tu amigo. (nosotras/de)

28 ¿Qué hiciste?

Trabajando con un(a) compañero/a de clase hagan mini-diálogos, tomando elementos de cada columna para hablar de lo que hiciste en días pasados.

MODELO **A:** ¿Adónde fuiste después de las clases?
B: Fui a la biblioteca.
A: ¿Quién fue contigo?
B: Mi hermano Pedro.

A

antes de venir aquí
ayer por la noche
después de las clases
el domingo por la mañana
el sábado por la noche
el viernes por la tarde
la semana pasada

B

la tienda por departamentos
de compras
la tienda de artículos electrónicos
el cine
el centro comercial
la biblioteca
el parquemi amigo/a

C

mis padres
nadie
mi hermano/a
mi tío/a
mis abuelos
mi primo/a

¿Fuiste al cine?

Notes

Point out the abbreviation *Nº* (for *número*) in activity 27.

Activity 27 develops higher-order thinking skills.

Comunicación

29 Fuimos de compras

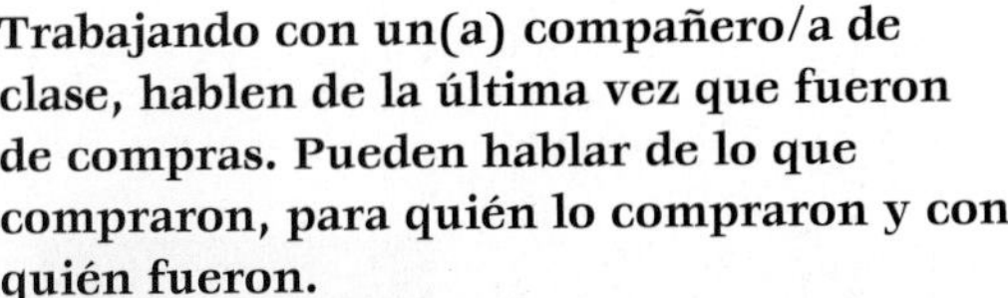

Trabajando con un(a) compañero/a de clase, hablen de la última vez que fueron de compras. Pueden hablar de lo que compraron, para quién lo compraron y con quién fueron.

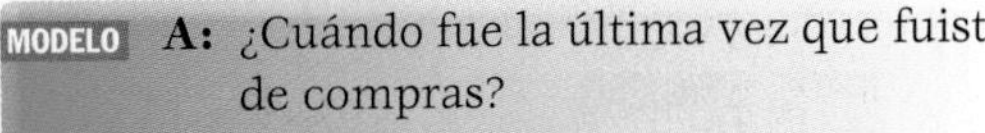

MODELO **A:** ¿Cuándo fue la última vez que fuiste de compras?
B: Fui el sábado pasado.
A: ¿Qué compraste y para quién?
B: Compré unos aretes para mi mamá.
A: ¿Con quién fuiste?
B: Fui contigo.

Fui de compras el sábado pasado.

30 De compras

Trabajando con un(a) compañero/a de clase, preparen un diálogo de cinco o seis oraciones sobre un día de compras. Uno de Uds. puede preguntar si la otra persona quiere ir contigo o no. Luego, pueden hablar de lo que van a comprar, el precio, la calidad, el tamaño y cómo van a pagar. Recuerden usar en forma apropiada las preposiciones.

MODELO **A:** ¿Te gustaría ir de compras conmigo al centro comercial?
B: Sí, claro, voy contigo. ¿Vas con tu hermana?
A: No, voy sin ella.
B: ¡Qué lástima! ¿Qué vas a comprar?

31 Seguimos de compras

In groups of six to eight, form concentric circles so three or four students in an inside circle face the same number of students in an outside circle. Then the opposing pairs of students should take turns asking and answering what each of you bought the last time you went shopping and what each of you would like to buy when you return there. Take notes as your partner speaks. Then students in the outer circle move one to the right and begin a similar conversation with the new partner. Continue until you have spoken with everyone in the other circle. One person from each circle should report the findings to the class.

MODELO **A:** ¿Qué compraste la última vez que fuiste de compras?
B: Compré un bolso de material sintético para mí.

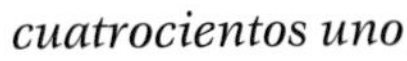

Answers

29 Creative self-expression.
30 Creative self-expression.
31 Creative self-expression.

Activities

Cooperative Learning
As an alternative to having one student from each circle report his or her findings for activity 31, have all students write a summary of their findings, which could be submitted for correction. (You may wish to have students number their summaries by group so you have a means of comparing answers.)

Multiple Intelligences (bodily-kinesthetic)
It is fun to act out activity 30 as a skit. Have students bring in all necessary props to make the skit more interesting and realistic.

National Standards

Communication
1.1, 1.3

Notes Inform students that you will be asking several pairs of students to present their dialogs in front of the class.

Set time limits for the paired activities on page 401 and keep a brisk pace.

Remember to circulate around the room as students complete these activities to keep students on task and to offer help as needed.

The circle technique used for activity 31 works anytime you would like to have students pair up to ask the same question of several people, but you prefer that students not be up and moving around the room.

Teacher Resources

Lectura personal
Activity 33

Answers

32 1. el sombrero "panamá"
2. el nombre verdadero del sombrero "panamá"
3. provincia de Ecuador en la costa y centro de producción de sombreros de jipijapa
4. pueblo colonial en Manabí donde se producen los mejores sombreros "panamá" llamados "superfinos"
5. la planta que se usa para tejer el sombrero "panamá"

33 Answers will vary.

Activities

Spanish for Spanish Speakers
Have students write a short composition in Spanish summarizing what they know about Ecuador. Expand the activity by having students seek out additional information about Ecuador at the library or on the Internet.

National Standards	
Communication 1.1	**Comparisons** 4.1
Cultures 2.2	
Connections 3.1, 3.2	

Lectura personal

Dirección http://www.emcp.com/músico/aventura1/

Archivo Edición Ver Favoritos Herramientas Ayuda

página principal | miembros | e-diario

Nombre: **Xavier Rodríguez Guerra**
Edad: **18 años**
País natal: **Estados Unidos**
Artículo de ropa favorito: **sombreros**
Artículo de ropa que nunca usa: **pantalones de cuero**

Estamos en Ecuador, un país muy lindo. Después del concierto, el grupo se fue de compras a Quito. Yo también me fui de compras pero no a una tienda por departamentos con escaleras mecánicas y todo eso. Yo me fui en avión a la provincia de Manabí, que está en el centro de las costas ecuatorianas. Manabí tiene playas lindas, pero ésa no es la razón por la cual fui. Estuve en el pueblo[1] colonial de Montecristi, para comprar un sombrero "panamá" para mi nuevo *"look."* Grandes personajes como Humphrey Bogart, Gary Cooper y Winston Churchill han usado sombreros "panamá." Creo que se ven muy elegantes.

Hacen sombreros "panamá" en Ecuador.

Saben, el sombrero "panamá" no es de Panamá; es un producto de Ecuador. Ecuador empezó a exportar estos sombreros en los años 1800s. En los años 40, era el producto de exportación número uno de Ecuador. Como se vendían[2] en los puertos[3] de Panamá, se les llamó sombreros "panamá," pero su verdadero[4] nombre es sombrero de jipijapa o sombrero de Montecristi. Montecristi produce los mejores sombreros "panamá" del mundo llamados "superfinos." Están hechos con la planta Carludovica palmata, que se hierve[5], se seca[6] y luego se teje[7]. Tardan tres meses en hacer un sólo sombrero. Son bastante caros, pero también son muy *"cool,"* ¿no creen?

[1]town [2]were sold [3]ports [4]real [5]boil [6]dry [7]weave

- **Panama hats are really from Ecuador. Can you think of other products (such as foods) that have a country in their names even though they did not originate from that country? How do you think this happens?**

¿Qué recuerdas?

Identifica cada uno.

1. el producto de exportación número uno de Ecuador en los cuarenta
2. sombrero de jipijapa
3. Manabí
4. Montecristi
5. Carludovica palmata

Algo personal

1. En tu opinión, ¿son los sombreros "panamá" elegantes? ¿Por qué sí o por qué no?
2. Donde tú vives, ¿hay un centro de producción de ropa? ¿Qué artículos de ropa hacen o venden?
3. Imagina que quieres tener un nuevo "look. " Describe tu nueva ropa.

Notes The *Lectura personal* and activity 32 are recorded and available in the *¡Aventura! 1* Audio Program.

Conduct a class discussion about clothing, using the questions in the *Algo personal* as your starting point.

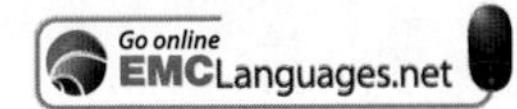

¿Qué aprendí?

Autoevaluación

As a review and self-check, respond to the following:

1. Name at least three items sold in a mall department store.
2. Name something that can be made of gold, silver or pearl.
3. Imagine you are buying a gift for your best friend. Describe the item you purchased.
4. Say at least three things you read, heard or saw yesterday.
5. The last time you made a purchase, did you pay cash or did you use credit?
6. Imagine you are shopping in a Spanish-speaking country. How would you ask how much an item costs and if it is on sale?
7. Say two things you learned about Ecuador.

Palabras y expresiones

How many of these words and expressions do you recognize?

Para describir
barato,-a
bastante
caro,-a
corto,-a
demasiado
largo,-a
lindo,-a
perfecto,-a
sintético,-a

En la tienda
el anillo
el arete
el ascensor
la billetera
el bolso
la bufanda
la caja
la calidad
el cambio
el cinturón
el collar
el crédito
el cuero
el dependiente, la dependienta
el efectivo
la escalera mecánica
la joya
el material
mecánico,-a
la oferta
el oro
el pañuelo
el paraguas
el perfume
la perla
la plata
la pulsera
el recibo
el regalo
el tamaño
la tarjeta (de crédito)

Verbos
ahorrar
cambiar
pagar
recibir
usar

Expresiones y otras palabras
a crédito
conmigo
contigo
en efectivo

Estructura

Do you remember the following grammar rules?

Preterite tense of irregular verbs: *leer, oír, ver, decir, hacer,* and *tener*

leer		oír	
leí	leímos	oí	oímos
leíste	leísteis	oíste	oísteis
leyó	leyeron	oyó	oyeron
ver		**decir**	
vi	vimos	dije	dijimos
viste	visteis	dijiste	dijisteis
vio	vieron	dijo	dijieron
hacer		**tener**	
hice	hicimos	tuve	tuvimos
hiciste	hicisteis	tuviste	tuvisteis
hizo	hicieron	tuvo	tuvieron

Notes Encourage students to find out more about Ecuador by going to the following Web sites:

Organization of American States
http://www.oas.org
Embassy of Ecuador
http://www.ecuador.org
General travel information
http://www.expedia.com
Virtual Countries, Inc.
http://www.ecuador.com/macie.html

Teacher Resources

 Activity 14

 pp. 62, 96

 Juegos

Flash Cards

Answers

Autoevaluación

Possible answers:

1. las bufandas, las billeteras, los paraguas
2. Un anillo puede ser de oro.
3. Le compré unos guantes de cuero.
4. Leí el periódico....
5. Pagué en efectivo por las cosas que compré.
6. ¿Cuánto cuesta? ¿Está en oferta especial?
7. La capital del Ecuador es Quito....

Activities

Pronunciation (*el sonido* ch)

In Spanish, *ch* sounds like the English *ch* in **church**. It never sounds like the combination *ch* in **machine** or in **chemistry**. Model these words with students: *archipiélago, chisme, chica, chorizo, Conchita, muchacho.*

Spanish for Spanish Speakers

Ecuador is one of the OPEC nations. Have students investigate and prepare a report on the impact that petroleum had on the Ecuadorean economy during the 1970s.

National Standards

Cultures
2.2
Connections
3.2
Comparisons
4.1

Teacher Resources

 *Las rebajas de Danté*

Answers

Preparación

1. A
2. C
3. B

Activities

Critical Thinking

To further reinforce the importance of visual organization to content, ask students to describe the typical format and related information for the following items: a job application, a recipe, a movie poster.

Multiple Intelligences (logical-mathematical)

Have students find out the value in dollars for the *balboa* (Panamanian currency) and for the *sucre* (currency of Ecuador). Sources for currency exchange rates include the business section of the local paper, the *Wall Street Journal*, other newspapers or the Internet. The school media specialist may be able to help students find other sources for exchange rates as well.

National Standards

Communication
1.2

Connections
3.1, 3.2

Tú lees

Estrategia

Using visual format to predict meaning
Visual details of printed information such as the style and format of printed media can tell you a lot about its probable content. For instance, the format of a letter will indicate whether it is for business or if it is personal. Similarly, cartoons are easily recognized by the style of the illustration and the way the contents appear on the page. Advertisements and brochures can differ greatly from one another depending on the intended population. Before starting to read, look at the layout, the artwork, the pictures, the titles and the format of the writing for hints about its content and meaning.

Preparación

Observa el título, el arte y la forma de esta lectura y contesta las siguientes preguntas.

1. ¿Qué tipo de lectura es ésta?
   A. Es un anuncio *(ad)*.
   B. Es un artículo *(article)* de periódico.
   C. Es una encuesta *(survey)*.
2. ¿Qué venden?
   A. Venden artículos electrónicos.
   B. Venden frutas y verduras.
   C. Venden ropa y servicios.
3. ¿Para quién es lo que venden?
   A. Para hombres.
   B. Para hombres, mujeres y jóvenes.
   C. Para mujeres.

Las rebajas de Danté

Las fabulosas rebajas de Danté te ofrecen grandes ahorros en ropa casual para todos. Tenemos grandes rebajas del 20%, 30%, 40% y hasta el 50%. Aquí puedes conseguir la ropa que necesitas para ir al cine, las fiestas y al colegio. Tenemos todos los estilos que te gustan en todas las marcas y colores.

Servicios generales

- ❖ Sastrería
- ❖ Pedidos especiales de vestidos
- ❖ Sorteos
- ❖ Danté Café
- ❖ Abrimos los domingos
- ❖ Tarjeta de crédito Danté

Notes *Almacenes Danté* is a large department store in Panama. You may wish to inform your students that they can visit the Web site for the store by searching the term *Almacenes Danté* in the search box of any browser. (See the *¡Aventura! 1* ATE Introduction for suggested browsers or use one of your choosing.)

¿Adónde vas de compras con más frecuencia?

centro comercial en Quito, Ecuador.

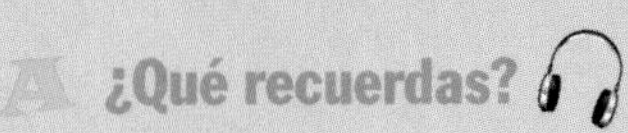

A ¿Qué recuerdas?

1. ¿En qué tipo de ropa puedes ahorrar dinero si la compras en esta tienda?
2. ¿De cuánto son las rebajas en esta tienda?
3. ¿Para ir a qué tipo de lugares puedes comprar ropa en Danté?
4. ¿Qué servicios tiene esta tienda?

B Algo personal

1. ¿Qué piensas del anuncio?
2. ¿Para qué tipo de personas piensas que es este anuncio?
3. ¿Buscas anuncios con rebajas antes de ir de compras? Explica.
4. ¿Qué tipo de anuncios te gustan?
5. ¿Adónde vas de compras con más frecuencia?

Teacher Resources

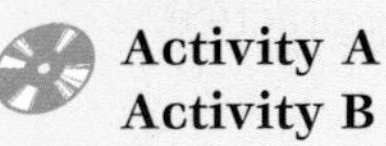

Activity A
Activity B

Answers

A 1. Puedo ahorrar dinero en ropa casual.
2. Las rebajas son del 20%, 30%, 40% y hasta el 50%.
3. Puedo comprar ropa para ir al cine, a las fiestas y al colegio.
4. Possible answers: sastrería, pedidos especiales de vestidos, sorteos, café, abren los domingos, tarjeta de crédito.

B Answers will vary.

Activities

Prereading Strategy
Note for students that it is not essential to understand every word to read in Spanish. Have students scan the advertisement to find cognates and other words they know. Be sure to cover the *Preparación* activity prior to beginning the reading.

National Standards

Communication
1.2

Connections
3.2

Notes Encourage students to find out more about Panama by going to the following Web sites:

Organization of American States
http://www.oas.org
Lonely Planet
http://www.lonelyplanet.com/destinations/central_america/panama/
Presidential Homepage
http://www.presidencia.gob.pa/
Panamainfo
http://www.panamainfo.com
General travel information
http://www.expedia.com

Answers

Creative writing practice.

Activities

Communities

In small groups, students prepare a survey *(encuesta)* about shopping. Have them send the survey via e-mail to a collaborating class and request a response. Share the results with the class. (Before assigning the activity, search the Internet for "Intercultural E-mail Connections" to find Spanish teachers in the United States or English teachers in other Spanish-speaking parts of the world.) As an alternative, you may prefer to have students survey just the class, your school or some segment of your community.

Critical Thinking

Ask students to identify appropriate gifts for each of the following people: *mi mejor amigo; mi mejor amiga; un abuelo o una abuela; una hermana de ocho años; un hermano de veinte años; el maestro/la maestra de español.* Then, in addition to naming the presents, students should justify the gift selection.

National Standards	
Communication 1.3	**Comparisons** 4.2
Cultures 2.1	
Connections 3.1	

Tú escribes

Estrategia

Indicating sequence

You have already learned to use transition words to make your writing flow smoothly. When writing about past activities or events, transition words can indicate the sequence in which actions occurred. Some sequence words you may want to use in your writing include the following: *primero* (first), *luego* (later, then), *antes de* (before), *después de* (after), *finalmente* (finally).

Shopping centers and malls are more than just convenient places to shop. Going to a *centro comercial* often turns into a social event that offers shoppers an opportunity to spend time with friends and to meet new people. What does shopping at the mall mean to you? Write a short composition telling about your last visit to the mall *(Mi última visita al centro comercial)*. Include when you went, with whom you went, what places you visited, if you visited a *tienda por departamentos*, what you did, whom you met, what you bought and any other information you wish. Be sure to use connecting words for making smooth transitions and for telling the sequence of events.

Compré una bolsa de cuero en la tienda por departamentos.

Notes Explain that when shopping in most Hispanic countries, shoppers will notice that the clerk who waits on the customer does not usually collect the money for the purchase. Instead, the clerk gives a copy of the bill to the customer. Another copy of the bill, along with the item being purchased, is given by the clerk to the cashier. The customer then stands in line at the cashier's register to pay for and receive the item purchased. Students should be aware that shopping in a store in Ecuador and in other Spanish-speaking countries may take more time and require more waiting in line.

Proyectos adicionales

A Conexión con la tecnología

You learned how to create a dialog journal in the *Tú escribes* activity in the *¡Viento en popa!* section of *Capítulo 2*. Create an electronic dialog journal entry to send to your teacher. Write about your last trip to a *tienda por departamentos* to shop for something special (e.g., clothing for yourself, a gift). You may wish to tell about where and with whom you went shopping, what you purchased and how much you paid. Include any other information you would like and e-mail the journal entry to your teacher.

B Conexión con otras disciplinas: arte y diseño

Imagine you work for an advertising agency. Cut out advertisements and pictures of different clothing items from fashion magazines and newspapers and design a poster-sized advertisement for clothing. Include in your collage various types of clothing in different colors and sizes. Then, working with a classmate, talk about fashion and clothing styles in the advertisement, including what the people are wearing, the colors of each article of clothing and whether you like the item or not. For what type of occasions is the clothing shown appropriate? What age and gender are you targeting with your advertisement?

C Comunidades

How do people in your community dress? Write a short composition describing how young people dress during a specific season of the year. What are the most popular colors and materials? What statement do you think they wish to convey by how they dress?

Unas mujeres en Otavalo, Ecuador.

Unos niños Amish en Ohio.

Teacher Resources

p. 75

Answers

A Creative self-expression.
B Creative self-expression.
C Creative self-expression.

Activities

Connections
Students can learn about both Spanish and science by investigating and preparing a report on the impact of ecotourism on the Galapagos Islands. Ask them to determine and justify whether ecotourism is good or bad for the islands.

Multiple Intelligences (bodily-kinesthetic)
Produce a fashion show. Divide the class into groups and have each group choose one or two students to be *los modelos*. The entire group writes a description of the style, articles of clothing and colors the models are wearing; then, one or two people in the group read the description as the model or models walk into the classroom. Videotape the production and save it to show as a model for future classes.

National Standards

Communication
1.1, 1.3

Connections
3.1, 3.2

Notes

For further practice with transition words, assign a composition about a real or imaginary trip to Panama or Ecuador. Students should include information on where they went and things that they did.

Connections. Activity B makes the cross-curricular connection to art and design.

Teacher Resources

Trabalenguas

Episode 9, DVD 2, Track 27

Answers

Resolviendo el misterio

1. José finds the key in an old jacket.
2. José finds a gold Aztec mask and an old map.
3. Conchita confirms that there is a gold mask and a map in the briefcase. She also tells Rafael that the key to the room can be found in don Pedro's library.

Activities

Multiple Intelligences (spatial/linguistic)
Have students prepare a travel brochure about the Galapagos Islands. Brochures should include what visitors can see, how to get there, lodging, etc. Students can use their own drawings or cut pictures from magazines.

Spanish for Spanish Speakers
Ask students to write an essay describing their favorite gift and stating who gave it to them and on what occasion (e.g., their birthday) they received it.

Trabalenguas
Ask students to rewrite the *Trabalenguas*, reassigning the adjectives that appear to different objects. Ask them to recite their new tongue twisters to the class.

National Standards

Communication
1.3

Connections
3.1, 3.2

REPASO

Now that I have completed this chapter, I can...	Go to these pages for help:
describe clothing.	364
identify parts of the body.	364
talk about the past.	370, 378
express disagreement.	374
discuss size and fit.	386
discuss price and payment.	394
I can also...	
talk about life in Panama and Ecuador.	367, 389
ask questions when I do not understand something.	368
talk about personal taste in clothing.	374
use affirmative and negative expressions in conversations.	381
use diminutives to express affection or that something is small.	390

Trabalenguas

Venancio vendía bonitas boinas, bonitas, baratas, embalaba baberos, bolillos, botas bellas y boinas buenas.

Resolviendo el misterio

After watching Episode 9 of *El cuarto misterioso*, answer the following questions.

1. How does José gain entrance to the briefcase?
2. What does José find in the briefcase?
3. What information does a confused Conchita let slip to Rafael about the treasure?

Notes

Review the functions and other objectives in the *Repaso* and assign the activities and answer questions so students can prepare for the Chapter Test. Follow up by reviewing the activities as a class.

Loose translation of the *Trabalenguas:* Venancio sold pretty berets, pretty cheap; he packed bibs, bobbins, beautiful boots and good berets.

Vocabulario

ahorrar to save *9B*
algo something, anything *9A*
el **algodón** cotton *9A*
alguien someone, anyone, somebody, anybody *9A*
algún, alguna some, any *9A*
alguno,-a some, any *9A*
anaranjado,-a orange (color) *9A*
el **anillo** ring *9B*
el **arete** earring *9B*
el **ascensor** elevator *9B*
barato,-a cheap *9B*
bastante rather, fairly, sufficiently, enough, sufficient *9B*
la **billetera** wallet *9B*
el **bolso** purse *9B*
la **bota** boot *9A*
el **brazo** arm *9A*
la **bufanda** scarf *9B*
la **cabeza** head
la **caja** cashier's desk *9B*
la **calidad** quality *9B*
cambiar to change, to exchange *9B*
el **cambio** change *9B*
caro,-a expensive *9B*
el **centro comercial** shopping center, mall *9A*
la **chaqueta** jacket *9A*
el **cinturón** belt *9B*
el **collar** necklace *9B*
combinar to combine *9A*
conmigo with me *9B*
contar (ue) to tell (a story) *9A*
contigo with you *9B*
la **corbata** tie *9A*
corto,-a short (not long) *9B*
el **crédito** credit *9B*
a crédito on credit *9B*
el **cuero** leather *9B*
el **cuerpo** body *9A*
el **dedo** finger *9A*
demasiado too (much) *9B*
el **departamento** department *9A*
el **dependiente, la dependienta** clerk *9B*
el **efectivo** effective *9B*
en efectivo in cash *9B*
la **escalera mecánica** escalator *9B*
estar en oferta to be on sale *9B*
el **guante** glove *9A*
la **joya** jewel *9B*
el **hombre** man *9A*
el **impermeable** raincoat *9A*
la **lana** wool *9A*
largo,-a long *9B*
lindo,-a pretty *9B*
la **mano** hand *9A*
marrón brown *9A*
el **material** material *9B*
las **medias** pantyhose, nylons *9A*
morado,-a purple *9A*
la **mujer** woman *9A*
nada nothing *9A*
nadie nobody *9A*
ni... ni neither... nor *9A*
ningún, ninguna none, not any *9A*
ninguno,-a none, not any *9A*
o... o either... or *9A*
la **oferta** offer *9B*
el **oro** gold *9B*
pagar pay *9B*
el **pañuelo** handkerchief, hanky *9B*
el **paraguas** umbrella *9B*
perfecto,-a perfect *9B*
el **perfume** perfume *9B*
la **perla** pearl *9B*
el **pie** foot *9A*
la **pierna** leg *9A*
el **pijama** pajamas *9A*
la **plata** silver *9B*
prometer to promise *9A*
la **pulsera** bracelet *9B*
quedar to remain, to stay *9A*
quedarle bien a uno to fit, to be becoming *9A*
recibir to receive *9B*
el **recibo** receipt *9B*
el **regalo** gift *9B*
la **ropa interior** underwear *9A*
rosado,-a pink *9A*
la **seda** silk *9A*
sintético,-a synthetic *9B*
el **sombrero** hat *9A*
el **suéter** sweater *9A*
el **tamaño** size *9B*
la **tarjeta (de crédito)** credit card *9B*
el **traje (de baño)** swimsuit *9A*
usar to use *9B*
las **vacaciones** vacation *9A*
vender to sell *9A*
el **vestido** dress *9A*
el **zapato bajo** flat shoe *9A*
el **zapato de tacón** high-heeled shoe *9A*

Llevamos las corbatas a la escuela.

Teacher Resources

Las aventuras de la familia Miranda

Repaso

¡Aventureros!, Ch. 9

Internet Activities

i-Culture

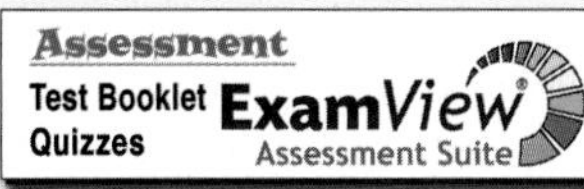

Activities

TPR

Try using TPR to teach and reinforce the parts of the body. Teach the following commands, combining them with the appropriate parts of the body: *toca, mueve, rasca, tira, levanta, baja, abre, cierra*. Parts of the body you may wish to include are: *el brazo, la cabeza, el dedo, la mano, el pie, la pierna*, which have been introduced in the book. In addition, you may want to teach other parts of the body including the following: *la boca, la cara, el codo, el cuello, el diente, el estómago, la garganta, el hombro, la lengua, la muñeca, la nariz, el ojo, la oreja, el pecho, el pelo, la rodilla, el tobillo.*

Notes

The Panama Canal has a fascinating history. After the canal was built by the United States, U.S. presence and control in the Panama Canal area became a source of increasing resentment in Panama. To ease the growing conflict, the United States and Panama signed the Panama Canal Neutrality Treaty in 1978 to increase Panamanian control gradually over the entire Canal Zone. The year 2000 marked the first year that Panama was in complete control of this important economic and political resource.

Remind students to return to either *Lección 9A* or *Lección 9B* (as indicated after each English equivalent) to review words and expressions they do not recognize.

National Standards

Connections
3.1

Teacher Resources

 *Capítulo 10*

TPRS *Capítulo 10*

 **Episode 10, DVD 2, Track 34**

Answers

El cuarto misterioso

1. Ver una película.
2. José entró en "el cuarto misterioso" nuevamente. Encontró la llave del maletín donde encontró una máscara de oro y un mapa.
3. José lleva un pantalón negro y una camisa. Francisco lleva un pantalón y una camisa roja. Conchita lleva una falda con una camiseta negra. Ana lleva una falda roja y una camisa negra.

Activities

Prior Knowledge

To review the chapter objectives ask: What is the time difference between saying that you are going to versus you will do something? What words and expressions indicate the use of the past tense? What words and body language are indicative of a polite person? Ask the following questions in Spanish: *¿Qué hiciste la semana pasada? ¿Qué haces todos los días?*

National Standards
Cultures 2.2.
Connections 3.1.

CAPÍTULO 10

Un año más

El cuarto misterioso

Contesta las siguientes preguntas sobre *Episodio 10–¿Dónde está la máscara?*

1. ¿Qué planes hicieron los chicos para la noche?
2. ¿Qué pasó en el último episodio?
3. Describe lo que José, Conchita, Ana y Francisco están llevando.

Mientras José, Conchita, Francisco y Ana caminaban a casa, algo sorprendente sucedió.

Objetivos

- discuss past actions and events
- talk about everyday activities
- express emotion
- indicate wishes and preferences
- write about past actions
- talk about the future
- make polite requests
- describe personal characteristics

Notes

Capítulo 10 offers a broad review of the content of *¡Aventura! 1*. This final chapter contains no new vocabulary or grammar. Therefore, select specific content you would like to review (e.g., the preterite tense, comparisons, expressions or vocabulary), complete the entire chapter or stop using the book after *Capítulo 9*. The authors have left the choice up to you to decide, according to time constraints and your own particular curricular needs.

You may choose to elicit information in Spanish from students. It is acceptable and natural for students to answer the questions with greater detail in English.

Activities

Connections
Using the maps at the front of the book, the *¡Aventura! 1* transparencies or a wall map, conduct a class discussion about some of the geographical features of Peru and Guatemala.

Contexto cultural

Perú
Nombre oficial: República del Perú
Población: 29.248.000
Capital: Lima
Ciudades importantes: Arequipa, Trujillo
Unidad monetaria: el nuevo sol
Fiesta nacional: 28 de julio, Día de la Independencia
Gente famosa: Mario Vargas Llosa, César Vallejo (escritores)

Guatemala
Nombre oficial: República de Guatemala
Población: 13.824.000
Capital: Ciudad de Guatemala
Ciudades importantes: Antigua, Chichicastenango, Quetzaltenango
Unidad monetaria: el quetzal
Fiesta nacional: 15 de septiembre, Día de la Independencia
Gente famosa: Rigoberta Menchú (líder popular)

Notes If you decide to use this chapter, you may skip activities or expand your review of a particular topic, according to the time you have available and according to student needs. *Capítulo 10* offers your students an opportunity to do interesting projects in which they talk about the past year (what they have learned, what they have done, what some of their favorite classes were). They also will have an opportunity to consider careers, future travel, relationships and other topics that are challenging and enjoyable.

National Standards
Connections 3.1
Communities 5.2

Lección A Diálogo
Fue un año divertido

Teacher Resources

Diálogo
Fue un año divertido
Activity 1
Activity 2
Activity 3

Activity 67

Activity 1

Activity 1

p. 40

Activity 1
Activity 2

Activities 1–2

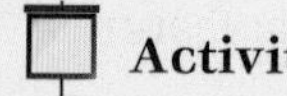

Content reviewed in *Lección A*
- talking about the past
- school
- leisure activities
- talking about the future
- *gustar*

Answers

1
1. No hay más tareas.
2. Mario estudió mucho.
3. Le gustó más jugar al fútbol y las clases de historia.
4. Le gustó más la clase de biología.
5. No le gusta la biología.
6. Silvia tiene amigos en el equipo de voleibol.

2 Answers will vary.

3
1. Falso. ...divertido.
2. Cierto.
3. Falso. ...biología.
4. Cierto.

National Standards

Communities
5.1

MARIO: ¡Un año más! No hay más tareas por unos meses.
SILVIA: ¡Qué bueno! Fue un año divertido.
MARIO: Estudié mucho.

SILVIA: ¿Qué fue lo que más te gustó?
MARIO: ¡Jugar al fútbol y las clases de historia!
SILVIA: A mí me gustó más la clase de biología.

MARIO: A mí la biología no me gusta.
SILVIA: Sí, yo sé. Bueno, también hice nuevos amigos.
MARIO: ¿Tus amigos del equipo de voleibol?
SILVIA: Sí, y voy a verlos ahora. Adiós.

1 ¿Qué recuerdas?

1. ¿Qué no hay por unos meses?
2. ¿Quién estudió mucho?
3. ¿Qué fue lo que más le gustó a Mario?
4. ¿Qué le gustó más a Silvia?
5. ¿Qué no le gusta a Mario?
6. ¿Quién tiene amigos en el equipo de voleibol?

2 Algo personal

1. ¿Fue tu año divertido? Explica.
2. ¿Te gusta hacer tareas? ¿Por qué?
3. ¿Qué fue lo que más te gustó del colegio este año?
4. ¿Qué deporte jugaste más este año?

3 ¡Fue un año divertido!

Di si lo que oyes es cierto o falso, según el Diálogo. Si es falso, corrige la información.

Notes

Capítulo 10 offers you the choice of whether to teach the contents to the entire class or to individuals based upon their interests, abilities or needs. For example, graduating seniors may benefit from some of the topics covered as they prepare for college, work or travel. Gifted and highly motivated students may enjoy doing portions of the chapter independently. In addition, you may have one or two students in class who are planning a trip to Peru or Guatemala and would like to learn about those countries.

Ask students to review the vocabulary from the previous page and then scan the dialog for familiar words or phrases.

Cultura viva

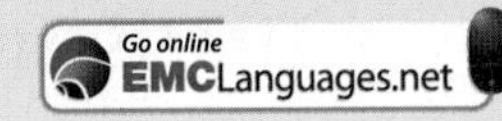

El Perú, centro del imperio inca

Peru formed the center point of the Incan Empire *(el imperio inca)*. Located on the Pacific Ocean along the western shores of South America, and situated between Ecuador and Chile, Peru, with its rich gold and silver deposits, quickly attracted many Spanish explorers in the sixteenth century. Although the Spaniards introduced their language and religion, the influence of the Inca civilization is evident throughout the modern-day culture of Peru. Descendants of the Incas still populate the Andean *(Andes)* highlands and the eastern jungles *(selvas del este)*. Many of them do not speak Spanish and they continue to live as their ancestors did centuries ago.

Descendientes de los incas viven en Perú.

Somos del Perú.

In direct contrast to Peru's indigenous past is the country's contemporary capital, Lima, where 30 percent of Peru's population lives and works. Lima is the most important area of development in the country. However, remnants of the past can be found even in this modern city. One example is the University of San Marcos, which is one of the oldest universities in the world.

La iglesia Santo Domingo en Cuzco, Perú.

4 El Perú

Contesta las siguientes preguntas sobre el Perú.

1. ¿De qué imperio fue Perú el centro?
2. ¿Por qué vinieron los exploradores españoles al Perú?
3. ¿En qué zona del Perú viven todavía los descendientes de los incas?
4. ¿Cómo se llama la capital del Perú?
5. ¿Cómo se llama una de las universidades más viejas del mundo?

5 ¡A viajar!

Imagina que te gustaría visitar Perú para practicar tu español. ¿Qué te gustaría ver o hacer allí? Busca información sobre Perú en la Internet. Luego, haz un itinerario con fechas, hoteles, restaurantes, lugares interesantes para visitar, precios, etc. Prepara un póster de viaje sobre el lugar y presenta la información a la clase.

¡Oportunidades!

En otro país

Have you ever visited another country? What did you see? What did you do there? After studying Spanish for a year, you probably realize the many opportunities that are available to you to use your language skills. Have you ever considered attending school in a different country for a year? Studying and living in a Spanish-speaking country could increase the Spanish skills you acquired this year.

Notes

Founded in 1551, the University of San Marcos is the oldest university in South America.

Peru's indigenous peoples comprise nearly half of the population. Peru has more indigenous people than any other country in South America. Most indigenous people live in Peru's *Altiplano*, all areas of the Andes above 6,500 feet.

Teacher Resources

 Activity 4

 Activities 2–4

 p. 126

 Activity 3

Answers

4 1. Fue el centro del imperio inca.
2. Vinieron por el oro y la plata.
3. Viven todavía en las zonas de los Andes y las selvas del este del Perú.
4. Se llama Lima.
5. Se llama la universidad de San Marcos.

5 Creative self-expression.

Activities

Cooperative Learning

Have students work in pairs preparing a dialog in which two people are talking about a trip one of them has just taken to Peru.

Expansion

Ask the following questions for discussion: *¿Qué países conoces?; ¿Qué hiciste en ese país/esos países?; ¿Qué lugares visitaste?; ¿Qué país(es) te gustaría visitar? ¿Por qué?; ¿En qué país te gustaría estudiar? ¿Por qué?; ¿Por qué es importante el español?*

Multiple Intelligences (musical)

Play Andean music to students and have them compare it to their favorite music.

National Standards	
Communication 1.1, 1.3	Comparisons 4.2
Cultures 2.2	Communities 5.1, 5.2
Connections 3.1, 3.2	

Teacher Resources

 Activities 5–7

 Activities 2–3

 Activity 4

 Activities 3–4

Answers

6 Creative self-expression.
7 Creative writing practice.
8 Answers will vary. You may also want to conduct the poll again with groups composed of all males and all females. Then compare the results to those of the mixed groups.

Activities

Cooperative Learning

After completing activity 8, have students conduct a similar survey on an issue of interest in your school.

Expansion

Select several students to summarize for the class what they learned about their partner in activity 6.

Spanish for Spanish Speakers

Pair bilingual and nonbilingual speakers for activity 6.

National Standards

Communication
1.1, 1.3

Connections
3.1

Proyectos

6 Una entrevista para el periódico del colegio

Prepara una entrevista para hacerla a un(a) compañero/a de clase para saber sobre sus experiencias y actividades durante este año. Pregúntale sobre las cosas más importantes que hizo, las más divertidas, las más aburridas, lo que más le gustó del año, lo que menos le gustó, algo interesante que le pasó y cualquier otra información de su vida en el colegio o en su casa. Luego, escribe un artículo en español de una página y preséntalo a la clase.

7 Tus experiencias

Escribe un ensayo *(essay)* en español de uno o dos párrafos sobre algo especial que te pasó durante tu vida escolar este año. En tu composición puedes hablar por ejemplo sobre alguien interesante que conociste, una actividad importante que hiciste, una clase que te gustó mucho, un deporte que hiciste o un evento al que fuiste. Añade detalles *(details)* importantes que rodearon *(surrounded)* el hecho *(event)*, como por ejemplo, la fecha en que pasó, el lugar, el tiempo que hizo, lo que pasó antes y lo que pasó después, etc.

Estrategia

The importance of reviewing

It is important to review what you have learned. No one remembers everything they have studied. You have made progress this year with Spanish, and reviewing will help keep everything fresh in your mind.

8 Encuesta estudiantil

Haz la siguiente encuesta a diez compañeros(as) de clase para averiguar *(to find out)* cuáles fueron las clases favoritas de tus compañeros(as) este año. Primero, completa la encuesta en cualquier clase que no sea la de español y hazte la encuesta a ti mismo y luego a tus compañeros(as) de español del grupo, compartan los resultados. Finalmente, reporten los resultados del grupo a la clase.

Encuesta sobre las clases favoritas del año

Por cada una de las siguientes clases di el número que representa mejor tu opinión.

1. el arte	0	1	2	3	4
2. las ciencias (biología, química, etc.)	0	1	2	3	4
3. la computación	0	1	2	3	4
4. la educación física	0	1	2	3	4
5. el español	0	1	2	3	4
6. los estudios sociales	0	1	2	3	4
7. la historia	0	1	2	3	4
8. el inglés	0	1	2	3	4
9. las matemáticas (álgebra, geometría, etc.)	0	1	2	3	4
10. la música (banda, orquestra, coro, etc.)	0	1	2	3	4
11. (¿otras?) ______	0	1	2	3	4

0 = No sé. No tengo una opinión.
1 = Fue horrible. Me disgustó (disliked) mucho.
2 = Fue aburrida. No me gustó mucho.
3 = Fue buena. Me gustó.
4 = Fue excelente. Me gustó mucho.

Notes

Review. Review the preterite tense with students before assigning activity 6.

Before assigning activity 7, review some of the writing strategies students have learned over the course of the year. Tell students they should apply as many of these strategies as possible when writing their essay.

Review classes and the use of *gustar* before assigning activity 8.

9 Encuesta electrónica

Prepara un e-mail o una página de la Web con una encuesta como la que hiciste en la actividad anterior sobre las clases favoritas. Envíala a otra clase (de tu colegio, de cualquier otro colegio del país o de un país de habla hispana), pidiendo a los estudiantes contestarla también por la Internet. Comparte los resultados con la clase, comparando y contrastando los resultados de la encuesta.

10 Un país hispanohablante

Crea un collage que represente al país hispanohablante que encontraste *(found)* más interesante durante tu año de clases de español. Luego, muéstralo a la clase y da una corta explicación del collage.

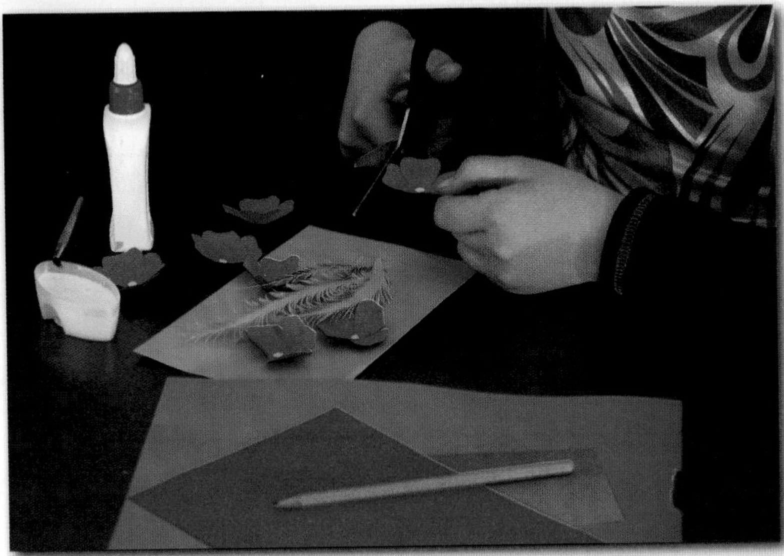

Mi collage trata de Perú.

11 Tu poesía

Escribe un poema o una canción en español sobre algún tema que aprendiste este año. Después, puedes leer tu poema o cantar tu canción a la clase.

Estoy escribiendo un poema.

Teacher Resources

 Activities 8–9

 Activities 4–6

Answers

9 Creative self-expression.
10 Creative self-expression.
11 Creative self-expression.

Activities

Cooperative Learning
Tell the class that it is time for a role-reversal: Instead of answering the teacher's questions or a partner's questions, it is their opportunity to ask questions of the teacher. The students should work in pairs to develop appropriate questions; the interview session follows.

Multiple Intelligences (musical)
Ask for volunteers to teach the class a song they know in Spanish. The song may be traditional or contemporary. As an alternative, ask if anyone in class would like to recite the poem or perform the song they wrote for activity 11.

Notes Activity 10 is meant to provide an additional opportunity for visual and artistic learners to excel and show what they have learned during the year.

Ask permission of students to place some of the better collages and poems on the wall or in a public display in the school. You may also wish to contact the editor and supervisor of the school newspaper to arrange to print one or two of the poems.

National Standards	
Communication 1.1, 1.2, 1.3	**Comparisons** 4.2
Cultures 2.2	
Connections 3.1	

Teacher Resources

Lectura cultural
Machu Picchu
Activity 12
Activity 13

 p. 157

Answers

12 1. no
2. sí
3. sí
4. sí
5. no

13 Answers will vary.

Activities

Expansion

Have students look in the media center for pictures of Machu Picchu and bring them in to share with the class.

National Standards

Cultures
2.2

Connections
3.1

Comparisons
4.2

Lectura cultural

Machu Picchu

Miles de turistas visitan este sitio arqueológico cerca de Cuzco, Perú. ¿Por qué?

Belleza[1]...

Los incas construyeron[2] Machu Picchu entre dos picos[3] altos. Las construcciones de piedra[4] parecen desplegarse[5] sobre la montaña. Abajo, el torrencial río[6] Urubamba corre por la selva amazónica. Es un lugar mágico.

Historia...

Machu Picchu fue construida[7] en el siglo XV cuando el imperio inca se extendía desde Ecuador a Argentina. Se la conoce como la Ciudad Perdida porque permaneció[8] escondida[9] hasta 1911 cuando Hiram Bingham la descubrió[10] intacta.

Misterio...

Machu Picchu, en quechua, quiere decir "Cima[11] Vieja" pero su verdadero nombre no se conoce. Tampoco se sabe la historia o la función de esta ciudad fortificada inca. Algunos creen que fue un monasterio pero como los incas no tenían escritura[12], este lugar estará siempre rodeado[13] de misterio.

Respeto...

La perfección de las paredes de Machu Picchu sorprende[14]. No usaron argamasa[15], y sin embargo[16], la unión entre las piedras es tan perfecta que no se puede introducir ni la hoja[17] de un cuchillo. La construcción de Machu Picchu—con sus paredes perfectas, acueductos, terrazas, observatorios, reloj solar—es evidencia de la sabiduría[18] de los incas.

[1]Beauty [2]built [3]peaks [4]stone [5]unfold [6]river [7]built [8]remained [9]hidden [10]discovered [11]Peak [12]writing [13]surrounded [14]amazes [15]mortar [16]however [17]blade [18]wisdom

12 ¿Qué recuerdas?

¿Sí o no?

1. Machu Picchu fue la capital secreta del imperio inca en el siglo XV.
2. Hiram Bingham descubrió las ruinas de Machu Picchu en 1911.
3. La geografía de Machu Picchu incluye montañas y selva.
4. La construcción de las paredes de Machu Picchu es perfecta.
5. Los incas sabían escribir y leer.

- **Compare and contrast the architecture and landscape of Machu Picchu with that of the city in which you live.**

13 Algo personal

1. ¿Qué más sabes sobre Machu Picchu? Comparte algunos datos con la clase.
2. ¿Por qué crees que nadie, ni los conquistadores españoles, descubrieron Machu Picchu hasta 1911? ¿Cuál crees que fue la función de esa ciudad inca?

Notes

Before beginning the *Lectura cultural* have students identify cognates and known words.

The Incas were the rulers of the largest native empire of the Americas. At the time of their demise, the Incas consisted of and ruled an estimated twelve million people in much of what is now Peru and Ecuador, as well as in large parts of Chile, Bolivia and Argentina.

¿Qué aprendí?

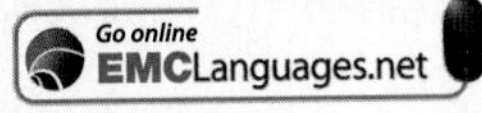

Autoevaluación

As a review and self-check, respond to the following:

1. Use the preterite tense to state six things you did this year.
2. State four things you learned about Peru.
3. Name two opportunities you have because you know Spanish.
4. Why is it important to review what you have learned?
5. Summarize the results of the surveys you did about favorite classes for activities 8 and 9.
6. State two things you learned about Machu Picchu.

Lima, la capital de Perú.

Unas paredes en Machu Picchu.

¡Aprendimos mucho este año!

Notes Students can find out more about Cuzco and Machu Picchu by visiting these Web sites:

Cuzco http://www.peru.com/cuzco/
Machu Picchu general information
http://www.machupicchu.org

Teacher Resources

 **Activity 10**

 **pp. 63, 97**

 **Activity 5**

Answers

Autoevaluación
Answers will vary.

Activities

Pronunciation
(las letras l e y, y el sonido ll)
The sound of *l* in Spanish is similar to the sound of **l** in English, but shorter. Model several words for students: *la, lavar, limpiar, lista, lugar, el, abril, telenovela.* In Spanish, *ll* has a sound that is similar to the English **y** as in **yet**. Have students practice the sound by having them pronounce the following words: *ella, paella, silla, olla, llueve, cuchillo, llegan, Guillermo, vainilla.* The letter *y* in Spanish is similar to the English **y** in **yet**, when preceding a vowel: *ayudar, ya, yo, mayo, playa, oyendo, leyendo.* When following a vowel, the Spanish *y* sounds like an *i*. This usually happens at the end of the word: *soy, estoy, hoy, hay, doy, voy, muy*.

National Standards
Cultures 2.1, 2.2
Connections 3.2
Comparisons 4.1

Teacher Resources

Diálogo
¿Adónde van de vacaciones?
Activity 1
Activity 2
Activity 3

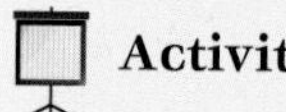

Activity 68

Activities 1–2

Activities 1–2

p. 41

Activity 1
Activity 2
Activity 3

Activity 1

Content reviewed in *Lección B*

- talking about the past
- *tener que*
- talking about the future
- adjective/noun agreement
- leisure activities
- careers that use Spanish

Answers

1
1. Tuvo que ayudar a sus padres.
2. Va a ir a las ruinas de Tikal.
3. Fue a Tikal.
4. Le gustaría ir a California a la casa de su tía.

2 Answers will vary.

3 1. Luis; 2. Luis; 3. Inés; 4. Inés; 5. Luis

National Standards

Communication
1.2

Connections
3.1

Diálogo
¿Adónde van de vacaciones?

Guatemala

LUIS: Hola, Inés.
INÉS: Hola, Luis. ¿Qué hiciste el sábado?
LUIS: Tuve que ayudar a mis padres.

INÉS: ¿Van a ir de vacaciones?
LUIS: Vamos a ir a las ruinas de Tikal.
INÉS: Fui a Tikal el año pasado. Me gustó mucho.

LUIS: Y tú, ¿qué vas a hacer en las vacaciones?
INÉS: No sé. Me gustaría ir a California a la casa de mi tía, o trabajar en la tienda de mi padre.
LUIS: Pienso que debes ir a California. Va a ser más divertido.

¿Qué recuerdas?

1. ¿Qué hizo Luis el sábado pasado?
2. ¿Adónde va Luis de vacaciones?
3. ¿Adónde fue Inés el año pasado?
4. ¿Adónde le gustaría a Inés ir de vacaciones?

Algo personal

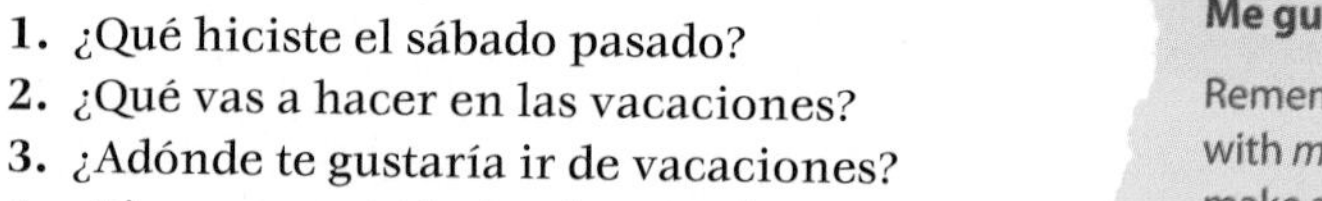

1. ¿Qué hiciste el sábado pasado?
2. ¿Qué vas a hacer en las vacaciones?
3. ¿Adónde te gustaría ir de vacaciones?
4. ¿Piensas que trabajar durante las vacaciones es una buena idea?

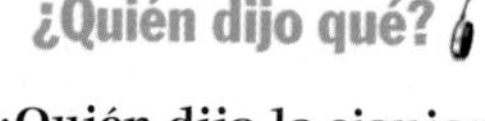

¿Quién dijo qué?

¿Quién dijo lo siguiente, Inés o Luis?

¡Extra!

Me gustaría

Remember to use *gustaría* combined with *me, te, les, nos* and *les* in order to make a request, to politely express a wish or to ask about another person's wishes.

Me gustaría ir a California.
¿**Te gustaría** ir de vacaciones?

Notes

Before beginning the dialog, review the preterite tense, family vocabulary, the use of *tener que*, the *futuro próximo* and adjective-noun agreement.

Ask students to review the vocabulary from the previous page and then scan the dialog for familiar words or phrases.

Cultura viva

Tikal, Guatemala.

Guatemala, tierra maya

One aspect of Guatemala that fascinates anyone who visits the country is that Guatemala is the land of the Maya Indian civilization. Although the ancient Mayan civilization disappeared mysteriously, traces of the advanced Mayan culture remain today. The Mayans had an extensive knowledge of astronomy, mathematics and architecture. Tikal, one of the most well-known Mayan cities, was founded around 700 B.C. The Mayan languages (mainly *quiché*) and traditions are still very much alive among the Mayans in today's Guatemala. The colors and patterns of the traditional ceremonial costumes that many Mayan descendants wear are visible evidence of one tradition that has been passed on for many years from one generation to the next.

The cities of *Antigua*, *Chichicastenango*, *Huehuetenango* and *Quetzaltenango* still contain remnants of the Spanish colonial period, which started in 1524. The capital, Guatemala City *(Ciudad de Guatemala)*, was founded in 1776, and in 1821 the region declared its independence from Spain.

Today Guatemala offers a mix of old and new, rustic and urban. The modern capital is the commercial, industrial, educational and governmental center of the country. However, Guatemala's rich farmland serves as the main source of income for the country's 14 million inhabitants, just as it has for centuries.

Los colores de Guatemala.

Unas chicas mayas.

4 Guatemala, tierra maya

Di si las siguientes oraciones sobre Guatemala son ciertas o falsas.

1. Guatemala es un centro de la civilización maya.
2. Los mayas estudiaron astronomía, matemáticas y biología.
3. La ciudad más famosa del imperio maya es Tikal.
4. La lengua maya es el español.
5. Antigua es una ciudad muy moderna.
6. La capital de Guatemala es la Ciudad de Guatemala.

Notes

Belize, situated to the east of Guatemala, is the only English-speaking country in Central America.

Antigua's Spanish colonial architecture, particularly its churches, is a major tourist attraction. A major earthquake struck the city in 1976.

Tell students that numerous Mayan ruins are located in Mexico's Yucatan Peninsula near Cancún. They include Chichén Itzá, Uxmal and Tulum.

Chichicastenango is known for its colorful market held every Sunday and Thursday. The market is described later in this chapter in the *Lectura personal*.

Teacher Resources

 Activity 4

 Activity 4

 p. 125

 Activity 4

 Activity 2

Answers

4
1. Cierta.
2. Falsa.
3. Cierta.
4. Falsa.
5. Falsa.
6. Cierta.

Activities

Expansion

Assign students to research and write a report on the work of Nobel Peace Prize winner Rigoberta Menchú.

Spanish for Spanish Speakers

Students should write a short composition in Spanish summarizing what they know about Guatemala. Expand the activity by having students seek out additional information about Guatemala on the Internet and at the library.

Technology

Ask students to search the Internet for pictures of the sites mentioned here. They should print them out on a color printer and bring them in to share with the class. Display the best ones on a bulletin board.

National Standards

Communication	Comparisons
1.3	4.2
Cultures	
2.2	
Connections	
3.1, 3.2	

Teacher Resources

GV Activities 3–5

Activity 3

Answers

5 Answers will vary.
6 Creative writing practice.
7 Answers will vary.

Activities

Cooperative Learning
As follow-up to activity 6, ask students to make predictions about their lives in ten to fifteen years: *¿Qué carreras van a tener?; ¿Dónde van a vivir y trabajar?; ¿Van a usar el español en sus carreras?*

Multiple Intelligences (linguistic/spatial)
Have students do a variation on the theme for activity 6 by assigning a composition in the past tense to tell what they did last summer. Have them attach a picture or a visual to make their paragraph more interesting and display their work on a bulletin board.

National Standards

Communication
1.1, 1.3

Connections
3.1

Communities
5.1, 5.2

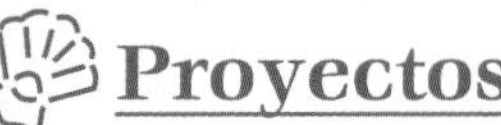

Proyectos

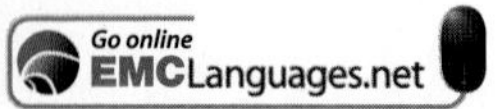

5 Otra entrevista para el periódico del colegio

Trabajando con un(a) compañero/a de clase, hazle las siguientes preguntas en combinación con cinco preguntas originales para saber sobre sus planes para el verano. Después de la entrevista, escribe un artículo de uno o dos párrafos sobre los planes de tu compañero/a y léelo a la clase.

1. ¿Cuál de los trabajos de la lista te gustaría hacer este verano?
2. ¿Qué otro trabajo de la lista te gustaría hacer?
3. ¿Tienes experiencia en alguno de estos trabajos? ¿En cuál? ¿Cuánta experiencia tienes?
4. ¿En cuáles de los trabajos de la lista no te gustaría trabajar? Explica.
5. ¿Vas a viajar durante tus vacaciones? ¿Adónde?
6. – 10. ¿...?

- cuidar a niños
- ser salvavidas de una piscina o de una playa
- hacer trabajos de jardinería
- trabajar en un restaurante
- limpiar casas
- trabajar en un supermercado
- pintar casas
- trabajar en una oficina
- reparar autos
- trabajar en una tienda

6 Tus vacaciones de verano

Escribe un ensayo en español de uno o dos párrafos sobre tus planes para las vacaciones. Di qué actividades piensas hacer, con quién las piensas hacer, cuál es la actividad que más te gusta hacer durante el verano, etc. Añade detalles relevantes asociados con cada actividad, como por ejemplo, cuándo piensas hacer la actividad, en dónde, por cuánto tiempo, etc.

7 Otra encuesta

Haz la siguiente encuesta a diez compañeros(as) de clase para averiguar cuáles son las actividades favoritas de tus compañeros(as) durante el verano. Hazte la encuesta a ti mismo y luego a tus compañeros(as). Añade otras actividades a la encuesta si es necesario. Después, en grupos de cuatro o cinco estudiantes compartan los resultados. Finalmente, reporten los resultados del grupo a la clase.

Encuesta sobre las actividades favoritas durante el verano

Por cada una de las siguientes actividades di el número que representa mejor tu opinión.

dormir	0	1	2	3	4
hacer deportes	0	1	2	3	4
hacer quehaceres	0	1	2	3	4
ir a la playa	0	1	2	3	4
ir al centro comercial	0	1	2	3	4
ir al cine	0	1	2	3	4
jugar a videojuegos	0	1	2	3	4
leer	0	1	2	3	4
nadar en una piscina	0	1	2	3	4
navegar en la internet	0	1	2	3	4
ver la televisión	0	1	2	3	4
viajar	0	1	2	3	4
(¿otras?) ________________	0	1	2	3	4

0 = No sé. No tengo una opinión.
1 = Es horrible. Me disgusta mucho.
2 = Es aburrida. No me gusta mucho.
3 = Es buena. Me gusta.
4 = Es excelente. Me gusta mucho.

Notes Communities. Activities 5, 10 and 11 provide the basis for a class discussion about career options and work opportunities that students have available to them because of their Spanish skills.

8 Las próximas vacaciones

Trabajando en los mismos grupos de la actividad anterior, creen un collage que represente las actividades favoritas del grupo durante las vacaciones y luego, preséntenlo a la clase.

9 Un proyecto en la Internet

Trabajando en grupos de tres a cinco estudiantes, busquen información en la Internet sobre algún lugar en un país hispanohablante adonde les gustaría ir de vacaciones. Luego, preparen un póster sobre el lugar, indicando las principales actividades que se pueden hacer allí y creando un slogan para decir por qué creen Uds. que este lugar es el mejor para ir de vacaciones. Finalmente, presenten el póster a la clase.

10 ¿Qué te gustaría ser?

Numera del 1 al 12 las siguientes profesiones en el orden de tu preferencia, siendo la número 1 la que más te gusta y la número 12 la que menos te gusta. Luego, en grupos de tres, compara los resultados de cada persona. Explica por qué crees que ciertas carreras y profesiones son más populares que otras, considerando el salario, los beneficios, las condiciones de trabajo, el horario, etc. Reporta los resultados de tu grupo a la clase.

agricultor/a	hombre/mujer de negocios
arquitecto/a	ingeniero/a
artista	maestro/a
banquero/a	médico/a
cocinero/a	programador/a
enfermero/a	veterinario/a

¡Oportunidades!

Pensando en el futuro, las carreras y el español

You are already aware that knowing how to communicate in a foreign language can enhance your career *(carrera)* opportunities. The following are some interesting careers requiring foreign language expertise that you may want to consider investigating:

border patrol agent	journalist
court interpreter	language teacher
customer service representative	lawyer
foreign broadcaster	travel agent
foreign diplomat	
hotel sales manager	
imported clothing merchandiser	

11 Tu futuro

Escribe uno o dos párrafos en español sobre la carrera que te gustaría estudiar. En tu composición, debes decir por qué te gustaría estudiar esa carrera y qué características piensas que tienes y son importantes para poder trabajar en esa profesión.

Notes

Extend activities 8 and 9 by having students summarize their work in writing.

Communities. Try to locate someone in your community who uses Spanish in his or her job and ask the person to speak to the class. Be sure to have students prepare questions in advance to keep the discussion going.

Review some of the writing strategies students have learned over the course of the year. Encourage students to apply as many of these strategies as possible in the composition for activity 11.

Teacher Resources

 Activities 4–5

 Activities 6–7

 Activity 5
Activity 6

 Activity 4

Answers

8 Creative self-expression.
9 Creative self-expression.
10 Creative self-expression.
11 Creative writing practice.

Activities

Communities
Suggest to students that they talk with their parents about ways they may use Spanish and communication skills they have developed during the year to volunteer in the community. Start a class discussion of other ways students may be able to participate in community service.

Multiple Intelligences (interpersonal/intrapersonal/linguistic)
Begin a discussion about how students intend to use Spanish in the future. Ask questions and let them express thoughts about places they would like to visit, careers they are now considering and contributions they will be able to make to their community because they know Spanish.

National Standards
Communication 1.1, 1.3
Connections 3.1
Communities 5.1, 5.2

Teacher Resources

Lectura personal
Activity 12
Activity 13

Answers

12 1. En Guatemala viven seis millones de mayas.
2. El libro sagrado de los mayas quichés se llama el Popol Vuh.
3. La blusa que usan las mujeres mayas se llama el huipil.
4. Los días de mercado en Chichicastenango son los jueves y los domingos.
5. El mercado de Chichicastenango es interesante porque se presencia la cultura maya: los trajes coloridos, las diferentes lenguas, los rituales.

13 Answers will vary.

Activities

Expansion

Ask students to summarize what they have learned to date about Guatemala. Then conduct a class discussion about places in Guatemala and elsewhere in the Spanish-speaking world that they would like to visit.

National Standards	
Communication 1.1	**Comparisons** 4.2
Cultures 2.1, 2.2	**Communities** 5.1
Connections 3.1	

Lectura personal

Nombre: **Ceci Eugenia Madrigal**
Edad: **18 años**
País natal: **Uruguay**
Pasatiempos: **dormir, comer, escuchar música**

Mercado de Chichicastenango.

Iglesia de San Tomás, Chichicastenango.

El domingo, tempranito por la mañana, tomamos un bus de la Ciudad de Guatemala a Chichicastenango. Nosotros hemos viajado[1] mucho este año y hemos visto[2] muchos mercados pero ninguno como el mercado de Chichicastenango. Es más que un mercado: es un impresionante espectáculo de colores, sonidos y aromas. Miles de indígenas de la región llegan al mercado cada jueves y domingo a vender, comprar, hablar, comer, reír, regatear. Chichicastenango se distingue por sus tejidos[3], particularmente el huipil, blusa femenina de los mayas. Yo me compré una muy colorida y después fui a la plaza. Allí está la iglesia[4] de San Tomás, construída[5] en 1540. Fue en esta iglesia donde un español vio por primera vez el Popul Vuh, el libro sagrado[6] de los mayas quichés. Aunque[7] es una iglesia católica, muchas de las ceremonias y los rituales son mayas. En las escaleras, vi a un hombre maya quemar[8] incienso[9]. En Guatemala viven 6 millones de mayas y hablan 20 lenguas mayas. Presenciar[10] la cultura maya fue una gran manera de concluir nuestra gira mundial.

[1]have traveled [2]have seen [3]weavings [4]church [5]built [6]sacred [7]Although [8]burn [9]incense [10]To witness

12 ¿Qué recuerdas?

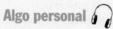

1. ¿Cuántos mayas viven en Guatemala?
2. ¿Cómo se llama el libro sagrado de los mayas quichés?
3. ¿Cómo se llama la blusa que usan la mujeres mayas?
4. ¿Cuáles son los días de mercado en Chichicastenango?
5. ¿Por qué es el mercado de Chichicastenango interesante?

- Compare the market in Chichicastenango with a place in your town where people go to buy, talk, eat, laugh. What are the similarities? What are the differences?

13 Algo personal

1. ¿Hay un mercado en tu comunidad? ¿Qué venden allí?
2. ¿Existe una cultura indígena en tu comunidad? ¿Cómo es su traje tradicional?
3. ¿Cuándo fue la última vez que oliste incienso? ¿Dónde fue?

Notes

Connections. This activity makes cross-curricular connections to geography and history.

The embroidered garments that are worn by the Maya today have a signature pattern that identifies them as members of a particular community. Each village has a characteristic woven or embroidered design. Often these ornate designs form a cross when the blouse or shirt is open and flat. The cross shape represents eternal life and the four cardinal points, the four winds and the four phases of the moon.

Autoevaluación

As a review and self-check, respond to the following:

1. Where is Tikal?
2. State four things you learned about Guatemala.
3. Tell what you are going to do this summer. Say where you are going to go, whom you are going to be with and what you are going to do there.
4. Summarize the results of the survey you did about favorite summer activities for Activity 7.
5. Name a place in a Spanish-speaking country you would like to go for vacation. Why would you like to go there?
6. Name three careers that may be open to you because you know Spanish.
7. What do you know about Chichicastenango?

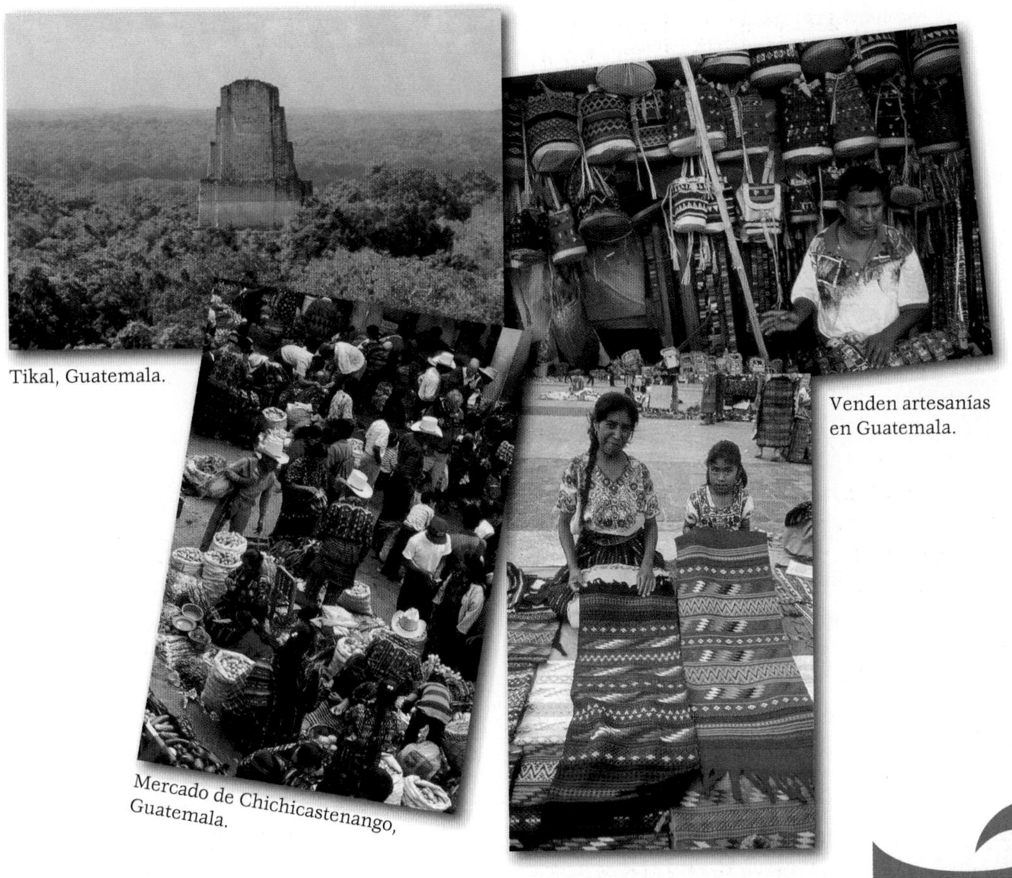

Tikal, Guatemala.

Venden artesanías en Guatemala.

Mercado de Chichicastenango, Guatemala.

Notes Rigoberta Menchú and Miguel Ángel Asturias are two well-known Guatemalans. Menchú is an advocate for the indigenous people of her country and the winner of the 1992 Nobel Peace Prize; Asturias received the Nobel Prize in literature in 1967.

The currency of Guatemala is the *quetzal*, which is also a typical bird of the region.

Teacher Resources

 Activities 6–8

 pp. 64, 98

 Activities 4–5

 Juegos

Flash Cards

 **Answers**

Autoevaluación

Possible answers:

1. Está en Guatemala.

2–7. Answers will vary.

 **Activities**

Pronunciation (*las letras* d y t)

The letter *d* is similar in Spanish and in English, but in Spanish the tip of the tongue touches the inside of the upper front teeth, not the palate. Have students try these words: *damas, deber, décimo, deportista, desde, día, dibujar, donde.* After a vowel, *d* is pronounced much like the **th** in the English word **mother**. Have students practice the sound by saying these words: *nublado, poder, rápidamente, todavía, vida, usted.* The Spanish *t* is also formed by touching the tip of the tongue to the inside of the upper front teeth. The sound is much like the **t** in the English word **stop**. Students can practice the sound by saying the following words: *continuar, estación, carta, tener, tiempo, tonto.*

National Standards

Cultures
2.1, 2.2

Connections
3.1

Comparisons
4.1

Teacher Resources

Es sólo una cuestión de actitud

Answers

Preparación

1. Answers will vary.
2. El tema principal es la actitud.

Activities

Cooperative Learning

In pairs, ask students to take turns interviewing one another about their immediate wishes or long-term desires and then report the results back to the class. Some questions to get students started: *¿Qué te gustaría hacer hoy después de las clases?; ¿Qué te gustaría hacer esta noche?; ¿Qué te gustaría hacer este fin de semana?; ¿Qué países te gustaría visitar?*

Prereading Strategy

Remind students that it is not essential to understand every word to read Spanish. Discuss factors and strategies that can help facilitate their reading comprehension.

National Standards
Communication 1.1
Cultures 2.2
Connections 3.1

Tú lees

Estrategia

Strategy summary

You have learned several ways of understanding different types of Spanish narratives. You know how to use cognates, you have learned to anticipate possible vocabulary and you have learned to gather information by skimming the content before starting to read. Use these techniques to read *Es sólo una cuestión de actitud* sung by La Ola.

Preparación

Contesta las siguientes preguntas como preparación para la lectura de la canción.

1. ¿Qué crees que quiere decir el título de la canción?
2. ¿Cuál es el tema principal de la canción?

Es sólo una cuestión[1] de actitud

Por Fito Páez

Es sólo una cuestión de actitud,
si lo cuentas no se cumple el deseo[2].
Es sólo una cuestión de actitud,
caballero, ¿me podría[3] dar fuego[4]?

Es sólo una cuestión de actitud
atreverse[5] a desplazarse[6] en el tiempo.
Es sólo una cuestión de actitud
entender[7] lo que está escrito en el viento.

Es sólo una cuestión de actitud
ir con taco aguja[8] en pista de hielo[9].
Es sólo una cuestión de actitud
recibir los golpes[10], no tener miedo.

Es sólo una cuestión de actitud
y no quejarse[11] más de todo, por cierto.
Es sólo una cuestión de actitud
atreverse a atravesar[12] el desierto[13].

Notes

The song *Es sólo una cuestión de actitud* has been recorded and is included in the Audio Program. Consider playing the recording as students follow the words in the *Tú lees*.

Hay un pozo profundo[14] en la esquina[15] del sol,
si caés[16], la vida te muele a palos[17].
Tengo rabia[18], que todo se pase y adiós
mis peleas[19] por estar a tu lado.

Cuando vos decidís elegir[20] la razón
yo prefiero siempre un poco de caos.
Soy tu rey[21], soy tu perro, soy tu esclavo[22]
y soy tu amor,
soy tu espejo[23] mirando el otro lado.

Es sólo una cuestión de actitud
reírse[24] del fracaso[25] y del oro.
Es sólo una cuestión de actitud
no tener nada y tenerlo todo.

Es sólo una cuestión de actitud
y nunca nadie sabe nunca nada,
para colmo[26].
Es sólo una cuestión de actitud,
espada[27], capa[28], torero[29] y toro[30].

[1]It's only a matter of [2]the wish will not come true [3]could [4]light [5]to dare [6]to travel [7]understand [8]stiletto heels [9]ice arena [10]receive a beating [11]not complain [12]to cross [13]the desert [14]deep well [15]corner [16]if you fall [17]life gives you a beating [18]I am mad [19]fights [20]to choose [21]king [22]slave [23]mirror [24]to laugh [25]failure [26]to top it all off [27]sword [28]cape [29]bullfighter [30]bull

A ¿Qué recuerdas?

Completa las frases de la izquierda con una de las frases de la derecha, según la canción *Es sólo una cuestión de actitud*.

1.	si lo cuentas...	**A.**	...¿me podría dar fuego?
2.	caballero,...	**B.**	...lo que está escrito en el viento
3.	atreverse a...	**C.**	...mirando el otro lado
4.	entender...	**D.**	...que todo se pase y adiós
5.	recibir los golpes,...	**E.**	...no se cumple el deseo
6.	Tengo rabia,...	**F.**	...desplazarse en el tiempo
7.	soy tu espejo...	**G.**	...del fracaso y del oro
8.	reírse...	**H.**	...no tener miedo

B Algo personal

1. ¿Qué piensas de esta canción? ¿Te gusta? Explica.
2. ¿Piensas que en la vida todo es cuestión de actitud? Explica.
3. ¿Qué actitud puedes cambiar hoy para hacer tu vida mejor?
4. ¿Te gustan las canciones con mensajes para pensar? ¿Por qué sí? ¿Por qué no?

Notes Rodolfo "Fito" Páez (born in Rosario, Argentina) is the composer of this song. He is very famous throughout the Spanish-speaking world. Fito started his first rock band (Staff) during his teen years. His songs and lyrics have been popular for more than thirty years and both new and old Hispanic rock bands often borrow his materials.

Teacher Resources

Activity B

Answers

A 1. E; 2. A; 3. F; 4. B; 5. H; 6. D; 7. C; 8. G

B Answers will vary.

Activities

Pronunciation
(las letras* ca, co, cu, que *y* qui*)
Practice the sound of the letter combinations *ca, co, cu, que* and *qui* by noting for students that the English sound of the consonant **k**, just like the sound of **p**, is explosive: that is, if you hold your hand over your mouth when you pronounce them, you will feel a slight puff of air. Note, however, that in Spanish this does not occur. Have students say and compare the English words **café, capital, card, kiss** and **quality** with the Spanish words *cada, cocina, cuarto, que* and *quince*, which begin with a similar sound, but without the puff of air that occurs in the English words. To help students who are experiencing difficulty avoiding the explosive burst of air, have them repeat *tatatata*, then *cocococo*, until they are able to say *taco* without the puff of air. Then have students practice the following sentences: *¿Quién está comiendo en el comedor?; No sé, pero Carlota está comiendo coco en la cocina.*

National Standards

Cultures
2.2

Connections
3.1

Answers

Creative writing practice.

Activities

Expansion

Give students this additional example of an acrostic poem and have them try to write their own poem following the model:

***M**oreno y muy romántico,*
***A**rtístico, mis amigos me describen.*
***R**esponsable y cooperativo con mis maestros.*
***I**mpulsivo, cómico y popular con mis compañeros.*
***O**ptimista de mi carrera de artista gráfico.*

Multiple Intelligences (linguistic/spatial)

Have artistic students create an interesting visual for the poem about Mario mentioned in the preceding ATE activity. They might rewrite the poem in the center of a collage of items, either cut from newspapers and magazines or hand drawn, that depict some aspect of the poem (for example, artist's supplies like paintbrushes, graphic pens).

National Standards

Connections
3.1

Tú escribes

Estrategia

Defining your purpose for writing

Before you begin a writing assignment, it is a good idea to identify your purpose. Then keep your purpose in mind throughout the writing process as you brainstorm your topic, formulate your rough draft and edit your finished product.

The purpose of this writing assignment is to describe yourself, using the format of an acrostic poem. In an acrostic poem, certain letters of each line spell out the letters of a specific word the author has in mind.

Use the letters of your name or nickname, in their correct order, as your acrostic word. Design the pattern for placing a letter of your name in each line. For instance, you might choose to highlight the first letter of each line, the first letter of the last word in each line, etc.

Then, in the lines, include some personal information you have learned this year to describe your personality, your appearance and your preferences. Also, work in some information about what you are going to do in the future. Be sure to make the letters of your acrostic word stand out in the poem (as was done in the poem on this page). Finally, you may wish to accompany your poem with artwork or graphics to make it more visually appealing.

Juego al fútbol, al básquetbol, y mucho más.
Soy un jugador, fuerte y rápido.
Quiero jugar al fútbol profesional algún día.
Las matemáticas, no me gustan ni un poquito.

Notes

Inform students how you will be grading their poems.

Allow some time for students to recite their poems in front of the class. You might ask students to vote for the best work as they would in a poetry slam or competition.

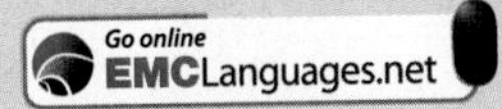

Proyectos adicionales

A Conexión con la tecnología

Prepare an electronic survey about favorite careers or jobs, using an e-mail or a Web page similar to the surveys you completed in this chapter. Ask another class (preferably in a different state or country) to complete the survey and send the results back to you via the Internet. Share the information with your classmates, comparing and contrasting the results of your survey.

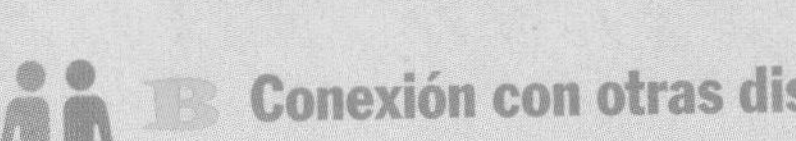

B Conexión con otras disciplinas: música

Working in pairs, find a song in any language you like. Using the music for the song, create lyrics in Spanish about some aspect of your life (school, vacations, family, etc.). Sing the song to the class.

C Conexión cultural

In groups of three to five students, research a group or culture that is native to your state or region. Find out the name of the group, where they lived, their social activities, number of inhabitants and where any ruins or remains may be found. Share the results with another group of students (a class in another region of the world, for example) and request the same information about civilizations that inhabited their region of the world.

Un indígena de North Dakota.

Ruinas de un pueblo de los Anasazi, indígenas de norteamérica. (Mesa Verde National Park, Colorado, EE.UU.)

Notes Activities A, B and C provide opportunities in keeping with the philosophy and goals of *¡Aventura! 1* for students as they become lifelong learners. These activities encourage students to learn about communities in the world where Spanish is spoken and to begin to make comparisons between the student's background knowledge and the reality of life in the Spanish-speaking world. In addition, students are invited to use what they have learned in Spanish class to establish connections with their neighborhood and with the larger world community.

Teacher Resources

p. 76

Answers

A Creative self-expression.
B Creative self-expression.
C Creative self-expression.

Activities

Critical Thinking

Have students complete a culture project in which they look back on the countries studied this year and make a collage that reflects what they have learned about one or more of the nations. A possible theme for the collage is *Mirando hacia el pasado*.

Multiple Intelligences (interpersonal/linguistic/logical-mathematical/spatial)

In groups of four, students should decide what are the main contributions of the Mayas, Aztecs and Incas. Then have them create posters showing the contributions.

National Standards

Communication
1.1, 1.3

Connections
3.1, 3.2

Comparisons
4.2

Communities
5.1, 5.2

Teacher Resources

 *Trabalenguas*

 Episode 10, DVD 1, Track 34

Answers

Resolviendo el misterio

1. Answers will vary.
2. Answers will vary.
3. Answers will vary.

Activities

Expansion

Review adjective-noun agreement by having students write a composition describing a favorite relative. The composition should address the subject's personality, appearance and typical activities. Encourage students to include a photo or drawing of the relative as well.

Trabalenguas

Ask students to answer the following questions in complete sentences. *¿Quién pide permiso para partir para París? ¿Para qué quiere partir para Paris? ¿Qué parece Pedro Pérez?*

National Standards

Communication
1.3

Connections
3.1, 3.2

Now that I have completed this chapter, I can...	Go to these pages for help:
discuss past actions and events.	412
talk about everyday activities.	412
express emotion.	418
indicate wishes and preferences.	418
write about past actions.	418
make polite requests.	418
talk about the future.	421
describe personal characteristics.	426
I can also...	
talk about Peru and Guatemala.	413, 419
research a topic in the library and on the Internet.	413
name some personal benefits to learning Spanish.	413
recognize some benefits to reviewing what I have already learned.	414
recognize the importance of reviewing what I have learned.	414
talk about Machu Picchu and Chichicastenango.	416, 422
identify some careers that use Spanish.	421
express myself artistically about what I have learned.	426

Trabalenguas

Pedro Pérez pide permiso para partir para París, para ponerse peluca postiza porque parece puerco pelado.

Resolviendo el misterio

After watching Episode 10 of *El cuarto misterioso*, answer the following questions.

1. Who do you think took the suitcase from the mysterious room?
2. Do you think that the police will be able to help José?
3. What explanation do you think that don Pedro will give about the gold mask and map that were in the suitcase?

Notes

Students can find out more about Peru by visiting these Web sites:

Organization of American States
http://www.oas.org
Peru Gateway
http://www.peru-explorer.com
PromPerú http://www.peru.org.pe

General information
http://www.expedia.com

Loose translation of the *Trabalenguas:* Pedro Pérez asks for permission to leave for Paris, to get a wig since he looks like a hairless pig.

El Angelito, México, D.F.

Go online EMCLanguages.net

Café de Colombia.

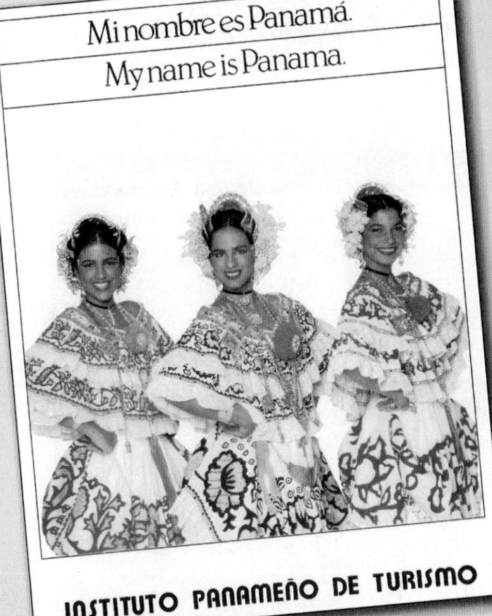
¡Vamos a esquiar!

Mi nombre es Panamá.
My name is Panama.

INSTITUTO PANAMEÑO DE TURISMO

El Morro, San Juan, Puerto Rico.

Teacher Resources

 *Las aventuras de la familia Miranda*

 Repaso

 *¡Aventureros!*, Ch. 10

 Internet Activities

 i-Culture

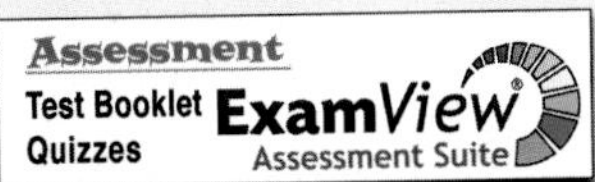

Activities

Communities
Ask students if they know people who use a foreign language in their professions. Encourage students to interview these individuals and share their findings with the class.

Expansion
Ask students personalized questions that require them to practice forms of *tener que* (they may make up any answers they wish): *¿Qué tienes que hacer hoy?; ¿Qué tienes que hacer mañana?; ¿Qué tienes que hacer este fin de semana?*

Spanish for Spanish Speakers
Have students write a short composition in Spanish summarizing what they know about Peru. Expand the activity by having students seek out additional information about the country on the Internet and at the library.

National Standards	
Communication 1.1, 1.3	**Communities** 5.1
Cultures 2.2	
Connections 3.1, 3.2	

Notes Students can find out more about Guatemala by visiting these Web sites:

Organization of American States
http://www.oas.org
Visita Guatemala
http://www.terra.com.gt/turismogt/
General information
http://www.expedia.com/

Appendices

Appendix A

Grammar Review

Definite articles

	Singular	Plural
Masculine	el	los
Feminine	la	las

Indefinite articles

	Singular	Plural
Masculine	un	unos
Feminine	una	unas

Adjective/noun agreement

	Singular	Plural
Masculine	El chico es alto.	Los chicos son altos.
Feminine	La chica es alta.	Las chicas son altas.

Pronouns

Singular	Subject	Direct object	Indirect object	Object of preposition
1st person	yo	me	me	mí
2nd person	tú Ud.	te lo/la	te le	ti Ud.
3rd person	él ella	lo la	le le	él ella
Plural				
1st person	nosotros nosotras	nos nos	nos nos	nosotros nosotras
2nd person	vosotros vosotras	os os	os os	vosotros vosotras
3rd person	Uds. ellos ellas	los/las los las	les les les	Uds. ellos ellas

Interrogatives

qué	what
cómo	how
dónde	where
cuándo	when
cuánto, -a, -os, -as	how much, how many
cuál/cuáles	which (one)
quién/quiénes	who, whom
por qué	why
para qué	why, what for

Demonstrative adjectives

Singular		Plural	
Masculine	**Feminine**	**Masculine**	**Feminine**
este	esta	estos	estas
ese	esa	esos	esas
aquel	aquella	aquellos	aquellas

Possessive adjectives

Singular	Singular nouns	Plural nouns
1st person	mi hermano mi hermana	mis hermanos mis hermanas
2nd person	tu hermano tu hermana	tus hermanos tus hermanas
3rd person	su hermano su hermana	sus hermanos sus hermanas
Singular	Singular nouns	Plural nouns
1st person	nuestro hermano nuestra hermana	nuestros hermanos nuestras hermanas
2nd person	vuestro hermano vuestra hermana	vuestros hermanos vuestras hermanas
3rd person	su hermano su hermana	sus hermanos sus hermanas

Appendix B

Verbs

Present tense (indicative)

Regular present tense		
hablar ***(to speak)***	hablo hablas habla	hablamos habláis hablan
comer ***(to eat)***	como comes come	comemos coméis comen
escribir ***(to write)***	escribo escribes escribe	escribimos escribís escriben

Preterite tense (indicative)

hablar ***(to speak)***	hablé hablaste habló	hablamos hablasteis hablaron
comer ***(to eat)***	comí comiste comió	comimos comisteis comieron
escribir ***(to write)***	escribí escribiste escribió	escribimos escribisteis escribieron

Present participle

The present participle is formed by replacing the *-ar* of the infinitive with *-ando* and the *-er* or *-ir* with *-iendo.*

hablar	hablando
comer	comiendo
vivir	viviendo

Progressive tenses

The present participle is used with the verbs *estar, continuar, seguir, andar* and some other motion verbs to produce the progressive tenses. They are reserved for recounting actions that are or were in progress at the time in question.

432

Present tense of stem-changing verbs

Stem-changing verbs are identified in this book by the presence of vowels in parentheses after the infinitive. If these verbs end in *-ar* or *-er*, they have only one change. If they end in *-ir*, they have two changes. The stem change of *-ar* and *-er* verbs and the first stem change of *-ir* verbs occur in all forms of the present tense, except *nosotros* and *vosotros*.

cerrar (ie) *(to close)*	e → ie	cierro cierras cierra	cerramos cerráis cierran

Verbs like **cerrar:** calentar *(to heat)*, comenzar *(to begin)*, despertar *(to wake up)*, despertarse *(to awaken)*, empezar *(to begin)*, encerrar *(to lock up)*, nevar *(to snow)*, pensar *(to think)*, recomendar *(to recommend)*, sentarse *(to sit down)*

contar (ue) *(to tell)*	o→ ue	cuento cuentas cuenta	contamos contáis cuentan

Verbs like **contar:** acordar *(to agree)*, acordarse *(to remember)*, almorzar *(to have lunch)*, colgar *(to hang)*, costar *(to cost)*, demostrar *(to demonstrate)*, encontrar *(to find, to meet someone)*, probar *(to taste, to try)*, recordar *(to remember)*

jugar (ue) *(to play)*	u → ue	juego juegas juega	jugamos jugáis juegan

perder (ie) *(to lose)*	e → ie	pierdo pierdes pierde	perdemos perdéis pierden

Verbs like **perder:** defender *(to defend)*, descender *(to descend, to go down)*, encender *(to light, to turn on)*, entender *(to understand)*, extender *(to extend)*, tender *(to spread out)*

volver (ue) *(to return)*	o → ue	vuelvo vuelves vuelve	volvemos volvéis vuelven

Verbs like **volver:** devolver *(to return something)*, doler *(to hurt)*, llover *(to rain)*, morder *(to bite)*, mover *(to move)*, resolver *(to resolve)*, soler *(to be in the habit of)*, torcer *(to twist)*

pedir (i, i) *(to ask for)*	e → i	pido pides pide	pedimos pedís piden

Verbs like **pedir:** conseguir *(to obtain, to attain, to get)*, despedirse *(to say good-bye)*, elegir *(to choose, to elect)*, medir *(to measure)*, perseguir *(to pursue)*, repetir *(to repeat)*

433

sentir (ie, i) *(to feel)*	e → ie	siento sientes siente	sentimos sentís sienten

Verbs like **sentir:** advertir *(to warn)*, arrepentirse *(to regret)*, convertir *(to convert)*, convertirse *(to become)*, divertirse *(to have fun)*, herir *(to wound)*, invertir *(to invest)*, mentir *(to lie)*, preferir *(to prefer)*, requerir *(to require)*, sugerir *(to suggest)*

dormir (ue, u) *(to sleep)*	o → ue	duermo duermes duerme	dormimos dormís duermen

Another verb like **dormir**: morir *(to die)*

Present participle of stem-changing verbs

Stem-changing verbs that end in *-ir* use the second stem change in the present participle.

dormir (ue, u)	durmiendo
seguir (i, i)	siguiendo
sentir (ie, i)	sintiendo

Preterite tense of stem-changing verbs

Stem-changing verbs that end in *-ar* and *-er* are regular in the preterite tense. That is, they do not require a spelling change, and they use the regular preterite endings.

pensar (ie)	
pensé	pensamos
pensaste	pensasteis
pensó	pensaron

volver (ue)	
volví	volvimos
volviste	volvisteis
volvió	volvieron

Stem-changing verbs ending in *-ir* change their third-person forms in the preterite tense, but they still require the regular preterite endings.

sentir (ie, i)	
sentí	sentimos
sentiste	sentisteis
sintió	sintieron

dormir (ue, u)	
dormí	dormimos
dormiste	dormisteis
durmió	durmieron

Verbs with irregularities

The following charts provide some frequently used Spanish verbs with irregularities.

buscar (to look for)	
preterite	busqué, buscaste, buscó, buscamos, buscasteis, buscaron
Similar to:	explicar *(to explain)*, sacar *(to take out)*, tocar *(to touch, to play an instrument)*

dar (to give)	
present	doy, das, da, damos, dais, dan
preterite	di, diste, dio, dimos, disteis, dieron

434

decir *(to say, to tell)*	
present	digo, dices, dice, decimos, decís, dicen
preterite	dije, dijiste, dijo, dijimos, dijisteis, dijeron
present participle	diciendo

enviar *(to send)*	
present	envío, envías, envía, enviamos, enviáis, envían
Similar to:	esquiar *(to ski)*

estar *(to be)*	
present	estoy, estás, está, estamos, estáis, están
preterite	estuve, estuviste, estuvo, estuvimos, estuvisteis, estuvieron

hacer *(to do, to make)*	
present	hago, haces, hace, hacemos, hacéis, hacen
preterite	hice, hiciste, hizo, hicimos, hicisteis, hicieron

ir *(to go)*	
present	voy, vas, va, vamos, vais, van
preterite	fui, fuiste, fue, fuimos, fuisteis, fueron
present participle	yendo

leer *(to read)*	
preterite	leí, leíste, leyó, leímos, leísteis, leyeron
present participle	leyendo

llegar *(to arrive)*	
preterite	llegué, llegaste, llegó, llegamos, llegasteis, llegaron
Similar to:	colgar *(to hang)*, pagar *(to pay)*

oír *(to hear, to listen)*	
present	oigo, oyes, oye, oímos, oís, oyen
preterite	oí, oíste, oyó, oímos, oísteis, oyeron
present participle	oyendo

poder *(to be able)*	
present	puedo, puedes, puede, podemos, podéis, pueden
preterite	pude, pudiste, pudo, pudimos, pudisteis, pudieron
present participle	pudiendo

poner *(to put, to place, to set)*	
present	pongo, pones, pone, ponemos, ponéis, ponen
preterite	puse, pusiste, puso, pusimos, pusisteis, pusieron

435

querer *(to love, to want)*	
present	quiero, quieres, quiere, queremos, queréis, quieren
preterite	quise, quisiste, quiso, quisimos, quisisteis, quisieron

saber *(to know)*	
present	sé, sabes, sabe, sabemos, sabéis, saben
preterite	supe, supiste, supo, supimos, supisteis, supieron

salir *(to go out, to leave)*	
present	salgo, sales, sale, salimos, salís, salen

ser *(to be)*	
present	soy, eres, es, somos, sois, son
preterite	fui, fuiste, fue, fuimos, fuisteis, fueron

tener *(to have)*	
present	tengo, tienes, tiene, tenemos, tenéis, tienen
preterite	tuve, tuviste, tuvo, tuvimos, tuvisteis, tuvieron

traer *(to bring)*	
present	traigo, traes, trae, traemos, traéis, traen
preterite	traje, trajiste, trajo, trajimos, trajisteis, trajeron
present participle	trayendo

venir *(to come)*	
present	vengo, vienes, viene, venimos, venís, vienen
preterite	vine, viniste, vino, vinimos, vinisteis, vinieron
present participle	viniendo

ver *(to see, to watch)*	
present	veo, ves, ve, vemos, veis, ven
preterite	vi, viste, vio, vimos, visteis, vieron

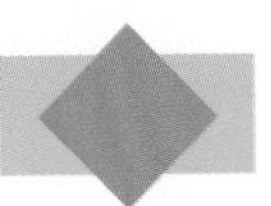

Appendix C

Numbers

Cardinal numbers 0–1.000

0—cero	13—trece	26—veintiséis	90—noventa
1—uno	14—catorce	27—veintisiete	100—cien/ciento
2—dos	15—quince	28—veintiocho	200—doscientos,-as
3—tres	16—dieciséis	29—veintinueve	300—trescientos,-as
4—cuatro	17—diecisiete	30—treinta	400—cuatrocientos,-as
5—cinco	18—dieciocho	31—treinta y uno	500—quinientos,-as
6—seis	19—diecinueve	32—treinta y dos	600—seiscientos,-as
7—siete	20—veinte	33—treinta y tres, etc.	700—setecientos,-as
8—ocho	21—veintiuno	40—cuarenta	800—ochocientos,-as
9—nueve	22—veintidós	50—cincuenta	900—novecientos,-as
10—diez	23—veintitrés	60—sesenta	1.000—mil
11—once	24—veinticuatro	70—setenta	
12—doce	25—veinticinco	80—ochenta	

Ordinal numbers

1—primero,-a (primer)	6—sexto,-a
2—segundo,-a	7—séptimo,-a
3—tercero,-a (tercer)	8—octavo,-a
4—cuarto,-a	9—noveno,-a
5—quinto,-a	10—décimo,-a

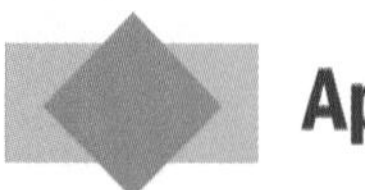

Appendix D

Syllabification

Spanish vowels may be weak or strong. The vowels *a*, *e* and *o* are strong, whereas *i* (and sometimes *y*) and *u* are weak. The combination of one weak and one strong vowel or of two weak vowels produces a diphthong, two vowels pronounced as one.

A word in Spanish has as many syllables as it has vowels or diphthongs.

al-gu-nas
lue-go
pa-la-bra

A single consonant (including *ch, ll, rr*) between two vowels accompanies the second vowel and begins a syllable.

a-mi-ga
fa-vo-ri-to
mu-cho

Two consonants are divided, the first going with the previous vowel and the second going with the following vowel.

an-tes
quin-ce
ter-mi-nar

A consonant plus *l* or *r* is inseparable except for *rl, sl* and *sr*.

ma-dre
pa-la-bra
com-ple-tar
Car-los
is-la

If three consonants occur together, the last, or any inseparable combination, accompanies the following vowel to begin another syllable.

es-cri-bir
som-bre-ro
trans-por-te

Prefixes should remain intact.

re-es-cri-bir

Appendix E

Accentuation

Words that end in *a, e, i, o, u, n* or *s* are pronounced with the major stress on the next-to-the-last syllable. No accent mark is needed to show this emphasis.

octubre
refresco
señora

Words that end in any consonant except *n* or *s* are pronounced with the major stress on the last syllable. No accent mark is needed to show this emphasis.

escribir
papel
reloj

Words that are not pronounced according to the above two rules must have a written accent mark.

lógico
canción
después
lápiz

An accent mark may be necessary to distinguish identical words with different meanings.

dé/de
qué/que
sí/si
sólo/solo

An accent mark is often used to divide a diphthong into two separate syllables.

día
frío
Raúl

439

Vocabulary Spanish / English

All active words introduced in *EMC Español 1, ¡Aventura!* appear in this end vocabulary. The number and letter following an entry indicate the lesson in which an item is first actively used. Additional words and expressions are included for reference and have no number. Obvious cognates and expressions that occur as passive vocabulary for recognition only have been excluded from this end vocabulary.

Abbreviations:
d.o. direct object
f. feminine
i.o. indirect object
m. masculine
pl. plural
s. singular

A

a to, at, in *2B; a caballo* on horseback *3A; a crédito* on credit *9B; a pie* on foot *3A; a propósito* by the way *1A; ¿a qué hora?* at what time? *2B; a veces* sometimes, at times *5B; a ver* let's see, hello (telephone greeting)
abierto,-a open *4A*
abran: see *abrir*
el **abrazo** hug *6B*
abre: see *abrir*
la **abreviatura** abbreviation
el **abrigo** coat *8A*
abril April *5B*
abrir to open *5A; abran* (*Uds.* command) open; *abre* (*tú* command) open
la **abuela** grandmother *4A*
el **abuelo** grandfather *4A*
aburrido,-a bored, boring *4B*
acabar to finish, to complete, to terminate *8A; acabar de* (+ infinitive) to have just *8A*
el **aceite** oil *6A*
la **aceituna** olive
el **acento** accent *1A*
la **acentuación** accentuation
aclarar to make clear, to explain
la **actividad** activity *5A*, exercise
el **acuerdo** accord; *de acuerdo* agreed, okay *3B*
adiós good-bye *1A*
el **adjetivo** adjective; *adjetivo posesivo* possessive adjective
¿adónde? (to) where? *3A*
adoptar to adopt
adornar to decorate *8A*
el **adverbio** adverb
los **aeróbicos** aerobics *7A*
el **aeropuerto** airport
la **agencia** agency; *agencia de viajes* travel agency
agosto August *5B*
el **agricultor** farmer
el **agua** *f.* water *3B; agua mineral* mineral water *3B*
el **aguacate** avocado *8B*
ahora now *3B; ahora mismo* right now *7A*
ahorrar to save *9B*
el **ajedrez** chess *7A*
el **ajo** garlic *8B*
al to the *3A; al lado de* next to, beside *6B*
alegre happy, merry, lively
el **alfabeto** alphabet
el **álgebra** algebra
algo something, anything *8A*
el **algodón** cotton *9A*
alguien someone, anyone, somebody, anybody *9A*
algún, alguna some, any *9A*
alguno,-a some, any *9A*
allá over there *6A*
allí there *2B*
la **almeja** clam
el **almuerzo** lunch *2B*
aló hello (telephone greeting) *2B*
alquilar to rent *7A*
alterna alternate (*tú* command)
alternen alternate (*Uds.* command)
alto,-a tall, high *4B*
amable kind, nice *4A*
amarillo,-a yellow *2B*
ambiguo,-a ambiguous
la **América** America; *América Central* Central America; *América del Sur* South America
americano,-a American *7A; el fútbol americano* football *7A*
el **amigo,** la **amiga** friend *2A; amigo/a por correspondencia* pen pal
el **amor** love *5A*
anaranjado,-a orange (color) *9A*
andino,-a Andean, of the Andes Mountains
el **anillo** ring *9B*
anteayer the day before yesterday *5B*
anterior preceding
antes de before *7A*
añade: see *añadir*
añadir to add *8B; añade* (*tú* command) add
el **año** year *5B; Año Nuevo* New Year's Day *5B; ¿Cuántos años tienes?* How old are you? *1A; tener* (+ number) *años* to be (+ number) years old *5A*
apagar to turn off *7A*
el **apartamento** apartment

el **apellido** last name, surname
el **apodo** nickname
aprender to learn
apropiado,-a appropriate
apunta: see *apuntar*
apuntar to point; *apunta* (*tú* command) point (at); *apunten* (*Uds.* command) point (at)
apunten: see *apuntar*
apurado,-a in a hurry *4A*
aquel, aquella that (far away) *6A*
aquellos, aquellas those (far away) *6A*
aquí here *1A; Aquí se habla español.* Spanish is spoken here.
el **árbol** tree; *árbol genealógico* family tree
el **arete** earring *9B*
la **Argentina** Argentina *1A*
arreglar to arrange, to straighten, to fix *8A*
arroba (@) at *(the symbol (@) used for e-mail addresses) 2B*
el **arroz** rice *8B*
el **arte** art *2B*
el **artesanía** handicrafts, artisanry
el **artículo** article *5A*
el **artista** artist
el **ascensor** elevator *9B*
la **asignatura** subject
la **aspiradora** vacuum *7A; pasar la aspiradora* to vacuum *8A*
el **Atlántico** Atlantic Ocean
la **atracción** attraction
aunque although
el **autobús** bus *3A*
la **avenida** avenue *3B*
aventurero,-a adventurous
el **avión** airplane *3A*
¡ay! oh! *2A*
ayer yesterday *5B*
la **ayuda** help
ayudar to help *6A*
el **azafrán** saffron
los **aztecas** Aztecs
el **azúcar** sugar *6A*
azul blue *2B*

bailar to dace *4B*
bajo,-a short (not tall), low *4B; planta baja* floor level *6B*
balanceado,-a balanced
el **baloncesto** basketball
el **banco** bank *3A*
el **baño** bathroom *6B; traje de baño* swimsuit *9A*
barato,-a cheap *9B*
el **barco** boat, ship *3A*
barrer to sweep *8A*
el **barril** barrel
basado,-a based
el **básquetbol** basketball *7A*
el **basquetbolista, la basquetbolista** basketball player *7B*
bastante rather, fairly, sufficiently; enough, sufficient *9B*
la **basura** garbage *8A*
la **bebida** drink
el **béisbol** baseball *4B*
la **biblioteca** library *3A*
la **bicicleta** bicycle, bike *3A*
bien well *1B*
bienvenido,-a welcome
la **billetera** wallet *9B*
la **biología** biology *2B*
blanco,-a white *2B*
la **blusa** blouse *2B*
la **boda** wedding
el **bolígrafo** pen *2A*
Bolivia Bolivia *1A*
el **bolo** ball; *jugar a los bolos* to bowl
el **bolso** handbag, purse *9B*
bonito,-a pretty, good-looking, attractive *4A*
borra: see *borrar*
el **borrador** eraser *2A*
borrar to erase; *borra* (*tú* command) erase; *borren* (*Uds.* command) erase
borren: see *borrar*
la **bota** boot *9A*
el **brazo** arm *9A*
buen good (form of *bueno* before a *m., s.* noun) *7B*
bueno well, okay (pause in speech) *3B;* hello (telephone greeting)
bueno,-a good *4B; buena suerte* good luck; *buenas noches* good night *1B; buenas tardes* good afternoon *1B; buenos días* good morning *1B*
la **bufanda** scarf *9B*
buscar to look for *5A*

el **caballero** gentleman
el **caballo** horse *3A; a caballo* on horseback *3A*
la **cabeza** head *9A*
cada each, every *5A*
el **café** coffee *8B*
la **cafetería** cafeteria
la **caja** cashier's desk *9B*
el **calcetín** sock *2B*
el **calendario** calendar
la **calidad** quality *9B*
caliente hot *4A*
la **calle** street *3B*
el **calor** heat *6B; hace calor* it is hot *7B; tener calor* to be hot *6B*
calvo,-a bald *4B*
la **cama** bed *8A*
el **camarón** shrimp
cambiar to change, to exchange *9B*
el **cambio** change *9B; en cambio* on the other hand *7B*
caminar to walk *3A*
el **camión** truck *3A*; bus (Mexico); *en camión* by truck *3A*
la **camisa** shirt *2B*
la **camiseta** jersey, polo, t-shirt *2B*
la **canción** song *5A*
canoso,-a white-haired *4B*
cansado,-a tired *4A*
el **cantante,** la **cantante** singer *3B*
cantar to sing *4B*
la **cantidad** quantity
la **capital** capital *1A*
el **capitán** captain
el **capítulo** chapter
la **cara** face
la **característica** characteristic, trait; *características de personalidad* personality traits; *características físicas* physical traits
¡caramba! wow! *5A*
cariñoso,-a affectionate *4A*
el **carnaval** carnival
la **carne** meat *8B*
caro,-a expensive *9B*
la **carrera** career, race
el **carro** car *3A; en carro* by car *3A*

441

la **carta** letter *6B,* playing card *7A*
la **casa** home, house *4A; en casa* at home
el **casete** cassette *5A*
casi almost *7A*
catorce fourteen *1A*
el **CD** CD (compact disc) *2B*
la **cebolla** onion *8B*
celebrar to celebrate *5B*
el **censo** census
el **centavo** cent
el **centro** downtown, center *3B; centro comercial* shopping center, mall *9A*
cerca (de) near *3A*
cero zero *1A*
cerrado,-a closed *4A*
cerrar (ie) to close *6A; cierra* (*tú* command) close; *cierren (Uds.* command) close
el **cesto de papeles** wastebasket *2A*
chao bye
la **chaqueta** jacket *9A*
charlando talking, chatting
la **chica** girl *2A*
el **chico** boy *2A,* man, buddy
Chile Chile *1A*
el **chisme** gossip *6B*
el **chocolate** chocolate *8B*
el **chorizo** sausage (seasoned with red peppers) *8B*
el **ciclismo** cycling
cien one hundred *1B*
la **ciencia** science
ciento one hundred (when followed by another number) *5B*
cierra: see *cerrar*
cierren: see *cerrar*
cinco five *1A*
cincuenta fifty *1B*
el **cine** movie theater *3A*
el **cinturón** belt *9B*
la **ciudad** city *3A*
la **civilización** civilization
el **clarinete** clarinet
¡claro! of course! *3A*
la **clase** class *2A*
el **clima** climate
el **coche** car; *en coche* by car
la **cocina** kitchen *6A*
cocinar to cook *8A*
el **cognado** cognate
el **colegio** school *2B*
colgar (ue) to hang *8A*
el **collar** necklace *9B*
Colombia Colombia *1A*
la **colonia** colony
el **color** color *2B*
combinar to combine *9A*
el **comedor** dining room *6A*
comer to eat *3B; dar de comer* to feed *8A*
cómico,-a comical, funny *4B*
la **comida** food *3B,* dinner
como like, since, as
¿cómo? how?, what? *1A; ¿Cómo?* What (did you say)? *2B; ¿Cómo está (Ud.)?* How are you (formal)? *1B; ¿Cómo están (Uds.)?* How are you *(pl.)? 1B; ¿Cómo estás (tú)?* How are you (informal)? *1B; ¡Cómo no!* Of course! *3B; ¿Cómo se dice...?* How do you say...? *2A; ¿Cómo se escribe...?* How do you write (spell)...? *1A; ¿Cómo se llama (Ud./él/ella)?* What is (your/his/ her) name? *1A; ¿Cómo te llamas?* What is your name? *2A*
comodidad comfort
cómodo,-a comfortable *6B*
el **compañero,** la **compañera** classmate, partner *5A*
comparando comparing
la **competencia** competition
completa: see *completar*
completar to complete; *completa (tú* command) complete
la **compra** purchase *4B; ir de compras* to go shopping *4B*
comprar to buy *4B*
comprender to understand *2A; comprendo* I understand *2A*
comprendo: see *comprender*
la **computadora** computer (machine) *2B*
la **computación** computer science *2B*
común common
con with *1A; con (mucho) gusto* I would be (very) glad to *1B; con permiso* excuse me (with your permission), may I *1B*
el **concierto** concert *3B*
la **conjunción** conjunction
conmigo with me *9B*
conquistar to conquer
conseguir (i, i) to obtain, to attain, to get
la **contaminación** contamination, pollution; *contaminación ambiental* environmental pollution
contar (ue) to tell (a story) *9A; cuenta* (*tú* command) tell; *cuenten* (*Uds.* command) tell; to count
contento,-a happy, glad *4A; estar contento,-a (con)* to be satisfied (with) *4A*
contesta: see *contestar*
contestar to answer *4B; contesta* (*tú* command) answer; *contesten* (*Uds.* command) answer
contesten: see *contestar*
el **contexto** context
contigo with you (*tú*) *9B*
continúa: see *continuar*
continuar to continue *7B; continúa* (*tú* command) continue; *continúen* (*Uds.* command) continue
continúen: see *continuar*
la **contracción** contraction
el **control remoto** remote control *7A*
copiar to copy *7B*
la **corbata** tie *9A*
correcto,-a right, correct
el **corredor,** la **corredora** runner *7B*
el **correo** mail; *correo electrónico* e-mail *2B*
correr to run *6B*
la **cortesía** courtesy
corto,-a short (not long) *9B*
la **cosa** thing *6A*
la **costa** coast
Costa Rica Costa Rica *1A*
costar (ue) to cost *7A*
crear to create
el **crédito** credit *9B; a crédito* on credit *9B; la tarjeta de crédito* credit card *9B*
creer to believe
el **crucero** cruise ship
cruzar to cross
el **cuaderno** notebook *2A*
¿cuál? which?, what?, which

one? *(pl. ¿cuáles?)* which ones? *2B*

la **cualidad** quality

cualquier any

cuando when *6B*

¿cuándo? when? *3A*

¿cuánto,-a? how much? *2B* *(pl. ¿cuántos,-as?)* how many? *2B; ¿Cuántos años tienes?* How old are you? *1A; ¿Cuánto* (+ time expression) *hace que* (+ present tense of verb)...? How long...? *7A*

cuarenta forty *1B*

el **cuarto** quarter *1B,* room, bedroom *6B; cuarto de baño* bathroom; *menos cuarto* a quarter to, a quarter before *1B; y cuarto* a quarter after, a quarter past *1B*

cuarto,-a fourth *7B*

cuatro four *1A*

cuatrocientos,-as four hundred *5B*

Cuba Cuba *1A*

los **cubiertos** silverware *6A*

la **cuchara** tablespoon *6A*

la **cucharita** teaspoon *6A*

el **cuchillo** knife *6A*

cuenta: see *contar*

cuenten: see *contar*

el **cuero** leather *9B*

el **cuerpo** body *9A*

cuidar to take care of

el **cumpleaños** birthday *5B; ¡Feliz cumpleaños!* Happy birthday! *5B*

cumplir to become, to become (+ number) years old, to reach *5B; cumplir años* to have a birthday *5B*

la **dama** lady

las **damas** checkers *7A*

dar to give *7A; dar de comer* to feed *8A; dar un paseo* to go for a walk, to go for a ride *7B; dé* (*Ud.* command) give

de from, of *1A; de acuerdo* agreed, okay *3B; ¿de dónde?* from where? *1A; ¿De dónde eres?* Where are you from? *1A; de la mañana* in the morning, A.M. *1B; de la noche* at night, P.M. *1B; de la tarde* in the afternoon, P.M. *1B; de nada* you are welcome, not at all *1B; de todos los días* everyday *6A; ¿de veras?* really? *5B; ¿Eres (tú) de...?* Are you from...? *1A*

dé: see *dar*

deber should, to have to, must, ought (expressing a moral duty) *6A*

décimo,-a tenth *7B*

decir to tell, to say *6B; ¿Cómo se dice...?* How do you say...? *2A; di* (*tú* command) say, tell; *díganme* (*Uds.* command) tell me; *dime* (*tú* command) tell me; *¿Qué quiere decir...?* What is the meaning (of)...? *2A; querer decir* to mean *6B; quiere decir* it means *2A; se dice* one says *2A*

el **dedo** finger, toe *9A*

dejar to leave *8A*

del of the, from the *3A*

delgado,-a thin *4B*

demasiado too (much) *9B*

la **democracia** democracy

el **dentista,** la **dentista** dentist *3A*

el **departamento** department *9A*

el **dependiente,** la **dependienta** clerk *9B*

el **deporte** sport *5A*

el **deportista,** la **deportista** athlete *7B*

desaparecido,-a missing

el **desastre** disaster

el **desayuno** breakfast

describe *(tú* command) describe

descubrir to discover

desde since, from *6B*

desear to wish

el **deseo** wish

la **despedida** farewell

después afterwards, later, then *6A; después de* after *7A*

di: see *decir*

el **día** day *2B; buenos días* good morning *1B; de todos los días* everyday *5A; todos los días* every day *5A*

el **diálogo** dialog

diario,-a daily

dibuja: see *dibujar*

dibujar to draw, to sketch *7A; dibuja* (*tú* command) draw; *dibujen* (*Uds.* command) draw

dibujen: see *dibujar*

el **dibujo** drawing, sketch *6B*

diciembre December *5B*

el **dictado** dictation

diecinueve nineteen *1A*

dieciocho eighteen *1A*

dieciséis sixteen *1A*

diecisiete seventeen *1A*

diez ten *1A*

la **diferencia** difference

diferente different

difícil difficult, hard *4B*

diga hello (telephone greeting)

dígame tell me, hello (telephone greeting)

díganme: see *decir*

dime: see *decir*

el **dinero** money *5A*

la **dirección** address *2B; dirección de correo electrónico* e-mail *2B*

el **director,** la **directora** director

dirigir to direct

el **disco** disc *2B; disco compacto (CD)* compact disk *2B*

disfrutar to enjoy

diskette diskette *2B*

divertido,-a fun *4A*

doblar to fold *8A*

doce twelve *1A*

el **doctor,** la **doctora** doctor

el **dólar** dollar

domingo Sunday *2B; el domingo* on Sunday

don title of respect used before a man's first name

donde where *6B*

¿dónde? where? *1A*

doña title of respect used before a woman's first name

dormir (ue, u) to sleep *7A*

dos two *1A*

doscientos,-as two hundred *5B*

Dr. abbreviation for *doctor*

Dra. abbreviation for *doctora*

durante during

el **DVD** DVD (digital video disc) *5A; el reproductor de DVDs* DVD player *5A*

e and (used before a word beginning with *i* or *hi*) *6B*
la **ecología** ecology
el **Ecuador** Ecuador *1A*
la **edad** age
el **edificio** building *3B*
la **educación física** physical education
el **efectivo** cash *9B; en efectivo* in cash *9B*
egoísta selfish *4B*
el **ejemplo** example*; por ejemplo* for example
el the *(m., s.) 2A*
él he *2A;* him (after a preposition) *4B; Él se llama....* His name is.... *2A*
eléctrico,-a electric
electrónico,-a electronic *2B*
El Salvador El Salvador *1A*
ella she *2A;* her (after a preposition) *4B; Ella se llama....* Her name is.... *2A*
ellos,-as they *2A;* them (after a preposition) *4B*
empatados: see *empate*
el **empate** tie; *los partidos empatados* games tied
empezar (ie) to begin, to start *6A*
en in, on, at *2A; en* (+ vehicle) by (+ vehicle) *3A; en cambio* on the other hand *7B; en casa* at home*; en efectivo* in cash *9B; en resumen* in short
encantado,-a delighted, the pleasure is mine *3A*
encender (ie) to light, to turn on (a light) *6A*
encontrar (ue) to find
la **encuesta** survey, poll
enero January *5B*
el **énfasis** emphasis
el **enfermero,** la **enfermera** nurse
enfermo,-a sick *4A*
la **ensalada** salad *3B*
enseñar to teach, to show
entero,-a whole
entonces then *6A*
entrar to go in, to come in *5A*
entre between, among
la **entrevista** interview
enviar to send *7B*
el **equipo** team *7A; equipo de sonido* sound system, stereo *5A*
equivocado mistaken; *número equivocado* wrong number *2B*
eres: see *ser*
es: see *ser*
escalar to climb
la **escalera** stairway, stairs *6B; escalera mecánica* escalator *9B*
la **escena** scene
escoger to choose *8B; escogiendo* choosing
escogiendo: see *escoger*
escriban: see *escribir*
escribe: see *escribir*
escribir to write *6B; ¿Cómo se escribe...?* How do you write (spell)...? *1A; escriban* (*Uds.* command) write; *escribe* (*tú* command) write; *se escribe* it is written *1A*
el **escritorio** desk *2A*
escucha: see *escuchar*
escuchar to listen (to) *4B; escucha* (*tú* command) listen; *escuchen* (*Uds.* command) listen
escuchen: see *escuchar*
la **escuela** school *3A*
ese, esa that *6A*
eso that (neuter form)
esos, esas those *6A*
el **espacio** space
España Spain *1A*
el **español** Spanish (language) *2B*
español, española Spanish
especial special *6A*
especializado,-a specialized
el **espectáculo** showcase
la **esposa** wife, spouse *4A*
el **esposo** husband, spouse *4A*
el **esquiador,** la **esquiadora** skier *7B*
esquiar to ski *7B*
está: see *estar*
establecieron settled down
la **estación** season *7B*
el **estadio** stadium
el **Estado Libre Asociado** Commonwealth
los **Estados Unidos (EE.UU.)** United States of America *1A*
están: see *estar*
estar to be *2B;¿Cómo está (Ud.)?* How are you (formal)? *1B; ¿Cómo están (Uds.)?* How are you (pl.)? *1B; ¿Cómo estás (tú)?* How are are you (informal)? *1B; está nublado,-a* it's cloudy *7B; está soleado,-a* it's sunny *7B; están* they are *1B; estar contento,-a (con)* to be satisfied (with) *4A; estar en oferta* to be on sale *9B; estar listo,-a* to be ready *7B; estás* you (informal) are *1B; estoy* I am *1B*
estás: see *estar*
este well, so (pause in speech)
este, esta this *6A; esta noche* tonight *7A*
el **estéreo** stereo
estos, estas these *6A*
estoy: see *estar*
la **estructura** structure
estudia: see *estudiar*
el **estudiante,** la **estudiante** student *2A*
estudiar to study *2B; estudia* (*tú* command) study; *estudien* (*Uds.* command) study
estudien: see *estudiar*
el **estudio** study
la **estufa** stove *6A*
estupendo,-a wonderful, marvellous *7A*
el **examen** exam, test *2B*
excelente excellent *7B*
el **éxito** success
explica: see *explicar*
la **explicación** explanation
explicar to explain; *explica* (*tú* command) explain
el **explorador,** la **exploradora** explorer
la **exportación** exportation
el **exportador,** la **exportadora** exporter
expresar to express
la **expresión** expression
la **extensión** extension

fácil easy *4B*
la **falda** skirt *2B*
falso,-a false
la **familia** family *4A*
famoso,-a famous
fantástico,-a fantastic, great *3A*

444

el **favor** favor; *por favor* please *1B*
favorito,-a favorite *3B*
febrero February *5B*
la **fecha** date *5B*
felicitaciones congratulations
feliz happy *(pl. felices) 5B; ¡Feliz cumpleaños!* Happy birthday! *5B*
femenino,-a feminine
feo,-a ugly *4B*
el **ferrocarril** railway, railroad
la **fiesta** party *3A*
la **filosofía** philosophy
el **fin** end *5A; fin de semana* weekend *5A*
la **física** physics *6A*
la **flauta** flute
la **flor** flower *7B*
la **florcita** small flower
la **forma** form
la **foto(grafía)** photo *4A*
la **frase** phrase, sentence
el **fregadero** sink *6A*
la **fresa** strawberry *8B*
el **fresco** cool *7B; hace fresco* it is cool *7B*
fresco,-a fresh, chilly *8B*
los **frijoles** beans *3B*
el **frío** cold *4A; hace frío* it is cold *7B; tener frío* to be cold *6B*
frío,-a cold *4A*
la **fruta** fruit *8B*
fue: see *ser*
fuerte strong
el **fútbol** soccer *4B; fútbol americano* football *7A*
el **futbolista,** la **futbolista** soccer player *7B*
el **futuro** future

G

la **gana** desire *6B; tener ganas de* to feel like *6B*
ganados: see *ganar*
ganar to win; *los partidos ganados* games won
el **garaje** garage *6B*
el **gato,** la **gata** cat *5A*
el **género** gender
generoso,-a generous *4B*
la **gente** people *8A*
la **geografía** geography
la **geometría** geometry
el **gerundio** present participle
el **gesto** gesture
el **gimnasio** gym
la **gira** tour
el **gobernador,** la **gobernadora** governor
gordo,-a fat *4B*
la **grabadora** tape recorder *5A*
gracias thanks *1B; muchas gracias* thank you very much *1B*
el **grado** degree *7B*
gran big (form of *grande* before a *m., s.* noun)
grande big *3B*
gris gray *2B*
el **grupo** group; *grupo musical* musical group
el **guante** glove *9A*
guapo,-a good-looking, attractive, handsome, pretty *4A*
Guatemala Guatemala *1A*
el **guía,** la **guía** guide
Guinea Ecuatorial Equatorial Guinea *1A*
el **guisante** pea *8B*
la **guitarra** guitar
gusta: see *gustar*
gustar to like, to be pleasing to *4B; me/te/le/nos/vos/les gustaría...* I/you/he/she/ it/ we/they would like... *6B*
gustaría: see *gustar*
el **gusto** pleasure, delight, taste *3A; con (mucho) gusto* I would be (very) glad to *1B; el gusto es mío* the pleasure is mine *3A; ¡Mucho gusto!* Glad to meet you! *1A; Tanto gusto.* So glad to meet you. *3A*

H

la **habichuela** green bean *8B*
la **habitación** room, bedroom
el **habitante,** la **habitante** inhabitant
habla: see *hablar*
hablar to speak *2B; habla (tú* command) speak; *hablen (Uds. command)* speak; *Se habla español.* Spanish is spoken.
hablen: see *hablar*
hace: see *hacer*
hacer to do, to make *3B; ¿Cuánto* (+ time expression) *hace que* (+ present tense of verb)...? How long...? *7A; hace buen (mal) tiempo* the weather is nice (bad) *7B; hace fresco* it is cool *7B; hace frío (calor)* it is cold (hot) *7B; hace* (+ time expression) *que* ago *7A; hace sol* it is sunny *7B; hace viento* it is windy *7B; hacer aeróbicos* to do aerobics *7A; hacer falta* to be necessary, to be lacking *8B; hacer un viaje* to take a trip *5A; hacer una pregunta* to ask a question *3B; hagan (Uds.* command) do, make; *haz (tú* command) do, make; *haz el papel* play the part; *hecha* made
hagan: see *hacer*
el **hambre** *f.* hunger *6B; tener hambre* to be hungry *6B*
hasta until, up to, down to *1A; hasta la vista* so long, see you later; *hasta luego* so long, see you later *1A; hasta mañana* see you tomorrow *1B; hasta pronto* see you soon *1B*
hay there is, there are *2A; hay neblina* it is misting *7B; hay sol* it is sunny *7B*
haz: see *hacer*
hecha: see *hacer*
el **helado** ice cream *8B*
la **hermana** sister *4A*
el **hermano** brother *4A*
el **hielo** ice *7B; patinar sobre hielo* to ice skate *7B*
la **hija** daughter *4A*
el **hijo** son *4A*
hispano,-a Hispanic
hispanohablante Spanish-speaking
la **historia** history *2B*
la **hoja** sheet*; hoja de papel* sheet of paper; leaf
hola hi, hello *1A*
el **hombre** man *9A*
Honduras Honduras *1A*
la **hora** hour *1B; ¿a qué hora?* at what time? *2B; ¿Qué hora es?* What time is it? *1B*
el **horario** schedule *2B*
el **horno microondas** microwave oven *6A*
horrible horrible *4B*

el **hotel** hotel *3A*
hoy today *3B*
el **huevo** egg *8B*

la **idea** idea *5B*
ideal ideal *4B*
ignorar to not know
imagina: see *imaginar*
la **imaginación** imagination
imaginar to imagine; *imagina* (*tú* command) imagine
el **impermeable** raincoat *9A*
importante important *4B*
importar to be important, to matter *8B*
la **impresora (láser)** (laser) printer *2B*
los **incas** Incas
incluir to include
indefinido,-a indefinite
la **independencia** independence
indica: see *indicar*
la **indicación** cue
indicado,-a indicated
indicar to indicate; *indica* (*tú* command) indicate
indígena native
el **informe** report
el **inglés** English (language) *2B*
el **ingrediente** ingredient *8B*
inicial initial
inmenso,-a immense
la **inspiración** inspiration
inteligente intelligent *4B*
interesante interesting *4B*
interrogativo,-a interrogative
el **invierno** winter *7B*
la **invitación** invitation
invitar to invite
ir to go *3A; ir a* (+ infinitive) to be going to (do something) *3B; ir de compras* to go shopping *4B; ¡vamos!* let's go! *3A; ¡vamos a* (+ infinitive)! let's (+ infinitive)! *3B; vayan* (*Uds.* command) go to; *ve* (*tú* command) go to
la **isla** island

el **jamón** ham *8B*
el **jardín** garden *8A*
la **jirafa** giraffe
los **jeans** jeans, blue jeans *2B*
joven young *5B*
la **joya** jewel *9B*
el **juego** game
jueves Thursday *2B; el jueves* on Thursday
el **jugador,** la **jugadora** player *7B*
jugar (ue) to play *4B, jugar a* (+ sport/game) *4B*
el **jugo** juice *3B*
julio July *5B*
junio June *5B*
junto,-a together *8A*

el **kilo (kg.)** kilogram *8B*

la the *(f., s.) 2A;* her, it, you *(d.o.) 5A; a la...* at...o'clock *2B*
el **lado** side *6B; al lado (de)* next to, beside *6B; por todos lados* everywhere *7B*
la **lámpara** lamp *6A*
la **lana** wool *9A*
la **langosta** lobster
lanzar to throw
el **lápiz** pencil *(pl. lápices) 2A*
largo,-a long *9B*
las the *(f., pl.) 2A;* them, you *(d.o.) 5A; a las...* at...o'clock *2B*
la **lástima** shame; *¡Qué lástima!* What a shame! *5A*
la **lata** can *8B*
el **lavaplatos** dishwasher *6A*
lavar to wash *8A*
le (to, for) him, (to, for) her, (to, for) it, (to, for) you (formal)*(i.o.) 3A*
lean: see *leer*
la **lección** lesson
la **leche** milk *8A*
la **lechuga** lettuce *8B*
la **lectura** reading
lee: see *leer*
leer to read *3B; lean* (*Uds.* command) read; *lee* (*tú* command) read
lejos (de) far (from) *3A*
la **lengua** language
lento,-a slow *4B*
les (to, for) them, (to, for) you *(pl.)(i.o.) 3A*
la **letra** letter
levantarse to get up, to rise; *levántate* (*tú* command) get up; *levántense* (*Uds.* command) get up
levántate: see *levantarse*
levántense: see *levantarse*
la **libertad** liberty, freedom
la **libra** pound
libre free *4A*
la **librería** bookstore *5A*
el **libro** book *2A*
el **líder** leader
limitar to limit
limpiar to clean *8A*
limpio,-a clean *4A*
lindo,-a pretty *9B*
la **lista** list *7A*
listo,-a ready *7B,* smart *8A; estar listo,-a* to be ready *7B; ser listo,-a* to be smart *8A*
la **literatura** literature
llama: see *llamar*
llamar to call, to telephone *5A; ¿Cómo se llama (Ud./él/ella)?* What is (your/his/her) name? *2A; ¿Cómo te llamas?* What is your name? *1A; llamaron* they called (preterite of *llamar*); *me llamo* my name is *1A; se llaman* their names are; *te llamas* your name is *1A; (Ud./Él/Ella) se llama....* (Your [formal]/His/Her) name is.... *2A*
llamaron: see *llamar*
llamas: see *llamar*
llamo: see *llamar*
llegar to arrive *8A; llegó* arrived (preterite of *llegar*)
llegó: see *llegar*
llevar to wear *2B;* to take, to carry *5A*
llover (ue) to rain *7B*
la **lluvia** rain *7B*
lo him, it, you *(d.o.) 5A; lo que,* that which *6B; lo siento* I am sorry *1B*
loco,-a crazy *4A*
lógicamente logically
lógico,-a logical
los the *(m., pl.) 2A;* them, you *(d.o.) 5A*
luego then, later, soon *1A; hasta luego* so long, see you later *1A*
el **lugar** place *7B*

lunes Monday *2B; el lunes* on Monday
la **luz** light *(pl. luces) 6A*

la **madrastra** stepmother
la **madre** mother *4A*
maduro,-a ripe *8B*
el **maestro** teacher, master; *La práctica hace al maestro.* Practice makes perfect.
el **maíz** corn *8B*
mal badly *1B;* bad *7B*
la **maleta** suitcase *5A*
malo,-a bad *4B*
la **mamá** mother, mom
la **manera** manner, way
la **mano** hand *9A*
el **mantel** tablecloth *6A*
la **mantequilla** butter *6A*
la **manzana** apple *8B*
mañana tomorrow *1B; hasta mañana* see you tomorrow *1B; pasado mañana* the day after tomorrow *5B*
la **mañana** morning *1B; de la mañana* A.M., in the morning *1B; por la mañana* in the morning *7A*
el **mapa** map *2A*
la **maravilla** wonder, marvel
mariachi popular Mexican music and orchestra
el **marisco** seafood, shellfish
marrón brown *9A*
martes Tuesday *2B; el martes* on Tuesday
marzo March *5B*
más more, else *4A; el/la/los/las* (+ noun) *más* (+ adjective) the most (+ adjective) *8B; lo más* (+ adverb) *posible* as (+ adverb + noun) as possible *8B; más* (+ noun/ adjective/ adverb) *que* more (+ noun/ adjective/adverb) than *8B*
masculino,-a masculine
las **matemáticas** mathematics *2B*
el **material** material *9B*
máximo,-a maximum *7B*
maya Mayan
los **mayas** Mayans
mayo May *5B*
mayor older, oldest *5B,* greater, greatest *8B*
la **mayúscula** capital letter *1A*
me (to, for) me *(i.o.) 4B;* me *(d.o.) 5A; me llaman* they call me; *me llamo* my name is *1A*
mecánico,-a mechanic *9B; la escalera mecánica* escalator *9B*
la **medianoche** midnight *1B; Es medianoche.* It is midnight. *1B*
mediante by means of
las **medias** pantyhose, nylons *9A*
el **médico,** la **médica** doctor *3A*
medio,-a half; *y media* half past *1B*
medio tiempo (trabajo) part-time (work)
el **mediodía** noon; *Es mediodía.* It is noon. *1B*
mejor better *8B; el/la/los/las mejor/mejores* (+ noun) the best (+ noun) *8B*
menor younger, youngest *5B,* lesser, least *8B*
menos minus, until, before, to (to express time) *1B,* less *8B; el/la/los/las* (+ noun) *menos* (+ adjective) the least (+ adjective + noun) *8B; lo menos* (+ adverb) *posible* as (+ adverb) as possible *8B; menos* (+ noun/adjective/ adverb) *que* less (+ noun/ adjective/adverb) than *8B; por lo menos* at least
mentir (ie, i) to lie
la **mentira** lie *6B*
el **menú** menu *3B*
el **mercado** market *8B*
el **merengue** merengue (dance music)
el **mes** month *5B*
la **mesa** table *6A; poner la mesa* to set the table *6A; recoger la mesa* to clear the table *8A*
el **mesero,** la **mesara** food server *3B*
el **metro** subway *3A*
mexicano,-a Mexican
México Mexico *1A*
mi my *2A; (pl. mis)* my *4A*
mí me *4B;* (after a preposition) *4B*
el **miedo** fear *6B; tener miedo de* to be afraid of *6B*
el **miembro** member, part
mientras que while
miércoles Wednesday *2B; el miércoles* on Wednesday
mil thousand *5B*
mínimo,-a minimum *7B*
la **minúscula** lowercase *1A*
el **minuto** minute *7A*
mío,-a my, mine; *el gusto es mío* the pleasure is mine *3A*
mira: see *mirar*
mirar to look (at) *4B; mira* (*tú* command) look *2B;* hey, look (pause in speech); *miren* (*Uds.* command) look; hey, look (pause in speech)
miren: see *mirar*
mismo right (in the very moment, place, etc.) *7A; ahora mismo* right now *7A*
mismo,-a same *7A*
el **misterio** mystery
la **mochila** backpack *2A*
el **modelo** model
moderno,-a modern
el **momento** moment *3B*
el **mono** monkey
montar to ride *5A; montar en patineta* to skateboard *7B*
morado,-a purple *9A*
moreno,-a brunet, brunette, dark-haired, dark-skinned *4B*
la **moto(cicleta)** motorcycle *3A*
la **muchacha** girl, young woman *1A*
el **muchacho** boy, guy *1A*
muchísimo very much, a lot
mucho much, a lot of, very much *4A*
mucho,-a much, a lot of, very *3B; (pl. muchos,-as)* many *3B; con (mucho) gusto* I would be (very) glad to *1B; muchas gracias* thank you very much *1B; ¡Mucho gusto!* Glad to meet you! *1A*
la **mujer** woman *9A*
el **mundo** world; *todo el mundo* everyone, everybody
la **muralla** wall
el **museo** museum *3B*
la **música** music *2B*
muy very *1B*

la **nación** nation
nacional national
nada nothing *9A; de nada* you are welcome, not at all *1B*
nadar to swim *4B*
nadie nobody *9A*
la **naranja** orange *3B*
natal birth
la **Navidad** Christmas *5B*
la **neblina** mist *7B; hay neblina* it is misting *7B*
necesitar to need *2B*
negativo,-a negative
el **negocio** business; *el hombre de negocios* businessman; *la mujer de negocios* businesswoman
negro,-a black *2B*
nervioso,-a nervous *4A*
nevar (ie) to snow *7B*
ni not even *5B; ni...ni* neither...nor *9A*
Nicaragua Nicaragua *1A*
la **nieta** granddaughter *4A*
el **nieto** grandson *4A*
la **nieve** snow *7B*
ningún, ninguna none, not any *9A*
ninguno,-a none, not any *9A*
el niño boy (child)
la niña girl (child)
no no *1A*
la **noche** night *1B; buenas noches* good night *1B; de la noche* P.M., at night *1B; esta noche* tonight *7A; por la noche* at night *6B*
el **nombre** name
el **norte** north
nos (to, for) us *(i.o.) 4B;* us *(d.o.) 5A*
nosotros,-as we *2A;* us (after a preposition) *4B*
la **nota** grade
la **noticia** news
novecientos,-as nine hundred *5B*
noveno,-a ninth *7B*
noventa ninety *1B*
la **novia** girlfriend
noviembre November *5B*
el **novio** boyfriend
nublado,-a cloudy *7B; está nublado* it is cloudy *7B*
nuestro,-a our *4A*
nueve nine *1A*
nuevo,-a new *2A; el Año Nuevo* New Year's Day *5B*
el **número** number *2B; número de teléfono/de fax/de teléfono celular* telephone/fax/cellular telephone number *2B, número equivocado* wrong number *2B*
nunca never *4A*

o or *2B; o...o* either...or *9A*
la **obra** work, play
ochenta eighty *1B*
ocho eight *1A*
ochocientos,-as eight hundred *5B*
octavo,-a eighth *7B*
octubre October *5B*
ocupado,-a busy, occupied *4A*
ocupar to occupy
la **odisea** odyssey
la **oferta** sale *9B; estar en oferta* to be on sale *9B*
oficial official
la **oficina** office *3A*
oigan hey, listen (pause in speech)
oigo hello (telephone greeting)
oír to hear, to listen *8A; oigan* hey, listen (pause in speech); *oigo* hello (telephone greeting); *oye* hey, listen (pause in speech) *3B*
la **olla** pot, saucepan *8A*
olvidar to forget *8B*
la **omisión** omission
once eleven *1A*
el **opuesto** opposite
la **oración** sentence
el **orden** order
la **organización** organization
el **órgano** organ
el **oro** gold *9B*
os (to, for) you (Spain, informal, *pl., i.o.),* you (Spain, informal, *pl., d.o.)*
el **otoño** autumn *7B*
otro,-a other, another *(pl. otros,-as) 4A; otra vez* again, another time *6A*
oye hey, listen (pause in speech) *3B*

el **Pacífico** Pacific (Ocean)
el **padrastro** stepfather
el **padre** father *4A; (pl. padres)* parents
la **paella** paella (traditional Spanish dish with rice, meat, seafood and vegetables) *8B*
pagar to pay *9B*
la **página** page *2A*
el **país** country *1A*
la **palabra** word *2A; palabra interrogativa* question word; *palabras antónimas* antonyms, opposite words
el **pan** bread *6A*
Panamá Panama *1A*
la **pantalla** screen *2B*
el **pantalón** pants *2B*
el **pañuelo** handkerchief, hanky *9B*
la **papa** potato *8B*
el **papá** father, dad
los **papás** parents
el **papel** paper *2A,* role; *haz el papel* play the role; *la hoja de papel* sheet of paper
para for, to, in order to *3A*
el **paraguas** umbrella *9B*
el **Paraguay** Paraguay *1A*
parecer to seem *8B*
la **pared** wall *2A*
la **pareja** pair, couple
el **pariente,** la **pariente** relative *4A*
parientes políticos in-laws
el **parque** park *3A*
el **párrafo** paragraph
la **parte** part
el **partido** game, match *4B; partidos empatados* games tied; *partidos ganados* games won; *partidos perdidos* games lost
pasado,-a past, last *5B; pasado mañana* the day after tomorrow *5B*
pásame: see *pasar*
pasar to pass, to spend (time) *5A,* to happen, to occur; *pásame* pass me *6A; pasar la aspiradora* to vacuum *8A; ¿Qué te pasa?* What is wrong with you?

el **pasatiempo** pastime, leisure activity *7A*
la **Pascua** Easter
el **paseo** walk, ride, trip *7B; dar un paseo* to go for a walk, to go for a ride *7B*
el **patinador,** la **patinadora** skater *7B*
patinar to skate *4B; patinar sobre ruedas* to in-line skate *4B; patinar sobre hielo* to ice skate *7B*
la **patineta** skateboard *7b*
el **patio** courtyard, patio, yard *6B*
pedir (i, i) to ask for, to order, to request *6B; pedir perdón* to say you are sorry *6B; pedir permiso (para)* to ask for permission (to do something) *6B; pedir prestado,-a* to borrow *6B*
la **película** movie, film *5A*
pelirrojo,-a red-haired *4B*
la **pelota** ball
pensar (ie) to think, to intend, to plan *6A; pensar de* to think about (i.e., to have an opinion) *6A; pensar en* to think about (i.e., to focus one's thoughts on) *6A; pensar en* (+ infinitive) to think about (doing something)
peor worse *8B; el/la/los/las peor/peores* (+ noun) the worst (+ noun) *8B*
pequeño,-a small *6B*
perder (ie) to lose; *los partidos perdidos* games lost
perdidos: see *perder*
perdón excuse me, pardon me *1B; pedir perdón* to say you are sorry *6B*
perezoso,-a lazy
perfecto,-a perfect *9B*
el **perfume** perfume *9B*
el **periódico** newspaper *2A*
el **periodista,** la **periodista** journalist, reporter
el **período** period
la **perla** pearl *9B*
el **permiso** permission, permit *7A; con permiso* excuse me (with your permission), may I *1B; pedir permiso (para)* to ask for permission (to do something) *6B*
permitir to permit *7A*
pero but *3B*
el **perro,** la **perra** dog *5A*
la **persona** person *8A*
personal personal*; el pronombre personal* subject pronoun
el **Perú** Peru *1A*
el **pescado** fish *3B*
el **petróleo** oil
el **piano** piano *4B*
el **pie** foot *9A; a pie* on foot *3A*
la **pierna** leg *9A*
el **pijama** pajamas *9A*
la **pimienta** pepper (seasoning) *6A*
el **pimiento** bell pepper *8B*
pintar to paint
la **pirámide** pyramid
la **piscina** swimming pool *6B*
el **piso** floor *6B; el primer piso* first floor *6B*
la **pista** clue
la **pizarra** blackboard *2A*
la **planta** plant *6B; planta baja* ground floor *6B*
la **plata** silver *9B*
el **plátano** banana *8B*
el **plato** dish, plate *6A; plato de sopa* soup bowl *6A*
la **playa** beach *4A*
la **plaza** plaza, public square *3B*
poco,-a not very, little, few *6B; un poco* a little (bit) *5A*
poder (ue) to be able *7A*
políticamente politically
el **pollo** chicken *3B*
poner to put, to place *6A;* to turn on (an appliance)*; poner la mesa* to set the table *6A*
popular popular *4A*
un **poquito** a very little (bit)
por for *4A*, through, by *6B*, in *7A*, along *7B; por ejemplo* for example*; por favor* please *1B; por la mañana* in the morning *7A; por la noche* at night *6B; por la tarde* in the afternoon *7A; por teléfono* by telephone, on the telephone *6B; por todos lados* everywhere *7B; por lo general* generally
¿por qué? why? *3A*
porque because *3A*
la **posibilidad** possibility
la **posición** position, place
el **póster** poster
el **postre** dessert *6A*
la **práctica** practice *5A; La práctica hace al maestro.* Practice makes perfect.
el **precio** price *8B*
preferir (ie, i) to prefer *6A*
la **pregunta** question *3B; hacer una pregunta* to ask a question *3B*
preguntar to ask *3B*
el **premio** award, prize
la **preparación** preparation
preparar to prepare *8A*
el **preparativo** preparation
la **preposición** preposition
presenciar to witness
la **presentación** introduction
presentar to introduce, to present*; le presento a* let me introduce you (formal, *s.*) to *3A; les presento a* let me introduce you *(pl.)* to *3A; te presento a* let me introduce you (informal, *s.*) to *3A*
presente present
presento: see *presentar*
prestado,-a on loan *6B; pedir prestado,-a* to borrow *6B*
prestar to lend *8B*
la **primavera** spring *7B*
primer first (form of *primero* before a *m., s.* noun) *6B; el primer piso* first floor *6B*
primero,-a first *5B*
primero first (adverb) *5A*
el **primo,** la **prima** cousin *4A*
principal main
la **prisa** rush, hurry, haste *6B; tener prisa* to be in a hurry *6B*
el **problema** problem *3A*
produce produces
el **producto** product
el **profesor,** la **profesora** teacher *2A; el profe* teacher
el **programa** program, show *7A*
prometer to promise *9A*
el **pronombre** pronoun; *pronombre personal* subject pronoun
el **pronóstico** forecast

449

pronto soon, quickly *1B; hasta pronto* see you soon *1B*
la **pronunciación** pronunciation
el **propósito** aim, purpose; *A propósito* by the way *1A*
próximo,-a next
la **publicidad** publicity
público,-a public
la **puerta** door *2A*
Puerto Rico Puerto Rico *1A*
pues thus, well, so, then (pause in speech) *3B*
la **pulsera** bracelet *9B*
el **punto** point, dot *(term used in Internet addresses) 2B*
la **puntuación** punctuation
el **pupitre** desk *2A*

que that, which *5A; lo que* what, that which *6B; más* (+ noun/adjective/adverb) *que* more (+ noun/ adjective/ adverb) than *8B; que viene* upcoming, next *5A*
¡qué (+ adjective)! how (+ adjective)! *4A*
¡qué (+ noun)! what a (+ noun)! *5A*
¿qué? what? *2A; ¿a qué hora?* at what time? *2B; ¿Qué comprendiste?* What did you understand?; *¿Qué hora es?* What time is it? *1B; ¿Qué quiere decir...?* What is the meaning (of)...? *2A; ¿Qué tal?* How are you? *1B; ¿Qué te pasa?* What is wrong with you?; *¿Qué temperatura hace?* What is the temperature? *7B; ¿Qué (+ tener)?* What is wrong with (someone)? *6B; ¿Qué tiempo hace?* How is the weather? *7B*
quedar to remain, to stay *9A; quedarle bien a uno* to fit, to be becoming *9A*
el **quehacer** chore *8A*
el **quemador de discos compactos (CDs)** compact disc (CD) burner 5A
querer (ie) to love, to want, to like *6A; ¿Qué quiere decir...?* What is the meaning (of)...? *2A; querer decir* to mean *6B; quiere decir* it means *2A; quiero* I love *4A;* I want *3A*
querido,-a dear *6B*
el **queso** cheese *8B*
¿quién? who? *2A; (pl. ¿quiénes?)* who? *3A*
quiere: see *querer*
quiero: see *querer*
la **química** chemistry
quince fifteen *1A*
quinientos,-as five hundred *5B*
quinto,-a fifth *7B*
quisiera would like
quizás perhaps *8A*

la **radio** radio (broadcast) *4B; el radio* radio (apparatus)
rápidamente rapidly *5B*
rápido,-a rapid, fast *4B*
el **rascacielos** skyscraper
el **ratón** mouse (pl. *ratones*) *2B*
la **razón** reason
real royal
la **realidad** reality
la **receta** recipe *8B*
recibir to receive *9B*
el **recibo** receipt *9B*
recoger to pick up *8A; recoger la mesa* to clear the table *8A*
recordar (ue) to remember *7A*
redondo,-a round
el **refresco** soft drink, refreshment *3B*
el **refrigerador** refrigerator *6A*
el **regalo** gift *9B*
regañar to scold
regatear to bargain, to haggle
la **regla** ruler *2A*
regresar to return, to go back
regular average, okay, so-so, regular *1B*
relacionado,-a related
el **reloj** clock, watch *2A*
remoto,-a remote *7A*
repasar to reexamine, to review
el **repaso** review
repetir (i, i) to repeat *6B; repitan* (*Uds.* command) repeat; *repite* (*tú* command) repeat
repitan: see *repetir*
repite: see *repetir*
reportando reporting
el **reproductor** player *5A; reproductor de CDs* CD player *5A; reproductor de DVDs* DVD player *5A; reproductor de MP3* MP3 player *5A*
la **República Dominicana** Dominican Republic *1A*
resolver (ue) to resolve, to solve
responder to answer
la **respuesta** answer
el **restaurante** restaurant *3A*
el **resultado** result
el **resumen** summary; *en resumen* in short
la **reunión** meeting
la **revista** magazine *2A*
rico,-a rich
el **riel** rail
el **río** river
el **ritmo** rhythm
rojo,-a red *2B*
la **ropa** clothing *2B; ropa interior* underwear *9A*
rosado,-a pink *9A*
rubio,-a blond, blonde *4B*
la **rutina** routine

sábado Saturday *2B; el sábado* on Saturday
saber to know *3B; sabes* you know *3B; sé* I know *2A*
sabes: see *saber*
el **sacapuntas** pencil sharpener *2A*
sacar to take out *8A*; *sacar fotos* to take photographs
la **sal** salt *6A*
la **sala** living room *6B*
salir to go out *4A*
la **salsa** salsa (dance music)
la **salud** health
el **saludo** greeting
el **salvavidas** lifeguard
la **sangre** blood
el **santo** saint's day; *Todos los Santos* All Saints' Day
el **saxofón** saxophone
se *¿Cómo se dice...?* How do you say...? *2A; ¿Cómo se escribe...?* How do you write (spell)...? *1A; ¿Cómo se*

llama (Ud./él/ ella)? What is (your/his/her) name? *2A; se considera* it is considered; *se dice* one says *2A; se escribe* it is written *1A; Se habla español.* Spanish is spoken.; *se llaman* their names are; *(Ud./Él/Ella) se llama....* (Your [formal]/His/ Her) name is.... *2A*

sé: see *saber*

sea: see *ser*

la **sed** thirst *6B; tener sed* to be thirsty *6B*

la **seda** silk *9A*

seguir (i, i) to follow, to continue, to keep on*; sigan* (*Uds.* command) follow; *sigue* (*tú* command) follow

según according to

el **segundo** second *7B*

segundo,-a second *7A*

seguro,-a safe

seis six *1A*

seiscientos,-as six hundred *5B*

selecciona select (*tú* command)

la **selva** jungle; *selva tropical* tropical rain forest

la **semana** week *5A; el fin de semana* weekend *5A; Semana Santa* Holy Week

sentarse (ie) to sit (down); *siéntate* (*tú* command) sit (down); *siéntense* (*Uds.* command) sit (down)

sentir (ie, i) to be sorry, to feel sorry, to regret *6A; lo siento* I am sorry *1B*

señalar to point to, to point at, to point out; *señalen* (*Uds.* command) point to

señalen: see *señalar*

el **señor** gentleman, sir, Mr. *1B*

la **señora** lady, madame, Mrs. *1B*

la **señorita** young lady, Miss *1B*

septiembre September *5B*

séptimo,-a seventh *7B*

ser to be *2A; eres* you are *1A; ¿Eres (tú) de...?* Are you from...? *1A; es* you (formal) are, he/she/it is *1B; es la una* it is one o'clock *1B; Es medianoche.* It is midnight. *1B; Es mediodía.* It is noon. *1B; fue* you (formal) were, he/she/it was (preterite of *ser*) *5B; ¿Qué hora es?* What time is it? *1B; sea* it is; *son* they are *1B; son las* (+ number) it is (+ number) o'clock *1B; soy* I am *1A*

serio,-a serious

la **servilleta** napkin *6A*

sesenta sixty *1B*

setecientos,-as seven hundred *5B*

setenta seventy *1B*

sexto,-a sixth *7B*

si if *5A*

sí yes *1A*

siempre always *3B*

siéntate: see *sentarse*

siéntense: see *sentarse*

siento: see *sentir*

siete seven *1A*

sigan: see *seguir*

el **siglo** century *7A*

los **signos de puntuación** punctuation marks

sigue: see *seguir*

siguiente following; *lo siguiente* the following

la **silabificación** syllabification

el **silencio** silence

la **silla** chair *2A*

el **símbolo** symbol

similar alike, similar

simpático,-a nice, pleasant *3A*

sin without *8B*

sintético,-a synthetic *9B*

la **situación** situation

sobre on, over, on top of *2B*, about*; patinar sobre hielo* to ice skate *4B; patinar sobre ruedas* in-line skate *4B*

la **sobrina** niece *4A*

el **sobrino** nephew *4A*

el **sol** sun *7B; hace sol, hay sol* it is sunny *7B*

solamente only

soleado,-a sunny *7B; está soleado* it is sunny *7B*

solo, -a alone

sólo only, just *8A*

el **sombrero** hat *9A*

son: see *ser*

el **sondeo** poll

el **sonido** sound; *equipo de sonido* sound system *5A*

la **sopa** soup *6A*

la **sorpresa** surprise *5A*

soy: see *ser*

Sr. abbreviation for *señor 1B*

Sra. abbreviation for *señora 1B*

Srta. abbreviation for *señorita 1B*

su, sus his, her, its, your *(Ud./Uds.),* their *4A*

suave smooth, soft

el **subdesarrollo** under-development

subir to climb, to go up, to go upstairs, to take up, to bring up, to carry up *8A*

el **suceso** happening

sucio,-a dirty *4A*

el **sueño** sleep *6B; tener sueño* to be sleepy *6B*

el **suéter** sweater *9A*

el **supermercado** supermarket *8B*

el **sur** south

el **sustantivo** noun

tal such, as, so; *¿Qué tal?* How are you? *1B*

el **tamal** tamale

el **tamaño** size *9B*

también also, too *3A*

el **tambor** drum

tampoco either, neither *2B*

tan so *5A; tan* (+ adjective/ adverb) *como* (+ person/ item) as (+ adjective/adverb) as (+ person/item) *8B*

tanto,-a so much *3A; tanto,-a* (+ noun) *como* (+ person/ item) as much/many (+ noun) as (+ person/item) *8B; tanto como* as much as *8B; Tanto gusto.* So glad to meet you. *3A*

la **tapa** tidbit, appetizer

la **tarde** afternoon *1B; buenas tardes* good afternoon *1A; de la tarde* P.M., in the afternoon *1B; por la tarde* in the afternoon *7A;* late

la **tarea** homework *4B*

la **tarjeta** card *9B; tarjeta de crédito* credit card *9B*

el **taxi** taxi *3A*

la **taza** cup *6A*

451

te (to, for) you *(i.o.) 3A;* you *(d.o.) 5A; ¿Cómo te llamas?* What is your name? *1A; te llamas* your name is *1A*
el **teatro** theater *3B*
el **teclado** keyboard *2B*
el **teléfono** telephone *2B; el número de teléfono* telephone number *2B; por teléfono* by the telephone, on the telephone *6B*
la **telenovela** soap opera *7A*
la **televisión** television *4B; ver la televisión* to watch television *4B*
el **televisor** television set *7A*
el **tema** theme, topic
la **temperatura** temperature *7B; ¿Qué temperatura hace?* What is the temperature? *7B*
temprano early *5B*
el **tenedor** fork *6A*
tener to have *5A; ¿Cuántos años tienes?* How old are you? *1A; ¿Qué (+ tener)?* What is wrong with (person)? *6B; tener calor* to be hot *6B; tener frío* to be cold *6B; tener ganas de* to feel like *6B; tener hambre* to be hungry *6B; tener miedo de* to be afraid *6B; tener* (+ number) *años* to be (+ number) years old *5A; tener prisa* to be in a hurry *6B; tener que* to have to *6A; tener sed* to be thirsty *6B; tener sueño* to be sleepy *6B; tengo* I have *1A; tengo* (+ number) *años* I am (+ number) years old *1A; tiene* it has; *tienes* you have *1A*
tengo: see *tener*
el **tenis** tennis *4B*
el **tenista,** la **tenista** tennis player *7B*
tercer third (form of *tercero* before a *m., s.* noun) *7B*
tercero,-a third *7B*
terminar to end, to finish *2B*
ti you (after a preposition) *4B*
la **tía** aunt *4A*
el **tiempo** time *4A,* weather *7B,* verb tense; *Hace buen (mal) tiempo.* The weather is nice (bad). *7B; ¿Qué tiempo hace?* How is the weather? *7B*
la **tienda** store *3B*
tiene: see *tener*
tienes: see *tener*
el **tío** uncle *4A*
típico,-a typical
el **tipo** type, kind
la **tiza** chalk *2A*
toca: see *tocar*
tocar to play (a musical instrument) *4B,* to touch; *toca* (*tú* command) touch; *toquen* (*Uds.* command) touch
todavía yet *7A,* still *7B*
todo,-a all, every, whole, entire *4A; de todos los días* everyday *6A; por todos lados* everywhere *7B; todo el mundo* everyone, everybody; *todos los días* every day *5A*
todos,-as everyone, everybody
tolerante tolerant
tomar to take *3A,* to drink, to have *3B*
el **tomate** tomato *8B*
tonto,-a silly *4B*
el **tópico** theme
toquen: see *tocar*
trabajar to work *8A; trabajando en parejas* working in pairs
el **trabajo** work *8A*
traer to bring *8A*
el **traje** suit *9A; traje de baño* swimsuit *9A*
el **transporte** transportation *3A*
tratar (de) to try (to do something)
trece thirteen *1A*
treinta thirty *1B*
el **tren** train *3A*
tres three *1A*
trescientos,-as three hundred *5B*
triste sad *4A*
el **trombón** trombone
la **trompeta** trumpet
tu your (informal) *2B; (pl. tus)* your (informal) *4A*
tú you (informal) *1A*
la **tumba** tomb
el **turista,** la **turista** tourist

u or (used before a word that starts with *o* or *ho*) *6B*
Ud. you (abbreviation of *usted*) *1B;* you (after a preposition) *4B; Ud. se llama....* Your name is.... *2A*
Uds. you (abbreviation of *ustedes*) *1B;* you (after a preposition) *4B*
último,-a last
un, una a, an, one *2A*
único,-a only, unique *4A*
unido,-a united
la **universidad** university
uno one *1A*
unos, unas some, any, a few *2A*
el **Uruguay** Uruguay *1A*
usar to use *9B*
usted you (formal, *s.*) *1B;* you (after a preposition) *4B*
ustedes you *(pl.) 1B;* you (after a preposition) *4B*
la **uva** grape *8B*

las **vacaciones** vacation *9A*
Vallenato a combination of African, European and Colombian folkloric sounds
¡vamos! let's go! *3A; ¡vamos a* (+ infinitive)*!* let's (+ infinitive)! *3B*
varios,-as several
el **vaso** glass *6A*
vayan: see *ir*
ve: see *ir*
veinte twenty *1A*
veinticinco twenty-five *1B*
veinticuatro twenty-four *1B*
veintidós twenty-two *1B*
veintinueve twenty-nine *1B*
veintiocho twenty-eight *1B*
veintiséis twenty-six *1B*
veintisiete twenty-seven *1B*
veintitrés twenty-three *1B*
veintiuno twenty-one *1B*
vender to sell *9A*
Venezuela Venezuela *1A*
vengan: see *venir*
venir to come *5B; vengan* (*Uds.* command) come
la **ventana** window *2A*

ver to see, to watch *3B; a ver* let's see, hello (telephone greeting); *ver la televisión* to watch television *4B*

el **verano** summer *4A*

el **verbo** verb

verdad true

la **verdad** truth *6B*

¿verdad? right? *3A*

verde green *2B*

la **verdura** greens, vegetables *8B*

ves: see *ver*

el **vestido** dress *9A*

la **vez** time *(pl. veces) 5B; a veces* at times, sometimes *5B;* (number +) *vez/veces al/a la* (+ time expression) (number +) time(s) per (+ time expression)*; otra vez* again, another time *6A*

viajar to travel *6A*

el **viaje** trip *5A; hacer un viaje* to take a trip *5A*; *la agencia de viajes* travel agency

la **vida** life *7A*

el **videojuego** video game *7A*

viejo,-a old *5B*

el **viento** wind *7B; hace viento* it is windy *7B*

viernes Friday *2B; el viernes* on Friday

el **vinagre** vinegar *8B*

la **vista** view; *hasta la vista* so long, see you later

vivir to live *4A*

el **vocabulario** vocabulary

la **vocal** vowel; *vocales abiertas* open vowels; *vocales cerradas* closed vowels

el **voleibol** volleyball *7A*

volver (ue) to return, to go back, to come back *7A*

vosotros,-as you (Spain, informal, *pl.*) *1B*

vuestro,-a,-os,-as your (Spain, informal, *pl.*)

y and *1A; y cuarto* a quarter past, a quarter after *1B; y media* half past *1B*

ya already *6A; ¡ya lo veo!* I see it!

yo I *1A*

la **zanahoria** carrot *8B*

el **zapato** shoe *2B; zapato bajo* flats *9A; zapato de tacón* high-heel shoe *9A*

Vocabulary English / Spanish

a un, una *1B*; *a few* unos, unas *1B*; *a lot (of)* mucho *4B*, muchísimo
about sobre
accent el acento *1A*
activity la actividad *5A*
to **add** añadir *8B*
address la dirección *2B*
to **adopt** adoptar
aerobics los aeróbicos *7A*; *to do aerobics* hacer aeróbicos *7A*
affectionate cariñoso,-a *4A*
afraid asustado,-a; *to be afraid of* tener miedo de *6B*
after después de *7A*
afternoon la tarde *1B*; *good afternoon* buenas tardes *1A*; *in the afternoon* de la tarde *1B*; por la tarde *7A*
afterwards después *7A*
again otra vez *6A*
age la edad
agency la agencia; *travel agency* agencia de viajes
ago hace *(+ time expression)* que *7A*
agreed de acuerdo *3B*
airplane el avión *3A*; *by airplane* en avión *3A*
airport el aeropuerto
algebra el álgebra
all todo,-a *4A*
almost casi *7A*
alone solo,-a
along por *7B*
already ya *6A*
also también *3A*
alternate alterna (tú *command*); alternen (Uds. *command*)
although aunque
always siempre *3B*
American americano,-a *7A*
an un, una *2A*
and y *1A*; e *(used before a word beginning with i or hi) 6B*
another otro,-a *2A*; *another time* otra vez *4B*
answer la respuesta
to **answer** contestar *4B*
any unos, unas *2A*; alguno,-a, algún, alguna *8A*, cualquier
anybody alguien *9A*
anyone alguien *9A*
anything algo *9A*
apartment el apartamento
apple la manzana *8B*
April abril *5B*
Argentina la Argentina *1A*
arm el brazo *9A*
to **arrange** arreglar *8A*
to **arrive** llegar *8A*
art el arte *2B*
article el artículo *5A*
artist el artista, la artista
as tal *1B*, como; *as (+ adverb) as possible* lo más/menos *(+ adverb)* posible *8B*; *as (+ adjective/adverb) as (+ person/ item)* tan *(+ adjective/ adverb)* como *(+ person/item) 8B*; *as much/many (+ noun) as (+ person/item)* tanto,-a *(+ noun)* como *(+ person/item) 8B*; *as much as* tanto como *8B*
to **ask** preguntar *3B*; *to ask a question* hacer una pregunta *3B*; *to ask for* pedir (i, i) *6B*; pedir permiso (para) *to ask for permission (to do something) 6B*
at en; (@) *symbol for e-mail address* arroba *2B*; *at home* en casa *9B*; *at night* de la noche *1B*, por la noche *6B*; *at... o'clock* a la(s)... *2B*; *at times* a veces *5B*; *at what time?* ¿a qué hora? *2B*
athlete el deportista, la deportista *7B*
to **attain** conseguir *(i, i)*
attractive bonito,-a, guapo,-a *4A*
August agosto *5B*
aunt la tía *4A*
autumn el otoño *7B*
avenue la avenida *3B*
average regular *1B*
avocado el aguacate *8B*
award el premio

backpack la mochila *2A*
bad malo,-a *4B*
bald calvo,-a *4B*
ball pelota, bola; *to bowl* jugar a los bolos
banana el plátano *8B*
bank el banco *3A*
to **bargain** regatear
baseball el béisbol *4B*
basketball el básquetbol *7A*, el baloncesto; *basketball player* el basquetbolista, la basquetbolista *7B*
bathroom el baño *6B*, el cuarto de baño
to **be** ser *2A*; *to be able to* poder *(ue) 7A*; *to be afraid of* tener miedo de *6B*; *to be hot* tener calor *6B*; *to be hungry* tener hambre *6B*; *to be important* importar *8B*; *to be in a hurry* tener prisa *6B*; *to be lacking* hacer falta *8B*; *to be necessary* hacer falta *8B*; *to be (+ number) years old* tener *(+ number)* años *5A*; *to be pleasing to* gustar *4B*; *to be ready* estar listo,-a *7B*; *to be satisfied (with)* estar contento,-a (con) *4A*; *to be sleepy* tener sueño *6B*; *to be smart* ser listo,-a *8A*; *to be sorry* sentir *6A*; *to be thirsty* tener sed *6B*
beach la playa *4A*
beans los frijoles *3B*

because porque *3A*
to **become** cumplir *5B*; *to become (+ number) years old* cumplir *(+ number)* años *5B*
bed la cama *8A*
bedroom el cuarto *6B*, la habitación
before antes de *7A*
to **begin** empezar *(ie) 6A*
to **believe** creer
belt el cinturón *9B*
beside al lado (de) *6B*
best mejor *8B*; *the best (+ noun)* el/la/los/las mejor/mejores *(+ noun) 8B*
better mejor *8B*
between entre
bicycle la bicicleta *3A*
big grande *3B*, gran *(form of grande before a m., s. noun)*
bike la bicicleta *3A*
biology la biología *2B*
birthday el cumpleaños *5B*; *Happy birthday!* ¡Feliz cumpleaños! *5B*; *to have a birthday* cumplir años *5B*
black negro,-a *2B*
blackboard la pizarra *2A*
blond, blonde rubio,-a *4B*
blouse la blusa *2B*
blue azul *2B; blue jeans* los jeans *2B*
boat el barco *3A*
body el cuerpo *9A*
Bolivia Bolivia *1A*
book el libro *2A*
bookstore la librería *5A*
boot la bota *9A*
bored aburrido,-a *4B*
boring aburrido,-a *4B*
to **borrow** pedir prestado,-a *6B*
boy el chico *2A*, el muchacho *1A*, el niño
boyfriend el novio
bracelet la pulsera *9B*
bread el pan *6A*
breakfast el desayuno
to **bring** traer *8A*
to **bring up** subir *8A*
brother el hermano *4A*
brown marrón *9A*
brunet, brunette moreno,-a *4B*
building el edificio *3B*
bus el autobús *3A*
busy ocupado,-a *4A*
but pero *3B*
butter la mantequilla *6A*
to **buy** comprar *4B*
by por *4A*; *by (+ vehicle)* en *(+ vehicle) 3A*; *by telephone* por teléfono *6B*; *By the way* A propósito; *by means of* mediante

C

cafeteria la cafetería
calendar el calendario
to **call** llamar *5A*
can la lata *8B*
capital la capital *1A*
car el carro *3A*, el coche; *by car* en carro *3A*, en coche
card la tarjeta *9B*; *credit card* tarjeta de crédito *9B*; *playing card* la carta *7A*
carrot la zanahoria *8B*
to **carry** llevar *5A*; *to carry up* subir *8A*
cash el efectivo *9B*; *in cash* en efectivo *9B*
cash register la caja *9B*
cassette el casete *5A*
cat el gato, la gata *5A*
CD el CD, el disco compacto *2B; CD player* el reproductor de CDs *5A; CD burner* el quemador de CDs *5A*
to **celebrate** celebrar *5B*
census el censo
center el centro *3B*; *shopping center* centro comercial *9A*
century el siglo *7A*
chair la silla *2A*
chalk la tiza *2A*
change el cambio *9B*
to **change** cambiar *9B*
cheap barato,-a *9B*
checkers las damas *7A*
cheese el queso *8B*
chemistry la química
chess el ajedrez *7A*
chicken el pollo *3B*
child el niño, la niña
Chile Chile *1A*
chilly fresco,-a *7B*
chocolate el chocolate *8B*
to **choose** escoger *8B*
chore el quehacer *8A*
Christmas la Navidad *5B*
city la ciudad *3A*
clam la almeja
clarinet el clarinete
class la clase *2A*
classmate el compañero, la compañera *5A*
clean limpio,-a *4A*
to **clean** limpiar *8A*
clerk el dependiente, la dependienta *9B*
to **climb** subir *8A;* escalar
clock el reloj *2A*
to **close** cerrar *(ie) 6A*
closed cerrado,-a *4A*
clothing la ropa *2B*
cloudy nublado,-a *7B*; *it is cloudy* está nublado *7B*
coat el abrigo *8A*
coffee el café *8B*
cold frío,-a *4A*; el frío *4A*; *it is cold* hace frío *7B*; *to be cold* tener frío *6B*
Colombia Colombia *1A*
color el color *7B*
to **combine** combinar *9A*
to **come** venir *5B*; *to come back* volver *(ue) 7A*; *to come in* entrar *5A*
comfort comodidad
comfortable cómodo,-a *6B*
comical cómico,-a *4B*
common común
compact disc el disco compacto (CD) *2B*; *CD player* el reproductor de discos compactos (CDs) *5A; CD burner* el quemador de discos compactos (CDs) *5A*
competition la competencia
to **complete** completar, acabar *8A*
computer la computadora *2B*
computer science la computación *2B*
concert el concierto *3B*
congratulations felicitaciones
to **conquer** conquistar
to **continue** continuar *7B*, seguir *(i, i)*
to **cook** cocinar *8A*
cool el fresco *7B*; *it is cool* hace fresco *7B*
to **copy** copiar *7B*
corn el maíz *8B*
to **cost** costar *(ue) 7A*
Costa Rica Costa Rica *1A*
cotton el algodón *9A*
to **count** contar

country el país *1A*
couple la pareja
courtyard el patio *6B*
cousin el primo, la prima *4A*
crazy loco,-a *4A*
to create crear
credit el crédito *9B*; *credit card* la tarjeta de crédito *9B*; *on credit* a crédito *9B*
to cross cruzar
Cuba Cuba *1A*
cup la taza *6A*
cycling ciclismo

dad el papá
to dance bailar *4B*
dark obscuro,-a; *dark-haired, dark-skinned* moreno,-a *4B*
date la fecha *5B*
daughter la hija *4A*
day el día 2B; *every day* todos los días *6A*; *the day after tomorrow* pasado mañana *5B*; *the day before yesterday* anteayer *5B*
dear querido,-a *5B*
December diciembre *5B*
to decorate adornar *8A*
degree el grado *7B*
delighted encantado,-a *3A*
dentist el dentista, la dentista *3A*
department el departamento *9A*
desire la gana *6B*
desk el escritorio, el pupitre *2A*
dessert el postre *6A*
difficult difícil *4B*
dinner la comida
to direct dirigir
director el director, la directora
dirty sucio,-a *4A*
disaster el desastre
disc el disco *2B; compact disc* (CD) el disco compacto *2B; CD player* el reproductor de discos compactos (CDs) *5A; CD burner* el quemador de discos compactos (CDs) *5A*
to discover descubrir
dish el plato *6A*
dishwasher el lavaplatos *6A*
diskette el diskette *2B*
to do hacer *3B*; *to do aerobics* hacer aeróbicos *7A*
doctor el médico, la médica *3A*, el doctor, la doctora
dog el perro, la perra *5A*
dollar el dólar
Dominican Republic la República Dominicana *1A*
door la puerta *2A*
dot punto *2B*
downtown el centro *3B*
to draw dibujar *7A*
drawing el dibujo *6B*
dress el vestido *9A*
drink el refresco *3B*, la bebida
to drink tomar *3B*
drum el tambor
during durante
DVD el DVD *5A; DVD player* el reproductor de DVDs *5A*

e-mail correo electrónico *2B*
each cada 5A
early temprano *5B*
earring el arete *2B*
Easter la Pascua
easy fácil *4B*
to eat comer *3B*
Ecuador el Ecuador *1A*
egg el huevo *8B*
eight ocho *1A*
eight hundred ochocientos, -as *5B*
eighteen dieciocho *1A*
eighth octavo,-a *7B*
eighty ochenta *1B*
either tampoco *2B*; *either...or* o...o *9A*
electric eléctrico,-a *6A*
electronic electrónico,-a *2B*
elevator el ascensor *9B*
eleven once *1A*
El Salvador El Salvador *1A*
else más *4A*
end el fin *5A*
to end terminar *2B*
English el inglés *(language) 2B*
to enjoy disfrutar
enough bastante *9B*
to erase borrar
eraser el borrador *2A*
escalator la escalera mecánica *9B*
every todo,-a *4A*, cada 5A; *every day* todos los días *5A*
everybody todo el mundo, todos,-as
everyday de todos los días *5A*
everyone todo el mundo, todos,-as
everywhere por todos lados *7B*
exam el examen *5A*
example el ejemplo; *for example* por ejemplo
excellent excelente *7B*
to exchange cambiar *9B*
excuse me perdón, con permiso *1B*
expensive caro,-a *9B*
to explain explicar, aclarar
explanation la explicación
exporter el exportador, la exportadora

face la cara
fairly bastante
family la familia *4A*; *family tree* el árbol genealógico
famous famoso,-a
fantastic fantástico,-a *3A*
far (from) lejos (de) *3A*
fast rápido,-a *4B*
fat gordo,-a *4B*
father el padre *4A*
favorite favorito,-a *3B*
fear el miedo *6B*; *to be afraid of* tener miedo de *6B*
February febrero *5B*
to feed dar de comer *8A*
to feel like tener ganas de *6B*
to feel sorry sentir *(ie) 6A*
few poco,-a *6A*
fifteen quince *1A*
fifth quinto,-a *7B*
fifty cincuenta *1B*
film la película *5A*
to find encontrar *(ue)*
finger el dedo *9A*
to finish terminar 2B, acabar *8A*
first primero,-a *5B*, primer *(form of primero before a m., s. noun) 6B*, primero *(adverb) 5B*; *first floor* el primer piso *6B*
fish el pescado *3B*
to fit quedarle bien a uno *9A*
five cinco *1A*
five hundred quinientos,-as *5B*

to fix arreglar *8A*
floor el piso *6B*; *first floor* el primer piso *6B*; *ground floor* la planta baja *6B*
flower la flor *7B*
flute la flauta
to fold doblar *8A*
to follow seguir (i, i); *the following* lo siguiente
food la comida *3B*; *food server* el mesero, la mesera *3B*
foot el pie *9A*; *on foot* a pie *3A*
football el fútbol americano *7A*
for por, para 3*A*; *for example* por ejemplo *1B*
to forget olvidar *8B*
fork el tenedor *6A*
forty cuarenta *1B*
four cuatro *1A*
four hundred cuatrocientos, -as *5B*
fourteen catorce *1A*
fourth cuarto,-a *7B*
free libre *4A*
fresh fresco,-a *8B*
Friday viernes *2B*; *on Friday* el viernes
friend el amigo, la amiga *2A*
from de *1A*, desde *6B*; *from the* de la/del (de + el) *3A*; *from where?* ¿de dónde? *1A*
fruit la fruta *8B*
fun divertido,-a *4A*
funny cómico,-a *4B*

G

game el partido *4B*, el juego
garage el garaje *6B*
garbage la basura *8A*
garden el jardín *8A*
garlic el ajo *8B*
generally generalmente
generous generoso,-a *4B*
geography la geografía
geometry la geometría
to get conseguir *(i, i)*
to get together reunir
gift el regalo *9B*
girl la chica 2*A*, la muchacha *1A*, la niña
girlfriend la novia
to give dar *7A*
glad contento,-a *2A*; *Glad to meet you!* ¡Mucho gusto! *1A*; *I would be glad to* con (mucho) gusto *1A*; *So glad to meet you.* Tanto gusto. *1A*
glass el vaso *4B*
glove el guante *9A*
to go ir *3A*; *let's go!* ¡vamos! *3A*; *to be going to (do something)* ir a *(+ infinitive) 3B*; *to go back* regresar, volver *(ue) 7A*; *to go in* entrar *5A*; *to go out* salir *4A*; *to go shopping* ir de compras *4B*; *to go up* subir *8A*; *to go upstairs* subir *8A*
gold el oro *9B*
good bueno,-a *4B*, buen *(form of* bueno *before a m., s. noun) 7B*; *good afternoon* buenas tardes *1B*; *good luck* buena suerte; *good morning* buenos días *1B*; *good night* buenas noches *1B*
good-bye adiós *1A*
good-looking guapo,-a 4A, bonito,-a *4A*
gossip el chisme *6B*
grade la nota, la calificación
granddaughter la nieta *4A*
grandfather el abuelo *4A*
grandmother la abuela *4A*
grandson el nieto *4A*
grape la uva *8B*
gray gris *2B*
great fantástico,-a *3A*
greater mayor *8B*
greatest mayor *8B*
green verde *2B*
green bean la habichuela *8B*
greens la verdura *8B*
group el grupo; *musical group* grupo musical
Guatemala Guatemala *1A*
guitar la guitarra
guy el muchacho *1A*
gym el gimnasio

H

half medio,-a; *half past* y media *1B*
ham el jamón *8B*
hand la mano *9A*; *on the other hand* en cambio *7B*
handbag el bolso *9B*
handkerchief el pañuelo *9B*
handsome guapo,-a *4A*
to hang colgar *(ue) 8A*
to happen pasar
happy contento,-a 4A, feliz *(pl.* felices) *5B*, alegre; *Happy birthday!* ¡Feliz cumpleaños! *5B*
hard difícil *4B*
hat el sombrero *9A*
to have tomar *3B*, tener *5A*; *to have a birthday* cumplir años *5B*; *to have just* acabar de *(+ infinitive) 8A*; *to have to* deber, tener que *6A*
he él *2A*
head la cabeza *9A*
health la salud
to hear oír *8A*
heat el calor *6B*
hello hola 1A; *hello (telephone greeting)* aló 2B, diga, oigo
help la ayuda
to help ayudar *6A*
her su, sus *4A*; la *(d.o.) 5A*; le *(i.o.) 1A*; *(after a preposition)* ella 4B
here aquí *1A*
hey mira, miren, oye, oigan
hi hola *1A*
him lo *(d.o.)* 5A; le *(i.o.) 3A*; *(after a preposition)* él *4B*
his su, sus *4A*
hispanic hispano,-a
history la historia *2B*
hockey el hockey
home la casa *4A*; *at home* en casa
homework la tarea *4B*
Honduras Honduras *1A*
horrible horrible *4B*
horse el caballo *3A*; *on horseback* a caballo *3A*
hot caliente *4A*; *it is hot* hace calor *7B*; *to be hot* tener calor *6B*
hotel hotel *3A*
hour la hora *1B*
house la casa *4A*
how? ¿cómo? *1A*; *How are you?* ¿Qué tal? *1B*; *How are you (formal)?* ¿Cómo está (Ud.)? *1B*; *How are you (informal)?* ¿Cómo estás (tú)? *1B*; *How are you (pl.)?* ¿Cómo están (Uds.)? *1B*; *How do you say...?* ¿Cómo se dice...? *2A*; *How do you write (spell)...?* ¿Cómo se escribe...? *1A*; *How is the weather?* ¿Qué tiempo hace? *7B*; *How long...?*

.¿Cuánto *(+ time expression)* hace que *(+ present tense of verb)...? 7A*; *how many?* ¿cuántos,-as? *2B*; *how much?* ¿cuánto,-a? *2B*; *How old are you?* ¿Cuántos años tienes? *1A*
how (+ adjective)! ¡qué *(+ adjective)!* 4A
hug el abrazo *6B*
hunger el hambre *f. 6B*
hungry: to be hungry tener hambre *6B*
hurry la prisa *6B*; *in a hurry* apurado,-a *4A*; *to be in a hurry* tener prisa *6B*
husband el esposo *4A*

I yo *1A*
ice el hielo *7B*; *to ice skate* patinar sobre hielo *7B*
ice cream el helado *8B*
idea la idea *5B*
ideal ideal *4B*
if si *5A*
to **imagine** imaginar
important importante *4B*
in en *2A*, por *4A*
in-laws los parientes políticos
ingredient el ingrediente *8B*
in order to para *3A*
intelligent inteligente *4B*
to **intend** pensar *(ie) 6A*
interesting interesante *4B*
to **introduce** presentar *3A*; *let me introduce you (formal, s.) to* le presento a *3A*; *let me introduce you (informal, s.) to* te presento a *3A*; *let me introduce you (pl.) to* les presento a *3A*
invitation la invitación
to **invite** invitar
island la isla
it la *(d.o.)*, lo *(d.o.) 5A*
its su, sus *4A*

jacket la chaqueta *9A*
January enero *5B*
jeans los jeans *2B*
jersey la camiseta *2B*
jewel la joya *9B*
juice el jugo *3B*
July julio *5B*
June junio *5B*
just sólo

to **keep on** seguir *(i,i)*
keyboard el teclado *2B*
kilogram el kilo (kg.)
kind amable *4A*, el tipo
kitchen la cocina *6A*
knife el cuchillo *6A*
to **know** saber *3B*

lady la señora, Sra. *1B*, la dama; *young lady* la señorita *1B*
lamp la lámpara *6A*
language la lengua, el idioma
last pasado,-a *5B*, último,-a
late tarde
later luego *1A*, después *6A*; *see you later* hasta luego *1A*, hasta la vista
lazy perezoso,-a
to **learn** aprender
leather el cuero *9B*
to **leave** dejar *8A*
leg la pierna *9A*
to **lend** prestar *8B*
less menos 8B; *less (+ noun/ adjective/adverb) than* menos *(+ noun/adjective/adverb)* que 8B; *the least (+ adjective + noun)* el/la/los/las *(+ noun)* menos *(+ adjective) 8B*
let's (+ infinitive)! ¡vamos a *(+ infinitive)*! *3B*
let's go! ¡vamos! *3A*
letter la carta *6B*, la letra; *capital letter* la mayúscula *1A*; *lowercase letter* la minúscula *1A*
lettuce la lechuga *8B*
library la biblioteca *3A*
lie la mentira *6B*
to **lie** mentir *(ie, i)*
life la vida *7A*
light la luz *(pl. luces) 6A*
to **light** encender *(ie) 6A*
like como
to **like** gustar *4B*; querer *6A*; *I/ you/he/she/it/we/they would like...* me/te/le/nos/vos/les gustaría... *6B*
list la lista *7A*
to **listen (to)** escuchar *4B*
little poco,-a *6B*; *a little (bit)* un poco *5A*; *a very little (bit)* un poquito
to **live** vivir *4A*
living room la sala *6B*
lobster la langosta
long largo,-a *9B*
to **look (at)** mirar *4B*; *to look for* buscar *3A*
to **lose** perder *(ie)*
love el amor *5A*
to **love** querer *6A*
lunch el almuerzo *2B*

magazine la revista *2A*
to **make** hacer *3B*
mall el centro comercial *9A*
man el hombre *9A*
many mucho,-a *3B*
map el mapa *2A*
March marzo *5B*
market el mercado *8B*
match el partido *4B*
material el material *9B*
mathematics las matemáticas *2B*
to **matter** importar *8B*
maximum máximo,-a *7B*
May mayo *5B*
me me *(i.o.) 4B*; me *(d.o.) 5A*; *they call me* me llaman; *(after a preposition)* mí
to **mean** querer decir *6B*; *it means* quiere decir *2A*; *What is the meaning (of)...?* ¿Qué quiere decir...? *2A*
meat la carne *8B*
mechanic mecánico,-a *9B;* la escalera mecánica *9B*
menu el menú *3B*
Mexico México *1A*
microwave oven horno microondas *6A*
midnight la medianoche *1B; It is midnight.* Es medianoche. *1B*
milk la leche *8A*
mine mío,-a; *the pleasure is mine* el gusto es mío *3A*
minimum mínimo,-a *7B*
minus menos *1B*
minute el minuto *7A*
Miss la señorita, Srta. *1B*
mist la neblina *7B*
mistaken equivocado
modern moderno,-a
mom la mamá

moment el momento *3B*
Monday lunes *2B*; *on Monday* el lunes
money el dinero *5A*
month el mes *5B*
more más *4A*; *more (+ noun/adjective/adverb) than* más (*+ noun/adjective/adverb*) que *8B*
morning la mañana *1B*; *good morning* buenos días *1B*; *in the morning* de la mañana *1B*, por la mañana *7A*
most: the most (+ adjective + noun) el/la/los/las *(+ noun)* más *(+ adjective) 8B*
mother la madre *4A*
motorcycle la moto(cicleta) *3A*
mouse ratón (*pl.* ratones) *2B*
movie la película *5A*; *movie theater* el cine *3A*
Mr. el señor, Sr. *1B*
Mrs. la señora, Sra. *1B*
much mucho,-a, mucho *4B*; *very much* muchísimo
museum el museo *3B*
music la música *2B*
must deber *6A*
my mi *2A*, *(pl. my)* mis *4A*; *my name is* me llamo *1A*

name el nombre; *last name* el apellido; *my name is* me llamo *1A*; *their names are* se llaman; *What is your name?* ¿Cómo te llamas? *2A*; *What is (your/his/ her) name?* ¿Cómo se llama (Ud./él/ella)? *1A*; *(Your [formal]/His/Her) name is....*(Ud./Él/Ella) se llama.... *2A*; *your name is* te llamas *1A*
napkin la servilleta *6A*
near cerca (de) *3A*
necklace el collar *9B*
to **need** necesitar *2B*
neither tampoco 2B; *neither... nor* ni...ni *9A*
nephew el sobrino *4A*
nervous nervioso,-a *4A*
never nunca *4A*
new nuevo,-a *2A*; *New Year's Day* el Año Nuevo *5B*
news la noticia
newspaper el periódico *2A*
next próximo,-a, que viene *5A*; *next to* al lado (de) *6B*
Nicaragua Nicaragua *1A*
nice simpático,-a *3A*, amable *4A*; *the weather is nice* hace buen tiempo *7B*
nickname el apodo
niece la sobrina *4A*
night la noche *1B*; *at night* de la noche *1B*, por la noche *6B*; *good night* buenas noches *1B*
nine nueve *1A*
nine hundred novecientos, -as *5B*
nineteen diecenueve *1A*
ninety noventa *1B*
ninth noveno,-a *7B*
no no *1A*
nobody nadie *9A*
none ninguno,-a, ningún, ninguna *9A*
noon el mediodía; *It is noon.* Es mediodía. *1B*
north el norte
not: not any ninguno,-a, ningún, ninguna *9A*; *not even* ni *5B*; *not very* poco,-a *6B*
notebook el cuaderno *2A*
nothing nada *9A*
November noviembre *5B*
now ahora *2B*; *right now* ahora mismo *7A*
number el número *2B*; *telephone/fax/cellular telephone number* número de teléfono/ de fax/de teléfono celular *2B*; *wrong number* número equivocado *2B*

to **obtain** conseguir *(i, i)*
occupied ocupado,-a *4A*
to **occur** pasar
October octubre *5B*
of de *1A*; *of the* de la/del (de + el) *1A*
of course! ¡claro! *3A*, ¡Cómo no! *3B*
office la oficina *3A*
official oficial
oh! ¡ay! *2A*
oil el aceite *6A*, el petróleo
okay de acuerdo *3B*, regular *1B*; *(pause in speech)* bueno *3B*
old viejo,-a *5B*; *How old are you?* ¿Cuántos años tienes? *1A*; *to be (+ number) years old* tener *(+ number)* años *5A*
older mayor *5B*
oldest el/la mayor *5B*
on en *2A*, sobre *2B*; *on credit* a crédito *9B*; *on foot* a pie *3A*; *on loan* prestado,-a *6B*; *on the other hand* en cambio *7B*; *on the telephone* por teléfono *6B*
one un, una, uno *2A*
one hundred cien *1B*; *(when followed by another number)* ciento *5B*
onion la cebolla *8B*
only único,-a *4A*, sólo *8A*, solamente
open abierto,-a *4A*
to **open** abrir *5A*
or o *2B*, u *(used before a word that starts with o or ho) 6B*; *either...or* o...o *9A*
orange la naranja *3B*; anaranjado,-a *(color) 9A*
to **order** pedir *(i, i) 6B*
organ el órgano
other otro,-a *4A*
ought deber *6A*
our nuestro,-a *4A*
over sobre *2B*; *over there* allá *6A*

paella la paella *8B*
page la página *2A*
pair la pareja
pajamas el pijama *9A*
Panama Panamá *1A*
pants el pantalón *2B*
pantyhose las medias *9A*
paper el papel *2A*; *sheet of paper* la hoja de papel
Paraguay el Paraguay *1A*
pardon me perdón *1B*
parents los padres *2A*, los papás
park el parque *3A*
part-time (work) medio tiempo (trabajo)
partner el compañero, la compañera *5A*
party la fiesta *3A*
to **pass** pasar *5A*; *pass me* pásame *6A*

past pasado,-a *5B*; *half past* y media *1B*
pastime el pasatiempo *7A*
patio el patio *6B*
to **pay** pagar *9B*
pea el guisante *8B*
pearl la perla *9B*
pen el bolígrafo *2A*
pencil el lápiz (*pl.* lápices) *2A*; *pencil sharpener* el sacapuntas *2A*
people la gente *8A*
pepper la pimienta *(seasoning) 6A*; *bell pepper* el pimiento *8B*
perfect perfecto,-a *9B*
perfume el perfume *9B*
perhaps quizás *8A*
permission el permiso *7A*; *to ask for permission (to do something)* pedir permiso (para) *6B*
permit el permiso *7A*
to **permit** permitir *7A*
person la persona *7A*
personal personal
Peru el Perú *1A*
philosophy la filosofía
photo la foto(grafía) *4A*
physics la física *6A*
piano el piano *4B*
to **pick up** recoger *8A*
pink rosado,-a *9A*
place el lugar *7B*, la posición
to **place** poner *6A*
to **plan** pensar (ie) *6A*
plant la planta *6B*
plate el plato *6A*
to **play** jugar *(ue) 4B*; *(a musical instrument)* tocar *4B*; *(+ a sport/game)* jugar a *4B*
player: el jugador, la jugadora *7B; CD player* el reproductor de CDs *5A; DVD player* el reproductor de DVDs *5A; MP3 player* el reproductor de MP3 *5A*
playing card la carta *7A*
plaza la plaza *3B*
pleasant simpático,-a *3A*
please por favor *1B*
pleasure el gusto *3A*; *the pleasure is mine* encantado,-a, el gusto es mío *3A*
plural el plural
point el punto
to **point** apuntar; *to point to (at, out)* señalar
politically políticamente
pollution la contaminación ambiental
polo la camiseta *2B*
popular popular *4A*
pot la olla *8A*
potato la papa *8B*
pound la libra
practice la práctica *5A*
to **prefer** preferir *(ie, i) 6A*
to **prepare** preparar *8A*
pretty bonito,-a *2A*, guapo,-a *2A*, lindo,-a *8B*
price el precio *8B*
printer (laser) la impresora (láser) *2B*
problem el problema *3A*
program el programa *7A*
to **promise** prometer *9A*
public público,-a; *public square* la plaza *3B*
Puerto Rico Puerto Rico *1A*
purchase la compra *4B*
purple morado,-a *9A*
purpose el propósito
purse el bolso *9B*
to **put** poner *6A*

quality la calidad *9B*
quarter el cuarto *1B*; *a quarter after, a quarter past* y cuarto *1B*; *a quarter to, a quarter before* menos cuarto *1B*
question la pregunta *3B*; *to ask a question* hacer una pregunta *3B*
quickly pronto *1B*

R

radio (broadcast) la radio *4B*; el radio
rain la lluvia *7B*
to **rain** llover *(ue) 7B*
raincoat el impermeable *9A*
rapid rápido *4B*
rapidly rápidamente *5B*
rather bastante *9B*
to **reach** cumplir *5B*
to **read** leer *3B*
reading la lectura
ready listo,-a 7B; *to be ready* estar listo,-a *7B*
really? ¿de veras? *5B*
receipt el recibo *9B*
to **receive** recibir *9B*
recipe la receta *8B*
red rojo,-a *2B*
red-haired pelirrojo,-a *4B*
refreshment el refresco *3B*
refrigerator el refrigerador *2B*
to **regret** sentir *(ie,i) 6A*
regular regular *1B*
relative el pariente, la pariente *4A*
to **remain** quedar *9A*
remains restos
to **remember** recordar *(ue) 7A*
remote remoto,-a *7A*; *remote control* el control remoto *7A*
to **rent** alquilar *7A*
to **repeat** repetir *(i, i) 6B*
report el informe
reporter el periodista, la periodista
to **request** pedir *(i,i) 6B*
to **resolve** resolver *(ue)*
restaurant el restaurante *3A*
to **return** volver *(ue) 4A*, regresar
to **review** repasar
rice el arroz *8B*
ride el paseo *7B; to go for a ride* dar un paseo *7B*
to **ride** montar *5A*
right correcto,-a; *right now* ahora mismo *7A*
right? ¿verdad? *3A*
ring el anillo *9B*
ripe maduro,-a *8B*
river el río
room el cuarto *6B*; *dining room* el comedor *6A*; *living room* la sala *6B*
ruler la regla *2A*
to **run** correr *6B*
runner el corredor, la corredora *7B*
rush la prisa *6B*

sad triste *4A*
safe seguro,-a
saint's day el santo; *All Saints' Day* Todos los Santos
salad la ensalada *3B*
sale la oferta *9B*; *to be on sale* estar en oferta *9B*
salt la sal *6A*
same mismo,-a *7A*
satisfied: *to be satisfied (with)* estar contento,-a (con) *4A*

Saturday sábado *2B*; *on Saturday* el sábado
saucepan la olla *8A*
sausage el chorizo *(seasoned with red peppers) 8B*
to **save** ahorrar *9B*
saxophone el saxofón
to **say** decir *6B*; *How do you say...?* ¿Cómo se dice...? *2A*; *one says* se dice *2A*; *to say you are sorry* pedir perdón *6B*
scarf la bufanda *9B*
schedule el horario *2B*
school el colegio *2B*, la escuela *3A*
science la ciencia
to **scold** regañar
screen la pantalla *2B*
season la estación *7B*
second el segundo *7B*; segundo,-a *7A*
to **see** ver *3B*; *I see it!* ¡ya lo veo!; *let's see* a ver; *see you later* hasta la vista, hasta luego *1A*; *see you soon* hasta pronto *1B*; *see you tomorrow* hasta mañana *1B*; *you see* ves
to **seem** parecer *8B*
selfish egoísta *4B*
to **sell** vender *9A*
to **send** enviar *7B*
sentence la oración, la frase
September septiembre *5B*
settled down establecieron
seven siete *1A*
seven hundred setecientos,-as *5B*
seventeen diecisiete *1A*
seventh séptimo,-a *7B*
seventy setenta *1B*
several varios,-as
shame la lástima; *What a shame!* ¡Qué lástima! *5A*
she ella *2A*
sheet la hoja; *sheet of paper* hoja de papel
ship el barco *3A*
shirt la camisa *2B*
shoe el zapato *2B*; *high-heel shoe* zapato de tacón *9A*; *low-heel shoe* zapato bajo *8A*
short bajo,-a *(not tall) 4B*, corto,-a *(not long) 9B*; *in short* en resumen
should deber *6A*
show el programa *7A*
to **show** enseñar
shrimp el camarón
sick enfermo,-a *4A*
side el lado *6B*
silk la seda *9A*
silly tonto,-a *4B*
silver la plata 9B
silverware los cubiertos *6A*
since desde *6B*, como
to **sing** cantar *4B*
singer el cantante, la cantante *3B*
sink el fregadero *6A*
sir el señor, Sr. *1B*
sister la hermana *4A*
six seis *1A*
six hundred seiscientos,-a *5B*
sixteen dieciséis *1A*
sixth sexto,-a *7B*
sixty sesenta *1B*
size el tamaño *9B*
to **skate** patinar *4B*; *to ice skate* patinar sobre hielo *7B*; *to in-line skate* patinar sobre ruedas *4B*
skateboard la patineta *7B*
to **skateboard** montar en patineta *7B*
skater el patinador, la patinadora *7B*
sketch el dibujo *6B*
to **sketch** dibujar *7A*
to **ski** esquiar *7B*
skier el esquiador, la esquiadora *7B*
skirt la falda *2B*
skyscraper el rascacielos
sleep el sueño *6B*
to **sleep** dormir *(ue, u) 7A*
slow lento,-a *4B*
small pequeño,-a *6B*
smart listo,-a *8A*; *to be smart* ser listo,-a *8A*
smooth suave
snow la nieve *7B*
to **snow** nevar *(ie) 7B*
so tal, tan *5A*
soap opera la telenovela *7A*
soccer el fútbol *4B*; *soccer player* el futbolista, la futbolista *7B*
sock el calcetín *2B*
soft suave; *soft drink* el refresco *3B*
so long hasta luego *1A*
to **solve** resolver *(ue)*
some unos, unas 2A; alguno,-a, algún, alguna *9A*
somebody alguien *9A*
someone alguien *9A*
something algo *9A*
sometimes a veces *5B*
son el hijo *4A*
song la canción *5A*
soon luego *1A*, pronto *1B*; *see you soon* hasta pronto *1B*
sorry: *I am sorry* lo siento *1B*; *to feel sorry* sentir *(ie, i) 6A*; *to say you are sorry* pedir perdón *6B*
so-so regular *1B*
sound system el equipo de sonido *5A*
soup la sopa *6A*; *soup bowl* el plato de sopa *6A*
south el sur
Spain España *1A*
Spanish el español *(language) 2B*, español, española; *Spanish-speaking* hispanohablante
to **speak** hablar *2B*
special especial *6A*
to **spend (time)** pasar *5A*
sport el deporte *5A*
spouse el esposo, la esposa *4A*
spring la primavera *7B*
stadium el estadio
stairway la escalera *6B*
to **start** empezar *(ie) 6A*
to **stay** quedar *9A*
stepfather el padrastro
stepmother la madrastra
stereo el estéreo
still todavía *7B*
store la tienda *3B*
stove la estufa *6A*
to **straighten** arreglar *8A*
strawberry la fresa *8B*
street la calle *3B*
strong fuerte
student el estudiante, la estudiante *2A*
study el estudio
to **study** estudiar *2B*
subject la asignatura *8A*
subway el metro *3A*
such tal
sufficient bastante *9B*
sufficiently bastante
sugar el azúcar *6A*
suit el traje *9A*
suitcase la maleta *5A*

461

summer el verano *4A*
sun el sol *7B*
Sunday domingo *2B*; *on Sunday* el domingo
sunny soleado,-a *7B*; *it is sunny* está soleado *7B*, hay sol *7B*, hace sol *7B*
supermarket el supermercado *8B*
surprise la sorpresa *5A*
sweater el suéter *9A*
to **sweep** barrer *8A*
to **swim** nadar *4B*
swimming pool la piscina *6B*
swimsuit el traje de baño *9A*
synthetic sintético,-a *9B*

T

table la mesa *6A*; *to clear the table* recoger la mesa *8A*; *to set the table* poner la mesa *6A*
tablecloth el mantel *6A*
tablespoon la cuchara *6A*
to **take** tomar *3A*, llevar *5A*; *take turns* alterna (tú *command*); alternen (Uds. *command*); *to take a trip* hacer un viaje *5A; to take out* sacar *8A*; *to take up* subir *8A*
tall alto,-a *4B*
tape recorder la grabadora *5A*
taste gusto
to **taste** probar
to **teach** enseñar
teacher el profesor, la profesora *2A*
team el equipo *7A*
teaspoon la cucharita *6A*
telephone el teléfono *2B*; *by the telephone, on the telephone* por teléfono *6B*; *telephone number* el número de teléfono *2B*; *cellular telephone number* número de teléfono celular
to **telephone** llamar *5A*
television la televisión *4B*; *to watch television* ver la televisión *4B*
television set el televisor *7A*
to **tell** decir *6B*; *(a story)* contar *(ue) 9A*; *tell me* dígame (Ud. *command*)
temperature la temperatura *7B*; *What is the temperature?* ¿Qué temperatura hace? *7B*
ten diez *1A*
tennis el tenis *4B*
tennis player el tenista, la tenista *7B*
tenth décimo,-a *7B*
to **terminate** acabar *8A*
test el examen *2B*
than: more (+ noun/ adjective/adverb) than más *(+ noun/adjective/adverb)* que *8B*
thanks gracias *1B*; *thank you very much* muchas gracias *1B*
that que *5A*, ese, esa *6A*, *(far away)* aquel, aquella *6A*, *(neuter form)* eso; *that which* lo que *6B*
the el *(m., s.) 2A*, la *(f., s.) 2A*, las *(f., pl.) 2A*, los *(m., pl.) 2A*; *to the* al *3A*
theater el teatro *3B*
their su, sus *4A*
them les *(i.o.) 3A*; los/las *(d.o.) 5A*; *(after a preposition)* ellos,-as *4B*
theme el tema, el tópico
then luego *1A*, después *6A*, entonces *6A*; *(pause in speech)* pues *3B*
there allí *2A*; *there is, there are* hay *2A*; *over there* allá *6A*
these estos, estas *6A*
they ellos,-as *2A*; *they are* son *2A*; *they were* fueron
thin delgado,-a *4B*
thing la cosa *6A*
to **think** pensar *(ie) 6A*; *to think about (i.e., to have an opinion)* pensar de *6A*; *to think about (i.e., to focus one's thoughts)* pensar en *6A*; *to think about (doing something)* pensar en *(+ infinitive)*
third tercero,-a,tercer *(form of* tercero *before a m., s. noun) 7B*
thirst la sed *6B*; *to be thirsty* tener sed *6B*
thirteen trece *1A*
thirty treinta *1B*
this este *(m., s.)*, esta *(f., s.) 6A*
those esos, esas 6A, *(far away)* aquellos, aquellas *6A*
thousand mil *5B*
three tres *1A*
three hundred trescientos,-as *5B*
through por *6B*
to **throw** lanzar
Thursday jueves *2B*; *on Thursday* el jueves
thus pues *3B*
tie la corbata *9A*
time el tiempo *4A*, la vez (pl. veces) *5B*; *at times, sometimes* a veces *5B*; *at what time?* ¿a qué hora? *2B*; *(number +) time(s) per (+ time expression) (number +)* vez/veces al/a la *(+ time expression)*; *What time is it?* ¿Qué hora es? *1B*
tired cansado,-a *4A*
to a *2B*
today hoy *3B*
toe el dedo *9A*
together junto,-a
tomato el tomate *8B*
tomorrow mañana *1B*; *see you tomorrow* hasta mañana *1B*; *the day after tomorrow* pasado mañana *5B*
tonight esta noche *7A*
too también *3A*, *too (much)* demasiado *9B*
to **touch** tocar
train el tren *3A*
transportation el transporte *3A*
to **travel** viajar *6A*
tree el árbol; *family tree* árbol genealógico
trip el paseo *7B*, el viaje *5A*; *to take a trip* hacer un viaje *5A*
trombone el trombón
truck el camión
trumpet la trompeta
truth la verdad *6B*
to **try (to do something)** tratar (de)
t-shirt la camiseta *2B*
Tuesday martes *2B*; *on Tuesday* el martes
to **turn off** apagar *7A*
to **turn on** encender *(ie) 6A*, poner
twelve doce *1A*
twenty veinte *1A*
twenty-eight veintiocho *1B*
twenty-five veinticinco *1B*
twenty-four veinticuatro *1B*
twenty-nine veintinueve *1B*
twenty-one veintiuno *1B*
twenty-seven veintisiete *1B*
twenty-six veintiséis *1B*
twenty-three veintitrés *1B*
twenty-two veintidós *1B*

two dos *1A*
two hundred doscientos,-as *5B*
typical típico, -a

ugly feo,-a *4B*
umbrella el paraguas *9B*
uncle el tío *4A*
to **understand** comprender *2A*; *I understand* comprendo *2A*
underwear la ropa interior *9A*
unique único,-a *4A*
united unido,-a
United States of America los Estados Unidos (EE.UU.) *1A*
university la universidad
until hasta *1A*, *(to express time)* menos *1B*
upcoming que viene *5A*
Uruguay el Uruguay *1A*
us nos *(i.o.) 4B*; nos *(d.o.) 5A*; *(after a preposition)* nosotros *4B*
to **use** usar *9B*

vacation las vacaciones *9A*
vacuum la aspiradora *7A*; *to vacuum* pasar la aspiradora *8A*
vegetable la verdura *8B*
Venezuela Venezuela *1A*
verb el verbo
very muy, mucho,-a *3B*; *very much* mucho, muchísimo *4A*; *not very* poco,-a *6B*
video game el videojuego *7A*
vinegar el vinagre *8B*
volleyball el voleibol *7A*

walk el paseo *7B*; *to go for a walk* dar un paseo *7B*; *to walk* caminar *3A*
wall la pared *2A*, la muralla
wallet la billetera *9B*
to **want** querer *6A*
to **wash** lavar *8A*
wastebasket el cesto de papeles *2A*
watch el reloj *2A*
to **watch** ver *3B*; *to watch television* ver la televisión
water el agua *f. 4B*; *mineral water* agua mineral *3B*
way la manera; *By the way* A propósito *1A*
we nosotros *2A*
to **wear** llevar *2B*
weather el tiempo *7B*; *How is the weather?* ¿Qué tiempo hace? *7B*; *the weather is nice (bad)* hace buen (mal) tiempo *7B*
Wednesday miércoles *2B*; *on Wednesday* el miércoles
week la semana *5A*
weekend el fin de semana *5A*
welcome bienvenido,-a; *you are welcome* de nada *1B*
well bien *1B*; *(pause in speech)* bueno, este, pues *3B*
what a (+ noun)! ¡qué *(+ noun)*! *5A*
what? ¿qué? *2A*, ¿cuál? *2B*; *at what time?* ¿a qué hora? *2B*; *What is the meaning (of)...?* ¿Qué quiere decir...? *2A*; *What is the temperature?* ¿Qué temperatura hace? *7B*; *What is wrong with (someone)?* ¿Qué (+ tener)? *6B*; *What is wrong with you?* ¿Qué te pasa?; *What is your name?* ¿Cómo te llamas? *2A*; *What is (your/his/her) name?* ¿Cómo se llama (Ud./él/ella)? 1A; *What time is it?* ¿Qué hora es? *1B*
when cuando *6B*
when? ¿cuándo? *3A*
where donde *6B*
where? ¿dónde? 1A; *from where?* ¿de dónde? *1A*; *(to) where?* ¿adónde? *3A*
which que *5A*; *that which* lo que *6B*
which? ¿cuál? *2B*; *which one?* ¿cuál? *2B*; *which ones?* ¿cuáles? *2B*
white blanco,-a *2B*
white-haired canoso,-a *4B*
who? ¿quién? *2A*, *(pl.)* ¿quiénes? *3A*
whole entero,-a
why? ¿por qué? *3A*
wife la esposa *4A*
to **win** ganar; *games won* los partidos ganados
wind el viento *7B*; *it is windy* hace viento *7B*
window la ventana *2A*
winter el invierno *7B*
to **wish** desear
with con *1A*; *with me* conmigo *9B*; *with you* (tú) contigo *9B*
without sin *8B*
to **witness** presenciar
woman la mujer *9A*
wonderful estupendo,-a *7A*
wool la lana *9A*
word la palabra *2A*
work el trabajo *8A*, la obra
to **work** trabajar *8A*
world el mundo
worse peor *8B*
worst: the worst (+ noun) el/la/los/las peor/peores *8B*
wow! ¡caramba! *5A*
to **write** escribir *6B*; *How do you write...?* ¿Cómo se escribe...? *1A*; *it is written* se escribe *1A*

yard el patio *6B*
year el año *5B*; *New Year's Day* el Año Nuevo *5B*; *to be (+ number) years old* tener *(+ number)* años *5A*
yellow amarillo,-a *8A*
yes sí *1A*
yesterday ayer 5B; *the day before yesterday* anteayer *5B*
yet todavía *7A*
you tú *(informal) 1A*, usted (Ud.) *(formal, s.) 1B*, ustedes (Uds.) *(pl.) 1B*, vosotros,-as *(Spain, informal, pl.) 1B*; *(after a preposition)* ti *4B*, usted (Ud.), ustedes (Uds.), vosotros,-as *1B*; la, lo, *(d.o.) 5A*, las, los, *(d.o.) 5A*, te *(d.o.) 6A*, os *(Spain, informal, pl., d.o.)*, le *(formal, i.o.)*, les *(pl., i.o.) 1A*, os *(Spain, informal, pl., i.o.)*, te *(i.o.) 3A*; *Are you from...?* ¿Eres (tú) de...? *1A*; *you are* eres *1A*; *you (formal) are* es *1B*; *you (pl.) were* fueron
young joven *5B*; *young lady* la señorita *1B*; *young woman* la muchacha *3A*
younger menor *5B*
youngest el/la menor *5B*
your tu *(informal) 2B*, tus *(informal, pl.) 4A*, su, sus (Ud./Uds.) *4A*, vuestro,-a,-os, -as *(Spain, informal, pl.)*

zero cero *1A*

Index

465

Acknowledgments

The authors wish to thank the many people of the Caribbean Islands, Central America, South America, Spain and the United States who assisted in the photography used in the textbook and videos. Also helpful in providing photos and materials were the National Tourist Offices of Argentina, Chile, Costa Rica, Colombia, Ecuador, Guatemala, the Dominican Republic, Honduras, Mexico, Nicaragua, Panamá, Perú, Puerto Rico, Spain and Venezuela. We would like to thank the Bilingual Press/Editorial Bilingüe, Arizona State University, Tempe, AZ, for permission to reprint *Coplas 1* and *9* from *Puentes y Fronteras/Bridges and Borders* (1996) by Gina Valdés, appearing on page 83 of this textbook. We would also like to thank the following institutions for permission to reproduce the paintings by Frida Kahlo on page 127 (*Autorretrato con mono,* 1938, and *Raíces,* 1943): Banco de México Diego Rivera and Frida Kahlo Museums Trust, Av. 5 de Mayo No. 2, Col. a Centro, Del. Cuauhtémoc 06059, México, D.F. Instituto Nacional de Bellas Artes y Literatura, Dirección de Asuntos Jurídicos, Edificio "La Nacional" 8o Piso, Av. Juárez No. 4 esq. Eje Central Lázaro Cárdenas, Col. Centro, 06050, México, D.F. Photographs of these paintings are © Albright-Knox Art Gallery / CORBIS and © SuperStock, Inc., respectively. Finally, we would like to thank Nicaraguan artist Rosa Delia López and her representatives, Americas' Arts L.L.C. [P.O. Box 4404, Gettysburg, PA, 17325], for permission to reproduce her painting *La Gritería* (© 1997), which appears on page 180.

Photo Credits

3alexd / iStockphoto: 227 (1D, 1E; Actividad 2, #1; Actividad 2, #3), 228 (bl, br), 238 (t)
4774344sean / iStockphoto: 320
aabejon / iStockphoto: 171 (bl)
abalcazar / iStockphoto: 111 (1E)
Aguinaldo, Louis / iStockphoto: 213 (24-2), 395 (18A)
ajt / iStockphoto: 387 (A)
albalcazar / iStockphoto: 392 (#6)
Albuquerque / iStockphoto: 387 (B)
Almeida, Helder / iStockphoto: 5 (b), 21 (b)
Alpamayo Software, Inc. / iStockphoto: 97
Anderson, Jennifer J.: 105 (#2), 185 (r), 219 (l, c), 301 (tl), 389 (tl), 407 (l, c) AFP/CORBIS
Anderson, Leslie: Cover (car)
Andresr / iStockphoto: 23 (Activity 10, #4), 191 (E), 191 (F)
Antagain / iStockphoto: 387 (C)
AP / WideWorldPhotos: v (t), xxi (br), xxii (tl), 15 (Penélope Cruz), 46 (Shakira), 78 (b), 82, 85 (Pablo Picasso), 132 (San Juan, Puerto Rico), 151 (Salma Hayek), 168 (Juan Pablo Montoya), 172 (Sammy Sosa), 174 (Pedro Martínez), 175 (t: Ramón and Pedro Martínez), 211 (tl), 220, 310, 354 (c, r), 407 (r)
apomares / iStockphoto: 180-181
Arruza, Tony / CORBIS: 170 (#2)
artpipi / iStockphoto: 283 (#3)
Ashwin82 / iStockphoto: 15 (b)
asiseeit / iStockphoto: 303 (#4)
Aula Photo / iStockphoto: 306 (Rosa)
Barry Austin Photogrphy: 287 (b)
Barton, Paul / CORBIS: Cover (female)
beemore / iStockphoto: 368
Béjar Latonda, Mónica: 30 (l, r), 58 (l), 80 (l), 92 (tl, tc, tr), 102 (tl, tc, tr), 112 (l, c, r), 118 (l, c, r), 124 (l), 172 (l), 216 (l), 228 (tl, tc, tr), 236 (tl, tc, tr), 246 (l, c, r), 254 (l, c, r), 260 (l), 272 (l, c, r), 278 (l, c, r), 292 (l, c, r), 300 (l, c, r), 308 (l), 320 (l, c, r), 330 (l, c, r), 340 (l, c, r), 341, 350 (l, c, r), 354 (l), 366 (l, c, r), 376 (l, c, r), 388 (l, c, r), 396 (tl, tc, tr), 402 (l), 422 (l), 424, 425
benmm / iStockphoto: 369 (#6)
Berg, Sanne / iStockphoto: 380 (#5)
Berry, Doug / iStockphoto: 294, 306 (Alejandro)
Bettmann / CORBIS: 126 (Frida Kahlo)
bikeriderlondon / Shutterstock: 325 (#1)
Blend Images / iStockphoto: 9 (t), 210 (c), 241 (tl)
Blondeau, Olivera / iStockphoto: 227 (2-4)
bluestocking / iStockphoto: 387 (E)
bo1982 / iStockphoto: 281 (br)
Boncina, Matjaz / iStockphoto: 159 (8-1), 212 (22-4), 213 (24-3)
Brand X Pictures: 268-9
Brey, James / iStockphoto: 392 (#5)
Brown, Katrina / iStockphoto: 111 (1A)
btrenkel / iStockphoto: 275 (#2)
BVDC / iStockphoto: 65
carebott / iStockphoto: 329 (#3)
Carlos Photos / iStockphoto: 417 (t)
CEFutcher / iStockphoto: 271 (F)
Chen, Chun Wu / iStockphoto: 112 (6C)
chictype / iStockphoto: 369 (modelo), 369 (#3)
Chilean Ministry of Tourism (Ministerio de Turismo de Chile): x (t), 293 (tr)
Chu, Andrea: 331 (l)
Cimmerian / iStockphoto: 316-317
Coburn, Stephen / Shutterstock: 54 (#2), 122 (b)
Cohen, Stewart: 410-411
Colita / CORBIS: 147 (Gabriel García Márquez)
contour99 / iStockphoto: 66 (#3)
Corbis Royalty-Free: vi (l), x (b), xxv (br), 14 (A), 23 (Activity 10, #2; Activity 11, #3), 47 ("tú," "Pablo"), 56 (tr), 56 (#8), 64, 74, 78 ("Josefina, Kathy, y yo"), 100 ("en bicicleta"), 142, 155 (A, B, C, E, F), 156 (b), 165 (#2, #6, #8), 171 (br), 189 (#2, #3, #4, #6), 193 (frog), 204, 207 (bl, br), 223 (l, r), 227 (1D), 228 (bc), 229 (pearl in shell), 243 (l, r), 263 (l, r), 271 (A), 275 (#1), 277, 280, 287 (t), 292, 293 (tl), 297, 299 (A, B, E), 303 (Modelo, #3), 304, 327, 329 (Activity 19, C), 336, 367 (b), 377 (tr), 384 (r), 396 (c), 401, 427 (l, r)
Corporación Nacional de Turismo-Colombia: xxvi (tr)
Costea, Adrian / Fotolia.com: 392 (#4)
Creatas Images: 10 (Modelo, #1, #2 in Activity 18), 23 (Activity 10, #3; Activity 11, #2), 76 (l), 77 (r), 78 ("Mi tía Sandra"), 165 (#7), 193 (r), 221 (br), 371 (r), 372, 377 (tl)
CREATISTA / Shutterstock: 281 (t)
CSP / Shutterstock: 113 (b)
Cummins, Jim / CORBIS: 302
Dapino, Carlo / Shutterstock: 122 (Actividad 24, #1)
dashek / iStockphoto: 283 (#1)
D'Cruz, Sam / Fotolia.com: 392 (#3)
DeGrie Photo Illustration / iStockphoto: 122 (Actividad 24, #6)
Des Varre, Pierre / iStockphoto: 283 (#2)
Dias, Mark: 216 (r)
Digital Savant / iStockphoto: 9 (b)
Digital Skillet / iStockphoto: 124

Digital Stock: 215
Digital Vision: 272 (b), 296
Dimdok /Shutterstock:Cover (farm scene background)
dmbaker / iStockphoto: 323
Dndavis / iStockphoto: 35 (r)
doram / iStockphoto: 373 (#2)
Dougall Photography / iStockphoto: 247 (tr)
Dr B Images / iStockphoto: 146
Dra Schwartz / iStockphoto: 271 (E)
drxy / iStockphoto: 379 (#6)
Duomo / CORBIS: 299 (D)
Dydynski, Krzysztof / LonelyPlanetImages: xxvi (bl)
Dyellalova, Kateryna / Shutterstock: 239 (modelo)
EasyBuy4U / iStockphoto: 326
edelweiss7227 / iStockphoto: 227 (1C)
Edwards, Jeremy / iStockphoto: 111 (1G)
Eisele, Reinhard / CORBIS: 157 (b)
Englebert, Victor: viii (t), ix (r), xiii (r), xxviii (l), 5 (t), 25, 93 (l), 100 ("en metro"), 105 (#5), 113 (t), 189 (#5), 197, 242 (t, b), 247 (c), 255 (t), 260 (r), 273 (b), 275 (#4), 311 (c), 331 (r), 384 (l), 402 (c, r), 413 (t, bl, br), 429 (tl)
Enlenathewise / iStockphoto: 378
Ersler, Dmitry / Fotolia.com: 379 (#4)
Etchison, Sonya / Shutterstock: 196
Etsey, Juan / iStockphoto: 42 (#2)
Eye Design Photo Team / iStockphoto: 21 (tr)
Facotria Singular / iStockphoto: 122 (Actividad 24, #2)
Federación Argentina de Pato: 288 (l, r)
Feketa, Petro / Shutterstock: 56 (b)
felinda / iStockphoto: 392 (#2)
Filzi, Fabio / iStockphoto: 229 (tl)
Fire & Earth / iStockphoto: 106 (Actividad 31, #1)
Fisher, Peter M. / CORBIS: xii (b)
Flap, Toni / iStockphoto: 256
Floortje / iStockphoto: 66 (#7)
Fnsy / Shutterstock: 191 (C)
Fotokostic / Shutterstock: 283 (#4)
Francisco, Timothy: 4 (l, c, r), 5 (c), 10 (tl, tc, tr), 20 (l, c, r), 26 (l, c, r), 42 (l, c, r), 50 (l, c, r), 56 (#2, #6), 62 (l, c, r), 68, 74 (l, c, r), 100 ("a pie," "en moto," "en camión"), 102 (B), 105 (#6), 106, 136 (l, c, r), 146 (l, c, r), 146 (b), 156 (l, c, r), 166 (l, c, r), 179, 184 (l, c, r), 192 (l, c, r), 202 (l, r), 210 (l, c, r), 275 (#3), 383, 412 (l, c, r), 418 (l, c, r)
Franken, Owen / CORBIS: Cover (landscape), xxi (tr), 23 (Activity 10, #6), 311 (t)
Free, Nick: 227 (2-5)
Frei, Franz-Marc / CORBIS: 161
French, Gerald / CORBIS: 100 ("en tren")
Fried, Robert: iv (b), vi (r), xi (l), xiii (l), xxii (bl), xxiii (bl), xxiv (tr), xxv (bl), xxvi (br), xxviii–1, 47 ("Jorge y Luisa" and "la Srta. Muñoz"), 51, 56 (#1, #5), 76–77, 78 ("Pedro y Francisco"), 91 (C, E), 98, 101 (B), 102 (Activity 26, C), 105 (Modelo, #1, #4), 119 (t), 124 (r), 137 (l), 148 (#4), 211 (c), 213, 236 (b), 255 (c), 273 (t), 278 (b), 279 (tr), 293 (b), 301 (b), 316–317, 321 (tl, b), 329 (A), 343, 347, 361 (l, r), 376 (b), 389 (tr), 397 (tr, b), 405 (l, r), 416 (r), 417 (r), 419 (tr), 422 (ct, cb), 423 (tr, br), 429 (br)
Friedman, David / CORBIS: 172 (r)
Frontpage / Shutterstock: 121
Funston, James: 41 (Activity 1, C), 101 (G), 102 (D)
Fuste Raga, José / CORBIS: xxv (tl)
Gabowski, Rafa / iStockphoto: 212 (22-3)
Gagne, Lise / iStockphoto: 254 (22C)
Gardel, Betrand / Getty Images: 88-89
Gareeva, Elina / Fotolia.com: 379 (#2)
garysludden / iStockphoto: 392 (#1)
gedhaul67 / iStockphoto: 362-363
Giardino, Patrick / CORBIS: 170 (#1)
Gil, Joey / iStockphoto: 191 (B)
glesik / iStockphoto: 344
Goldberg, Beryl: xxiii (tl), xxiv (bl), xxvii (tr), 171 (t), 237 (t), 285, 416 (tl), 419 (b), 422 (r), 423 (tl, bl), 429 (c)
Gordons Life / iStockphoto: 192 (b)
Gos Photo Design / Shutterstock: 114
Grace / CORBIS: Cover (two males)
Greenberg, Jeff / eStockPhoto: 75 (t)
griffre / iStockphoto: 99 (c)
Gurkan, Zelihav / iStockphoto: 395 (18 B)
Gvozdikov, Anton / Shutterstock: 27
H3 Photography / iStockphoto: 306 (Ana)
Hamurishi / iStockphoto: 106 (Actividad 31, #3)
Hawlan, Dieter / iStockphoto: 254 (22F)
Heavenman / Shutterstock: 380 (modelo)
hemorton / iStockphoto: xx (tl)
Henley, John / CORBIS: xxi (tl)
Hermira / Shutterstock: 373 (#3)
Hildebrand, Karin / Fotolia.com: 379 (modelo)
Hiroyuki, Matsumoto / Getty Images: 103 (r)
Hiser, David / Getty Images: 99 (b)
Hogan, Dale / iStockphoto: 212 (22-6) Honduras Tourism Institute (Instituto Hondureño de Turismo): 35 (l)
Hola Imagees / Getty Images: 0-1
holicow / iStockphoto: 369 (#2)
Hollingsworth, Jack: 132-133, 138, 253, 332
Horowitz, Ted / CORBIS: 207 (t)
Houser, Dave G. / CORBIS: xxvii (bl)
Hutchinson, Justin / CORBIS: 274
ILLYCH / iStockphoto: 415 (c)
imacon / iStockphoto: 369 (#5)
Image Depot Pro / iStockphoto: 66 (#5)
Image More Co. Ltd. / Getty Images: 122 (Actividad 24, modelo)
Image Source / iStockphoto: 122 (Actividad 24, #5)
iofoto / iStockphoto: 54 (modelo)
Iserg / iStockphoto: 210 (b)
iStockphoto: 111 (1B), 111 (1C), 213 (24-modelo), 213 (24-6), 227 (2), 258 (b), 259, 395 (18D)
Ivan Cholakov Gostock-dot-net / Shutterstock: 106 (Actividad 31, #6)
IvanWuPI / iStockphoto: 183 (1E), 187 (modelo)
jcamilobernal / iStockphoto: 224-225
jcarillet / iStockphoto: 248
Jen Takes Pictures / iStockphoto: 195 (t)
JerryPDX / iStockphoto: 247 (tl)
jhorrocks / iStockphoto: 151 (bl), 329 (#1)
Jitalia17 / iStockphoto: 380 (#3)
jlocke / iStockphoto: 325 (#2)
JMF Design / iStockphoto: 183 (1A)
jobhopper / iStockphoto: 66 (#1)
Joe Potato Photo / iStockphoto: 106 (Actividad 31, modelo)
Jonas / iStockphoto: 183 (1C), 187 (#4), 213 (#6)
Jostaphot / iStockphoto: 369 (#1)
Jung, Michael / Shutterstock: 23 (Activity 11, #4), 70, 166 (b)
Jupiterimages / Getty Images: 11 (tl), 11 (br), 11 (bl), 122 (Actividad 24, #4), 191 (A), 207 (bc), 303 (#2)
Jurica, Jim / iStockphoto: 254 (22D)
Kali9 / iStockphoto: 38-39
kamil / iStockphoto: 295 (b)
Kashi, Ed / CORBIS: 84 (Isabel Allende)
kcline / iStockphoto: 329 (#6)
Kemter / iStockphoto: 371 (l)
Kester, Boris / traveladventures.org: 203 (c)
Klune, Joseph / iStockphoto: 395 (18F)
Knaupe / iStockphoto: 387 (F)
Kotlov, Alex / iStockphoto: 183 (1B)
Kraft, Wolfgang: 23 (Activity 11, Modelo), 101 (A)
Kzuma / iStockphoto: 54 (#4)
Lady Minnie / iStockphoto: 155 (1A)
Landau, Robert / CORBIS: 58 (r)
Large, Timothy / iStockphoto: 212 (22-1)
largeformat4x5 / iStockphoto: 369 (#4)
lathuric / iStockphoto: xxiii (tr)
Latif, Andrees / CORBIS: 162 (b)
Lau, Karin / iStockphoto: 111 (1F)
lawcaim / iStockphoto: 250
Lena S / Shutterstock: 122 (Actividad 24, #3)
Lenars, Charles and Josette / CORBIS: 108 (Pino Suárez Station)
Lewine, Rob / CORBIS: vii, 132–133, 176, 249
Lichtmeister / Shutterstock: 148 (Actividad 25, #6)
Linke, Heinz / iStockphoto: 112 (6B)
lisafx / iStockphoto: 395 (18E)
Lite Motifs Design / iStockphoto: 106 (Actividad 31, #5)
Lobo, Guillermo / iStockphoto: 227 (1F), (2-2)
Locke, Sean / iStockphoto: 278 (b)
Look GMBH / eStockPhoto: 264

467

LUGO / iStockphoto: 387 (D)
Luxner, Larry: 396 (b)
LWA-Stephen Welstead / CORBIS: 391
lypnyk2 / istockphoto: 373 (#5), 380 (#1), 392 (#7)
Maica / iStockphoto: 163
Mangostock / iStockphoto: 283 (modelo)
Manning, Lawrence / CORBIS: 167 (t)
MAPS.com / CORBIS: 229 (map of Venezuela)
MarFot / iStockphoto: 380 (#4)
Mariday / iStockphoto: 306 (Carmen)
Marshall, James / CORBIS: 16 (b)
mashabuba / iStockphoto: 241 (b)
Massimo Mastrorillo / CORBIS: 279 (b)
Mays, Buddy / CORBIS: 203 (tl)
McInnich / iStockphoto: 322
McVay, Ryan: 292 (b), 400
Medioimages/Photodisc: 157 (t), 335
Memory, Jelani / iStockphoto: 254 (22B)
mikered / iStockphoto: 155 (1E)
Milan Foto / iStockphoto: 333 (modelo)
Milner, Gary / iStockphoto: 306 (Pedro)
Mlekuz, Peter / iStockphoto: 187 (#1)
Mmbirdy / iStockphoto: 29, 54 (#6)
moniaphoto / iStockphoto: 373 (modelo)
Monkey Business Images / Shutterstock, iStockphoto: 148 (Actividad 25, #2), 149
Moos, Viviane / CORBIS: 101 (D)
Mr Pliskin / iStockphoto: 325 (modelo)
Mug Shots / CORBIS: 329 (B)
Murdo / iStockphoto: 43 (l)
Murillo, Aldo / iStockphoto: 54 (#1), 151 (br), 417 (b)
Nemese, Maria Marta / iStockphoto: 187 (#5)
Ney, Nancy / CORBIS: 41 (Activity 1, D)
Nguyen, Nhuan / iStockphoto: 227 (1A)
Nichols, Don / iStockphoto: 183 (1F), 187 (#2), 212 (#4), 213 (#3)
niknikon / iStockphoto: 333 (#5)
ollo / iStockphoto: 183 (1D)
One Word / iStockphoto: 324
Oralleff / iStockphoto: 419 (l)
Orange Lime Media / Shutterstock: 95
ozgurdonmaz / iStockphoto: 392 (#8)
PackShot / Fotolia.com: 379 (#5)
Pallardo del Rio, Miguel Ángel / iStockphoto: 112 (6D)
Pawlowska, Edyta / Shutterstock: 23 (Activity 11, #5)
Pelaez, José Luis, Inc. / CORBIS: 152 (b), 170 (#3), 188
Peterson, Chip and Rosa María de la Cueva: v (b), xx (tr), xxi (bl), 10 (Activity 18, #4), 69, 78 ("Felipe"), 100 ("en avión," "a caballo"), 101 (F), 102 (E), 138, 145, 148 (#1), 165 (#1), 203 (tr), 229 (tr: oil derricks), 230, 237 (b), 268 (l), 271 (B, D), 326, 397 (tl), 406
Peterson, Lisa / ChipandRosaMariadelaCueva: 273 (c)
Photo Talk / iStockphoto: 47 ("Alicia")
Photosindiacom, LLC / Shutterstock: 41 (b)
Pierini, Javier / CORBIS: 279 (tl)
Pitamitz, Sergio / CORBIS: xii (t), 367 (t)
Pixland: 306 (Esteban), 409
Preston, Neal / CORBIS: 14 (Wilmer Valderrama, Activity 26, B)
Prill / iStockphoto: 333 (#2)
Ramirez Lee, Rafae / iStockphoto: 111 (1H)
Rangel, Francisco: iv (t), 43 (r), 84 (César Chávez), 91 (F), 93 (r), 94, 100 ("en autobús"), 103 (l), 148 (#3, #6), 171 (c), 271 (C)
RapidEye / iStockphoto: 329 (#2)
REDAV / Shutterstock: 241 (tr)
Reuters NewMedia Inc. / CORBIS: 162 (Ricky Martin), 167 (Juan Luis Guerra), 184 (Alejandro Sanz), 229 (cacao beans)
Rihak, Jan / iStockphoto: 212 (22-2)
Rivero, Eduardo / Shutterstock: 13
RLJi / iStockphoto: 106 (Actividad 31, #2)
robynmac / iStockphoto: 333 (#4)
Rodrigo, Kote / CORBIS: 170 (Jennifer López)
Rogers, Martin / CORBIS: 185 (l)
Roset, Jamie / iStockphoto: 205
Rowell, Galen / CORBIS: 307
Russ, Kevin / iStockphoto: 45
Sacks, David: 325 (#3)
Salsera, Anika / iStockphoto: 373 (#6)
Sanger, David: xxv (tr), xxvii (tl), 10 (Activity 18, #3), 356, 357 (b)
sashagala / iStockphoto: 382
scanrail / iStockphoto: 333 (#3)
Schaefer, Norbert / CORBIS: 329 (D)
Schafer, Kevin / CORBIS: xxiv (tl), xxvii (br), 308 (r)
Schmidt, Chris / iStockphoto: 258 (t)
Schulte Productions / iStockphoto: 329 (#4)
Sean M / Fotolia.com: 392 (modelo)
Serrabassa, Eva / iStockphoto: 42 (#1)
shbjug / iStockphoto: 329 (#5)
Shelego, Olga / iStockphoto: 159 (8-3)
Shironosov / iStockphoto: 162 (t)
Silva, Nuno / iStockphoto: 7
SimpleFoto / iStockphoto: 101 (H)
Simson, David: viii (b), ix (l), xi (r), xx (br), xxii (tr, br), xxiii (br), 23 (Activity 10, #5; Activity 11, #1), 41 (Activity 1, B), 45, 47 ("Luis"), 53, 56 (tl, #4, #7), 75 (b), 80 (r), 91 (D), 92 (A, B, C, D), 100 ("en carro," "en barco," "en taxi"), 102 (A), 105 (#3), 119 (bl), 137 (r), 155 (D), 195 (b), 221, 236 (c), 253, 282, 301 (tr), 321 (tr), 324, 357 (t), 377 (b), 390, 429 (t)
Sirotina, Anna / iStockphoto: 213 (24-5)
skvoor / Fotolia.com: 379 (#1)
Smirnoff, Debbi / iStockphoto: 333 (#6)
Smith, Johnathan; Cordaiy Photo Library Ltd. / CORBIS: 232
snagfoto / iStockphoto: 106 (Actividad 31, #4)
SochAnam / iStockphoto: 325 (#4)
Songbird839 / iStockphoto: 305
Specht Jarvis and Associates: 159 (8-4)
Stanczak, Norber / iStockphoto: 227 (1B)
Steidl, James / iStockphoto: 159 (8-modelo)
Stephens, Jacom / iStockphoto: 69
Stevanovic, Ivan / iStockphoto: 212 (22-5)
Stewart, Tom / CORBIS: 205 (b), 311 (b)
Stitt, Jason / iStockphoto: 254 (22E)
Stock Machine / iStockphoto: 283 (#5)
Stockbyte Images: 14 (Activity 26, C and D), 23 (Activity 10, #1), 47 ("Daniel" and "yo"), 56 (#3), 91 (A, B), 165 (#3, #4, #5), 189 (Modelo; #1), 281 (bl), 299 (C, F)
Stockcam / iStockphoto: 96
Stoffberg, Werner / iStockphoto: 147 (lc)
Strauss, Curtis / CORBIS: 41 (Activity 1, A)
Suljo / iStockphoto: 373 (#1)
technotr / iStockphoto: 303 (#6)
The Final Miracle / iStockphoto: 155 ("Ver (la) televisión")
Thinkstock Royalty-Free: 63, 213 (t), 255 (b), 258 (b), 303 (#5), 346, 373 (#4)
Thompson, Leah-Anne / iStockphoto: 223 (bl)
Thompson, Tim / CORBIS: 101 (Activity 21, C)
Tiller, Wellford / Shutterstock: 54 (#3)
Tomlin, Graham / iStockphoto: 212 (22-modelo)
Torrens, Lee / Shutterstock: 285
Tourist Office of Spain: xxiv (br), 351 (t, c, b), 359 (t, b)
Track5 / iStockphoto: 78 ("María" and "Amalia y Virginia"), 99 (t)
Trigger Photo / iStockphoto: 191 (D)
Tsibikaki, Sophiav / iStockphoto: 183 (l)
Turudu, Emrah / iStockphoto: 213 (24-4)
Ultra Pro / iStockphoto: 322 (#1)
van Elzelingen, Corstiaan / iStockphoto: 205 (t)
Vargas Bonilla, Alejandro: 47 ("el Sr. y la Sra. Vargas")
Varvaki, Vasiliki / iStockphoto: 111 (1D)
Vera, Cesár / CORBIS: iv (t)
Villaflor, Francisco / CORBIS: 152 (t)
Viorika / iStockphoto: 54 (#5)
vlorzor / Fotolia.com: 379 (#3)
Walls, Stephen / iStockphoto: 254 (22A)
Werner, Tom / iStockphoto: 159 (8-6)
Westmorland, Stuart / CORBIS: xxvi (tl), 169
Wheeler, Nik / CORBIS: 101 (Activity 21, E)
Wojcik, Jaroslaw / iStockphoto: 213 (24-1)
Woraput / iStockphoto: 148 (Actividad 25, #5)
Wright, Lewis / iStockphoto: 395 (18C)
Yin Yang / iStockphoto: 303 (#1)
Zoom Studio / iStockphoto: 380 (#2)
Zuckerman, Jim / CORBIS: 219 (r)